ADULT DEVELOPMENT & AGING:
BIOPSYCHOSOCIAL PERSPECTIVES, SECOND EDITION

Susan Krauss Whitbourne, Ph.D.
University of Massachusetts at Amherst

WILEY

JOHN WILEY & SONS, INC.

EXECUTIVE EDITOR	Ryan Flahive
ASSOCIATE EDITOR	Lili DeGrasse
EDITORIAL ASSISTANT	Deepa Chungi
MARKETING MANAGER	Kate Stewart
PRODUCTION MANAGER	Pam Kennedy
PRODUCTION EDITOR	Sarah Wolfman-Robichaud
SENIOR DESIGNER	Harry Nolan
ILLLUSTRATION EDITOR	Anna Melhorn
SENIOR PHOTO EDITOR	Lisa Gee
PHOTO RESEARCHER	Lisa Passmore

COVER ART: Henri Matisse, *Polynesia, the Sea*, 1946. Musée National d'Art Moderne, Centre Georges Pompidou, Paris/ ©CNAC/MNAM/Dist. Réunion des Musées Nationaux/ Art Resource/ ©2003 Succession H. Matisse, Paris/Artists Rights Society (ARS), New York.

This book was set in 10.5/12.5 Berkeley Old Style Book by John Wiley & Sons Australia, Ltd and printed and bound by R.R. Donnelley-Crawfordsville. The cover was printed by Lehigh Press.

This book is printed on acid free paper. ∞

Printed in the United States of America

10 9 8 7 6 5 4 3 2 1

ISBN: 0-471-45821-X

Preface

I teach this course for two reasons. One is because I love the field and think that it is the most interesting and important subject matter imaginable. To understand the aging process is to understand the very essence of life itself. Without getting morbid, think about what it means to understand why we age. It is to understand, also, why we die, since death is the natural ending of the aging process. The biological, psychological, and sociocultural aspects of adult development and aging can provide us with some very important keys to existence.

Stepping down to a more practical level, I hope I will convince you of the field's importance as you start to learn about how you can apply what scientists know about adult development and aging to your own life. This is the second reason I love to teach the course to undergraduates. For students who are entering their 20s, there are many preventive steps that can be taken now. Once you have this knowledge, you can delay or perhaps even avoid altogether some of the changes associated with aging that are within your power to control. For students who are older than their 20s, it is not too late to apply this knowledge about aging, in fact, having gone through some changes already, the information may be taken even closer to heart. Older students will also be able to relate to many of the phenomena described in this text about adult life, including relationships, work, and involvement in the larger community.

The first time I was given the opportunity to develop a course on adult development and aging, I was just starting out as an assistant professor. It was a thrill to have the chance to share with my students (some of whom were older than I was) the excitement I felt about this new and increasingly important field of study within psychology. After all, this was the 1970s, and it was clear that the field would grow by leaps and bounds in no time. Students needed to learn this vital information so that they could apply it to their jobs and future studies. I was right about the second point but a little premature about the first. Information about adulthood and aging is of vital importance, even more so now that the Baby Boomers are booming into their 50s. However, the optimism I felt about the growth of the field is only now beginning to be justified. It is impossible to turn on a news program, open the paper, or even pick up a popular magazine while waiting in line at the supermarket without reading something about the aging process and how it is affecting us all. I have also been encouraged by the strong and continued interest that students have shown over the years in this topic. If their desire to learn about the aging of their elders (and the aging of themselves) is any indication, the field has no where to go but up, and very shortly.

Themes of the Book

The book is based on a biopsychosocial model, a term that reflects the growing tendency in the study of development to examine the multiple interactions among the domains of biology, psychology, and sociology. According to this model, changes in one domain have effects on changes in other domains. The centerpiece of this model is identity, the individual's self-definition. Interactions between the individual and environment are interpreted through the framework provided by identity. These interactions, in turn, shape identity throughout the adult years and beyond. Terms and concepts relevant to this model will be introduced and elaborated upon throughout the text and will be focused on specifically through featured Biopsychosocial Perspective boxes (see below).

This is an exciting time to be studying developmental processes in adulthood. Not only is the topic gaining increasing media attention, but it is also gaining tremendous momentum as an academic discipline within life-span development. The biopsychosocial model fits within the framework of several new approaches that emphasize the impact of social context on individuals throughout all periods of life. Entirely new concepts, sets of data, and practical applications of these models are resulting in a realization of the dreams of many of the classic developmental psychologists whose work shaped the field in the early twentieth century.

Organization

The text is organized in a manner that reflects the biopsychosocial theme. The opening chapters present introductory material, including basic concepts, demography, theoretical models, and research methods. The next section of chapters covers the physical aging process in adulthood and old age as well as the major health problems encountered by adults during these years. The middle section of the book includes topics within the psychology of adult development and aging, including cognitive and personality changes. The next set of chapters covers sociocultural aspects of adulthood aging, including relationships, vocational development, and retirement. Throughout these chapters biopsychosocial interactions are emphasized. In the final two chapters, these perspectives are brought together in a chapter on death and dying, and a final chapter on successful aging. This final chapter includes a discussion of creativity and productivity in the latter years of life.

Features

The topics and features in this text are intended to involve the student at multiple levels. The Biopsychosocial Perspective boxes present focused examples of research and theory that illustrate the biopsychosocial model. Interactions among sociocultural factors, physical age-related changes, and personality and identity are given emphasis. These boxes also present recent data on issues that are of practical as well as theoretical relevance, such as the topic of aging and driving.

The Behind the Research boxes follow the format of popular music video channels that highlight the work of particular individuals who have been influential in the field. Although there were many notable individuals who could have been chosen for these boxes, I decided to feature people whose research provided a good example of the biopsychosocial theme. Each of these experts provided me with insightful commentaries about the aspects of their research that are most exciting or compelling for them, what they see as the major challenges, and what their predictions are about future research in this area. Their answers are presented as they were written by each individual, so you have their personal views truly in their own words. Photographs of each researcher provide you with a visual image of who this person is, a fact that should help enliven even further your understanding of what the researcher is trying to accomplish.

Finally, I decided to have a little fun with the Assess Yourself boxes. As I was conducting research on the topics in the book and looking for additional lecture material to use in my class, I came across some interesting quizzes and exercises on the Web that were developed by both popular and professional sources. I would love to be able to have you enter these Web sites directly and look at these exercises, but given the limitations of a textbook that must be printed on paper (rather than on the Web) I thought I would try the next best thing. The Assess Yourself boxes give you a chance to test your knowledge and attitudes in each of the book's substantive content areas, with one of these tests per chapter. Short of being able to score yourself as you would on a Web-based test, you at least will be able to get some idea of how much you know or what your attitudes are toward the topic. Where the data were available, I summarized the answers of people who took these surveys.

New to the second edition are introductory quotes that open each chapter. These are observations about aging that I have found to be particularly useful in teaching my course. My students enjoy the sentiments expressed in these quotes, which range from the humorous to the profound. The individuals quoted are people who have lived to ripe old ages themselves and reflect the wisdom that has accompanied their own journeys through life.

A second new feature is the interspersing of "What Do You Think?" questions throughout each chapter. These are lead-ins to discussions that I have found to be particularly stimulating when posed to my own students. You can answer these questions yourself or, even better, ask your fellow students, family, and friends. I think you will find these questions to be engaging, thought-provoking, and challenging. By thinking about them, you will gain an even more in-depth understanding of the relevant chapter material.

You will see little blue Web icons interspersed throughout the text. These icons will allow you to enter the virtual world of adult development and aging, by going to the John Wiley & Sons Web site that is specific to this book (www.wiley.com/whitbourne), and investigating the source that I have selected for that section of the book. Some of these sources contain updates of statistics, and others are the sources for the Assess Yourself boxes (or ones that are similar to the boxes when they become outdated). I encourage both student and instructor to visit the Web site frequently because new material will continue to be added and updated. The Web icons may also be thought of as interactive, in that I would greatly appreciate receiving updates from users that I may post on the site. Students have found some of the best Web sites for me to use in my own teaching, and I hope readers will become involved at a similar level.

Learning Aids

Each chapter contains several pedagogical features, including a numbered summary, glossary terms, and suggested readings. These will assist students in reviewing the important material from the chapter and in pursuing further areas in more depth. Furthermore, the chapters have been written with ample illustrations, particularly tables and figures. These will help the student organize the information and can be used by the instructor as a basis for lecture material (see below).

Instructor's Manual and Test Bank

The *Instructor's Manual* and *Test Bank* were written by me and reflect my 25-plus years of teaching the course. The *Instructor's Manual* provides chapter outlines, key terms, learning objectives, and lecture "talking points," extenders, and launchers. Material taken from what is now a rather vast movie and video collection that I possess is also described in the *Instructor's Manual*. More importantly, suggestions for incorporating new material as it becomes available, including documentaries, movies, and even pop music, are described. Quotes that can be used in teaching each lecture topic are also provided.

Instructors will also be able to benefit from a set of PowerPoint slides that can be used for lectures and overhead transparencies. These are available from the Wiley sales representative after a decision has been made to adopt the text for a course. Contained on the slides are highlights of chapters and extensive visual illustrations of chapter concepts and key terms.

I also wrote the *Test Bank*, and like the *Instructor's Manual*, it reflects my many years of teaching the course. The test bank includes at least 50 to 70 questions in each chapter. Each multiple-choice question is labeled according to which concept it tests, along with its difficulty level. There are also short-answer and essay questions corresponding to each section of the chapter.

Changes in the Second Edition

The first edition of *Adult Development and Aging: Biopsychosocial Perspectives* was intended to provide a fresh and engaging approach to the field of the psychology of adult development and aging by focusing on three themes: a multidisciplinary approach, positive images of aging, and the newest and most relevant research. The second edition maintains these three themes, as they have proven to be well received by adopters and students. In addition, the second edition highlights further the sociocultural theme. New features enhance the text's ability to stimulate critical thinking among students.

The topics covered in this text have been chosen and refined over the years to reflect areas that attract students, and it has the pedagogical aids to make it student friendly. In the second edition, I shortened some chapters and recombined the material in others so that the material is even more accessible to students. The following summary of changes describes the specific changes that I made in writing this edition. The chapter on mental health and treatment was divided to separate the traditional area of abnormal psychology as applied to adult development and aging from issues relating to institutionalization and the financing of long-term care. Additional changes in the text provided important refinements, such as moving the section on "The Aging Context" from the first to the second chapter, adding more material on prevention to the chapter on health, adding a section specifically devoted to wisdom to Chapter 7 (cognition), shortening the description of research in Chapter 8 (personality) but enhancing the treatment of midlife, and reducing the descriptions of statistics in the chapters on family, work, and death and dying.

Throughout the second edition, references have been substantially updated. There are approximately 2000 references, 1300 of which are from the years 2000–2003. To maintain the same length of the text, outdated references were deleted and sections were updated to reflect the new research. For example, the report in July 2002 discrediting the use of hormone replacement therapy (HRT) required completely rewriting the section in Chapter 4 ("Physical and Sensory Changes") in which the benefits of HRT were described. New research on the role of obesity in causing heart disease, diabetes, and cancer was incorporated into Chapter 4 ("Health and Prevention"). Census 2000 data have been completely integrated into demographic material presented throughout the text, as have special reports on older adults published by the Administration on Aging and the U.S. Department of Health and Human Services. New information on Alzheimer's disease associated with publications on the caspase theory was incorporated into Chapter 5. Extensive new information on mental health, with new studies on depression and anxiety, was incorporated into Chapter 12. Updates were also made in examples provided in photographs and within the text to make the material more current for undergraduates. Changes throughout the text include focusing more on prevention when describing age-related changes and diseases, incorporating international data, expanding the treatment of midlife, and condensing the level of detail provided in descriptions of statistics and research studies.

Acknowledgments

My first set of acknowledgments go to my long-suffering family, who put up with the hours I spent holed away in my study preparing this second edition. Writing a text also places an emotional burden on one's family, and my case was no exception. My husband, Richard O'Brien, as always, not only provided important substantive help (his field is biology) but also continued to encourage me at every step along the way. My college-age daughter, Jennifer O'Brien, provided a constant source of humor and inspiration to make this book appealing to students. My older daughter, Stacey Whitbourne, is now herself completing a doctoral program at Brandeis University studying the field of gerontology. Not only were both of my daughters students in my Psychology of Aging course (an interesting experience!) but they have continued to provide me with feedback and challenges about my

approach to teaching and thinking about, among other things, the aging process. Finally, my mother, Lisa Rock, deserves a special merit award for not only providing regular companionship around the dinner table but also continuing to demonstrate so many of the qualities of creativity that make up successful aging.

It is customary to thank the editorial and production staff of a publishing house, but in my case, I would like to go beyond the usual custom. Every individual from John Wiley & Sons who has been involved in this book has shown unusual dedication, care, and professionalism. The most centrally involved of these individuals has been Lili DeGrasse, assistant editor, whose good sense and good cheer provided constant support and encouragement throughout the revision process. Anne Smith, publisher, has also shown an unusual dedication to this project, being involved in providing guidance virtually from the inception through the very last phase of the revision.

Perhaps the best indication of the tremendous attitude at Wiley is the instantaneous speed with which e-mails are returned from everyone involved with this book. An author can hardly ask for more!

My final thanks go to the reviewers who provided helpful comments and suggestions throughout the revision process. Their insightful observations and thoughtful proposals for changes helped me to tighten and focus the manuscript and to enhance the discussion of several key areas of interest in the field: Katie E. Cherry, Louisiana University; Lisa C. McGuire, Georgia State University.

In conclusion, I hope that I have given you something to look forward to as you venture into the fascinating field of adult development and aging, and that the subsequent pages of this book will fulfill these expectations. I have tried to present a comprehensive but clear picture of the area and hope that you will be able to apply this knowledge to improving your own life and the lives of the older adults with whom you may be preparing to work. I hope you will come away from the course with a positive feeling about what older adults can do to "age better" and with a positive feeling about the potentialities of later life. And maybe, just maybe, a few of you will decide to pursue this field more seriously, and I can welcome you as colleagues in the coming years.

Susan Krauss Whitbourne, Ph.D.

January, 2004

About the Author

Susan Krauss Whitbourne, Ph.D., Professor of Psychology at the University of Massachusetts Amherst, received her Ph.D. in Developmental Psychology from Columbia University in 1974 and completed a postdoctoral training program in Clinical Psychology at the University of Massachusetts at Amherst, having joined the faculty there in 1984. Her previous positions were as an Associate Professor of Education and Psychology at the University of Rochester (1975–84) and an Assistant Professor of Psychology at SUNY College at Geneseo. Currently Psychology Departmental Honors Coordinator at the University of Massachusetts at Amherst and Director of the Office of National Scholarship Advisement, she is also Faculty Advisor to the University of Massachusetts Chapter of Psi Chi, a position for which she was recognized as the Eastern Regional Outstanding Advisor for the year 2001 and as the Florence Denmark National Faculty Advisor in 2002. Her teaching has been recognized by the College Outstanding Teacher Award in 1995 and the University Distinguished Teaching Award in 2001. In 2003, she received the American Psychological Association (APA) Division 20 (Adult Development and Aging) Master Mentor Award and the Gerontological Society of America (GSA) Behavioral and Social Sciences Distinguished Mentorship award.

During the past 20 years, Dr. Whitbourne has held a variety of elected and appointed positions in APA Division 20 including president (1995–96), treasurer (1986–89), secretary (1981–84), Program Chair (1997–98), Education Committee Chair (1979–80), Student Awards Committee Chair (1993–94), Continuing Education Committee Chair (1981–82), and Elections Committee Chair (1992–93). She is a Fellow of Divisions 1 (General Psychology), 2 (Teaching of Psychology), 12 (Clinical Psychology), and 20. She is the Division 20 Representative to the APA Council, a member of the Committee for the Structure and Function of Council, and Chair of the APA Coalition of Academic, Scientific, and Applied Psychologists.

Dr. Whitbourne is also a Fellow of the Gerontological Society of America, having served as Chair of the Student Awards Committee. A founding member of the Society for the Study of Human Development, she is currently the President-elect. She also serves on the Board of Directors of the National Association of Fellowship Advisors.

Her publications include 14 published books and nearly 100 journal articles and chapters, including articles in *Psychology and Aging*, *Psychotherapy*, *Developmental Psychology*, *Journal of Gerontology*, *Journal of Personality and Social Psychology*, and *Teaching of Psychology*, and chapters in the *Handbook of the Psychology of Aging*, *Clinical Geropsychology*, *Comprehensive Clinical Psychology (Geropsychology)*, the *Encyclopedia of Psychology* and the *International Encyclopedia of the Social and Behavioral Sciences*. She has been a consulting editor for *Psychology and Aging* and serves on the editorial board of the *Journal of Gerontology*. Her presentations at professional conferences number more than 175 and include several invited addresses, among them the APA G. Stanley Hall Lecture in 1995, the EPA Psi Chi Distinguished Lecture in 2001, and the SEPA Invited Lecture in 2002.

Contents

Chapter One

Themes and Issues in Adult Development and Aging

> **"**I had to wait 110 years to become famous. I wanted to enjoy it as long as possible.**"**
>
> Jeanne Louise Calment
> (1875–1997)

If you are reading this book, you are an "adult." Even if you are, by all accounts, an average-aged college student, you nevertheless fit many of the criteria for this age category of human beings. The term "adult," which may conjure up the image of someone who is a "grown-up," refers to all individuals who have reached a certain level of physical, psychological, and social maturity. You and your fellow students may have difficulty entering certain commercial establishments without valid proof of age. Nevertheless, you are considered in many ways able to enjoy the privileges and carry out the responsibilities of those whom you tend to think of as from the "older generation." For those of you reading this book who have no difficulty thinking of yourselves as adults, you may be struggling with the issue of whether you are a "young" or "middle-aged" version of this

category of humans. And for those students who clearly identify themselves as members of the older generation of adults, the issues you face with regard to self-definition may involve contemplating your status as a "senior citizen."

Questions involving self-definition based on age are very relevant to the scope and coverage of this book. We will be examining definitions of adulthood, the meaning and definition of "age," and the approaches researchers have taken to understanding the biological, psychological, and social changes that take place from the years of adolescence through old age. Readers will find that this information is of personal as well as theoretical and professional interest. We will explore the many ways individuals can affect their own aging processes through incorporating into their daily lives behaviors and activities that can maintain maximum levels of functioning well into the later decades of life. For college students of traditional age (18–22) taking the course, we will see that it is never too early to begin to make these adaptations. For those college students of nontraditional age, we will see that it is never too late to initiate these important interventions.

THE BIOPSYCHOSOCIAL PERSPECTIVE

The theme of this book is based on a **biopsychosocial perspective**, a view of development as a complex interaction of biological, psychosocial, and social processes (Fig. 1.1). Biological processes incorporate the changes within the body associated with the passage of time that alter the body's functions and structures. Psychological processes are those that involve cognition,

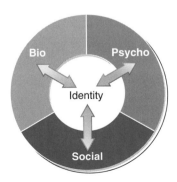

<u>FIGURE 1.1</u>
Biopsychosocial model

personality, and emotions. The social processes in development are those that reflect the environment or context, and they include indicators that reflect the individual's position within the social structure. Theories and models of life-span development, discussed in Chapter 2, attempt to sort out the relative influence of these sets of factors on the individual's progression through life.

The biopsychosocial model implies that biology, medicine, nursing, sociology, history, and even the arts and literature provide crucial perspectives to the psychology of adulthood and aging. Knowledge, theories, and perspectives from a variety of areas each contribute importantly to the study of the individual over time. Within this model, the concept of **identity** will have a central role. An individual's identity is defined as a composite of self-representations in biological, psychological, and social domains. The interaction of these domains as interpreted in terms of the individual's view of the self forms a central organizing concept within the biopsychosocial perspective.

PRINCIPLES OF ADULT DEVELOPMENT AND AGING

The field of adult development and aging is built on a set of principles that form the foundation of this book. Although theoretical differences exist within the discipline, there is general agreement on these underlying premises.

Continuity of Changes over the Life Span

The first principle of the study of adult development and aging is that changes over the life span occur in a continuous fashion. In other words, the changes that occur in later adulthood build on those that have occurred over the previous years of life. This principle has theoretical as well as practical implications.

BIOPSYCHOSOCIAL PERSPECTIVE

THROUGHOUT THIS BOOK, clear interactions will be apparent between the biological changes taking place as a function of normal aging and the actions people engage in either to speed up or to slow down the aging process. The role of psychological and sociocultural factors as they affect the physical functioning of the middle-aged adult is also crucial to consider. As further research driven by an integrative perspective incorporating biological, psychological, and sociocultural factors accrues, the study of physical functioning, health, social status, and identity processes will be further enhanced. Throughout this book, many tantalizing possibilities will emerge regarding how and whether adults can alter the rate of aging. Ultimately, these possibilities will continue to be explored as researchers find ways to suggest how the actions of individuals and the contribution of society can influence not only the length of life but also its quality throughout the middle years and beyond.

Biopsychosocial Perspective boxes in each chapter will explore a particular area in which there are intersections among the domains of biological, psychological, and sociocultural processes. In some cases, these processes will be examined from the standpoint of how all three jointly affect the individual's development. As will become evident in Chapter 2, individuals can affect their development as well as be affected by forces related to the passage of time. Furthermore, in adulthood many changes in these areas converge to affect the individual's personal sense of self, which in turn can affect the actions people take to alter their own developmental processes. By examining these complex and fascinating interactions, researchers and theorists can make significant progress in understanding how people maneuver through the challenges presented by life in the middle and later years.

Although people change in outward appearance over their lifetimes, they still feel that they are the same person on the "inside."

Theories of adulthood and aging, from the biological to the sociological, take it as a given that the changes in old age occur against the backdrop of a prior developmental history of the individual. For example, in the biological realm, changes that occur in a particular organ system in later life depend in many ways on the prior functioning of that system throughout life.

The practical implications of the continuity principle relate to the ways that individuals feel about themselves and the ways that others feel about them. Adults do not feel that they become different people because they reach a certain birthday. In fact, older adults often say that they do not feel they have changed very much on the "inside" and that they still feel the same way they always have. Unfortunately, outward appearance plays a large role in the ways we are perceived by others. Consequently, when others look at a middle-aged or older adult, they are likely to focus on that person's age rather than on some other characteristic of personality or ability. It is important to keep in mind that as people develop through adulthood they think of themselves as the "same," but older, and that many of them will resent being treated in a particular way because of their age. Think of the way you feel when you are lumped together with all other college students (for better or for worse) on the basis of your age and position in life rather than who you are as an individual.

"What do you think?" | **1-1**

Have you ever heard anyone say that they don't feel any older but when they look in the mirror they see that they appear this way?

It Is the Survivors Who Grow Old

The second principle of adult development and aging that will be encountered throughout this book is one that is perhaps obvious but worth pointing out nevertheless. Simply put, in order for people to become old, they have to not die. Think about the ramifications of this principle. The people who have become old (and not died) are the ones who survived the many threats to life that cause other people to not survive. Such threats include car accidents, natural disasters, genetic vulnerabilities to diseases, and risky behaviors such as excessive drug use (see Table 1-1). The fact that people manage to avoid death from these conditions suggests that they have inherited a good set of genes, made wise choices in lifestyles, and managed to avoid misfortune.

When you consider what it takes to become old, then you realize that, indeed, these people have some special characteristics. This fact has implications for the way that we make sense out of scientific data on human aging. All older people are survivors of the conditions that took away the lives of others. With increasing age

TABLE 1-1
Five Ways to Shorten Your Life

The Centers for Disease Prevention and Control regards these five behaviors as the major obstacles that prevent people from living a longer and healthier life

1	Being overweight
2	Drinking and driving
3	Eating inadequate amounts of fruit and vegetables
4	Being physically inactive
5	Smoking

Source: Kamimoto, Easton, Maurice, Husten & Macera, 1999.

into later life, they become even more select on important characteristics such as physical functioning, health, intelligence, and probably even personality style. Consequently, if you are looking at the differences between younger and older people on any given characteristic, you should realize that the older people are a more restricted (and perhaps superior) group than the younger ones. The younger ones have not been subjected yet to the same conditions that could threaten their lives.

A concrete example might help illustrate this principle. Consider the data on the psychological characteristic of cautiousness. Many studies have found that older people are less likely to take risks than are younger people. Along similar lines, older adults are also less likely to engage in criminal behavior. Why is this? One possibility is that people do in fact learn to moderate their behavior as they get older. They choose not to engage in behaviors that will bring them harm or get them arrested. The other possibility is that the high risk-takers are no longer in the population because their risky behavior led to an early accidental death. The criminals are no longer in the population for study because they were either killed in their professional exploits or were imprisoned and could no longer commit these acts. These examples are worth keeping in mind as you read about some of the subtler age-related "changes" in behavior reported as associated with the aging process.

Individual Differences Must Be Recognized

A long-held myth regarding development in adulthood and old age is that as people age, their individuality fades as the aging process takes its toll on the body and the mind. This view is refuted by this third principle of adult development and aging: that as people grow older, they become more different, not more alike. Middle-aged and especially older adults are a highly diverse segment of the population in terms of their physical functioning, psychological performance, and conditions of living. Supporting this point, in one study researchers examined a large number of studies of aging and compared the amount of variability in measures of older compared to younger adults. The researchers found that the variability was far greater in measures taken from older adults, suggesting increasing diversity over the adult years (Nelson & Dannefer, 1992).

This finding of increasing diversity with age in adulthood points to the importance of experiences in adulthood as shaping development. As people get older, their lives diverge increasingly from one another because of the many choice points that are offered to them and the many different choices they make. They may have gone to college or not gone to college, they may have joined the Army or not joined the Army, they may have moved to New York City or landed in Wichita, Kansas. They may have gotten married or not, had children or not, and as a result, they might have had grandchildren

or not. Even little decisions can affect later outcomes in life, such as whether one chooses to go out to a movie on a stormy night and perhaps ends up with a broken leg after the car skids through an intersection. The possibilities in life are endless, and as a result, each individual's personal history moves in increasingly idiosyncratic directions with each passing day, year, and decade of life.

The principle that people become more different from each other with age relates to the notion of **inter-individual differences**. Another aspect of the principle of individual differences relates to differences within the individual, or **intra-individual differences**. This principle is also referred to as the **multidirectionality of development** (Baltes & Graf, 1996). According to this principle, not all systems develop at the same rate within the person—over time some functions may show positive changes; and others, negative changes. Even within the same

United States Senator and astronaut John Glenn, training for his flight on the Space Shuttle Discovery in October 1998 at the age of 77. At the time of the mission, Glenn was by far the world's oldest astronaut. This was clearly a non-normative event.

function, such as intelligence, the same individual may show gains in one area, losses in another, and stability in yet a third domain.

One important and very intriguing consequence of the principle of individual differences is that it is possible to find older adults whose performance on a given measure is superior to that of younger people. Average-age college students may think that they can run faster, lift heavier weights, or solve crossword puzzles faster than a person two or three times their age. However, a middle-aged or older adult who exercises and remains active may very well be quicker, stronger, and mentally more adept than a sedentary or inactive younger person. There is no reason for all functions to "go downhill" as people get older.

"Normal" Aging Is Different from Disease

The fourth principle of adult development is the need to differentiate among **normal**, **impaired**, and **optimal** aging (Rowe & Kahn, 1987). A set of normal aging changes built into the hardwiring of the organism occur more or less in all individuals (although at different rates) and are different from those changes associated with disease. **Impaired aging** implies the existence of changes that result from diseases and do not occur in all individuals. Optimal aging is also called "successful aging." This concept implies that the individual has avoided changes that would otherwise occur with age through preventative and compensatory strategies.

Another term for normal aging is **primary aging**, referring to age-related changes that are universal, intrinsic, and progressive. The term **secondary aging** is then used to refer to changes that are due to disease (Aldwin & Gilmer, 1999). The basis for this distinction is the need to differentiate between normal age-related changes that occur throughout life and

the disease or diseases that eventually cause death by leading a vital life function to shut down. Many people remain healthy well into their later adult years, acquiring the disease that ends their life only close to the time of their death.

It is important for practical as well as scientific reasons to distinguish between normal aging and disease. Practitioners who work with middle-aged and older adults must be able to recognize and treat a disease when it occurs rather than attribute it to the normal aging process or simply "getting older." For example, a 60-year-old adult who suffers from symptoms of depression can be successfully treated but only if the practitioner is aware that the symptoms of depression are not simply a feature of normal aging. Personality development in adulthood does not inevitably lead to symptoms of lowered self-esteem, excessive guilt, changes in appetite, or lack of interest in activities. If a clinician mistakenly thinks that these symptoms are part of the aging process, he or she will fail to provide the necessary therapy that could ultimately alleviate the depressed person's suffering.

THE MEANING OF AGE

What does chronological age represent? It is simply the difference between the date of our birth and the present date, usually measured in years. Our society uses this number to describe us because it is convenient to calculate, but what does it actually mean? After all, chronological age is a number based on events in the universe that occur independently of events inside our body. If you think even further about the meaning of age, you come to the realization that age, like time, is a purely human invention. Scientists on our planet have decided to use seconds, minutes, days, weeks, and years as the way to segment units of the dimension called time, but these numbers are in some ways arbitrary. Our bodies do not "keep time" in these units, and although some of our biological functions do seem to operate according to an internal clock, we don't know yet if these functions have anything to do with the aging process or with changes that take place over many years. To say that chronological age (or time) "means" anything with regard to the status of our body's functioning is, based on current questionable evidence.

Using Age to Define "Adult"

One of the most difficult words to define is the very basic term "adult." As indicated at the very opening of this chapter, this term is synonymous with the word "mature." We assume that a person who has become an adult has achieved some degree of full-fledged growth. When we think of the term "mature," we might think of an apple that is ready to be eaten or a dog that is no longer a puppy. Fortunately or unfortunately, people are not like apples or dogs, and the point of reaching maturity is much harder to quantify.

We cannot use physical maturity alone as a criterion for maturity because then we might consider a 15-year-old or even a 13-year-old who has reached full physical growth to be an adult. Can we use some other criterion based on ability? This might lead us to use the age of 16 years, which is when people can legally drive. Alternatively, maturity in the eyes of the U.S. government is 18 because that is when a person is eligible to vote. However, states may use other criteria for adulthood, such as the "age of consent," which is when a person can marry without the consent of a parent. In South Carolina, this is 14, but in most other states it is 16 or 18. Alternatively, the age of 21 years may be the final mark of maturity because that is when

it is legal to drink in most states in the U.S. However, it may seem inappropriate or unjustifiable to consider the age of legal drinking as an overall criterion of adulthood.

Because of all these contradictory definitions, it might be wise to recommend that the age given as the crossing-over point into adulthood depends on the individual's having reached the chronological age that has associated with it the expectations and privileges of a given society or subculture. For example, in a particular state, individuals may be considered to have reached adulthood at the age when they are eligible to vote, drink, drive, and get married. In that state, the age of 21 would be considered the threshold to adulthood. In another state, these criteria may be reached at the age of 18. In any case, the first three or four years of adulthood represent a transition prior to assuming the responsibilities associated with adulthood. These may either be the years that follow college graduation or, for those individuals who are not in college, more quickly as they face the need to find full employment or make family commitments.

Divisions by Age of the Over-65 Population

Traditionally, 65 years of age has been seen as the entry point for "old age." However, it is being increasingly recognized that those individuals who are close to the age of 65 face some very different issues and challenges than those who are close to the age of 85 or older. These issues and challenges relate mainly to the quality of physical functioning and health, but they also involve different economic constraints and social opportunities. The demarcations, then, are **young-old**, which incorporates ages 65 to 74, **old-old**, which includes ages 75 to 84, and **oldest-old**, or ages 85 and older. A person does not magically shift on the seventy-fifth birthday, of course. However, there is an understanding in this system that some changes will become apparent within a year or two of that birthday that may lead to some significant changes in functioning. Furthermore, even if the use of precise age categories may seem arbitrary, it is considered advantageous to have some type of categorization system. These demarcations draw attention to the need to differentiate among the older population rather than to place them all in one category. They also have implications for planning policy decisions regarding older adults. For example, as will be discussed in Chapter 12, the majority of individuals who receive home health services are between the ages of 75 and 84. They are in need of assistance to maintain themselves but are nevertheless able to live independently in the community.

Alternative Indices of Age

As an alternative to chronological age, researchers have suggested indices of age based on specific aspects of functioning. Using this system, we would find that an individual may have more than one "age," based on each of these indices. The advantage of using these alternative indices of aging would be that the individual would be more accurately characterized than through the simple chronological system used now. Many people use these indices informally when talking about other people, as when you say that someone is "young for her age."

The quality of functioning of the individual's organ systems would be used to determine **biological age**. Standards of performance on various biological measures for an individual can be compared to the age norms for those measures. For example, a 50-year-old may have the blood pressure values of those in the 25–30 segment of the population and therefore would have a youthful biological age on that measure.

> ### "What do you think?" 1-2
>
> How could the alternative indices of age be implemented in a practical sense so that they would replace chronological age?

A similar logic would form the basis for calculating **psychological age**, which represents the quality of an individual's functioning on psychological measures such as intelligence, memory, and learning ability. People would be classified according to their abilities to perform cognitive tasks, which are important aspects of functioning in everyday life. Since such performance is known to be affected by the aging process, an index of psychological age would accurately characterize a person's ability to meet the cognitive demands of the environment.

The third component of the equation for calculating age according to alternative indices would be **social age**-characterization of a person's age based on occupying certain social roles. Social age would take into account the person's family, work, and possibly community roles. For example, a grandparent would have an older social age than would a parent, although the grandparent might be chronologically younger than the parent. Similarly, a retiree would have an older social age than would a person still working.

As previously stated, the advantage of using these alternative indices of aging would be that the individual would be more accurately characterized than through the chronological system currently used. However, a major disadvantage is the fact that these indices require frequent upgrading to make sure that they are still accurate. For example, a biological index based in part on blood pressure may have to be adjusted as successive generations change in the distribution of values. In the area of social age, the fact that there are diverse subcultures within a single society means that social age has to be defined according to the particular group of which the individual is a part. Furthermore, given the fact that people are making major life decisions based on their own expectations of what is appropriate rather than by what society believes, social age may be becoming increasingly irrelevant. With all its faults, chronological age may be the more expedient index for most uses.

Personal versus Social Aging

Researchers in developmental psychology face the challenge of attempting to separate processes intrinsic to the individual theorized to be responsible for changes in behavior over time from changes due to exposure to events in the world. Changes within the individual are referred to as **personal aging**, or more formally, *ontogenetic* change (with *onto* referring to being, and *genesis* to development). Theoretically, it should be possible to isolate the changes within the cells of the individual's body that are tied to alterations with time in structure and function. This process would then lead to an understanding of the inherent nature of aging.

However, people exist within the context of their societies, and therefore changes that occur in societies over time can have an impact on the individuals within those societies. Changes in societies over time are responsible for the process of **social aging**, in which people change along with or perhaps as the result of historical change. Factors extrinsic to the individual can cause direct changes in the individual or can interact with personal aging. For example, as people are exposed to improvements in health care and education over their lifetimes, their rate of personal aging may slow down because they are able to take advantage of preventative strategies, such as avoiding the poor health habits listed in Table 1-1.

The term "normative," as used in this categorization system, implies that the influence is one that occurs as the "norm"—in other words, that it is expected to happen in the lives of the majority of individuals within a given culture or society. Normative changes, then, are those that happen to most people within that social group. Nonnormative changes are those that are idiosyncratic to the life of the individual. Combining the concepts of normative and nonnormative influences specific to the individual and more general to historical time provides a set of three interacting systems of influence that regulate the nature of life-span development. These influences, developed by the influential psychologist Paul Baltes (1979), are normative age-graded influences, normative history-graded influences, and nonnormative influences.

The first set of normative influences to consider is in some ways the easiest to understand in relation to age. They are the **normative age-graded influences** on life that lead individuals to choose certain experiences that their culture and historical period attach to certain ages or points in the life span. In Western society, individuals are affected by normative age-graded influences that lead them to graduate from college in the early 20s, get married at some later point, begin a family in the 20s or 30s, retire in their 60s, and become grandparents in their middle to later years. We expect that people will have these experiences at these ages because most people do, and we do not think it is unusual when they happen. These expectable life events may not occur to everyone, but when they do, they are typically associated with certain ages.

Events that occur in response to normative age-graded influences occur in part because a given society has developed expectations about what is desirable for people of certain ages. The decision to retire at the age of 65 years can be seen as a response to the norm regarding when it is appropriate and desirable to leave the labor market. Graduation from high school occurs at about the age of 18 years for most people because in our society, children start school at the age of 5 or 6, and the educational system is based on 12 grades. Biological factors also play a role in the optimal timing of certain events, however, such as parenthood, which has traditionally been limited to the years between 20 and 40, at the peak of a woman's years of fertility. Some normative age-graded events set the pattern for later events to occur in response, so that if an adult becomes a parent at the age of 30, a lower limit is set on the age at which he or she can become a grandparent. If the child also follows a normative age-graded influence, the parent will become a grandparent for the first time somewhere between the ages of 55 and 65 years.

Normative age-graded influences are associated, then, with the life span of the individual, even though they may reflect environmental or social factors. By contrast, influences that transcend the individual's life and are associated with changes in society as a whole are referred to as **normative history-graded influences**. These are events that occur to everyone within a certain culture or geopolitical unit and include large-scale occurrences such as world wars, economic trends, or sociocultural changes in attitudes and values. The impact of these events on people's lives may be felt immediately, but they can have continuing impact for many years on subsequent patterns of work, family, and quality of life (Elder, Shanahan, & Clipp, 1994). For example, men who entered the military after their families were already established were more likely upon their return to get divorced or separated, suffer career setbacks, and even experience poorer physical health after they turned 50. Interestingly, however, men who entered the military at a younger age were more positively affected and returned to their civilian lives with improved chances for success in all areas of experience through the middle adult years.

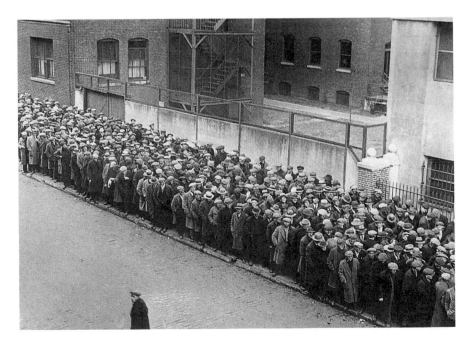

During the Depression of the 1930's, it was common for large numbers of unemployed to wait in long lines to be served a free dinner.

In some cases, these influences may be specific to a particular part of the world, such as the winter 2003 floods in Mozambique that affected 100,000 people. In other cases, the event may occur in one part of a country but have an impact on the nation as a whole, such as the September 11, 2001, World Trade Center attacks. The historical events may not even directly affect the individual, but they may have an indirect influence by virtue of the changes they stimulate in social awareness, anxiety, or sensitivity. For example, similar personality changes over time that outweighed individual differences were observed in a longitudinal study of adolescents who were exposed to the turmoil of the Vietnam years in the late 1960s and early 1970s (Nesselroade & Baltes, 1974). Such findings point to the importance of contextual factors in influencing the course of development and add substance to the point made earlier regarding the need to look beyond the individual's immediate environment.

If the course of life were influenced only by the two types of normative changes just examined, it would be very easy to predict the route of development taken by people of the same age living in the same culture. However, each individual's life is also affected by random, chance factors that occur due to a combination of coincidence, the impact of earlier decisions made on later events, and relationships with other people. Little is written about these **nonnormative influences** in the developmental literature because there is virtually no way of predicting their occurrence. Developmentalists can only observe these phenomena when they occur and then attempt to draw generalizations about the impact of certain unpredictable life events on individuals more or less after the fact.

Examples of nonnormative influences include events that have an effect on subsequent life paths. Some are due to good luck, such as winning the lottery or making a smart investment.

Anne Martindell, Smith College's oldest graduate at the age of 87. For Martindell, college graduation at this age was definitely a non-normative event.

It is not just that one may become wealthier as the result of these events, but that one's life may take a different turn because the money makes certain activities possible. For instance, a lottery winner might make a few thousand dollars that she decides to spend on a vacation. On that vacation, she might have experiences that change her life after she returns. Maybe she takes up a new hobby or makes a permanent change in her lifestyle, such as exercising more or eating different foods. Nonnormative influences can also be negative, such as a car accident, a fire, or the accidental death of a relative. One moment a person's life is normal, and the next moment everything is ruined. Other nonnormative influences may unfold over a gradual period, such as being fired from one's job (due to personal reasons), developing a chronic illness not related to aging, or getting divorced.

As you were reading about these three types of influences on life, surely you were also thinking about ways that they may interact with each other. Consider the example of getting divorced. Although society's norms are changing, many would still consider this a nonnormative event because the norm (and certainly the hope) of married couples is to remain married. And although it is a very personal occurrence, a divorce may be seen in part as a response to larger social forces. Social-historical changes that have sensitized one of the marital partners to problematic areas within the marriage may give the individual the impetus to seek an end to the relationship. The wife may realize that her husband's resistance to her seeking outside employment has restricted her independence, or, conversely, the husband may wish that his wife would become more independent like the women he knows at work. In either case, the sensitivity of a partner in the relationship to such social issues may lead to a decision that permanently alters the course of the lives of all people involved including, of course, the children.

It is also interesting to consider what happens when individuals have experiences that would normatively occur at one age but instead occur at a different age. In a sense these are "nonnormative," because, although they are normative events, they have happened at an age when most people do not experience them. Such is the case when an individual marries for the first time in late adulthood, becomes a grandparent at age 30, enters the job market at age 60, or retires at age 18. Examples of such nonnormative events are often the basis for human interest stories in the news, and some of these can have wide-ranging impact. Consider the 1997 case of the California woman who gave birth to her first child when she was 63 years old. This event aroused interest all over the world and not a small degree of controversy. People were amazed that such a seemingly impossible act could be accomplished, but the event also raised issues of whether it was "right" for a woman of such advanced years to bring a child into the world. Interestingly, this occurred at about the same time that an even older man, the actor Tony Randall, became a first-time father at the age of 77 years.

He was the target of far less criticism from the media, reflecting perhaps the interaction of normative beliefs regarding gender roles with those regarding age.

SOCIAL FACTORS IN ADULT DEVELOPMENT AND AGING

The study of adult development and aging involves an understanding of concepts that describe the characteristics of individuals according to certain social factors or indicators. Along with age, these social factors help to shape the structures of opportunities available to people throughout their lives.

Sex and Gender

The term **gender** refers to the individual's identification as being male or female. It is generally considered distinct from a person's biological **sex**, which typically refers to an individual's anatomy. Both sex and gender are important in the study of adult development and aging.

Physiological factors relevant to sex influence the timing and nature of physical aging processes, primarily through the operation of sex hormones (see Chapter 4). For example, the female sex hormone estrogen is thought to play at least some role for premenopausal women in lowering the risks of heart disease, bone loss, and cognitive changes.

Social and cultural factors relevant to gender are important to the extent that the individual assumes a certain role in society based on being viewed as a male or female. Opportunities in education and employment are the main areas in which gender influences the course of adult development. Although improvements have occurred in both of these domains, women nevertheless face a restricted range of choices and the prospects of lower earnings than do men. Furthermore, these differences were particularly likely to have affected older cohorts who were raised in an era with more traditional gender expectations than currently exist.

Race

A person's **race** is defined in biological terms as the classification within species based on physical and structural characteristics. However, the concept of race as commonly used is broader than these biological features. Race has come to be used in a broad fashion to refer to the cultural background associated with being born within a particular biologically defined segment of the population. The "race" that a person uses to identify himself or herself is more likely to be socially than biologically determined. In addition, because few people are purely of one race in a biological sense, social and cultural background factors assume even greater prominence. The U.S. Census 2000 used a similar approach in characterizing race on the basis of a person's self-identification. In addition to using race, the census also included categories based on national origin, shown in Table 1-2.

To the extent that race is biologically determined, however, racial differences in functioning in adulthood and aging may reflect differences in genetic inheritance. People who have inherited a risk factor that has been found to be higher within a certain race are more likely to be at risk for developing that illness during their adult years. Racial differences in risk factors may also interact with different cultural backgrounds associated with a particular race. For example, people with a high risk factor for a disease with a metabolic basis (such as inability to metabolize fats) will be more likely to develop that disease depending on whether high-fat foods are a part of their culture.

Social and cultural aspects of race may also alter an individual's development in adulthood through the structure of a society and based on whether there are systematic biases against people who identify with that race. As will be shown repeatedly throughout this book, health problems and mortality rates are higher for African Americans than for whites. Part of the differences in health may be attributed to lack of opportunities for education and well-paying jobs, but it is thought that systematic discrimination also takes its toll on health by increasing the levels of stress experienced by African Americans (Clark, Anderson, Clark, & Williams, 1999).

Ethnicity

The concept of **ethnicity** captures the cultural background of an individual, reflecting the predominant values, attitudes, and expectations in which the individual has been raised. Along with race, ethnicity is often studied in adult development and aging as an influence on a person's family attitudes and experiences. For example, people of certain ethnic backgrounds are thought to show greater respect for older adults and feel a stronger sense of obligation to care for their aging parents (discussed in Chapter 9). Ethnicity also may play a role in influencing the aging of various physiological functions, in part through genetic inheritance and in part through exposure to cultural habits and traditions. Finally, discrimination against people of certain ethnic backgrounds may serve the same function as race in limiting the opportunities for educational and occupational achievements.

"What do you think?"	*1-3*

Do you feel that your ethnicity is an important influence on your development?

TABLE 1-2
Racial Categories used in the U.S. Census 2000

Racial category	Definition
White	A person having origins in any of the original peoples of Europe, the Middle East, or North Africa. It includes people who indicate their race as "White" or report entries such as Irish, German, Italian, Lebanese, Near Easterner, Arab, or Polish.
Black or African-American	A person having origins in any of the black racial groups of Africa. It includes people who indicate their race as "Black, African American, or Negro," or provide written entries such as African American, Afro American, Kenyan, Nigerian, or Haitian.
Hispanic or Latino	People who identify with the terms "Hispanic" or "Latino" are those who classify themselves in one of the specific Hispanic or Latino categories listed on the questionnaire—"Mexican," "Puerto Rican," or "Cuban"—as well as those who indicate that they are "other Spanish, Hispanic, or Latino." Origin can be viewed as the heritage, nationality group, lineage, or country of birth of the person or the person's parents or ancestors before their arrival in the United States. People who identify their origin as Spanish, Hispanic, or Latino may be of any race.
American Indian and Alaska Native	A person having origins in any of the original peoples of North and South America (including Central America), and who maintain tribal affiliation or community attachment.
Asian	A person having origins in any of the original peoples of the Far East, Southeast Asia, or the Indian subcontinent including, for example, Cambodia, China, India, Japan, Korea, Malaysia, Pakistan, the Philippine Islands, Thailand, and Vietnam. It includes "Asian Indian," "Chinese," "Filipino," "Korean," "Japanese," "Vietnamese," and "Other Asian."
Native Hawaiian and Other Pacific Islander	A person having origins in any of the original peoples of Hawaii, Guam, Samoa, or other Pacific Islands. It includes people who indicate their race as "Native Hawaiian," "Guamanian or Chamorro," "Samoan," and "Other Pacific Islander."
Some Other Race	Includes all other responses not included in the "White," "Black or African American," "American Indian and Alaska Native," "Asian," and the "Native Hawaiian and Other Pacific Islander" race categories described above. Respondents providing write-in entries such as multiracial, mixed, interracial, or a Hispanic/Latino group (for example, Mexican, Puerto Rican, or Cuban) in the "Some other race" category are included in this category.
Two or More Races	People may have chosen to provide two or more races either by checking two or more race response check boxes, by providing multiple write-in responses, or by some combination of check boxes and write-in responses. "Two or more races" refers to combinations of two or more of the following race categories: • White • Black or African American • American Indian and Alaska Native • Asian • Native Hawaiian and Other Pacific Islander • Some other race

Source: U.S. Bureau of the Census, 2001f

Socioeconomic Status

An individual's **socioeconomic status**, or "social class," is a function of level of education and level of occupation. Various researchers have developed scales of socioeconomic status (Featherman & Stevens, 1982). Although the exact calculations may vary, these scales weight some combination of education and occupational level in ranking people from low to high. Higher education and a higher level of occupation, in terms of prestige and status, contribute to a higher socioeconomic status. Income levels are not necessarily associated with socioeconomic status because high-prestige jobs (such as teacher) often are associated with mid- or even low-level salaries.

Along with race, socioeconomic status has a strong association with health in adulthood. Race and socioeconomic status are clearly related, particularly for African Americans, who tend to have lower socioeconomic status. Attempts to partial out the contributions of these factors in the equation become very complicated (Clark et al., 1999), particularly when age and gender are added to the mix. However, education is associated with greater access to information about health care and more opportunities to take advantage of preventative measures. Consequently, it is thought that socioeconomic status contributes independently to the prediction of health and physical functioning in adulthood.

Religion

Although relatively uninvestigated, **religion**, which is an individual's identification with an organized belief system, is being given increasing attention as a factor influencing development in adulthood. Organized religions form an alternative set of social structures that is at least partly connected with race and ethnicity. More importantly, however, from the standpoint of aging, for many people religion provides a source of coping strategies, social support in

times of crisis, and a systematic basis for interpreting one's life experiences (George, 2000; Van Ness & Larson, 2002).

THE BABY BOOMERS GROW UP: CHANGES IN THE MIDDLE-AGED AND OLDER POPULATIONS IN THE UNITED STATES AND THE WORLD

The age structure of the U.S. population, shown in Fig. 1.2, provides a quick snapshot of the current distribution of males and females in the country. In this figure, the number of people (in millions) by sex for each 5-year age group is depicted in the bars along the middle axis. The comparison of the 1990 and 2000 census estimates, shown in this figure, reveal two interesting facts. First, there is a "bulge" in the middle of this structure, reflecting the **baby boom** generation of people who were born between 1945 and 1964. Second, comparison of the 1990 and 2000 census figures shows that the biggest population increases have been for the age groups between 40 and 54. As this bulge continues to move upward, this generation will have a continued impact on the nature of society, as indeed it already has.

The number of Americans over the age of 65 years grew from 3.1 million in 1900 (about 4% of the population) to 35.3 million in the year 2001, equaling 12.4% of the total U.S. population (see Fig. 1.3). This number is estimated to rise to 70.3 million by the year 2030, or 20% of the total U.S. population (U.S. Bureau of the Census, 2003). The highest rate of increase within the 65 and older population is of the oldest-old, those who are 85 years of age and older. This age group is projected to increase from 4.4 million now (1.5% of the total U.S. population) to 8.9 million (2.5% of the population) by 2030 and even higher, to 19.4 million, by 2050 (4.8% of the population). The oldest group of people, **centenarians** (people

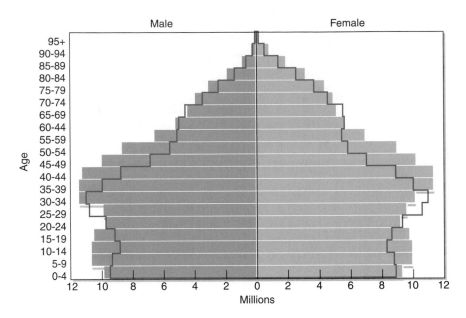

Source: Meyer J. (2001).

FIGURE 1.2

Age-sex structure in U.S. Census 2000

100 and older) will actually be the fastest growing of all older age groups (see Fig. 1.4). In 1990, it was estimated that there were 37,306 centenarians in the U.S. By 2000 this number increased by 35% to 50,545 (Administration on Aging, 2001a) and by 2050, there will be 1.1 million centenarians (0.3% of the population) (U.S. Bureau of the Census, 2003a).

The major reason for these large increases in the 65 and older population is the movement of the Baby Boomers through the years of middle and later adulthood. However, it is not just that those people were born but that they are expected to continue to live into their 80s, 90s, and 100s, and hence will increase the numbers of very-old individuals well into the twenty-first century. Such

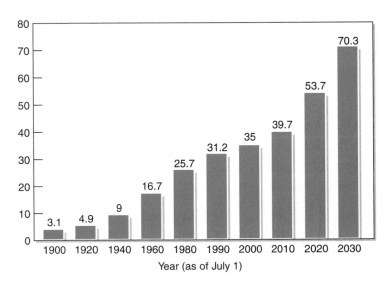

FIGURE 1.3

Growth of the 65+ Population in the United States

Source: Administration on Aging (2003).

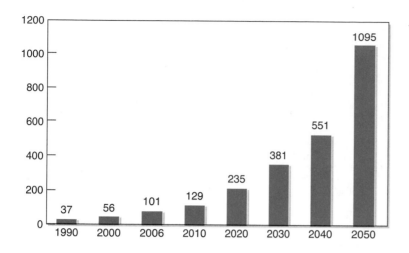

FIGURE 1.4
Projected Growth of Centenarians in the United States

Source: U.S Bureau of the Census, 2001e (Krach and Veloff, 1999).

increases represent huge gains in **life expectancy**, the average number of years of life remaining to the people born within a similar period of time. The values of life expectancy for a given year are based on a given set of age-specific death rates, generally the mortality conditions existing in the period mentioned. Life expectancy may be determined by race, sex, or other characteristics using age-specific death rates for the population with that characteristic. Life expectancy from birth rose overall from 62.9 years in 1940 to 77.2 years in 2001. Many factors have contributed to increases in life expectancy, including reduced death rates for children and young adults. In addition, however, people are living longer once they make it to age 65, with the life expectancy from age 65 (which is always higher than life expectancy from birth) estimated to be about 18 years (Arias, Anderson, Kung, Murphy, and Kochanek, 2003).

"What do you think?"   **1-4**

What do you think the world will be like when you are 65?

Within the United States, the population is aging at a differential rate of growth. As shown in Fig. 1.5, there are higher proportions of individuals over the age of 65 clustered in certain states. As of 2000, slightly over one-half of persons 65 and over lived in nine states. The city with the highest proportion of people over 65 is Clearwater, Florida, where 21% of the population is 65 or older. The high percentages in the Midwest reflect the migration of younger adults from rural areas to more populous areas, leaving relatively higher numbers of older people behind. Between the years 1990 and 2000, the population of people 65 and over increased by 14% or more in 11 states: Nevada, Alaska, Hawaii, Arizona, Utah, Colorado, New Mexico, Wyoming, Delaware, North Carolina, and Texas. You may wonder why California does not show up as having a high percentage of adults over 65. This is because older people are the most numerous in this state, but they are not as large a proportion of the total population. It is also interesting that a state such as Florida, associated with large numbers of retirees, has a percentage of over-65 similar to that of some midwestern states (Administration on Aging, 2004). This population continues to increase; of all the U.S. States, Florida had the highest number of people 65 and older who have migrated from other states within the United States (He & Schachter, 2003).

BEHIND THE RESEARCH

THOMAS PERLS, M.D., & MARGERY
SILVER, ED.D., HARVARD MEDICAL
SCHOOL, CENTENARIAN STUDY

What is most exciting to you about research in this field?

It's hard to pick out what's *most* exciting about exploring the boundaries of the human life span with centenarians, the pioneers of aging. They include:

Helping to change scientific and societal views of aging. Aging has too often been seen as a time of sickness, and inevitable dementia. The discovery that people can be physically and cognitively healthy at the age of 100 is turning this perception around.

Helping to change the idea that extreme old age is to be dreaded to the sense that it can be a time not only of health, but enjoyable pursuits and meaningful relationships.

Learning from the study of 100-year-olds the factors that have enabled them to live the majority of their lives in good health. Although not all of us have the genetic endowment to live to 100, these factors can help people to live to their maximum aging potential in good health.

Getting to know wonderful individuals, who are exemplars of healthy aging and who demonstrate that the self is ageless.

Learning from the centenarians that we have the potential for many more productive, satisfying years after age 65. This means that we have to rethink traditional ideas about retirement and how we want to spend these bonus years.

What do you see as the major challenges?

The greatest challenges arise from the fact that this is a new research population. Until recently, there were few centenarians to study. Now, with 100-year-olds representing the fastest growing population group—and with 3 million Baby Boomers living to be 100—it is important to know about a group that will have

such an impact on society. And there are now plenty of them to study.

Also, the study of the extreme old is pioneering research, tests are not generally designed for them, and there is little normative data available. This makes differentiating between what is cognitive aging and what is disease more difficult and adds a greater degree of complexity and difficulty to cognitive research with the extreme old. A similar challenge is presented in evaluating the impact of genetic factors versus lifestyle/psychological factors.

Where do you see this field headed in the next decade?

There is burgeoning interest in the field, in response to the demographic realities of a larger and larger population of centenarians and the "oldest old," those over 85. This will draw more and more researchers into the field. With increased research activity, it is likely there will be very major findings regarding how the aging process is slowed in centenarians—or how they avoid diseases associated with aging, either through genetic inheritance or psychological/lifestyle factors.

Even more importantly, the visibility of a much larger group of centenarians to show the possibilities of remaining physically and cognitively healthy will begin to change the stereotypes of old age, drawing more researchers and changing public views of aging. This change will reduce ageism and at the same time have a far-reaching impact on the development of new products that are "elder friendly," as well as how they are advertised and how older people are portrayed in the media.

FIGURE 1.5

Percentage of 65+ Population by State

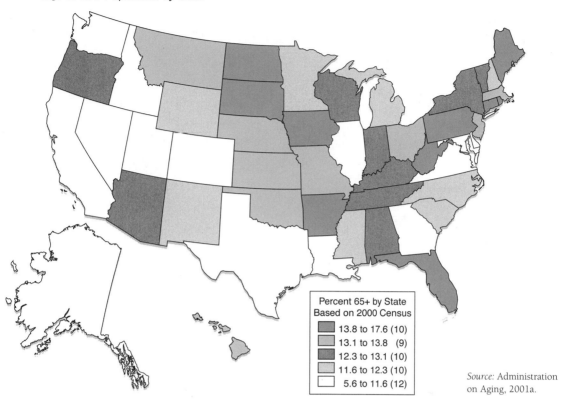

Percent 65+ by State
Based on 2000 Census

- 13.8 to 17.6 (10)
- 13.1 to 13.8   (9)
- 12.3 to 13.1 (10)
- 11.6 to 12.3 (10)
- 5.6 to 11.6 (12)

Source: Administration
on Aging, 2001a.

Women over age 65 currently outnumber men, amounting to about 59% of the total over-65 population. The "gender gap" widens for those in the 85 and over category, with 71% females and 29% males, and extends even further to 79% females of all those over 100 compared with 21% males (Krach & Veloff, 1999; Meyer, 2001). Thus, with each older group of individuals over age 65, the imbalance between females and males grows even greater. This disparity between the genders is expected to diminish by 2030, when the Baby Boomers reach advanced old age. At that time, there will be 56% females and 44% males in the total over-65 population, and 64% females and 36% males among those over age 85 (U.S. Bureau of the Census, 2001e).

Changes are also occurring in the distribution of white and minority segments of the population (see Fig. 1.6). According to the U.S. Census 2000, about 16% of the over-65 population was made up of members of racial and ethnic minorities, but this number will rise to 36% by 2050. The Hispanic population of older adults is expected to grow at the fastest rate, increasing from less than 2 million in 2000 to more than 13 million by 2050. It is expected that by 2028, the Hispanic population will outnumber non-Hispanic blacks in the 65-plus age group (Adminstration on Aging, 2002).

The statistics from around the world confirm the picture of an increasingly older population in the twenty-first century. As of 2000, there were 420 million people worldwide over

FIGURE 1.6

Changes in the Racial and Ethnic Composition of U.S. Population, 2000–2050

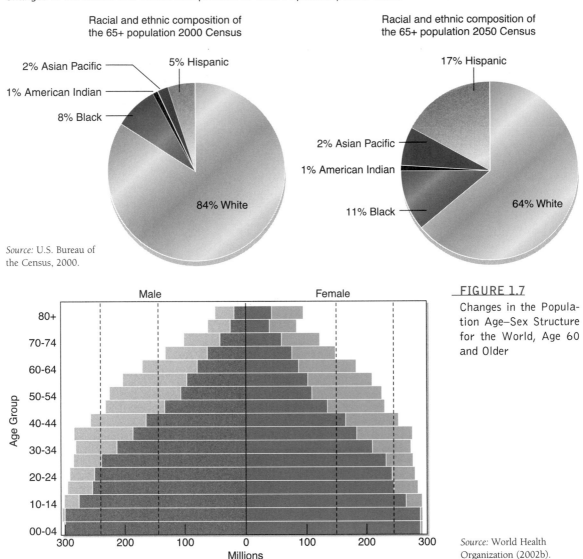

Racial and ethnic composition of the 65+ population 2000 Census

2% Asian Pacific
1% American Indian
8% Black
5% Hispanic
84% White

Source: U.S. Bureau of the Census, 2000.

Racial and ethnic composition of the 65+ population 2050 Census

17% Hispanic
2% Asian Pacific
1% American Indian
11% Black
64% White

Male   Female

Age Group: 80+, 70-74, 60-64, 50-54, 40-44, 30-34, 20-24, 10-14, 00-04

Millions: 300, 200, 100, 0, 100, 200, 300

FIGURE 1.7

Changes in the Population Age–Sex Structure for the World, Age 60 and Older

Source: World Health Organization (2002b).

age 65, and their numbers are increasing by about 800,000 each month (Kinsella & Veloff, 2001). The United Nations, which uses the age of 60 as the cutoff for defining the aging population, estimated that in 2000 there were 629 million people worldwide who fit into this age bracket and that the number will rise precipi-

tously to over 1.9 billion by 2050 (United Nations, 2002). These changes are reflected in Fig. 1.7, which contrasts the 1995 age–sex structure with that projected for 2025.

World population statistics are often reported in terms of "more developed" and "less developed" countries or "developing" countries.

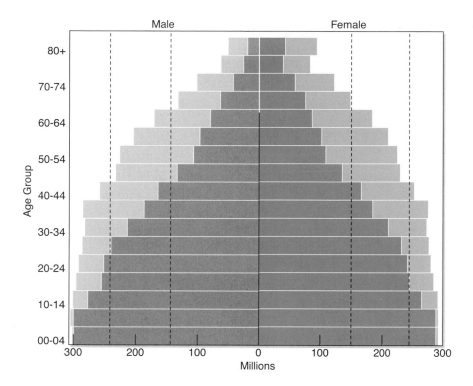

FIGURE 1.8

Changes in the Proportion of 65+ in Developed versus Developing Nations

The more developed countries represent the industrialized nations, and the less developed countries are those that have an agrarian-based economy, typically with low levels of health care, education, and income. As can be seen in Fig. 1.8, projections of world population trends estimate that the proportion of the population of adults 65 years and over living in the less developed countries will rise disproportionately between now and the year 2050. Although Italy now has the highest percentage of individuals 65 and older (18.1%), it will show about 5% to 10% of the growth in older adults as developing countries such as Singapore, Malaysia, and Colombia. In these countries, the older populations will grow to about triple the size they were in 2000 (Kinsella & Veloff, 2001).

What are the implications of these figures for your future as you move into your adult years? First, you will be more likely to have friends and associates to socialize with than is true of the current older population. And if you are a man, the news is encouraging: You will be more likely to live into old age than was true for current cohorts of older adults. For those of you who are younger than the Baby Boomers, the statistics are encouraging if you are considering a career related to the field of aging: The older clientele is definitely going to be on the increase. Changes in various aspects of lifestyle can also be expected in the next decades, as adjustments are made to an aging population in the entertainment world and the media. Just as we are getting used to the idea of an aging Mick Jagger, many others will follow in his footsteps to change the way we regard prominent celebrities in Western society and indeed, around the world.

Assess Yourself

Are you a Baby Boomer?

This is one of many e-mails that people in their 40s and 50s send to each other, containing a "Baby Boomer Trivia Quiz." See how you do on these questions:

The Age Test—NO cheating by skipping to the answers!

1. Name the Beatles.

   _____

   _____

   _____

   _____

2. Finish the line: "Lions and Tigers and Bears, _____ _____!"

3. "Hey kids, what time is it?" _____ _____ _____ _____!

4. What do M&M's do? _____ _____ _____ _____ _____ _____ _____ _____.

5. What helps build strong bodies 12 ways? _____ _____.

6. Long before he was Mohammed Ali, we knew him as _____ _____.

7. You'll wonder where the yellow went, _____ _____ _____ _____ _____ _____ _____.

8. Post–Baby Boomers know Bob Denver as the Skipper's "little buddy." But we know that Bob Denver is actually Dobie's closest friend, _____ G. _____.

9. M-I-C: See ya' real soon; K-E-Y: _____? _____ _____ _____ _____!

10. "Brylcream: _____ _____ _____ _____ _____."

11. Jerry Rubin advised us never to trust anyone _____ _____.

12. From the early days of our music, real rock 'n roll, finish this line: "I wonder, wonder, wonder . . . wonder who; _____ _____ _____ _____ _____ _____?"

13. And while we're remembering rock n' roll, try this one: "War . . . uh-huh,huh . . . yea; what's it good for?, _____ _____!"

Assess Yourself *(continued)*

14. Meanwhile, back home in Metropolis, Superman fights a never-ending battle for truth, justice, and _____ _____ _____.

15. He came out of the University of Alabama and became one of the best quarterbacks in the history of the NFL. He later went on to appear in a television commercial wearing women's stockings. He is Broadway _____ _____.

16. "I'm Popeye the sailor man; I'm Popeye the sailor man. I'm strong to the finish, _____ _____ _____ _____ _____. I'm Popeye the sailor man."

17. Your children probably recall that Peter Pan was recently played by Robin Williams, but we will always remember when Peter was played by _____ _____.

18. In a movie from the late 1960s, Paul Newman played Luke, a ne'er do well who was sent to a prison camp for cutting off the heads of parking meters with a pipe cutter. When he was captured after an unsuccessful attempt to escape, the camp commander (played by Strother Martin) used this experience as a lesson for the other prisoners, and explained, "What we have here, _____ _____ _____ _____ _____."

19. In 1962, a dejected politician chastised the press after losing a race for governor while announcing his retirement from politics. "Just think, you won't have _____ _____ to kick around anymore."

20. "Every morning, at the mine, you could see him arrive; He stood six foot, six, weighed 245. Kinda' broad at the shoulder, and narrow at the hip. And everybody knew you didn't give no lip, _____ _____ _____, _____ _____, _____ _____, _____ _____ _____."

21. "I found my thrill, _____ _____ _____"

22. _____ _____ said, "Good night, Mrs.Calabash, _____ _____ _____."

23. "Good night, David." " _____ _____, _____."

24. "Liar, liar, _____ _____ _____."

25. "When it's least expected, you're elected. You're the star today. _____ _____ _____ _____ _____! ."

26. It was Pogo, the comic strip character, who said, "We have met the enemy, and _____ _____ _____."

Assess Yourself (continued)

Answers:

1. John, Paul, George, Ringo
2. Oh, my
3. It's Howdy Doody Time!
4. They melt in your mouth, not in your hand.
5. Wonder Bread
6. Cassius Clay
7. when you brush your teeth with Pepsodent
8. Maynard G. Krebbs
9. Why? Because we like you.
10. A little dab'll do ya.
11. over 30
12. who wrote the book of love
13. Absolutely nothin'
14. the American way
15. Joe Namath
16. "cause I eats me spinach"
17. Mary Martin
18. is a failure to communicate
19. Richard Nixon
20. to Big John, Big John, Big John, Big Bad John
21. On Blueberry Hill
22. Jimmy Durante ... Wherever you are.
23. Good night, Chet.
24. pants on fire
25. Smile! You're on Candid Camera
26. he is us

Scoring:
24–26 correct:50+ years old
20–23 correct:40s (or 60s)
15–19 correct:30s (or 70s)
10–14 correct:20s (or 80s)
1–9 correct:You're, like, sorta a teenage dude? (or 90s)
0 correct:OVER THE HILL!! (or dead)

SUMMARY

1. This book is based on the biopsychosocial model, which regards development as a complex interaction of biological, psychological, and social processes.

2. The four principles of adult development and aging are that changes are continuous over the life span, the survivors grow old, individual differences must be recognized, and "normal" aging is different from disease. Dis-

tinctions must be drawn between primary and secondary aging.

3. It is difficult to define the term "adult," and there are many possible criteria. In this book, the age of 18 for individuals not in college and the postcollege years for individuals who attend college from 18 to 22 will serve as a rough guideline. The over-65 population is generally divided into subcategories of young-old (65–74), old-old (75–84), and oldest-old(85 and over). These divisions have

policy implications and they draw attention to the need to distinguish among those over 65. Biological, psychological, and social age all provide alternative ways to describe an individual. Personal aging refers to changes within the individual over time. Social aging can be viewed as reflecting normative age-graded influences, normative history-graded influences, and nonnormative influences.

4. Social factors that are important in the study of adult development and aging include gender, race, ethnicity, socioeconomic status, and religion.

5. The world and the United States are "graying." There are 35 million people in the United States over age 65, which constituted 12% of the total U.S. population in 2000. This number will rise to 20% by 2030. The highest growth rate in the United States is among the 45–54 population (the Baby Boomers), and there are an increasing number of centenarians. Increases in the older age groups are due to increases in life expectancy, which rose to 77.2 in 2001. About one-half of the over-65 population in the United States is clustered in nine states. Women outnumber men, a gender gap that widens with each older age category. The number of minorities in the over-65 population will rise from 16% to 36% by 2050. The largest increases in minorities will be for Hispanics. Countries around the world will show increases in the over-65 population as well, with the highest percentage of growth occurring in the developing countries.

GLOSSARY TERMS

Baby boom: generation who currently are between the ages of 35 and 54 years old, born between 1945 and 1965.

Biological age: the age of the individual based on the quality of functioning of the individual's organ systems.

Biopsychosocial perspective: a view of development as a complex interaction of biological, psychosocial, and social processes.

Ethnicity: the cultural background of an individual, reflecting the predominant values, attitudes, and expectations in which the individual has been raised.

Gender: the individual's identification as being male or female.

Identity: a composite of the individual's self-representations in biological, psychological, and social domains.

Impaired aging: processes that result from diseases that do not occur in all individuals.

Inter-individual differences: differences between individuals in developmental processes.

Intra-individual differences (also called multi-directionality of development): differences within individuals in developmental processes.

Life expectancy: the average number of years of life remaining to the people born within a similar period of time.

Multidirectionality of development: the principle that not all systems develop at the same rate within the person—over time some functions may show positive changes; and others, negative changes. Even within the same function, the same individual may show gains in one area, losses in another, and stability in yet a third domain.

Nonnormative influences: random, chance factors that occur due to a combination of coincidence, the impact of earlier decisions on later events, and relationships with other people.

Normal aging: changes built into the hard-wiring of the organism that occur more or less in all individuals (although at different rates) and are distinct from those changes associated with disease.

Normative age-graded influences: the influences on life that are linked to chronological age and associated with a society's expectations for people of a given age.

Normative history-graded influences: influences that transcend the individual's life and are associated with changes in a given culture or geopolitical unit as a whole.

Oldest-old: portion of the over-65 population ages 85 and older.

Old-old: portion of the over-65 population ages 75 to 84.

Optimal aging (also called "successful aging"): avoidance of changes that would otherwise occur with age through preventative and compensatory strategies.

Personal aging: changes occurring over time within the individual, also referred to as onto-genetic change.

Primary aging (also called normal aging): age-related changes that are universal, intrinsic, and progressive.

Psychological age: the age of the individual based on psychological measures such as intelligence, memory, and learning ability.

Race: a biological term for classifications within species based on physical and structural characteristics.

Religion: an individual's identification with an organized belief system.

Secondary aging (also called impaired aging): changes in later life that are due to disease.

Sex: the individual's biological designation as male or female.

Social age: the age of the individual based on occupying certain social roles, including family, work, and possibly community roles.

Social aging: changes in people that occur along with or perhaps as the result of historical change.

Socioeconomic status (or social class): an index of a person's position in society based on level of education and level of occupation.

Young-old: portion of the over-65 population ages 65 to 74.

Chapter Two

Models of Development: Nature and Nurture in Adulthood

"Too many people, when they get old, think that they have to live by the calendar."

John Glenn, at age 77

The study of adult development and aging has evolved as an expansion of the field of developmental psychology to incorporate the years past childhood and adolescence into a unified view of the life span. For many years, the field of developmental psychology was synonymous with the field of child development, but starting in the 1960s, the emphasis began to shift to models that would explain changes within the individual from "cradle to grave." It did not make sense to designate a point in life when people stopped developing. To a certain extent, traditional developmental psychology retains a focus on youth, but as knowledge about and interest in the adult years expands, the emphasis is slowly shifting toward a more all-encompassing view of change

(Baltes & Schaie, 1976). This shift toward understanding development as continuous from childhood through old age is reflected in the **life-span perspective** that increasingly is replacing the focus on youth.

Along with a shift from the early years of life to the middle and later portions of the life span has been an expansion of developmental psychology to include social or **contextual influences on development**. This shift arose out of the now outdated "nature versus nurture" debate concerning whether development reflected genetic inheritance ("nature") or the effects of parenting and society ("nurture"). With movement away from the "versus" in this debate, developmental psychology began to incorporate the increasing recognition that change is a function of both sets of factors. More recently, the term **developmental science** rather than "developmental psychology" has come into use to reflect the need to take a broad, interdisciplinary approach to understanding patterns of change in life (Magnusson, 1996).

"What do you think?"   **2-1**

Why is a life-span perspective necessary to understanding development in adulthood and later life?

Taking the word "psychology" out of the term "developmental science" reflects the fact that researchers and theorists wish to look at multiple factors in the individual's development. On the one hand, this means expanding the study of processes within the individual from psychological domains such as cognition and personality to areas of functioning that fall more traditionally into biology. On the other hand, the broadening of the term to developmental science means that it is no longer considered sufficient to look in the individual's immediate environment. By incorporating the study of context into development, this newer approach attempts to expand the understanding of the individual to see that individual as part of a community and society (Ford & Lerner, 1992). Furthermore, developmental scientists

assume that development involves dynamic interactions among and within each level of analysis of change, from the biological to the contextual (Lerner, 2003).

A second implication of the term "developmental science" is that the field is moving away from description of age-related changes and more and more toward attempts to explain the mechanisms or underlying processes of development. In a descriptive approach to development, researchers attempt to establish the ages at which different events occur within the individual. This approach characterized the work of the early child psychologist Arnold Gesell, who wrote books on "the child at two," "the child at three," and so on. Developmental scientists are clearly attempting to discover orderly principles underlying growth through life: the "why's" and not just the "what's."

MODELS OF INDIVIDUAL–ENVIRONMENT INTERACTIONS

Classic developmental psychology evolved around the notion that growth in childhood occurred primarily as a result of "nature." This was the assumption of some of the earliest writers who, like Gesell, believed that their task was to chronicle accurately and thoroughly the changes that occurred from birth onward. These changes, it was thought, would reflect the influence of ontogenesis, or maturational processes, as it unfolded within the child. The role of the environment (specifically the parents) was to understand this sequence of changes and then provide the right growing conditions, much as one provides water and light to a seedling. However, it was not long until the "nurture" position began to emerge among child psychologists. The founder of behaviorism, John B. Watson, claimed that a child's future could be molded entirely by the environment provided by the parents.

Models of Development

Many investigations were stimulated by the nature–nurture debate, and many findings were presented on either side to provide support for one position or the other. Gradually, it became increasingly evident that both sets of factors interact to influence the course of early development. Moreover, it became clear that the interaction was not just a matter of *X*% of genetics and *X*% of the environment (although such data certainly were presented). With the introduction of the concept of **niche-picking** (Scarr & McCartney, 1983), the notion began to take hold that the interaction of nature and nurture is an active and dynamic one. According to the idea of niche-picking, genetic and environmental factors work together to influence the direction that children's lives take. The process works this way. A child has the genetic potential to be talented in a particular area, such as dancing. She has a great deal of flexibility, poise, and a good sense of rhythm. Let's say she has strong "dance" genes. Now, at the age of 4, she is taken to a ballet performance by her parents. The child sits glued to her seat, fascinated by the pirouettes and leaps of the performers. This event triggers her to beg her parents to let her start ballet lessons, and soon they do. The child has chosen her "niche" of dancing, having been exposed to the sight of ballet dancers, and now that she has found her niche, she has continued to thrive. Thus, her "dance genes" led her to develop an interest in exactly the activity that would allow her talents to flourish.

At the same time these changes were being suggested by researchers and theorists in the area of child development, others were beginning to look at expanding the focus of child development to incorporate the years of adulthood. The middle years of adulthood, which were being studied primarily by educators in the field of adult learning, became swept along in the general movement to integrate the previously disparate studies of development. People in the field of **gerontology**, the study of the aging process, became interested in general issues pertaining to development prior to old

These young children are expressing an interest in dance, which will become a "niche" as they continue to develop further their interests and abilities.

age, and a unified view of the life span began to emerge.

Out of the general philosophical and theoretical discussions revolving around the expansion of child psychology to life-span development emerged some very clear statements of the underlying models into which the nature–nurture debate had evolved. These models represent broad views or positions regarding the nature of development. Table 2-1 presents the essential elements of these models. The **organismic model** (taken from the term "organism") is based on the notion that nature is the prime mover of development. Growth in childhood and beyond is seen as the manifestation of genetic predisposition as it is expressed in the physical and mental development of the individual. Changes are proposed to occur through qualitative or structural alterations in the individual's psychological qualities (such as intelligence and personality), reflecting movement from one stage of development to the next. This model is, then, the basis for stage theories of development, which postulate that change over the life span occurs in leaps rather than in a continuous fashion.

The **mechanistic model** of development (taken from the word "machine") is based on the premise that nurture is the primary force in development. Growth throughout life is postulated to occur through the individual's exposure to experiences that present new learning opportunities. Because this exposure is gradual, there are no clear-cut or identifiable stages according to this model. Instead, development is seen as a smooth, continuous set of gradations as the individual acquires experience.

On the column in the extreme right of Table 2-1 is the **interactionist model**, the perspective that is represented by the evolving field of developmental science. According to this model, not only do genetics and environments interact in complex ways (as suggested by the niche-picking concept), but the individual actively participates in his or her development through reciprocal relations with the environment. Another important aspect of this model is the proposition of multidirectionality, a term introduced in Chapter 1. According to the principle of multidirectionality, there are multiple paths in development, so that it is not possible to describe development according to a series of linear stages. **Multidimensionality** is another principle of the interactionist model, meaning that there are multiple processes in development. Finally, the model is based on the assumption that there is **plasticity** in development, meaning that the course of development may be altered depending on the nature of the individual's specific interactions in the environment.

TABLE 2-1
Models of Individual–Environmental Interactions

	Organismic	*Mechanistic*	*Interactionist*
Nature of Change	Qualitative	Quantitative	Multidirectional Multidimensional
Contribution of organism	Active	Passive	Active
Main force in development	Biological–intrinsic maturational changes	External stimulus environment	Reciprocal relations with environment

Source: Adapted from Lerner, 1995.

BEHIND THE RESEARCH

RICHARD M. LERNER, BERGSTROM CHAIR IN APPLIED
DEVELOPMENTAL SCIENCE, TUFTS UNIVERSITY

What is most exciting to you about research in this field?

Developmental theory has changed in several significant ways in the past two decades. Scholars, whose work is focused on different age periods from across the life span, ranging from the neonate and infant to the adult and the old-old, have embraced models of development that involve the breadth of the system of relations between individuals and the complex context, or ecology, of human development. Theories that approached development through mechanistic or reductionist lenses have receded in importance, and scholars are considering how the integration of variables from levels of organization that include biology, psychology, social relationships (e.g., with family members and peers), institutions (e.g., schools and businesses), neighborhoods and communities, culture, the physical ecology, and history combine to create development across life. In short, we have entered into an era wherein developmental systems theories have come to the forefront of scholarly interest.

What do you see as the major challenges?

Systems models indicate that variables from multiple levels of organization are integrated in the development of human behavior and that, as such, longitudinal research that assesses relations among both micro- and macro-variables must be involved in developmental research.

However, no one scholar and in fact no one discipline has expertise in all the levels of organization involved in the developmental system. As such, a key challenge is to forge the multidisciplinary and multiprofessional collaborations that will be needed to bring the needed expertise to bear on the design and analysis of the longitudinal research that may be framed by developmental systems theories.

Where do you see this field headed in the next decade?

Because behavioral development is seen as an outcome of the relations among multiple levels of organization, and because changes at any level can result in alterations at all others, developmental systems models take an optimistic stance in regard to the potential for systematic change (plasticity) in human development. As a consequence, these models are similarly optimistic about the potential to develop means—interventions, or programs and policies—to promote positive development across the life span. Consistent with Kurt Lewin's (1943) famous observation that "there is nothing as practical as a good theory," I believe that scholars will use developmental systems theories to apply developmental science in the service of enhancing the lives of individuals, families, and communities across the life span.

Specific theories of development, which are the basis for specific hypotheses about life-span changes, fall within these models. Theories that propose that development is the result of ontogenetic changes within the individual fall within the organismic model. Learning theory, which proposes that development proceeds according to environmental influences, falls within the mechanistic model. Theories that regard development as the product of joint influences, such as the contextual theories that will be discussed later, fit within the interactionist model. A less formal term than "theory" is **perspective**, which presents a position or set of ideas. The biopsychosocial perspective falls within the interactionist model of development.

As we explore the processes of development in adulthood and old age, the usefulness of the concepts of multidimensionality, multidirectionality, and plasticity will become apparent. We have already discussed the need to examine the aging process from a multidimensional point of view, and along with this notion goes the idea that development can proceed in multiple dimensions across life. The concept of plasticity fits very well with the notion of compensation and modifiability of the aging process through actions taken by the individual, another point that will be explored throughout this book. The interactionist model, then, provides an excellent backdrop for the biopsychosocial perspective and a basis for viewing the processes of development in later life on a continuum with developmental processes in the early years.

Reciprocity in Development

As emphasized by the interactionist model, adults are, at least in part, products of their experiences. However, adults also shape their own experiences, both through active interpretation of the events that happen to them and through actions they take. These propositions emphasize the **reciprocal nature of development**, meaning that people both influence and are influenced by the events in their lives (Bronfenbrenner & Ceci, 1994).

Consider the reciprocal process as it has affected your own life. You were influenced by earlier events to choose a particular course of action that has brought you to your current point in life. Perhaps your best friend from high school chose to go to the college you are attending now, and that influenced you to attend this school. Perhaps you chose this college because you knew you wanted to major in psychology and you were impressed by the reputation of the faculty in your department. Or, just perhaps, your choice was made randomly, and you're not sure what led to your being in this place at this time. In any case, you are now at this school, having been influenced one way or another by your prior life events. That is one piece of the reciprocal process.

The next piece of the reciprocal process has to do with the effect you will have on your environment, which in turn will affect subsequent events in your life. By virtue of your very own existence, you are having an effect on the people who know you. Their lives may be forever altered by their relationship with you. Furthermore, you may be having an impact on your school that will alter the events that happen to you as a function of your being a student here. We all know of great student athletes, scholars, or musicians who bring renown to their institutions. Even if you are not fortunate enough to have such vast and recognized talents, your contributions to the school may alter it nevertheless. You may ask a question in class that stimulates your professor to investigate a new research question, and the investigation may ultimately produce new knowledge in the field, drawing attention to your school's contributions to the area. For example, a student at the University of Massachusetts brought his history professor a World War II political cartoon drawn by Dr. Seuss. Intrigued by this item, the professor went on to conduct research on the early political cartoon career of this well-known children's writer.

Thus, individuals are not passive recipients of environmental effects. Instead, their choices and behaviors leave a mark on the environment of which they are a part. Subsequently, the changes in that environment may further alter individuals in significant ways, who in turn affect their surroundings.

Ecological Perspective in Development

The **ecological perspective** (Bronfenbrenner, 1979, 2001) emphasizes that changes occur throughout life in the relations between the individual and these multiple levels of the environment. At the first level is the inner biological level, which refers to physiological processes. Next is the level of individual functioning, including cognition, personality, and other processes of adaptation. The third level is the **proximal social relational level**, involving the individual's relationships with significant others, peers, and nuclear families. At the fourth level, the **sociocultural level**, are relations with the larger social institutions of educational, public policy, governmental, and economic systems. Although interactions at both social levels occur throughout development, because those that occur at the proximal level happen over time, they are regarded as having the greatest impact on the individual's life (Bronfenbrenner, 1995; Lerner, 1995).

> ### *"What do you think?"*   2-2
>
> What are influences on your development from each of the three levels described within the ecological perspective?

BIOLOGICAL APPROACHES TO AGING IN ADULTHOOD

Biological changes throughout later life, as is true of those in the years of infancy, childhood, and adolescence, are based on certain genetically determined events or at least changes in physiological functioning brought about by intrinsic changes within the organism. As just shown, the interactionist model of development predicts that environmental factors influence the expression of biological or genetic predispositions. According to the principle of reciprocity, the individual's activities, both in direct relation to these changes and through the more general behaviors we call "lifestyle," interact with the preset biological program. The result is that large individual differences occur in the nature and timing of age-related changes in physical and cognitive functioning. Ultimately, however, it is the aging of the body that sets the limit to the life span. Individuals can compensate through behavioral measures for many of the changes associated with the aging process. Yet, an inevitability is associated with the passage of time. The body's biological clock continues to record the passage of time.

Having acknowledged this fact of life regarding the biological aging process, next we can turn to the question of why it happens. Why must organisms grow old and die? Science fiction fans enjoy stories of worlds in which biological aging does not occur, or at least not at the rate it does on our planet, and people live forever or for hundreds of years. If we contemplate such a world or think about how these worlds are portrayed in fiction, we can think of some obvious problems associated with prolonged or eternal life. Overpopulation, lack of resources, intergenerational strife (lasting hundreds, not tens of years) are just some of the possible outcomes. Alternatively, the birth rate may be reduced to a virtual standstill in one of these planets to avoid some of those problems.

Another futuristic possibility, as the "X Files" often suggested, is that perhaps people can constantly be reborn and the same individual can live on in multiple bodies despite apparent physical death. In any case, the problems of a static society may be just as unpleasant as the alternatives. Perhaps it is far more efficient to have a world such as ours, in which the older generations are constantly being swept aside to make room for the new ones whose entry into the population assures its vitality.

But can we assume that there is some advantage to aging and death that has led to its association with life? Although some of the biological theories are based on this assumption, maybe those fictional worlds in which death did not occur had some other advantages that we will not be able to enjoy until we unlock the secret of eternal life. Perhaps it is preferable to have a society in which people's wisdom and experience continue to accumulate and the lessons of history don't need to be painfully relearned with every generation. Perhaps being old and full of years is the ideal state, and being young and naive is an unpleasant hurdle that must be suffered through by each new flock of young people. Maybe we were not meant to die after all, and aging is some terrible accident that can ultimately be corrected.

The idea that aging is the result of some kind of correctable defect in living things is a premise that underlies some of the major biological theories. Or, as a third possibility reflected in theories, perhaps organisms are programmed to survive until reaching sexual maturity. Having guaranteed the survival of their species, either organisms are programmed to deteriorate, or they simply fade away because there are no genes programmed to keep them alive past that point.

When we speak of inherited characteristics, we are talking about the components of the genome, the complete set of instructions for building all the cells that make up an organism (see Fig. 2.1). The human genome is found in each nucleus of a person's many trillions of cells. The genome for each living creature consists of tightly coiled threads of the molecule deoxyribonucleic acid (**DNA**). The DNA resides in the nucleus of the body's cells as two long, paired strands spiraled into a double helix, a shape that resembles a twisted ladder. The components of DNA encode the information needed to manufacture proteins, which are large, complex molecules made up of long chains of subunits called amino acids. Protein is the primary component of all living things. There are many kinds of proteins, each with different functions. Some proteins provide structure to the cells of the body, whereas others called enzymes assist biochemical reactions that take place within the cells. Antibodies are proteins that function in the immune system to identify foreign invaders that need to be removed from the body. The entire process of protein manufacture is orchestrated by the genetic code contained in the DNA.

A **gene** is a functional unit of a DNA molecule carrying a particular set of instructions for producing a specific protein. Human genes vary widely in length, but only about 10% of the genome actually contains sequences of genes used to code proteins. The rest of the genome contains sequences of bases that have no apparent coding or any other function. Some of the proteins that the genes encode provide very basic housekeeping functions in the cell. These genes stay active all the time in many types of cells. More typically, however, a cell activates just the genes it needs at the moment and suppresses the rest. Through this process of selective activation of genes, the cell obtains its character as a skin cell, for example, rather than a bone cell.

The genome is organized into **chromosomes**, which are distinct, physically separate

FIGURE 2.1
Genes, Chromosomes and DNA

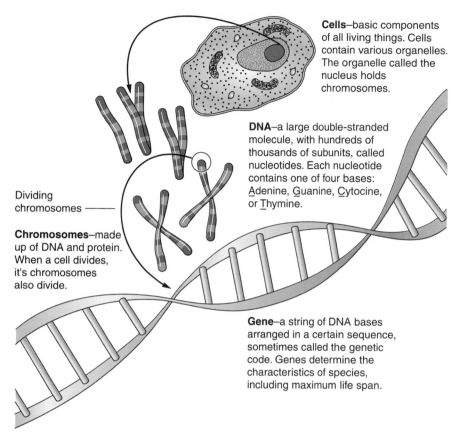

Cells—basic components of all living things. Cells contain various organelles. The organelle called the nucleus holds chromosomes.

DNA—a large double-stranded molecule, with hundreds of thousands of subunits, called nucleotides. Each nucleotide contains one of four bases: Adenine, Guanine, Cytocine, or Thymine.

Dividing chromosomes ———

Chromosomes—made up of DNA and protein. When a cell divides, it's chromosomes also divide.

Gene—a string of DNA bases arranged in a certain sequence, sometimes called the genetic code. Genes determine the characteristics of species, including maximum life span.

Source: National Institute on Aging, 1998.

units of coiled threads of deoxyribonucleic acid (DNA) and associated protein molecules. In humans, there are two sets of 23 chromosomes, one set contributed by each parent. Each set has 23 single chromosomes: 22 are called "autosomes" and contain nonsex-linked information, and the twenty-third is the X or Y sex chromosome. A normal female has a pair of X chromosomes, and a male has an X and Y pair. The presence of the Y chromosome determines maleness. Although each chromosome always has the same genes on it, there is no rhyme or reason to the distribution of genes on chromosomes. A gene that produces a protein that influences eye color may be next to a gene that is involved in cellular energy production. The locus of a gene is its place along the chromosome.

Genes may undergo alterations, called **mutations**, when DNA reproduces itself. When a gene contains a mutation, the protein encoded by that gene is likely to be abnormal. Sometimes the protein will be able to function even though it is damaged, but in other cases, it will be totally disabled. If a protein that is vital to survival becomes severely damaged, the results of the mutation are obviously going to be very serious. Genetic mutations can be either inherited from a parent or acquired over the course of one's life. Inherited mutations originate from the DNA of the cells involved in reproduction (sperm and egg). When reproductive cells containing mutations are combined in one's offspring, the mutation will be in all the bodily cells of that offspring. Inherited mutations are responsible for diseases such as cystic fibrosis and sickle cell anemia or may predispose an individual to cancer, major psychiatric illnesses, and other complex diseases.

Acquired mutations are changes in DNA that develop throughout a person's lifetime. Remarkably, cells possess the ability to repair many of these mutations. If these repair mechanisms fail, however, the mutation can be passed along to future copies of the altered cell. Mutations can also occur in the mitochondrial DNA, which is the DNA found in the tiny structures within the cell called mitochondria. These structures are crucial to the functioning of the cell because they are involved in producing cellular energy.

The process of genetic mapping involves starting with known genes and looking for traits that seem to be inherited along with those genes. The frequency with which they are passed along together provides an indication of how far apart they are likely to be on the chromosome. Having located the site of a gene, the next job is to describe its structure. This is the ultimate goal of geneticists who are attempting to provide a high-resolution map of the human genome. Researchers around the world have mapped the entire human genome in a massive effort called the Human Genome Project.

Biologists have provided many fascinating perspectives on the aging process. Their theories share the common thread of being attempts to solve one of, if not the greatest, mysteries of life.

This scientist, working in a laboratory in Cambridge, Massachusetts, is contributing to the Human Genome Project. Here she studies a map of the human Y chromosome, which by 1994 had been fully mapped.

PROGRAMMED AGING THEORIES

The biological theories of aging are divided into two categories (Hayflick, 1994): programmed aging and random error. Programmed aging theories are based on the assumption that aging and death are built into the hard-wiring of all organisms. Following from this assumption is the notion that there are "aging genes" that count off the years past maturity as surely as "development genes" lead to the point of maturity in youth. One argument long used in support of this assumption is based on the fact that the life span varies according to species, suggesting that life span is part of an organism's genetic makeup. For example, butterflies have life spans of 12 weeks, and giant tortoises have life spans of 180 years. Humans, the mammals with the longest life spans, are in between these points with life spans of 120 years. The relationship between the age span of a species and the age of its death (or life span), is expressed in the **Gompertz equation** shown in Fig. 2.2 (Sacher, 1977). More recently, biologists have been able to manipulate genetically the longevity of fruit flies, laboratory worms, yeast, and mice (Jazwinski, 2000).

In humans, large population studies in Sweden have demonstrated that longevity has a **heritability index** (indicating the degree to which a characteristic is inherited) of .26 in men and .23 in women. These figures were replicated over three birth cohorts and were not accounted for by smoking or degree of body fat (Herskind, McGue, Holm, Sorensen, Harvald, et al., 1996; Herskind, McGue, Iachine, Holm, Sorensen, et al., 1996). These findings in support of genetic theories are particularly intriguing in view of the considerable progress being made in the field of genetics in general, culminating perhaps in the 1997 cloning of Dolly the sheep. The ability to identify and then

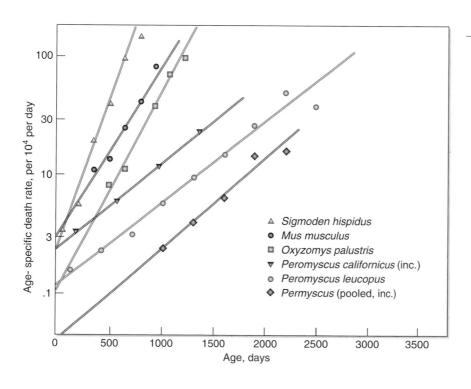

FIGURE 2.3
Gompertz Curve

Source: Sacher, 1977.

control the "aging" gene (if it indeed exists) would go a long way toward changing the very nature of aging.

Despite the appeal of a genetic theory based on the concept that one or multiple genes control the aging process from birth to death, such a simple genetic theory is not considered viable. It would imply that evolution has selected for the aging process along the lines of the preceding argument (i.e., old generations must die to make room for new ones). The fact is that, historically, few species survived until they were old enough to grow old and be exposed to the evolutionary selection process. A more defensible variant of the genetic theory is that evolution has selected for species that are vigorous up to the point that sexual maturity has passed. In the postreproductive years, "good genes gone bad" (Hayflick, 1994) take over and lead to the ultimate destruction of the organism.

One recent theory that has attracted considerable attention provides a possibly revolutionary new view of the genetics of aging. The **telomere** theory proposes that defects develop in gene

Assess Yourself

Ten Tips for Healthy Aging

The following Ten Tips for Healthy Aging are recommended by the U.S. National Institute on Aging. Assess yourself by asking *honestly* whether you follow these tips:

1. Eat a balanced diet, including five helpings of fruits and vegetables a day.
2. Exercise regularly (check with a doctor before starting an exercise program).
3. Get regular health check-ups.
4. Don't smoke (it's never too late to quit).
5. Practice safety habits at home to prevent falls and fractures. Always wear your seatbelt in a car.
6. Stay in contact with family and friends. Stay active through work, play, and community.
7. Avoid overexposure to the sun and the cold.
8. If you drink, make moderation the key. When you drink, let someone else drive.
9. Keep personal and financial records in order to simplify budgeting and investing. Plan long-term housing and money needs.
10. Keep a positive attitude toward life. Do things that make you happy.

Resources
The National Institute on Aging Information Center
P.O. Box 8057
Gaithersburg, MD 20898-8057
1-800-222-2225 1-800-222-4225 (TTY)

expression within cells that cause them to lose their ability to reproduce (Stewart & Weinberg, 2002). The loss of the ability to reproduce is called **replicative senescence**. Many laboratory investigations of aging involve the study of the number of times that cells divide. It has long been known that there are a finite number of times (about 50) that normal human cells proliferate in culture before they enter a state in which they are terminally incapable of further division (Hayflick & Moorhead, 1961). The telomere is the terminal region or tail of a chromosome that is made up of DNA but that contains no genetic information. Telomeres protect the ends of chromosomes from being degraded and fusing with other chromosome ends. The telomere theory of aging is based on the fact that every time a cell replicates, it loses part of its telomere. The older the cell (the more times it has divided), the shorter the length of the telomeres. As the length of a telomere decreases, changes may occur in patterns of gene expression that could affect both the functioning of the cell and the organ system in which it operates (Baur, Zou, Shay, & Wright, 2001). There is direct evidence linking telomere length to mortality in humans (Cawthon, Smith, O'Brien, Sivatchenko, & Kerber, 2003).

"What do you think?"   **2-3**

Will the telomere theory hold the key to aging?

According to the telomere theory, cells stop dividing when the short telomere length is sensed as damage to the DNA. Some cells do not show this reduction of telomere length; for example, tumor cells do not show replicative senescence, and when added to normal cells, they replicate indefinitely. Because of the danger posed by indefinitely replicating tumor cells, senescence may be thought of as a form of protection against cancer (Tominaga, Olgun, Smith, & Pereira-Smith, 2002). The trick

in extending life span would be finding a way to keep cells replicating longer without increasing the risk of cancer cell proliferation (Weinstein & Ciszek, 2002).

Two of the older programmed aging theories focus on specific organ systems whose aging is hypothesized to lead to deleterious changes in the entire body. According to the first of these theories, the neuroendocrine theory, changes in the hypothalamus, which mediates between the nervous and endocrine systems, are responsible for age changes in the hormones that eventually bring about the aging of the organism. If the hypothalamus were, in fact, the ultimate biological clock, it might explain why restriction of calorie intake might have some life-extending effects as some biologists claim. The theory would also have some relevance to the presumed age-retarding effects of the hormone dehydroepiandrosterone (DHEA), which will be discussed more extensively later in the book. Another point in favor of a neuroendocrine theory is the fact that menopause, the end of the woman's reproductive capacity, is associated with many aging changes throughout the body. However, the obvious problem with this line of argument is that although men age, they do not lose their reproductive abilities. For this reason, and the fact that there is no direct support, the theory is not generally accepted.

Similarly, the neuron theory, which states that loss of neurons in the brain is the cause of aging, is not seen as a plausible explanation of aging. It is true that the nervous system controls almost every other system in the body. Furthermore, it is known that brain weight is positively correlated with life spans across species. This evidence has led proponents of this theory to suggest that there are signaling pathways within the brain that regulate life span (Mattson, Duan, & Maswood, 2002). However, arguing against this theory is the fact that aging occurs in animals with very primitive brains that are not known to undergo the type of cell loss that is documented in higher species (Hayflick, 1994). In humans, there is more reason to believe that loss of neurons in the brain is the result rather than the cause of the aging process more generally.

Random Error Theories

Random error theories are based on the assumption that aging reflects unplanned changes in an organism over time. The wear and tear theory of aging is a theory that many people implicitly refer to when they speak of "falling apart" as they get older. According to this theory, the body, like a used Chevy sedan, acquires more and more damage as it is exposed to the use and abuse it takes on a daily basis. Eventually, as more and more of its parts give out, it stops running altogether.

The rate of living theory is another one with some intuitive appeal, as well as a kind of common-sense view that if you "live fast" you will "die young." This theory also allows a continuation of the automobile metaphor in that it implies that once your "gas tank" is empty, you will have depleted your energy supplies and your life will be over. The theory, which can be traced back to the early 1900s, has no empirical backing, however. It also conflicts with another common-sense notion, but one that is supported by the literature—namely, the "use it or lose it" principle. The implication of the rate of living theory is that you shouldn't "waste" yourself by engaging in too much activity.

The waste product accumulation theory also has a kind of metaphoric appeal, conjuring up images of bodily products building up year after year without release until the cells of the body suffocate in their own residue. Lipofuscin, a mixture of lipoproteins and waste products, is seen as the most likely candidate for causing this deleterious waste. A yellowish-brown pigment, lipofuscin accumulates in a number of cells throughout the body with increasing age, including neurons and skin cells (Porta, 2002). There is no evidence, however, that the lipofuscin actually does any damage.

The cross-linking theory involves another kind of substance found throughout the body—**collagen**—which makes up about one-third of all bodily proteins. The process that alters the nature of the collagen molecule increasingly with age is known as "cross-linking," hence, the name of the theory that attributes deleterious changes with aging to this process. Cross-links are the horizontal strands, like the rungs of a ladder that connect the two parallel molecules that form the collagen protein. Increasingly with age, the rungs of one ladder start to connect to the rungs of another ladder through the development of more cross-links, so that the ladders start to resemble larger and larger scaffolds within the structure of the tissue. These changes, when they occur within the skin, cause it to become increasingly rigid and to shrink in size. It is also proposed that cross-links form within the DNA, leading to deleterious changes in the genes. In evaluating this theory, it seems likely that the process it describes may have importance in affecting structures that contain cross-linked molecules, but it is unlikely that the process is a primary cause of aging.

Another theory that has received popular attention is the **free radical** theory, also known as the oxidative stress theory (Sohal, 2002). As described in Table 2-2, free radicals are produced by a reaction of certain molecules in cells to the presence of oxygen, which causes them to break apart and form molecular fragments. These fragments, called free radicals, seek to bind to other molecules. When this binding takes place, the molecule to which the free radical has become attached loses its functioning. Some of the havoc that can be wreaked by free radicals includes the formation of age pigments and cross-links described above, as well as possible damage to the nervous system. Although proposed as a random error theory, the free radical theory is is now beginning to incorporate concepts from genetic theories (Melov, 2000). One proposal links oxidative stress to telomeres, suggesting that telomeres are shortened when cells are exposed to oxidative damage (von Zglinicki, 2002). Another theory suggests that mutations in the mitochondrial DNA cause oxidative damage (Wei & Lee, 2002).

TABLE 2-2
Biological Theories of Aging

	Theory	Description
PROGRAMMED AGING	Genetic life-span theory	Length of life is genetically programmed.
	Genetic postreproduction theory	Aging is programmed to begin after the organism cannot reproduce. Selective survival applies to survival of the fittest when the species is still able to reproduce; after that point, the cells are programmed to deteriorate and die.
	Telomere theory	Changes in gene expression cause molecular changes in parts of the cells (telomeres) that cause cellular "senescence" in which the cell has lost its ability to divide.
	Specific system theories	Neuroendocrine theory: Changes occur in neural structures that regulate endocrine activity (the hypothalamus). Neuron loss: Loss of neurons controls the rate of the body's aging.
RANDOM EVENTS	Wear and tear theory	Stress of everyday life erodes biochemical processes that take place in the cells, ultimately causing them to die.
	Rate of living theory	Organisms begin life with only a finite amount of physiological capacity, and once it is "used up" the organism can no longer live.
	Waste product accumulation theory	Metabolic waste builds up in the cells and interfered with their operation of basic functions.
	Cross-linking theory	Collagen develops "cross-links", interfering with cellular metabolism and causing increasing rigidity of bodily tissues.
	Free radical theory	Chemical reaction with oxygen causes unstable "free radicals" that unite with other molecules and interfere with their functioning.
	Autoimmune theory	Immune cells lose the ability to produce antibodies and mistakenly produce antibodies against the body's own proteins (autoimmunity).
	Error theories	Errors occur in cellular reproduction and are less efficiently repaired in aging cells. Error catastrophe theory proposes that crucial errors occur that cause many cells to malfunction and die.
	Order to disorder theory	After sexual maturation, the organism loses efficiency due to a droposs in the energy needed to maintain the system. Increasing disorder causes it to develop errors that ultimately lead to death.

Source:　Based on Hayflick, 1994.

There is some experimental support for the free radical theory. Some of this support comes from research involving antioxidants, which are chemicals that prevent the formation of free radicals. A well-known antioxidant that is being widely advertised as an anti-aging substance is vitamin E; another antioxidant vitamin that is receiving increasing attention is vitamin C. Free radicals can also be destroyed by superoxide dismutase (SOD), which is being sold as an anti-aging drug. Longer-living species have higher levels of SOD, and feeding antioxidants such as those used in food preservatives can extend the lives of laboratory animals. (Melov, Ravenscroft, Malik, Gill, Walker, et al., 2000). However, many scientists remain skeptical about whether these supplements will ultimately deliver what they promise (Biesalski, 2002).

One implication of the free radical theory relates to caloric restriction, referred to earlier as a condition that seems to extend the life span. Biologist Roy Walford has devoted his career to proving the hypothesis that restriction of caloric intake can prolong life (Walford, Mock, Verdery, & MacCallum, 2002). There is evidence to support this hypothesis but no clear explanation of how it works (if in fact it does). Proponents of the free radical theory propose

Biologist Roy Walford, shown in this 1991 photo at the age of 67, proposes that caloric restriction can slow the aging process.

that the effects of caloric restriction may be attributed to a reduction in the process of free radical formation (Barja, 2002). Benefits of caloric restriction are thought to include protection of the hippocampus, an area of the brain involved in memory (Patel & Finch, 2002). Critics argue that there still is not sufficient evidence directly linking oxidative stress to the aging process (Sohal, Mockett, & Orr, 2002).

The autoimmune theory proposes changes that involve an accumulation of mistakes in how the immune system functions with increasing age. One set of problems involves changes in the immune system's ability to fight off the invasion of bacteria and viruses into the body. As we shall see later in the book, there is mixed evidence regarding the effects of aging on the immune system, but there is some support for the loss of certain functions. Another set of changes are the formation of antibodies by the immune system in response to the body's own cells. This autoimmunity is at the heart of certain diseases that become more prevalent in older adults (but are not restricted to them), such as some forms of arthritis. But because a strong case cannot be made that changes in immune functioning underlie the changes in the body as a whole, this theory has not received strong support.

Error theories are based on the proposal that mutations occur in the somatic cells of the body (those that are not involved in reproduction), causing a set of changes associated with aging. According to one variant of this theory, the error catastrophe theory (Orgel, 1963), it is not just random errors that lead to the changes associated with aging, but errors that play a key role in the maintenance of the body's cells. These are errors in the manufacturing of proteins. Such errors would accumulate at an exponential rate, leading many of the molecules in a cell to become dysfunctional. Like a collapsed bridge that has suddenly failed after gradually accumulating damage over the years, the impairment in the cell would lead to widespread tissue and organ malfunction.

Finally, the order to disorder theory proposes that energy is required to maintain order in the body's cells by repairing damage when it occurs and, in general, ensuring the integrity of the system. After the organism has "fulfilled" its function by reproducing (or passing reproductive age), the energy put into maintenance of the organism is no longer needed and the system displays increasing disorganization or entropy. The problem with this theory is that the laws of thermodynamics do not translate well from a closed system to a living organism.

In looking at perspectives on the aging process that derive from the social sciences, it will be important to keep in mind the central role of biological factors. These factors form the nature component to the complex nature–nurture interactions assumed to characterize development in the adult years.

PSYCHOLOGICAL MODELS OF DEVELOPMENT IN ADULTHOOD

Recognizing the role of biology, but not attempting to explain it, are psychological approaches to development in the adult years. In the broadest sense, psychological models attempt to explain the development of the "person" in the person–environment equation from the standpoint of how adaptive abilities unfold over the course of life. It is taken as a given that the body undergoes significant changes, but of interest within the psychological approaches are the changes that occur in the individual's self-understanding, ability to adjust to life's challenges, and perspective on the world.

Erikson's Psychosocial Theory

Perhaps the best known life-span psychological theory is Erik Erikson's (1963), which focuses on the development of the ego through a series of eight stages. In this theory, each stage of development is defined as a crisis in which particular stage-specific issues present themselves as challenges to the individual's ego. The theory is called **psychosocial**, but it could easily be characterized by the more contemporary term "biopsychosocial." Erikson proposed that individuals pass through a series of transitions in which they are particularly sensitive or vulnerable to a complex interaction of biological, psychological, and social forces characteristic of their period of life. For example, during the intimacy versus isolation stage, the young adult is biologically capable of engaging in sexual relationships, psychologically capable of serious emotional involvement with another adult, and socially expected to "settle down" and find a partner. The "crisis" is not truly a crisis in the sense of being a catastrophe. Instead, each psychosocial stage is a time during which the individual may move closer to a positive or negative resolution of the psychosocial issue. This is why each stage is described in terms of a favorable attribute versus an unfavorable attribute. These attributes are qualities of the ego that will develop based on how the crisis is resolved.

Another crucial aspect of Erikson's theory is the **epigenetic principle**, which means in this context that each stage unfolds from the previous stage. Furthermore, like Freud's psychosexual theory, Erikson's characterizes these stages as evolving according to a predestined order. These stages, according to Erikson, are set in much the same manner as is the program for the biological development of the individual throughout life. They are built, according to Erikson, into the hard-wiring of the human being.

Erikson's theory has fascinated researchers and developmental theorists, in part because his writing is so compelling and in part because it presents an organized, cohesive view of development from birth to death. The matrix of ages by stages, which forms the heart of the theory, is shown in Fig. 2.3. This chart is elegant but deceptively simple. At first glance, it might appear that development proceeds in a series of steps from childhood to old age. A more careful inspection of the table shows that the diagonal line is not the only possibility for development of the ego, although it may be the most straightforward. The matrix format of this chart implies that there may be developments occurring in boxes that lie outside the diagonal line. Thus, the issues characterizing each stage (such as "trust versus mistrust" for infancy) may coexist as relevant concerns throughout adulthood. Any stage may reach ascendancy in response to events that stimulate its reappearance. For example, an 80-year-old victim of a mugging in a park may reexperience the trust versus mistrust crisis again in attempting to overcome the tremendous fear and trauma associated with the crime. Autonomy may be revisited as an issue in later adulthood when the individual begins to experience limitations in

FIGURE 2.3

Stages in Erikson's Psychosocial Theory

Stage	1	2	3	4	5	6	7	8
Later adulthood								Ego integrity vs. despair
Middle adulthood							Gener-activity vs. stagnation	
Young adulthood						Intimacy vs. isolation		
Adolescence					Identity achievement vs. identity diffusion			
Middle childhood				Industry vs. inferiority				
Early childhood			Initiative vs. guilt					
Todler		Autonomy vs. shame doubt						
Early infancy	Basic trust vs. mistrust							

Source: Adapted from Erikson, 1963.

mobility associated with the physical aging process (Erikson, Erikson, & Kivnick, 1986).

Another implication of the matrix concept is that a crisis may be experienced before its "time." A 35-year-old woman diagnosed with breast cancer may become faced with issues relevant to **Ego Integrity versus Despair**, the psychosocial crisis normally reserved for a much older person. The crisis stages are best thought of as "critical periods" during which certain issues are likely to become prominent, but they are not meant to be discrete, age-related segments of the life span.

Given these qualifications regarding the correspondence of the stages with chronological age, the essence of each crisis stage can be used as a basis for describing major themes in the development of the adult's personality and functioning in society. The first of the eight stages that is directly relevant to adulthood is **Identity Achievement versus Identity Diffusion**. This stage first emerges in adolescence, but it persists in importance throughout adulthood and forms a cornerstone of subsequent adult psychosocial crises (Erikson, 1959; Whitbourne & Connolly, 1999). An individual who achieves a clear identity has a coherent sense of purpose regarding the future and a sense of continuity with the past. Identity diffusion, the opposite to identity achievement, involves a lack of direction, vagueness about life's purposes, and an unclear sense of self.

The next stage, which emerges in early adulthood, is **Intimacy versus Isolation**. The attainment of intimacy involves establishing a mutually satisfying close relationship with another person (traditionally, one's marital partner). It is the intersection of two identities but not a total overlap. In a truly intimate relationship, each partner preserves a sense of separateness and has the ability to retain his or her unique qualities. An individual who is isolated fails to achieve true mutuality. Theoretically, isolation is more likely to occur in an individual who lacks a strong identity because an individual must be secure from within in order to establish a close relationship with others.

The motive for caring for the next generation emerges from the successful resolution of the intimacy stage. The stage of **Generativity versus Stagnation** focuses on the psychosocial issues of procreation, productivity, and creativity. The most common route to generativity is through becoming a parent and in this way becoming involved in care of the next generation. However, even those who do not have children may express their generativity through means such as teaching or mentoring. A career that involves producing something of value that future generations can enjoy is another form of generativity. The main feature of generativity is a feeling of concern over what happens to the young and a desire to make the world a better place for them. Stagnation, by contrast, occurs when the individual turns

Adults who serve as mentors for younger persons are thought by Erikson to be expressing a sense of generativity.

concern and energy inward or solely to others of one's own age group rather than to the young. A person who is high on the quality of stagnation lacks interest or may even go so far as to reject the younger generation. Of course, being a parent is no guarantee of achieving generativity; the crucial component of generativity is concern and care for the people who will follow one's own generation.

Toward the end of adulthood, the individual faces psychosocial issues related to aging and growing closer to death, as manifested in the stage of Ego Integrity versus Despair. The older individual who establishes a strong sense of ego integrity can look back over the years lived thus far with acceptance. Ego integrity also involves an ability to look at and accept the positive and negative attributes of one's own self, even if it may be painful to acknowledge some of those unfavorable characteristics. This sense of acceptance of the past and present self allows the individual who has attained ego integrity to look upon the future (i.e., mortality) similarly with acceptance of the inevitable. It may be difficult for a young person to imagine how a person who is happy with life could also be happy (or at least not devastated) by the thought of his or her own death. However, according to Erikson, it is this acceptance of past, present, and future that comes late in life when a person has achieved successful resolution of all psychosocial crises. In contrast, despair is the outcome of realizing that death is unavoidable and that it will come too soon to make possible a righting of previous wrongs. The individual in a state of despair feels discontent with life and is unhappy, if not panicky, at the thought of death. Even though one's daily existence is filled with complaints and misery, the thought of ending that life before past mistakes can be corrected is even more frightening.

Erikson regarded the stages of Intimacy versus Isolation, Generativity versus Stagnation, and Ego Integrity versus Despair as resulting in the development of new qualities of the ego; specifically, love, care, and wisdom. However, the ego is, in effect, equivalent to identity in that it reflects the self. Does identity change as the individual passes through the stages of adulthood that involve romantic involvement with a partner, investment in career and family, and the approaching of end-of-life issues? As will become clear in the later chapters of the book, it seems more likely that identity affects the choice of partner, career, and approach to mortality. In keeping with this view, it seems more reasonable to regard the stages of intimacy, generativity, and ego integrity as "developmental tasks" (Havighurst, 1972). This would mean that the stages are viewed as demands that must be confronted as individuals grow older rather than as stages that present the possibility of fundamental alterations in identity (Whitbourne & Connolly, 1999).

Piaget's Cognitive-Developmental Theory

Jean Piaget was a Swiss psychologist who described the development of intelligence in terms of the reciprocal relationship of the child to the environment. The focus of Piaget's theory was cognitive development in childhood, but the terms and concepts central to this theory can be applied more generally to life-span models.

A major feature of Piaget's theory was his description of a series of stages in childhood cognition. More generally, however, the developmental processes identified in the theory have a great deal of relevance to adult development and aging and the way that individuals interpret and react to their experiences. The process of **assimilation** is engaged when individuals interpret new experiences in terms of their existing mental structures, or **schemas**. The term "assimilation," in this context, does not have its common meaning, as when we say that a person has become assimilated to a new culture. In Piaget's model, assimilation has the opposite meaning; rather, it refers to the situation in which individuals are trying to fit their experiences into their current ways of viewing the world.

As an example of assimilation, let's say that you have a very meager understanding of different varieties of birds, and you call all little birds "sparrows" and all large birds "crows." You are forcing into two categories what actually may be eight or ten different varieties of birds in your neighborhood. According to Piaget, individuals engage in this assimilative process until they are able to gain experiences that allow them to refine their concepts or schemas. If you go for a walk with an avid bird lover who points out the differences between sparrows, finches, and chickadees (all small birds), you will emerge with a refinement to your previous categorization system. In Piaget's terms, this process of change in an existing schema is referred to as **accommodation**.

In Piaget's theory, the development of intelligence proceeds through alterations between assimilation and accommodation. The ideal state is one in which individuals are able to interpret their experiences through a consistent framework (assimilation) but are able to change this framework when it no longer is helpful in organizing experiences (accommodation). Such an ideal state is referred to as an **equilibrium**, and the process of achieving this balance is called **equilibration**.

Identity Process Theory

Integrating Erikson's and Piaget's theories provides an excellent vantage point for making predictions about psychosocial development in adulthood, and in particular, the way that individuals react to the aging process. According to **identity process theory** (Whitbourne, 2002), the processes of assimilation and accommodation can account for interactions between the individual and experiences through the framework provided by identity (see Fig. 2.4).

FIGURE 2.4
Identity Process Theory

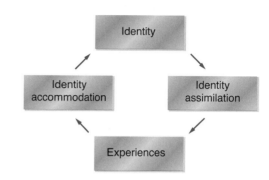

In identity process theory, it is assumed that individuals approach their experiences from the vantage point provided by their personal identities—their ideas or concepts about the self. Adult identity, as discussed in Chapter 1, is defined as a composite of the individual's self-representation in a variety of substantive areas. These areas include identity with regard to physical appearance and functioning, cognitive abilities, personality traits, relationships with others, and social roles. Thus, individuals define themselves as looking a certain way, having certain abilities, behaving in accordance with certain dispositions, relating to others in certain ways, and having a set of particular social roles that define them within their particular communities and contexts. There is a certain bias within identity to view the self in a favorable light. For psychologically healthy adults, this bias is to regard the self as physically and mentally competent, to be regarded positively by others, and as adhering to ethical principles such as being honest and concerned for others.

Applying assimilation to adult identity produces the term **identity assimilation**, which refers to the tendency of individuals to interpret new experiences relevant to the self in terms of their existing self-schemas or identities. The process of identity assimilation can lead people to twist their perception of experiences so that they do not have to change their views of themselves. For example, the experience of failing a test has the potential to challenge the view of the self as competent. Identity assimilation would lead this individual to attribute that failure to a fault in the test rather than to a personal lack of ability.

Although identity assimilation preserves a positive view of the self, continued failure experiences that the individual refuses to incorporate into self-appraisals or changes in behavior can ultimately have negative consequences. As with the example of the bird classification, a discrepancy between a certain way of viewing the self or the world and the reality of an experience that is incongruent or inconsistent with that view at some point may need to be resolved. When experiences and identity are consistent, there is not much incentive for the identity processes of assimilation or accommodation to come into play because the individual is in balance or equilibrium. Adjustments are needed when the person's identity does not match the experience.

It is through the process of **identity accommodation** that changes eventually occur in the individual's view of the self. Given the generally positive bias toward seeing the self in a favorable light, identity accommodation often involves acknowledging areas of personal weakness. After repeatedly failing the exams in a given course, a student may decide that it is time to study harder or perhaps to switch majors to an area more compatible with his or her abilities. In a more general sense, however, identity accommodation involves changes in response to new experiences, and so any type of redefinition of the self would fall into this category. A person may learn that he or she possesses an ability that was not previously recognized. For example, people who are able to cope successfully with a tragedy may find that they have inner strength that they did not

know had existed. As with identity assimilation, however, it is possible to rely too heavily on identity accommodation. Individuals who define themselves entirely on the basis of their experiences, such as how others treat them, have the potential to be devastated by a negative event such as rejection by a romantic partner.

> ### "What do you think?" 2-4
> Can you give an example of identity assimilation and identity accommodation from your own life or from examples in literature or film?

Ideally, as in Piaget's theory, there is a balance or dynamic equilibrium between identity assimilation and identity accommodation in adulthood. Although individuals may tend to use assimilation as a first approach to a new experience, seeing it from the perspective of their current views of the self, they should theoretically be able to make accommodations when the situation warrants changes.

Major stimuli for the activity of identity processes in adulthood are age-related changes in physical and cognitive functioning. The multiple threshold model proposes that personal recognition of aging occurs in a stepwise process across the years of adulthood (Whitbourne & Collins, 1998). Individuals pass through a threshold of feeling "old" at different times for different systems of the body. Each new age-related change brings with it the potential for another threshold to be crossed. The area or areas that are of greatest significance to an adult's identity are likely to be observed with great care or vigilance. Some thresholds are crossed without creating a challenge for identity because they are in areas that are not of particular importance to that individual. You may find that the gray hair provides a

According to the Multiple Threshold Model, age-related changes in appearance can lead some adults to undergo changes in their identity.

threshold for you, but that you don't care much that your muscles have gotten somewhat weaker than they used to be. Someone else may disregard the gray hair entirely but become obsessed with the first signs of loss of muscle strength. At the point of crossing a threshold, the individual is stimulated to recognize the reality of the aging process in that particular area of functioning. At that point, the individual moves from identity assimilation to identity accommodation in an attempt to adjust to the crossing of the threshold and reach a new state of balance.

A term that has recently gained popularity is the "senior moment," generally used humorously by a middle-aged person to refer to the forgetting of a well-known piece of information such as someone's name or telephone number. This term can easily be regarded in connection with the multiple threshold model as a point of crossing into recognition that a valued ability is at risk of being lost. It is interesting that this term is almost always used in a joking manner, but it can have more ominous overtones in people who are seriously concerned that their memory is taking an irreversible turn for the worse.

In keeping with the notion of reciprocity, identity process theory also assumes that identity influences the actions people take to improve their health and longevity and to avoid the behaviors that detract from their functioning and years of life. Many studies that will be cited in this book demonstrate the value of an active use it or lose it approach to the aging process. Such an approach applies to strategies designed to ward off negative changes, ranging from loss of muscle strength to memory. On the other hand, there are many bad habits or ways in which a person's behavior can accelerate the aging process. Some of the most well-known of these negative behaviors were described in Chapter 1 (see Table 1-1); another that is not on that list but important nevertheless is excessive exposure to the sun. Ideal adaptation to the aging process is theorized to involve maintaining a positive identity through identity assimilation. At the same time, however, the individual must take advantage of the use it or lose it approach and avoid the bad habits. These behavioral adaptations can maximize one's health and competence without threatening one's overall sense of self.

BIOPSYCHOSOCIAL PERSPECTIVE

THE IDENTITY PROCESS theory describes a complex process of adaptation to the changes involved in aging. The aging of appearance provides a very good example of how this process might operate. Appearance of the face is an important part of one's self-concept, and changes in the face with age present a potentially important threat to the older person's overall identity (Cash, 1990; Fedok, 1996). Interestingly, people who are concerned about the aging of their facial appearance also seem to be more likely to worry about a related problem, which is the possible effect of weight gain on aging (Gupta, 1995).

An older person using identity assimilation in response to aging of the face would be one who refuses to acknowledge that these changes are occurring. This tactic helps the individual maintain a youthful, if inaccurate, view of the self. By contrast, an older adult using identity accommodation would be one who becomes alarmed and distressed over even small changes in appearance, feeling a direct threat to a positive self-image. A person adopting a more balanced approach to these changes would acknowledge that the face is undergoing changes but not become overly preoccupied with them.

What are the implications of these three different styles of response to changes in appearance? First, consider the individual's sense of personal happiness. The individual who refuses to acknowledge changes in appearance of the face, by definition, will not be overly preoccupied with aging. An adult who adopts a more accommodative style would be at the opposite extreme, concerned to the point of despondency over the least little wrinkle or gray hair. Finally, the individual with a balanced identity style may suffer temporary setbacks as new realizations about aging must be faced, but in the end, this person will achieve a favorable adaptation in terms of feelings about the self.

Of course, appearance is not equally important to everyone. An adult's response to the aging process largely reflects the attitudes of the greater society and culture. In a society where age rather than youth was considered beautiful, people would aspire to having as many gray hairs and wrinkles as they could. They would never consider dyeing their hair (unless it were to bleach it pure white), and they would try to accentuate rather than cover up the bags and sags that develop around their face. Unfortunately, we do not live in such a society; in fact, with the advent of "botox" (botulinum) as a way to paralyze facial muscles and remove the associated frown lines, social trends are moving toward less acceptance of a wrinkled facial appearance. It is therefore far more common for people (especially women) to find that aging of appearance represents a significant threat to their positive feelings about themselves. In this respect, then, sociocultural influences interact with identity and with biological changes taking place within the individual under the control of genetic factors.

SOCIOCULTURAL MODELS OF DEVELOPMENT

In the field of social gerontology, the influence of social context has been examined in terms of demographic variables such as age and sex structures within the population, income levels, and social class (Cavanaugh, 1999). The **life course perspective** in social gerontology emphasizes the importance of age-based norms, roles, and attitudes as influences that shape events throughout development (Ryff, Marshall, & Clarke, 1999). Through the life course perspective, sociologists and social gerontologists are attempting to forge links between these broad social factors and individual adjustment.

Aging in Society: Influence of Social Context on the Individual

Disengagement theory is a topic which was at one time of great interest in the psychology of middle adulthood and aging (Cumming & Henry, 1961). According to this theory, not only does society withdraw support and interest in the individual during these years, but starting in late middle age, the individual chooses to disengage from social involvements. Successful aging, according to this view, involves this process of mutual withdrawal of the individual from society. This theory was considered a direct assault on the underlying tenets of the prevailing views in social gerontology, specifically, that it is harmful to the well-being of older adults to force them out of productive social roles, a view referred to as **activity theory** (Cavan, Burgess, Havighurst, & Goldhamer, 1949). Following considerable debate and further research, **continuity theory** (Atchley, 1989) provided a resolution of the issue. According to this view, older adults will suffer a loss of well-being and negative effects of ageism if they are not allowed to maintain their desired level of involvement in society. The implication of continuity theory is that either forced retirement or forced activity will lead to lower adjustment and self-esteem in middle-aged and older adults.

Social Meaning of Age: Social Clocks and Ageism

Apart from its meaning as an index of functioning, a person's age is an important social cue. The degree of interest that others have in this one piece of data about a person is evident from the amount of attention given by the media to learning the age of a particular celebrity. There is even an interest in the ages of non-celebrities, as indicated by the fact that most newspaper articles include age immediately following the name of everyone from newlyweds to murderers. A person's age seems to hold intrinsic interest for others. Furthermore, many people give considerable attention to their own ages. An upcoming birthday, particularly at a decade marker, may be the source of intense scrutiny about the value of one's life thus far.

At least some of the preoccupation that people have about age is based on a process known as the **social clock**, the normative expectations for the ages at which major life events should occur (Hagestad & Neugarten, 1985). Events such as parenthood have a biological component; others are based on calendars that are set by society, such as the need to make progress up the career ladder by the early 30s. Such events in one's own life and the lives of others are evaluated according to whether they are "on-time" or "off-time" with regard to the social clock. When a person's life is off-time, the individual may feel a great deal of personal distress and perhaps criticism from others who expect that people will follow the normative prescriptions for their age group. Non-events, which are the failure to experience an expected life change, may have as much of an influence on an individual's life as actual events.

Increasingly, however, individuals are setting their own unique social clocks, as exemplified by people like John Glenn, quoted at the beginning of this chapter. At the age of 77, Glenn joined the Space Shuttle Discovery crew on a nine-day orbital mission. His ability to meet the arduous physical requirements of the voyage supports the notion that, as he asserted in the quote, people should not be limited by "the calendar."

As with the "isms" of racism and sexism, ageism is a set of beliefs, attitudes, social institutions, and acts that denigrate individuals or groups based on their chronological age. The components of ageism represent stereotyped views of different age groups and theoretically could apply to teenagers as well as to older persons. However, for all practical purposes, ageism is used as a term referring to stereotyped views of the over-65.

The negative feature of ageism is that, like other stereotypes, it involves making overgeneralizations about individuals based on an outward characteristic that they possess. However, ageism may take the form of overly positive attitudes as well as attitudes that are more negatively valenced (Hummert, Garstka, Shaner, & Strahm, 1994). For example, older adults may be seen as "cute" or "kindly," labels that, though perhaps favorable (if not patronizing), cannot possibly apply to each and every older person. For the most part, however, ageist views portray older adults in a negative light—as cranky, senile, ridiculous, and incapable of effective action. Closeness to an older person is seen as disgusting or frightening, and consequently, young people attempt to avoid direct or prolonged contact.

Ageism may also take the form of making older adults invisible, that is, as not included in representations of people in general. For example, the August 2003 issue of *Vogue* magazine, in its yearly "age issue," failed to include pictures of women in their 50s, 60s, and 70s. Ironically, the fashion photographs featured in the magazine showed a model in her 20s wearing the clothing considered appropriate for each age decade.

There are many possible causes of ageism, but one plausible notion is that negative attitudes toward aging represent fear of death and dying. By their presence, the old remind younger people of the inevitability of their own mortality. Unlike the case for the other "isms," people who hold these stereotypes will eventually become the targets of their own negative beliefs as they themselves grow old.

Although there is ample evidence for ageism, there is little consensus on its cause. One prominent theory of ageism proposes that the status of older adults is negatively related to the degree of industrial development in a given society. According to the **modernization hypothesis**, the increasing urbanization and industrialization of Western society have led to lower social value for older persons (Cowgill & Holmes, 1972).

However, this hypothesis is somewhat simplistic (Luborsky & McMullen, 1999). For example, in the United States, attitudes toward the aged were not consistently positive, even when life expectancy was much lower and the prevalence of older persons in the population was less common than in modern times (Achenbaum, 1978).

Furthermore, evidence for negative attitudes toward elders are found in current pre-industrialized societies. Conversely, in some highly developed countries, older adults are more likely to be treated with reverence and respect and are well provided for through health care and economic security programs. The status of older adults in a given society is determined by many complex factors.

Related to the concept of ageism is the **multiple jeopardy hypothesis** (Ferraro & Farmer, 1996). According to this view, older individuals who are of minority status, particularly women, are affected by additional biases beyond those caused by ageism. Systematic biases against women, minorities, and working-class people are thought to interact with age to produce greater risk for discrimination in attitudes and the provision of services to specific subgroups of older adults. Alternatives also exist to the multiple jeopardy hypothesis, however. One alternative is the **age-as-leveler** view, which proposes that as people become older, age overrides the other "isms." All older adults, including the supposedly favored white males, become victim of the same stereotypes. Therefore, minorities and women are no more disadvantaged than are other persons of their age. A second alternative is the **inoculation hypothesis**. According to this view, older minorities and women have become immune to the effects of ageism through years of exposure to discrimination and stereotyping. Therefore, they are in a better position than white males to withstand the negative attitudes they experience as older adults.

These views of ageism become important in examining the health and well-being of older adults. Interestingly enough, neither ageism nor multiple jeopardy appears to have deleterious effects on feelings of happiness and well-being, as will be seen in Chapter 14. However, the effects of less access to health care and exposure to negative views of aging on those who are subjected to the "isms" may take their toll on physical health and therefore are a matter of vital concern.

As the field of developmental science moves toward placing greater emphasis on contextual influences on development, the nature and role of the environment in shaping the life of the individual is a topic that is gaining increased attention. Social factors such as the context of aging and the effects of gender, race, ethnicity, and socioeconomic status are incorporated into these models, which attempt to understand how the individual's life is affected by these socially determined distinctions and definitions.

The sociocultural models provide an important balance to the biological and psychological models, which emphasize inner processes of change. The individual's interaction with social forces at all levels of the environment provides infinite opportunities for variations and change throughout the period of adulthood. Clearly, all three models must be brought to bear in attempting to understand the complexities of nature and nurture.

SUMMARY

1. The life-span perspective is increasingly replacing the view of development as ending in adolescence. Current life-span models emphasize contextual influences on development, and the term "developmental science" is emerging to reflect the need to take a broad, interdisciplinary approach to the study of change over time.

2. Interactionist models of development emphasize processes such as niche-picking in which there is a reciprocal interaction between the individual and the environment. Organismic models regard development as an unfolding of genetic processes, and mechanistic models emphasize the role of the environment in shaping development. Interactionist models include the concepts of multidimensionality and multidirectionality, and they regard plasticity as an important element of development. Reciprocal processes in which individuals affect and are affected by their environment are a focus of interactionist models. The biopsychosocial perspective fits within the interactionist model.

3. There are two major categories of biological theories, all of which regard aging as the result of changes in the biological makeup of the organism. Programmed aging theories are based on the observation that species differ in life spans (represented by the Gompertz equation) and propose that aging is genetically determined. The telomere theory, which emerged in part from observations of replicative senescence, proposes that cells are limited in the number of times they can reproduce by the fact that each replication involves a loss of the protective ends of chromosomes known as telomeres. Other programmed aging theories regard changes in organ systems, such as the endocrine and nervous systems, as the cause of aging. Random error theories view aging as an accident resulting from cellular processes that have gone awry. Included in random error theories are the wear and tear theory, the rate of living theory, the waste product accumulation theory, the cross-linking theory, and the free radical theory. Studies on caloric restriction provide support for the free radical theory, which also proposes that antioxidants can slow down the aging process.

The autoimmune, error catastrophe, and order to disorder theories are additional random error theories (see Table 2-2 for a summary).

4. Erikson's psychosocial development theory is an important psychological model of development in adulthood. It proposes a series of eight psychosocial crisis stages that correspond roughly to age periods in life in the growth of psychological functions. The eight stages follow the epigenetic principle, which means that each stage builds on the ones that come before it. However, later stages can appear at earlier ages, and early stages can reappear later in life. The four psychosocial crisis stages of adulthood are Identity versus Identity Diffusion, Intimacy versus Isolation, Generativity versus Stagnation, and Ego Integrity versus Despair. According to Piaget's theory of development, individuals gain in the ability to adapt to the environment through the processes of assimilation and accommodation. The ideal state of development is one of equilibrium or balance. According to the identity process theory, identity assimilation and identity accommodation operate throughout development in adulthood as the individual interacts with experiences. The multiple threshold model was proposed as an explanation of how identity processes influence the interpretation of age-related events such as changes in physical or cognitive functioning.

5. Ageism is a set of stereotyped views about older adults, reflected in negative as well as positive images. Some historians believe that older adults were more highly regarded in preindustrial societies, a view known as the modernization hypothesis. However, it appears that mixed views of aging have existed throughout history and across cultures. Theories that relate the well-being of the older individual to level of social involvement include disengagement theory, activity theory, and continuity theory. These propose different relationships between individuals and society. According to the multiple jeopardy hypothesis of aging, older adults who are of minority status and are female face more discrimination than white male individuals. The age-as-leveler hypothesis and the inoculation hypothesis provide alternatives to the multiple jeopardy hypothesis.

6. Age provides an important social cue about an individual. Social clocks describe the life course in terms of "on-time" and "off-time" events as well as "non-events" that do not happen at expected ages.

7. Sociocultural models of development emphasize the effects of the environment on individuals, focusing on variables such as age and sex structures within the population, income, and social class. The life course perspective highlights age-related norms, roles, and attitudes as influences on individuals. Ecological perspectives examine multiple levels of organization within the environment, such as the proximal social relational level and the sociocultural level.

GLOSSARY TERMS

Accommodation: process in Piagetian theory in which individuals change their existing mental structures to incorporate information from experiences.

Activity theory: the prevailing view in social gerontology that it is harmful to the well-being of older adults to force them out of productive social roles.

Age-as-leveler: the proposal that as people become older, age overrides the other "isms."

Ageism: a set of beliefs, attitudes, social institutions, and acts that denigrate individuals or groups based on their chronological age.

Assimilation: process in Piagetian theory in which individuals interpret new experiences in terms of their existing mental structures.

Chromosomes: distinct, physically separate units of coiled threads of deoxyribonucleic acid (DNA) and associated protein molecules.

Collagen: substance found throughout the body, which makes up about one-third of all bodily proteins.

Contextual influences on development: the effects of social processes on changes within the individual.

Continuity theory: the proposal that older adults will suffer a loss of well-being and only the negative effects of ageism if they are not allowed to maintain their desired level of involvement in society.

Developmental science: term replacing "developmental psychology" to reflect the need to take a broad, interdisciplinary approach to understanding patterns of change in life.

DNA (deoxyribonucleic acid): the basic unit of genetics that carries inherited information and that controls the functioning of the cell.

Disengagement theory: the proposal that successful aging involves a process of mutual withdrawal of the individual from society.

Ecological perspective: theoretical model emphasizing that changes occur throughout life in the relations between the individual and multiple levels of the environment.

Ego Integrity versus Despair: stage in Erikson's psychosocial development theory in which the individual attempts to establish a sense of acceptance and integration.

Epigenetic principle: the principle in Erikson's theory that states that each stage unfolds from the previous stage.

Equilibration: process in Piagetian theory through which individuals are able to interpret their experiences through a consistent framework but are able to change this framework when it no longer is helpful in organizing experiences.

Equilibrium: state in Piagetian theory through which individuals are able to interpret their experiences through a consistent framework but are able to change this framework when it no longer is helpful in organizing experiences.

Free radical: molecular fragment that seeks to bind to other molecules.

Gene: a functional unit of a DNA molecule carrying a particular set of instructions for producing a specific protein or other molecules needed by the body's cells.

Generativity versus Stagnation: stage in Erikson's psychosocial development theory in which the individual focuses on the issues of procreation, productivity, and creativity.

Gerontology: the scientific study of the aging process.

Gompertz equation: a function that expresses the relationship between age of the organism and age of death.

Heritability index: the degree to which a characteristic is inherited.

Identity accommodation: the process through which changes occur in the individual's view of the self.

Identity Achievement versus Identity Diffusion: stage in Erikson's psychosocial development theory in which the individual attempts to establish a sense of self.

Identity assimilation: the process through which individuals interpret new experiences relevant to the self in terms of their existing self-schemas or identities.

Identity process theory: theoretical perspective describing interactions between the individual and experiences.

Inoculation hypothesis: the proposal that older minorities and women have become immune to the effects of ageism through years of exposure to discrimination and stereotyping.

Interactionist model: view that genetics and environments interact in complex ways and that the individual actively participates in his or her development through reciprocal relations with the environment.

Intimacy versus Isolation: stage in Erikson's psychosocial development theory in which the individual attempts to establish an intimate relationship with another adult.

Life course perspective: theoretical model in social gerontology that emphasizes the importance of age-based norms, roles, and attitudes as influences that shape events throughout development.

Life-span perspective: the understanding of development as continuous from childhood through old age.

Mechanistic model: view in which "nurture" or the environment is regarded as the prime mover in development.

Model: a broad view or position regarding the nature of development.

Multidimensionality: the principle that there are multiple processes in development.

Multidirectionality of development: the principle that not all systems develop at the same rate within the person—over time, some functions may show positive changes; and others, negative changes. Even within the same function, the same individual may show gains in one area, losses in another, and stability in yet a third domain.

Multiple jeopardy hypothesis: the proposal that older individuals of minority status, particularly women, are affected by additional biases beyond those caused by ageism.

Multiple threshold model: theoretical perspective proposing that personal recognition of aging occurs in a stepwise process across the years of adulthood.

Mutations: alterations in genes that lead to changes in their functions.

Niche-picking: the notion that a child's genetically based abilities lead that child to select certain activities that further enhance the development of those abilities.

Organismic model: view in which "nature" or genetics is regarded as the prime mover in development.

Perspective: a proposal that presents a position or set of ideas to account for a set of processes; less formal than a theory.

Plasticity: the proposal that the course of development may be altered depending on the nature of the specific interactions of the individual in the environment.

Proximal social relational level: level of interaction in the ecological perspective involving the individual's relationships with significant others, peers, and nuclear families.

Psychosocial: term used by Erikson to refer to developmental processes that involve a combination of psychological and social forces.

Reciprocal nature of development: the principle that people both influence and are influenced by the events in their lives.

Replicative senescence: the loss of the ability to reproduce.

Schema: term used by Piaget to refer to the individual's existing mental structures.

Social clock: normative expectations for the ages at which major life events should occur.

Sociocultural level: level of interaction in the ecological perspective involving relations with the larger social institutions of educational, public policy, governmental, and economic systems.

Telomere: the terminal region or tail of a chromosome that is made up of DNA but that contains no genetic information.

Chapter Three

The Study of Adult Development and Aging: Research Methods

> **"**Nature gives you the face you have at twenty; it is up to you to merit the face you have at fifty.**"**
>
> Coco Chanel
> 1883–1971

A ging is intimately tied up with the passage of time. It is this intrinsic relationship between age and time that researchers in adult development and aging must struggle with in designing their studies. As difficult as questions are regarding the nature of change over time, it is crucial that such research be conducted. Without empirical data, there would be no solid ground for establishing a basis for gathering a clear view of how aging affects people. In this chapter, we examine the many innovative strategies that researchers have devised to provide the information needed to gain an accurate view of the processes of development in adulthood and later life.

VARIABLES IN DEVELOPMENTAL RESEARCH

A **variable** is a characteristic that "varies" from individual to individual. Behavioral scientists attempt to understand why some people are high on a particular variable and some people are low. This is the **dependent variable**, the variable on which people differ. The **independent variable** is the variable that explains or "causes" the range of scores in the dependent variable. Although developmental psychologists treat age as an independent variable, it is not technically correct to do so because the experimenter cannot control its value.

An **experimental design** involves the manipulation of an independent variable followed by the measurement of scores on the dependent variable. Respondents are randomly assigned to treatment and control groups. It is assumed that people vary on the dependent measure because they were exposed to different levels of the independent variable. Since age is not an independent variable, we cannot state that aging "caused" people to receive the scores they did on a dependent variable of interest.

In cases where the characteristics of a group cannot be manipulated experimentally, the design is said to be **quasi-experimental**. In a quasi-experimental design, groups are compared on predetermined characteristics. We cannot conclude that the predetermined characteristic caused the variations in the dependent variable, but we can describe the differences. If we feel that other explanations have been ruled out, and if we can repeatedly demonstrate differences based on age, we can make the cautious inference that aging had something to do with the variations in people's scores. Solid theories and careful ruling out of alternative explanations are the key to drawing conclusions about the "effect" of age on variables of interest.

DESCRIPTIVE RESEARCH DESIGNS

The research designs used in studies on adult development involve manipulation in quasi-experimental fashion of the variables of age, cohort, and time of measurement (see Table 3-1).

TABLE 3-1
Age, Cohort and Time of Measurement

Term	Definition	Index of
Age	Chronological age, measured in years	Change within individual
Cohort	Year of period of birth	Influences relative to history
Time of measurement	Time of testing	Current influences on individuals being tested

These three factors are thought to influence jointly the individual's performance on any given psychological measure at any point in life. As we will see, these variables are highly related to each other, making the task of conducting research in adult development and aging a challenging enterprise.

Age, Cohort, and Time of Measurement

Age is measured as chronological age, usually in years. As an objectively determined measure based on the passage of time, age is not a direct measure of an individual's internal characteristics. The older a person is, the more calendar years that person has experienced. There may or may not be a direct connection between the movement of the calendar and changes going on within the person. Developmental psychologists use age as a convenient shorthand but understand that age is an imperfect index of the phenomena being investigated.

> **"What do you think?"** 3-1
>
> Why is it that cohort, time of measurement, and age cannot truly be separated from each other?

Social aging is represented by the two factors of cohort and time of measurement. **Cohort** is determined by the year of the individual's birth, and this term is used in studies on adult development and aging to signify the general era in which a person was born. Conceptually, the term "cohort" may represent the more familiar term "generation" in that it is intended to refer to people who were born (and hence lived through) some of the same social influences. For example, members of the 1950 cohort were in college during the Vietnam War era and shared certain experiences specific to this period of history. By contrast, the college experiences of people born in the 1960 cohort were far more quiescent.

Time of measurement is the year or period in which testing has occurred. It is a convenient way of representing the social and historical influences on the individual at the point when data are collected. Time of measurement is linked to cohort in that people of a certain age being tested at a particular time were born within the same cohort. However, conceptually, time of measurement is intended to be an index of current environmental conditions. For instance, adults tested now are more proficient at using computers than were adults tested in the 1980s, when personal computers were far less available or accessible. A measure of development that depends on being able to use the computer, then, would be highly influenced by the year in which the study is conducted, apart from any effects attributable to the aging process. The inherent connection between time of measurement and cohort creates logical difficulties when investigators attempt to disentangle these indices of social and historical context.

Although the three variables of age, cohort, and time of measurement may be separately described, they are interdependent because when two are known, the third is determined.

In this spy movie spoof, Austin Powers proves to be a good example of what might happen when a person becomes separated in time from other members of his cohort.

Therefore, researchers cannot conclude with certainty that an effect appearing to be caused by age is not due to the operation of one of these other factors.

Early findings in psychology on adult development and aging involved simple one-factor designs in which people of different ages were compared on the variable of age. No efforts were made in these studies to investigate contextual effects relating to historical or social contextual factors. The two variants of these descriptive research designs are **longitudinal**, which involves comparing the same people at different ages, and **cross-sectional**, which involves comparisons between people of different ages at the same point of measurement. Many current researchers also base their work on these designs, but there is greater awareness of their limitations than was true in the past. A summary of these designs is shown in Table 3-2.

<u>TABLE 3-2</u>
Characteristics of Descriptive Research Designs

	Design Advantages	*Disadvantages*	*Corrective Step*
LONGITUDINAL	Measures age changes and therefore "development"	Effects of aging cannot be separated from historical change. Takes many years to complete. Expensive. Researcher will not have publishable results. Selective attrition of respondents. Practice effects on tests may lead to improved performance. Original test may become outdated.	Devote administrative resources to maintaining the respondents in the study. Use alternate forms of the test to avoid practice effects. Re-score outdated measures using newer theoretical frameworks. Examine data from multiple studies conducted at different time periods.
CROSS-SECTIONAL	Quick and inexpensive. Latest theories can be tested	Measure differences between age groups and not changes over time. Results may reflect cohort differences and not differences due to aging. Tasks may not be equivalent for different cohorts. Survivor problems exist because the older adults are a select group. Appropriate age ranges are difficult to determine.	Control for cohort differences by careful attention to selection of samples. Validate test procedures on different age groups before comparing them. Regard results as tentative rather than conclusive. Replicate studies, preferably with more sophisticated methods.

Longitudinal Designs

The goal of a longitudinal study is to examine age changes. By observing and studying people as they get older, researchers feel confident that they have changed as the result of intrinsic aging changes that have occurred with the passage of time. The longitudinal study is analogous to attending a high school reunion. You and everyone else are wearing badges with your copies of your senior yearbook photos displayed over your names. As you compare the faces of the people on the badges with the faces of the people as they appear in person now, you are struck by the way some people look the same and others look like completely different individuals. This, in effect, is your own "longitudinal" study. You are comparing people with the way they were at one point in time with the way they are now on the rather obvious (and subjective) variable of physical appearance. You may wonder why Jane, the former prom queen, now looks somewhat faded and frumpy, or how Harold, the former math freak, has evolved into a charming and desirable stockbroker. As you speak to these people, you learn more about how they have changed over the years. That prom queen has gotten a great deal more serious than she was in high school, and the math freak has now become a great deal worldlier. The hypotheses you spin out regarding these people are the kinds of inferences that researchers interested in adult development and aging attempt to make based on similar observations of people over time.

As intuitively appealing as is the longitudinal design, it has serious drawbacks. From a theoretical point of view, researchers cannot know with certainty that the changes observed over time are the results of the person's own aging versus the result of the person having been subjected to a changing environment. The individual cannot be removed from the environment to see what would happen in a different set of circumstances. In longitudinal studies, there is an inevitable coincidence of personal and historical time.

Practical problems also plague longitudinal research. The most obvious problem is that longitudinal research takes many years. To be of value as a study of adult development and aging, a longitudinal study should span at least a decade or more. Both patience and a solid research budget are required because the study will be costly. Furthermore, the results of the study will not be available for many years, which may create problems for researchers whose careers depend on their publication records. The study may even outlive at least its original investigator.

The participants in a longitudinal study are also likely to be lost over time, a problem referred to as **subject attrition**. The loss of participants from the original sample creates a host of practical and theoretical problems. From a practical point of view, as the number of subjects dwindles, it becomes increasingly difficult to complete statistical analyses on the data. Even if there are a respectable number in the total sample, there may be too few to permit more refined analysis of, for example, differences according to sex, social class, or race.

Participants in a high school reunion have a chance to witness their own longitudinal study as they watch the aging of their fellow classmates.

The loss of participants also creates difficulties when the investigator wants to draw inferences from the sample to the population as a whole. The people remaining at the end of the study are the "survivors" who did not become ill, die, lose interest, or move away without leaving a forwarding address. The people who did disappear from the sample did so for one of those reasons. If the reason pertained to their health, social class, or motivation, then it means that the ones remaining in the study are higher on all or some of these factors. Conclusions made about the "survivors" may not apply to the general population. Data from a longitudinal study are likely to be skewed by the fact that different types of people are present in the samples at Time 1 and Time 2 (or later testings). If both the dropouts and the survivors are included in the data set for Time 1 but only the survivors are present for Time 2, the scores on positively oriented measures are likely to be higher at Time 2 than they were at Time 1. The researcher may erroneously conclude that people in the sample "improved" from Time 1 to Time 2, when all that happened was that the sicker and less motivated ones died off or dropped out between testings. The survivors may not have changed at all.

How do researchers tackle these problems of attrition? First, let's look at the practical side. Large-scale longitudinal studies are often housed in established institutions or agencies that provide clerical help to the investigator. It is then possible to set aside administrative resources to provide for the "care and feeding" of the sample in between test occasions. The research staff may send out greeting cards every year (birthday and holiday), as well as newsletters keeping them up to date on progress in the study, or may make telephone calls to establish a more personal touch. These special efforts not only keep the respondents more motivated, but they also make it more likely that the research team will find out when a person has moved or is no longer available due to illness or death.

Another way to tackle this problem is to conduct a simulated longitudinal design in which several cohorts are followed up over a 5- or 10-year period. For example, one study would include people in their 30s, 40s, and 50s, who would be followed up over a 10-year period. The second study would include people in their 50s, 60s, and 70s. Then the results would be combined to produce a simulated longitudinal design from ages 30 to 70. Sophisticated statistical methods are now making these types of analyses more feasible.

Practice effects are another complication in longitudinal studies. The survivors have had at least one, if not several, opportunities to practice taking the tests they are being given. If the test is one of intelligence, they may learn the answers in between testings. The same problem may plague personality studies, should a participant suspect or find out later that a certain response means admitting to a personality flaw. On the next test occasion, the respondent will be less likely to admit to having that particular problem. Researchers may use alternate forms of their tests on different test occasions to avoid these problems.

Another problem relating to the test itself is that the original test may become outdated. One option to get around this problem is to find a way to reanalyze or rescale the test scores to correspond to contemporary ways of thinking about the variable under scrutiny. This was the strategy used in studies of personality development by researchers at the Institute for Human Development in Berkeley, who have followed the same samples from infancy to old age. Previous measures were rescored using newer theoretical and empirical frameworks to allow analysis over time to be conducted without sacrificing data. Some of these studies will be described in Chapter 8.

Despite these limitations, longitudinal studies have the potential to add invaluable data on psychological changes in adulthood and old age. Furthermore, as data accumulate from multiple investigations concerning related variables, it is possible to overcome the limitations of any one particular study.

Cross-Sectional Designs

In a cross-sectional design, the researcher compares the performance of people selected on the basis of their ages. The goal of cross-sectional research is to describe age differences, but it is assumed that performance differences between age groups are the result of changes associated with the aging process. To ensure that such an assumption is valid, the researcher attempts to control for cohort differences that would obscure or exaggerate the effects of age. This control is achieved by selecting samples comparable in important factors such as amount of education and social class.

Like the longitudinal design, the cross-sectional design has the problem of providing results applicable to only one historical period. The age differences obtained in this study are specific to the cohorts of people compared. People born in the 1950s and tested in the 1990s at the age of 40 may be higher on an attribute than people born in the 1970s and tested in the 1990s at the age of 20 due to environmental factors. A similar difference between 20- and 40-year-olds may not be encountered among people compared in a study conducted in the 1980s, when the samples were born 10 years earlier. For example, although common-sense wisdom regards young adults as less conservative than middle-aged adults, it is possible that middle-agers who lived through the 1960s are less conservative than young people growing up in the 1980s. The same difference between age groups may not show up if the study is conducted in a different historical era.

Practical problems also beset the cross-sectional study. One is the matter of the survivors. Although participants might not die in the middle of the study, as is true in a longitudinal study, the fact that they are around for testing in their 60s, 70s, 80s, or beyond means that they are, by definition, survivors compared to their age peers who have died already. Thus, they may represent a healthier or luckier group of people. They may also be the people who are more cautious, perhaps smarter, and born with sturdier genes that have enabled them to avoid the many diseases that could have killed them off prior to old age. As a result, the older adults in a cross-sectional study may look different from the younger ones because the two groups are drawn from two different populations—those who will die young (but are still represented in the young adult group) and those who will live to be old. If young adults are drawn exclusively from a college population, they may not be representative of their cohort either.

The next practical problem has to do with the ages selected for the samples. How do researchers decide on the age spans for the different samples? If they are working with a young adult college student sample, then the age range will be 18 to 22 or perhaps 25 at most. This is a span of four to seven years. The older adult sample is rarely defined so narrowly. Older adult volunteers are difficult to entice into the laboratory, and most researchers have to settle for an age range that is larger than they would prefer. That age range may be as high, in some studies, as 20 to 30 years. Moreover, the "older" sample may be defined as including all respondents over the age of 50 or 60.

Related somewhat to this problem of acceptable age ranges is the question of how to divide the adult age range when selecting samples. Is it better to divide samples of people in cross-sectional studies into decades and then examine age differences continuously across the adult years? Or is it better to compare people at the two extremes of the adult span? Another possibility is to use three groups: young adult, middle-aged, and older adult. With three groups there is a greater sense of confidence in the appropriateness of "connecting the dots" between their scores on measures of psychological functioning.

With regard to test procedures, researchers conducting cross-sectional studies must also be sensitive to how different age groups will react to the test materials. In studies of memory, for example, there is a risk that the older adults will find some of the measures too challenging and perhaps intimidating. Young adults are far more comfortable with test situations because they are in school or were recently in school where they were frequently tested. To an older adult, particularly one who is sensitive to memory loss, anxiety alone about the situation can result in lowered performance than would otherwise be obtained (see below, in the section on laboratory studies).

Task equivalence also applies to the way different cohorts react to measures of personality and social attitudes. The same item may have very different meanings to people of different generations or people of different educational or cultural backgrounds. One common problem that occurs in research on personality and mental health is that a measure of, for example, depression, may have been tested for use on a young adult sample but not on an older sample. Items on such a scale that concern physical changes, such as alterations in sleep patterns presumably related to depression, may in fact reflect normal age-related differences. Therefore, older adults will receive a higher score on the depression scale by virtue of changes in their sleep patterns alone, not because of higher levels of depression. Researchers must attempt to validate their measures on samples of different ages before attempting to make conclusions about differences between age groups on that measure. More about this issue follows in the section on measurement issues in research on adult development and aging.

These problems aside, cross-sectional studies are relatively quick and inexpensive compared to the alternative. Another advantage is that they can be used with the latest technology, whether in the biomedical area or in the psychological and social domains. If a new tool comes out one year, it can be tested cross-sectionally the next. Researchers are not tied to obsolete methods that were in vogue some 30 or 40 years ago.

Perhaps the best that can be said about cross-sectional studies is that they provide descriptions of differences between groups of varying ages. The more effort the investigators put into controlling for differences other than age, the greater the likelihood that the age differences are not the result of differences in the backgrounds or life experiences of the participants. Furthermore, most researchers regard their cross-sectional findings as tentative descriptions of the effects of aging on the function of interest. There is great sensitivity in the field to the need for their findings to be replicated and, ultimately, verified through studies employing a longitudinal element.

SEQUENTIAL RESEARCH DESIGNS

It should be clear by now that the perfect study on aging is virtually impossible to conduct. Age can never be a true independent variable because it cannot be manipulated. Furthermore, age is inherently linked with time, and so personal aging can never be separated from social aging. However, considerable progress in some areas of research has been made through the application of **sequential designs**. These designs consist of different combinations of the variables age, cohort, and time of measurement. A sequential design involves a "sequence" of studies, such as a cross-sectional study carried out twice (two sequences) over a span of 10 years. The sequential nature of these designs is what makes them superior to the truly descriptive designs conducted on one sample, followed over time (longitudinal design) or on different-aged samples, tested on one occasion (cross-sectional design).

BEHIND THE RESEARCH

ROGER A. DIXON, CANADA RESEARCH CHAIR,
UNIVERSITY OF ALBERTA (EDMONTON, ALBERTA, CANADA)

What is most exciting to you about research in this field?

It is exciting for me to see the development of many new and improved research methods for investigating developmental change. It is even more exciting to see them implemented in a growing number of studies of adult development. For example, I have been impressed by the increasing number of high-quality longitudinal studies of aging. Examining actual changes with aging (using various longitudinal designs) in addition to age differences (using cross-sectional designs) has provided researchers with important new insights about aging processes. Interestingly, the results of longitudinal research do not always match the expectations based on earlier cross-sectional studies. Moreover, it is fascinating to chart actual changes in processes such as the normal decline in some aspects of memory and the gradual emergence of pathogenic diseases such as Alzheimer's. Using change-oriented designs together with new statistical techniques (such as structural equation modeling) can help us understand better why some adults change more rapidly than others and whether there are early indicators of who will decline and who will not.

What do you see as the major challenges?

Human aging is a complex phenomenon, and both our theories and methods must reflect this assumption. Accordingly, large longitudinal studies of aging often collect information from a wide variety of domains, such as health, social status, personality, and cognition. An important challenge is to develop theoretically meaningful linkages among these domains and to implement methodologically appropriate techniques for evaluating these hypothesized linkages. For example, some aspects of health (such as nutrition, education, head injury, sensory status) may be crucial predictors of late life changes in everyday memory performance. Not only must one collect specific indicators of both health and memory over a particular phase of adulthood, but one must also use sophisticated statistical techniques to test the predicted linkages against alternatives. For this reason, research teams are often deployed such that different team members have expertise in one or more aspects of the study. In the present example, a research team with expertise in health, cognitive, and methodological aspects of aging may be necessary. Appropriate matching of research questions with methodological tools will remain an important challenge for psychologists interested in aging.

Where do you see this field headed in the next decade?

I see two major directions for the future of research methods in aging. First, more young researchers will acquire a sophisticated understanding of the challenging designs and statistical techniques appropriate to the study of aging. In addition, methodologists will continue to develop new software and instructional materials, so that these techniques will become more widely available and easier to learn. Second, more research on aging will be conducted with multidisciplinary team members—many of whom may be at different locations throughout the world. Research conducted at multiple sites provides an opportunity to compare aging changes along such dimensions as urban-rural, gender, ethnicity, and culture. Such comparisons require further theoretical and methodological advances, but these advances may be "just around the corner."

The Most Efficient Design

One of the most crucial articles to be published in the field of adult development and aging was the landmark work by psychologist K. Warner Schaie (1965) in which he outlined the **Most Efficient Design**, a set of three designs manipulating the variables of age, cohort, and time of measurement.

The general layout for the Most Efficient Design is shown in Table 3-3. Researchers organize their data by constructing this table, which combines year of birth (cohort) with year of testing (time of measurement). The three designs that make up the Most Efficient Design (and the factors they include) are the time-sequential design (age by time of measurement), the cohort-sequential design (cohort by age), and the cross-sequential design (cohort by time of measurement). When all three designs are analyzed, they theoretically make it possible for the researcher to obtain separate estimates of the effects of each of the three factors.

Depending on the pattern of significant effects, the researcher may be able to make some conclusions about the relative influence of personal and historical aging. For example, if age effects are significant in the time-sequential and cohort-sequential designs, and there are no significant effects of time of measurement or cohort in the cross-sequential design, then a strong argument can be made for the possibility of "true" aging effects. Another scenario involves significant effects of time of measurement in both the time-sequential and cross-sequential designs. If there are no age effects, then the researcher may be able to make the case that the variable being studied was sensitive to current historical influences. Similarly, if the cohort factor is significant in the two designs in which it is used, and there are no significant age or time of measurement effects, then the researcher may look toward environmental factors specific to the early years of childhood in these samples.

Unfortunately, the patterns of findings are unlikely to be this clear, and it may be expected that the results show patterns of interactions (the joint effects) of the factors manipulated in each of the designs. Depending on the specific pattern of effects, along with predictions derived from the researcher's theoretical model, it may be possible to interpret the relative influence of both aging and environmental factors on the variables under study.

Of course, this process takes time. For the effort to be worthwhile there must be a respectable span of years between testing occasions. Schaie's research team has worked with seven-year intervals between measurements, with cohorts divided into five-year periods. Nevertheless, he saved time compared to what he would have needed to complete a longitudinal study on the entire span of adulthood (which would, of course, have suffered the flaws of

TABLE 3-3
Layout for Sequential Studies

Year of Birth (Cohort)	Year of Testing (Time of Measurement)			
	1980	1990	2000	2010
1940	40 years old	50 years old	60 years old	70 years old
1930	50 years old	60 years old	70 years old	80 years old
1920	60 years old	70 years old	80 years old	90 years old

simple longitudinal studies). Very early into the research, Schaie began to construct **age gradients**, or patterns of scores from individuals at each of the age points tested.

Figure 3.1 shows a very clear version of an age gradient from early in the Schaie study of intelligence (the "within-cohort gradient") in which the scores from one cohort are traced over the three times that they were tested (Schaie, Labouvie, & Buech, 1973). The legend in the lower left-hand corner shows the symbols that were used to represent each of the three times of measurement (1956, 1963, and 1970). Each group of three symbols shows the scores of people in one cohort over those three test occasions (as they grew older). At each age shown on the horizontal axis of the figure, there are at least two data points representing the scores of a given cohort when they were that age. If you visually smooth out the points in the figure, you see an overall downward trend with increasing age, starting in the 50s and accelerating in the later years.

For the moment, we need not concern ourselves with the meaning of these age patterns.

Instead, just consider the fact that Schaie was able to construct a graph of performance across the adult years after having completed just 14 years of testing rather than the 56 that would have been required to cover the years from 25 to 81. The data are superior to what would have been obtained through traditional longitudinal methods because they were based on the study of more than one cohort over more than one test occasion.

ALTERNATIVE SEQUENTIAL DESIGNS

A simpler and, according to some, clearer alternative to the three designs proposed by Schaie are the "sequences" designs proposed by Schaie's colleague, Paul Baltes (1968). According to Baltes, it is not that essential to the aging enterprise to divide social-historical aging into effects relevant to time of birth (cohort) versus effects relevant to time of measurement. It is enough to know that environmental factors contribute to the overall pattern of findings so

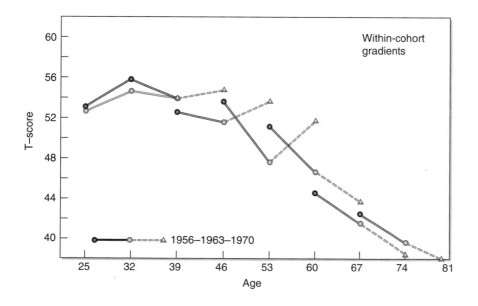

FIGURE 3.1

Age Gradient in a Sequential Study

Source: Schaie et al., 1973.

that results are not erroneously attributed to the effects of the aging process. Again, Baltes points to the weaknesses of one-shot cross-sectional or longitudinal designs, but he suggests that to correct these weaknesses, it is enough to conduct replications.

"What do you think?"   **3-2**

Why are sequential designs referred to as "sequential"?

Following from this logic, a **cross-sectional sequences design** is one in which there is a "sequence" (two or more) of cross-sectional studies. Age groups are compared, for example, on a measure of intelligence with testing completed in 1980, 1990, and perhaps 2000 (although only two testings are necessary). If the same pattern of cross-sectional findings is observed at each year of testing, then the researcher will be on firmer ground with claims of age effects than if only a single data point were used. Recall that in the comparable time-sequential design, a similar claim is made, but the researcher would attempt to determine whether effects other than age are due to time of birth or time of testing.

Similarly, in a **longitudinal-sequences design**, the researcher repeats a longitudinal study once or twice and analyzes the data to determine whether the pattern of age changes can be replicated from study to study. If the same pattern shows up repeatedly, then the attribution of age effects can be made with some confidence. However, if one pattern of longitudinal changes turns upward and another turns downward, then it would appear that the effect is not very stable and that environmental factors must play a role. This design would be comparable to the cohort-sequential design, but, again, the researcher would not be interested in

partitioning effects due to time of birth from those due to time of testing.

Both of these designs can easily be seen within Table 3-3. The cross-sectional sequences design would consist of comparisons between two times of measurement of the scores of different cohorts. Look vertically at the columns in this table. Two cross-sectional studies would be completed in, for example, 1990 and 2000, comparing 70- and 60-year-olds. If the same pattern of findings were obtained in both times of measurement, then the evidence in favor of age as a factor would be much stronger than if one set of age differences were found in one year and another set of age differences found in another year. The longitudinal sequences design would consist of two longitudinal studies conducted on two different cohorts. The 1920 cohort could be followed from 1970 to 1990, and the 1930 cohort could be followed from 1980 to 2000. If both sets of age changes showed the same patterns, then it would be safe to conclude that a true aging trend accounted for the findings. However, if one cohort's scores went up and the other cohort's went down over those times of measurement, then it would be more likely that there were historical influences in play.

No design in the Baltes framework is comparable to the cross-sequential design because, according to his position, such an analysis is neither of interest nor likely to produce clear results. It is sufficient to have shown that an effect is attributable to aging, to the environment, or to some interaction between the two.

CORRELATIONAL DESIGNS

An alternative to describing group differences using the quasi-experimental design is the correlational approach, in which relationships are observed among variables as they exist in the world. The researcher makes no attempt to divide participants into groups or to manipulate variables.

Simple Correlational Designs

Comparisons of age groups or groups based on divisions such as year of birth or time of measurement are useful for many research questions in the field of gerontology. However, in some situations this approach is neither the most efficient nor the most informative. Recall that at the beginning of the discussion about variables, it was mentioned that researchers attempt to "explain" or account for the reasons that people differ in their performance. We want to know why someone is higher on the variable of response speed than someone else. If we suspect that age differences can "explain" this difference in response speed, then we might set up a cross-sectional study in which we compare groups of people who differ in age and see if they also differ in response speed. This approach, based on the model of the experimental method (although it is not an experimental design, for reasons discussed above) is clear and intuitively sensible. However, apart from all of the problems involved in cross-sectional studies, another problem is directly tied in with the notion of grouping people according to age. The variable of age is a continuous variable, meaning that it does not have natural cutoff points (as does grade in school). When we put people into groups based on their age, we are losing information. There may be a difference between people of 42 and people of 45 years of age, but when they are all grouped in the "40-year-olds" this distinction is obscured.

In the **correlational design**, the relationship is observed between two or more variables, producing the statistic known as the **correlation** (represented as the letter r) whose value can range from +1.0 to −1.0. A correlation greater than zero indicates that the two variables are positively related so that when the value of one variable increases, the other one does as well. A correlation less than zero indicates that the two variables are negatively related so that when one increases in value the other one decreases. A correlation of zero indicates no relationship between the variables.

One advantage of the correlational design for the study of aging is that age can be treated as a continuous variable, and so there is no loss of information owing to the necessity of collapsing people into age groups. In the example of the study on the relationship between aging and response speed, the values of age can be directly inserted into the equation, as can the values of response speed. Examples of positive, negative, and zero correlations are shown in Fig. 3.2. This displays the positive correlation between age and response speed (meaning that older adults are slower than younger adults), the negative correlation between age and depression (meaning that older adults are less likely to be depressed), and the fictitious zero correlation between age and liking of cats.

Studies based on the correlational design differ not only in the statistics that are used to analyze the data but also in the underlying assumptions about the nature of the variables under scrutiny. In experimental designs, researchers explain the variance in the dependent variable by assuming that differences among people in their scores are caused by their differences on the independent variable. By manipulating the values of the independent variable, the researcher has caused people to differ on the dependent variable. In a correlational study, the researcher makes no assumptions about what caused what—there are no "independent" or "dependent" variables. A correlation between two variables indicates simply that the two variables are related, but like the proverbial chicken and egg, the researcher cannot say which came "first."

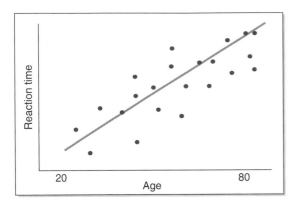

FIGURE 3.2a
Simple Correlation—Positive

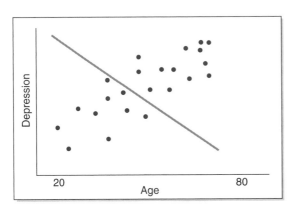

FIGURE 3.2b
Simple Correlation—Negative

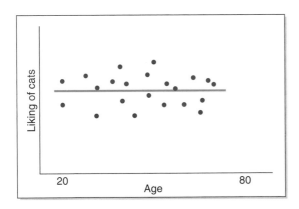

FIGURE 3.2c
Simple Correlation—Zero Value

"What do you think?" | **3-3**

Can you think of an example in which two variables that have a correlation are related to each other due to the influence of a third variable?

Let's return to the example of the relationship between age and response speed. The correlation between these variables would quite likely be found to be positive; when age increases, response speed increases as well. (A higher response speed indicates slower performance.) When interpreting this relationship, the researcher may be tempted to conclude that age "caused" the increase in response speed. However, this conclusion is not justified because age was not experimentally manipulated. In a correlational study, since there are no independent or dependent variables, the possibility that variable *a* accounts for variable *b* is equal to the possibility that *b* accounts for *a*. Now, you are probably saying to yourself, "Response speed can't cause age, it must be the other way around!" However, the truth is that because an experiment was not conducted, even the apparently silly possibility that increased response speed caused aging cannot be ruled out. Think of another example that might help firm up this point. There is a correlation between certain personality characteristics known as Type A behavior and cardiovascular disease. People with the Type A personality, who are hard-driving, competitive, somewhat hostile, and impatient, are more likely to have heart disease. Does the personality type cause heart disease (which might seem logical to you), or does heart disease cause people to have personality problems? Because the design is correlational, neither possibility can be excluded.

You may have learned these facts about correlational studies already; it is probably fair to say that most psychology students have ingrained into their nervous systems the phrase "correlation does not equal causation." The possibility that either of the two variables could have "caused" the other is part of the basis for this statement. There is yet another alternative; namely, that a third but unmeasured variable accounts for the apparent relationship between the two observed variables. In the case of the relationship between age and response speed, this third variable might be "number of functioning brain cells." Age may be related to number of brain cells, and number of brain cells may be related to response speed. The apparent correlation between age and response speed might disappear entirely when number of brain cells is measured and factored into the relationship. Similarly, the correlation between Type A behavior and heart disease might be accounted for entirely by an unmeasured third variable such as cigarette smoking. Perhaps people with certain personality types are more likely to smoke cigarettes, and cigarette smoking is related to heart disease. This unmeasured variable could be responsible for the apparent relationship between the other two.

When examining the data from a typical correlational study, then, it is essential to repeat to yourself like a mantra "correlation does not equal causation" and be on the lookout for competing hypotheses related to unmeasured variables. This is no less true of gerontology as it is for all the other sciences, but in gerontology it is particularly easy to fall into the trap because arguments related to age seem so compelling. Interestingly, however, the need to look for possible third variables is not all that different from the problems we reviewed in quasi-experimental studies when groups of different ages are compared. In these cases, generational differences in important background variables

(education, health status, environmental stimulation) could account for age differences rather than age per se. In those studies, particularly cross-sectional studies, we must also be aware of potential confounds with age that could account for older and younger groups showing different levels of performance.

Correlational studies can contain a wealth of information, despite their limitations in terms of determining cause and effect. The value of the correlation itself provides a useful indication of the strength of the relationship. Furthermore, it is possible to manipulate a larger number of variables at one time than is generally true in studies involving group comparisons. Finally, within the last 20 years, advanced correlational methods have become increasingly available that allow researchers to get around the problems involved in causality with traditional correlational methods.

Multivariate Correlational Designs

In contrast to simple correlational designs, which involve determining the statistical relationship between two variables (also called a bivariate relationship), a multivariate correlational design involves the analysis of relationships among multiple variables. A multivariate design makes it possible for the researcher to analyze a set of complex interconnections among variables. Instead of being restricted to the study of two variables, which can result in the researcher overlooking an important third (or fourth) variable, the researcher using a multivariate design can evaluate simultaneously the effects of many potentially important factors.

The simplest multivariate correlational design is one in which the researcher measures the relationship among three variables by studying the correlations of all possible pairs. This makes it possible to use a partial correlation to estimate the correlation between the two variables of interest, while the third, confounding, variable is controlled. Let us return to the example of Type A behavior and heart disease. The researcher may measure all three variables: Type A behavior, cardiovascular functioning (perhaps through blood pressure), and number of cigarettes smoked per day. The relationship between Type A personality and heart disease can then be estimated with a partial correlation that controls for number of cigarettes smoked.

Multivariate correlational methods also enable researchers to test models in which a set of variables is used to "predict" scores on another variable. In **multiple regression analysis**, the predictor variables are regarded as equivalent to the independent variables used in experiments, and the variable that is predicted is regarded as equivalent to a dependent variable. Although the design is still correlational in that the experimenter makes no actual manipulation of the independent variable, the statistics involved enable investigators to suggest and test inferences about cause-effect relationships.

Multivariate correlational designs have the potential to test complex models in which there are relationships predicted among age and scores on measures predicted to have a relationship to age. In **structural equation modeling** (SEM), researchers develop hypotheses regarding the relations among observed (measured) and latent (underlying) variables or factors (Hoyle, 1995). SEM serves purposes similar to multiple regression, but in a more powerful way, taking into account the possibility that there may be complex relationships among the variables and factors of interest.

Although SEM requires an advanced background in statistics both to use and to understand, the basics of the method can be seen from the path diagram presented in Fig. 3.3. The models produced by SEM have three principal elements, each represented by a different shape in a path diagram. Latent constructs (shown here as circles or ellipses) are abstract theoretical concepts such as "personality" or "intelligence," which cannot be directly measured but must be inferred from scores on measures that can be directly observed. These are usually the key

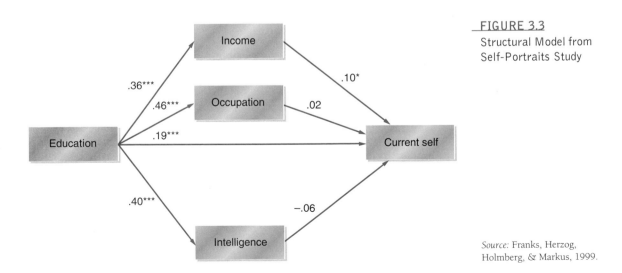

FIGURE 3.3
Structural Model from Self-Portraits Study

Source: Franks, Herzog, Holmberg, & Markus, 1999.

variables of interest. The second set of elements in a path diagram contains the relationships among latent constructs, shown by arrows. These in turn are labeled with a value (ranging from −1 to +1) indicating how strong the path is found to be in the analysis. Straight arrows point in one direction and represent the direction of prediction from predictor to outcome; curved arrows point in two directions and represent correlations. The third elements are the observed or manifest variables (the ones that are measured), and these are represented by squares or rectangles. Each latent variable is usually associated with a set of measures. For example,

the latent construct of "health" may be measured by subjective and objective ratings of various physical functions. Taken into account in a SEM diagram is measurement error, that is, the fact that measures of the latent constructs are never 100% accurate.

The simple path analysis shown in Fig. 3.3 illustrates the basic elements of this method. The circles represent the latent constructs of health, physical fitness, and self-esteem. Each of these has two or three measures. The paths illustrated in this model show the kinds of paths that would be specified in an actual model, which are direct and indirect. The model

BIOPSYCHOSOCIAL PERSPECTIVE

THE BIOPSYCHOSOCIAL MODEL is a multidimensional approach to understanding development that requires the complex research methods available through the procedure of structural equation modeling, which is based on the correlational method. An example of this type of research is provided by analysis of data from the Self Portraits Study, an investigation of factors contributing to the complexity of the self-concept in a large sample of adults spanning the years of middle and later adulthood (Franks, Herzog, Holmberg, & Markus, 1999).

In the Self Portraits Study, respondents were asked to describe themselves in their own words, and their answers were coded according to the number of different descriptors they used about themselves. Ratings were also made of descriptors developed by the researchers. Examples of some of these descriptors were "organized," "curious," "independent," "aware of race or ethnic background," and "physically attractive." The total number of descriptors that respondents used to apply to themselves were then counted and used in subsequent analysis. The larger the number of descriptors, the more complex the individual's self-representation was considered to be.

The results of this study for the 679 adults over the age of 65, summarized in Fig. 3.3, indicate that education has a direct effect on the complexity of self-representations of these older adults. Through testing the model shown in this figure, the researchers were able to establish that, although education is related to income, occupation, and intelligence, only income had a slightly positive effect on self-complexity. Education alone, independently of the other related factors, predicted a fuller representation of the self, as indicated by the +.19 relationship between education and current self. Income (.10), occupation (.02), and intelligence (−.06) had smaller values in predicting the quality of self-descriptions. This study provides a good example both of structural modeling and of biopsychosocial factors by relating sociocultural factors such as education, income, and occupation to self-concept. Biological factors are indirectly incorporated into this model, given the researcher's interest in finding out how older adults adjust their self-concepts in view of changes in physical functioning. Complex modeling approaches such as this one enable researchers to provide important information on the intersection of multiple developmental processes in middle and later adulthood.

hypothesizes that there is a direct effect of health on self-esteem, and also an indirect effect of health on self-esteem through the variable of physical fitness.

The steps to be followed in SEM are to define the structural equations linking the constructs (structural model), specify the variable(s) that will be used to measure the constructs (measurement model), and identify the mathematical matrices that define the hypothesized correlations among constructs. Eventually, the researcher will test the extent to which the data collected in the study actually fit the theoretical model (called, appropriately, "goodness of fit"). The final step is for the researcher to replicate the findings with other samples, a step important in all research but particularly in this method, in which many assumptions are made about the measures and the samples that require verification.

The newest multivariate method to be introduced into developmental research is **hierarchical linear modeling** (HLM), a method used for longitudinal studies (Raudenbush & Bryk, 2002). In this method, researchers investigate individual patterns of change rather than simply compare mean scores. This is important because in a longitudinal study, not every participant shows the same changes over time. Some individuals' scores may increase, others may decrease, and some may not change at all. Looking at the overall mean scores fails to capture this individual variation. In HLM, researchers can investigate these individual patterns statistically and examine whether particular variables affect some individuals more than others. For example, the scores obtained by people with initially high intelligence may increase more over the course of adulthood than those for people with initially lower scores, because the people with the higher abilities take advantage of more opportunities to expand their intellectual horizons. Researchers can

therefore use HLM to test their ideas about the factors that influence growth or decline of individuals over the adult years.

TYPES OF RESEARCH METHODS

Data on adult development and aging can be gained using one or more of the following types of studies. Each has advantages and disadvantages that must be weighed according to the particular field of study, the nature of the sample, available resources, and desired applications.

Laboratory Studies

The majority of information about physical and cognitive changes associated with the aging process through adulthood comes from **laboratory studies**, in which participants are tested in a systematic fashion using standardized procedures. This method is considered the most objective way of collecting data because each participant is exposed to the same treatment, using the same equipment and the same data recording procedures. For example, in a study of memory, participants would be given a set of items to be recalled, probably shown on a computer. Then they would be asked at some later point to recall as many of those items as possible, again using some type of automated response system.

There are obvious advantages to a laboratory study. The objective and systematic way in which data are recorded provides the investigator with assurance that the results are due to the variables being studied rather than to extraneous factors. In the memory study, for instance, all participants would be presented with the items to be remembered in a way that does not depend on the voice inflections of the researcher, the quality of the visual stimuli, or the amount of time used to present the items.

On the negative side, the laboratory study is removed from the reality of most adults. It is possible that the older person feels uncomfortable when tested in an impersonal and possibly intimidating manner using equipment that is unfamiliar. Consequently, the findings may underestimate the individual's abilities in everyday life.

Qualitative Studies

There are often instances in which researchers wish to explore a phenomenon of interest in an open-ended fashion. The investigation of contextual factors in adult development such as, for example, personal relationships, may demand the researcher use a method that makes it possible to identify potentially relevant factors within a broad spectrum of possible influences (Allen & Walker, 2000). Qualitative methods allow for the exploration of such complex relationships without the restrictions and assumptions of the scientific model. In other cases, researchers may be working in an area in which conventional methods are neither practical nor appropriate for the problem under investigation. Qualitative methods are also used in the analysis of life history information, which is likely to be highly varied from person to person and not easily translated into numbers. The main point in using qualitative methods is that they provide researchers with alternative ways to test their ideas and that the method can be adapted in a flexible manner to the nature of the problem at hand.

Archival Research

In **archival research**, investigators use existing resources that contain data relevant to a question about aging. The archives might consist of a governmental data bank or the records

kept by an institution, school, or employer. Another source of archival data is newspaper or magazine reports.

An advantage of archival research is that the information is readily accessible, especially given the growth of Web-based data sets including those of the U.S. Census. Data files can be downloaded directly from the internet, and publications can be accessed using portable document files (PDFs) that are easily read and searched. One disadvantage is that the researcher does not necessarily have control over the form of the data. For instance, a governmental agency may keep records of employment by age that do not include information on specific occupations of interest to the researcher. Another disadvantage is that the material may not be systematically collected or recorded. Newspaper or school records, for example, may have information that is biased or incomplete.

Surveys

Researchers rely on the **survey** method to gain information from a sample that can be generalized to a larger population. Surveys typically are short and easily administered with simple rating scales to use for answers, for example, the surveys used to poll voters on whom they will be casting their ballots for in upcoming elections. Occasionally, more intensive surveys may be given to gain in-depth knowledge about aging and its relationship to health behaviors, health risks, and symptoms. The U.S. Census, mentioned above as an archival data source, was collected through survey methodology. However, it is considered archival in that it is far more comprehensive than the average survey, and it has extensive historical records going back to the year 1750, when the first U.S. Census was conducted.

Assess Yourself

Behavioral Risk Factors Survey

National trends in health and aging are tracked by surveys conducted by the Centers for Disease Control and Prevention (CDC). The information collected through this method provides important information on behavioral health patterns and risk factors for diseases that become more prevalent in later life. The Behavioral Risk Factor Surveillance System (BRFSS) is a collaborative project of the Centers for Disease Control and Prevention, and U.S. states and territories. The BRFSS, administered and supported by CDC's Behavioral Surveillance Branch, is an ongoing data collection program designed to measure behavioral risk factors in the adult population, 18 years of age or older, living in households. The BRFSS was initiated in 1984, with 15 states collecting surveillance data on risk behaviors through monthly telephone interviews. The number of states participating in the survey increased, so that by 2001, 50 States, the District of Columbia, Puerto Rico, Guam, and the Virgin Islands were participating in the BRFSS.

The objective of the BRFSS is to collect uniform, state-specific data on preventive health practices and risk behaviors that are linked to chronic diseases, injuries, and preventable infectious diseases in the adult population. Factors assessed by the BRFSS include tobacco use, health care coverage, HIV/AIDS knowledge or prevention, physical activity, and fruit and vegetable consumption. Data are collected from a random sample of adults (one per household) through a telephone survey.

Examples of the questions included in a recent BRFSS survey are listed below. See what answers you would provide about your health and health habits:

Eating Risk Factors

How often do you eat bacon or sausage?
How often do you eat beef other than hamburger, cheeseburger, or meat loaf?
How often do you usually add butter or margarine to bread, rolls, or vegetables?
How often do you eat carrots?
How often do you eat cheese or cheese spreads, not including cottage cheese?
Including breakfast, lunch, and dinner, how many days per week, if any, do you eat red meat such as beef, pork, hamburger, or sausage but not including chicken or fish?
How often do you eat doughnuts, cookies, cake, pastry, or pies?
How often do you eat french fries or fried potatoes?
How often do you eat fried chicken?
Not counting juice, how often do you eat fruit?
How often do you eat green salad?
How often do you eat hot dogs or lunch meats such as ham or other cold cuts?
How many glasses (8 oz.) of whole milk do you usually drink?

Assess Yourself *(continued)*

Physical Activity

What type of physical activity or exercise did you spend the most time doing during the past month?

During the past month, did you participate in any physical activities or exercises such as running, calisthenics, golf, gardening, or walking for exercise?

Health Problems

Have you ever been told by a doctor, nurse, or other health professional that you have high blood pressure?

Have you ever been told by a doctor that you have diabetes?

Would you say that in general your health is: excellent, very good, good, fair, or poor?

Health Prevention

Have you ever had your blood cholesterol checked?

About how long has it been since you last visited a doctor for a routine checkup?

When was the last time you had an eye exam in which the pupils were dilated?

Have you had a flu shot in the last 12 months?

About how long has it been since you had your last mammogram?

How long has it been since you last visited the dentist or a dental clinic?

When did you have your last Pap smear?

When did you have your last proctoscopic exam?

About how many times in the last year has a health professional checked your feet for any sores or irritations?

Alcohol Consumption and Related Risk Factors

During the past month, how many days per week or per month did you drink any alcoholic beverages, on the average?

Considering all types of alcoholic beverages, that is beer, wine, wine coolers, cocktails, and liquor, as drinks, how many times during the past month did you have five or more drinks on an occasion?

During the past month, how many times have you driven when you've had perhaps too much to drink?

Activity Limitations

Because of any impairment or health problem, do you need the help of other persons with your personal care needs, such as eating, bathing, dressing, or getting around the house?

What is the major impairment or health problem that limits your activities?

Are you limited in any way in any activities because of any impairment or health problem?

Assess Yourself *(continued)*

Mental Health

During the past 30 days, for about how many days have you felt sad, blue, or depressed?

During the past 30 days, for about how many days have you felt you did not get enough rest or sleep?

Now thinking about your mental health, which includes stress, depression, and problems with emotions, for how many days during the past 30 days was your mental health not good?

Are you now doing any of the following to lose weight or to keep from gaining weight: causing yourself to vomit after you eat?

Vision Impairments

How often do you have trouble telling the difference between a one dollar bill and a five dollar bill?

While stopped in a vehicle at a traffic light, how often do you have trouble reading the license plate on the car in front of you? (This means when wearing glasses or contacts if needed.)

Other Risk Factors

Are there any loaded or unloaded firearms in your home or the car, van, or truck you usually drive? Is there a working smoke detector in your household?

Can you swim or tread water for 5 minutes in water that is over your head?

Information on trends in specific states and in the United States as a whole is available on the BRFSS web site (http://www.cdc.gov/brfss/index.htm). An example of the type of information that can be obtained from the prevalence data on this site is shown in Fig. 3.4.

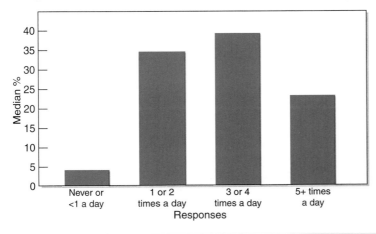

FIGURE 3.4
Fruit and Vegetable
Consumption
Nationwide—2000

Surveys have the advantage of providing data that allow the researcher to gain insight into the behavior of more people than it would be possible to study in the laboratory or other testing site. Surveys can be administered over the telephone or, increasingly, in a Web browser. Interview-based surveys given by trained administrators provide knowledge that is easily coded and analyzed while still providing comprehensive information about the behavior in question. Typically, however, surveys tend to be short, with questions that are subject to bias by respondents, who may attempt to provide a favorable impression to the researcher. Consequently, although the data may be generalizable to a large population, the quality of the data may be limited.

Case Reports

When researchers want to provide an in-depth analysis of particular individuals, they use the **case report**, which summarizes the findings from multiple sources for those individuals. Data may be drawn from interviews, psychological tests, observations, archival records, or even journal and diary entries. The focus of the case report is on the characteristics of the individual and what has influenced his or her development and life experiences. Personal narratives may also be obtained in this method, in which individuals describe their lives as they have experienced them along with their ideas about why their lives have evolved in a given manner.

Although the case report has the benefit of providing insights into the lives of individuals as they change over time, it relies heavily on the clinical judgments by the researcher. Therefore, for a case report to provide valuable information, a high level of expertise is required so that the findings are presented in a manner that balances the objective facts with the subjective analysis of the researcher.

Focus Groups

A less formal research method is a **focus group**, which is a meeting of a group of respondents oriented around a particular topic of interest. In a focus group, an investigator tries to identify important themes in the discussion and keep the conversation oriented to these themes. By the time the focus group ends, concrete research questions to pursue in subsequent studies will be identified. For example, attitudes toward mental health providers may be assessed by a focus group in which participants share their concerns and experiences with counselors and therapists.

An advantage of the focus group is that issues can be identified through a focus group prior to conducting a more systematic investigation. This approach is particularly useful when there is little preexisting research on the topic. An obvious disadvantage is that the method is not particularly systematic, so the data cannot readily be analyzed or systematically interpreted.

Observational Methods

In the **observational method**, researchers draw conclusions about behavior through careful and systematic examination in particular settings. Recordings may be made using either videotapes or behavioral records. In one type of observational method known as the participant-observation method, the researcher participates in the activities of the respondents. For example, a researcher may wish to find out about the behavior of staff in a nursing home. In participant observation, the researcher would spend several days living with people in the nursing home. The researcher's subjective experiences would become part of the "data."

There are elaborate procedures available for making behavioral records in which the researcher defines precisely the behavior to be

Clinician recording behaviors of people in a group setting.

observed (the number of particular acts) and specifies the times during which records will be made. This procedure may be used to find out if an intervention is having its intended effects. If an investigator is testing a method to reduce wandering in people with Alzheimer's disease, behavioral records could be made before and after the intervention is introduced. After observing the effects of the intervention, a final check on the method's effectiveness would involve a return to baseline condition to determine whether wandering increases without the intervention.

MEASUREMENT ISSUES IN ADULT DEVELOPMENT AND AGING

Research designs, no matter how cleverly engineered, cannot yield worthwhile results if the methods used to collect the data are flawed. Researchers in adult development and aging, like all other scientists, must concern themselves with the quality of the data-gathering instruments. The task is made more difficult because the instruments must be usable with people who are likely to vary in ability, educational background, and sophistication with research instruments. Earlier we pointed out the problems involved in comparing older and younger adults on measures used in cross-sectional studies. Here we will look specifically at some of the ways developmental researchers can ensure that their measures are equivalent across age groups.

The first measurement issue to consider is that of **reliability**. A measure is reliable if it yields consistent results every time it is used. The importance of reliability can be seen if you consider the analogy of a measure that you would use in cooking. If your tablespoon were unreliable (e.g., if it were made of soft plastic), you would be adding different amounts of ingredients every time you used it. Your brownies might come out flat and soggy one day but sky high the next. A psychological test must also provide the same scores every time it is given, or at least, it should result in a similar placement of individuals along the scale of measurement on each occasion. Thus, the first quality that psychologists look for in a measure is its ability to provide consistent scores. Reliability can be assessed by **test-retest reliability**, which is based on giving the test on two occasions and determining whether respondents receive similar scores on both occasions. The **internal consistency** of the measure is another form of reliability, indicating whether respondents are giving similar answers to similar items.

"What do you think?"   **3-4**

How might psychological measures vary in their psychometric qualities when applied to adults of different ages?

The second criterion used to evaluate a test is **validity**, meaning that the test measures what it is supposed to measure. A test of intelligence should measure intelligence, not how good your vision is. Returning to the example in the kitchen, if the tablespoon were marked "teaspoon," it would not be measuring what it is supposed to measure, and your baking products would definitely be ruined.

Tablespoons are fairly easy to assess for validity, but unfortunately psychological tests present a far greater challenge. In fact, validity is a much more elusive quality than is reliability. Furthermore, there are different kinds of validity, depending on the potential use of the measure. **Content validity** provides an indication of whether a test that assesses factual material is correctly measuring that material, as would be the case in a test of a student's knowledge of psychology that includes questions about experimental methods. **Criterion validity** indicates whether a test score accurately predicts performance on a "criterion" measure, as would be used in a test of vocational ability that claims to predict success on the job. Finally, **construct validity** is used to assess the extent to which a measure that is intended to assess a psychological construct appears to be able to do so. Construct validity is difficult to establish and requires two types of evidence. **Convergent validity** is needed to show that the measure relates to other measures

A good test is one that provides scores that are both reliable and valid.

that are theoretically similar to it. A test of intelligence should have a positive relationship to another test of intelligence that has already been validated. **Divergent validity** is needed to show that the measure does not relate to other measures that have no theoretical relationship to it. A test of intelligence should not be correlated with a test of personality unless the personality test assesses some aspect of intelligence.

The determination of a measure's ability to meet the criteria of reliability and validity is a process referred to as **psychometrics** (literally, "measurement of the mind"), and it forms a crucial part of any methodologically sound design. Although psychologists are generally aware of the need to establish the reliability and validity of their measures as used in both research and practical settings, less attention tends to be paid to psychometrics when used in gerontological research. Measures whose reliability and validity were established on young adult samples are often used, inappropriately, without testing their applicability to samples of adults of varying ages. The process can become very complicated, as you can imagine. If "Form A" of a measure is found to be psychometrically sound with college students, but only "Form B" has adequate reliability and validity for older adults, the researcher is faced with the prospect of having to use different forms of a test for different samples within the same study. Nevertheless, sensitivity to measurement issues is crucial if the conclusions drawn from the research are to have value.

ETHICAL ISSUES IN RESEARCH

All scientists who engage in research with living organisms must take precautions to protect the rights of their participants. In extreme cases, such as medical research, the life of an individual may be at stake. Equally important for other reasons, research in which respondents are being tested or put through an experimental manipulation also requires that the researcher follow a certain protocol. Recognizing the importance of these considerations, the American Psychological Association developed a comprehensive set of guidelines for psychologists that includes the appropriate treatment of human subjects in research (Americal Psychological Association, 2003) (see Table 3-4).

Researchers must present a potential respondent as full a disclosure as possible of the risks and benefits of becoming involved in any research project. When the individual is a minor child or an adult who is not able to make independent decisions, the researcher is obligated to inform the legal guardian of that individual about the nature of the study. Having provided information about the study, the researcher must then obtain a legal signature indicating that the subject understands the risks and benefits involved in the study. At this point, the researcher is able to obtain the full **informed consent** of the respondent or the respondent's legal representative. When the individual is an animal, the researcher is similarly bound to ensure that the animal is not mishandled or subjected to unnecessary harm, although different protective procedures are followed.

Research participants are also entitled to know what the study was about after it has been completed, a process called **debriefing**. If you have ever been a participant yourself, then you were probably curious during the course of the study to know what was being tested. In some cases, you might have been surprised to find out about the "real" purpose of the study. Perhaps you were told that you were going to be asked to fill out a series of questionnaires in a quiet laboratory room. In the middle of the questionnaire, you hear a loud noise out in the hallway, and then you hear a man scream. The researcher is really interested in finding out if

TABLE 3-4
Summary of Ethical Principles in Research

Guideline	Definition	Example
Informed consent	Explain risks and benefits of participation.	Prior to completing a memory test, the participant is told that the test may be difficult and challenging.
Debriefing	Describe the study after it is over.	Participants are told that an experiment in which they participated supposedly testing intelligence was actually testing agreement with stereotypes.
Suggest resources	Provide sources of help if needed.	In a study on reactions to loss of a spouse, participants who become emotionally distressed are told about mental health services they can obtain.
Right to withdraw	Participants can withdraw without any penalties.	Residents of a nursing home are told that no services will be withheld from them should they decide not to participate in a study on a new medication to treat hypertension.
Confidentiality of data	Responses will not be revealed to anyone outside the research team.	In a study in which participants are asked about their income, assurance is given that the responses will be kept in sealed or password-protected files.

you will get up from your chair and see what is wrong with the man. The questionnaires were just a ruse. After the experiment is over, the researcher is obligated to give you the correct information about the purpose of the study. You may not feel very good about yourself if you in fact did not get up to help, but at least you have a right to know that you were being tested on this attribute.

As this example illustrates, research participants may learn information about themselves that is potentially upsetting or damaging. In fact, ethical guidelines for research in psychology dictate that the researcher not only provide feedback (debriefing) but also be ready to suggest support or counseling for people who become distressed while involved in the experiment. Respondents are also entitled to withdraw from a study without risk of penalty should they choose to do so. The experimenter should not coerce them into completing the study, and even if they decide to discontinue participation, they should still receive whatever reimbursement they were initially promised. If they are students in a class or clients receiving services (such as hospital patients), they should not fear having their grades lowered or services withheld from them.

Finally, research participants are entitled to know what will happen to their data. In all cases, the data must be kept confidential, meaning that only the research team will have access to the information provided by the participants. The other condition usually attached to the data is that of anonymity. Participants are guaranteed that their names will not be associated with their responses. The condition of anonymity obviously cannot be kept if the study is a longitudinal one because the researchers must maintain access to names for followup purposes. In this case, the condition of confidentiality applies, and the researchers are obligated to ensure that all records are kept private.

These ethical standards are enforced in all institutions receiving federal funding for research through Institutional Review Boards (IRBs), which review all proposed studies to be carried out at that institution or by anyone employed by that institution. These reviews ensure that the rights of research participants are adequately protected according to the criteria discussed here. In addition, the American Psychological Association's ethical guidelines ensure that studies specifically in the field of psychology meet predetermined criteria for protection of human and animal subjects. An important development in the area of protection of human participants was the implementation in April 2003 of national standards within the United States to protect the privacy of personal health information. The Health Insurance Portability and Accountability Act, referred to as HIPAA, is the first-ever set of federal privacy standards to protect patients' medical records and other health information provided to health plans, doctors, hospitals, and other health care providers. HIPAA protects research participants by ensuring that a researcher must meet standards to maintain the privacy of health-related information. With these guidelines in place, there is assurance that respondents in research will be appropriately treated.

SUMMARY

1. The study of aging is intimately tied up with the passage of time, and researchers on aging have attempted to develop innovative methods to increase the reliability of their findings. The variables in developmental research are age, cohort, and time of measurement. Age represents processes going on within the individual, and cohort and time of measurement are regarded as measures of social aging. These three variables are interdependent because as soon as two are known, the third is determined.

2. Descriptive research designs include longitudinal and cross-sectional. Both of these designs are quasi-experimental because they do not involve the manipulation of age as an independent variable. Each has advantages and disadvantages (see Table 3-1), but the main problem is that they do not allow for generalizations to be made beyond a single cohort or period of history. Sequential designs are necessary to attempt to control for the effects of social aging because they allow researchers to make estimates of the influence of factors other than age on performance. The Most Efficient Design was developed by Schaie to provide a framework for three types of sequential studies. Baltes developed an alternative strategy that involves two types of sequential research designs.

3. Correlational designs involve studying the relationship between age (or another variable) and other measures of interest. A simple correlational design involves two variables, and a multivariate correlational design involves analyzing relationships among multiple variables. Structural equation modeling is a form of multivariate correlational analysis in which complex models involving age can be statistically evaluated. In hierarchical linear modeling, patterns of change over time

are analyzed, taking into account individual differences in change.

4. There are several methods of research available to investigators who study aging. In the laboratory study, conditions are controlled and data are collected in an objective manner. Archival research uses existing records, such as census data or newspaper records. Surveys involve asking a sample of people to provide answers to structured questions, with the intention of generalizing the collected data to larger populations. Case reports are used to provide in-depth analyses of an individual or small group of individuals. Focus groups gather information about people's views on particular topics. Observational methods provide objective data on people in specific settings and under specific conditions.

5. Researchers in adult development and aging must concern themselves with finding the most appropriate measurement tools available. The science of studying measurement instruments is known as psychometrics. Of particular concern is the need to establish the appropriateness of the same measurement instrument for adults of different ages. Reliability refers to the consistency of a measurement instrument, and validity assesses whether the instrument measures what it is intended to measure.

6. Ethical issues in research address the proper treatment of participants by researchers. Informed consent is the requirement that respondents be given adequate knowledge about a study's procedures before they participate. Debriefing refers to notification of participants about the study's real purpose. Respondents also have the right to withdraw at any time without penalty. Finally, respondents must be told what will happen to their data, but at all times it must be kept confidential. All research institutions in the United States are required by federal law to guarantee the rights of human and animal participants.

GLOSSARY

Age gradients: patterns of scores from individuals at each of the age points tested.

Archival research: a method of research in which investigators use existing resources that contain data relevant to a question about aging.

Case report: a method of research in which an in-depth analysis of particular individuals is done.

Cohort: variable in developmental research used to signify the general era in which a person was born.

Construct validity: an indication of whether a measure that is intended to assess a psychological construct appears to be able to do so.

Content validity: an indication of whether a test that assesses factual material is correctly measuring that material.

Convergent validity: an indication of whether a measure corresponds to other measures that are theoretically similar to it.

Correlation: statistic whose value can range from $+1.0$ to -1.0, indicating the strength of the relationship between two variables.

Correlational design: research design in which the relationship is observed between two or more variables.

Criterion validity: an indication of whether a test score accurately predicts performance.

Cross-sectional sequences design: developmental research design in which there is a sequence of cross-sectional studies.

Cross-sectional: developmental research design in which people of different ages are compared at the same point of measurement.

Debriefing: providing a research participant with information about the study's real purpose, after the participation has ended.

Dependent variable: the variable on which people differ.

Divergent validity: an indication that a measure does not relate to other measures that have no theoretical relationship to it.

Experimental design: a research method in which an independent variable is manipulated and scores are then measured on the dependent variable. Involves random assignment of respondents to treatment and control groups.

Focus group: a meeting of a group of respondents oriented around a particular topic of interest.

Laboratory study: a research method in which participants are tested in a systematic fashion, using standardized procedures.

Hierarchical linear modeling: a method used for longitudinal studies in which researchers investigate individual patterns of change rather than simply compare mean scores.

Informed consent: written agreement to participate in research based on knowing what that participation will involve.

Longitudinal: developmental research design in which the same people are compared at different ages.

Longitudinal-sequences design: developmental research design in which there are a sequence of longitudinal studies.

Most Efficient Design: framework originated by Schaie to organize the collection of sequential data.

Multiple regression analysis: multivariate correlational research design in which a set of variables is used to predict scores on another variable.

Multivariate correlational design: research design that involves the analysis of relationships among multiple variables.

Observational method: a research method in which conclusions are drawn about behavior through careful and systematic examination in particular settings.

Psychometrics: the science of studying measures of mental functioning.

Quasi-experimental: a research method in which groups are compared on predetermined characteristics.

Reliability: the consistency of a measurement procedure.

Sequential designs: developmental research design in which the researcher conducts a sequence of cross-sectional or longitudinal studies.

Structural equation modeling: multivariate correlational research in which a set of relationships among variables are tested to determine whether the variables provide a good fit to the data.

Subject attrition: loss of respondents over time in a longitudinal study.

Survey: a research method that involves asking a sample of people to provide answers to structured questions, with the intention of generalizing the collected data to larger populations.

Test-retest reliability: the extent to which a measurement produces the same scores on two occasions.

Time of measurement: the year or period in which testing has occurred.

Validity: the extent to which a test measures what it is supposed to measure.

Variable: a characteristic that varies from individual to individual.

Chapter Four

Physical and Sensory Changes in Adulthood and Old Age

> **"**I have reached an age when, if someone tells me to wear socks, I don't have to. **"**
>
> Albert Einstein
> 1879–1955

ccording to the biopsychosocial perspective, changes in physical functioning have psychological and social interactions. Biologically based changes have an effect on an individual's behaviors, which in turn can modify the expression of these changes. Furthermore, these changes occur in a social context, which affects their rate of progression as well as their meaning to the individual and others. Identity plays an important role in this process, for the way that individuals feel about themselves is affected in part by their physical appearance and competence. In this chapter, changes in the body, brain, and sensory functions throughout middle and later adulthood are examined, with an emphasis on their interactions with the individual's actions and identity processes. Special attention is paid to preventive measures that individuals can begin to take in young and middle adulthood.

APPEARANCE

Outward appearance is our first cue when we look at a person and make guesses about age. The face provides the most information, but there are other hints based on body build and the appearance of the skin in the hands and other exposed areas. Guesses about age are based on experience and on learning how people of different ages are likely to look and function. However, it is often surprising to learn someone's age when he or she looks prematurely old or seems to possess the secret of eternal youth. Unfortunately, as discussed in the Chapter 2 Biopsychosocial Perspective box, people in Western society have very negative attitudes toward the aging of appearance. Consequently, people can become highly sensitive to these outward signs of aging, even though they do not interfere significantly with their everyday activities.

When you ask someone about the most obvious physical changes associated with the aging process, chances are that the person will mention wrinkles and gray hair. These outward signs are not necessarily good indices of the aging of what's inside the body. However, starting in middle age many adults regard these as some of the most important aspects of the changes that occur as they get older.

Skin

The wrinkling and sagging of the skin are processes that take on significance in early adulthood, although they are hardly evident in most people at that time. Gradually, however, the number and depth of skin wrinkles increase. The skin starts to lose its firmness and elasticity, leading to the formation of sagging areas such as the infamous "double chin." Other changes in the skin involve the development of discolored areas, colloquially referred to as "age spots" (officially called *lentigo senilus*). These areas of brown pigmentation (on fair-skinned people) are more likely to develop in the exposed areas of skin on the face, hands, and arms.

With increasing age, the cells of the epidermis become less regularly arranged (Kligman, Grove, & Balin, 1985), accounting for part of the visual changes in the appearance of the skin. The majority of changes in the skin,

however, are due to a loss of the skin's flexibility and ability to conform to the changing shape of the skin as the limbs move. The skin is more likely to sag because it cannot return to its original state of tension after it has been stretched out through movement.

Two other components of the dermis show age-related changes that ultimately affect the skin's function and appearance. The sweat glands become less active, and as we shall see later, this results in a loss of the ability to tolerate heat. The sebaceous glands, which normally provide oils that lubricate the skin, become less active. Consequently, the skin surface becomes drier and more vulnerable to damage from being rubbed or chafed.

Changes also occur with increasing age in adulthood in the layer of subcutaneous fat, which becomes diminished in thickness. In young adults, the subcutaneous fat gives the skin its opacity and smoothes the curves of the arms, legs, and face. When it begins to thin in middle adulthood, the skin is more likely to sag and become more translucent. The fat does not disappear, however, but shifts as it begins to collect as fatty deposits around the torso.

Other changes in the coloring of the skin occur through the development of pigmented outgrowths ("moles") and elevations of small blood vessels on the skin surface ("angiomas"). Capillaries and arteries in the skin may become dilated and in general are more visible due to the loss of subcutaneous fat. Large irregularities in the blood vessels known as varicose veins may develop and appear on the skin of the legs.

Technically parts of the skin are the nails, which also show signs of aging. Their growth rate slows down, and they become yellowed in color. The toenails especially are likely to develop ridges and thickened areas, and they may even become curved to the point of looking like hooks.Facial appearance is affected by changes that start to accumulate in middle adulthood in the skin as well as the teeth, which become somewhat discolored due to loss of their enamel surface and staining from coffee, tea, food, and tobacco. Current generations of middle-aged adults may suffer less from problems related to tooth loss, because of improvements in dental hygiene in the past several decades, particularly flossing. Changes in the eyes also begin in middle adulthood, affecting the face's appearance. In addition to eyeglasses, which many middle-aged adults must wear for reading, if not distance, the areas around the eyes become baggy in their appearance through the accumulation of fat, fluid, and dark pigmentation.

Although genetic contributions to the apparent age of the skin are apparently quite significant (Guinot, Malvy, Ambroisine, Latreille, Mauger, et al., 2002), there are also important contributions made by the individual's lifestyle. Primary among these lifestyle factors is **photoaging**, age changes caused by exposure to the sun's harmful radiation (Scharffetter-Kochanek, Brenneisen, Wenk, Herrmann, Ma, et al., 2000). Parts of the body that are more exposed to the sun, such as the face and arms, are more likely to show the microscopic changes described here than are parts of the body that are not exposed (Takema, Yorimoto, Ohsu, Osanai, & Kawai, 1997). Sunscreen that effectively blocks the rays of the sun (at least level 15 SPF) is the most effective prevention (Dreher & Maibach, 2001; Griffiths, 1999). Cigarette smoking is also harmful to the skin.

In addition to preventive measures, adults can compensate for age-related changes in the skin in the years of middle adulthood. To counteract the fragility, sensitivity, and dryness of the skin, the individual can use sunscreens, emollients, and fragrance-free cosmetics. Vitamin A treatment can also be beneficial in

preserving the collagen matrix of the skin (Varani, Warner, Gharaee-Kermani, Phan, Kang, et al., 2000). Increasingly, chemical treatments are becoming available, including the prescription medications oral isotretinoin (Accutane), (Hernandez-Perez, Khawaja, & Alvarez, 2000), retinaldehyde (Boisnic, Branchet-Gumila, Le Charpentier, & Segard, 1999), and tretinoin (Renova) peeling (Cuce, Bertino, Scattone, & Birkenhauer, 2001). These treatment methods can be beneficial, and although they may have some unintended negative side effects (redness, irritation), they are not as extreme as laser treatment, plastic surgery, or the newest trend, injection with "Botox" (botulinum), which is a toxic substance that paralyzes facial muscles. Unfortunately, the long-term side effects of Botox are not known, and although some individuals may develop extremely painful headaches (Alam, Arndt, & Dover, 2002), it is still not known whether repeated injection of this toxin will have harmful effects on other bodily functions.

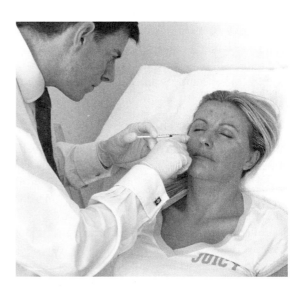

A woman receiving a Botox injection, a commonplace office procedure performed by cosmetic dermatologists.

Hair

As people get older, their hair becomes gray and eventually turns white. Equally likely, but especially of course for men, the hair also gets thinner. Changes in the color of the hair are due not to the accumulation of gray but to the increasing loss of pigmentation in the hairs that remain on the head as the production of melanin ceases. The actual shade of gray in one's hair color is the result of the mixture of the white (unpigmented) hairs with the remaining pigmented hairs. Eventually, for most people, all the hairs are unpigmented, and the overall hair color is white. People vary tremendously in the rate at which their hair changes color

The thinning of the hair, though more obvious in men, actually occurs in both sexes. Over one-third of women also experience pattern hair loss by the age of 70 years (Birch, Messenger, & Messenger, 2001) Hair loss in general results from the destruction of the germination centers that produce the hair under the surface of the skin. In **male pattern baldness**, the hair follicles continue to produce hair, but this hair is not visible. Although hair stops growing or becomes less visible where it is desired, it may appear in larger amounts in places where it is not welcome, such as the chin on women, the ears, and in thicker clumps around the eyebrows.

According to current knowledge, age changes in the hair are unpreventable. This is unfortunate, particularly for men, who are judged to be less attractive when they are bald unless they are highly attractive in other ways (Muscarella & Cunningham, 1996). It is also unfortunate that the hair dyes designed "just for men" may have opposite effects than are intended, because people tend to look more negatively upon men who use these cosmetics (Harris, 1994). This would appear to be the classic "Catch 22"! For women, estrogen replacement has been found to extend the life of the hair follicle (Brincat, 2000); the benefits of this treatment must be weighed against risks, as will become evident throughout the book in the context of hormone replacement therapy.

However, pharmaceutical companies are actively working on the solution to the problem of baldness, and improvements in hair stimulation products are probably not far off in the future.

BODY BUILD

Throughout adulthood, the body is a dynamic entity, changing size and shape continuously over the years of adulthood. People are used to considering themselves fully grown by the early 20s, although their height and weight will change significantly over the course of their adult years. A gradual loss of height takes place throughout adulthood as is demonstrated in cross-sectional and longitudinal studies; it is more pronounced for women, however (de Groot, Perdigao, & Deurenberg, 1996; Pini, Tonon, Cavallini, Bencini, Di Bari, et al., 2001). Loss of bone material in the vertebrae causes women's spines to collapse and shorten in length.

Two measures are used to quantify body composition. One is fat-free mass (FFM), which is an index of the amount of lean tissue in the body. The second is body mass index (BMI), which equals weight (in kilograms) divided by height squared (in meters). An ideal BMI is one that is about 23 in men and 21 in women. Total body weight increases from the 20s until the mid-50s, but declines after that. Most of the weight gain that occurs through the years of middle adulthood is due to an increase in BMI, which is manifested mainly as the accumulation of body fat around the waist and hips (appropriately called "middle-aged spread"). The loss of body weight in the later years of adulthood is not due to loss of this accumulated fat. Older adults lose pounds because they suffer a reduction of FFM, losing lean body mass consisting of muscle and bone (Baumgartner, Heymsfield, & Roche, 1995).

Even people well into middle age can take preventive and compensatory measures to offset these changes. Regular involvement in aerobic exercise can help the individual maintain muscle tone and reduce the fat deposits of middle-aged spread. Particularly important in the positive effects of exercise for middle-aged adults is the prevention of the increase in BMI that occurs in sedentary individuals (Kyle, Gremion, Genton, Slosman, Golay, et al., 2001). Exercise in which resistance training (weight lifting or Nautilus) is used can help to offset age losses in bone content that contribute to the loss of height. By engaging in vigorous walking, jogging, or cycling for 30 to 60 minutes a day three to four days a week, the sedentary adult can see positive results within two to three months (Vitiello, Wilkinson, Merriam, Moe, Prinz, et al., 1997).

"What do you think?"	4-1

What will future generations of older adults (who exercised when young) look like compared to current older adults?

A wealth of data supports these claims about the benefits of exercise, some of which comes from studies of long-term endurance athletes and their performance in old age compared to untrained men of equal or younger ages. One particularly impressive study (Horber, Kohler, Lippuner, & Jaeger, 1996) compared highly trained men in their late 60s with untrained men of similar age and sedentary men in their early 30s. The older athletes had been running at least 15 miles (30 km) each week for 10 years. They were regular participants in an annual race, the Grand Prix of Berne. There was no difference in lean body mass or body fat mass between the older trained men and the young sedentary men, but the older untrained

men had lower lean body mass and higher fat. Longitudinal studies provide similar supportive data for the value of endurance training even in later life. In one study of track athletes followed from ages 80 to 89 years, age-related changes in body composition were found to be reduced compared to what is observed in healthy people of similar age (Pollock, Mengelkoch, Graves, Lowenthal, Limacher, et al., 1997).

It is also important to consider interactions with identity when discussing the individual's decision to take advantage of exercise as a preventive measure against negative changes in body build. In one intriguing study, older adults were tested on a measure of "social physique anxiety," the extent to which one is afraid of what other people think of one's body. Over the course of a six-month exercise training study, social physique anxiety significantly decreased along with improvements in feelings of fitness and a measure of self-efficacy, or the feelings of confidence in being able to complete physically demanding tasks (McAuley, Marquez, Jerome, Blissmer, & Katula, 2002). These findings may be interpreted in terms of the identity process theory as indicating the advantages of helping older adults to achieve a balanced and self-accepting instead of accommodative approach to the changes associated with the aging process in physical appearance and fitness.

MOBILITY

The structures that support movement are the bones, joints, tendons, and ligaments that connect the muscles to the bones, and the muscles that control flexion and extension. In the average person, all these structures undergo age-related changes that compromise their ability to function effectively. Beginning in the 40s, or earlier in the case of injury, each component of mobility undergoes significant age-related losses. Consequently, there is a gradual reduction of the speed of walking (Bohannon, 1997), and joint pain develops, leading to restriction of movement in daily activities (Grimby & Wiklund, 1994). You may be aware of some of these changes from your own experience or your experience with older relatives or friends, who probably take longer than you do to reach the same destination.

Muscles

The adult years are characterized by a progressive loss of muscle mass, a process known as **sarcopenia**. There is a reduction in the number and size of muscle fibers, especially the fast-twitch fibers involved in speed and strength (Morley, Baumgartner, Roubenoff, Mayer, & Nair, 2001). As muscle mass decreases, it is replaced at first by connective tissue and then ultimately by fat. Estimates are that sarcopenia significantly affects 13–24% of people 65–70 to over 50% of persons over 80 years old (Roubenoff & Hughes, 2000). Variations in the rate of sarcopenia exist by gender and race. Among average men and women, the process is more pronounced in men (Gallagher, Ruts, Visser, Heshka, Baumgartner, et al., 2000; Goodpaster, Carlson, Visser, Kelley, Scherzinger, et al., 2001). However, there are no gender differences in athletes over the course of adulthood (Wiswell, Jaque, Marcell, Hawkins, Tarpenning, et al., 2000). Racial differences among women have been identified. Compared to white women, black women lose muscle as a lower rate.(Aloia, Vaswani, Feuerman, Mikhail, & Ma, 2000)

As indicated in cross-sectional studies, muscle strength as measured by maximum force reaches a peak in the 20s and 30s, remains at a plateau until the 40s to 50s, and then declines at a rate of 12% to 15% per decade (Hurley, 1995). Longitudinal studies confirm the existence of this pattern of loss of muscle strength in later life (Frontera, Hughes, Fielding, Fiatarone, Evans, et al., 2000). By contrast, muscular endurance as measured by isometric strength, is generally maintained throughout adulthood (Bemben, Massey, Bemben, Misner, & Boileau, 1996). There are also relatively minor effects of age on eccentric strength, involved in lowering arm weights, slowing down while walking, and going down the stairs. Eccentric strength is preserved through the 70s and 80s in men and women (Hortobagyi, Zheng, Weidner, Lambert, Westbrook, et al., 1995) (Horstmann, Maschmann, Mayer, Heitkamp, Handel, et al., 1999). These findings are consistent with the known patterns of atrophy of the fast-twitch and slow-twitch fibers.

Muscle mass changes do not completely predict age-related reductions in strength in adulthood (Hughes, Frontera, Wood, Evans, Dallal, et al., 2001). There are also disruptions in the signals the nervous system sends to the muscles, telling them to contract (Akima, Kano, Enomoto, Ishizu, Okada, et al., 2001). For example, in one study comparing men in their 20s with men in their late 50s, age differences were not observed in tests involving small muscle groups. These small muscle groups test (such as those used in a one-arm cranking device) are estimated to have a small component of central nervous system functioning (Aminoff, Smolander, Korhonen, & Louhevaara, 1996). Another factor contributing to muscle strength loss other than sarcopenia is a reduced sensitivity in the sensory receptors in the skin of the hand (Kinoshita & Francis, 1996).

Strength training is the number one preventative measure that can counteract the process of sarcopenia in adulthood, potentially doubling muscle strength (McCartney, Hicks, Martin, & Webber, 1995; McCartney, Hicks, Martin, & Webber, 1996). People as old as 100 years of age can benefit from this form of exercise. Effective training typically involves 8 to 12 weeks, three to four times per week at 70% to 90% of the one-repetition maximum. Even a short break from an exercise program can be compensated for in a brief time (Taaffe & Marcus, 1997).

Bones

Bone consists of living tissue that is constantly reconstructing itself through a process of bone remodeling in which old cells are destroyed and replaced by new cells (Fig. 4.1). The remodeling process is controlled partly by hormones and partly by the amount of mechanical pressure placed on the bone. The greater the amount of stress placed on the bone, the more the growth of new bone cells is stimulated. The general pattern of bone development in adulthood involves an increase in the rate of bone destruction compared to renewal and greater porosity of the calcium matrix, leading to loss of bone mineral content.

Estimates of the decrease in bone mineral content over adulthood are 5% to 12% per decade from the 20s through the 90s (McCalden, McGeough, Barker, & Court-Brown, 1993), with an accompanying decrease in strength of 8.5% per decade (McCalden, McGeough, & Court-Brown, 1997). Adding to this process, microcracks develop in response to stress placed on the bones and further contributes to the likelihood of fracture (Courtney, Hayes, & Gibson, 1996). Part of the older bone's increased susceptibility to fracture can be accounted for by a loss of collagen, which means that the bone is less able to bend when pressure is put upon it (Zioupos, Currey, & Hamer, 1999).

Variations exist in the rate of bone loss according to a number of other factors. First of all, the rate of bone loss is greater in women, particularly those who are past reproductive age and are no longer producing the hormone estrogen in monthly cycles (Garnero, Sornay Rendu, Chapuy, & Delmas, 1996). Heavier people in general have higher bone mineral content, and so they lose less in adulthood, particularly in the weight-bearing limbs that are involved in mobility (Edelstein & Barrett-Connor, 1993). Higher muscle mass, at least in older men, also contributes positively to bone density (Ravaglia, Forti, Maioli, Bastagli, Facchini, et al., 2000).

Genetic factors are estimated to account for about about 80% of bone mineral content in adulthood (Sagiv, Vogelaere, Soudry, & Ehrsam, 2000). Among women, African American women have higher bone mineral content than whites (Perry, Horowitz, Morley, Fleming, Jensen, et al., 1996), and among whites, bone loss is greater in those with fair skin (May,

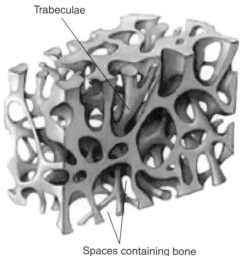

Trabeculae

Spaces containing bone
marrow and blood vessels

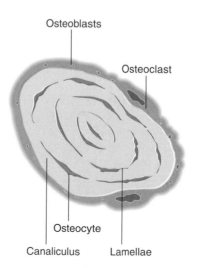

Osteoblasts

Osteoclast

Osteocyte

Canaliculus   Lamellae

FIGURE 4.1

Diagram of the Bone

Murphy, & Khaw, 1995). Still, bone loss is generally higher in women of all races studied (Krall, Dawson-Hughes, Hirst, Gallagher, Sherman, et al., 1997), including whites, African Americans (Perry, et al., 1996), and Chinese (Xu, Huang, & Ren, 1997). Hispanic women show similar patterns of bone loss as non-Hispanic whites, even though the risk of hip fracture among Hispanic women is lower (Villa, Marcus, Ramirez Delay, & Kelsey, 1995).

BIOPSYCHOSOCIAL PERSPECTIVE

AGE-RELATED CHANGES in the bones, joints, and muscles greatly increase the risk of accidental falls in later adulthood, particularly for women. Estimates in the United States place the rate at about 7% of the over-65 population per year (U.S. Bureau of the Census, 2003a). Fractures are the most serious consequence of falls, occurring in 5% of all people who fall. The most common fractures from falls are those of the pelvis, hip, femur, vertebrae, humerus, hand, forearm, leg, and ankle. Of these, hip fractures are the most serious. Both the rates of falling and hip fractures are more common in older women than in older men. It is estimated that hip fractures resulting from falls account for 40% of admissions to nursing homes. The injury sustained in a fall can also lead to death. For people aged 65 and older, accidents are the ninth leading cause of death, and falls account for one-third of all of injury-related deaths (Minino, Arias, Kochanek, Murphy, & Smith, 2002).

One fact important to keep in mind when looking at the apparent relationship between hip fracture and falling is that a person may fall as the result of a hip fracture. In other words, the hip breaks due to internal weakening, and consequently the person is unable to stand.

Loss of muscle strength is another risk factor for falling (Evans, 1995; Schwendner, Mikesky, Holt, Peacock, & Burr, 1997), as are declines in the ability to make quick adjustments after losing one's footing (Thelen, Schultz, Alexander, & Ashton-Miller, 1996). Sensory and cognitive changes also appear to play important roles in increasing the risk of falling. Women who experience pain in their joints or muscles are at heightened risk for falling, particularly if the pain is untreated (Leveille, Bean, Bandeen-Roche, Jones, Hochberg, et al., 2002). Yet another risk factor is the wearing of high heels, which make it more difficult for older women to maintain their balance (Lord & Bashford, 1996).

In addition to the many contributions already seen to the increased likelihood of falls among older people is evidence that reduced proprioception in the lower limbs is an additional risk factor for falling (Bergin, Bronstein, Murray, Sancovic, & Zeppenfeld, 1995). Although not a major addition to the formula of age-related changes that contribute to loss of balance, the ability to sense the position of the feet and legs seems to add at least a measurable element to the risk of falling (Era, Schroll, Ytting, Gause-Nilsson, Heikkinen, et al., 1996).

A woman who has the painful and perhaps frightening experience of a fall may become anxious the next time she is in a situation where she feels insecure and become even more unsteady in her gait (Brown, Gage, Polych, Sleik, & Winder, 2002). The "fear of falling", or what is also called "low self-efficacy" about avoiding a fall (Tinetti, Mendes de Leon, Doucette, & Baker, 1994), can create a vicious cycle in which the older individual increasingly restricts her movements, further increasing the risk of losing strength.

Sociocultural factors may also be seen to contribute to the risk of falling. The culture in which current elders were raised did not promote activity or exercise in women. It is therefore more likely that they will have lower muscle and bone strength than would have been the case if they had enjoyed a lifetime of strength-building activity. Furthermore, many environments are not particularly conducive to the mobility of older adults and can contribute to the risk of falling (Connell, 1996). The typical urban sidewalk and street are filled with many potential traps for young and old alike; unfortunately, older people have a lower chance of surviving a stumble over a high curb than do healthy, fit young people.

The process of bone loss is not a significant problem until at least the 50s or 60s. However, actions that are taken prior to this age can have important preventive consequences. These actions are particularly important for women. Smoking, alcohol use, and poor diet exacerbate bone loss in later adulthood, while bone loss can be slowed by aerobic activity, resistance training with weights, increased calcium intake prior to menopause, and use of vitamin D (Dawson-Hughes, Harris, Krall, & Dallal, 2000; Murphy, Khaw, May, & Compston, 1994; Sinaki, 1996; Welten, Kemper, Post, & van Staveren, 1995). Bone loss also reflects a variety of environmental factors. People who live in climates with sharp demarcations between the seasons appear to be more likely to suffer from earlier onset of bone loss (Belkin, Livshits, Otremski, & Kobyliansky, 1998). A disease known as osteoporosis, which will be discussed in Chapter 5, occurs when the rate of bone loss significantly exceeds the norm.

Joints

Although most adults do not notice changes in joint functioning until their 40s, deleterious processes are at work even before the age of skeletal maturity, continuing steadily throughout the adult years (Tuite, Renstrom, & O'Brien, 1997). Structural changes occur with age in virtually every component of the joint. By the 20s and 30s, the arterial cartilage that protects the joints begins to degenerate, and as it does so, the bone underneath begins to wear away. This is because, over time, the cells in the arterial cartilage lose the ability to repair themselves (Verbruggen, Cornelissen, Almqvist, Wang, Elewaut, et al., 2000). Over the course of adulthood, problems are exacerbated by outgrowths of cartilage that begin to develop, further interfering with the smooth movement of the bones against each other. The fibers in the joint capsule become less pliable, reducing flexibility (Ralphs & Benjamin, 1994).

Unlike muscles, joints do not benefit from constant use. On the contrary, these deterioration processes are directly related to the amount of stress placed on the joints, a problem that particularly affects the knees (Kettunen, Kujala, Kaprio, Koskenvuo, & Sarna, 2001). Exercise cannot compensate for or prevent age-related changes. However, there are a number of measures that older individuals can take to help reduce joint pain, stiffness, and limitation of movement. Strength training that focuses on the muscles that support the joints can be beneficial in helping the individual to use those joints while placing less stress upon impaired tendons, figments, and arterial surfaces. Because obesity is related to reduced joint flexion range of the hips, knees (Escalante, Lichtenstein, Dhanda, Cornell, & Hazuda, 1999), shoulders, and elbows (Escalante, Lichtenstein, & Hazuda, 1999), an exercise program should also focus on lowering body fat. Particularly important is flexibility training that increases the range of motion of the joint (O'Grady, Fletcher, & Ortiz, 2000).

Precautions taken in early adulthood can reduce the chance of losses in middle age and beyond. Most important is proper footwear, particularly during exercise. People who engage in occupational activities that involve repetitive motions of the wrist should attempt to minimize damage by the use of ergonomically designed accessories. Middle-aged individuals already experiencing joint damage can benefit from flexibility exercises that expand a stiff joint's range of motion. Exercise that strengthens the muscles supporting the joint also helps to improve its functioning (Blanpied & Smidt, 1993). Both kinds of exercise have the additional benefit of stimulating circulation to the joints, thereby enhancing the blood supply that promotes repair processes in the tendons, ligaments, and surfaces of the exercising areas.

VITAL BODILY FUNCTIONS

Age-related changes throughout adulthood in the bodily systems that support life ultimately determine the individual's survival. Figure 4.2 summarizes early cross-sectional studies on the functioning of a number of key systems throughout adulthood. As we will see in this section of the chapter, there is much that individuals can do to reduce or offset the impact on aging on the majority of these functions.

Cardiovascular System

Aging of the cardiovascular system involves changes that begin in middle age in both the heart itself and the arteries that circulate blood throughout the body (see Fig. 4.3). The component of the heart that has the most relevance to aging is the left ventricle, which loses muscle mass and strength and increases in fat and connective tissue. The wall of the left ventricle becomes thicker and less compliant during each contraction, leading the left ventricle to lose its effectiveness as a pumping mechanism. Therefore, less blood is ejected into the aorta with each contraction of the heart. The arteries become less able to accommodate the flow of blood that spews from the left ventricle. This loss of flexibility in the arteries is referred to as **vasculopathology of aging** (Bilato & Crow, 1996). Adding to these changes is the continuing deposit of plaque along the arterial walls of fatty substances, consisting of cholesterol, cellular waste products, calcium, and fibrin (a clotting material in the blood).

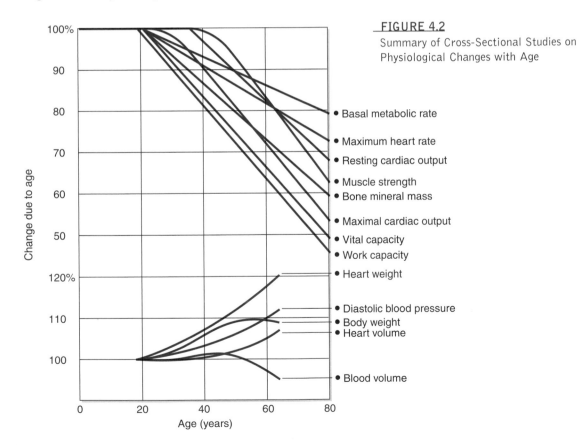

FIGURE 4.2

Summary of Cross-Sectional Studies on Physiological Changes with Age

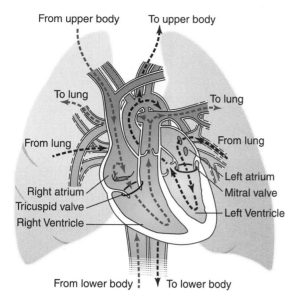

From upper body   To upper body

To lung   To lung

From lung   From lung

Left atrium

Right atrium   Mitral valve
Tricuspid valve
Left Ventricle
Right Ventricle

From lower body   To lower body

FIGURE 4.3
Heart and Circulation

The primary indicators of cardiovascular efficiency are **aerobic capacity**, the maximum amount of oxygen that can be delivered through the blood, and **cardiac output**, the amount of blood that the heart pumps per minute. Both indices decline consistently at a rate of about 10% per decade from age 25 and up, so that the average 65-year-old has 40% lower cardiovascular efficiency than the young adult. **Maximum heart rate**, the heart rate achieved at the point of maximum oxygen consumption, also shows a linear decrease across the years of adulthood (Whitbourne, 2002). Howeve, women show a less pronounced decrease in aerobic capacity (Neder, Nery, Silva, Andreoni, & Whipp, 1999).

Many studies show that declines in aerobic capacity occur even in highly trained athletes, but that their loss of cardiovascular functioning is about half of that in sedentary individuals (Kasch, Boyer, Schmidt, Wells, Wallace, et al., 1999; Pollock et al., 1997). However, some researchers suggest that continued activity into later adulthood does not offer a guaranteed protection against loss of aerobic capacity. One comprehensive analysis of all of the available literature on exercise and aerobic capacity in 4,884 women ranging from 18 to 89 years of age and number of subjects revealed declines in aerobic capacity greater for active than for sedentary women (Fitzgerald, Tanaka, Tran, & Seals, 1997). Even though the active women may have lost an estimated 10% of their aerobic power per decade, they still were functioning at higher levels than the sedentary women, who started off at a lower level before losing even more. Thus, the absolute but not the relative rate of decline was greater in active women. When the analyses on women were replicated on an even larger set of studies on men ($N = 13,828$), similar findings were obtained. Comparisons were made among men who were endurance-trained, actively exercising, and sedentary on aerobic capacity and a set of related measures. There was no advantage at all in cardiovascular functioning for the athletes or exercising men (Wilson & Tanaka, 2000). One of the positive features of the cardiovascular functioning of the active women was that they did not experience the stiffness in their central arteries shown by sedentary women of the same age (Tanaka, DeSouza, & Seals, 1998). The benefits of exercise according to these analyses did not, however, extend to protection against deleterious changes in the carotid artery, which supplies the blood supply to the head (Tanaka, Seals, Monahan, Clevenger, DeSouza, et al., 2002).

Continued involvement in exercise throughout adulthood therefore does not appear to result in stopping the biological clock. However, there are other benefits in terms of improvements in functional capacity, lifestyle, and control over body mass. Add to this the benefits of avoiding cigarette smoking, and the impact on cardiovascular functioning and hence the quality of daily life of these positive health habits can be significant (Shephard, 1999).

BEHIND THE RESEARCH

CAROLYN ALDWIN, PH.D., PROFESSOR OF HUMAN
DEVELOPMENT, UNIVERSITY OF CALIFORNIA, DAVIS

What is most exciting to you about research in this field?

The most exciting area of research in the field of aging and health concerns the plasticity of aging. While genetics plays a role in how we age, the majority of the variance in both morbidity and mortality is related to factors that can be controlled. Although everyone will eventually become ill and die, we can affect the rate at which we age through exercise, moderate drinking, quitting smoking, eating a healthy diet, and decreasing hostile attitudes. This also affects our quality of life in old age. For example, osteoporosis is a particularly debilitating disease that afflicts nearly half of all women over the age of 65. Adequate intake of calcium, vitamin D, and weight-bearing exercises earlier in life can decrease the rate of bone loss in late life, delaying the onset of osteoporosis and thus increasing the quality of life.

What do you see as the major challenges?

It is ironic that as our knowledge of how to control the aging process is increasing, we appear to be losing the battle to change the health behavior habits of the larger population. Obesity rates are at an all-time high: One out of every three Americans is at least 30% overweight. Furthermore, studies have shown that the increase in longevity is seen primarily in higher socioeconomic status groups; there has been little, if any, change in lower socioeconomic status groups. Thus, there is a widening gap in health status among the social classes, and it is important to try to decrease this disparity.

The other major challenge will be the strain on Medicare when the Baby Boomers turn 65. The demand for high-quality health care will create tremendous financial problems for the society as a whole. We need either to keep the population healthier through prevention or to institute some sort of rationing system, which is not a particularly palatable alternative. Thus, gerontologists must not only do research on factors that modulate the rate of aging, but also make sure that information is applied to as broad a segment of the population as possible.

Where do you see this field headed in the next decade?

There will be more research on the mechanisms through which psychosocial factors affect health. For example, while we know that stress affects the immune system and that the state of our immune system impacts our susceptibility to both acute and chronic diseases, establishing links among stress, immune status, and illness in humans has been problematic (although there is abundant evidence in laboratory animals). The effect of stress on brain aging will be another hot area. The hippocampus seems particularly susceptible to the effects of stress, and we are beginning to see a great deal more work on stress and cognitive status.

On the cellular level, more work will be done on the genetic regulation of aging. While we may not find a "death gene" that regulates all aging, some of the most interesting work is on deoxyribonucleic acid (DNA) repair mechanisms and genes that regulate antioxidant factors. If stress does affect DNA repair mechanisms, then this might be another link through which stress affects health and aging.

BEHIND THE RESEARCH *(continued)*

It is also interesting that social class differences in morbidity and mortality exist in every country in the world, even those, like Britain, that have universal health care. Although this relationship is partially mediated through factors such as health behavior habits, perhaps social class differences in neonatal health may have life-long effects.

Finally, Baby Boomer aging will be another important topic. Most of what we know about aging has been learned from the World War II generation, but the Baby Boomers may be very different. They are more educated and have better access to medical care and nutrition, but they are also more sedentary and more obese than previous cohorts. Thus, it is not clear whether we can keep projecting increases in longevity for this cohort. Baby Boomers will also demand more services and better quality ones. I am eagerly awaiting the first sit-down strike or takeover of the administration in a nursing home!

Short-term training studies provide more consistent findings about the value of exercise for middle-aged and older adults. To be maximally effective, exercise must stimulate the heart rate to rise to 60%–75% of maximum capacity, and this training must take place three to four times a week. Some recommended aerobic activities are walking, hiking, jogging, bicycling, swimming, jumping rope, and roller skating. The chart in Fig. 4.4 is commonly displayed in health clubs to help people estimate the rate their heart should be in order to gain benefits from exercise (maximum heart rate = 220 minus your age; target zone = 50%–80% of this number). However, even moderate or low-intensity exercise can have positive effects on older people who have never been active.

Evidence accumulating over the past 20 years clearly supports the value of aerobic exercise training. The American Heart Association (Fletcher, Balady, Blair, Blumenthal, Caspersen, et al., 1996) and the American College of Sports Medicine (1998) published a position paper based on this evidence recommending that older adults participate in both aerobic and strength training. Positive effects of training have been demonstrated in middle-aged and older adult men and women, including individuals in their 70s and 80s, that can approximate the improvement in fitness levels achieved by younger adults (Petrella, Cunningham, & Paterson, 1997). An exercise program as short as six months can have dramatic effects, improving an older adult's fitness level to that of a person 25 years younger (Tsuji, Tamagawa, Nagatomi, Irie, Ohkubo, et al., 2000).

Even moderate or low-intensity exercise can have beneficial effects on healthy sedentary

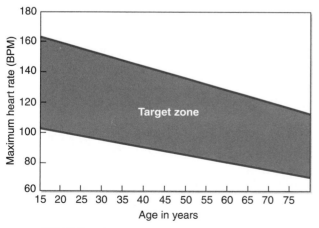

FIGURE 4.4
Compute Your Target Zone

older men and women. Part of the benefits of short-term exercise training can be attributed to improvements in the arteries. As a result, people who begin to participate in exercise can lower their blood pressure (Cameron, Rajkumar, Kingwell, Jennings, & Dart, 1999; Kelley & Sharpe Kelley, 2001; Turner, Spina, Kohrt, & Ehsani, 2000).

In part, improvements in blood pressure associated with short-term training may reflect the favorable effect that exercise has on enhancing lipid metabolism. Exercise increases the fraction of **high-density lipoproteins (HDLs)**, the plasma lipid transport mechanism responsible for carrying lipids from the peripheral tissues to the liver where they are excreted or synthesized into bile acids. Older adults who exercise therefore benefit from enhanced lipid metabolism compared to their sedentary counterparts (Hunter, Wetzstein, Fields, Brown, & Bamman, 2000) As is true for the effects of exercise on aerobic power and muscle strength, even moderate levels of exercise can have a beneficial impact on cholesterol metabolism (Knight, Bermingham, & Mahajan, 1999).

"What do you think?"   **4-2**

Do you know people who exercise extensively? How much do you think a desire to avoid negative cardiovascular changes fits into their exercise goals?

Respiratory System

Respiration includes the mechanical process of breathing, the exchange of gases in the innermost reaches of tiny airways in the lungs, and the transport of gases to and from the body's cells that occur in these airways. Aging affects this process in part through a reduced strength of the respiratory muscles and an increased rigidity of the connective tissue in the chest wall to be expanded during inspiration and contracted during expiration. These changes have the effect of reducing the amount of air that can be pumped in and out of the lungs (Teramoto, Fukuchi, Nagase, Matsuse, & Orimo, 1995). Aging is also associated with a **failing lung** (Rossi, Ganassini, Tantucci, & Grassi, 1996) that causes the lung tissue itself to lose its ability to expand and contract to the maximum possible levels (Babb & Rodarte, 2000). Consequently, all measures of lung functioning in adulthood show age-related losses from about age 40 and on (Rossi et al., 1996), particularly under conditions of exertion (DeLorey & Babb, 1999; Ishida, Sato, Katayama, & Miyamura, 2000).

Exercise can strengthen the chest wall and thereby compensate for some loss of pumping capacity of the respiratory muscles. However, no measure is available to offset changes that occur in the lung tissue itself, even aerobic exercise (Womack, Harris, Katzel, Hagberg, Bleecker, et al., 2000). The best that can be hoped for is to minimize the effects of aging on the lungs, and this is done by not smoking cigarettes (Rossi et al., 1996). People who smoke show a greater loss of forced expiratory volume in later adulthood than those who do not (Morgan & Reger, 2000), and the cessation of smoking is clearly associated with improvements in lung functioning in adults over 50. In a large-scale study of almost 1400 adults from ages 51 to 95 years, lung functioning was significantly lower in smokers than nonsmokers across people of all ages (Frette, Barrett-Connor, & Clausen, 1996). Interestingly, in this study, people who quit smoking before the age of 40 were no different on this index of respiratory functioning than people who had never smoked. Those who quit smoking after the age of 60 years were no different in functioning than current smokers of the same age.

Urinary System

The urinary system is composed of the kidneys, bladder, ureters, and urethra (see Figure 4.5). The nephron cells in the kidneys filter out the harmful waste products of metabolism, which pass through the ureters and into the bladder. In the bladder, the waste products are combined with excess water from the blood and are eliminated as urine through the urethra. Studies dating back to the late 1940s conducted as part of the initial phases of the Baltimore Longitudinal Study on Aging showed that nephron loss occurs consistently throughout adulthood at a rate of 6% per decade and that virtually all measures of renal efficiency show a steady and consistent dropoff over time (Davies & Shock, 1950). This view has been challenged by more refined studies that indicate normal aging is not associated with impaired kidney functioning (Epstein, 1996; Fliser, Franek, Joest, Block, Mutschler, et al., 1997). Moreover, it is known that cigarette smoking can cause damage to the kidneys, leading in some cases to serious kidney

disease in older adults with other risk factors (Stengel, Couchoud, Cenee, & Hemon, 2000). Studies conducted on samples in the past may have yielded exaggerated estimates of the effects of normal aging, reflecting instead the unhealthy effects of smoking at a time when people were more likely to engage in this habit. However, when the kidney is placed under stress, such as caused by illness, extreme exertion, or during a heat wave, declines in functioning become evident (Fuiano, Sund, Mazza, Rosa, Caglioti, et al., 2001). Because of the risk of lower excretion rates, medication levels must be carefully monitored in middle-aged and older adults who may have such conditions (Zubenko & Sunderland, 2000).

Changes with aging may also occur in the elastic tissue of the bladder such that it can no longer efficiently retain or expel urine. Older adults also experience some changes in the perception that they need to urinate. Adding to intrinsic changes in the bladder which lower the rate of urinary flow in men (Kitagawa, Ichikawa, Akimoto, & Shimazaki, 1994) is the fact that

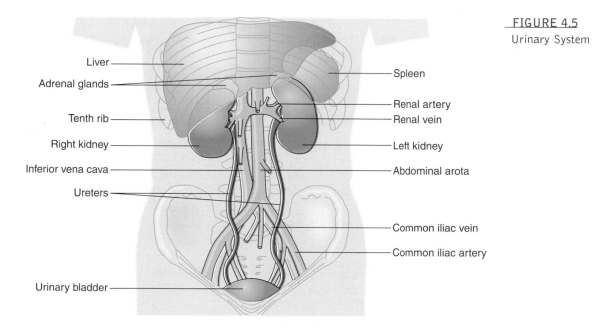

FIGURE 4.5
Urinary System

Liver — Spleen — Adrenal glands — Renal artery — Renal vein — Tenth rib — Right kidney — Left kidney — Inferior vena cava — Abdominal arota — Ureters — Common iliac vein — Common iliac artery — Urinary bladder

many men experience hypertrophy (overgrowth) of the prostate, a gland that sits on top of the bladder. This puts pressure on the bladder and can lead men to feel frequent urges to urinate, particularly at night.

Despite these changes, the majority of older adults do not experience significant problems in the area of bladder functioning. The latest available statistics indicate that 10%–35% of all adults suffer from urinary incontinence (AHCPR, 1996). Although nearly half of those 65 and older living in nursing homes are incontinent, the percentage in the community is about 6%–8% (Iqbal & Castleden, 1997). Stress incontinence, which is loss of urine during a sudden physical action, is more likely to occur in women due to the effects of childbirth or age-related decreases in estrogen. Urge incontinence, which involves loss of control over urinary sphincters, is associated with prostate disease in men.

Older adults with urinary incontinence, particularly women, are more likely to use disposable pads than to use other methods of control (Johnson, Kincade, Bernard, Busby-Whitehead, & DeFriese, 2000), primarily because they are not aware of alternatives. Behavioral controls alone or combined with medication are often successful in treating incontinence (Burgio, Locher, & Goode, 2000). The "Kegel" exercise is particularly effective for this purpose. In this exercise, the individual contracts and relaxes the urinary sphincters for about one minute at a time (both men and women can engage in this exercise). Apart from these strategies, the older individual can avoid some of the behaviors that can exacerbate renal dysfunction such as not becoming dehydrated, particularly during hot weather or while exercising. Unfortunately, although older adults do not find it particularly difficult to talk to their physicians about incontinence, they may fail to bring it up as a symptom due to the mistaken belief that it

is a normal part of aging (Dugan, Roberts, Cohen, Preisser, Davis, et al., 2001). Furthermore, adult diaper ads convey the impression that incontinence can be corrected only through purchase of these products, and they erroneously portray middle-aged women as prime sufferers of this condition. Making the problem even worse is the fact that there are mental health costs to this condition. Among the 5700 women ages 50–69 in the Health and Retirement Study, those with incontinence were significantly more likely to meet the criteria for major depressive disorder (Nygaard, Turvey, Burns, Crischelles, & Wallace, 2003).

Digestive System

Physiological changes in the digestive system in middle and later adulthood appear to be relatively minor. Apparently maintained is the functioning of the salivary glands (Ship, Nolan, & Puckett, 1995), esophagus (Nishimura, Hongo, Yamada, Kawakami, Ueno, et al., 1996), and (for people in good health) the remaining organs consisting of the stomach and lower digestive tract (Bharucha & Camilleri, 2001). There are general patterns of changes in such functions as gastric juice secretion, stomach emptying, and blood flow through the liver (Altman, 1990). However, the effects of aging on these processes is highly variable, showing a great deal of individual differences and a strong relationship to overall health.

Many lifestyle factors that can change in middle and later adulthood contribute to digestive functioning in middle and later adulthood. These factors include family composition, financial resources, and age-related mobility and cognitive problems. All of these factors can detract from the motivation to eat, adding to whatever health and/or age-related changes occur in the physiological process of digestion. Other factors reflect the individuals' exposure through the media to the need for dietary supplements, digestive aids, and laxatives after the age of 40 or 50. Despite the image propagated by the media, problems such as fecal incontinence affect only a small fraction of even the over-65 population (7%).

BODILY CONTROL SYSTEMS

The regulation of metabolism, reproduction, and control against infection is accomplished through the actions of intricate networks of organ systems and tissues controlled by the endocrine and immune system.

Endocrine System

The endocrine system incorporates the set of glands that regulate the actions of the body's other organ systems (called "target" organs) by producing and releasing hormones into the bloodstream. Changes in the endocrine system in adulthood can occur at many levels. There can be alterations in the endocrine glands, hormone levels, or the response of target organs to stimulation. Furthermore, the endocrine system is highly sensitive to levels of stress and physical illness. Alterations that appear to be due to normal aging in adulthood may instead reflect the effects of disease.

The major hormonal system involves the hypothalamus and anterior (front) section of the pituitary gland. Hypothalamus-releasing factors (HRFs) act on specific cell types within the anterior pituitary gland to regulate the secretion of one or more anterior pituitary hormones. Pituitary hormones may also be triggered by signals from target organs carried through the blood indicating that more of the necessary substance must be produced. HRFs may also be stimulated by information sent from other parts of the nervous system.

Six hormones are produced by the anterior pituitary: thyroid-stimulating hormone (TSH), adrenocorticotropic hormone (ACTH), follicle-stimulating hormone (FSH), luteinizing hormone (LH), growth hormone (GH, also called

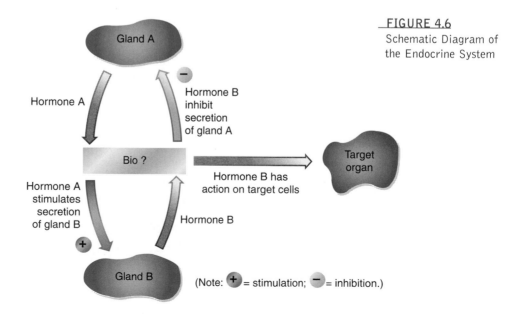

FIGURE 4.6

Schematic Diagram of the Endocrine System

somatotropin), and prolactin. Each of these hormones acts on specific target cells within the body and some (such as TSH) stimulate the production of other hormones.

Growth Hormone. The secretion of growth hormone declines at an estimated 14% per decade over adulthood (Kern, Dodt, Born, & Fehm, 1996; Toogood, O' Neill, & Shalet, 1996). A related hormone produced by the liver, IGF-I (insulin-like growth factor-1), also shows an age-related decrease across adulthood. IGF-1 stimulates muscle cells to increase in size and number, perhaps by stimulating their genes to increase the production of muscle-specific proteins. This decline in the somatotrophic axis (GH and IGF-1) is called **somatopause**. Because GH production affects the metabolism of proteins, lipids, and carbohydrates, the somatopause is thought to account for a number of age-related changes in body composition across adulthood, including loss of bone mineral content (Boonen, Lesaffre, Dequeker, Aerssens, Nijs, et al., 1996), increases in fat, and decrease in muscle mass (Bjorntorp, 1996). Normally, GH production shows regularly timed peaks during nighttime sleep; in older adults, this peak is smaller (Russell-Aulet, Dimaraki, Jaffe, DeMott-Friberg, & Barkan, 2001). GH also rises during heavy resistance exercise, and in adults over 70 this response is attenuated (Hakkinen & Pakarinen, 1995).

"What do you think?"   **4-3**

Why might hormones be thought of as the key to aging?

Media attention given to hormones and aging includes claims that GH replacement therapy is the magic potion that can stop the aging process (Hermann & Berger, 2001). In addition to being

extremely expensive (over $1000 per month), there is also evidence that the side effects of this treatment outweigh any of its possible advantages (van den Beld & Lamberts, 2002). Growth hormone is linked to joint pain, enlargement of the heart, enlargement of the bones, diabetes, and pooling of fluid in the skin and other tissues, which can lead to high blood pressure and heart failure. Diabetes and glucose intolerance are also linked to GH therapy (Blackman, Sorkin, Munzer, Bellantoni, Busby-Whitehead, et al., 2002). A safer and cheaper alternative is exercise, which can accomplish some of the positive effects of growth hormone replacement therapy, including favorable effects on growth hormone secretion and bodily composition (Lamberts, 2000).

Cortisol. The production of ACTH by the anterior pituitary gland stimulates the adrenal gland to produce **cortisol**, a glucocorticoid hormone that provides energy to the muscles during times of stress. Cortisol production is regulated by a series of checks built into the system intended to protect the body from damage caused by unchecked rises. Such damage would include destruction of tissue in the thymus gland, depression of immune responses in general, breakdown of proteins, formation of fat deposits (Seaton, 1995) and impairments in sleep (Prinz, Bailey, & Woods, 2000). Increases in circulating cortisol in the blood may also be linked to damage to cells in the hippocampus, a brain structure involved in short-term memory (Hibberd, Yau, & Seckl, 2000).

The so-called **glucocorticoid cascade hypothesis** proposes that aging causes dangerous increases in cortisol levels affecting immune response, fat deposits, and cognition (O'Brien, Schweitzer, Ames, Tuckwell, & Mastwyk, 1994; Wilkinson, Peskind, & Raskind, 1997). In support of this hypothesis, researchers have estimated that cortisol levels rise from 20% to 50% between the years of 20 and 80 at a rate of 5% to 7% per decade. Based on these data, cortisol, which is also called the stress hormone, would merit the role of a number one player in promoting the body's wear and tear in response to accumulation of life stresses (Van Cauter, Leproult, & Kupfer, 1996). Adding weight to this hypothesis is evidence for a heightened cortisol response of older people to stress, physiological stimulation, and fasting, (Bergendahl, Iranmanesh, Mulligan, & Veldhuis, 2000; Laughlin & Barrett-Connor, 2000) particularly in women (Seeman, Singer, Wilkinson, & McEwen, 2001). In turn, cortisol increases have a negative effect on memory and other forms of cognitive functioning in older adults (Greendale, Kritz-Silverstein, Seeman, & Barrett-Connor, 2000; Kelly & Hayslip, 2000) Finally, sleep impairments, which are more common in older adults, are also related to higher cortisol levels (Prinz et al., 2000).

However, not all studies support the idea of a general collapse of the hypothalamus-pituitary-adrenal system. Some find that there are no age differences under normal conditions (Gotthardt, Schweiger, Fahrenberg, Lauer, Holsboer, et al., 1995) or that age differences in cortisol are minimal (Ferrari, Cravello, Muzzoni, Casarotti, Paltro, et al., 2001; Nicolson, Storms, Ponds, & Sulon, 1997). Furthermore, not all researchers find age differences in the reaction to stress (Kudielka, Schmidt-Reinwald, Hellhammer, Schurmeyer, & Kirschbaum, 2000). Most significant is the fact that when the data are collected longitudinally rather than cross-sectionally (which is true for all of the above studies), individual variations exist in the pattern of changes over time. Yearly testing of healthy older adults over a three- to six-year period revealed that some older individuals increase, some decrease, and some remain stable in cortisol levels (Lupien, Lecours, Schwartz, Sharma, Hauger, et al., 1996). Interestingly,

positive associations were found in this longitudinal study between anxiety and cortisol, suggesting that variations in time in cortisol level may relate to individual differences in personality. Another factor that may play a role in cross-sectional studies is obesity, which is positively related to cortisol levels, at least in middle-aged men (Field, Colditz, Willett, Longcope, & McKinlay, 1994). Of course, it is impossible to determine whether increases in obesity reflect cause or effect in relation to cortisol levels. Nevertheless, these findings create doubt regarding the validity of the glucocorticoid cascade hypothesis.

Thyroid Hormones. **Thyroid hormones** regulate the body's basal metabolic rate (the BMR), which begins to slow in middle age and is responsible for weight gain occurring even when a person's caloric intake remains stable. Despite the presumed importance in this process of the thyroid hormones and their regulators in the pituitary gland and hypothalamus, very few studies have been conducted on adults, and the existing findings are contradictory. Some researchers suggest that the pituitary gland declines (Erfurth & Hagmar, 1995), and others maintain that the problem originates in the hypothalamus (Monzani, Del Guerra, Caraccio, Del Corso, Casolaro, et al., 1996). Another argument is that there are deficiencies in the absorption of thyroid hormones by the tissues so that more remains in the blood (Hays & Nielsen, 1994). This last finding supports the argument that changes in thyroid functioning are due to loss of muscle mass and therefore the demand for thyroid hormones decreases. Further support for this position is the fact that there are higher levels of T3 in men who are physically active and who therefore have higher muscle mass and a higher demand for thyroid hormones (Ravaglia, Forti, Maioli, Pratelli, Vettori, et al., 2001).

Melatonin. Manufactured by the pineal gland, **melatonin** is involved in the synchronization of **circadian rhythm** (daily variations in various bodily functions), the regulation of other hormones, and possibly the protection of cells against free radical damage (Touitou, 2001). The production of melatonin declines across adulthood, and circulating melatonin levels are affected by certain environmental conditions, such as food restriction, which increases melatonin levels and prevents its age-related decline. The only exception to this pattern is an increase during menopause (Okatani, Morioka, & Wakatsuki, 2000).

Some researchers believe that melatonin supplements can reduce the effects of aging and age-associated diseases, especially in the brain and immune system. Melatonin supplements for women have been shown to lead to improved pituitary and thyroid functions (Bellipanni, Bianchi, Pierpaoli, Bulian, & Ilyia, 2001) and to reduce the incidence of sleep problems (Pawlikowski, Kolomecka, Wojtczak, & Karasek, 2002). However, the weight of the evidence does not favor this strategy. There are insufficient data on humans, the side effects have still not been completely identified, and the purity of the available supplements on the market has not been assured. Melatonin supplements can also interfere with sleep cycles if taken at the wrong time. Other side effects include confusion, drowsiness, headaches, and constriction of blood vessels, which would be dangerous in people with high blood pressure. Finally, the dosages usually sold in over-the-counter medications may be as high as 40 times the amount normally found in the body, and the effect of such large doses taken over a long term has not been determined.

DHEA. One adrenal hormone outside the control of the hypothalamus-anterior pituitary axis that has been the target of considerable recent attention with regard to aging is **dehydroepiandrosterone (DHEA)**. This hormone is a weak male steroid (androgen) produced by the adrenal glands located adjacent to the kidneys. It is a precursor to the sex hormones testosterone and estrogen and is believed to have a variety of functions in the body. Some of these functions include increasing production of other sex steroids and availability of IGF-1 and positively influencing some central nervous system functions.

DHEA, which is higher in males than females, shows a pronounced decrease over the adult years, reducing by 80% to 90% between the years of 20 and 80. This phenomenon, termed **adrenopause** (Lamberts, van den Beld, & van der Lely, 1997), is greater in men, although men continue to have higher levels than women because they start at a higher baseline. There is some evidence that loss of DHEA is related to functional declines in various measures of physical and mental health, particularly for women (Berr, Lafont, Debuire, Dartigues, & Baulieu, 1996). Extremely low levels of DHEA have been linked to cardiovascular disease in men, some forms of cancer, trauma, and stress. Low levels of DHEA are also linked to smaller hippocampal size (Laughlin & Barrett-Connor, 2000) and are more likely to be found in older adults with Alzheimer's disease (Murialdo, Barreca, Nobili, Rollero, Timossi, et al., 2001).

In animal studies, DHEA replacement has led to impressive increases in the strength and vigor of older animals. It is not clear how DHEA has these effects. It circulates through the blood in an inactive form, called DHEA sulfate, and becomes active when it comes in contact with a specific cell or tissue that "needs" it. When this happens, the sulfate is removed. Researchers have attempted to determine whether changes in DHEA are related to the reductions, with age, of insulin sensitivity (Denti, Pasolini, Sanfelici, Ablondi, Freddi, et al., 1997) and immune system functioning (James,

Premchand, Skibinska, Skibinski, Nicol, et al., 1997).

Although there are no definitive answers other than the fact that the decline in DHEA is probably a reliable one, DHEA replacement therapy is rivaling GH and melatonin in the anti-aging industry. However, the opinion of the medical community is that the utility and safety of DHEA replacement has not been established (Allolio & Arlt, 2002; Johnson, Bebb, & Sirrs, 2002). Like GH therapy, there are health risks, notably liver problems and an increase in risk of prostate and breast cancer. Furthermore, as was true for GH replacement therapy, a natural substitute for DHEA replacement therapy is exercise, which can help to compensate for its loss in the later adult years (Proctor, 1998; Ravaglia, 2001).

Estrogen and the Menopause. Technically speaking, **menopause** is the point in a woman's life when menstruation stops permanently. As used in common speech, however, menopause has come to mean a phase in middle adulthood covering the years in which reproductive capacity diminishes. The more precise term for this gradual winding down of reproductive ability is **climacteric**, a term that applies to men as well. For women, the climacteric occurs over a three- to five-year span called the perimenopause, ending in the menopause when the woman has not had her menstrual period for one year. The average age of menopause is 50 years, but the timing varies among individuals. Menopause occurs earlier in women who are thin, malnourished, or smoke.

Throughout the perimenopause, there is a diminution in the production of **estrogen**, the primary female sex hormone, by the ovarian follicles. Since the other female hormone, progesterone, is produced in response to ovulation, progesterone levels also decline during this time. The process of estrogen decline begins about 10 to 15 years before menopause, at some point in the mid-30s. By the mid-40s, the ovaries have begun to function less effectively and produce fewer hormones. Eventually, menstrual cycles by the early to middle 50s have ended altogether. There is still some production of estrogen, however, as the ovaries continue to produce small amounts and the adrenal glands stimulate the production of estrogen in fat tissue.

FSH and LH levels rise dramatically during the perimenopausal period as the anterior pituitary sends out signals to produce more ovarian hormones. In turn, the hypothalamus produces less gonadotropin-releasing factor (GnRH). It is not clear which part of the system is responsible for triggering the start of menopause: a reduction in ovarian follicles or changes in the central nervous system that cause the hypothalamus to reduce its production of GnRh (Wise, Krajnak, & Kashon, 1996).

Although women vary considerably in their progression through the menopause (as is true during puberty), there are certain characteristic symptoms. One of the most prominent is the occurrence of "hot flashes," which are sudden sensations of intense heat and sweating that can last from a few moments to half an hour. Over half of women experience hot flashes over the course of a two-year period. These changes in perceived body temperature are the result of decreases in estrogen levels, which cause the endocrine system to release higher amounts of other hormones that affect the temperature control centers in the brain. Fatigue, headaches, night sweats, and insomnia are other physiological symptoms thought to be the result of fluctuating estrogen levels. Psychological symptoms are also reported, such as irritability, mood swings, depression, memory loss, and difficulty concentrating, but the evidence regarding the connection between these symptoms and the physiological changes involved in menopause is far from conclusive. Along with these hormonal changes are alterations in the reproductive tract. The tissues throughout the system become thinner, less elastic, and altered in position and shape. Because of lower estrogen levels, there is a reduction in the supply of blood to the vagina and surrounding nerves and glands. The tissues become thinner, drier, and less able to produce secretions to lubricate before and during intercourse. The result is the possibility of discomfort during intercourse and greater susceptibility to infection, which is more prevalent among women over 50 (Laumann, Paik, & Rosen, 1999). In addition, the woman may become more susceptible to urinary problems such as infections and stress incontinence (as discussed earlier).

More widespread throughout the body are other effects of menopause associated with the impact of decreasing estrogen levels on other bodily systems. Loss of bone strength, atherosclerosis, high blood pressure, and cardiovascular disease become more prevalent among postmenopausal women. It appears that estrogen provides protection against these diseases during the reproductive years which is lost at menopause. There are also changes in cholesterol levels in the blood associated with menopause, causing postmenopausal women to be at higher risk of atherosclerosis and associated conditions.

Estrogen-replacement therapy (**ERT**) was introduced in the 1940s to counteract the negative effects of estrogen loss on postmenopausal women. However, this strategy had serious drawbacks. The administration of estrogen can lead to an overgrowth of the uterine lining, which increases the risk of cancer and blood clots. Women receiving estrogen were therefore given lower doses along with progestin (called **hormone replacement therapy**, or **HRT**) to reduce the cancer risk. Progestin causes the uterine lining to shed, triggering a few days of menstrual-like bleeding each month. An alternative to HRT is **selective estrogen replacement modulaters** (**SERM**) such as raloxifene. This form of hormone-replacement therapy is targeted at bone loss. Early studies on HRT's effects on the body provided enthusiastic support, a support that has since been challenged. Estrogen enhances the skin's tone and appearance by improving the content and quality of collagen, and can thicken the skin and increase the blood supply to the skin. The thickness and texture of the hair is increased by lengthening the life cycle of the hair follicle (Brincat, 2000). Improvements in the immune system (Porter, Greendale, Schocken, Zhu, & Effros, 2001) were also associated with HRT. A reduction in inflammatory and neuroendocrine reactions to tissue damage was found to be lessened in postmenopausal women receiving estrogen replacement (Puder, Freda, Goland, & Wardlaw, 2001). Another potential benefit of HRT was a reduced risk of opacities in the lens of the eye (Worzala, Hiller, Sperduto, Mutalik, Murabito, et al., 2001). Most clearly established was the improvement in bone mineral density shown in women given HRT (Villareal, Binder, Williams, Schechtman, Yarasheski, et al., 2001). Women on HRT were found to be less likely to fall (Randell, Honkanen, Komulainen, Tuppurainen, Kroger, et al., 2001) and to experience stress-related sleep problems (Prinz, Bailey, Moe, Wilkinson, & Scanlan, 2001).

Another area of research on HRT investigated its positive effects on cognitive functioning. Specifically, estrogen was reported to decrease the risk of disease or injury to neurons (Wise, Dubal, Wilson, Rau, & Bottner, 2001) and in animal studies to have favorable effects on the formation of synapses in the hippocampus (Janowsky, Chavez, & Orwoll, 2000). However, the effects of estrogen on cognitive functions in humans is now being questioned (Binder, Schechtman, Birge, Williams, & Kohrt, 2001;

Fillenbaum, Hanlon, Landerman, & Schmader, 2001). The effects on verbal memory, abstract reasoning, and information processing are small and inconsistent and may reflect differences in health and social status rather than estrogen use itself. Some researchers have claimed that estrogen serves a protective function for Alzheimer's disease, but the beneficial effects of estrogen seem to diminish and may even reverse over time (Hogervorst, Williams, Budge, Riedel, & Jolles, 2000). Combined therapy of progesterone and estrogen may be more effective (Natale, Albertazzi, Zini, & Di Micco, 2001).

Claims were also made in earlier research that estrogen alone (Soares & Cohen, 2001) or the combination of estrogen and progesterone can alleviate depression (Paoletti, Pilia, Nannipieri, Bigini, & Melis, 2001). This would counteract the effect of changing hormone levels in women on mood, mediated possibly by the effect of estrogen levels on neurotransmitters involved in depression such as serotonin (Taylor, 2001).

Beginning in the summer of 2002, two serious blows were dealt to enthusiastic advocates of the benefits of HRT, following the publication of a major international study on the relative risks and benefits of hormone replacement therapy. This study, funded by the U.S. National Institutes of Health and an Italian medical foundation, involved 161,809 postmenopausal women ranging from 50 to 79 years. After a little over five years, the study was discontinued because rates of invasive breast cancer in women taking HRT rose to unacceptable levels. In addition, there was a higher risk of heart attacks among women taking HRT. The study's authors suggested that rather than prescribing HRT, physicians should provide postmenopausal women with medications designed to target specific conditions associated with estrogen loss (Rossouw, Anderson, Prentice, LaCroix, Kooperberg, et al., 2002).

The second major finding to call into question the benefits of HRT was in the area of well-being. A randomized clinical trial on over 16,000 women in the United States, 10% of whom were studied over a three-year period, showed that there were no significant effects of estrogen plus progestin on general health, vitality, mental health, depressive symptoms, or sexual satisfaction. Although small improvements were observed after one year in some quality-of-life symptoms, these were not clinically meaningful, nor did they persist in the group studied over the entire three years of the study. The New England Journal of Medicine, a leading medical journal in the United States, believed the results of this study to be so important that they took the unusual step of releasing the paper on the Internet two months before its publication in the print version of the journal (Hays, Ockene, Brunner, Kotchen, Manson, et al., 2003).

Other recommended approaches to use in addition to HRT to counteract the effect of hormonal changes include exercise, giving up smoking, lowering cholesterol in the diet, and perhaps more enjoyably, having one alcoholic drink a day. In addition, although generally regarded with skepticism among the aging community, DHEA may have some beneficial effects in women (Baulieu, Thomas, Legrain, Lahlou, Roger, et al., 2000).

Testosterone and the Andropause. The term **andropause** refers to age-related declines in the male sex hormone **testosterone**, a decrease observed both in African American and Caucasian samples (Perry, Miller, Patrick, & Morley, 2000) to equal 1% per year after the age of 40 years (de Lignieres, 1993; Morley, 2001), a decrease observed in longitudinal as well as cross-sectional studies (Harman, Metter, Tobin, Pearson, & Blackman, 2001). Thought to be related to the andropause are a number of changes in body composition and physiology, including reduced lean body mass, increases in body fat, a decrease in bone mineral density, and reduced numbers of red blood cells (Heaton & Morales, 2001; Longcope, Feldman, McKinlay, & Araujo, 2000). However, there are large individual variations in testosterone levels—about 25% of men over 75 years old have testosterone levels within the upper 25% of values for young men (Vermeulen, Goemaere, & Kaufman, 1999). These variations may reflect differences within older populations in cholesterol levels, percent of body fat, cigarette smoking, and behavioral tendencies that predispose an individual to developing cardiovascular disease (Zmuda, Cauley, Kriska, Glynn, Gutai, et al., 1997). There nevertheless remains an overall decrease in testosterone across adulthood even in healthy active men (van den Beld, de Jong, Grobbee, Pols, & Lamberts, 2000).

Although common wisdom for a number of years was that testosterone supplements for aging men are an unnecessary and potentially dangerous proposition, they are now gaining greater empirical support and acceptance in the medical community as long as this treatment is accompanied by regular medical screening (Schulman & Lunenfeld, 2002; Tenover, 2000). Benefits associated with testosterone supplements include maintenance or improvement in bone density; greater muscle strength; lowering of the ratio of fat to lean muscle mass; and increased strength, libido, and sexual function. Mood and cognitive functioning also seem to be positively affected. Most significantly, in contrast to the findings of early studies, there is no evidence that prostate mass is increased as long as the treatment maintains a man's testosterone within a normal range. Also, in contrast to early findings, a higher rather than a lower testosterone level is associated with lowered cardiovascular risk, including more favorable cholesterol levels (i.e., higher HDLs), lower blood pressure, and lower levels of substances in the blood that contribute to atherosclerosis (van den Beld, Bots, Janssen, Pols, Lamberts, et al., 2003; Vermeulen, 2000).

The implications of these changes in the male and female reproductive hormones for sexual functioning and relationships in the later adult years will be explored in Chapter 9 in the context of intimate relationships. We will see that, although bodily changes have important ramifications for sexuality, older men and women are able to maintain enjoyable and satisfying sexual relations.

Immune System

Psychologists have only in relatively recent decades become interested in the immune system, which is beginning to be understood as intimately connected to the nervous system and, consequently, behaviors, thoughts, and emotions. Conversely, stress and negative emotions are thought to have deleterious effects on immune functioning which, in turn, can result in the body's less efficient response to a variety of diseases that are more prevalent in older adults including cancer, heart disease, Alzheimer's disease, osteoporosis, and diabetes (Kiecolt-Glaser, McGuire, Robles, & Glaser, 2002; McGuire, Kiecolt-Glaser, & Glaser, 2002).

The immune system function that is of greatest interest to researchers in the field of aging is **acquired immunity**—acquired as the result of prior contact with an antigen. The mechanisms involved in acquired immunity are **lymphocytes**, specialized white blood cells that can develop the ability to destroy or neutralize specific antigens. Acquired immunity increases in strength and effectiveness through the ability to acquire memory for each antigen. Normally, the body's defenses do not attack tissues that carry a marker indicating that they are "self." Instead, immune cells reside peaceably with other body cells in a state known as self-tolerance.

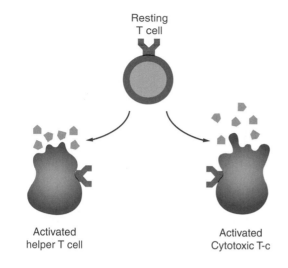

Resting
T cell

Activated
helper T cell

Activated
Cytotoxic T-c

FIGURE 4.7a

T Cells in the Immune System

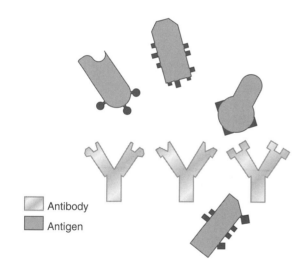

Antibody

Antigen

FIGURE 4.7b

B Cells in the Immune System

Two types of lymphocytes are involved in the immune response: T lymphocytes (also called T cells) and B lymphocytes (also called B cells) (see Fig. 4.7a and b). The two types of lymphocytes participate in different forms of the immune response. One form of T cells, known

as **cytotoxic T cells**, is primarily responsible for cell-mediated immunity in which invading antigens that have infected a bodily cell are identified and killed (Fig. 4.7a). **B cells** are involved in humoral immunity, in which they produce antibodies that bind to and neutralize the antigen (Fig. 4.7b). Certain T cells also participate in humoral immunity by either activating or suppressing the B cells. Macrophages are also involved in acquired immunity by processing substances to the T cells in a form suitable for initiating the immune response.

Another group of cells involved in cellular immunity are called natural killer (NK) cells, which have the ability to destroy a variety of infected or tumor cells. As the name implies, the NK cells do not require prior exposure to a substance in order to destroy it. Both T cells and NK cells contain granules filled with potent chemicals, and both types kill on contact. The chief weapons of the T cells are cytokines, hormone-like proteins secreted by the cells of the immune system. Cytokines encourage cell growth, promote cell activation, direct cellular traffic, and destroy target cells-including cancer cells. Because they serve as a messenger between white cells, or leukocytes, many cytokines are also known as interleukins. Whenever T cells and B cells are activated, some become memory cells. The next time an individual encounters that same antigen, the immune system is primed to destroy it quickly. The memory cells produced after the primary response may survive for decades, giving lifetime immunity to certain diseases.

Age-related declines in immune system functioning have been suspected for many years. However, much remains to be resolved, such as whether observed immune deficiencies in older adults are the result of normal aging or disease processes. In addition to the fact that the immune system is highly complex, it is also true that there is much disagreement in the published literature. Nevertheless, researchers feel so confident that the observed age effects are reliable that Miller coined the term **immune senescence** to describe the features of the aging immune system.

The primary features of immune senescence are a decline of T-cell functioning, including production of fewer T cells during cell-mediated immunity and fewer helper T cells in humoral immunity (Linton & Thoman, 2001). There are more memory T cells and fewer naïve T cells, and as a result, the system is less able to respond to new antigens (Miller, 1996). B cells are less able to produce antibodies. Interleukins, the substances produced by T cells, also undergo changes. One of these, interleukin-6, increases with age and as a result interferes with the immune response. By contrast, interleukin-2 diminishes with age, a fact that may account for decreases in T cells. The functioning of NK cells in the bloodstream is maintained in later life, but these cells may be less effective in the spleen and lymph node tissues, where they are most needed. There also may be important links between the immune and endocrine systems. For example, interleukin-2 is depressed when estrogen levels decrease.

The cause of immune senescence is commonly thought to be the involution of the thymus, which loses most of its functioning by early adulthood (Aspinall & Andrew, 2000). Thus, the T cells that circulate in the secondary lymphoid organs are mature T cells that were produced early in the individual's life during exposure to new antigens. Countering this fact is the suggestion that the system may have more dynamic properties than would be true if anatomy were the sole determinant of immune functioning. If the remaining T cells are able to retain or improve their responsiveness, this would compensate for their sheer loss of numbers (Born, Uthgenannt, Dodt, Nunninghoff, Ringvolt, et al., 1995). Nevertheless, the established

wisdom regards the immune system as a target of the aging process and, further, as a prime suspect in regulating length of life (Khanna & Markham, 1999).

This being said, there are many interactions between the immune system and other physical and psychological processes. Diet and exercise can either enhance or detract from various immune system indicators (Bruunsgaard & Pedersen, 2000). For example, additives such as zinc and vitamin E improve immune responsiveness (Lesourd, 1997; Sone, 1995) even in people over the age of 90 (Ravaglia et al., 2000). Conversely, older people who eat low-protein diets show deficient immune functioning, in addition to other serious losses in body composition (Castaneda, Charnley, Evans, & Crim, 1995). As is true for diet, exercise can improve immune responsiveness in older adults (Wang, Bashore, Tran, & Friedman, 2000) but this activity be maintained over the long term (Nieman, 2000).

Given this knowledge, it will be necessary to reevaluate the existing data on aging and the immune system, in which exercise and diet were not controlled. Previous findings may have presented an overly negative picture of the effects of aging. One study of healthy volunteers found no age differences in a variety of immune system measures as well as similar responses to vaccines (Carson, Nichol, O'Brien, Hilo, & Janoff, 2000).

For the present time, it is best to be aware of the potentially negative effect aging may have in people who do not maintain ideal levels of diet and exercise. A malfunctioning immune system, as in the case of cancer, is a major contributor to mortality in middle and later adulthood.

NERVOUS SYSTEM

The nervous system exerts control over all bodily systems and behavior. Within the central nervous system, events in the environment are monitored and responded to, thoughts are conceived and enacted, and connections are maintained with other bodily systems. The autonomic nervous system controls involuntary behaviors, response to stress, and actions of other organ systems that sustain life. The areas of greatest interest in nervous system functioning and aging include changes in neural structures and bodily control systems regulated by the autonomic system.

Central Nervous System

Early research on nervous system functioning in adulthood was based on the hypothesis that, because neurons do not reproduce, there is a progressive loss of brain tissue across the adult years that is noticeable by the age of 30. The model of aging based on this hypothesis was called the **neuronal fallout model**. However, in the years intervening since that early research, it has become clear that in the absence of disease, the aging brain maintains much of its structure and function. The first evidence in this direction was provided in the late 1970s by an innovative team of neuroanatomists who found that mental stimulation can compensate for loss of neurons. According to the **plasticity model**, although some neurons die, the remaining ones increase their synapses (Coleman & Flood, 1987). Research continues to accumulate supporting the notion of plasticity, including studies on the value of physical exercise as a way to maintain brain function and, consequently, cognitive functioning (Cotman & Berchtold, 2002). Improvements in methods, due to the availability of brain scans as well as experimental studies involving synaptic proliferation and neuron regeneration, are also responsible for the greater optimism regarding the nervous system in adulthood and old age. Furthermore, with refinements in the definition and diagnosis of Alzheimer's disease, researchers are increasingly

able to separate the effects of normal aging from the severe losses that occur in this disease and related conditions (see Chapters 5 and 11).

Studies using brain-imaging techniques are making it clear that there is considerable interindividual variability in patterns of brain changes across adulthood. In one large magnetic resonance imaging (MRI) study of adults, percentages of atrophy ranging from 6% to 8% per year were reported. However, there were wide individual variations in patterns of cortical atrophy and in ventricular enlargement (Coffey, Wilkinson, Parashos, Soady, Sullivan, et al., 1992). Some of this variability was related to health status. Adults in good health were spared some of the effects of aging, such as reductions in temporal lobe volume (DeCarli, Murphy, Gillette, Haxby, Teichberg, et al., 1994). There also may be significant gender variations in the effects of aging on the brain in adulthood. There are larger increases in the ventricular spaces in the brain for men than women (Matsumae, Kikinis, Morocz, Lorenzo, Sandor, et al., 1996). Men show greater reductions than women in the frontal and temporal lobes (Cowell, Turetsky, Gur, Grossman, Shtasel, et al., 1994) as well as in the parieto-occipital area (Coffey, Lucke, Saxton, Ratcliff, Unitas, et al., 1998). Conversely, men may be spared compared to women in the hippocampus and parietal lobes (Murphy, DeCarli, McIntosh, Daly, Mentis, et al., 1996).

In studies of the frontal lobes using brain scans, including magnetic resonance imaging (MRI) and positron-emission tomography (PET), age reductions are more consistent than in studies of other cortical areas (Raz, Gunning, Head, Dupuis, McQuain, et al., 1997). Estimates range from a low of 1% per decade (De Santi, de Leon, Convit, Tarshish, Rusinek, et al., 1995) to a high of around 10% (Eisen, Entezari-Taher, & Stewart, 1996). One PET scan study estimated a loss of 17% per decade from age 20 onward in the density of serotonin receptors, with a more pronounced decrease through the midlife years. Serotonin is thought to be involved in mood regulation. The areas most affected were the prefrontal cortex, hippocampus, and the occipital (visual) cortex (Sheline, Mintun, Moerlein, & Snyder, 2002). There is also evidence that the volume of the hippocampus becomes smaller with increasing age in adulthood (de Leon, George, Golomb, Tarshish, Convit, et al., 1997; Raz, Gunning-Dixon, Head, Dupuis, & Acker, 1998). These patterns of findings are interpreted as providing a neurological basis for the behavioral observations of memory changes in adulthood (Golomb, Kluger, de Leon, Ferris, Mittelman, et al., 1996; Nielsen Bohlman & Knight, 1995). One major exception to this general pattern is based on a replication of a study conducted in the 1970s involving a quantitative assessment of synaptic numbers (Huttenlocher, 1979). In this more recent study, brain autopsies were obtained from 37 cognitively normal individuals ranging in age from 20 to 89 years. There was no decline in the frontal cortex in otherwise normal individuals older than 65 (Scheff, Price, & Sparks, 2001).

Even if older adults suffer from brain deficits in one area, these deficits may be compensated by the increased activation of other brain regions. In one carefully conducted PET scan study, the regional cerebral blood flow was compared in men in their 70s and men in their 20s and 30s while they were performing memory tests (Cabeza, Grady, Nyberg, McIntosh, Tulving, et al., 1997). The younger men used regions of the brain better designed to meet the cognitive demands of the task, in contrast to the older men who showed more diffuse but higher levels of brain activation in other areas. For example, the younger men used the left half of their frontal lobes while they were learning new material and the right half when they were trying to recall the material. The older men showed very little activity of the frontal lobe while they were learning the material but then used both the right and left frontal lobes during recall. The authors concluded from this study that older adults are capable of mustering their resources when the situation demands it, even if those resources are less efficiently organized. There is also evidence that older adults maintain higher levels of activation overall, even on easy tasks, as a way of compensating for cognitive deficits. Rather than shifting to other cortical pathways, older adults in an attentional task were more likely to increase the activation of a visual processing pathway compared to younger adults, whose levels of activation increased only for a more difficult attentional task (Madden, Turkington, Provenzale, Denny, Langley, et al., 2002). Another possible source of age effects is the failure to inhibit irrelevant information, a phenomenon observed in the cognitive processes of attention, memory, and language (see Chapters 6 and 7). Researchers have found that increasing the levels of a neurotransmitter involved in brain inhibition resulted in improved the processing of information in the visual cortex of monkeys (Leventhal, Wang, Pu, Zhou, & Ma, 2003). This finding implies that changes in the aging brain involving inhibition underlie an important source of cognitive deficits.

The view that there are changes with aging in adulthood in the frontal lobes and the circuits between the limbic system and cortex is consistent with data on cognitive changes in adulthood. Nevertheless, it is important to remember both the plasticity of the brain throughout adulthood and the repeated demonstrations that older people find ways around some of their neural circuitry problems. Although their efficiency might be reduced, they have not by any means lost the ability to put their brains to work.

Sleep

The literature on sleep in adulthood clearly refutes a common myth about aging, namely, that as people grow older they need less sleep. Regardless of age, everyone requires seven to nine hours of sleep a night (Ancoli-Israel, 1997). In fact, sleeping eight hours or more a night has been found to be associated with higher mortality risks, as is use of prescription sleeping pills (Kripke, Garfinkel, Wingard, Klauber, & Marler, 2002). However, changes in various aspects of sleep-related behavior and sleep problems can affect the mental and physical well-being of the middle-aged and older adult (Moore, Adler, Williams, & Jackson, 2002). These changes relate in part to lifestyle as well as physiology. Middle-aged individuals who are experiencing high degrees of job-related stress face different challenges in their sleep patterns than do those whose lives have less pressure. Furthermore, hormonal changes, such as those associated with the menopause and growth hormone levels, affect the individual's sleep patterns throughout the adult years. Alcohol intake is another potentially negative factor affecting sleep patterns of older adults (Brower & Hall, 2001).

Changes in sleeping patterns emerge gradually in later adulthood. Older adults spend more time in bed relative to time spent asleep. They take longer to fall asleep, awaken more often during the night, lie in bed longer before rising, and have sleep that is shallower and fragmented, meaning that it is less efficient (Bliwise, 1992). EEG sleep patterns show some corresponding age alterations, including a rise in Stage 1 sleep and a large decrease in both Stage 4 and REM (rapid eye movement) sleep (Dijk, Duffy, Riel, Shanahan, & Czeisler, 1999). These changes occur even for people who are in excellent health. The relationship between melatonin and sleep phase timing also becomes altered in older adults such that sleep cycles become dissociated from the timing of peak melatonin production (Duffy, Zeitzer, Rimmer, Klerman, Dijk, et al., 2002). There is some evidence that sleep disturbances become evident by the age of 50 and are more prevalent in women than in men (Middelkoop, Smilde-van den Doel, Neven, Kamphuisen, & Springer, 1996). There is cross-national data to support the findings of problems with insomnia as revealed by the Honolulu-Asian Aging Study (Barbar, Enright, Boyle, Foley, Sharp, et al., 2000).

Perhaps related to the changes in circadian rhythms at night is the fact that at some point in middle to later adulthood, individuals shift from a preference to working in the later hours of the day and night to a preference for the morning. Several investigators have established the fact that the large majority of older (over 65-year-old) adults are "morning" people, and the large majority of younger adults are "evening" people (Duffy, Dijk, Hall, & Czeisler, 1999; Intons-Peterson, Rocchi, West, McLellan, & Hackney, 1998). The biological basis for this shift in preferences presumably occurs gradually throughout adulthood, along with changes in hormonal contributors to sleep and arousal patterns. However, given that upon college graduation most young adults must shift from evening to morning schedules of preferred work hours, the social contributors to daytime arousal patterns would seem to have their effect earlier in the adult years. One intriguing implication is that when studies of cognitive functioning take place in the afternoon, older adults perform more poorly (Hasher, Chung, May, & Foong, 2002). To the extent that researchers fail to take this into account, there is a systematic bias against the over-60 participants.

Changes in sleep patterns in middle and later adulthood may be prevented or corrected by one or more alterations in sleep-related behaviors. A sedentary lifestyle is a major contributor to sleep problems at night; therefore, exercise (during the day) can improve sleep at night. Using the bed or bedroom as a workplace is another behavior that can interfere with sleep. The bed and related areas become associated with work-related activities, some of which may be arousing and possibly stressful as well. The behavioral method used to counteract this contributor to sleep problems is referred to as "stimulus control." Other contributors to sleep problems are excessive intake of alcohol, an irregular sleep schedule, exercising too close to bedtime, and having coffee or smoking before going to bed. People in jobs that involve shift work or require frequent shifts in time zone are particularly likely to suffer from sleep disturbances.

A variety of psychological disorders and medical conditions can also interfere with the sleep of the middle-aged and older adults (Riedel & Lichstein, 2000). Depression, anxiety, and bereavement are psychological causes of sleep disturbance. Medical conditions that disturb sleep include arthritis, osteoporosis, cancer, chronic lung disease, congestive heart failure, and digestive disturbances. People with Parkinson's disease or Alzheimer's disease also suffer serious sleep problems. Finally, the normal age-related changes that occur in the bladder lead to a more frequent urge to urinate during the night and thereby cause sleep interruptions. Such problems are worse for men with prostate disease or for people who suffer from incontinence. During menopause, the hot flashes that come at night due to hormonal changes can cause breathing difficulties and lead to frequent awakenings. Periodic leg movements during sleep (also called nocturnal myoclonus) can awaken the individual. All of these conditions, when they interrupt sleep, can lead to daytime sleepiness and fatigue. A vicious cycle begins when the individual starts to establish a pattern of daytime napping, which increases the chances of sleep interruptions occurring at night.

One physical condition in particular that interferes with sleep at any age but is more prevalent in middle-aged and older adults is **sleep apnea**, also called sleep-related breathing

disturbance. People with this condition experience a particular form of snoring in which a partial obstruction in the back of the throat restricts airflow during inhalation. A loud snore is followed by a choking silence when breathing actually stops. When the airway closes, the lack of oxygen is registered by the respiratory control centers in the brain, and the sleeper awakens. There may be 100 such episodes a night, and to make up for the lack of oxygen that occurs during each one, the heart is forced to pump harder to circulate more blood. As a result, there are large spikes in blood pressure during the night as well as elevated blood pressure during the day. Over time, the person's risk of heart attack and stroke is increased. In addition, the individual experiences numerous periods of daytime sleepiness that interfere with everyday activities.

Sleep apnea is more common in older adults, perhaps affecting 8% to 10% of the over-65 population, although one comprehensive study of people monitored while asleep indicated a surprisingly high incidence of 27% (Philip, Dealberto, Dartigues, Guilleminault, & Bioulac, 1997). The causes of sleep apnea include allergies and colds that swell throat tissue, obesity, the use of alcohol, tranquilizers, and sedatives (which relax the throat muscles), and anatomical abnormalities, such as large soft palates or nasal malformations that restrict airflow. In addition to interference with sleep and possible risks of more serious medical conditions, sleep apnea seems to be related to poorer cognitive performance among people over 60 when it is accompanied by daytime drowsiness (Dealberto, Pajot, Courbon, & Alperovitch, 1996).

Although changes in sleep patterns occur as a normal feature of the aging process, severe sleep disturbances do not. Sleep specialists can offer innovative approaches such as light therapy, which "resets" an out of phase circadian rhythm, and encouragement of improvements in sleep habits (Klerman, Duffy, Dijk, & Czeisler, 2001). Exercise can also be helpful in resetting disturbed circadian rhythms (Van Someren, Lijzenga, Mirmiran, & Swaab, 1997). Melatonin has no proven value and may even be harmful, as discussed earlier. Furthermore, individuals must be careful to avoid the temptation of solving sleep problems with sedative-hypnotic drugs to which tolerance quickly develops and which can interfere with daytime alertness. These drugs may set up a cycle on top of a cycle and lead to an exacerbation of problems due to age-related changes in circadian rhythms (Vitiello, 1997).

Temperature Control

It is standard news fare that as parts of the country suffer extreme weather, older adults are at risk of dying from hyper- or hypothermia, conditions known together as **dysthermia**. In the 20-year period from 1979 to 1999, over 8000 deaths occurred in the United States due to heat exposure (http://www.cdc.gov/nceh/hsb/extremeheat/). Over a similar period (1979–1998), a total of 13,970 deaths were attributed to hypothermia. The majority of deaths due to dysthermia occur in people over the age of 65, and the percentages rise sharply with each age decade (Centers for Disease Control and Prevention, 2002b) (see Fig. 4.8).

Although these statistics are a cause for concern, there is reason to question the extent to which dysthermia is a function of the normal aging process. Researchers are challenging the common wisdom that age alone increases the risk of hyperthermia and hypothermia. Some of the factors known to contribute to dysthermia are amount of body fat (Inoue, Nakao, Araki, & Ueda, 1992), gender—that is, women preserve responses to cold better than do men with age—(Young, 1991), and physical fitness (Young, 1991). With regard to physical fitness, for example, older adults have an impaired ability to secrete sweat in conditions of extreme heat (Inoue, 1996). The lack of body-cooling mechanisms can lead to heat exhaustion and heat stroke in extreme heat conditions. However, men in their late 50s to early 70s who have greater

FIGURE 4.8

Deaths Due to Hypothermia in the United States, 1979–1998

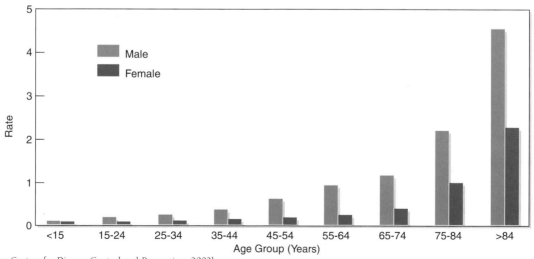

Source: Centers for Disease Control and Prevention, 2002b.

aerobic power have superior sweat gland functioning and blood flow to the skin, processes that improve body heat adaptation (Tankersley, Smolander, Kenney, & Fortney, 1991). More and more researchers seem to be concurring that, in the absence of disease and in the presence of a well-trained body, middle-aged and older adults may have some impairment in thermal regulation but not to the extent that was once believed.

Adding support to this proposition is the fact that a variety of chronic medical conditions prevalent in the older population are related to dysthermia. Hypothermia is more likely to occur in people who have experienced hypothyroidism or other disorders of the body's hormone system, stroke, severe arthritis or other diseases that limit mobility, and peripheral vascular disease, which limits blood flow throughout the limbs. Cognitive disorders, such as Alzheimer's disease, also increase a person's risk of hypothermia because people who are disoriented fail to take preventive action against the cold. Heat stroke and heat exhaustion are more likely to occur among people who are overweight, drink alcohol to excess, and suffer from diabetes, cardiovascular, or respiratory illnesses. The disorientation, confusion, and memory problems that characterize people with dementia also make them more vulnerable to hyperthermia because they fail to recognize that they are becoming overheated. Certain medications used in treating some of these diseases that are more prevalent among older adults also increase the risk of developing a heat-related disorder.

SENSATION AND PERCEPTION

A variety of changes occur in adulthood throughout individual sensory systems. These changes reduce the quality of input that reaches the brain to be integrated in subsequent stages of information processing.

TABLE 4-1

Data from the 1998 National Health Interview Survey on Hearing and Visual Impairments in Adults by Sex and Age

Age Group	Hearing		Vision
	A Little Trouble	A Lot of Trouble or Deaf	Trouble
25–44	9.02	1.07	4.52
45–64	23.11	3.99	10.57
65+	35.99	14.00	15.36
25–44	6.08	0.66	6.69
45–64	12.66	1.81	11.33
65+	27.09	7.80	19.93

Source: Pleis and Coles, 2002

Vision

As can be seen in Table 4-1, higher percentages of people report that they have visual problems in increasingly older age groups across adulthood. Visual acuity as measured by the Snellen chart (used in eye exams) shows a consistent drop across the years of adulthood so that the level of acuity in an 85-year-old is about 80% less than that of a person in the 40s. The loss of acuity is greater in African Americans than in whites, and it appears to be similar for men and women (West, Munoz, Rubin, Schein, Bandeen-Roche, et al., 1997). By raising the level of illumination, it is possible to compensate somewhat for this loss, but in dimly lit surroundings, older people have a great deal more trouble when they must observe details at a distance. On the other hand, adults over the age of 40 are sensitive to glare, so sudden increases in light or exposure to bright scattered light can impair rather than improve visual acuity. **Presbyopia**, the second major normative age-related change in the eye, is caused by a thickening and hardening of the lens, which makes it more difficult to focus on near objects. This condition must be corrected by wearing reading glasses or bifocals (see Fig. 4.9).

FIGURE 4.9
Normal Accommodation Process

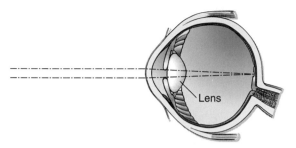

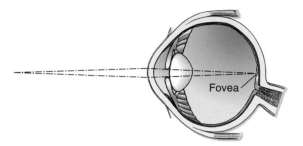

When looking at an object that is far away, the lens is relatively flattened and relaxed.

When looking at nearby objects, the lens gets fatter, causing the image of the object to be focused on to the retina in the fovea.

In addition to normal age-related changes in vision, the susceptibility to certain diseases increases in later life. About one-half of adults over the age of 65 report that they have experienced some form of visual impairment.

A **cataract** is clouding that has developed in the normally clear crystalline lens, resulting in blurred or distorted vision because the image cannot be focused clearly onto the retina. The term "cataract" reflects the previous view of this condition as a waterfall behind the eye that obscured vision. Cataracts usually start as a slight cloudiness that progressively grows more opaque (Fig. 4.10). They are usually white, but they may take on color such as yellow or brown. The photo on the next page shows the effects of cataracts on vision. Cataracts seem to develop as a normal part of the aging process, but other than the fact that they are due to changes in the lens fibers, the cause is not known. Heredity, prior injury, or disease such as diabetes may play roles in causing cataract formation. It has also been suggested that exposure to sunlight and cigarette smoking may increase a person's risk for developing cataracts.

Cataracts are the main visual impairment experienced by older adults in surveys of self-reported health status, affecting about 25% of the

over-65 population (Desai, Zhang, & Hennessy, 1999). The development of cataracts occurs gradually over a period of years during which the individual's vision becomes increasingly blurred

FIGURE 4.10
Effect of a Cataract on Vision

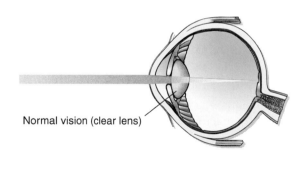

Normal vision (clear lens)

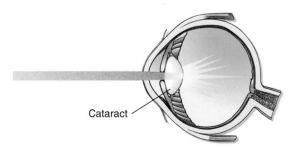

Cataract

and distorted. If the cataracts have a yellow or brown tone, colors will take on a yellow tinge similar to the effect of wearing colored sunglasses. Vision becomes increasingly difficult both under conditions of low light, as acuity is reduced, and under conditions of bright light, due to increased susceptibility to glare. Bright lights may seem to have a halo around them. These are significant limitations and can alter many aspects of the person's everyday life. It is more difficult to read, walk, watch television, drive, recognize faces, and perform one's work, hobbies, and leisure activities. Consequently, people with cataracts may suffer a reduction in independence, as they find it more difficult to drive or even go out at night with others.

Despite the common nature of cataracts and their pervasive effect on vision, they need not significantly impair the life of the older person who suffers from them. Enormous strides have been made in the treatment of cataracts due to advances in surgical procedures. Currently, cataract surgery is completed in about an hour or less, under local anesthesia, and with no hospital stay. Visual recovery is achieved usually within one to seven days, and for many people, vision is so improved that they rely only minimally on corrective lenses.

A second significant form of blindness that becomes more prevalent in later adulthood is **age-related macular degeneration**, one of the leading causes of blindness in those over the age of 65. It is estimated that there are 16,000 new cases of age-related macular degeneration annually, and that some development of abnormalities in the macula is common in those over the age of 75 (Klein, Klein, & Linton, 1992). An estimated 15% of people 80 and older have this disease (O'Neill, Jamison, McCulloch, & Smith, 2001).

Age-related macular degeneration involves destruction of the photoreceptors located in the central region of the retina known as the macula, leaving dark or empty areas in the center of the afflicted individual's vision. This area of the retina is normally used in reading, driving, and other visually demanding activities, so the selective damage to the receptors in the macula that occurs with this disease is particularly incapacitating. There is no known treatment for this disorder. Vitamin supplements containing antioxidant vitamins and/or zinc, once promoted as effective interventions, do not work (Cho, Stampfer, Seddon, Hung, Spiegelman, et al., 2001). However, there is a hopeful sign in that diet may play a role in prevention. People who eat diets high in omega-3 fatty acids (found in fish, e.g.) have a lower risk of developing age-related macular degeneration (Seddon, Rosner, Sperduto, Yannuzzi, Haller, et al., 2001).

The third form of blindness affecting middle-aged and older adults is **glaucoma**, a group of conditions in which the optic nerve is damaged. The most common type of glaucoma develops gradually and painlessly, without symptoms, meaning that it may not be detected until the disease reaches advanced stages. Eventually, glaucoma causes a loss of peripheral vision and, over time, may cause the remaining vision to diminish altogether. More rarely, the symptoms appear suddenly, including blurred vision, loss of side vision, perception of colored rings around lights, and experience of pain or redness in the eyes.

Glaucoma is the third most common cause of blindness in the United States, and the most common form is estimated to affect about 3 million Americans. It is diagnosed in 95,000 new patients each year, and over 80,000 Americans are estimated to have developed glaucoma-caused blindness. The risk of glaucoma is much higher in people over the age of 60. Blacks are at higher risk than whites, as are people who are nearsighted, have diabetes, or have a family history of glaucoma. Some forms of glaucoma can be controlled but not cured, and others can be treated successfully through surgery.

Hearing

The percentage of older adults who report that they have hearing loss increases across adulthood, as shown in Table 4-1. Two forms of hearing loss can occur in later life, and because they are so common, they are considered a normal component of the aging process. In sensorineural hearing loss, also known as **presbycusis**, degenerative changes occur in the cochlea or auditory nerve leading from the cochlea to the brain. Presbycusis is most often associated with loss of high-pitched sounds. In **conductive hearing loss**, damage occurs in one of the structures that transmits sounds within the ear, most often the tympanic membrane. Although hereditary factors, various health problems (diabetes, heart disease, high blood pressure), and the use of some medications (aspirin, antibiotics) can contribute to hearing loss in later adulthood, exposure to loud noise is the most frequent cause. Another hearing disturbance that is relatively common in older people is **tinnitus**, in which the individual perceives sounds in the head or ear (such as a ringing noise) when there is no external source for it. The condition can be temporarily associated with use of aspirin, antibiotics, and anti-inflammatory agents. Changes in the bones of the skull due to trauma and the buildup of wax in the ears may also contribute to tinnitus.

With the many improvements in hearing aids, much of the age-associated hearing loss can be corrected without need to rely on an outwardly detectable device. In addition, certain communication strategies can be used by others to ensure that they are heard, such as avoiding interference, speaking in low tones, facing the person while speaking, and remaining patient. Although prevention of hearing loss is obviously preferable to correction, certain devices and communication strategies are available to help older adults compensate for presbycusis. Just as surgery for cataracts has taken advantage of the latest technological innovations, so hearing aids have become increasingly compact and effective. These miniature devices, which are effectively invisible to the outside observer, reduce considerably the social stigma associated in many people's minds with the need to wear a hearing aid. In fact, the necessity for a middle-aged president of the United States (Bill Clinton) to wear such a device drew attention to the problem and may have helped lessen the embarrassment that ordinary adults might otherwise feel about being in a similar situation.

Other communication strategies can be of use to the individual and others close to the individual affected by hearing loss. The first such strategy is recognition of the problem. People who communicate with others who have experienced hearing loss can also take advantage of several strategies to ensure that they are heard. One is to face the person directly in a well-lit situation so that he or she can see the face of the person speaking. It is also important to avoid background noise such as a television or a radio in the room so there will be minimal interference from competing sources of sound. In restaurants and social gatherings, it is better to find a place to talk that is as far as possible from crowded or noisy areas. The speaker should not be chewing food or gum. Rather than shouting, which increases interference with the speech signal, the speaker should use a low, clear voice and be sure to enunciate carefully. It is especially important not to talk to the person as if he or she was a child and cannot understand the content of what is being said. Similarly, one should not talk about the individual in the third person or leave the person out, as this will tend to isolate him or her. It is helpful to provide clues to the person about the topic of the conversation whenever possible. Most importantly, the speaker should not become frustrated or upset with the listener and should try to maintain a positive and patient attitude.

Assess Yourself

Do You Suffer From Hearing Loss?

Many people experience hearing loss gradually, often as a result of the natural aging process or long exposure to loud noise. Hearing loss can also be a sign of more serious health problems. If you think you may have a hearing loss, take this five-minute hearing test. You will receive 3 points for each "almost always," 2 for every "half the time," 1 for every "occasionally," and 0 for every "never" answer.

1. I have a problem hearing over the telephone.

2. I have trouble following the conversation when two or more people are talking at the same time.

3. People complain that I turn the TV volume too high.

4. I have to strain to understand conversations.

5. I miss hearing some common sounds like the phone or doorbell ring.

6. I have trouble hearing conversations in a noisy background, such as a party.

7. I get confused about where sounds come from.

8. I misunderstand some words in a sentence and need to ask people to repeat themselves.

9. I especially have trouble understanding the speech of women and children.

10. I have worked in noisy environments (such as assembly lines, construction sites, or near jet engines).

11. Many people I talk to seem to mumble or don't speak clearly.

12. People get annoyed because I misunderstand what they say.

13. I misunderstand what others are saying and make inappropriate responses.

14. I avoid social activities because I cannot hear well and fear I'll make improper replies.

15. Ask a family member or friend to answer this question: Do you think this person has a hearing loss?

Balance

Age-related alterations in the vestibular system that controls balance contribute to increased risk of falling in older adults. In addition to muscular weakness, joint stiffness, and the loss of bone density discussed earlier, older individuals are more susceptible to dizziness, vertigo, and difficulty detecting body position. They are therefore more likely to lose their balance or fail to see a step or an obstacle in their path on a level surface. Furthermore, heightened body sway can lead to postural instability, which can cause the person to fall spontaneously.

The two symptoms most frequently associated with age-related vestibular dysfunction are dizziness and vertigo. **Dizziness** is a feeling of lightheadedness and the sense that one is floating. When you are dizzy, you might feel as though you are about to faint. **Vertigo** is a sense of movement when the body is actually at rest, usually the sense that one is spinning. Because the vestibular system is so intimately connected to other parts of the nervous system, symptoms of vestibular disturbance may also be experienced as problems such as headache, muscular aches in the neck and back, and increased sensitivity to noise and bright lights. Other problems can include fatigue, inability to concentrate, unsteadiness while walking, and difficulty with speech. Increased sensitivity to motion sickness is another common symptom. Some of these changes may come about with diseases that are not part of normal aging, and others may occur as the result of normative alterations in the vestibular receptors.

"What do you think?"   **4-4**

Can you balance for a minute on one foot holding onto the other foot behind you? If not, this is something you should work on to improve your own balance.

Compensation for deficits or abnormalities of the vestibular system involves ensuring proper eyeglass prescriptions, use of a prosthetic aid in walking, outfitting the home with balance aids such as handrails, and developing greater sensitivity to the need to take care while walking. Balance training, including Tai Chi, can also be an effective preventive method to lessen the likelihood of falling (Wong, Lin, Chou, Tang, & Wong, 2001), as can aqua aerobics (Simmons & Hansen, 1996).

It is also important to correct for sensory losses in other areas that could contribute to faulty balance. First, the proper eyeglass prescription is obviously very crucial because vision provides important cues to navigating the environment. Second, an older individual with vestibular problems can obtain an aid to balance such as a walking stick and learn how to use it. In the home, it is important to find ways to substitute sitting for standing in situations that might pose a risk. For example, a shower chair or bath bench can be used in the tub, and a hand-held shower head can be installed. The individual can also get used to sitting while performing ordinary grooming tasks around the bathroom. This further reduces the need to maintain balance while engaging in delicate operations such as shaving. Similar adaptations can be made in the kitchen, such as sitting down rather than standing at the counter to cut vegetables. Buying a cordless telephone is another useful strategy so that it is not necessary to run (and possibly fall) when trying to answer a phone in another room.

In addition to such practical remedies, older individuals can learn to develop greater sensitivity to the need to be careful when moving from one floor surface to another, such as onto a tile floor from a carpet. This type of adjustment is particularly important when the individual is in an unfamiliar environment. Similarly, the individual should develop the habit of waiting a minute or two when getting up from a horizontal position. Reminding oneself of the need to use railings on stairways is another useful adjustment, or if there is no railing, using the wall to balance oneself when moving up or down the stairs.

Smell and Taste

Smell and taste belong to the chemical sensing system referred to as **chemosensation**. The sensory receptors in these systems are triggered when molecules released by the substances around us stimulate special cells in the nose, mouth, or throat.

Despite the fact that the olfactory receptors responsible for smell constantly replace themselves, the area of the olfactory epithelium shrinks, and ultimately the total number of receptors becomes reduced throughout the adult years. At birth, the olfactory epithelium covers a wide area of the upper nasal cavities, but by the 20s and 30s, its area has begun to decrease. A corresponding decrease in odor sensitivity appears to develop across the years of adulthood. Data from the National Geographic Smell Survey, a massive investigation of smell sensitivity in 712,000 adults aged 20–79, revealed overall patterns of age differences indicating poorer smell sensitivity and smell identification. However, the effects of age varied according to the particular odor tested (Wysocki & Gilbert, 1989). A short-term longitudinal study of men and women over a similar age range backed up the cross-sectional study with evidence of losses in olfactory sensitivity in the oldest age group (Ship et al., 1995).

The loss of olfactory receptors that apparently accounts for these changes in smell sensitivity reflects an intrinsic change associated with the aging process as well as damage caused by disease, injury, and exposure to toxins. Viral infections destroy olfactory receptors, and although they often grow back, repeated injury to the olfactory receptors caused by viral infections eventually takes its toll. Exposure to harmful chemicals in the environment is another source of damage to the olfactory receptors. Those people in the National Geographic Smell Survey who had worked in factories all their lives were more likely to suffer from losses in odor sensitivity (Corwin, Loury, & Gilbert, 1995). Another common source of environmental damage is tobacco smoke. The sense of taste also suffers due to damage to the taste buds caused by smoking. Although people who quit smoking eventually experience an improvement in their sense of smell, this can take many years (equal to the number of years spent smoking). Permanent damage to the olfactory receptors can be caused by head injury. A blow to the back of the head can cause the brain to hit the front of the skull, damaging the cribriform plate that supports the olfactory neurons. Bleeding into the mucus membrane caused by head trauma can also damage these structures. In fact, the greatest losses in the National Geographic Survey occurred for older female factory workers who had suffered a head injury at some point in their work lives (Corwin et al., 1995). Finally, dentures are another cause of loss of taste sensitivity because these may block the receptor cells of the taste buds.

Cognitive changes also appear to be associated with loss of smell sensitivity. Individuals who show extreme memory deficits consistent with Alzheimer's disease also show an extreme loss of smell sensitivity (Wang, Tian, Huang, Qin, He, et al., 2002). There is some indication that genes may play a role in this relationship, as people with a genetic risk for developing Alzheimer's disease show more loss of smell sensitivity than those who do not have this risk (Royall, Chiodo, Polk, & Jaramillo, 2002).

The changes associated with the aging process and damage caused by exposure to toxins and injury lead to small but discernible loss of smell and taste sensitivity (Nakazato, Endo, Yoshimura, & Tomita, 2002) and potentially a diminished ability to enjoy food. However, the existence of diagnosed disorders of taste and smell is still relatively small, with estimates ranging from 2 to 4 million Americans (of all ages) who have ever been diagnosed with a disorder of taste or smell and a yearly count of 200,000 who seek medical attention. Some of these disorders are also associated with other diseases or conditions of poor health, including obesity, diabetes, hypertension, malnutrition, and some degenerative diseases of the nervous system such as Parkinson's or Alzheimer's disease.

Although nothing can be done to reverse age-related losses of smell and taste, individuals who are experiencing more than a normal amount of change in sensitivity in either of these two functions may benefit from medical evaluations and treatments for underlying conditions contributing to the sensory losses (Forde, Cantau, Delahunty, & Elsner, 2002). Apart from such interventions, older individuals can also take advantage of strategies to enhance the enjoyment of food, such as expanding food choices to vary temperature, color, and texture, planning meals in enjoyable environments, and finding good dining companions!

Somatosensory System

The somatosensory system, which in general is responsible for the transduction of physical stimuli into neural impulses, is divided into two major subsystems. One subsystem includes the skin senses of touch, pain, pressure, and temperature. The second subsystem allows for the detection of the position and movement of the body's limbs. Position is mediated by the sense called **proprioception**, which provides information about where the limbs are placed when the person is standing still. **Kinesthesis** applies to the knowledge that receptors in the limbs provide when the body is moving. Through proprioception, you would know that you are poised at the top of a staircase, ready to go, and through kinesthesis you would know that you are actually moving down those stairs.

Research on aging in these areas is very limited. The majority of studies on movement and movement perception are tied to studies of balance (see Biopsychosocial Perspective box); other than the findings reported here, little is known about how aging affects the bodily senses.

Touch. There is a well-established body of evidence linking loss of the ability to discriminate

touch with the aging process throughout adulthood. Age differences have been documented in such areas as the ability to discriminate the separation of two points of pressure on the skin and the detection of the location of a stimulus applied to the skin. One estimate places the loss at 1% per year over the years from 20 to 80 (Stevens & Cruz, 1996). However, these effects vary by body part. The hands and feet are particularly subject to the effects of aging compared to areas located more centrally, such as the lip and tongue. The increase in threshold (loss of acuity) on the big toe is estimated to be 400% over the course of the life span, at least from childhood to advanced old age. The fingertip loses 130% over the years from youth to old age (Stevens & Cruz, 1996). These are significant losses indeed, and they can compromise the adult's ability to grasp, maintain balance, and perform delicate handwork. Furthermore, the studies that have been conducted, though somewhat few in number, have involved some very large samples, including one consisting of almost 2000 males and females ranging from childhood to well into old age (Shimokata & Kuzuyam, 1995). Some of these losses related to age changes in the touch receptors known as Pacinian corpuscles (Gescheider, Beiles, Checkosky, Bolanowski, & Verrillo, 1994).

Pain. The question of whether older adults are more or less sensitive to pain is a topic of considerable concern for health practitioners. Changes in pain perception with age could make life either much harder or much easier for individuals who have an illness whose symptoms include pain. There is no evidence that older adults become somehow immune or at least protected from pain by virtue of age changes in this sensory system. Lower back pain, the most common form of chronic pain, is experienced as a chronic symptom in 3.7 million men and

6.5 million women 65 years and older, or about one third of all older adults (Pleis & Coles, 2002). A survey of over 3300 deaths at six of the nation's top medical centers (discussed in more detail in Chapter 13) revealed that in the last three days before they died, 35% to 45% of the patients were in severe pain (Lynn, 1996). Among people with osteoarthritis, pain is a constant feature of life regardless of age, being reported as a daily experience for about one-third of a sample that included adults ranging from 19 to 92 years old (Lethbridge-Cejku, Scott, Reichle, Ettinger, Zonderman, et al., 1995). Comparable pain thresholds across age groups, including people in their 90s, have also been reported among healthy individuals (Heft, Cooper, O. Brien, Hemp, & O'Brien, 1996). In one unusual longitudinal study, which covered a 24-year period from middle to old age, approximately half of the respondents stated that they were in pain on three out of the four test occasions. The experience of pain was more severe in women then men (Brattberg, Parker, & Thorslund, 1997). Fortunately, the need to monitor and manage pain in older adults is increasingly recognized as an area of appropriate medical intervention (Gagliese & Melzack, 1997).

The fact that older adults are not spared from the experience of pain does not address the question of whether their pain thresholds are more or less sensitive to painful stimuli. There is some evidence that in fact sensitivity to pain as measured in the laboratory is reduced in later adulthood. Higher pain thresholds among people over 65 years old compared to people under 65 were observed in a measure of the response to a painful stimulus placed within the esophagus. Some of the older respondents even reported feeling no pain at all to a stimulus that a group of younger adults clearly regarded as very uncomfortable (Lasch, Castell, & Castell, 1997). However, it is very difficult to draw

generalizations about pain thresholds in one part of the body based on evidence from another. In an investigation of response times of the Aδ (fast) nerve endings compared to the C (slow) nerves in arms and legs, no age differences in sensitivity in either type of nerve were found between younger and older adults in the arms. However, in the legs, response types were delayed for fast nerve fibers among older adults, who also had no slow fiber pain response at all (Harkins, Davis, Bush, & Kasberger, 1996). Another factor that can influence pain perception is cognitive functioning. Older men with cognitive impairments are less likely to report that they experience pain than are those with cognitive deficits (Pickering, Jourdan, Eschalier, & Dubray, 2002).

In summary, changes in physical functioning have important interactions with psychological and sociocultural factors, and can influence the individual's identity in the middle and later years of adulthood. Fortunately, there are many preventive and compensating steps that people can take to slow the rate of physical aging.

SUMMARY

1. Changes in the skin include wrinkling and sagging. Discolorations also occur in the nails and skin. Many age changes in the skin are the result of excessive exposure to the harmful rays of the sun, a phenomenon known as photoaging. The hair thins and becomes gray, and in men in particular, baldness can develop. There are significant changes in body build, including loss of height, increase of body weight to the 50s followed by a decrease, and changes in fat distribution. However, adults of all ages can benefit from exercise, which can maintain muscle and lower bodily fat.

2. Mobility reflects the quality of the muscles, bones, and joints. The process of sarcopenia involves loss of muscle mass, and there is a corresponding decrease in muscle strength. Again, exercise, particularly strength training, is the key to maintaining maximum muscle functioning in adulthood. Bones lose mineral content throughout adulthood, particularly in women. Diet and exercise are important areas of prevention. The joints encounter many deleterious changes, and exercise cannot prevent these. However, middle-aged and older adults can benefit from flexibility training, which maintains range of motion even in joints that are damaged.

3. The cardiovascular system undergoes changes due to alterations in the heart muscle and arteries that lower aerobic capacity, cardiac output, and maximum heart rate. It is crucial for adults to avoid harmful fats in the diet and to engage in a regular pattern of aerobic exercise to minimize changes in the cardiovascular system. The respiratory system loses functioning due to stiffening of lung tissue. The most important preventive action is to avoid (or quit) cigarette smoking. Changes in the urinary system make the kidney more vulnerable to stress and less able to metabolize toxins, including medications. The bladder of older adults becomes less able to retain and expel urine, but the majority of people do not become incontinent. Behavioral methods can correct normal age-related changes in urinary control. The digestive system becomes somewhat less efficient in older adults, but there is not a significant loss of functioning. Many older people are misinformed by the media and take unnecessary corrective medications to control their gastrointestinal functioning.

4. The endocrine system is the site of many changes in the amount and functioning of the body's hormones. Growth hormone levels decline significantly in adulthood, but GH therapy is not recommended. Cortisol levels show increases, a process thought to be related to deleterious changes in cognitive functioning. However, changes in both of these important hormones can be modulated by diet and exercise. Thyroid hormones become lower, most likely through loss of muscle mass. Melatonin levels decline, a phenomenon thought to be linked to alterations in circadian (daily) rhythms. DHEA levels decrease drastically in men, but DHEA replacement is not advisable. The climacteric is the period of gradual loss of reproductive abilities. After the menopause, women experience a reduction in estrogen, and although estrogen-replacement therapy was an accepted therapeutic intervention, studies published beginning in 2002 led to a reversal of position in the medical community on the advisability of HRT. Decreases in testosterone level in older men are not consistently observed. Replacement therapy, once thought of as having dangerous side effects, is now recommended for older men whose levels of testosterone are below normal. Changes in the immune system, referred to as immune senescence, are observed primarily in a decline in T-cell functioning. Diet and exercise can counteract loss of immune responsiveness in older adults.

5. Normal age-related changes in the nervous system were once thought of as neuronal fallout, but it is now recognized that there is much plasticity in the aging brain. Brain scans reveal considerable variation in age-related alterations in brain structure. There is a rise in Stage 1 and a decrease in Stage 4 and REM (dream-related) sleep. Changes in circadian rhythms lead older adults to awake earlier and prefer the morning for working. Poor sleep habits and the coexistence of psychological or physical disorders (such as sleep

apnea) can interfere further with the sleep patterns of middle-aged and older adults. In many cases, dysthermia is related to the presence of disease.

6. Visual acuity decreases across adulthood, and presbyopia leads to a loss of the ability to focus the eye on near objects. Cataracts, age-related macular degeneration, and glaucoma are medical conditions that can lead to reduced vision or blindness. Presbycusis is the gradual loss of hearing that occurs in later life, and along with conductive hearing loss and tinnitus, are conditions that can interfere with the ability to communicate. Older adults are more vulnerable to loss of balance, particularly when they suffer from dizziness and vertigo. Balance training can compensate for these changes. Smell and taste show some losses with age, but both senses are extremely vulnerable to negative effects from disease and environmental damage. Touch sensitivity decreases in adulthood, particularly in the fingertips and toes. Findings on pain are inconclusive. There is loss of the perception of the position of the feet and legs, adding to other age-related changes in balance.

GLOSSARY

Acquired immunity: form of immune response that develops as the result of prior contact with an antigen (foreign agent in the body).

Adrenopause: age-related decline in dehydroepiandrosterone (DHEA).

Aerobic capacity: the maximum amount of oxygen that can be delivered through the blood.

Age-related macular degeneration: progressive form of blindness in which there is a destruction of the photoreceptors located in the central region of the retina known as the macula.

Andropause: age-related decline in the male sex hormone testosterone.

B cells: also called B lymphocytes, cells in the immune system involved in humoral immunity, in which they produce antibodies that bind to and neutralize the antigen.

Cardiac output: the amount of blood that the heart pumps per minute.

Cataract: clouding that has developed in the normally clear crystalline lens of the eye, resulting in blurred or distorted vision because the image cannot be focused clearly onto the retina.

Chemosensation: chemical sensing system that includes smell and taste.

Circadian rhythm: daily variations in various bodily functions.

Climacteric: gradual winding down of reproductive ability.

Conductive hearing loss: form of hearing loss due to damage in one of the structures that transmits sounds within the ear.

Cortisol: a glucocorticoid hormone that provides energy to the muscles during times of stress.

Dehydroepiandrosterone (DHEA): hormone that is a weak male steroid (androgen) produced by the adrenal glands located adjacent to the kidneys.

Dizziness: feeling of lightheadedness and the sense that one is floating.

Dysthermia: conditions in which the individual shows excessive raising of body temperature (hyperthermia) or excessive lowering of body temperature (hypothermia).

Estrogen: the primary female sex hormone.

Estrogen replacement therapy (ERT): therapeutic administration of estrogen to counteract the negative effects of estrogen loss on postmenopausal women.

Failing lung: loss of expandability of lung tissue.

Glaucoma: a group of conditions in which the optic nerve is damaged, causing loss of visual function.

Glucocorticoid cascade hypothesis: proposal that aging causes dangerous increases in cortisol levels affecting immune response, fat deposits, and cognition.

Hormone replacement therapy (HRT): therapeutic administration of lower doses of estrogen than in ERT, along with progestin to reduce the cancer risk associated with ERT.

High-density lipoproteins (HDLs): the plasma lipid transport mechanism responsible for carrying lipids from the peripheral tissues to the liver where they are excreted or synthesized into bile acids.

Immune senescence: term used to refer to features of the aging immune system.

Kinesthesis: knowledge that receptors in the limbs provide when the body is moving.

Lymphocytes: specialized cells in the bloodstream that are involved in the immune response.

Male pattern baldness: the form of hair loss that is specific to males and is genetically determined in which the hair follicles continue to produce hair, but it is hair that is not visible.

Maximum heart rate: the heart rate achieved at the point of maximum oxygen consumption.

Melatonin: a hormone manufactured by the pineal gland involved in synchronization of circadian rhythm, the regulation of other hormones, and possibly the protection of cells against free radical damage.

Menopause: the point in a woman's life when menstruation stops permanently.

Neuronal fallout model: view of the aging nervous system as involving progressive loss of brain tissue across the adult years noticeable by the age of 30.

Perimenopause: three- to five-year span during which women gradually lose reproductive ability.

Photoaging: age changes caused by exposure to the sun's harmful radiation.

Presbycusis: age-related hearing loss due to degenerative changes in the cochlea or auditory nerve leading from the cochlea to the brain.

Presbyopia: age-related change in the eye involving loss of accommodative power of the crystalline lens resulting in loss of the ability to focus on near objects.

Proprioception: bodily sense that provides information about where the limbs are placed when the person is standing still.

Sarcopenia: progressive loss of muscle mass.

Selective estrogen replacement modulaters (SERM): therapeutic administration of estrogen with more targeted effects than ERT.

Sleep apnea: condition in which the individual experiences a particular form of snoring in which a partial obstruction in the back of the throat restricts airflow during inhalation.

Somatopause: age-related decline in the somatotrophic axis (GH and IGF-1) of the endocrine system.

T cells: also called T lymphocytes, cells in the immune system primarily responsible for cell-mediated immunity in which invading antigens that have infected a bodily cell are identified and killed.

Testosterone: the primary male sex hormone.

Thyroid hormones: hormones produced by the thyroid gland that regulate the body's basal metabolic rate (the BMR).

Tinnitus: condition in which the individual perceives sounds in the head or ear (such as a ringing noise) when there is no external source for it.

Vasculopathology of aging: loss of flexibility in the arteries.

Vertigo: a sense of movement when the body is actually at rest, usually the sense that one is spinning.

Chapter Five

Health and Prevention

Chronic illnesses can significantly interfere with the quality of the individual's daily activities and can present complicating factors in the diagnosis and treatment of psychological disorders among older adults. These illnesses are cases of secondary aging and, as pointed out in Chapter 1, need to be distinguished from primary aging because they are not an inherent part of the aging process.

In this chapter, physical diseases that affect the body's major organ systems are described (see Table 5-1). We also examine the set of conditions known as dementia in which individuals suffer cognitive changes due to neurological damage and diseases that may become prevalent in later life. Although all of these conditions have the potential to be highly disabling, individuals can take advantage of many preventive strategies starting early in the adult years.

DISEASES OF THE CARDIOVASCULAR SYSTEM

Cardiovascular diseases include diseases that affect the heart and arteries. These diseases, which include atherosclerosis, hypertension, myocardial infarction ("heart attack"), and congestive heart failure, are the number one cause of death throughout the world (Lenfant, 2001). Because the distribution of blood throughout the body is essential for the normal functioning of all other organ systems, diseases in this system can have widespread effects on health and everyday life.

TABLE 5-1
Chronic Health Conditions by Age Group and Sex, 2000 (Based on the National Health Interview Survey)

	Condition	<45	45–64	65–74	75+
MALES	Heart conditions	3.1%	13.4%	26.0%	39.5%
	Hypertension*	3.0%	21.5%	31.5%	27.1%
	Chronic bronchitis	4.8%	4.1%	5.8%	3.4%
	Arthritis	2.6%	19.3%	39.5%	43.8%
	Diabetes	.6%	5.7%	11.7%	12.9%
FEMALES	Heart conditions	3.6%	10.0%	22.1%	25.9%
	Hypertension*	3.0%	21.3%	39.0%	43.7%
	Chronic bronchitis	5.2%	7.6%	6.3%	8.8%
	Arthritis	3.6%	28.4%	50.0%	57.6%

* Blood Pressure > 140/90.

Source: U.S. Bureau of the Census, 2000b.

Cardiac and Cerebrovascular Conditions

In the normal aging process, as described in Chapter 4, fat and other substances accumulate in the walls of the arteries throughout the body. In the disease known as atherosclerosis (from the Greek words athero meaning "paste" and sclerosis meaning "hardness"), these deposits collect at an abnormally high rate, to the point that they substantially reduce the width of the arteries.

Atherogenesis is the term that refers to stimulation and acceleration of **atherosclerosis**. Atherosclerosis is a condition related to **arteriosclerosis**, which is a general term for the thickening and hardening of arteries. As is true for atherosclerosis, some degree of arteriosclerosis also occurs in normal aging. Many people live with atherosclerosis and do not encounter significant health problems. However, the progressive buildup of plaque that occurs with this disease may eventually lead to partial or total blockage of the blood's flow through an artery. The organs or tissues that are fed by that artery will then suffer serious damage due to the lack of blood supply. When this occurs in the arteries that feed the heart muscle, the condition is known as coronary artery disease (or coronary heart disease). A **myocardial infarction** occurs when the blood supply to part of the heart muscle (the myocardium) is severely reduced or blocked.

The condition known by the technical term **hypertension**, or high blood pressure, is defined as a blood pressure that is greater than or equal to the value of 140 mm Hg systolic pressure and 90 mm Hg diastolic pressure. Changes in the arteries associated with atherosclerosis are thought to be due to the damaging effects of hypertension. The fact that blood pressure is virtually always elevated means that the blood is constantly putting strain on the walls of the arteries. Eventually, the arterial walls develop areas of weakness and inflammation, particularly in the large arteries where the pressure is greatest. Damage to the walls of the arteries makes them vulnerable to the accumulation of substances that form plaques. Furthermore, hypertension increases the workload on the heart, which is forced to pump harder. Consequently, people with hypertension are more likely to develop hypertrophy of the left ventricle of the heart. It is estimated that as a result of this damage to the circulatory system, adults with even mild levels of hypertension have a greater likelihood of developing serious heart disease (O'Donnell & Kannel, 2002).

Congestive heart failure (or heart failure) is a condition in which the heart is unable to pump enough blood to meet the needs of the body's other organs. Blood flow out of the heart slows, and so the blood returning to the heart through the veins begins to back up, causing the tissues to become congested with fluid. This condition can result from **coronary artery disease**, scar tissue from a past myocardial infarction, hypertension, disease of the heart valves, disease of the heart muscle, infection of the heart, or heart defects present at birth. People experiencing this condition are unable to exert themselves without becoming short of breath and exhausted. They develop a condition known as edema, in which fluid builds up in their bodies, causing their legs to swell. They may also experience fluid buildup in their lungs and kidney problems.

The term "cerebrovascular disease" refers to the disorders of the circulation to the brain. This condition may lead to the onset of a **cerebrovascular accident**, also known as a "stroke" or "brain attack," an acute condition in which an artery leading to the brain bursts or is clogged by a blood clot or other particle. The larger the area in the brain that is deprived of blood, the more severe the deterioration of the physical and mental functions controlled by that area. Another condition caused by the development of clots in the cerebral arteries is a **transient ischemic attack (TIA)**, also called a "mini-stroke." The cause of a TIA is the same as that of a stroke, but in a TIA, the blockage of the artery is temporary. The tissues that were deprived of blood soon recover, but the chances are that another TIA will follow. People who have had a TIA are also likely to have a stroke at some later point.

Incidence Rates

Heart disease is stated to be the number one killer in the United States; this is factually correct, but only because it is the number one killer for people 75 and older, who account for over half of all deaths in the United States (Minino, Arias, Kochanek, Murphy, & Smith, 2002).

TABLE 5-2
Causes of Death by Age and Sex, United States, 2001 (% of deaths per age and sex group)

	Age Group	Heart Disease	Stroke	Cancer	Lung Disease	AIDS
Male	25–44	1.8	1.81	10.5	NA	6.7
	45–54	27.5	3.4	27.8	3.0	1.3
	65+	32.2	6.6	25.2	6.4	NA
Female	25–44	11.9	3.7	27.7	NA	4.5
	45–54	18.5	4.3	40.3	4.4	.5
	65+	32.6	9.2	18.9	5.6	NA

Source: Anderson & Smith, 2003

Although death rates due to heart disease have gone down dramatically in the past 20 years, it is still the case that these are major killers among this age group. Together, heart and cerebrovascular disease accounted for 41% of all deaths in the United States for people over the age of 65 in 2000 and about 36% in Canada (Arias et al., 2003; American Heart Association, 2003). (See Table 5-2.)

Worldwide, the figures are just as dramatic, with nearly 17 million deaths in 2000 occurring due to cardiovascular disease, amounting to nearly one-third of all deaths around the globe (World Health Organization, 2002c). The countries with the highest death rates from cardiovascular disease are Romania and Hungary (American Heart Association, 2003).

As can be seen in Table 5-3, there are substantial variations by sex and race in the risk of dying from heart and cerebrovascular disease. Men have a much higher chance of dying from heart disease than do women. The sex discrepancy is lower for cerebrovascular disease, although in all cases the rate is also higher for

TABLE 5-3

Age-Adjusted Death Rates by Race and Sex for Heart and Cerebrovascular Disease

Race	Sex	Heart Disease	Cerebrovascular Disease
Whites	Males	304.8	56.5
	Females	200	54.8
Blacks	Males	384.5	85.4
	Females	269.8	73.7
American Indian/Alaskan	Males	200.7	37.5
	Females	127	44
Asian/Pacific Islander	Males	169.8	55.3
	Females	112.9	48.2
Hispanic	Males	232.6	48.9
	Females	161	41.6

Source: National Center for Health Statistics, 2003a.

men. The highest death rate by far is for heart disease among black men, a rate that is more than double that of other age and sex groups. Black women also have an elevated death rate for this disease. The death rate for cerebrovascular disease is also highest for blacks, and again, it is much higher for men than all other sex and race groups. Looking at the other end of the spectrum, we find that the Asian/Pacific Islander groups have the lowest death rates of all groups for heart disease, although they do not fare quite so well compared to other groups in the rate of death for cerebrovascular disease.

Variations in stroke rates by race or ethnicity, social class, and poverty have emerged as causes of national concern in the United States (Hart, Hole, & Smith, 2000; Centers for Disease Control and Prevention, 2000). Non-Hispanic blacks under the age of 65 have a particularly elevated risk of dying from stroke as do, to a lesser extent, American Indians/Alaskan natives (see Fig. 5.1). As we will see when we explore the risk factors for heart and cerebrovascular disease, living and working in a high stress environment, diminished access to health care, and lack of resources to pursue a healthy life style are major factors contributing to these disparities.

Behavioral Risk Factors

Understanding the contribution of lifestyle factors to heart disease is one of the most heavily researched topics in the biomedical sciences. The available body of literature now includes a list of four major risk factors, but new evidence is constantly accumulating, and so the numbers are likely to change. At the same time, researchers are heavily engaged in the enterprise of determining what lifestyle choices people can make to reduce their risk of developing heart disease. The hope is that by communicating these results to the general population, adults at

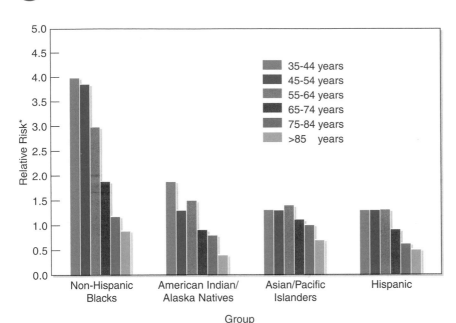

Source: Centers for Disease
Control and Prevention, 2000

FIGURE 5.1
Risk for Stroke Mortality among Racial/Ethnic Minority Groups Compared to Non-Hispanic Whites, by Age—United States, 1997

risk will be motivated to implement behavioral change strategies. Increasingly, these educational efforts are also being directed at younger and younger age groups, for developing health habits very early in life can minimize the risk of heart disease.

"What do you think?" **5-1**

Do you know people who have one or more of these diseases? How are their lives affected?

As was true of age-related normal cardiovascular changes, a sedentary lifestyle is the first major risk factor for heart disease. Many studies support this conclusion, but one carried out on a large sample of men in Finland is particularly impressive. Nearly 1400 men from 35 to 63 years of age were studied over an 11-year period, from 1980 to 1991 (Haapanen, Miilunpalo, Vuori, Oja, & Pasanen, 1996). During the

period of the study, 12% died, over half from cardiovascular disease. The men in the study reported involvement in a variety of activities, including some that are fairly specific to certain locales, such as weekend logging and ice fishing. The 27% of the sample who engaged in vigorous activity at least two times a week had about a 60% lower death rate from all causes, including cardiovascular disease, compared to those who did not participate regularly in vigorous activity. The lowest rates of death from cardiovascular disease were for men who spent their leisure time working in the forest. Gardening and repair work also had beneficial effects on mortality. The key to the success of an activity in terms of prevention of death from cardiovascular disease was the amount of calories burned per week in some type of physical activity. Those who burned fewer than 800 calories a week had almost five times the risk of dying from cardiovascular disease compared to those who burned 2100 calories or more.

Longevity calculators developed by insurance companies provide an estimate of a person's life expectancy based on gender, health, and lifestyle factors. See how you score on this parody of one of these tests.

Assess Yourself

Healthy Heart Quiz

1. Which one of the following is NOT a major risk factor for heart attack?
   A. Gender
   B. Age
   C. Heredity
   D. Vigorous exercise

2. If you have this experience, there is little cause for concern:
   A. Uncomfortable pressure, fullness, squeezing, or pain in the center of the chest that lasts more than a few minutes.
   B. Heartburn that is quickly relieved by antacids.
   C. Pain that spreads in the shoulders, neck, or arms.
   D. Discomfort in the chest accompanied by light-headedness, sweating, fainting, nausea, or shortness of breath.

3. Which of the statements below is true?
   A. Someone who has had a heart attack should not begin an exercise program.
   B. As you age, exercise becomes less important for your health.
   C. To be effective, an exercise program requires a significant investment of your time.
   D. You don't have to work out like an athlete to obtain physical fitness.

4. Keeping your weight at a healthy level is NOT likely to cause which one of the following:
   A. Reduce your chance of developing cardiovascular disease.
   B. Reduce your risk of developing diabetes.
   C. Reduce the likelihood that you will appear in an ad for underwear.
   D. Help control diabetes if you have the condition.

5. Where does dietary cholesterol come from?
   A. High fiber, whole-grain breads, and cereals.
   B. Nuts and seeds such as peanuts, cashews, and sunflower seeds.
   C. Animal products, most especially egg yolks and organ meats.
   D. Vegetable oils, particularly olive oil, safflower oil, and corn oil.

6. A high blood cholesterol level is one of three major risk factors for heart attack. What are the other two?
   A. Overexercise and lack of sleep.
   B. Excessive sweets and alcoholic beverages.
   C. Pregnancy and low blood pressure.
   D. High blood pressure and cigarette smoking.

Assess Yourself *(continued)*

7. Cholesterol is found in all your body's cells and is produced internally mostly by which organ in your body?
   A. Liver.
   B. Kidneys.
   C. Bone marrow.
   D. Pancreas.

8. Which of the three fatty acids, saturated, polyunsaturated, and monounsaturated, raise blood cholesterol?
   A. Saturated fats.
   B. Polyunsaturated fats.
   C. Monounsaturated fats.
   D. All of the above.

Answers: 1. D, 2. B, 3. D, 4. C, 5. C, 6. D, 7. A, 8. A

Unfortunately, the majority of adults at highest risk for heart disease (i.e., those 75 and older) are the least likely to exercise. As can be seen from Fig. 5.2, over 60% of women and slightly over 50% of men in this age group do not engage in leisure-time physical activity (Centers for Disease Control and Prevention, 2002a). Slightly under half of adults in the 65 to 74-year-old age group, similarly, fail to engage in this form of preventive behavior.

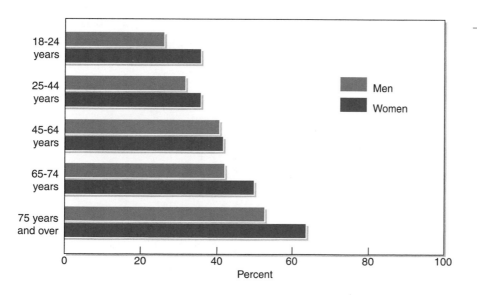

FIGURE 5.2
Adults Not Engaging in Leisure-Time Physical Activity by Age and Sex: United States, 2000

Source: Centers for Disease Control and Prevention, 2002a

The second risk factor is smoking. Although it is not known exactly why smoking increases the risk of heart disease, it is thought that it damages the arteries, making them more vulnerable to the passing fat cells that contribute to plaque formation. In one Japanese study cigarette smoking was found to interact with genetic predispositions for developing hypertension so that people at risk due to inheritance of a gene linked to hypertension who smoke have an even greater likelihood of developing the disease (Abe, Nakura, Yamamoto, Jin, Wu, et al., 2002). In a study of over 5000 Finnish adults 20 to 64 years of age, among smoking proved to be the most significant of all health-related behaviors in predicting most other health behaviors, meaning that if a person smoked, he or she was more likely to engage in other high-risk behaviors (Laaksonen, Luoto, Helakorpi, & Uutela, 2002).

Approximately one-quarter of all adults in the United States are current smokers, and a similar percentage are former smokers. The rates of current smokers decrease across cohorts of adults from rates of 24%–28% between the ages

of 18–64, down to 15% of those aged 65–74 and then 6.8% of those 75 and older (Schoenborn, Vickerie, & Barnes, 2003).

Body weight is the third risk factor for cardiovascular disease (Wilson, D'Agostino, Sullivan, Parise, & Kannel, 2002). According to the CDC, dramatic increases in overweight and obesity have occurred among U.S. adults in the years between 1987 and 2000. Currently, over 45 million adults are considered obese by government standards. As discussed in Chapter 4, the measure used to calculate risk based on the body weight to height ratio is the BMI (body mass index), which equals weight in kilograms divided by (height in meters) squared. An ideal BMI is one that is about 23 in men and 21 in women. According to U.S. government guidelines, which were recently revised to be consistent with those of other countries, the range for "overweight" is a BMI of 25 to 29.9 and that for obesity is a BMI of 30 or higher. These ranges vary slightly by race; Fig. 5.3 shows the range of weights and heights associated with BMI's in the overweight range for non-Asian/Pacific islanders,

If you are not Asian American or Pacific Islander At Risk BMI ≥ 25		If you are Asian American At Risk BMI ≥ 23		If you are Pacific Islander At Risk BMI ≥ 26	
Height	Weight	Height	Weight	Height	Weight
4'10"	119	4'10"	110	4'10"	124
4'11"	124	4'11"	114	4'11"	128
5'0"	128	5'0"	118	5'0"	133
5'1"	132	5'1"	122	5'1"	137
5'2"	136	5'2"	126	5'2"	142
5'3"	141	5'3"	130	5'3"	146
5'4"	145	5'4"	134	5'4"	151
5'5"	150	5'5"	138	5'5"	156
5'6"	155	5'6"	142	5'6"	161
5'7"	159	5'7"	146	5'7"	166
5'8"	164	5'8"	151	5'8"	171
5'9"	169	5'9"	155	5'9"	176
5'10"	174	5'10"	160	5'10"	181

FIGURE 5.3
Sample Age and Height for BMIs Considered Overweight by Race

Source: Centers for Disease Control and Prevention, 2003b

Asians, and Pacific Islanders. Using these criteria, as of 1998, over one-half of the United States population is overweight, and one-fifth is obese (U.S. Bureau of the Census, 2003).

The importance of BMI as a factor predicting health status extends beyond cardiovascular disease, as will be seen throughout this chapter. In addition to its relationship to a variety of chronic diseases, a high BMI is associated with declines in perceived health over time. A longitudinal study of nearly 8000 adults in their 50s revealed that people with high BMIs (30–35) were more likely to experience decreases in a measure of health-related quality of life. In addition to the impact on actual and subjective health, a high BMI was also associated with declines in mobility (Damush, Stump, & Clark, 2002).

The risk of mortality, particularly from cardiovascular disease, increases almost linearly with increasing levels of BMI. As can be seen in Figs. 5.4 and 5.5, mortality increases for men

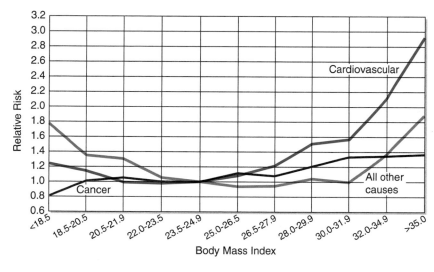

FIGURE 5.4

Body Mass Index and Mortality in Men

Source: American Cancer Society, 2002

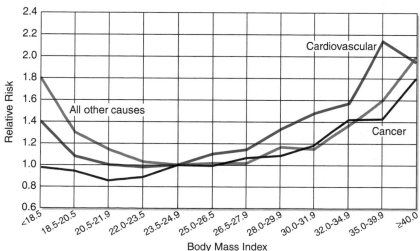

FIGURE 5.5

Body Mass Index and Mortality in Women

Source: American Cancer Society, 2002

and women from BMIs of 26 and above, with sharp increases particularly for men with BMIs of 30 and over. The increased risk of mortality extends throughout the adult years, not just in later life. Men in their 20s with severe levels of obesity are estimated to have a 22% shorter life span (a reduction of 13 years) compared to nonobese men (Fontaine, Redden, Wang, West-fall, & Allison, 2003). As will be seen later, it is not only cardiovascular disease, but also cancer and other causes of death that are associated with higher BMIs in adulthood.

Analyses of regional variations within the United States in diabetes risk identified a "stroke belt," located in the South, which reported the highest consumption of monounsaturated fatty acids, polyunsaturated fatty acids, cholesterol, and sodium, and the least amount of fiber. The South also consumed the least potassium; calcium; phosphorous; magnesium; copper; ribo-flavin; niacin; iron; and vitamins A, C, and B-6 (see Fig. 5.6).

The fourth factor is alcohol intake. This has been a controversial matter, with evidence accumulating pro and con about how much is "good" and how much is "bad." It is difficult to separate the effect of alcohol intake from the effect of diet (Barbaste, Berke, Dumas, Soulet, Delaunay, et al., 2002). In fact, in one large study of Finnish adults ages 15–64, high alcohol consumption was associated with healthier diets (Laaksonen, Prattala, & Karisto, 2001). However, it seems that moderate alcohol consumption has a protective effect on the risk of myocardial infarction (Mukamal, Conigrave, Mittleman, Camargo, Stampfer, et al., 2003) and stroke risk. Heavy alcohol intake (more than 60 grams of alcohol or two beers or two glasses of wine a day) may be associated with increased stroke risk (Reynolds, Lewis, Nolen, Kinney, Sathya, et al., 2003).

Behavioral factors related to stress on the job are a fifth factor related to heart disease. In a major study of Scandinavian workers (over 10,000 adults), the amount of job strain (daily stress experienced at work) was related to lower levels of high-density lipoproteins (HDLs), the so-called good cholesterol that is associated

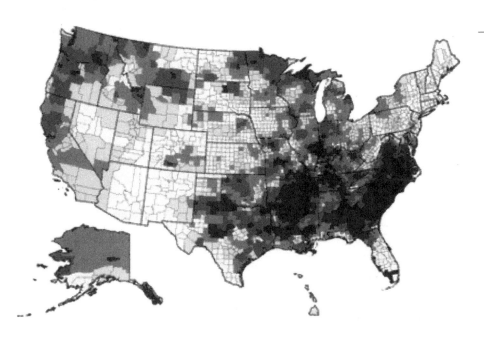

FIGURE 5.6
Stroke Death Rates, 1991–1995 Adults Aged 35 Years and Older, by County

Source: Casper et al., 2003

with lower risk of heart disease. Although men with high levels of job strain did not have a higher risk of hypertension, women in high-stress jobs were more likely to have hypertension (Alfredsson, Hammar, Fransson, de Faire, Hallqvist, et al., 2002).

Prevention of Heart Disease

Ultimately, the success of the vast research enterprise on the causes of heart disease will rest on its ability to provide the public with safe and effective medical or dietary supplements to lower the death rates due to this disease. Exercise, of course, remains an important preventive measure for reducing the risk of heart disease in middle-aged and older adults (Karani, McLaughlin, & Cassel, 2001; Seeman & Chen, 2002). Until 2002, estrogen-replacement therapy (ERT) was thought to provide a variety of benefits in terms of lowering harmful components of LDLs and increasing, but as mentioned in Chapter 4, the risks outweigh benefits, and other preventive or therapeutic measures are now being recommended instead.

For men, there is some evidence that DHEA and DHEAS can serve a protective function against the development of heart disease (Feldman, Johannes, Araujo, Mohr, Longcope, et al., 2001). Drugs called statins, which lower the levels of harmful cholesterol in the blood, are the newest agents to enter the war against heart disease (Morishita, Tomita, & Ogihara, 2002).

The simplest and cheapest measures that people can take to protect against heart disease involve diet and exercise (Krauss, Eckel, Howard, Appel, Daniels, et al., 2001). Dietary supplements, include Vitamin C (ascorbic acid), which is found in fruits (Khaw, Bingham, Welch, Luben, Wareham, et al., 2001) Certain foods have been found to lower harmful forms of cholesterol, including vegetables (Liu, Lee, Ajani, Cole, Buring, et al., 2001), food with high-fiber content such as cereal (Mozaffarian, Kumanyika, Lemaitre, Olson, Burke, et al., 2003), and folic acid (Wald, Bishop, Wald, Law, Hennessy, et al., 2001), which is found in yeast, liver, green vegetables, and certain fruits. The American Heart Association has engaged in

Participation in regular exercise, such as this step aerobics class, is one of the most important ways to maintain cardiovascular fitness.

a widespread campaign in recent years to inform people of the advantage of adding these components to their diet (Smith, Blair, Bonow, Brass, Cerqueira, et al., 2001). These are increasingly being seen as viable adjuncts to exercise and control over obesity. Of course, it is not only the availability of preventive treatments that counts. People have to be motivated to engage in these preventive measures and to maintain their motivation throughout any program of dietary improvements or exercise. The field of behavioral medicine is increasingly addressing these concerns, particularly as they apply to preventive and treatment measures in the later years of adulthood (Siegler, Bastian, Steffens, Bosworth, & Costa, 2002).

BIOPSYCHOSOCIAL PERSPECTIVE

INCOME, EDUCATION, OCCUPATION, race, gender, and ethnicity may contribute to the health and well-being of the individual in part through direct influences on the quality of life and opportunities to take advantage of age-related compensatory or preventative measures. In part, these influences are indirect, through influences of occupation, and quality of life and lifestyle choices.

Social status affects the rate of normal aging through actions taken by such behavior as exercise and smoking, which are known to affect many, if not all, systems covered in this chapter (Bjorntorp, 1995; Wister, 1996). These behaviors are technically within the individual's personal control and may reflect pervasive attitudes, opportunities, and normative behaviors of people in varying occupational and educational groups. One impressive study illustrating the potential dangers of these high-risk behaviors followed 1700 individuals over a 32-year period. The age of encountering disability was delayed by five years in the low-risk group who did not smoke, did not overeat, and exercised. High-risk participants, who smoked, were overweight, and did not exercise, had twice the rate of disability and death. Thus, these age-altering behaviors can not only lengthen life, but they can significantly reduce disability in the later years (Vita, Terry, Hubert, & Fries, 1998). Sociocultural influences can also include the values held by people that can contribute to the risk factors of diet and exercise. Even after controlling for relevant factors such as income, social support, and availability of services, education was found in one large sample of adults 55 and older to play a significant role in predicting health status (Murrell & Meeks, 2002). The role of education seems to be to increase the value that individuals place on maintaining a healthy diet and a regular pattern of exercise. In the United States exercise rates among those with a high school degree or better are just about double (52%) the rates of people with less than a high school education (26%). In the cultures of some developing nations, where concerns center on not starving rather than on staying thin voluntarily, people hold the opposite set of social values about weight.

Gender and age also play a role in the relationships among health and socioeconomic status (SES). In a study of comparing over 11,000 women in their 40s and over 9500 women in their 70s, SES was found to play a larger role in affecting health among the mid-life than the older adult women. However, within the older adult sample, education was associated with higher risk of specific health conditions (Mishra, Ball, Dobson, Byles, & Warner-Smith, 2002). Therefore, when looking at SES and health, gender and age need to be taken into account.

Negative emotions also seem to play a role in mediating the relationship between SES and health. People with low SES are more likely to experience negative emotions and perceptions of the world. Their lower SES means that they are exposed to more stressful situations, which in turn create more negative views of the world. These views, in turn, make them more vulnerable to negative health outcomes (Gallo & Matthews, 2003). Ethnicity may also interact with emotions in affecting illness. For example, in a study comparing Eastern Europeans with Americans of European descent, negative affect was found to increase the risk of arthritis in Eastern Europeans only. When comparing African Americans with Caribbeans, negative emotion had a greater impact among African Americans compared to Caribbeans (Consedine, Magai, Cohen, & Gillespie 2002).

In one particularly key international study, researchers investigated rates of hypertension among Africans in comparison to individuals of African heritage living in the United States and Caribbean countries (Cooper, Rotimi, & Ward, 1999). The purpose of this study was to investigate differences in health status according to the degree of urbanization and exposure to other environmental factors (including racial discrimination) among people of similar genetic backgrounds, at least in terms of race. Blood pressure was substantially higher among people living in the city of Ibadan, Nigeria, than in nearby rural areas, despite small differences in the groups' overall levels of obesity and sodium intake. Psychological stress and lack of physical activity were also seen as contributing to the increase in blood pressure.

In Chapter 13, the issue of SES and income will be revisited in terms of mortality rates, and once again, the role of stress, discrimination, and social structure will be examined. Clearly, these are complex issues, and researchers are only beginning to untangle the many intriguing connections among these variables.

CANCER

Cancer is a generic term for a group of more than 100 different diseases. Each type of cancer has its own symptoms, characteristics, treatment options, and overall effect on a person's life and health.

Types of Cancer

Most cancers are named for the type of cell or the organ in which they originate. A **carcinoma** is a cancer that begins in the lining or covering tissues of an organ. Squamous cell carcinomas begin in the flat scale-like cells in the skin and in tissues that line certain organs of the body. An **adenocarcinoma** begins in glandular tissue within an organ. When cancer spreads, the new tumor has the same kind of abnormal cells and the same name as the primary tumor, even though the cancer is found in a different organ or type of cell.

In 2002, it was estimated that about 1.3 million Americans received a diagnosis of cancer and that about 8.9 million are living with the disease (United States Cancer Statistics Working Group, 2002). Skin cancer is the most prevalent type of cancer in the United States, with about one million new cases occurring each year (American Cancer Society, 2002). It is estimated that one out of every five Americans will develop skin cancer at some point in his or her lifetime, and 40% to 50% of people who live to the age of 65 will have skin cancer at least once (http://www.nci.nih.gov/cancerinfo/wyntk/skin#2). The most common form of skin cancer is basal cell carcinoma, which is a slow-growing cancer that begins in the cells just below the surface of the skin. The most serious type of cancer that occurs in the skin is melanoma, which begins in melanocytes, the cells that produce the skin coloring or pigment known as melanin.

Breast cancer is the most frequent cancer that occurs in women and the second leading cause of cancer death (National Center for Health Statistics, 2002a). In 2001, there were an estimated 192,200 new cases reported and 40,200 deaths (U.S. Bureau of the Census, 2003). The most common type of breast cancer begins in the lining of the ducts that lead from the milk-producing glands (lobules) to the nipple. This kind of breast cancer is called ductal carcinoma. The cancer cells, which develop in a duct, spread through the wall of the duct and invade the fatty tissue of the breast. At this point, the cancer cells have the potential to metastasize through the blood and lymphatic system. The second most common form of breast cancer is lobular carcinoma, which arises in the milk-producing lobules.

Cancer of the reproductive organs of women is most likely to develop in the uterus, the cervix, and the ovary. The most frequently occurring of all these forms of cancer in women originates in the lining of the organ (epithelial or squamous cell carcinomas). Cancer in the reproductive organs of men most often affects the prostate gland. Cells in this gland often grow abnormally, leading to enlargement of the prostate in older men, but the tumor is very slow-growing, and the condition is usually benign.

A number of forms of cancer can develop in the digestive system. The most common are stomach, colon, and rectal cancer. Cancer can develop in any section of the stomach, and depending on which section is affected, the symptoms and outcomes will differ. Colon cancer and rectal cancer have many features in common and are referred to together as colorectal cancer. Polyps, which are small precancerous growths that develop in or just under the epithelium, usually develop first. When these become cancerous, they start to grow either inward toward the hollow part of the colon or rectum or outward through the wall of these organs. Most stomach and colorectal cancers are adenocarcinomas.

The most common form of lung cancer is called large cell cancer. This includes squamous cell or epidermoid carcinoma (also called bronchogenic carcinoma), which originates in cells that line the bronchi or their primary branches. Another form of lung cancer, adenocarcinoma, begins in the glandular cells that line the respiratory tract along the outer edges of the lung and under the lining of the bronchi. This is the most common type of lung cancer in people who have never smoked. Small cell carcinomas, also called "oat cell" cancers, usually begin in the bronchi. Many forms of cancer become particularly lethal when they spread to the lymph nodes and enter the lymphatic system. If the cancer has reached these nodes, it may mean that cancer cells have spread to other parts of the body-other lymph nodes and other organs, such as the bones, liver, or lungs. Tragically, it is not until many forms of cancer have metastasized that the afflicted individuals are aware that they have the disease because many cancers do not cause symptoms when they are growing within the organ that is primarily affected.

Risk Factors and Prevention

All cancer is the result of genetic causes in the sense that it reflects damage to the genes that control cell replication, most often due to random mutations that develop in the cells of the body. The mutations develop either as a mistake in cell division or in response to injuries from environmental agents such as radiation or chemicals. The progress of a cell or cells from normal to malignant to metastatic appears to follow a series of distinct steps, each controlled by a different gene or set of genes. In addition to damage caused by random mutations or exposure to harmful agents, there are gene mutations linked to an inherited tendency for developing common cancers, including breast and colon cancer. The risk of breast cancer increases for women whose first-degree relatives (mother, sister, or daughter) had the disease. Furthermore, about 5% of women with breast cancer have a hereditary form of this disease. Similarly, close relatives of a person with colorectal cancer are themselves at greater risk, particularly if it has affected many people within the extended family.

Most cancers become more prevalent with increasing age in adulthood because age is associated with greater cumulative exposure to harmful toxins (carcinogens) in the environment. People with certain lifestyles are particularly vulnerable to certain forms of cancer. The three greatest risk factors for the development of cancer during adulthood are exposure to the sun, cigarette smoking, and lack of control over diet. It is thought that many of the 1 million skin cancers diagnosed in 2001 in the United States could have been prevented by protection from the sun's rays. In 2001, the American Cancer Society estimated that about 172,000 cancer deaths were caused by tobacco use, and 19,000 deaths were related to excessive alcohol use, often used in combination with tobacco. Furthermore, one-third of the 553,400 cancer deaths that occurred in the United States in 2001 were thought to be related to lifestyle patterns such as poor nutrition and lack of physical activity (American Cancer Society, 2002).

Perhaps the most impressive evidence for the role of lifestyle comes from a nationwide study of over 900,000 adults in the United States who were studied prospectively (before they had cancer) from 1982 to 1998. During this period of time, there were 57,145 deaths from cancer. The people with the highest BMIs had death rates from cancer that were 52% higher for men and 62% higher for women compared to men and women of normal BMI. The types of cancer observed to be associated with BMI included cancer of the esophagus, colon and rectum, liver, gallbladder, pancreas and kidney. Significant trends of increasing risk with higher BMI values were observed for death from cancers of the stomach and prostate in men and for death from cancers of the breast, uterus, cervix, and ovary in women (Calle, Rodriguez, Walker-Thurmond, & Thun, 2003). We can conclude from this study that maintaining a low BMI is a critical preventive step in lowering an individual's risk of cancer.

"What do you think?" 5-2

How might public health efforts be better directed at reducing the risk for cancers in this country?

Skin cancer, the most common form of cancer in adults, is directly linked to exposure to ultraviolet (UV) radiation from the sun. In the United States, for example, melanoma is more common in Texas than it is in Minnesota, where the levels of UV radiation from the sun are weaker. Around the world, the highest rates of skin cancer are found in South Africa and Australia, areas that receive high amounts of UV radiation. Even artificial sources of UV radiation, such as sunlamps and tanning booths, can cause skin cancer despite the claims they make about their safety.

Cigarette smoking is the next greatest health risk, and in many ways it is more dangerous than UV exposure because the forms of cancer that are related to cigarettes are more likely to be lethal than skin cancer. It is known that most lung cancer is caused by cigarette smoking, and exposure to cigarette smoke is a risk factor for developing cancers of the mouth, throat, esophagus, larynx, bladder, kidney, cervix, pancreas, and stomach (see Fig. 5.7). The risk of lung cancer begins to diminish as soon as a person quits smoking. People who have had lung cancer and stop smoking are less likely to get a second lung cancer than are patients who continue to smoke. Exposure to cigarette smoke ("second-hand smoke") can be just as great a risk, if not greater, for lung cancer.

Diet is the third risk factor. Older women who are overweight are thought to have a greater risk of breast cancer. Although the link between diet and breast cancer has not been established, there is evidence that exercise and a low-fat diet combined with well-balanced meals

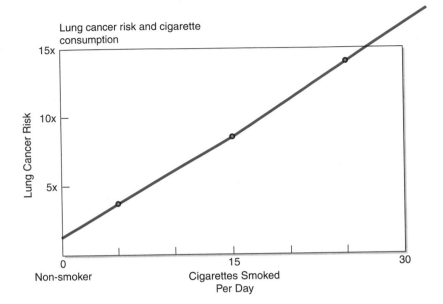

Lung cancer risk and cigarette consumption

FIGURE 5.7
Lung Cancer Risk and Cigarette Consumption

Source: National Cancer Institute, 2004

may be beneficial. For men, a diet high in fat is thought to increase the risk of prostate cancer and a diet high in fruits and vegetables to decrease the risk, although this has not been firmly established. Stomach and colon cancer also appear to be related to diet. Stomach cancer is more common in parts of the world—such as Japan, Korea, parts of Eastern Europe, and Latin America—in which people eat foods that are preserved by drying, smoking, salting, or pickling. By contrast, fresh foods, especially fresh fruits and vegetables, may help protect against stomach cancer. Similarly, the risk of developing colon cancer is thought to be higher in people whose diet is high in fat, low in fruits and vegetables, and low in high-fiber foods such as whole-grain breads and cereals. For instance, New Zealand and the United States have the higher rates of colon cancer and also consume the largest amount of meat (National Cancer Institute, 2004).

In addition to these three general risk factors, there are other specific types of experiences that seem to make certain people more vulnerable to cancer. Environmental toxins such as pesticides, electromagnetic fields, engine exhausts, and contaminants in water and food are being investigated for a possible role in the development of breast cancer. Carcinogens in the workplace, such as asbestos and radon (a radioactive gas), also increase the risk of lung cancer. The risk of prostate cancer may be increased by exposure to cadmium, a metal involved in welding, electroplating, and making batteries. Fumes and dust from an urban or workplace environment may also increase the risk of stomach and colorectal cancer.

Lifestyle habits and choices that people make can further contribute to the risk of developing cancer. In the intensive efforts being made to find the causes of breast cancer, various personal history factors have been suggested, such as amount of alcohol consumed or having an abortion or a miscarriage. The evidence is somewhat stronger for the effect of personal history in the case of cervical cancer, which has a higher risk among women who began having sexual intercourse before age 18 and/or have had many sexual partners. For men, efforts are under way to determine whether having had a vasectomy increases their risk for prostate cancer.

Having had a prior history of a related disease is another risk factor for cancer. For women who have had nonmetastatic lobular cancer in the past, there is a higher risk that they will develop an invasive form of cancer in the future. Other benign changes in breast tissues may also increase the subsequent risk of breast cancer. Similarly, there is a higher risk of uterine cancer among women who have had abnormal but benign growths within the endometrium and among women who have a history of colorectal or breast cancer. The higher risk for cervical cancer among women with a higher number of sexual partners may be related to the heightened risk they have for developing a sexually transmitted virus. This virus, in turn, can cause cells in the cervix to begin the series of changes that can lead to cancer. Women whose immune systems are weakened by disease, such as the human immunodeficiency virus (HIV), which causes acquired immune deficiency syndrome (AIDS), are also more at risk for cervical cancer. Similarly, the possibility is being investigated that sexually transmitted viruses increase the risk for prostate cancer.

Diseases that affect the stomach and intestine are also regarded as suspects for increasing the likelihood of cancers developing in these organs. A type of bacteria that causes stomach inflammation and ulcers may be an important risk factor for stomach cancer. Increased risk of cancer is also thought to be found in people who have had stomach surgery or who have diseases that reduce the amount of gastric acid. The presence of polyps in the colorectal area increases the risk of cancer, as does ulcerative colitis, which is a disease involving the development of ulcerated areas and inflammation within the lining of the colon.

In addition to a person's lifestyle and history of disease, variations due to race and ethnicity are observed among certain types of cancers. It is known that skin cancer is more likely to develop in people with fair skin that freckles easily, who often have red or blond hair and light-colored eyes. Black people are less likely to get any form of skin cancer. Other cancers that vary according to race are uterine cancer, which is more prevalent among whites, and prostate cancer, which is more prevalent among blacks. Stomach cancer is twice as prevalent in men and is more common in black people, as is colon cancer. However, rectal cancer is more prevalent among whites. Finally, hormonal factors are thought to play an important role in the risk of certain forms of cancer. Although the cause of prostate cancer is not known, it is known that the growth of cancer cells in the prostate, like that of normal cells, is stimulated by male hormones, especially testosterone. Along similar lines, estrogen is thought to increase the likelihood of a woman's developing uterine cancer. It is possible that the link between weight and uterine cancer in women may be due to the fact that women with a higher amount of body fat produce more estrogen and that it is the estrogen, not fat, that increases the risk of uterine cancer. Similarly, the finding that diabetes and high blood pressure increase the risk of uterine cancer may be related to the fact that these conditions are more likely to occur in overweight women who have higher levels of estrogen. Because of the link between estrogen and cancer, greater cautions have been taken to protect women who are taking estrogen-replacement therapy after menopause to offset other deleterious changes in the bones and cholesterol metabolism. Medical researchers are finding safer alternatives to traditional forms of estrogen-replacement therapy such as combining estrogen with progesterone and using other forms of estrogen (see below). Unfortunately, the breast cancer drug tamoxifen, which was approved by the FDA for use in this country in 1998, is known to increase the risk of developing uterine cancer presumably because of its estrogen-like effect on the uterus.

Treatments

Cancer detection with frequent screenings is the primary step in treatment. Organizations such as the American Cancer Society publicize the need for tests such as breast self-examination and mammograms for women, prostate examinations for men, and colon cancer screenings for both men and women. There is mixed evidence for the effectiveness of this publicity. In the case of mammograms, for example, it does appear that women have responded. The percentage of women in the U.S. population who have had this screening procedure in the past two years rose from 29% to 70% in the years between 1987 and 2000 (Centers for Disease Control and Prevention, 2002a). However, the distribution of women who take this preventive step varies by education and poverty status, as do so many other aspects of health care. In 2000, of those with less than a high school education, only 58% had gotten a mammogram compared to 76% of those with at least one year of college. A similar discrepancy exists in mammogram rates for those below the poverty line (55%) compared to those at or above the poverty level (72%). Some of these factors undoubtedly contribute to differences between white and black women in the stage of breast cancer reported at first diagnosis. Because they are less likely to have mammograms, black women are more likely to be diagnosed at a later stage in the progression of the disease (McCarthy, Burns, Coughlin, Freund, Rice, et al., 1998).

Depending on the stage of cancer progression at diagnosis, various treatment options are available. Surgery is the most common treatment for most types of cancer when it is likely that all of the tumor can be removed. Radiation therapy is the use of high-energy X-rays to damage cancer cells and stop their growth. Chemotherapy is the use of drugs to kill cancer cells. It is most often used when the cancer has metastasized to other parts of the body. Biological therapy is treatment involving substances called biological response modifiers that improve the way the body's immune system fights disease and may be used in combination with chemotherapy to treat cancer that has metastasized. As more information is gathered through the rapidly evolving program of research on cancer and its causes, new methods of treatment and prevention can be expected to emerge over the next few decades. Furthermore, as efforts grow to target populations at risk for the development of preventable cancers (such as lung cancer), it may be expected that cancer deaths will be reduced even further in the decades ahead.

AIDS

A disease of the immune system which has achieved global notoriety is **acquired immune deficiency syndrome** (**AIDS**). This disease is the number one killer of certain segments of the young adult population, but it is increasingly affecting older adults as well. The disease was first reported in the United States in 1981 and has since become a major worldwide epidemic.

Characteristics of AIDS

The term "AIDS" applies to the most advanced stages of infection by the **human immunodeficiency virus**, also known as HIV. This virus kills or impairs cells of the immune system, hence the term "immunodeficiency" (meaning

The scene "La Vie Boheme," from the Broadway musical *Rent* shows young people who have been affected by AIDS celebrating the appreciation for life that they have gained from this disease.

that the immune system is lacking one or more of its components). As HIV kills or impairs immune system cells, it progressively destroys the body's ability to fight infections and certain cancers. Consequently, individuals who are diagnosed with AIDS become vulnerable to certain life-threatening diseases (called **opportunistic infections**), which are caused by microorganisms that usually do not cause illness in healthy people. People with AIDS often suffer infections of the intestinal tract, lungs, brain, eyes, and other organs, as well as debilitating weight loss, diarrhea, neurologic conditions, and cancers such as Kaposi's sarcoma and lymphomas.

The cells destroyed by HIV are the helper T cells (called CD4+ T cells). An uninfected person in good health usually has 800 to 1200 CD4+ T cells per cubic millimeter (mm3) of blood. As a result of HIV infection, the number of CD4+ T cells progressively declines. When the count falls below 200/mm3, the person becomes particularly vulnerable to the opportunistic infections and cancers that typify AIDS. The HIV-mediated destruction of the lymph nodes and related immunologic organs also plays a major role in causing the immunosuppression seen in people with AIDS.

Symptoms generally do not appear when a person is first infected with HIV. Some people, however, develop a flu-like illness within a month or two after they are exposed to the virus, but the symptoms usually disappear and are mistaken for those of another viral infection. More persistent or severe symptoms may not surface for a decade or more after HIV first enters the body in adults and within two years in children born with HIV infection. This period of "asymptomatic" infection is highly variable, ranging from a few months to more than 10 years. Factors such as age, genetic differences, level of virulence of an individual strain of virus, and co-infection with other microorganisms may influence the rate and severity of disease progression.

As the immune system deteriorates, a variety of complications begins to emerge. These include enlargement of lymph nodes, lack of energy, weight loss, frequent fevers and sweats, persistent or frequent yeast infections, persistent skin rashes or flaky skin, pelvic inflammatory disease that does not respond to treatment, and short-term memory loss. Some people develop frequent and severe herpes infections that cause mouth, genital, or anal sores, or a painful nerve disease known as shingles. Children may have delayed development or failure to thrive.

In the end stages of the disease, opportunistic infections cause such symptoms as coughing, shortness of breath, seizures, dementia, severe and persistent diarrhea, fever, vision loss, severe headaches, wasting, extreme fatigue, nausea, vomiting, lack of coordination, coma, abdominal cramps, or difficult or painful swallowing. People with AIDS are particularly prone to developing various cancers such as Kaposi's sarcoma or cancers of the immune system known as lymphomas. These cancers are usually more aggressive and difficult to treat in people with AIDS. Signs of Kaposi's sarcoma are round pigmented spots that develop in the skin or in the mouth. Many people are so debilitated by the symptoms of AIDS that they are unable to hold steady employment or do household chores. Other people with AIDS may experience phases of intense life-threatening illness followed by phases of normal functioning.

Incidence

From the identification of the disease in the early 1980s through the year 2002, there were approximately 22 million deaths worldwide due to AIDS (http://www.avert.org/worldstats.htm); in 2002 alone, 3.1 million deaths were associated with this disease. It was estimated that 42 million people were living with the disease, and 5 million new cases of infected individuals were reported during that year. The vast majority of these new cases occurred in developing countries, with the highest number (29.4 million) in Sub-Saharan Africa, but the numbers are rising rapidly in Eastern Europe (World Health Organization, 2002a).

In the United States, 384,906 individuals were living with AIDS at the end of 2002. Through December 2002, 886,575 AIDS cases had been reported since the beginning of the epidemic, and of these, 501,669 (57%) had died. The epidemic is growing most rapidly among minority populations and is a leading killer of African-American males. Blacks and Hispanics are disproportionately represented in the AIDS statistics, with Blacks totaling 42% of people living with AIDS and Hispanics 20%. Whites are 37% of AIDS cases. There are dramatic regional variations in AIDS rates in the United States, with the highest annual rates in New York City (65.9 per 100,000) and Miami, Florida (53.8 per 100,000) (Centers for Disease Control and Prevention, 2003c).

Some positive indications of a slowing in the rates of incidence of AIDS began to appear in the late 1990s. The decrease in the number of new cases began in 1996, when there were 60,805 reported, and continued through 1998 (42,832 new cases). Incidence rates have leveled off since then, with 42,651 new cases reported in 2002. The peak death rate was in 1995 (51,670), and the number of deaths per year has steadily declined since then (16,371 in 2002). These decreases are attributed to a slowing of the epidemic overall and to improved treatments, which have lengthened the life span of people with HIV/AIDS.

Risk Factors and Prevention

HIV is spread most commonly by sexual contact with an infected partner. The virus can enter the body through the lining of the genitals, rectum, or mouth during sex. Having another sexually transmitted disease appears to make someone more susceptible to acquiring HIV infection during sex with an infected partner. HIV also is spread through contact with infected blood, and drug users who share needles or syringes contaminated with minute quantities of blood of someone infected with the virus can contract AIDS. Women can transmit HIV to their fetuses during pregnancy, birth, or breastfeeding.

Among men diagnosed with AIDS in the United States in 2002, male-to-male sexual contact accounted for the largest proportion of cases (58%), followed by injection drug use (23%). Among women diagnosed with AIDS in the United States in 2002, most acquired HIV infection through sexual contact with a man with HIV or at risk of HIV infection (61%) or through injection drug use (36%) (Centers for Disease Control and Prevention, 2003c). Although HIV can be detected in the saliva of infected individuals, there is no evidence that the virus is spread by contact with saliva because saliva has natural compounds that inhibit the infectiousness of HIV. However, the risk of infection from so-called deep kissing, involving the exchange of large amounts of saliva, is unknown. There is no evidence that HIV is spread through sweat, tears, urine, or feces, nor is HIV spread by biting insects such as mosquitoes or bedbugs. The most reliable form of prevention of HIV infection is use of a condom.

Treatment

When AIDS first appeared in the United States in the early 1980s, there were no drugs available to combat the underlying immune deficiency, and few treatments existed for the opportunistic diseases that resulted. A number of drugs have now been approved for the treatment of HIV infection, although they do not provide a cure. The first group of drugs used to treat HIV infection, called reverse transcriptase (RT) inhibitors, interrupts an early stage of virus replication. The most well known of this class of drugs is AZT (also known as zidovudine). These drugs may slow the spread of HIV in the body and delay the onset of opportunistic infections. A second class of drugs approved for

treating HIV infection are called protease inhibitors. These drugs interrupt virus replication at a later step in its life cycle. Because HIV can become resistant to both classes of drugs, combination treatment (the "AIDS cocktail") using both is necessary to effectively suppress the virus. The retrovirus drugs do have side effects, including a depletion of red or white blood cells (especially when taken in the later stages of the disease), inflammation of the pancreas, and painful nerve damage. The most common side effects associated with protease inhibitors include nausea, diarrhea, and other gastrointestinal symptoms. In addition, protease inhibitors can interact with other drugs, resulting in serious side effects. Drugs are also available to help treat the opportunistic infections to which people with HIV are especially prone.

AIDS in the Over-50 Population

Although most people who die from AIDS are in the 25–44 age range, it also affects people over the age of 50. In 2002, 11% of those reported to have AIDS were 50 or older. Cumulatively of those who died from AIDS, 8% were 55 or older (Centers for Disease Control and Prevention, 2003c) (see Fig. 5.8).

FIGURE 5.8

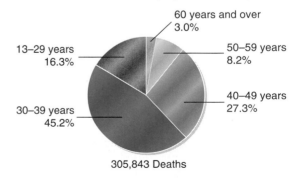

Distribution of AIDS Death, by Age: 1982 Through 1995

- 60 years and over 3.0%
- 13–29 years 16.3%
- 50–59 years 8.2%
- 30–39 years 45.2%
- 40–49 years 27.3%

305,843 Deaths

Source: National Center for Health Statistics, 1998.

In the early years of the epidemic, HIV infections were disproportionately high among people over 50 due to the contamination of blood or blood products received from blood donors. After 1985, as a result of improved blood-screening methods, the risk of contacting AIDS through contaminated blood decreased substantially; however, the risk of HIV infection associated with other methods of exposure increased in those over 50. The highest risk of HIV infection for those over 50 is for men having sex with men (36%). People over the age of 50 with HIV infection differ from younger adults in that they are more likely to have developed an AIDS-related opportunistic infection and are more likely to have died within one month of diagnosis. People over 50 with AIDS are less likely than younger people to be diagnosed as HIV positive and at risk for developing AIDS. It appears that physicians are less likely to consider HIV infection as the reason for an older person's symptoms because older people are not regarded as being at risk for AIDS. Furthermore, some of the opportunistic diseases that develop in people with AIDS may resemble other diseases associated with aging such as Alzheimer's disease, cancer, and depression. It is also likely that people over 50 do not perceive themselves as being at risk for HIV infection, and so they are less likely to follow the guidelines for "safe sex," which they may see as applicable only to young persons (Centers for Disease Control and Prevention, 1998).

DISORDERS OF THE MUSCULOSKELETAL SYSTEM

Although not usually fatal, musculoskeletal diseases can be crippling and may even lead to injury or bodily damage that does prove to take the afflicted individual's life. Two primary disorders of the musculoskeletal system affect middle-aged and older adults: arthritis and osteoporosis. These disorders, which unfortunately are quite common, can range in their effects on the individual from minor but annoying limitations to severe disability.

Osteoarthritis

Arthritis is a general term for conditions that affect the joints and surrounding tissues. It refers to any one of several diseases that can cause pain, stiffness, and swelling in joints and other connective tissues. The most common form of arthritis is known as **osteoarthritis**, a painful, degenerative joint disease that often involves the hips, knees, neck, lower back, or the small joints of the hands (see Fig. 5.9). Osteoarthritis typically develops in joints that are injured by repeated overuse in the performance of a particular job or a favorite sport or from obesity and the carrying of excess body weight. Eventually, this injury or repeated impact thins or wears away the cartilage that cushions the ends of the bones in the joint so that the bones rub together. The articular cartilage that protects the surfaces of the bones where they intersect at the joints wears down, and the synovial fluid that fills the joint loses its shock-absorbing properties. Joint flexibility is reduced, bony spurs develop, and the joint swells. These changes in the joint structures and tissues cause the individual to experience pain and loss of movement.

Pain management is an important feature of the treatment for osteoarthritis. The forms of pain medication usually prescribed include aspirin, acetaminophen, ibuprofen, and aspirin-like drugs called nonsteroidal anti-inflammatory drugs (NSAIDs). Unfortunately, the NSAIDs can cause stomach problems, including ulcers. Corticosteroids can also be injected directly into joints to reduce swelling and inflammation. These drugs are used sparingly, however,

Healthy knee in cross section

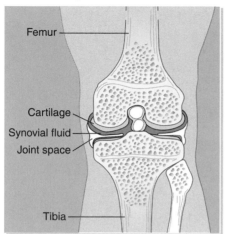

Osteoarthritic knee in cross section

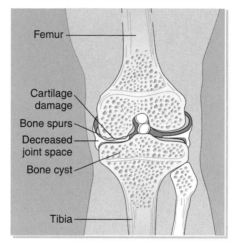

FIGURE 5.9
Normal Knee and Knee with Osteoarthritis

because chronic use can have destructive effects on bones and cartilage. Pain medications only alleviate symptoms; obviously they do not provide any kind of cure for the disease. More active forms of treatment are becoming available to people who have osteoarthritis, including injection of a synthetic material into an arthritic joint to replace the loss of synovial fluid. A second option is injection of sodium hyaluronate into the joint, an injectable version of a chemical normally present in high amounts in joints and fluids. Other forms of treatment that can help offset some of the damage caused by the disease include weight loss, which takes the stress off the joints. Increasingly common is the total replacement of an affected joint, such as a hip or a knee.

"What do you think?"　　5-3

Do you know anyone with arthritis? How is that person's life affected by the disease?

Osteoporosis

As we saw in Chapter 4, normal aging is associated with loss of bone mineral content due to an imbalance between bone resorption and bone growth (see Fig. 5.10). This loss of bone mineral content is called **osteoporosis** (literally, "porous bone") when it reaches the point at which bone mineral density is more than 2.5 standard deviations below the mean of young white, non-Hispanic women.

It is estimated that 10 million individuals in the United States have osteoporosis, 80% of them women (National Institutes of Health Osteoporosis and Related Bone Diseases National Resource Center, 2002). Women are at higher risk than men because they have lower bone mass in general, and menopause, with its accompanying decrease in estrogen production, accelerates the process. White and Asian women have the highest risk, and blacks and Hispanics the lowest. In addition, women who have small bone structures and are underweight have a higher risk than heavier women.

FIGURE 5.10
Processes Involved in Osteoporosis

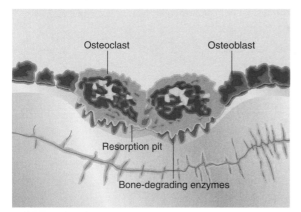

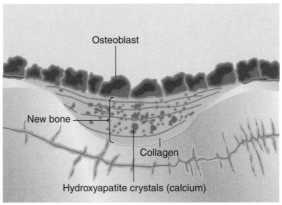

RESORPTION: Osteoclasts invade the bone surface and secrete bone-dissolving enzymes, which carve out cavities (resorption pits) to release calcium.

FORMATION: Osteoblasts fill in the cavities by building new bone. Osteoporosis occurs when osteoclasts carve too deeply or when osteoblasts fail to fill enough new bone.

Alcohol and cigarette smoking increase the risk of developing osteoporosis. This risk is reduced by an adequate intake of calcium through dairy products, dark green leafy vegetables, tofu, salmon, and foods fortified with calcium such as orange juice, bread, and cereal (a regimen similar to that recommended to prevent heart disease). Vitamin D, obtained through exposure to sunlight (while wearing sunblock of course) or as a dietary supplement, is another important preventive agent because it plays an important role in calcium absorption and bone health. Exercise and physical activity are also significant factors in reducing the risk of osteoporosis.

Prevention and treatment of osteoporosis involves attempting to restore bone strength through nutritional supplements and a regular program of weight-bearing exercise. Calcium and vitamin D are recommended supplements that, in addition to helping prevent osteoporosis, can help prevent bone loss in older adults (Krall, Wehler, Garcia, Harris, & Dawson-Hughes, 2001). Individuals with osteoporosis can also benefit from exposure to information about pre-

vention of falls. Medication may also be prescribed to slow or stop bone loss, increase bone density, and reduce fracture risk. Given the problems with HRT, other drugs have also begun to appear in the market that have the effect of reducing bone loss and therefore the risk of fractures. As mentioned in Chapter 4, these new drugs include raloxifene, which is a selective estrogen replacement modulator (SERM) that has specific effects on bone density. Alendronate is a bisphosphonate used to increase bone density, and calcitonin is a naturally occurring hormone involved in the regulation of calcium and bone metabolism. Each of these has advantages but also side effects that make them more or less useful for particular individuals.

DIABETES

A large fraction of the over-65 population suffers from Type II diabetes, a disease that begins in adulthood (also called "adult-onset"). **Diabetes** is associated with long-term complications that affect almost every organ system, contributing to blindness, heart disease, strokes, kidney failure, the necessity for limb amputations, and damage to the nervous system.

Characteristics of Diabetes

Diabetes is caused by a defect in the process of metabolizing **glucose**, a simple sugar that is a major source of energy for the body's cells. Normally, the digestive process breaks food down into components that can be transported through the blood to the cells of the body. The presence of glucose in the blood stimulates the beta cells of the pancreas to release insulin, a hormone that acts as a key at the cell receptors within the body to "open the cell doors" and let in the glucose. Excess glucose is stored in the liver, muscle, or fat. After it is disposed of through this mechanism, its level in the blood returns to normal. In the most common form of diabetes, Type 2, or noninsulin dependent diabetes (NIDDM), the pancreas produces some insulin, but the body's tissues fail to respond to the insulin signal, a condition known as insulin resistance. Insulin cannot bind to the cell's insulin receptor, and glucose cannot be transported into the body's cells to be used. Eventually, the excess glucose overflows into the urine through which it leaves the body. Thus, the body loses a main source of energy, although large amounts of glucose are potentially available in the blood.

The symptoms of diabetes include fatigue, frequent urination (especially at night), unusual thirst, weight loss, blurred vision, frequent infections, and slow healing of sores. These symptoms develop more gradually and are less noticeable in Type 2, compared to Type 1, diabetes. If blood sugar levels become too low (hypoglycemia), the individual can become nervous, jittery, faint, and confused. When this condition develops, the individual must eat or drink something with sugar in it as quickly as possible. The person can also become seriously

ill if blood sugar levels rise too high (hyperglycemia). Women who develop diabetes while pregnant are more likely to experience complications, and their infants are more likely to develop birth defects.

Incidence and Risk Factors

It is estimated that 10 million Americans have been diagnosed with diabetes, and there may be as many as 5 million people who have the disease but have not been diagnosed with it. The disease is estimated to afflict 7 million people over the age of 65, which is about 20% of adults in this age category (Centers for Disease Control and Prevention, 2002b). In 2000, diabetes was listed as the cause of death for 71,372 people in the United States, and 76% of these deaths occurred in the 65 and over age group (Arias et al., 2003).

According to the World Health Organization, the number of people suffering from diabetes worldwide is projected to grow by more than twofold from the 150 million reported in 2000 to 300 million by the year 2025. The rise in cases will approach 200% in developing countries and 45% in developed countries. Nearly 900,000 deaths worldwide in 2000 were due to this disease (World Health Organization, 2002c).

The main risk factors for diabetes are obesity and a sedentary lifestyle. Epidemiologists attribute the rise in diabetes to the increase in BMIs, noted earlier in the chapter as a risk factor for heart disease (Centers for Disease Control and Prevention, 2003a).

Other risk factors contributing to diabetes risk are race and ethnicity. The incidence of diabetes is about 60% higher in African Americans and 110 to 120 percent higher in Mexican Americans and Puerto Ricans compared to whites. The highest rates of diabetes in the world are found among Native Americans. Half of all Pima Indians living in the United States, for example, have adult-onset diabetes.

Prevention and Treatment

Given the clear relationship between obesity and diabetes, the most important means of preventing Type 2 diabetes is diet and weight control (Cowie, Harris, Stern, Boyko, Reiber, et al., 1995). As is true for heart disease, moderate alcohol consumption also seems to offer a protective effect (Nakanishi, Suzuki, & Tatara, 2003).

Once an individual has Type 2 diabetes, it can be managed by control of diet, participation in exercise, and frequent blood testing to monitor glucose levels. Much of this treatment involves trying to keep blood sugar at acceptable levels. Some people with Type 2 diabetes must take oral drugs or insulin to lower their blood glucose levels. In addition to medication and monitoring of diet, people with diabetes are advised to develop an exercise plan to manage their weight and to lower blood pressure and blood fats, which can lead to reductions in blood sugar levels.

RESPIRATORY DISEASES

The main form of respiratory disease, **chronic obstructive pulmonary disease** (**COPD**), is a group of diseases that involve obstruction of the airflow into the respiratory system. Two related diseases—chronic bronchitis and chronic emphysema—often occur together in this disease. People with COPD experience coughing, sputum, and difficulty breathing even when performing relatively easy tasks, such as putting on their clothes or walking on level ground. Over 10 million individuals in the United States suffered from COPD in 2000. Women are more likely to have this disease than men, and the rates increase linearly from about 39 to 96 per 1,000 in the 65–74 age group and 106 in those 75 and older (Mannino, Homa, Akinbami, Ford, & Redd, 2002).

Chronic bronchitis is a long-standing inflammation of the bronchi, the airways that lead into the lungs. The inflammation of the bronchi leads to increased production of mucus and other changes, which in turn lead to coughing and expectoration of sputum. People with this disorder are more likely to develop frequent and severe respiratory infections, narrowing and plugging of the bronchi, difficulty breathing, and disability. Chronic emphysema is a lung disease that causes permanent destruction of the alveoli. Elastin within the terminal bronchioles is destroyed, leading to collapse of the airway walls and an inability to exhale. The airways lose their ability to become enlarged during inspiration and to empty completely during expiration, leading to a lowering of the quality of gas exchange (see Fig. 5.11). Subjectively, the main symptom is shortness of breath. In addition to the symptoms associated with COPD, people with this disorder are at higher risk for developing lung cancer.

Although the cause of COPD is not known, it is generally agreed that cigarette smoking is a prime suspect. Exposure to environmental toxins such as air pollution and harmful substances in the occupational setting also may play a role, particularly for people who smoke. The specific mechanism involved in the link between smoking and emphysema is thought to involve the release of an enzyme known as **elastase**, which breaks down the elastin found in lung tissue. Cigarette smoke stimulates the release of this enzyme and results in other changes that make the cells of the lung less resistant to elastase. Normally, there is an inhibitant of elastase found in the lung, known as alpha-1 antitrypsin (AAT). However, cigarette smoke inactivates AAT and allows the elastase to destroy more lung tissue. Of course, not all smokers develop COPD, and not all people with COPD are or have been smokers. Heredity may also play a role. There is a rare genetic defect in

FIGURE 5.11

The Lungs in Chronic Obstructive Pulmonary Disease

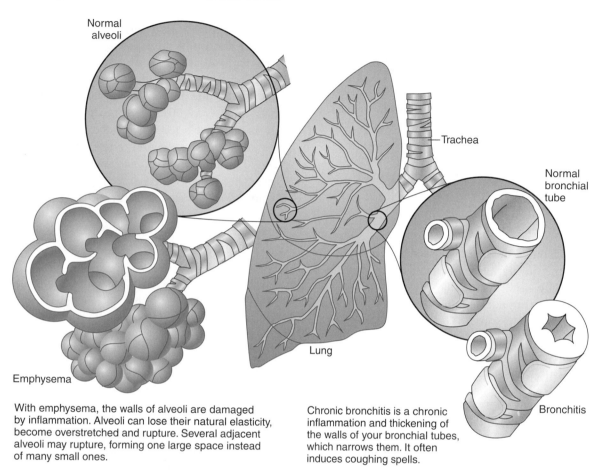

Normal alveoli

Trachea

Normal bronchial tube

Emphysema

Lung

Bronchitis

With emphysema, the walls of alveoli are damaged by inflammation. Alveoli can lose their natural elasticity, become overstretched and rupture. Several adjacent alveoli may rupture, forming one large space instead of many small ones.

Chronic bronchitis is a chronic inflammation and thickening of the walls of your bronchial tubes, which narrows them. It often induces coughing spells.

the production of AAT in about 2% to 3% of the population that is responsible for about 5% of all cases of COPD.

Apart from quitting smoking, which is obviously the necessary first step in prevention and treatment, individuals with COPD can benefit from medications and treatments. These include inhalers that open the airways to bring more oxygen into the lungs or reduce inflammation, machines that provide oxygen, or in extreme cases, lung surgery to remove damaged tissue.

In 2003 a pulmonary disease known as Severe Acute Respiratory Syndrome (SARS) spread rapidly throughout several countries and threatened to become a major health epidemic. Fortunately, the spread of the disease was halted by mid-2003, but in that short time it caused the deaths of nearly 800 people worldwide. The fatality rate associated with the disease was 50% for people 60 and older, compared to a fatality rate of 13% for people 60 and under. Many of the deaths occurred in older individuals who were already weakened by other diseases.

DEMENTIA AND RELATED NEUROLOGICAL DISORDERS

Dementia is a clinical condition in which the individual experiences a loss of cognitive function severe enough to interfere with normal daily activities and social relationships. Dementia can be caused by a number of diseases that affect the nervous system, including cardiovascular disorders, a variety of neurologically based disorders, and abnormalities in other bodily systems. The disorder that has received the most attention by far is Alzheimer's disease, which is also the most common cause of dementia.

Alzheimer's Disease

The disorder now known as **Alzheimer's disease** has been given many names over the years, including senile dementia, presenile dementia, senile dementia of the Alzheimer's type, and organic brain disorder. The current terminology reflects the identification of the condition as a disease by Alois Alzheimer (1864–1915), a German neurologist who was the first to link changes in brain tissue with observable symptoms. Alzheimer treated a patient, Auguste D., a woman in her 50s who suffered from progressive mental deterioration marked by increasing confusion and memory loss. Taking advantage of a then-new staining technique, he noticed an odd disorganization of the nerve cells in her cerebral cortex. In a medical journal article published in 1907, Alzheimer speculated that these microscopic changes were responsible for the woman's dementia. Recent discovery of brain slides from this patient confirmed that these changes were similar to those seen in the disease (Enserink, 1998). In 1910, as more autopsies of severely demented individuals showed the same abnormalities, one of the foremost psychiatrists of that era, Emil Kraepelin (1856–1926), gave the name described by his friend Alzheimer to the disease. Today, a definite diagnosis of Alzheimer's disease

is still only possible when an autopsy reveals these hallmarks of the disease.

Prevalence. A commonly quoted figure regarding the number of people in the United States with Alzheimer's disease is 4 million people, representing a rate of about 12% of the over-65. The rate among those over 85 years of age is quoted as 50%. The media and other sources have projected this number to soar into the mid-twenty-first century, reaching a staggering 14 million individuals unless a cure is found. These statistics have recently come under scrutiny however (Zarit & Zarit, 1998), however, and the figures for those currently suffering from Alzheimer's disease are now placed at about half that at 2.3 million (Brookmeyer & Kawas, 1998; Hy & Keller, 2000). Broken down by age group, estimates are 1% for ages 65–74; 7% for those aged 75–84; and 25% of those 85 or older. However, in the Baltimore Longitudinal Study on Aging, in which participants were studied longitudinally prior to the diagnosis of the disease, the incidence rates of new cases was far lower—less than 1% a year for those 60–65 to a high of 6.5% in those 85 and older (Kawas, Gray, Brookmeyer, Fozard, & Zonderman, 2000). The World Health Organization estimates the prevalence worldwide of people over 60 as 5% of men and 6% of women (World Health Organization, 2001).

The original 4 million estimate for the United States is based on a small sample of working-class residents of Italian descent from East Boston who were tested with relatively primitive diagnostic methods. The rates found in this sample were superimposed onto 1980 U.S. census figures and projections (Evans, Scherr, Cook, Albert, Funkenstein, et al., 1990) and have clearly led to an overestimation. The numbers presented in the media, though drawing attention to an important problem, present an unfortunate reinforcement of the notion that "senility" is an inevitable feature of aging.

Psychological Symptoms

The psychological symptoms of Alzheimer's disease evolve gradually over time. The earliest signs are occasional loss of memory for recent events or familiar tasks. Although changes in cognitive functioning are at the core of this disease's symptoms, changes in personality and behavior eventually become evident. By the time the disease has entered the final stage, the individual has lost the ability to perform even the simplest and most basic of everyday functions. The rate of progression in Alzheimer's disease varies from person to person, but there

is a fairly regular pattern of loss over the stages of the disease (Galasko, Edland, Morris, Clark, Mohs, et al., 1995). The survival time following the diagnosis is 7–10 years for people diagnosed in their 60s and 70s, but it drops to 3 years for people diagnosed in their 90s (Brookmeyer, Corrada, Curriero, & Kawas, 2002).

Biological changes

One set of changes that Alzheimer discovered in the brain of Auguste D. consisted of what looked like the accumulated waste products of collections of dead neurons (see Fig. 5.12).

FIGURE 5.12
Plaques and Tangles in Alzheimer's Disease

Normal

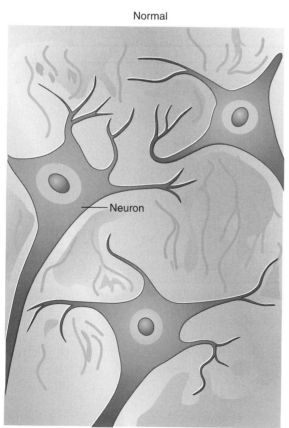

Alzheimer's

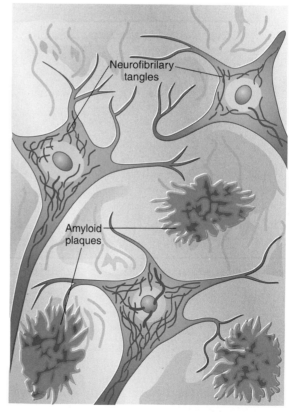

Now known as **amyloid plaques**, they develop as long as 10 to 20 years before symptoms become noticeable and are thought to be one of the first events in the pathology of the disease, and possibly at the root of the illness (Hardy & Selkoe, 2002). **Amyloid** is a generic name for protein fragments that collect together in a specific way to form insoluble deposits (meaning that they do not dissolve). The form of amyloid most closely linked with Alzheimer's disease consists of a string of 42 amino acids and is referred to as beta-amyloid-42.

Beta amyloid is formed from a larger protein found in the normal brain, referred to as **amyloid precursor protein** (**APP**). It is thought that APP, which is manufactured by neurons, plays a role in their growth and communication with each other, and perhaps contributes to the repair of injured brain cells. Beta-amyloid is formed when APP is being manufactured in the cell. Enzymes called proteases (BACE and secretase) snip the APP into fragments. If the APP is snipped at the wrong place, beta-amyloid (–42) is formed (Vassar, Bennett, Babu-Khan, Kahn, Mendiaz, et al., 1999). The fragments eventually clump together into abnormal deposits that the body cannot dispose of or recycle. Apart from its tendency to form insoluble plaques, beta amyloid seems to have the potential to kill neurons. A relatively new theory of Alzheimer's disease, called **caspase** theory, proposes that beta amyloid stimulates substances called caspases, which become enzymes that destroy neurons. The destruction of neurons, called apoptosis, is what then ultimately leads to the loss of cognitive functioning that occurs in Alzheimer's disease (Marx, 2001).

The second mysterious change observed in Auguste D.'s brain was a profusion of abnormally twisted fibers within the neurons themselves, known as **neurofibrillary tangles** (literally, tangled nerve fibers). It is now known that the neurofibrillary tangles are made up of a protein called **tau**, which seems to play a role in maintaining the stability of the microtubules that form the internal support structure of the axons. The microtubules are like train tracks that guide nutrients from the cell body down to the ends of the axon. The tau proteins are like the "railroad ties, " or crosspieces of the microtubule train tracks. In Alzheimer's disease, the tau is changed chemically and loses its ability to separate and support the microtubules. At that point, it twists into paired helical filaments, which resemble two threads wound around each other. This collapse of the transport system within the neuron may first result in malfunctions in communication between neurons and eventually may lead to the death of the neuron.

Like the formation of plaques, the development of neurofibrillary tangles seems to occur early in the disease process and may progress quite substantially before the individual shows any behavioral symptoms. The earliest changes in the disease appear to occur in the hippocampus and the entorhinal region of the cortex, which is the area near the hippocampus; these are the areas that play a critical role in memory and retention of learned information (Kaye, Swihart, Howieson, Dame, Moore, et al., 1997; Morys, Bobinski, Wegiel, Wisniewski, & Narkiewicz, 1996). Throughout the course of the disease, tangles continue to accumulate in the hippocampus along with the destruction of neurons in this critically important area of the brain (Kril, Patel, Harding, & Halliday, 2002).

Causes of Alzheimer's Disease

One certainty about Alzheimer's disease is that it is associated with the formation of plaques and tangles, particularly in areas of the brain controlling memory and other vital cognitive functions. The great uncertainty is what causes these changes. It is also not clear whether the development of plaques and tangles is the cause of neuron death or whether these changes are the result of another, even more elusive, underlying process that causes neurons to die and produces these abnormalities in neural tissue as a side product.

Genetic. The theory guiding most researchers is that genetic abnormalities are somehow responsible for the neuron death that is the hallmark of Alzheimer's disease (Ashford & Mortimer, 2002). This theory began to emerge after the discovery that certain families seemed more prone to a form of the disease that struck at the relatively young age of 40 to 50 years. These cases are now referred to as **early-onset familial Alzheimer's disease**, and though tragic, scientists have been able to learn a tremendous amount from studying the DNA of afflicted individuals. Since the discovery of the early-onset form of the disease, genetic analyses have also provided evidence of another gene involved in familial Alzheimer's disease that starts at a more conventional age of 60 or 65 years. This form of the disease is called **late-onset familial Alzheimer's disease**. The four genes that have been discovered so far, which are thought to account for about half of all early-onset familial Alzheimer's disease, are postulated to lead by different routes to the same end-product, namely, excess amounts of beta-amyloid protein. Furthermore, the changes in the brain produced by these genes are thought to be the same as those involved in nonfamilial, or **sporadic Alzheimer's disease**.

Aided by the discovery of familial patterns of early-onset Alzheimer's disease along with the burgeoning technology of genetic engineering, genetic research has led within a surprisingly short time to some very plausible suspects for genes that cause the brain changes associated with the disease. One of the prime candidates is involved in the late-onset familial pattern of the disorder. This is the **apolipoprotein E (ApoE) gene**, located on chromosome 19. ApoE is a protein that carries blood cholesterol throughout the body, but it also binds to beta-amyloid, and hence may play a role in plaque formation.

People who inherit the ApoE4 allele of the gene have at least double the risk of developing Alzheimer's disease than those who do not, especially women (Martinez, Campion, Brice, Hannequin, Dubois, et al., 1998). Higher risk has been found for groups other than whites in the United States, including people from China (Katzman, Zhang, Chen, Gu, Jiang, et al., 1997; Mak, Chiu, Woo, Kay, Chan, et al., 1996) and Finland (Lehtimaki, Pirttila, Mehta, Wisniewski, Frey, et al., 1995). However, among African Americans and people of Hispanic descent in the United States, the picture is not so clear. Regardless of their ApoE genotype, these groups have a heightened risk of Alzheimer's disease (Tang, Stern, Marker, Bell, Gurland, et al., 1998). Another variant of Apo, called ApoD, has also been identified in neurodegenerative diseases including late onset Alzheimer's disease. It is thought that a variation in this gene may be involved in the risk of Alzheimer's disease among African Americans (Desai, Hendrie, Evans, Murrell, DeKosky, et al., 2003).

Although the ApoE gene has received more attention, the first genetic defects found to be associated with familial Alzheimer's disease were on the **APP gene** on chromosome 21, which is now fully mapped (Hattori, Fujiyama, Taylor, Watanabe, Yada, et al., 2000). The APP gene appears to control the production of the protein that generates beta-amyloid. Mutations of this gene are believed responsible for about 2% to 3% of all published cases of familial Alzheimer's disease and a slightly higher proportion (5% to 7%) of early-onset cases (Tanzi, Kovacs, Kim, Moir, Guenette, et al., 1996). The age of onset for the disease among people with mutations in the APP gene is typically 50 to 60 years.

BEHIND THE RESEARCH

ROBERT L. KANE, ROSALIE A. KANE, UNIVERSITY
OF MINNESOTA SCHOOL OF PUBLIC HEALTH

What is most exciting to you about research in this field?

Long-term care is an area where little things can mean a lot. Small changes can produce big effects in the lives of people whose basic scope of activity has been greatly circumscribed. Research can help to reshape perspective about this field. The most exciting aspects of research in long-term care are the changes in conceptual models. We have some major shifts in the last decade that challenge prior assumptions. It is no longer believed necessary to subject people to the indignities of institutional care to get reasonable assistance. Quality of life is coming into parity with more traditional concerns about quality of care. Considerable emphasis is being given to consumer direction of care in all settings, the most extreme manifestation being cash payments to consumers in lieu of managed services. New forms of group residential care are being developed that allow older people to live more normal autonomous lives while still having access to the care they need. These new forms include apartment-style housing-with-service settings, often licensed as assisted living, and even radically changed nursing homes. "Culture change" is now a well established goal for nursing homes.

What do you see as the major challenges?

Culture change, power shifts, and redistribution of efforts are not easy. In the United States, we still persist in defining services by where they are provided rather than by the service tasks and what they accomplish. We have not found a way to address the disparities between the funding of nursing homes (which covers both room and board and services) and community care (which covers only services). One of the greatest challenges—redressing the balance of services so that most long-term care is provided in the community with the nursing home being the less used alternative—is rendered difficult because of the discrepant funding policies.

The problems are even more compounded in the area of post-acute care (PAC), which has not been well distinguished from long-term care because many of the same venues are used. PAC continues to operate in separate silos by type of care. Its relationship to hospital care in terms of both fiscal and quality accountability has not been well defined.

Long-term care (LTC) will never rise high on the policy agenda until its value is appreciated. It continues to be viewed as a socially necessary service but one where the relationship between inputs and outputs is hard to appreciate. One of the major problems in demonstrating the effectiveness of LTC is that its success is often measured as slowing the rate of decline. This relative achievement is invisible unless one has access to information about what would have been the rate of decline in the absence of the care provided. The failure to establish the necessary measures of effectiveness will have a chilling impact on societal enthusiasm for greater investments in LTC, but it will also have a negative effect on the morale of those who work in the field.

LTC has both a social and a medical dimension. Although medical and social care need not be merged, they do need to be integrated. Achieving this end will require that practitioners on the health and on the social side share a common set of goals

BEHIND THE RESEARCH *(continued)*

and at least understand each other's language. This collaboration between the health and social sides of care is a challenge for long-term care in every country. Related to this, we are challenged to offer older people the same flexibility and range of long-term care choices that are offered to younger adults with disabilities. Publicly funded long-term care for adults under 65 with physical disabilities or with intellectual impairments is much more user-friendly, and much less dependent on provider organizations than is care for older people. For example, younger people are more likely to have access to attendant services to assist them in an individualized way at home and in the community, whereas older people are more likely to be required to receive their assistance from home care agencies and be required to be at home for the help.

Finally, we are challenged to build a capable labor force for long-term care and remunerate direct service workers commensurately with their responsibilities. Personnel shortages rise to the status of major crisis in a cyclical way depending on the economy, but even in times of relatively high employment, the long-term care labor force needs nurturing and development.

Where do you see this field headed in the next decade?
We envision substantial developments in new forms of care, which synthesize elements of current approaches. Measurement will become more refined, especially for quality of life. A common set of outcome measures for PAC will be established. The regulations that have driven LTC will need to change. The growth of assisted living (AL) will catalyze that shift. Great efforts will be made to keep AL from becoming another variant of nursing homes, This step will require that AL not be as intensely regulated. Parity will, then, require less NH regulation.

Consumer directed models will become more commonplace for long-term care clientele of all ages. Because unionization of LTC workers will also be a trend, some friction will arise between the rights of consumers to direct their care and the labor movement's attention to traditional issues of seniority, working hours and conditions, and the like. Whether labor force shortages and quality problems endure will depend on how well health care providers, educational establishments, and governments work to address the problems.

Most early-onset familial Alzheimer's disease cases are associated with defects in the so-called **presenilin genes** (**PS1** and **PS2**). The mean age of onset in families with mutations in the PS1 gene is 45 years (ranging from 32 to 56 years) and 52 years for people with PS2 gene mutations (40 to 85 years). Researchers speculate that these genes somehow lead APP to increase its production of beta-amyloid. The PS1 gene is located on chromosome 14 and accounts for up to 50%–80% of early-onset cases. The PS2 gene, located on chromosome 1, accounts for a much smaller percentage of early-onset familial Alzheimer's disease cases

(Sherrington, Froelich, Sorbi, Campion, Chi, et al., 1996). The pattern of inheritance for the presenilin genes is autosomal dominant; this means that if one parent carries the disease, the offspring has a 50% chance of developing the disorder. Presenilin genes 1 and 2 are thought to interact with APP, beta-amyloid, plaques, and tangles.

Recently, researchers are beginning to consider the possibility that both neurofibrillary tangles and beta-amyloid plaques are caused by mutations of the APP gene or by beta-amyloid, the product of APP (Lewis, Dickson, Lin, Chisholm, Corral, et al., 2001). Another intriguing possibility is that PS2 is linked to caspase, the substance thought to accelerate the death of neurons in the brains of people with Alzheimer's disease (Hashimoto, Niikura, Ito, Kita, Terashita, et al., 2002).

Environmental. The available information on genetic contributions to Alzheimer's disease leaves unexplained about 60% of late-onset and up to 50% of the early-onset pattern. Some mechanism other than genetics is needed to explain what appears now to be the sporadic (nonfamilial) pattern as well as the fact that less than perfect correspondence exists between monozygotic twins in the development of the disease (Gatz, Pedersen, Berg, Johansson, Johansson, et al., 1997). Even when the disease strikes in both twins, it may occur many years apart.

Another piece of support for an environmental contribution to Alzheimer's disease comes from a highly unusual study of over 3700 men who were born between 1900 and 1919 in Japan but who lived in Honolulu during their adult lives. When studied in the years 1991–1993 (at the ages of 71 through 93), their rate of Alzheimer's disease was 5.4%, which is comparable to the rate in American and European men of that age. The surprising feature of this study was that among a similar group of men living in Japan, the rate of Alzheimer's disease was only 1.5%, a finding that reflects the lower prevalence of the disorder in Japan. Either something about the move itself or something unique to the environment of Hawaii caused the Japanese American men to be more vulnerable to the disease (White, Petrovitch, Ross, Masaki, Abbott, et al., 1996).

Serious injuries involving loss of consciousness increase the risk of developing the disease in late life. The mechanism postulated to account for this environmental contributor to Alzheimer's disease is damage to the blood-brain barrier, a lining in the blood vessels that protects the brain from foreign bodies or toxic agents circulating in the bloodstream outside the brain. The injury may activate the production of cytokines and other proteins, a process that ultimately destroys neurons (Griffin, Sheng, Royston, Gentleman, McKenzie, et al., 1998).

Higher education and continued mental activity throughout life are protective environmental factors. In addition to the statistical association between higher education and lower risk of Alzheimer's disease, as pointed out earlier, high levels of cognitive activity predict lower risk of Alzheimer's disease in an individual's later years. Two studies of older adults living in religious orders support this observation. One was a 7-year followup of Catholic clergy members (nuns, priests, and brothers). Those who engaged in cognitively stimulating activities such as reading, going to museums, playing games, and listening to music or television, had a lower chance of developing Alzheimer's disease than those who did not engage their minds (Wilson, Mendes De Leon, Barnes, Schneider, Bienias, et al., 2002). The second study is known as the Nun Study, and is an ongoing longitudinal study of 678 women living in the School Sisters of Notre Dame religious order (Snowdon, 2001). The Nun Study presented a particularly unusual design. The women were chosen for the study specifically because something about their lifestyle seemed to reduce their risk of developing Alzheimer's disease despite the fact that they were statistically at highest risk for the disorder because of their age (85 and over) and gender. Obviously, they did not share genetic inheritance, so it was thought that something about their living conditions offered them an unusual degree of protection against the disease. Many of the nuns had advanced academic degrees, but more importantly, they led an intellectually challenging life throughout their 80s and 90s. One of the women, "Sister Mary," retained high scores on the cognitive measures until her death at 101 years. Surprisingly, the autopsy revealed that she had many of the characteristic plaques and tangles usually found in the brains of people with profound behavioral deficits. The study also points out another fact that is often referred to in research in Alzheimer's disease, namely, that some people can function during life with no observable signs of the disease.

The extent to which the individual participates in exercise may be another lifestyle contributor to the development of or progression of Alzheimer's disease. In a 3-year longitudinal study, individuals with the E4 allele of the ApoE gene who did not participate in exercise were twice as likely as their more active counterparts with the same genetic susceptibility (Schuit, Feskens, Launer, & Kromhout, 2001) to develop symptoms of Alzheimer's dieease.

It might be expected that given its generally negative effects on other illnesses that cigarette smoking would quite naturally have a similar effect on the risk of developing dementia and specifically Alzheimer's disease. However, oddly enough, some findings revealed the opposite pattern. A review of a large number of studies showed that individuals who are current cigarette smokers are 50% less likely to have dementia due to Parkinson's disease (see below) or Alzheimer's disease (Fratiglioni & Wang, 2000). However, these findings have since been challenged, and it now appears that smoking, at best, has no effect and at worst may in fact increase the risk of developing this disease (Doll, Peto, Boreham, & Sutherland, 2000; Kukull, 2001).

Finally, as is true for cardiovascular and cerebrovascular disease, consumption of a moderate amount of alcohol (1 to 6 drinks per week) is associated with lower risk of dementia in older adults (Mukamal, Kuller, Fitzpatrick, Longstreth, Mittleman, et al., 2003). However, in the case of this particular research, a distinction was not made between dementia caused by Alzheimer's disease and dementia having other causes (see below), including cerebrovascular disease.

Diagnosis

The diagnosis of dementia is made by psychiatrists and clinical psychologists when the individual meets the criteria for clinical signs of dementia (American Psychiatric Association, 2000):

1. Memory loss—progressing from mild impairment to inability to remember familiar names, events, and places.
2. **Aphasia**—loss of the ability to use language.
3. **Apraxia**—loss of the ability to carry out coordinated bodily movements.
4. **Agnosia**—loss of the ability to recognize familiar objects.
5. Disturbance in executive functioning—loss of the ability to carry out complex cognitive activities such as planning and organizing.

The diagnosis of Alzheimer's disease through clinical methods is done by exclusion because there is no one specific test or clinical indicator that is unique to the disorder. In fact, patients and their families are not given the diagnosis of Alzheimer's disease. Instead they are told that other possible diagnoses have been dismissed, so that Alzheimer's disease is the most likely diagnosis by the process of elimination. As noted earlier, a definite diagnosis is possible only through autopsy, which identifies the characteristic neurofibrillary tangles and beta-amyloid plaques known to occur in the disease.

Guidelines established by a joint commission of the National Institute of Neurological and Communicative Disorders and Stroke and the Alzheimer's Disease and Related Diseases Association (NINCDS/ADRDA Guidelines) have significantly improved the chances of a correct diagnosis (McKhann, Drachman, Folstein, Katzman, Price, et al., 1984) to 85%–90% accuracy in the disease's later stages (Table 5-4). Diagnosis of Alzheimer's disease based on the NINCDS/ ADRDA criteria involves thorough medical and neuropsychological screenings in addition to behavioral and mental status ratings (see description of the Mental Status Exam in Chapter 11).

TABLE 5-4
NiNCDS/ADRDA* Criteria for Alzheimer's Disease

Criteria for Diagnosis of Probable Alzheimer's Disease:
- Dementia established by clinical examination, documented by a standard test of cognitive function (e.g., Mini-Mental State Examination, Blessed Dementia Scale, etc.), and confirmed by neuropsychological tests.
- Significant deficiencies in two or more areas of cognition, for example, word comprehension and task-completion ability.
- Progressive deterioration of memory and other cognitive functions.
- No loss of consciousness.
- Onset from age 40 to 90, typically after 65.
- No other diseases or disorders that could account for the loss of memory and cognition.

A Diagnosis of Probable Alzheimer's Disease Is Supported by:
- Progressive deterioration of specific cognitive functions: language (aphasia), motor skills (apraxia), and perception (agnosia).
- Impaired activities of daily living and altered patterns of behavior.
- A family history of similar problems, particularly if confirmed by neurological testing.
- The following laboratory results:
  Normal cerebrospinal fluid (lumbar puncture test).
  Normal electroencephalogram (EEG) test of brain activity.
  Evidence of cerebral atrophy in a series of CT scans.

Other Features Consistent with Alzheimer's Disease:
- Plateaus in the course of illness progression.
- CT findings normal for the person's age.
- Associated symptoms, including depression, insomnia, incontinence, delusions, hallucinations, weight loss, sex problems, and significant verbal, emotional, and physical outbursts.
- Other neurological abnormalities, especially in advanced disease, including increased muscle tone and a shuffling gait.

Features That Decrease the Likelihood of Alzheimer's Disease:
- Sudden onset.
- Such early symptoms as seizures, gait problems, and loss of vision and coordination.

* National Institute of Neurological and Communicative Disorders and Stroke and the Alzheimer's Disease and Related Disorders Association.

Source: Adapted from McKhann et al., 1984

Medical Treatments. Even as the search for the cause of Alzheimer's disease proceeds, researchers are attempting to find medications that will alleviate its symptoms. Although the drugs currently being tested have yet to produce significant improvements in Alzheimer's patients, they are seen as having the potential to lead to treatments that will.

The two drugs approved by the FDA for the treatment of Alzheimer's disease are those that target the neurotransmitter acetylcholine. These drugs are the **anticholinesterase treatments** given the names THA or tetrahydroaminoacridine (also called tacrine and given the brand name Cognex) and donepezil hydrochloride (Aricept). They are called anticholinesterase because they work by inhibiting the action of acetylcholinesterase (also called cholinesterase), the enzyme that normally destroys acetylcholine after its release into the synaptic cleft. Declines in the levels of acetylcholine, particularly in the hippocampus, are thought to be a factor in the memory loss shown by people with Alzheimer's disease. By inhibiting the action of acetylcholinesterase, these drugs slow the breakdown of acetylcholine, and therefore its higher levels remain in the brain.

"What do you think?" | 5-4

If a test is developed that can predict whether a person has a high chance of developing Alzheimer's disease, would you want to take that test and find out the results?

Initial excitement accompanying the approval of tacrine in 1993 was followed by disappointing reports that it could produce toxic effects in the liver if taken in required doses. Aricept was approved three years later, although it also has gastrointestinal side effects related to the effects of acetylcholinesterase inhibitors (diarrhea and nausea). However, its required dose is lower, and it does not interfere with liver function (Barner & Gray, 1998; Rogers & Friedhoff, 1998). Both drugs give the patient a few months to a year of relief from the troubling cognitive symptoms that occur in the early stages of the disease. Other drugs that inhibit acetylcholinesterase activity are citicoline, arecoline, and ENA 713 (Exelon). Rivastigmine (Exelon) is another medication in this category that operates in a similar manner but causes fewer gastrointestinal side effects (Grossberg & Desai, 2001). A combination of donepezil and memantine, a chemical that simulates aspartate (another neurotransmitter) may be more effective than donepezil alone (Tariot, Farlow, Grossberg, Graham, et al., 2004).

Anti-inflammatory agents are also being tested as treatment approaches. In particular, nonsteroidal anti-inflammatory drugs (NSAIDs) such as ibuprofen (Advil, Motrin), naproxen sodium (Aleve), and indomethacin (Indocin), among others, may offer some protection against the disease. In a study of nearly 1700 participants in the Baltimore Longitudinal Study of Aging, the risk of Alzheimer's disease was substantially lower among people who had been using NSAIDs for a period of two or more years. People who had been taking aspirin or acetaminophen as painkillers did not experience a similar benefit (Stewart, Kawas, Corrada, & Metter, 1997). One theory regarding the effectiveness of NSAIDs is that they exert some type of protective effect against damage to and death of neurons (Asanuma, Nishibayashi-Asanuma, Miyazaki, Kohno, & Ogawa, 2001; Deigner, Haberkorn, & Kinscherf, 2000). Prednisone is another anti-inflammatory agent being tested as a treatment to slow the progression of Alzheimer's disease by reducing the activation of cytokines (Aisen & Pasinetti, 1998).

In the late 1990s, researchers and clinicians were advocating the use of estrogen-replacement therapy (ERT) in the prevention of Alzheimer's disease in postmenopausal women. However, along with the other problems associated with hormone replacement therapy (HRT) for women already discussed in Chapter 4 and earlier in this chapter, there is now evidence that estrogen plus progestin treatment increases the risk for probable dementia and does not prevent mild cognitive declines (Shumaker, Legault, Rapp, Thal, Wallace, et al., 2003).

Several new approaches are now being tried that target the formation of beta amyloid plaques. Clioquinol is an antibiotic that breaks up the chemical bonds that hold the amyloid protein together (Melov, 2002). Antioxidants are also being experimented with, based on the theory that when beta-amyloid breaks into fragments, free radicals are formed that damage the surrounding neurons. One form of antioxidant is bioflavonoid, a substance that occurs naturally in wine, tea, fruits, and vegetables. A longitudinal study of over 1300 French people found benefits associated with bioflavonoids in reducing the risk of Alzheimer's disease (Commenges, Scotet, Renaud, Jacqmin-Gadda, Barberger-Gateau, et al., 2000). Finally, researchers are experimenting with an

Alzheimer's vaccine that would increase the body's immune response against beta-amyloid to prevent or reduce plaque formation (Nicolau, Greferath, Balaban, Lazarte, & Hopkins, 2002).

Psychosocial Treatments. As intensively as research is progressing on treatments for Alzheimer's disease, the sad truth is that there is no cure. Meanwhile, people with this disease and their families must find ways to deal, on a daily basis, with the incapacitating cognitive and sometimes physical symptoms that accompany the deterioration of brain tissue. Clearly, until a cure can be found, mental health workers will be needed to provide assistance in this difficult process, so that the individual's functioning can be preserved for as long as possible.

A critical step in providing this kind of management of symptoms is for health care professionals to recognize the fact that Alzheimer's disease involves families as much as it does individuals. Family members are most likely to be the ones providing care for the patient, especially wives and daughters. These individuals, called **caregivers**, have been the focus of considerable research efforts over the past two decades. It is now known that people in the role of caregivers are very likely to suffer adverse effects from the constant demands placed on them. The term **caregiver burden** is used to describe the stress that these people experience in the daily management of their afflicted relative. As the disease progresses, caregivers must provide physical assistance in basic life functions, such as eating, dressing, and toileting. As time goes by, the caregiver may experience health problems that make it harder and harder to provide the kind of care needed to keep the Alzheimer's patient at home.

Given the strain placed on caregivers, it should come as no surprise that health problems and rates of depression, stress, and isolation are higher among these individuals than among the population at large. Fortunately, support for caregivers of people with Alzheimer's disease has become widely available. Books such as *The 36-Hour Day* (Mace & Rabins, 1999) was the first of many to be published in the popular press. Local chapters of national organizations in the United States such as the Alzheimer's Association provide a variety of community support services for families in general and caregivers in particular. Caregivers can be taught ways to promote independence and reduce distressing behaviors in the patient, as well as learn ways to handle the emotional stress associated with their role.

An important goal in managing the symptoms of Alzheimer's disease is to teach caregivers behavioral methods to maintain functional independence in the patient. The idea behind this approach is that, by maintaining the patient's functioning for as long as possible, the caregiver's burden is at least somewhat reduced. For example, the patient can be given prompts, cues, and guidance in the steps involved in getting dressed and then be positively rewarded with praise and attention for having completed those steps. Modeling is another behavioral strategy, in which the caregiver performs the desired action (such as pouring a glass of water) so that the patient can see this action and imitate it. Again, positive reinforcement helps to maintain this behavior once it is learned (or more properly, relearned). Caregivers then have less work to do, and patients are given the cognitive stimulation involved in actively performing these tasks rather than having others take over their care completely.

Another strategy that a caregiver can use to maintain independence is to operate according to a strict daily schedule that the patient can learn to follow. The structure provided by a regular routine of everyday activities can give the patient additional cues to use as guides. In addition to increasing the extent to which people with Alzheimer's disease engage in independent activities, caregivers can also use behavioral strategies to eliminate, or at least reduce the frequency, of undesirable acts such as wandering or being aggressive. In some cases, this strategy may require ignoring problematic behaviors, with the idea that by eliminating the reinforcement for those behaviors in the form of attention, the patient will be less likely to engage in them. However, it is more likely that a more active approach will be needed, especially for a behavior such as wandering. In this case, the patient can be provided with positive reinforcement for not wandering. Even this may not be enough, however, and the caregiver may need to take precautions such as installing a protective device in doors and hallways.

It may also be possible for the caregiver to identify certain situations in which the patient becomes particularly disruptive, such as during bathing or riding in the car. In these cases, the caregiver can be given help in targeting those aspects of the situation that cause the patient to become upset and then modify it accordingly. For example, if the problem occurs while bathing, it may be that a simple alteration such as providing a terry cloth robe rather than a towel helps reduce the patient's feeling of alarm at being undressed in front of others.

Creative approaches to managing the recurrent stresses involved in the caregiver's role may help to reduce the feelings of burden and frustration that are so much a part of daily life. Along with the provision of community and institutional support services, such interventions can go a long way toward helping the caregiver and ultimately the patient.

Other Neurological Diseases That Can Cause Dementia

The condition known as dementia is frequently caused by Alzheimer's disease in later life, but many other conditions can affect the status of the brain and cause loss of memory, language, and motor functions. These can be very difficult to differentiate on the basis of behavioral evidence, although diagnostic tests are becoming more refined, agreeing about 90% of the time with autopsy findings (Gearing, Mirra, Hedreen, Sumi, Hansen, et al., 1995).

Vascular Dementia. In **vascular dementia**, progressive loss of cognitive functioning occurs as the result of damage to the arteries supplying the brain. Dementia can follow a stroke, in which case it is called acute onset vascular dementia, but the most common form of vascular dementia is **multi-infarct dementia** or **MID**, caused by transient ischemic attacks. In this case, a number of minor strokes (infarcts) occur in which blood flow to the brain is interrupted by a clogged or burst artery. Each infarct is too small to be noticed, but over time, the progressive damage caused by the infarcts leads the individual to lose cognitive abilities. The risk of developing this form of dementia begins in middle age among those with hypertension (Launer, Ross, Petrovitch, Masaki, Foley, et al., 2000) or the combination of hypertension and diabetes (Knopman, Boland, Mosley, Howard, Liao, et al., 2001).

There are important differences between MID and Alzheimer's disease. The development of MID tends to be more rapid than Alzheimer's disease, and personality changes are less pronounced. However, the two conditions may often coexist (Hulette, Nochlin, McKeel, & Morris, 1997) and, in fact, the presence of vascular dementia may intensify the severity of symptoms seen in Alzheimer's disease (Breteler, 2000). As with Alzheimer's disease, there is no treatment to reverse the cognitive losses in MID, although supplements of vitamin E and C may help to protect individuals against the development of vascular dementia (Masaki, Losonczy, Izmirlian, Foley, Ross, et al., 2000). Antihypertensive medications also seem to play a role in lowering the risk of an individual's developing this form of dementia (Veld, Ruitenberg, Hofman, Stricker, & Breteler, 2001; Jick, Zornberg, Jick, Seshadri, & Drachman, 2000).

Frontal lobe Dementia. Dementia that attacks specifically the frontal lobes of the brain is known as **frontal lobe dementia** and is reflected in personality changes such as apathy, lack of inhibition, obsessiveness, and loss of judgment. Eventually, the individual becomes neglectful of personal habits and loses the ability to communicate. The onset of frontal lobe dementia is slow and insidious, usually beginning in the 60s. In searching for causes of this form of dementia, researchers have identified possibilities in the tau gene, thought to be located on chromosome 17 (Knopman, 2001; Lee, Goedert, & Trojanowski, 2001).

Parkinson's Disease. People who develop **Parkinson's disease** show a variety of motor disturbances including tremors (shaking at rest), speech impediments, slowing of movement, muscular rigidity, shuffling gait, and postural instability or the inability to maintain balance. Dementia can develop during the later stages of the disease, and some people with Alzheimer's disease develop symptoms of Parkinson's disease. Patients typically survive 10 to 15 years after symptoms appear.

An abnormality on chromosome 2 has been identified as a possible locus of the gene, leading to dysfunction in the dopaminergic system that controls movement (Le, Xu, Jankovic, Jiang, Appel, et al., 2003). There is no cure for Parkinson's disease, but medications have been developed that have proved relatively successful in treating its symptoms. The primary drug being used is Levadopa (L-dopa), but over the years this medication loses its effect and may even be toxic. Major advances have also been made in surgical

Actor Michael J. Fox, waiting to testify before the U.S. Senate Appropriations Subcommittee in September, 1998. Fox and others suffering from Parkinson's disease spoke of the need to increase funding for research on treatment. In May 2000, Fox left his hit series *Spin City* to spend full time working on behalf of this cause.

techniques, including pallidotomy (Uitti, Wharen, Turk, Lucas, Finton, et al., 1997). In this procedure, a pearl-sized area in the globus pallidum is destroyed by electric current (carefully guided using precise brain imaging methods). "Turning off" this structure reduces the abnormal motor movements associated with the disease.

Lewy Body Dementia. **Lewy bodies** are tiny spherical structures consisting of deposits of protein found in dying nerve cells, in damaged regions deep within the brains of people with Parkinson's disease. Lewy body dementia, first

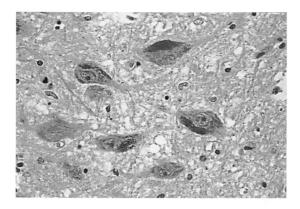

Neurons in the cerebral cortex containing Lewy bodies which show up as dark spots in this picture.

identified in 1961, is very similar to Alzheimer's disease with progressive loss of memory, language, calculation, and reasoning, as well as other higher-mental functions. Estimates are that this form of dementia is the second most common form of dementia following Alzheimer's disease (Kosaka, 2000).

The dementia associated with the accumulation of Lewy bodies fluctuates in severity, at least early in the disease. The disease also includes episodes of confusion and hallucinations, which are not typically found in Alzheimer's disease. Individuals with pure Lewy body dementia also show impairments in motor skills and in specific skills including tasks demanding concentrated attention, problem solving, and spatial abilities (McKeith, Galasko, Kosaka, Perry, Dickson, et al., 1996). However, their memory performance is less impaired than that of people with Alzheimer's disease (Salmon, Galasko, Hansen, Masliah, Butters, et al., 1996). Lewy body dementia has no cure.

Pick's Disease. A relatively rare cause of dementia is **Pick's disease**, which involves severe atrophy of the frontal and temporal lobes. This disease is distinct from fronterotemporal

dementia because, in addition to deterioration of these areas, there is an accumulation of unusual protein deposits (called Pick bodies). The symptoms of Pick's disease include disorientation and memory loss in the early stages, but the disorder eventually progresses to include pronounced personality changes and loss of social constraints, similar to frontal lobe dementia. Eventually, the individual becomes mute, immobile, and incontinent. Women are more likely to develop this disease, and the age of onset is typically 40 to 60 years.

Reversible Dementias. **Reversible dementias** are due to the presence of a medical condition that affects but does not destroy brain tissue. If the medical condition is allowed to go untreated, permanent damage may be done to the central nervous system and the opportunity for intervention will be lost. Furthermore, if the condition is misdiagnosed as Alzheimer's disease, the patient will be regarded as untreatable and not be given the appropriate care at the appropriate time.

A neurological disorder known as **normal-pressure hydrocephalus**, though rare, can cause cognitive impairment, dementia, urinary incontinence, and difficulty in walking. The disorder involves an obstruction in the flow of cerebrospinal fluid, which causes the fluid to accumulate in the brain. Early treatment can divert the fluid away from the brain before significant damage has occurred. Head injury can cause a **subdural haematoma**, which is a blood clot that creates pressure on brain tissue. Again, surgical intervention can relieve the symptoms and prevent further brain damage. The presence of a brain tumor can also cause cognitive deficits, which can be prevented from developing into a more severe condition through appropriate diagnosis and intervention.

Delirium is another cognitive disorder that is characterized by temporary but acute confusion that can be caused by diseases of the heart and lung, infection, or malnutrition. Unlike dementia, however, delirium has a sudden onset. Because this condition reflects a serious disturbance elsewhere in the body, such as infection, it requires immediate medical attention.

Prescribed medications given in too strong a dose or in harmful combinations are included as other potentially toxic substances that can cause dementia-like symptoms. The condition called **polypharmacy** in which the individual takes multiple drugs, sometimes without knowledge of the physician, can be particularly lethal. Recall that the excretion of medications is slower in older adults because of changes in the renal system, so that they are more vulnerable to such toxic effects of medications.

Chronic alcohol abuse can lead to severe permanent memory loss in **Korsakoff syndrome**, a form of dementia that occurs when there is a deficiency of vitamin B1 (thiamine). A related disorder, **Wernicke's disease**, is an acute condition involving delirium, eye movement disturbances, difficulties maintaining balance and movement, and deterioration of the nerves to the hands and feet. Providing the individual with thiamine can reverse this condition. Unfortunately, if it is not treated, Wernicke's disease progresses to Korsakoff syndrome. The individual develops **retrograde amnesia** (an inability to remember events from the past) and **anterograde amnesia** (an inability to learn new information). The chances of recovering from Korsakoff syndrome are less than 25%, and the symptoms become so debilitating that the individual must be permanently institutionalized.

Depression is another condition that can mimic the cognitive changes involved in Alzheimer's disease. In older adults, the symptoms may also include confusion, distraction, and irritable outbursts, and these symptoms may be mistaken for Alzheimer's disease. When these symptoms appear, causing impairment like that of dementia, the disorder is referred to as **pseudodementia**. Depression may also occur in conjunction with dementia, particularly in the early stages. In either case, the depression is treatable, and when appropriate interventions are made, the individual's cognitive functioning can show considerable improvement. (Depression will be discussed more fully in Chapter 11.)

Clearly, Alzheimer's disease and the variety of dementias described here are major potential limitations on the lives of older adults. Fortunately, they afflict a minority of people. Nevertheless, breakthroughs in their treatment along with contributions to understanding other major diseases will be among the most significant achievements of science in the next century.

SUMMARY

1. Diseases in middle and later adulthood can be highly disabling. However, many are preventable, starting with actions taken in early adulthood. Cardiovascular diseases in which there are pathological changes in the arteries are arteriosclerosis and atherosclerosis. Heart disease includes coronary artery disease, myocardial infarction, and congestive heart failure. Cerebrovascular accidents involve a cutting off of blood to the brain and may be acute or transient. Cardiovascular diseases are the leading cause of death in the over-75 population, with men having a higher risk, particularly African-American men. Behavioral risk factors include sedentary lifestyle, smoking, high BMI, and excessive alcohol intake. Heart disease can be largely prevented by careful monitoring of diet and exercise.

2. Cancer is a group of diseases in which there is abnormal cell growth. Skin cancer is the most prevalent form in the United States in the adult population overall. Breast cancer is the most frequent cancer in women. There are many behavioral risk factors for cancer,

including smoking, sun exposure, and lack of control over diet. Environmental toxins can increase cancer risk. Cancer treatment includes surgery, radiation therapy, chemotherapy, and biological therapy.

3. AIDS is a terminal immune system disease that occurs in the most advanced stages of HIV infection. Deaths from AIDS have decreased in the United States, but the epidemic is a leading killer of African American males. The slowing in the rates of death and new incidence of the disease reflect advances in prevention and treatment. AIDS is a concern for the over-50 population, although it is generally thought of as a younger person's disease.

4. Several musculoskeletal disorders are more common in older adults than in the younger population. Osteoarthritis is a degenerative joint disease in which the cartilage deteriorates. Osteoporosis is an extreme loss of bone mineral content that primarily affects women. Preventive steps include calcium intake, vitamin D, exercise, dietary control, and estrogen-replacement therapy.

5. Type 2 diabetes is an increasingly common chronic disease in older adults caused by a defect in metabolizing glucose. Prevention and treatment involves weight control and exercise.

6. Chronic respiratory diseases, including chronic emphysema and chronic bronchitis, are thought to be caused primarily by cigarette smoking. They have no cure at present.

7. Dementia is a clinical condition involving loss of memory and other cognitive functions. Alzheimer's disease is the most common form of dementia, affecting an estimated 7% of the over-65 population. Biological changes include development of amyloid plaques and neurofibrillary tangles. Alzheimer's disease is thought to have genetic causes, possibly involving abnormalities on the ApoE, APP, and presenilin genes that lead to formation of plaques and tangles. The caspase theory is the newest to emerge, focusing on the neurotoxic role of amyloid. Some researchers believe there are environmental causes such as head trauma. Diagnosis of Alzheimer's disease can be made only from autopsy, but NINCDS/ADRDA criteria have improved diagnostic accuracy. Medical treatments being tested include anticholinesterases, antioxidants, anti-inflammatory agents, and estrogen. Psychosocial treatments attempt to control behaviors and to provide support to caregivers. Other forms of dementia are vascular dementia, frontal lobe dementia, Parkinson's disease, Lewy body dementia, Pick's disease, and HIV. There are also reversible dementias, including pseudo-dementia, which if treated can lead to a return to normal cognitive functioning.

GLOSSARY

Acquired immune deficiency syndrome (AIDS): the most advanced stages of infection by the HIV virus.

Acute onset vascular dementia: dementia following a stroke.

Adenocarcinoma: a cancer that begins in glandular tissue within an organ.

Agnosia: loss of the ability to recognize familiar objects.

Alzheimer's disease: the most common form of dementia.

Amyloid plaque: collection of dead and dying neurons surrounding a central core amyloid.

Amyloid precursor protein (APP): protein manufactured by neurons that plays a role in their growth and communication with each other, and perhaps contributes to the repair of injured brain cells.

Amyloid: generic name for protein fragments that collect together in a specific way to form insoluble deposits.

Anterograde amnesia: inability to learn new information.

Anticholinesterase treatments: known as THA or tetrahydroaminoacridine, blocks the action of the enzyme cholinesterase, which destroys acetylcholine.

Aphasia: loss of the ability to use language.

Apolipoprotein E (ApoE) gene: gene located on chromosome 19 that controls the production of ApoE, a protein that carries blood cholesterol throughout the body.

APP gene: gene located on chromosome 21 that appears to control the production of the protein that generates beta-amyloid.

Apraxia: loss of the ability to carry out coordinated bodily movements.

Arteriosclerosis: a general term for the thickening and hardening of arteries.

Atherogenesis: the process that stimulates and accelerates atherosclerosis.

Atherosclerosis: a form of cardiovascular disease in which fat and other substances accumulate within the arteries at an abnormally high rate and substantially reduce the width of the arteries.

Carcinoma: a cancer that begins in the lining or covering tissues of an organ.

Caregiver burden: the stress that these people experience in the daily management of their afflicted relative.

Caregivers: family members most likely to be the ones providing care for the patient, and in particular, wives and daughters.

Cerebrovascular accident: (also known as a stroke or brain attack). An acute condition in which an artery leading to the brain bursts or is clogged by a blood clot or other particle.

Chronic obstructive pulmonary disease (COPD): respiratory disorder composed primarily of two related diseases, chronic emphysema and chronic bronchitis.

Congestive heart failure (or heart failure): a condition in which the heart is unable to pump enough blood to meet the needs of the body's other organs.

Coronary artery disease (or coronary heart disease): a form of cardiovascular disease in which there is a lack of blood supply to the arteries that feed the heart muscle.

Delirium: cognitive disorder characterized by temporary but acute confusion that can be caused by diseases of the heart and lung, infection, or malnutrition.

Dementia: clinical condition in which the individual experiences a loss of cognitive function severe enough to interfere with normal daily activities and social relationships.

Diabetes: a disease caused by a defect in the process of metabolizing glucose.

Early-onset familial Alzheimer's disease: form of Alzheimer's disease that begins in middle adulthood and shows an inherited pattern.

Elastase: enzyme that breaks down the elastin found in lung tissue.

Frontal lobe dementia: dementia that attacks specifically the frontal lobes of the brain and is reflected in personality changes such as apathy, lack of inhibition, obsessiveness, and loss of judgment.

Glucose: a simple sugar that is a major source of energy for the body's cells.

Human immunodeficiency virus (HIV): virus that kills or impairs cells of the immune system.

Hypertension: blood pressure that is chronically greater than or equal to the value of 140 mm Hg systolic pressure and 90 mm Hg diastolic pressure.

Korsakoff syndrome: a form of dementia that occurs when there is a deficiency of vitamin B1 (thiamine).

Late-onset familial Alzheimer's disease: inherited form of Alzheimer's disease that starts at the age of 60 or 65 years.

Lewy bodies: tiny spherical structures consisting of deposits of protein found in dying nerve cells in damaged regions deep within the brains of people with Parkinson's disease.

Multi-infarct dementia or MID: most common form of vascular dementia caused by transient ischemic attacks.

Myocardial infarction: acute form of cardiovascular disease that occurs when the blood supply to part of the heart muscle (the myocardium) is severely reduced or blocked.

Neurofibrillary tangles: tangled fibers within neurons.

Normal-pressure hydrocephalus: reversible form of dementia that can cause cognitive impairment, dementia, urinary incontinence, and difficulty in walking.

Opportunistic infections: life-threatening diseases in people with AIDS that are caused by microorganisms that usually do not cause illness in healthy people.

Osteoarthritis: a painful, degenerative joint disease that often involves the hips, knees, neck, lower back, or the small joints of the hands.

Osteoporosis: loss of bone mineral content of more than 2.5 standard deviations below the mean of young white, non-Hispanic women.

Parkinson's disease: progressive neurological disorder causing motor disturbances, including tremors (shaking at rest), speech impediments, slowing of movement, muscular rigidity, shuffling gait, and postural instability or the inability to maintain balance.

Pick's disease: form of dementia that involves severe atrophy of the frontal and temporal lobes.

Polypharmacy: condition in which the individual takes multiple drugs, sometimes without knowledge of the physician.

Presenilin genes (PS1 and PS2): PS1 gene, a gene that is located on chromosome 14 and accounts for up to 50% to 80% of early-onset cases. PS2 gene, a gene that is located on chromosome 1 and accounts for a much smaller percentage of early-onset familial Alzheimer's disease.

Pseudodementia: cognitive symptoms of depression that appear to be dementia.

Retrograde amnesia: inability to remember events from the past.

Reversible dementias: loss of cognitive functioning due to the presence of a medical condition that affects but does not destroy brain tissue.

Sporadic Alzheimer's disease: nonfamilial Alzheimer's disease.

Subdural haematoma: blood clot that creates pressure on brain tissue.

Tau: protein that seems to play a role in maintaining the stability of the microtubules which form the internal support structure of the axons.

Transient ischemic attack (TIA) (also called a mini-stroke): a condition caused by the development of clots in the cerebral arteries.

Vascular dementia: progressive loss of cognitive functioning that occurs as the result of damage to the arteries supplying the brain.

Wernicke's disease: an acute condition involving delirium, eye movement disturbances, difficulties maintaining balance and movement, and deterioration of nerves to the hands and feet.

Chapter Six

Basic Cognitive Functions: Information Processing, Attention and Memory

Study of the abilities to learn, remember, solve problems, and become knowledgeable about the world has a long history in psychology under the general category of cognition. Within the field of adult development and aging, researchers seek to apply new models, techniques, and methods of analysis to the question of how mental abilities change with age over the course of adulthood. This chapter examines the major approaches in the field.

The field of **cognition** in adulthood has important implications not only for psychologists, but also for the quality of ordinary people's lives and for society as a whole. As shown in Fig. 6.1, the poor design of the 2000 Florida election ballot may have changed the course of history. It was particularly confusing for older voters.

There are practical ramifications of changes in the ability to apply cognitive skills to situations in everyday life, ranging from job

> *"By the time you're eighty years old you've learned everything. You only have to remember it."*
>
> George Burns

performance to driving to the enjoyment of leisure activities. Some of these applications will be explored in this chapter; others will be discussed in Chapter 10 where age differences in job performance will be examined. Furthermore,

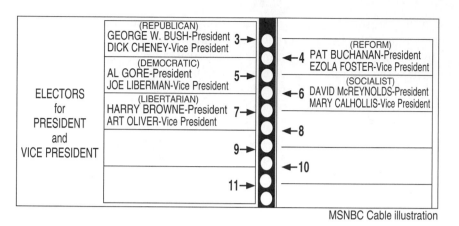

FIGURE 6.1

The 2000 Florida Election Ballot provides an outstanding example of a visually distracting stimulus such as those used in studies of information processing and aging.

cognitive abilities are important in terms of the way people feel about themselves and their own aging. The popular concept of the "senior moment" referred to in Chapter 2 is intended to be humorous, but it may relate to a more deep-seated anxiety that middle-aged individuals have about losing their memories for familiar knowledge. In this chapter, we will see whether or not such anxiety is warranted. As a preview, it is safe to say that although there are some losses in speed and memory toward the later adult years, normal age-related changes are not entirely negative. Furthermore, in terms of identity processes, there are many ways that individuals can compensate for memory changes as long as they manage to adopt a balanced approach to this important aspect of self-definition.

INFORMATION PROCESSING

Researchers working within the **information processing** perspective regard the cognitive functioning of humans as comparable to the functioning of a computer. The "data" from experience are entered into the brain through the various sensory routes, where they progress through a series of stages of analysis. Like a computer, the brain either stores the information or

prepares it to be used instantaneously. Studies of information processing in adulthood attempt to determine whether and how the aging process alters the efficiency and effectiveness of these analytical phases. As is evident from the research on driving covered in the Biopsychosocial Perspective box, findings from laboratory studies on information processing can have significant effects on daily life.

Psychomotor Speed

Theories about changes in the overall quality of information processing in adulthood are based on the results of studies on **psychomotor speed**, which is the amount of time it takes a person to process a signal, prepare a response, and then execute that response (Rabbitt, 1996). The basic framework of a study on psychomotor speed is fairly straightforward. The individual is given a stimulus array to study and is provided with instructions on how to respond when that stimulus array takes a certain form. Then the individual's time is calculated (to the millisecond) on each trial of the experiment. This measure is called **reaction time**. Although the reaction time study procedure sounds simple, what adds to the complexity and elegance of the research design is the experimenter's creation of various conditions intended to measure different facets of cognitive functioning. What happens if the individual is given a prompt that provides a clue regarding where the stimulus will appear? Conversely, what happens when the task is made more difficult by the presentation of a misleading or irrelevant cue? Such conditions may produce effects in terms of shorter or longer reaction times on the part of the individual. It is the observation of these effects in individuals of different ages that forms the basis for research on adult age differences in psychomotor speed.

Although this older female executive may be experiencing changes in her information processing abilities, she is nevertheless able to make use of high-tech equipment to meet the demands of her job.

The majority of studies that use reaction time as the index of interest involve visual stimuli. Individuals are shown a display on a computer screen and are told to push a button when certain stimuli appear. The stimulus to which the individual is told to respond is called a "target," and a stimulus to which a response should not be made is called a "distractor." On some of the experimental trials, the target is present, and on other trials the target is not present. The individual's accuracy in judging whether or not the target is present tends to be the main dependent measure of interest.

There are several basic variants of the reaction time study. In a study of **simple reaction time**, the target is either there or not there, and the individual must respond only when detecting its presence. In a **choice reaction time** task, the individual must perform one response for one stimulus and another response for another stimulus. For example, two shapes might be presented, one circle and one square. The individual would be told to push the "A" key for the circle and the "L" key for the square. In a **complex reaction time** task, the individual must make many decisions prior to responding. An example of a laboratory complex reaction time task would be a driving simulator or other similarly fast-moving display that requires a series of decisions and actions. Researchers in this area assume that the ability to react speedily is limited by biological factors. Sensory processing is one of these biological factors. If the information is more slowly brought into the central nervous system, there will be an inevitable delay in the ability to produce a response (Salthouse, 1996). A second limiting factor is the speed of neuronal transmission caused by loss of neurons or a slowing of synaptic communication (Birren, 1974). Another possibility is that information is lost at each synaptic transmission (Myerson, Hale, Wagstaff, Poon, & Smith, 1990).

BIOPSYCHOSOCIAL PERSPECTIVE

LOSS OF VISUAL ACUITY, increased sensitivity to glare, and difficulty seeing in the dark can contribute to impaired performance of older drivers. In addition, many driving situations involve rapid cognitive judgments that may present a challenge for older adults.

The very oldest (75 years plus) and the very youngest (15–24 years) drivers have similarly high death rates (about 28 to 30 per 100,000 population), about twice the rates for people in the middle years of 35 to 64 (see Figs. 6.1 and 6.2). However, compared to younger drivers (particularly those in the 20- to 24-year-old bracket), people over 65 drive far fewer miles, so their fatality rate (per mile) is higher (see Fig. 6.1).

Older people involved in collisions are more than three times as likely to die as younger people. Thus, it appears that older drivers are certainly a risk, particularly to themselves.

Younger people are involved in many more crashes than older drivers per number of licensed drivers, as can be seen from Fig. 6.2. However, on a per-mile basis (rather than per driver), the youngest and oldest drivers have the highest risks. In any given mile driven by a driver under 25 and a driver over 65, there is a greater chance of an accident occurring than when a middle-aged adult is driving.

There are age differences in the types of accidents involving older and younger drivers. Most crashes for all age groups occur when the vehicle is traveling in a straight direction just prior to the accident. Speed is a greater factor for young drivers: It is estimated to be involved in 15% of their crashes compared to 5% of accidents involving older adults. Young adults are also more likely to go through an intersection when there is a red light (75% of 18–25 versus 35% of 56 and older). By contrast, the older adult group is more likely to be involved in a crash at an intersection when making a left-hand turn. This is the cause of 17% to 21% of accidents involving age groups over 65 compared to 11% in the 15–24 year age category. Older drivers are also more likely to be involved in accidents in which they violate the right-of-way of another driver (18%) than are younger people (9%) and in failing to use proper signals at an intersection (14% versus 9%).

Although their sensory and decision-making capabilities may be limited by factors that they cannot alter, many older drivers take measures to reduce their risk of becoming involved in an accident. In 1990, the Nationwide Personal Transportation Survey (NPTS) was conducted on a random sample of nearly 48,000 residents from almost 22,000 households.

FIGURE 6.2

Fatal Crash Involvement per 100 Million Miles by Driver Age, 1995–1996

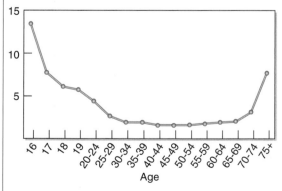

Source: Insurance Institute for Highway Safety, 2000.

FIGURE 6.3

Crash Involvement Rate per 1000 Drivers by Age Group

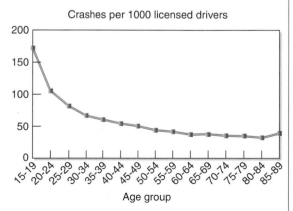

Source: National Highway Traffic Safety Administration, 2000.

BIOPSYCHOSOCIAL PERSPECTIVE *(continued)*

Respondents were asked to provide data on their driving habits during assigned 24-hour "travel days" over a two-week "travel period." The results of this comprehensive study provide clear evidence that older adults are aware that their driving abilities have changed and adjusted accordingly. In this study, "older drivers" were defined as people over the age of 65, and "mid-aged" drivers the ones between 25 and 64 years. "Young drivers" were those less than 24 years old.

The findings of the NPTS clearly indicate that older drivers take many precautions. They drive more slowly and fewer miles per day than mid-aged drivers. They may leave the house as often as younger drivers, but when they do, they take shorter trips. Older drivers are less likely to drive at night or during peak traffic hours. They try to avoid limited-access highways, such as the Interstate, and when they do, their speed is lower by 5 miles than that of mid-aged drivers and 10 miles lower than that of young drivers. They are much less likely to be involved in fatal accidents in which their blood alcohol level is at or above 0.10% (6% of older drivers compared with 26% to 27% of younger drivers).

Sociocultural factors add to biological and psychological processes to influence further the driving behavior of older adults. The link between driving and independence is highly reinforced in U.S. society, and loss of the ability to drive is seen as a major blow to a person's sense of autonomy. There are also practical implications of not being able to drive. Older adults who live in suburban or rural areas with limited or no public transportation lose an important connection to the outside world, and they risk becoming housebound and socially isolated. Prejudice against them by younger people can exacerbate whatever fears and concerns older drivers already have about their changing abilities.

Despite these problems, many older drivers seem to be able to adjust their behavior and attitudes so that they compensate for changes in cognitive and perceptual abilities. Younger people may not always like being on the road with an older driver who is a bit more slow and cautious, but the fact that older people have fewer accidents per person indicates that they are doing something right. Improvements are also being made on a broader scale in the United States as the number of older drivers continues to increase with the increased longevity of the Baby Boomer generation. Appropriate safeguards are being investigated, such as driving tests and safety classes for older drivers. Along with these safeguards, we can hope for changes in the attitudes of current middle-aged people as they themselves become the "older driver."

Countering the biological limitations presumed to affect reaction time are cognitive processes through which organisms learn to anticipate the future so that they can prepare with a rapid and effective response (Rabbitt, 1996). Moreover, as is also discussed later in the chapter, older adults can be trained to improve their performance on speeded tasks (Ball, Berch, Helmers, Jobe, Leveck, et al., 2002). However, biology appears to win out over experience in the area of reaction time and age. It is well established that reaction time increases with age in adulthood, at least within very short spans of time, on the order of several hundreds of milliseconds. This finding is the basis for the **general**
slowing hypothesis (Salthouse, 1996), which states that the increase in reaction time reflects a general decline of information processing speed within the aging nervous system. Related to this proposal is the **age-complexity hypothesis**, which proposes that through slowing of central processes in the nervous system, age differences increase with the increasing complexity of the task (Cerella, Poon, & Williams, 1980). As tasks become more difficult, older adults are disproportionately disadvantaged in their ability to respond. This disadvantage is reflected in their relatively poorer performance on complex reaction time tasks compared to simple reaction time tasks.

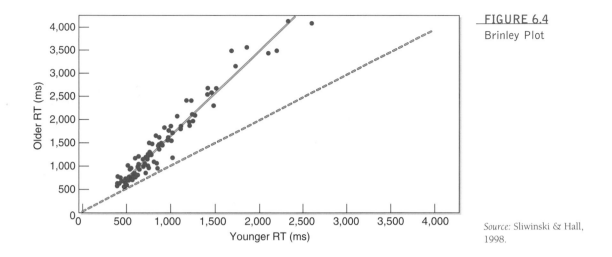

FIGURE 6.4
Brinley Plot

Source: Sliwinski & Hall, 1998.

The general slowing hypothesis was arrived at through observations in cross-sectional studies showing the reaction times of an older group of adults plotted against the times of younger adults on a graph called a **Brinley plot** (see Fig. 6.4). As you can see from this graph, older adults perform at similar speeds on tasks that can be completed relatively quickly by a young adult (500 ms). On tasks that take longer for young adults (1000 ms), older adults take proportionately longer (1500–2000 ms) than for the 500-ms tasks.

Although not particularly elegant in terms of a theoretical model, the general slowing hypothesis is consistent with a large body of data on reaction time performance in adulthood. Note that the main characteristic of this position is the claim that older adults do not become disadvantaged or deficient during any particular component of information processing tasks, but that they are simply slower. A further implication of the general slowing hypothesis is that loss of speed leads to other impairments in cognitive functioning caused essentially by a backlog in cognitive processes when multiple operations must be completed simultaneously or within a limited time.

Attention

The slowing of reaction time with age may be attributed to many factors, but one that has intrigued researchers is the possibility that older adults are particularly disadvantaged in the stage of information processing that involves input of the stimulus into the system. **Attention** involves the ability to focus or concentrate on a portion of experience while ignoring other features of experience, to be able to shift that focus as demanded by the situation, and to be able to coordinate information from multiple sources. Further cognitive operations, such as memory or problem solving, may then be performed on this information.

If you are one of the many people who has difficulty concentrating or focusing your attention for long periods of time, you are certainly aware of the price that you pay. It is annoying to others and frustrating to oneself to have an important piece of information fly by without having had the chance to absorb it. Attentional problems can have serious consequences, as is true for children and adults who have attention deficit disorder. Finally, a lapse in attention at a crucial moment of decision making, as in when to apply the brakes or turn the wheel of the car, can lead to disaster.

Researchers have examined adult age differences in attention by comparing people of different ages performing under various conditions, including when they must shift attention, divide attention among multiple inputs, and sustain their attention over an extended period of time (Hartley, 1992). Studies of attention are considered important for understanding the cognitive functions of adults of varying ages and their abilities to function in various real-life situations in which cognitive resources must be focused on some target or goal.

Shifts of Attention. Researchers have devised several ways to test the efficiency of shifts of attention in adulthood. In priming, the observer sees one stimulus that sets the stage for the subsequent response that will be required. The "prime" can be a word or signal of some sort that makes it more or less likely that the observer will make a speedy response. In "positive priming," the stimulus is one that makes it more likely that the observer will respond quickly. Suppose the task is one of deciding whether or not a five-letter sequence is a word. In positive priming, the target word (e.g., spoon) would be preceded by a word related to it (knife). The individual should be able to respond more quickly to the question of whether spoon is a word than if the target word is preceded by a word that is not related to it (chalk) or by a random string of digits. Many situations in life involve positive priming. For example, perhaps your classmate Jamie reminds you of another classmate, Jennifer. You are walking across campus and see Jamie. Moments later, you spot Jennifer heading in your direction. Having seen Jamie (who reminds you of Jennifer), you are quick to say "Hi, Jennifer!" because you have so recently been reminded of her.

FIGURE 6.5a
Consistent Mapping
TASK: Respond ONLY to X.

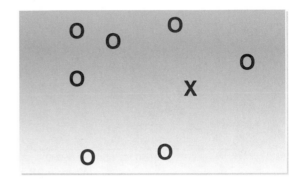

FIGURE 6.5b
Varied Mapping
TASK: Trial 1—Respond to X.

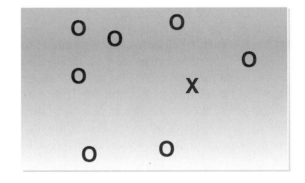

FIGURE 6.5c
Varied Mapping
TASK: Trial 2—Respond to 0.

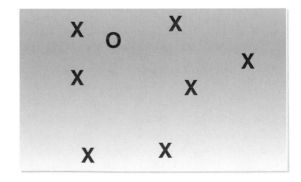

The opposite situation occurs in "negative priming," in which the observer is shown a stimulus that makes it more difficult to respond during the critical trial (See Fig. 6.5). In negative priming, the individual may be shown a pair of letters, one blue and one yellow. On the priming trial, a response would be required to a *blue* letter, and on the critical trial, the correct response would be to identify the presence of a *yellow* letter. Clearly, good performance on negative priming tasks involves the ability to ignore the fact that a distractor on one trial was a target on a previous trial. However, once primed not to respond to the yellow letter, the individual takes longer to respond to it as the target.

The Stroop color-word task is another example of negative priming. In this task, a word that refers to a color (e.g., red) is shown in a different color (e.g., in yellow ink). The task involves reading the color of the ink (yellow) in this example rather than the word itself (red). The Stroop effect refers to the fact that the observer takes longer to read the word when the color does not match the ink (incongruent condition) than when the color matches (congruent condition). Most of the evidence from the Stroop task supports the view that older adults have more difficulty in the incongruent condition and benefit relatively more from congruence between color and word content (Brink & McDowd, 1999; Hartley, 1992).

A **visual search** task requires that the observer examine a visual display to identify whether or not the target is present. In a single-feature condition, the observer is told to look for targets that have one characteristic, such as being of a certain color or shape. In a conjunction condition, targets are identified by a combination of features such as, for example, all red roses from among a set of distractors consisting of red roses, purple roses, red lilies, and purple lilies. A **memory search** task involves a delay between the presentation of the stimulus and the request to identify whether or not the target was present. The observer sees a display containing an array of stimuli and is asked to try to remember it. Then, when the display is no longer visible, the individual is asked to indicate whether or not the target was present.

There are two major variations in the memory search task. In consistent mapping, the targets and distractor items come from two distinct sets, so that a target on one trial is never a distractor on another trial. For example, if X is a target item, it is not ever used as a distractor for any trial in the series. In varied mapping, a target on one trial may serve as a distractor on another trial (Tipper, 1985). The letter X may be a target in one display and a distractor in a later display. In general, as the number of items to be searched in memory becomes larger (contains more items), the search time increases. However, under consistent mapping, reaction time becomes independent of the size of the display and the number of items to be remembered. The search is said to be automatic or effortless, for the target items "pop out" at the observer almost immediately. Under conditions of consistent mapping, older adults are able to develop automatic and effective searches (Ho & Scialfa, 2002). In varied mapping, reaction times increase significantly with increases in the size of the set of items to be remembered and the size of the display. The difference between older and younger adults in varied mapping conditions is greater than that observed in consistent mapping (Hartley, 1992).

"What do you think?" **6-1**

What real-life situations are comparable to those used in studies involving shifts of attention?

In another experimental manipulation called inhibition of return (IOR), participants are given a cue to look at a particular location, but then the target does not actually appear in that location. The next time a cue is presented to attend to that location, people are less likely to look in that direction again. Older adults show a particular deficit in this task, which is that they are able to refrain from looking at a previously viewed location, but are not able to refrain from looking at a previously viewed object that was incorrectly cued (McCrae & Abrams, 2001).

Divided Attention. So far, the types of situations described here involving attention are those in which the observer looks for a single target within a display but does so one display at a time. Although this situation corresponds to many in the real world in which an individual must search for a desired item, in many other situations people must monitor more than one situation at a time. For example, if someone calls you on the telephone while you are waiting for a weather forecast on the television, you must attend to both sets of auditory stimuli at the same time. In a **divided attention** task, the individual is given information from two input sources. One commonly used experimental situation is the dichotic listening experiment in which the individual being tested has earphones connected to two channels of audio input. Each channel sends a different set of stimuli such as letters to each ear. Various experimental conditions can be tested with this arrangement, but commonly, individuals may be asked to report the input from each ear. The dichotic listening procedure is based on a filter model of attention (Broadbent, 1958). According to this model, a filter regulates the amount of incoming information into the mind's central processor. This filter allows the processor to be set to the channel (ear) that the person is to report first. Although

the digits' input to that ear are being reported, the digits sent to the other channel undergo decay.

Divided attention as measured by the dichotic listening method appears to be a process that is negatively affected by aging over the course of adulthood (Hartley, 1992). However, other factors than the process of allocating attention across tasks seem to account for the age differences observed on dichotic listening. One possibility is that older adults have more difficulty on the individual components of a dual-task operation, and as a result, their performance suffers disproportionately compared to the young when they must switch between two operations. One particularly well-controlled study that many subsequent researchers cite to support this point was conducted by Somberg and Salthouse (1982). They compared older and younger adults on a divided attention task in which participants were given enough practice so that they achieved almost perfect performance on each of the component tasks. Under these conditions, younger and older adults were affected similarly by the need to shift their focus of attention from one task to the other. In a later study involving the division of attention between a memory and a reaction time task, the magnitude of age differences observed between older and younger adults on the dual task was greatly reduced when controlling for performance on the individual tasks.

Sustained Attention. Another frequently encountered attentional situation involves examining a stimulus array and waiting for a certain target to appear. In this situation, which is referred to as **sustained attention**, efficient performance depends on the ability to make a quick response even after a long delay of waiting for the target to appear. This is the sort of task that is required of a person who is fishing in a quiet stream who must sit and wait for the occasional tug of a bite on the end of the line. Laboratory tasks involve a comparable setup, with observers required to watch a computer display for targets to which they are instructed to respond, such as identifying a letter that is presented among other stimuli. Another term for this type of experimental task is "vigilance," meaning that the observer's ability to watch and wait before responding is being tested. Performance is measured in terms of decreases in the chances of correct detection of a target as the amount of time spent on the task increases (the vigilance decrement). Of particular interest in this type of task is the extent to which the observer's accuracy of detection is affected by the frequency of the presentation of the target stimulus and the degree to which the target appears in the same location on each trial.

Compared to younger persons, older adults appear to have more difficulty when there is a high rate of the target's presentation and when its location on the screen is less predictable (Mouloua & Parasuraman, 1995).

Theories to explain this variety of findings will be discussed in the next section. To help you organize the material so far, the results are summarized in Table 6-1.

Theories of Attention and Aging in Adulthood

Tasks involving attention require that the individual focus or shift cognitive resources onto one specific task or stimulus input. Many of the findings on age differences in adulthood provide evidence for a reduction in the efficiency of

TABLE 6-1
Effects of Age on Attention

Type of Attention	Example	Age Effects
Positive priming	Prime decreases search time for target.	Should benefit older adults.
Negative priming	Target on one trial is distractor on another.	Significant.
Cuing	Cue indicates where the target will appear.	Results not clear.
Memory search—consistent mapping	Hold target in memory and respond when it appears—target does not change.	Older adults can develop automatic search.
Memory search—varied mapping	Hold target in memory and respond when it appears—targets may become distractors.	Older adults perform more poorly compared to consistent mapping.
Divided attention	Dichotic listening task.	Older adults do more poorly but not when performance on separate tasks is controlled.
Sustained attention	Watch screen for appearance of target.	Negative effects of aging increase with increasing frequency of event and unpredictability of target.

these attentional processes. One view of aging and attention regards attention as a process reflecting the allocation of cognitive resources. When you must focus on a particular object, you must dedicate a certain proportion of your mental operations to that object. The theory of **attentional resources** and aging proposes that older adults have a limited amount of energy

BEHIND THE RESEARCH

**TIMOTHY A. SALTHOUSE, PROFESSOR OF PSYCHOLOGY
UNIVERSITY OF VIRGINIA**

What is most exciting about research in this field?
Cognitive abilities are among the most valued individual difference characteristics in society because they not only involve memory, but also reasoning, problem solving, and decision making. Considerable research suggests that many of these cognitive abilities appear to decrease with increased age; if so, these decreases may have important consequences for one's quality of life and eventually perhaps even for the ability to live independently. The possibility of preventing these reductions in cognitive functioning from occurring in the future is probably one of the primary motivations for many researchers studying effects of aging on cognition. There are many different approaches to studying cognition, but the analytical perspective views cognition as dependent upon presumably more basic components such as attention and working memory. To the extent that this reductionistic assumption is valid, the study of age-related effects on attention, working memory, and other cognitive "primitives" may be the key to discovering why increased age is often associated with lower levels of certain cognitive abilities.

What are the major challenges?
In my opinion one of the major challenges facing researchers in this field concerns the level of analysis likely to be most productive in understanding age-related differences in attention,

memory, and other cognitive abilities. Most prior research has focused on one or two behavioral measures from a single task, but it is possible that either higher or lower levels of analysis may be more meaningful. A higher level of analysis may be informative because a large number of different types of cognitive variables have been found to be related to age, and there is evidence that the age-related effects on those variables are not independent of one another. However, a lower level of analysis focusing on neuroanatomical and neurophysiological substrates of cognition would likely also be informative because regardless of the distal causes, all behavior must ultimately be represented biologically in one form or another.

Where is the field headed in the next decade?
Predictions are always risky, but if forced to speculate I would guess that the challenges mentioned in the previous paragraph will begin to be addressed and perhaps resolved over the next 10 years. One manifestation of this may be more integrated or systemic approaches to research in which the effects of aging on specific variables are examined in the context of effects on other variables. Another manifestation will almost certainly be a greater neuroscience emphasis in research on aging and cognition in order to identify the neural bases of age-related differences in cognitive functioning.

available for cognitive operations due to reductions in central nervous system capacity (Salthouse, 1985). This theory is based on the notion that only a limited amount of capacity is available for cognitive operations (Kahneman, 1973). Following from this theory is the **inhibitory deficit hypothesis**, which proposes that aging involves a reduction in the cognitive resources available for controlling or inhibiting attention. These are the processes required in the search and the screening out of irrelevant stimuli such as distractors (Hasher & Zacks, 1988). According to this view, selective attention involves two processes: activation and inhibition. Activation or excitation is needed to engage the search process, and inhibition is needed to restrict attention to irrelevant or distractor information. The inhibitory deficit hypothesis proposes that activation is spared but inhibition is negatively affected by aging over the course of adulthood.

The experimental tasks used as tests of the interference hypothesis are the negative priming method, the Stroop test, and the inhibition of return (IOR) task. With some exceptions (Gamboz, Russo, & Fox, 2002), the inhibitory deficit hypothesis receives strong support. Furthermore, there is evidence that inability to inhibit irrelevant information may have a neurological basis. Studies of event-related potentials, which measure the brain's electrical activity in response to stimuli, show that older adults are less able to block out distracting stimuli during an attentional task. Such a pattern of responding suggests that there are deficits in the prefrontal cortex, which is involved in the control of inhibiting irrelevant information (Gaeta, Friedman, Ritter, & Cheng, 2001). Neuropsychological tasks also support this interpretation (Persad, Abeles, Zacks, & Denburg, 2002).

These theories have important implications for understanding the performance of adults of varying ages in tasks requiring the allocation of attention. The interference theory would imply that middle-aged and older adults are able to focus more effectively when distractions are kept to a minimum. Some of these distractions might, ironically enough, involve concern over the quality of one's performance. An air traffic controller who is anxious about the possibility of being laid off or reassigned because of problems in performance may find it more difficult to concentrate on the task at hand. Attention, by definition, is a fleeting cognitive state, a necessary step prior to subsequent and more detailed analysis of incoming information. Factors that can serve to limit its effectiveness, such as concern over the quality of one's functioning, will make it even more difficult for the individual to put it to use in further cognitive operations.

Many of the lessons learned from studies on attention in adulthood are usefully applied to studies of memory in adulthood, which increasingly are borrowing concepts and theories from this area in understanding the effects of aging. The theories of memory changes across adulthood are becoming increasingly focused on the speed, efficiency, and clarity of the processing operations needed to encode information for long-term use.

MEMORY

Simply defined, memory refers to the acquisition, storage, and retrieval of information. Most cognitive psychologists regard memory as involving a sequence of stages through which information is initially processed, maintained in a holding pattern, and then either discarded or moved into more or less permanent storage. Like the cognitive models of attention, current conceptualizations of memory compare the human mind to the operation of a computer, although increasing attention is being paid to neuropsychology and links to brain functioning. Researchers working in both the cognitive and neuropsychological perspectives agree that what people experience as memories are based on the establishment of patterns of neuronal activity in the brain.

Components of Memory

Researchers who work in the field of adult development generally agree that the aging process has negative effects on most memory functions. However, it is also realized that not all aspects of memory are affected in the same way by aging and that people vary considerably in which memory functions show significant decrements. Although theories of aging and memory loss are not in agreement regarding the cause of age differences in patterns of performance, these theories share common ground regarding the underlying model of human memory. This model is shown in Fig. 6.6.

Sensory memory involves a very brief passage of information from the senses into the central nervous system, on the order of no more than a few seconds. There are different kinds of

sensory memory, including iconic (visual) and echoic (auditory). Auditory sensory memory might be involved in your recall of a bar of a song you hear on the radio. The characteristic of sensory memory is that information will be lost as new information enters the sense unless the individual makes a deliberate attempt to remember the incoming material. Age differences in adulthood and old age have generally not been investigated in this area of memory functioning.

As rapidly as information enters sensory memory, just as quickly is it forgotten unless it undergoes additional processing in working memory. Formerly called short-term or immediate memory, **working memory** refers to the system that keeps information temporarily available and active while the information is being used in other cognitive tasks (Baddeley, 1986). These tasks may involve solving a problem, following a plan of action, or understanding written or spoken language. The key to a working memory task is that it requires the individual to perform a cognitive task while

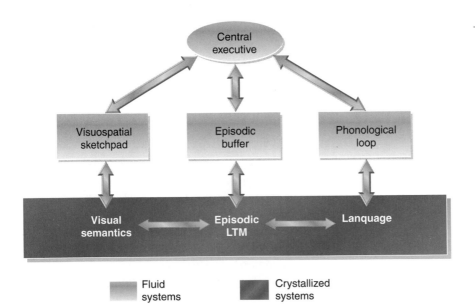

Source: Baddeley, Chincotta, and Adlam, 2001.

FIGURE 6.6
Schematic Diagram of Memory

simultaneously trying to remember some of the information for a later memory task. For example, in computational working memory, the individual is given a set of simple addition problems to solve (e.g., 4 + 7 = ?). As shown in Fig. 6.7, the working memory task involves asking the individual to remember the second number of each pair (e.g., 7) while solving the arithmetic problems.

Three components are theorized to be part of working memory. The **phonological loop** consists of a memory store for speech-based information called the phonological store, along with an articulatory control process that rehearses this information. In the phonological loop, one might hear a name (phonological store) and then keep saying it over and over again subvocally (articulatory control process), to keep from forgetting that name. A comparable set of structures are involved in visual memory. The **visuospatial scratch pad** makes it possible to manipulate and maintain visual and spatial images. For instance, the visuospatial scratch pad may be used when figuring out a shorter route between home and the

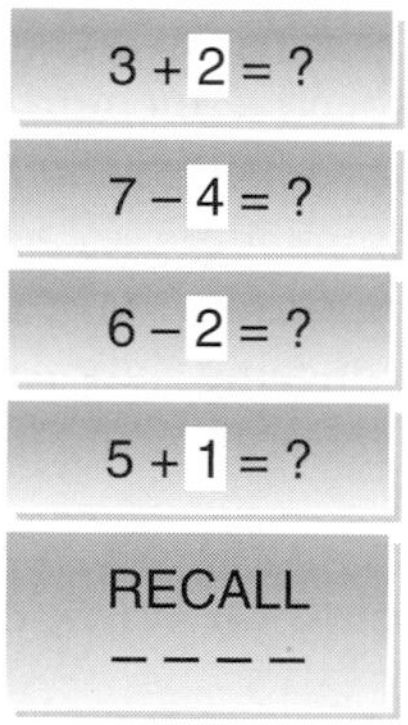

<u>FIGURE 6.7</u>

Computational Span Task for Working Memory
Instructions:
1. Complete these problems
2. Recall the second digit from each problem.

closest convenience store. The third component of working memory puts this all together. The **central executive** is responsible for deciding how to allocate cognitive resources such as whether to rehearse that name or to form a mental street map. Through the central executive, attentional resources are allocated to specific operations.

Information does not remain in working memory forever, and eventually it is either forgotten or consolidated in **long-term memory**, the repository of information that is held for a period of time ranging from several minutes to a lifetime. Long-term memory contains information ranging from within the recent past, such as where one lay down a pen, to information from many years ago, such as the events surrounding one's fourth birthday party. The model of working memory shown in Fig. 6.6 shows the relationships among the components of working memory and long-term memory.

The episodic buffer integrates information from the phonological and visuospatial components of working memory with information pulled out of long-term memory. Essentially, it is the information brought into conscious awareness, either from experiences being processed anew or from memories retrieved from long-term memory. For example, when trying to get directions to a friend's house in a familiar part of town, one would listen to and perhaps visualize the new instructions as well as integrate that information with knowledge about the town from previous visits to nearby locations.

Episodic memory is memory for events (episodes) and can include the recall of material presented in a memory experiment such as a word list. **Semantic memory** is the equivalent of "knowledge," and it includes the words and definitions of words found in one's vocabulary or storehouse of historical facts. The method of semantic **priming** is used to assess this aspect of long-term memory. The individual being tested might be asked to pronounce a word (the target) that has been preceded by either a semantically related word or sentence fragment (the prime). Semantic priming is shown when the response to the target is faster following a semantically related rather than a semantically unrelated word. Recall from semantic memory is theorized to involve the activation of networks of associated or linked words and facts. Nonverbal memories are stored in **procedural memory**, which is the knowledge of how to perform certain activities such as using a complicated computer program, sewing on a button, or cooking up a batch of chocolate chip cookies.

Contemporary researchers believe procedural memory is a variant of what is known as **implicit memory**, the recall of information that was acquired unintentionally. To test implicit memory, the individual may be shown a list of words containing, for example, the word "apple." When asked to name three fruits, the individual is more likely to include "apple" as one of those fruits. Another way to test implicit memory is through repetition priming. Here the individual would be shown the list of words containing the word "apple." Then a word fragment such as "a _ p _ _" would be presented and the individual would be asked to fill in the remaining three blanks. Implicit memory is shown when the individual says "apple" rather than "ample." The majority of verbal memory tasks involve **explicit memory**, in which the individual consciously or deliberately attempts to recall a list of words or other stimuli. Cognitive researchers regard procedural memory as a variant or form of implicit memory because it involves the recall of information that is not available to conscious awareness (Cohen, 1996). To illustrate this point, consider what you would say to someone if you were trying to describe the processes involved in tying a shoelace. Although you are very familiar with these actions, it is hard to put these actions into words because they are not thought of in verbal terms.

The study of aging and memory involves efforts to determine how well the theorized divisions of long-term memory hold up throughout adulthood into old age. Researchers also study various functions of long-term memory as tapped by different procedures. In source memory, also called source monitoring, the individual is asked to state where information was heard or seen. In everyday life, **source memory** may be required when you are trying to recall who told you where you could buy concert tickets or where you saw a drug store coupon for one dollar off on disposable shavers. A problem in retrieval from long-term memory, reflected in the common experience of not being able to retrieve a well-known piece of information, such as someone's name, is known as the **tip-of-the-tongue phenomenon**, also referred to as a word-finding deficit. Two other long-term memory phenomena relate to recall of information from the past. **Remote memory** involves, as the term implies, recall of information from the distant past, and **autobiographical memory** is recall of information from your own past. Finally, there is another form of memory, which is the recall of events to be performed in the future, or **prospective memory**. In this type of memory, the individual must retrieve from long-term memory an intention to perform an action. Often, this retrieval must take place during the course of an ongoing task, which must be interrupted to perform the intended action.

Effects of Aging on Working Memory in Adulthood

Although there are variations across studies, most measures of working memory span show clear age-related deficits, in verbal and visuo-spatial tasks (Park, Lautenschlager, Hedden, Davidson, Smith, et al., 2002). In terms of the components of working memory, it appears that the articulation rate slows in adulthood, which could affect the processing of information in the phonological loop (Multhaup, Balota, & Cowan, 1996). The visuospatial sketch pad also suffers from the effects of aging, as is evident from studies demonstrating deficits in spatial memory in older adults (Smith, 1996; Wilkniss, Jones, Korol, Gold, & Manning, 1997). These effects are present even when the factor of expertise with the stimulus materials is taken into account. In one intriguing study, musicians and nonmusicians of various ages in adulthood were compared in their memory for the patterns of musical notes. The age effects in spatial memory were equally pronounced in both groups (Meinz & Salthouse, 1998).

"What do you think?"   **6-2**

Why is working memory an important aspect of cognition?

A surprising and potentially dangerous side effect of a reduction in the efficiency of the visuospatial sketch pad in later adulthood is greater difficulty maintaining one's balance while standing. In one study, middle-aged and older adults were given a working memory task involving spatial memory while their postural stability was measured. The older sample had more trouble maintaining their balance during this task than did the sample of middle-aged individuals (Maylor, 1996). Placing cognitive demands on an older individual who may be more vulnerable to falling can therefore have very unfortunate consequences. Trying to keep the bus route straight while walking down an icy sidewalk could place too severe a demand on a person who is at high risk of falling.

Turning now to the theoretical explanations of the effects of aging on working memory, it

may come as no surprise that they closely parallel those on aging and attention. Reductions in the ability to hold information in storage while simultaneously processing new information are seen as the result of reduced speed or a deficit in inhibition. Both attention and working memory are seen within these theoretical perspectives as limited-capacity processing resources whose efficiency determines the outcome of cognitive operations. The aging process is seen as compromising this efficiency, although through different mechanisms as postulated by each theory.

According to the speed deficit hypothesis, age-related declines in working memory span across adulthood are a result of reduced processing speed, as indexed by the slower reaction time in middle-aged and older adults. Salthouse, the main advocate of the speed hypothesis, has consistently shown that perceptual speed accounts for over 80% of the age-related variation in measures of recall (Salthouse, 1993). The slowing of response speed can account for memory loss through two mechanisms, the limited-time and the simultaneity mechanisms (Salthouse, 1996). According to the limited-time mechanism, the aging adult simply runs out of time while performing working memory tasks and cannot complete the necessary operations. According to the simultaneity mechanism, the older individual is unable to complete tasks that require the results of one memory operation to be available during the completion of another necessary set of processes. As a result of these mechanisms, it is more difficult for middle-aged and older people to hold information in memory while processing incoming input.

The second explanation of age effects on memory, developed by Hasher and Zacks, relies on the inhibitory deficit hypothesis (Hasher, Zacks, & May, 1999). According to this view, efficient working memory requires the individual to inhibit information that is not relevant to the task by preventing such information from entering into awareness and by removing information that is no longer of use. As was true for attention, the inhibitory deficit theory of memory proposes that older adults are more likely to activate irrelevant information and are less efficient in suppressing such information once it enters working memory (Hedden & Park, 2001; Malmstrom & LaVoie, 2002). This irrelevant information, called "mental clutter," is thought to interfere with processing in working memory and in the processes of encoding material into and retrieval from long-term memory. In support of this approach, researchers in the area of cognitive neuroscience have identified deficits in the prefrontal cortex that would provide the biological basis for the lack of inhibition seen in older adults (Braver, Barch, Keys, Carter, Cohen, et al., 2001; Simensky & Abeles, 2002). Others have argued, however, that it is simply inability to recall rather than failure to inhibit that causes increased susceptibility to the effects of interference on memory (Jacoby, Debner, & Hay, 2001).

Autobiographical memories about the teenage years may be stimulated by looking through one's high school yearbook.

Effects of Aging on Long-Term Memory in Adulthood

If working memory is thought of as the individual's capacity for "mental work" (Zacks & Hasher, 1997), then it would make sense that a reduction in this capacity would have widespread effects on the acquisition and storage of new information. Indeed, cognitive aging researchers assume that the effects of aging on working memory can be viewed as deficits in processing resources that account for other age differences in episodic memory for information acquired during the course of experiments. Because older adults are deficient in processing newly presented information, they do not engage in effective encoding and retrieval of this material, and so their recall suffers as a result.

Perspective on the effect of working memory deficits on long-term memory is provided by

the **environmental support hypothesis**. This hypothesis proposes that age differences in adulthood appear on tasks that provide little context or support and demand high levels of self-initiated processing in which participants must work hard to try to encode and remember the material (Craik, 1994; Naveh-Benjamin, Craik, & Ben-Shaul, 2002). When these heavy demands are placed on working memory, older adults do not have the ability to process the material as efficiently or effectively. For example, age differences across adulthood are typically shown in tasks involving **free recall**, in which the individual must generate a list of words previously presented in the experiment. By contrast, **recognition tasks**, in which the participant must simply indicate whether a word was presented, show minimal age differences in adulthood. According to the environmental support hypothesis, these variations in results are due to the fact that recognition tasks provide more context and require less self-initiated processing by the participant than do recall tasks. Another example of the effect of context is provided by the results of memory for visual scenes. Because scenes are rich in contextual cues, older and younger adults tend to perform at similar levels (Smith, 1996). Researchers hypothesize that the benefits of increased environmental support in tasks involving spatial memory come from its facilitation of encoding processes rather than retrieval (Sharps & Martin, 1998).

Assess Yourself

Memory Quiz: How Sharp Are You?

The following quick, easy, screening memory tests were developed by the Memory Assessment Clinic in Bethesda, Maryland, and by Thomas Cook, former chief of the Geriatric Psychopharmacology Program at the National Institute of Mental Health.

I. The Shopping List

II. Read the following list carefully just once. Then look away and write down all the items you remember.

onions	shrimp	mangoes
plums	tonic water	pasta
eggs	mayonnaise	ham
blackberries	basil	brownies
hazelnuts	zucchini	oatmeal

Scoring:
The average 18–39-year-old recalls 10 of the 15 items.
The average 40–49-year-old recalls nine.
The average 50–59-year-old also recalls nine.
The average 60–69-year-old recalls eight.
The average person 70 or older recalls seven.

II. The Shopping List
Read the list once every five minutes. After your fifth reading, put it away and wait 30 minutes. Then try to recall the list.

Scoring:
The average 18–39-year-old recalls 13 of the 15 items.
The average 40–49-year-old recalls 12.
The average 50–59-year-old also recalls 12.
The average 60–69-year-old recalls 11.
The average person 70 or older recalls 10.

Assess Yourself *(continued)*

III. Phone Fun

Read a 10-digit phone number aloud (the area code plus the number). Then dial it from memory. When it rings (or if it's busy), hang up and redial it from memory. How many digits can you recall?

Scoring:

The average 18–39-year-old recalls six of the 10 digits correctly.
The average 40–49-year-old recalls five or six.
The average 50–59-year-old recalls five.
The average 60–69-year-old recalls four or five.
The average person 70 or older recalls three.

IV. The Name Game

A tester reads you six names, both first and last. Then the tester scrambles the list and reads you just the last name. Your job is to remember the first name. The tester rescrambles the list four more times, for a total of 30 tries. Each time, the tester gives you the last name, and you try to come up with the first.

Scoring:

The average 18–39-year-old identifies 21 of the 30 names correctly.
The average 40–49-year-old identifies 17.
The average 50–59-year-old identifies 16.
The average 60–69-year-old identifies 15.
The average person 70 or older identifies 12.

IV. Name That Face

At one-second intervals, a tester shows you six photographs, each of one person's face, with their first names attached. Then the tester removes the names, shuffles the photos, and presents them at one-second intervals. You name each face.

Scoring:

The average 18–39-year-old recalls four of the six names correctly.
The average 40–49-year-old recalls three.
The average 50–59-year-old recalls three.
The average 60–69-year-old recalls two.
The average person 70 or older recalls two.

The theorized reduction across adulthood in processing resources and in being able to engage in self-initiated processing is reflected primarily in age differences in episodic memory rather than in semantic memory (Wingfield & Kahana, 2002). Age comparisons on free recall tasks consistently favor young adults, and many other laboratory tasks of episodic memory show a similar fate with regard to aging (Craik & Jennings, 1992). Older adults are both slower and less accurate in performing episodic memory tasks (Verhaeghen, Vandenbroucke, & Dierckx, 1998). Although the vast majority of memory studies on aging are cross-sectional and hence subject to cohort effects, longitudinal data are available to confirm the general pattern of negative age effects in recall memory after the age of 55 (Davis, Trussell, & Klebe, 2001; Zelinski & Burnight, 1997). Furthermore, the memory deficits of older adults appear in everyday life as well as in the laboratory. Consider the case of "flashbulb" memories, which are important and distinctive events personally experienced by the individual. When they form such memories, older adults are as likely as younger adults to recall them correctly, even after as long as 50 years. However, compared to young adults, older individuals are less likely to form these memories in the first place (Tekcan & Peynircioglu, 2002).

Semantic memory, by contrast, is theorized to be spared from the negative effects of the aging process (Wingfield & Kahana, 2002). In fact, older adults appear to be better able to take advantage of semantic priming than are their younger counterparts. Rather than an impairment, there appears to be greater activation throughout links of associated words through the structure of semantic memory (Laver & Burke, 1993). Here is where greater experience pays off for the older person, who "knows more" than a younger adult and therefore has a richer and more elaborated semantic network (MacKay & Abrams, 1996).

In the area of procedural memory, it appears that adults retain well-learned and practiced motor skills such as playing an instrument, touch typing, or riding a bicycle for as long as they are able to perform these actions. However, people become slower with age in acquiring new procedural knowledge, such as the steps to the solution of a nonverbal problem even though they may reach comparable levels of performance (Vakil & Agmon-Ashkenazi, 1997). Furthermore, there is evidence that the greater experience of older adults can serve to compensate for changes in working memory in areas involving procedural expertise such as bridge-playing, chess, reading, cooking, gardening, and typing (Mireles & Charness, 2002). People with high levels of expertise reach the point of extreme familiarity with the requirements of these tasks so that the knowledge they have effectively becomes proceduralized (Charness, 1989; Cohen, 1996). The experienced bridge player is able to whip through a round of cards without giving each individual card a great deal of thought. Through years of playing, many of the choices about which card to play follow established conventions and rules, so that the older bridge player does not have to remember as much about each hand of cards.

The findings on procedural memory are important in pointing to an area that appears to be spared from the effects of aging. As mentioned earlier, procedural memory is regarded as a form of implicit memory. The results of research on age differences in implicit memory parallel the findings on procedural memory in adulthood. Tasks such as repetition priming that involve no conscious effort at recall show no age differences (Zacks, Hasher, & Li, 1998). Similar findings are observed when individuals with amnesia are tested on implicit memory tasks (Schugens, Daum, Spindler, & Birbaumer, 1997). In terms of normal aging processes, however, the implicit-explicit distinction may have a connection to the fact that word retrieval (tip-of-the-tongue) but not semantic memory activation is affected negatively by aging (Kemper, 1992).

By contrast, older adults seem to have greater difficulty on memory tasks that require judging an item's source (Hedden & Park, 2003). The task of judging an item's source becomes increasingly difficult for older adults as items become more similar (Henkel, Johnson, & De Leonardis, 1998) and when they are placed under pressure to respond quickly (Benjamin & Craik, 2001). Not only are older persons less able to remember where or how information was presented, but they also are more likely to have illusory memories in which they recall something that never happened. For example, in one study older and younger adults were shown a videotape and then shown photographs that they were asked to judge as having been in the videotape or not. Older adults were more likely to state that an event shown in a photograph had been in the videotape when in fact it was not there at all (Schacter, Koutstaal, Johnson, Gross, & Angell, 1997). Along similar lines, older adults are more susceptible to the implanting of false memories in which they incorrectly recall seeing a stimulus that was not actually presented to them (Schacter, Norman, & Koutstaal, 1998).

A related problem occurs with the phenomenon known as ironic memory (Wegner, 1994) in which a thought or image is suggested and the individual is instructed not to think about it. In the classic experiment on ironic memory, the respondent is told not to think about white bears. Following this suggestion, it is very difficult to rid the mind of this image. Older adults are more susceptible to the effects of ironic memory under some conditions, suggesting that they experience greater difficulties in controlling their recollection of information (Jacoby, 1999).

Problems in retrieval from long-term memory appear in research on the tip-of-the-tongue phenomenon in adulthood. This situation is most likely to occur when trying to remember the name of a person, place, or movie. The effect is observed more in older adults in both laboratory and everyday life situations (Burke & Mackay, 1997). Young adults occasionally experience this effect when trying to retrieve an abstract word, but for older persons, it is more likely to occur when trying to remember a person's name (Evrard, 2002). Although the information eventually can be recalled (Burke, MacKay, Worthley, & Wade, 1991), the experience can lead to inconvenience and embarrassment, as when one cannot greet an acquaintance by name.

Information that is stored and not accessed from remote memory appears to become increasingly difficult to retrieve, however, with the passing years. It is often assumed that older people can remember information from many years in the past better than they can remember information to which they have more recently been exposed. However, this apparent truism is not supported by data on remote memory (Piolino, Desgranges, Benali, & Eustache, 2002). For example, when older adults were asked to recall events from television shows, their memory for recent programs was superior to that of programs in the more distant past (Squire, 1989). Over time, the memory for past events becomes less vivid and loses detail (Cohen, 1996). The exception to this finding on remote memory is in the area of autobiographical memory, or recall of one's own past. Events that have a great deal of personal relevance and are rehearsed many times, such as the birth of a child or the achievement of an important career goal, do retain their clarity (Cohen, 1998). Particularly salient to many adults is a "reminiscence bump" of memories from the ages of 10 to 30 (Rubin, Rahhal, & Poon, 1998), especially happy memories (Berntsen & Rubin, 2002). People show higher levels of recall for memories from this period of life, memories that are marked by their distinctiveness and heightened personal importance. These memories are preserved because people often think and talk about them. For those remote memories that do not have the same personal relevance, the effect of aging and time is for those memories to fade.

The ability to remember to "do" something, or prospective memory, is another area of interest with regard to changes in adulthood. A common complaint of older adults is that they become absent-minded, such as forgetting what they were intending to get when going from one room to another. In event-based prospective memory, the individual attempts to remember to do something such as going to a friend's house after dinner. In time-based prospective memory, the individual attempts to remember to do something at a particular time, such as meeting that friend at 7:00 P.M. Prospective memory is important in everyday life because it is a nuisance, both to oneself and to others, when one forgets to be at a certain place at a certain time. For instance, if you forget your dental appointment, you are inconveniencing the dentist, who now has an unfilled time slot, and yourself, because it will probably take you months to reschedule your appointment. There are also potential health risks associated with a decrease in prospective memory, as when an individual forgets to take medication at the right time or, as in many cases, with a meal.

It appears that there are minimal age differences across adulthood in the ability to perform tasks involving event-based prospective memory as long as there is no time delay between the reminder and the performance of the task (Einstein, McDaniel, Manzi, Cochran, & Baker, 2000). However, older adults are disadvantaged when they must perform time-based prospective memory tasks. One possible explanation for the disparity between time-based and event-based prospective memory is that older adults lack some kind of time-monitoring mechanism (Park & Jones, 1997). Age differences in prospective memory are also more likely to occur when the individual is performing a cognitive task that must be interrupted. For example, while being tested on working memory, the individual may be instructed to perform an action at the point when a specific background pattern appears on the screen. In one such experiment, the performance of older adults on the prospective memory task deteriorated as the task became more demanding (Kidder, Park, Hertzog, & Morrell, 1997).

Similarly, in another study in which participants were asked to press a key one time during the completion of each of 11 tasks, older adults were more likely than younger adults to forget to perform this action (Einstein, McDaniel, Smith, & Shaw, 1998). In another prospective memory study, participants ranging in age from 35 to 80 years old were told to remind the experimenter to sign a paper at the end of a two-hour testing session. There was a progressive decrease across adulthood in scores on this task (Maentylae & Nilsson, 1997).

A final variable to consider in evaluating prospective memory is that of individual differences in memory ability and education. Older adults with fewer resources in these domains are more likely to suffer from deficits in event-based prospective memory (Cherry & LeCompte, 1999; Cherry, Martin, Simmons-D'Gerolamo, Pinkston, Griffing, et al., 2001).

A summary of the findings of research on memory and aging in adulthood is presented in Table 6-2. As can be seen from this table, certain cognitive functions are immune to the negative effects of aging, such as semantic memory, implicit memory, and autobiographical memory. In particular, memory for information that is highly familiar and is frequently retrieved remains preserved, as does memory that occurs without conscious processing. Tasks with a heavy reliance on the type of processing involved in working memory, which places high demands on cognitive resources, appear to be negatively affected by the changes involved in the aging process.

TABLE 6-2
Effects of Age on Types of Memory

Type of Memory	Example	Age Effects
Working memory span	Remember the second set of digits from a series of addition problems	Significant
Episodic memory	Free recall of a list of words	Significant
Flashbulb memory	Remember details of a distinctive historical event	Significant
Semantic memory	Semantic priming	None
Procedural memory	Riding a bicycle	None or small
Implicit memory	Repetition priming	None or small
Source memory	Recall whether word was spoken or read	Significant
Tip-of-the-tongue phenomenon	Recall a well-known name or word	Significant
Remote memory	Remember the details of a historical event	Significant
Autobiographical memory	Remember the details of a personal event	None if the information is of great importance
Prospective memory	Remember to do something in the future	None for event-based but significant for time-based

Researchers attempting to understand the patterns of age and memory performance invoke the concepts of working memory capacity and inhibitory deficits as psychological explanations, but there are also increasing efforts to integrate cognitive or computer-based models with evidence from brain imaging and other neuro-physiological data. For example, age deficits in implicit memory were mirrored in age differences in event-related potentials (ERPs), with young adults showing more positive waves (indicating greater activation) than older adults during an explicit memory task (Swick & Knight, 1997). One possible area of age-related effects are the frontal lobes, which may play a role in the encoding of new memories, working memory and source memory (Stebbins, Carrillo, Dorfman, Dirksen, Desmond, et al., 2002). A second area is the hippocampus-medial temporal lobe areas, which may be involved in memory encoding and retrieval from explicit memory (Henkel et al., 1998; Raz, Gunning-Dixon, Head, Dupuis, & Acker, 1998; Smith, 1996). Individual differences in brain volumes are beginning to be investigated as correlates of attention, speed, and memory (Coffey, Ratcliff, Saxton, Bryan, Fried, et al., 2001). Such investigations may eventually hold promise as a way of understanding brain-behavior relationships in later adulthood.

Other physiological factors are also cited as possible sources of age-related memory changes. Inspired perhaps by research on possible hormonal contributions to Alzheimer's disease, investigators have examined the effects of estrogen-replacement therapy on memory functioning in older adults who do not have dementia. Women receiving estrogen or estrogen and progesterone together have higher performance on memory tests than women who did not, presumably due to positive effects of hormone levels of hippocampal functioning (Resnick, Metter, & Zonderman, 1997; Sandstrom & Williams, 2001). A relationship also has been observed between higher levels of cortisol, the "stress hormone," and lower levels of memory performance (Lupien, de Leon, De Santi, Convit, Tarshish, et al., 1998; Seeman, McEwen, Singer, Albert, & Rowe, 1997). Chronically heightened blood glucose also appears to be related to memory losses in older adults due, it is thought, to the negative effects of high levels of insulin (Vanhanen, Koivisto, Kuusisto, Mykkanen, Helkala, et al., 1998). On the positive side, older people who have high levels of aerobic fitness show a small (5%) but significant improvement on complex speed-based cognitive measures (van Boxtel, Paas, Houx, Adam, Teeken, et al., 1997). A little more dubious but nevertheless intriguing is the finding in an older adult Swiss sample that high levels of antioxidants in the blood (ascorbic acid and beta-carotene) were associated with enhanced memory functioning over a 22-year period (Perrig, Perrig, & Stahelin, 1997). The provision of vitamins and trace elements (such as zinc) in the diet of older adults over a period of a year was found in one study to lead to improved short-term memory performance (Chandra, 2001). Other studies have pointed to a relationship between levels of vitamin B12 in the blood and enhanced cognitive functioning (Calvaresi & Bryan, 2001).

Metamemory

As researchers in the area of memory and aging continue to develop greater refinement in their understanding of cognitive changes among older adults, they are also searching for compensatory strategies and techniques that would help individuals with memory losses. The study of **metamemory**, or knowledge about memory processes, may provide suggestions for such methods of compensation. Researchers are interested in evaluating the effects of aging on the ability of adults to predict accurately their memory performance, which is one component of metamemory. A second component of metamemory is knowledge about what one needs to do in order to improve that performance. In combination with research relating specific memory functions to aging in adulthood, such as decreases in time-based prospective memory, it would then be possible to give middle-aged and older adults concrete suggestions that could lead to enhanced performance. There are also some interesting and potentially important implications of this research for understanding the relationship between identity and memory in later adulthood. Of particular interest in this regard is the related area of memory-control strategies.

The many reported studies showing that older adults have poorer episodic memory might lead you to expect people in this age group to scale downward their predictions about how well they would do on a particular task. Older adults are in fact sensitive to memory losses (Loewen, Shaw, & Craik, 1990), and those who are experiencing memory declines rate their memory processing as less efficient than do younger adults (Johansson, Allen-Burge, & Zarit, 1997; Jonker, Launer, Hooijer, & Lindeboom, 1996).

There are varying reports in the literature regarding changes in older people's accuracy in making specific predictions about their performance on a given task, however. In several studies it has been shown that older adults are less able to estimate how well they would remember, typically overestimating the level of their performance. For example, in one study, researchers investigated the surprisingly challenging task of remembering the details of a penny and a telephone dial. Older adults were more often incorrect in judging how well they would perform on this task than were younger adults, predicting that they performed better than they actually did (Foos, 1989). An overconfident tendency among the older adults led them to make incautious responses because they assumed that they knew the components of these highly familiar stimuli. Other researchers found a similar tendency for older adults to be overconfident about their abilities on standard episodic memory tasks, such as free recall of words (Dobbs & Rule, 1987). Another metamemory problem was observed in a study comparing age groups in the amount of time allocated to studying word pairs prior to recall. Although older adults were able to predict their performance as accurately as did younger adults, the older group failed to gauge correctly the amount of time they would need to study the materials (Dunlosky & Connor, 1997).

Other findings, however, further confuse the issue of whether metamemory is better or worse in later adulthood. Over the course of three experiments, older adults were found to be accurate in their predictions of both how well they would perform overall and how well they would be able to remember individual items (Connor, Dunlosky, & Hertzog, 1997). Furthermore, they were able to improve the accuracy of their predictions as they progressed through the memory tests. This result also conflicts with the findings of earlier studies showing an inability of older adults to take into account their own level of performance when predicting future scores on a memory test (Bieman-Copland & Charness, 1994).

Some of the discrepancies regarding the accuracy of performance predictions may be accounted for by individual differences among adults in personality and self-perceptions (Cavanaugh & Murphy, 1986; Dixon & Hultsch, 1983). Specifically, individuals who have low self-esteem and suffer from depressed mood are more likely to underestimate their memory abilities (Cipolli, Neri, De Vreese, & Pinelli, 1996; Scogin, Storandt, & Lott, 1985). Conversely, those who view themselves more favorably are perhaps more forgiving in assessing the quality of their memory abilities (Rabbitt & Abson, 1990). Self-efficacy with regard to memory performance, or the degree to which an individual feels that he or she can successfully complete a memory task, seems to be one particularly important factor in this process (Cavanaugh, 1989; Ryan & See, 1993). The higher one's self-efficacy, the greater the chance that the individual will be able to perform to maximum ability. Although one's self-efficacy may be too high, and thereby lead to inflated memory predictions, the alternative is much more likely. Unfortunately, for many older persons, self-efficacy with regard to memory functioning is diminished by the so-called implicit theory about aging and memory that many people have: namely, that memory functioning inevitably declines in later life (McDonald-Miszczak, Hertzog, & Hultsch, 1995). In fact, there is evidence to suggest that these beliefs apply to people as young as 40 years of age (Whitbourne & Collins, 1998). A related suggestion, that the instructions in memory tests present a threat to older but not younger adults, was tested in a study comparing traditional and nontraditional instructional conditions in relation to memory for trivia (Rahhal, Colcombe, & Hasher, 2001). Differences were observed in the traditional, but not the nontraditional, instructional condition. In a subsequent investigation, it was found that older adults who value their memories were more vulnerable to this effect of threat on memory (Itess, Auman, Colcombe, & Rahhal, 2003).

This analysis of aging and metamemory readily fits into the identity model. The assumption that aging (or middle-aging) causes one's memory to go downhill sets the stage for the individual to engage in an overuse of identity accommodation processes after an episode of forgetting. A downward spiral may set in such that the individual now starts to be painfully aware of each instance of forgetting and on each occasion becomes more pessimistic about future memory performance. As a result of the overuse of identity accommodation, individuals may be less likely to engage in preventive and compensatory strategies and therefore suffer further, preventable losses. However, there is evidence that older adults do in fact engage in identity assimilation. When asked to judge the likelihood of suffering memory decline with age, older adults were more likely to believe that such negative changes would occur for others than for themselves (Jin, Ryan, & Anas, 2001).

Related to the concepts of memory self-efficacy and identity with regard to memory abilities is the notion of control over memory functioning. In addition to having lower feelings of confidence about the quality of their memory performance, adults may come to believe that there is nothing they can do to control the eventual decline of their abilities (Hultsch, Hertzog, & Dixon, 1987). They interpret memory failures as due to an uncontrollable loss of capacity (Bieman-Copland & Ryan, 1998). People who have this belief, and feel that the forces that determine their memory functioning are outside their control, are more likely in fact to have lower memory test scores (Riggs, Lachman, &

Wingfield, 1997). Again, if this belief in external control is thought of in terms of identity accommodation, it seems reasonable to regard identity processes as linked in important ways to actual memory performance.

Memory-Training Studies

It seems safe to say that one mission of researchers who study adult memory is to find ways to help older adults offset deleterious changes in working memory, episodic memory, and other functions of long-term memory. Many of the researchers in this field are true "gerontological optimists" who believe that their work can help improve cognitive functioning in older adults. They have established, for example, the fact that even simple practice can produce significant improvements in memory task performance, offsetting the negative effects of mental inactivity (Lachman, Weaver, Bandura, Elliott, & Lewkowicz, 1992). Other strategies also appear to help maintain memory functioning. These include teaching older people to form images or associations to new material, to organize new material more efficiently, and to take advantage of a mnemonic trick known as the method of loci in which one forms associations between new material and the location of objects in a familiar setting (Anschutz, Camp, Markley, & Kramer, 1985; Yesavage, Rose, & Bower, 1983). Another approach is to increase the degree of environmental support. In a series of studies on techniques to increase comprehension and recall of information about medications, researchers found improvement for older adults through techniques such as providing instructions in lists rather than paragraphs and icons for remembering timelines (Morrow, Hier, Menard, & Leirer, 1998; Morrow, Leirer, Andrassy, Hier, & Menard, 1998). The simple act of notetaking can also enhance memory, even for complex material, such as the evidence presented in a courtroom (Fitzgerald, 2000).

One of the most ambitious cognitive training interventions was a multisite study known as Advanced Cognitive Training for Independent and Vital Elderly (ACTIVE) carried out over a 2-year period on over 2800 adults 65 to 94 years of age (Ball et al., 2002). Training sessions consisted of 10 sessions lasting about an hour over a 5- to 6-week period. The participants were trained in one of three types of cognitive skills—memory, reasoning, or speed of processing. The control group received no training. These types of training were selected because in small laboratory studies these methods showed the most promise. Also, these were cognitive functions related to everyday living tasks (e.g., telephone use, shopping, food preparation, housekeeping, laundry, transportation, medication use, and management of personal finances). For instance, those who received memory training were taught ways to remember word lists and sequences of items, text, and the main ideas and details of stories. Training in the area of reasoning involved learning how to solve problems that follow patterns such as reading a bus schedule or filling out an order sheet. Training in speed of processing involved learning how to identify and locate visual information quickly for use in tasks such as looking up a phone number, finding information on medicine bottles, and responding to traffic signs. In testing at the end of the training period, the majority of participants in the speed (87%) and reasoning (74%) groups showed improvement; about one quarter (26%) in the memory group showed improvement. Two years later, the gains were still maintained, although these were larger for participants who participated in booster sessions.

As can be seen, there may be limitations to the effectiveness of training programs in which older adults receive instructions in traditional memory improvement strategies. In one investigation, older adults were given training in the method of loci to learn how to remember the items on a shopping list (i.e., learn to associate the items to be remembered with a specific location such as the rooms of one's home). Although initially effective, three years later the method proved to have no beneficial impact. The participants remembered the technique itself, but they had not put it to practical use (Anschutz, Camp, Markley, & Kramer, 1987). Furthermore, even when training is effective, it does not allow older adults to achieve the levels of performance shown by younger persons (Baltes & Kliegl, 1992). Rather than giving formal training in mnemonics, the more successful memory training studies seem to involve allowing older persons to be given help in devising their own memory enhancement strategies (Park, Smith, & Cavanaugh, 1990). Self-guided practice provides a more positive training effect (Kotler-Cope & Camp, 1990) and has the added advantage of boosting the older adult's feelings of efficacy and mastery (Cavanaugh & Green, 1990). Another important factor in ensuring the effectiveness of training is consistency with the individual's preferred learning style. In one study involving training in the use of imagery as a memory improvement technique, researchers found that older persons high in the trait of openness to experience were more likely to benefit from instructions to make up novel visual associations to verbal materials (Gratzinger, Sheikh, Friedman, & Yesavage, 1990).

"What do you think?"　　　**6-3**

If you were going to open a memory clinic for older adults, what types of strategies would you teach? Why?

Researchers have also investigated training methods based on the accumulating evidence regarding the potential influence of memory control beliefs on memory functioning in later adulthood. In the technique known as cognitive restructuring, a method developed in cognitively based psychotherapy, attempts are made to challenge and thereby change an individual's low feelings of self-efficacy. In memory enhancement programs using this method, older adults are encouraged to adopt a more positive view of memory functioning in later adulthood. Although the first study using this method of training provided positive effects on memory control beliefs but not on actual performance (Lachman et al., 1992), later research provided more encouraging findings. After 10 weeks of such training, their memory scores in fact showed significant improvement compared to a comparable group of individuals who received traditional memory training (Caprio-Prevette & Fry, 1996).

In conclusion, attentional and memory processes in adulthood are important in everyday life. Older adults appear to suffer some deleterious changes but these changes are by no means universally or irreversibly negative. Identity seems to play an important role in determining whether individuals are able to take advantage of compensatory strategies. Future research will help uncover the personality-memory linkages as well as identify which strategies can be most effective in maximizing cognitive performance throughout middle and later adulthood.

SUMMARY

1. Cognitive functions are an important component of an individual's identity, and in middle and later adulthood, individuals become concerned about the loss of these abilities. However, many cognitive abilities are maintained well into later life, and there are preventative strategies individuals can use. Psychomotor speed, measured by reaction time, is an important variable in research on cognitive aging. There is a consistent increase of reaction time throughout adulthood. The general slowing hypothesis explains this increase as a decline of information processing speed, and the related age-complexity hypothesis proposes that the loss is greater for more difficult tasks. Studies of attention and aging involve the tasks of priming, search, divided attention, and sustained attention. Patterns of age differences on these tasks are interpreted in terms of the theory of attentional resources and aging, which proposes that older adults have limited resources, and by the inhibitory deficit hypothesis, according to which older adults are less able to inhibit irrelevant information in attentional tasks.

2. Memory is studied in terms of its components. The study of aging and memory involves attempts to determine how each component is affected by age-related changes in the processes of storing, encoding, and retrieving information. Working memory is significantly poorer in older adults, both in terms of the phonological loop and the visuospatial sketch pad. The speed deficit hypothesis regards the poorer memory of older adults as a function of reduced processing speed, a similar mechanism that is used to account for the poorer attentional performance of older adults. The alternative explanation is the inhibitory deficit hypothesis, which is also used in understanding aging and attention.

3. The effects of age on long-term memory are understood in terms of the environmental support hypothesis, which proposes that

older adults have more difficulty when they must engage in self-initiated processing, as in free recall. Tasks of episodic memory are most sensitive to age effects, and older adults have more difficulty in everyday memory tasks as well as in standard laboratory experiments. Semantic memory, however, is not affected by the normal aging process. Procedural memory is also retained in older adults, as is implicit memory. However, older adults have more difficulty with tasks involving source memory, tip-of-the-tongue, and remote memory. Certain personal memories are well-retained into later life, particularly those from adolescence and early adulthood. Prospective memory is retained when an individual can be prompted by the time rather than by an event. Consult Table 6-2 for a summary of results on aging and memory. Researchers are attempting to establish connections between changes in the nervous system and age-related deficits in working memory.

4. Metamemory shows varying results with regard to aging. Older adults are sensitive to memory loss, but not all individuals are able to predict their performance on a memory task accurately. Some provide overly optimistic and some overly pessimistic predictions about how well they will do in a laboratory task. Memory self-efficacy seems to be an important aspect of this process, and it is suggested that identity with regard to an individual's cognitive abilities may also play a role.

5. Memory training studies show that older adults can improve their memory performance on a variety of tasks, particularly if they are allowed to devise their own strategies. Cognitive restructuring about memory abilities, in which individuals are encouraged to develop a more positive view, seems to have positive effects as well.

GLOSSARY

Age-complexity hypothesis: proposal that due to slowing of central processes in the nervous system, age differences increase with increasing complexity of the task.

Attention: ability to focus or concentrate on a portion of experience while ignoring other features of experience, to be able to shift that focus as demanded by the situation, and to be able to coordinate information from multiple sources.

Attentional resources hypothesis: proposal that older adults have a limited amount of energy available for cognitive operations because of reductions in central nervous system capacity.

Autobiographical memory: recall of information from one's own past.

Brinley plot: graph in which reaction times of older adults are plotted against reaction times of younger adults.

Central executive: component of working memory responsible for deciding how to allocate cognitive resources.

Choice reaction time: measure of reaction time in which the individual must make a choice before responding.

Cognition: study of the abilities to learn, remember, solve problems, and become knowledgeable about the world.

Complex reaction time: measure of reaction time in which the individual must make many decisions prior to responding.

Divided attention: task in which the individual is given information from two input sources.

Environmental support hypothesis: proposal that age differences in adulthood appear on tasks that provide little context or support and demand high levels of self-initiated processing in which participants must work hard to try to remember the material.

Episodic memory: memory for events (episodes), which can include the recall of material presented in a memory experiment such as a word list.

Explicit memory: recall of information that the individual has consciously or deliberately attempted to recall.

Free recall: memory task in which the individual must generate a list of words previously presented in the experiment.

General slowing hypothesis: proposal that the age-related increase in reaction time reflects a general decline of information processing speed within the aging nervous system.

Implicit memory: recall of information acquired unintentionally.

Information processing: perspective in psychology in which cognitive functioning of humans is regarded as comparable to the functioning of a computer.

Inhibitory deficit hypothesis: proposal that aging involves a reduction in the cognitive resources available for controlling or inhibiting attention.

Long-term memory: repository of information that is held for a period of time ranging from several minutes to a lifetime.

Memory search: measure of attention in which there is a delay between the presentation of the stimulus and the request to identify whether or not the target was present.

Metamemory: knowledge about memory processes.

Phonological loop: memory store in working memory for speech-based information.

Priming: measure of attention in which the observer sees one stimulus that sets the stage for the subsequent response that will be required.

Procedural memory: knowledge of how to perform previously acquired activities.

Prospective memory: recall of events to be performed in the future.

Psychomotor speed: amount of time it takes a person to process a signal, prepare a response, and then execute that response.

Reaction time: time calculated for an individual to study a stimulus array and then respond when that stimulus array takes a certain form.

Recognition tasks: tasks in which the participant must simply indicate whether or not a word was presented on a previous occasion.

Remote memory: recall of information from the distant past.

Semantic memory: equivalent to "knowledge," and includes the words and definitions of words found in one's vocabulary or storehouse of historical facts.

Simple reaction time: measure of reaction time in which the target is either there or not there, and the individual must respond only when detecting its presence.

Source memory (source monitoring): recall of where information was heard or seen.

Sustained attention: measure in which efficient performance depends on the ability to make a quick response even after a long delay of waiting for the target to appear.

Tip-of-the-tongue phenomenon: problem in retrieval from long-term memory, reflected in the common experience of not being able to retrieve a well-known piece of information, such as someone's name.

Visual search: measure of attention in which the observer examines a visual display to identify whether or not the target is present.

Visuospatial scratch pad: memory store in working memory that makes it possible to manipulate and maintain visual and spatial images.

Working memory: system that keeps information temporarily available and active while the information is being used in other cognitive tasks.

Chapter Seven

Language, Problem Solving and Intelligence

> *"The wiser mind mourns less for what age takes away than what it leaves behind."*
>
> William Wordsworth
> 1770–1850

Traditionally considered the higher cognitive functions are the use of language, the ability to solve problems, and the application of mental abilities broadly known as intelligence. As critical as information processing and memory are to the ability to adapt to everyday life, the ability to analyze, reason, and communicate with others guides your use of judgment, knowledge, and decision making. Moreover, without these abilities, your potential to learn new information and integrate it with your existing body of knowledge would be highly limited.

Researchers have a great interest in finding out about the higher level cognitive functions in adulthood and later life. Such findings help address the practical need to determine how well older workers can perform (as will be discussed in Chapter 10). Furthermore, information on thinking and learning in later adulthood can provide a greater understanding of the potential for, as it is termed, *lifelong learning*.

LANGUAGE

The use of language involves a wide range of cognitive functions, including comprehension, memory, and decision making. As shown in Chapter 6, many of these functions are negatively affected by the aging process. Somewhat surprisingly, then, most researchers believe that, overall, the average healthy older adult does not suffer significant losses in the ability to use language effectively (Burke, 1997). The basic abilities to carry on a conversation, read, and write are maintained throughout later life.

206

Cognitive Aspects of Language

Given an overall picture of stability in language, there are nevertheless changes with age in cognitive processes that may affect an older adult's ability to use language effectively (MacKay & Abrams, 1996). At the most basic level, reading rate slows down in later adulthood, even in people with good visual acuity (Lott, Schneck, Haegerstrom-Portnoy, Brabyn, Gildengorin, et al., 2001). The changes in hearing and speech perception described in Chapter 4 may influence language use in later adulthood (Tun & Wingfield, 1997). When conversing, older adults may find it more difficult to hear particular words, so that there are gaps in the sentences they must try to process and interpret. The slowing of cognitive processing also affects the quality of interpretations that older adults derive from spoken language. Retrieval deficits can cause older adults to make mistakes in spelling causing them to be unable to recall the proper spelling of a word they once knew (Burke & Mackay, 1997). Compared to young adults, they may speak in simpler sentences (Kemper, Marquis, & Thompson, 2001). Their writing also becomes simpler, both in terms of expression of ideas and in terms of grammatical complexity (Kemper, Greiner, Marquis, Prenovost, & Mitzner, 2001). Furthermore, their speech may become more ambiguous, as in not using the proper referents to pronouns (such as not indicating who "they" are in a sentence) (Shadden, 1997). A major cognitive factor influencing spoken and written language is the existence of working memory deficits (Just & Carpenter, 1992; Kemper & Sumner, 2001). Working memory is the ability to hold one piece of information in mind while processing other information. Declines in this capacity can cause older adults to lose track of what they wish to say as they speak.

"What do you think?" | **7-1**

When have you seen older people spoken to with elderspeak? How do you think this makes them feel?

These older adults, participating in an Elder Hostel educational program in Washington, D.C., are clearly enjoying their ability to communicate about shared experiences through language.

On the other hand, there are compensating factors that can counteract the negative effects of aging on the processes involved in speech production and comprehension. A major benefit for older adults is the fact that they do not lose the ability to understand individual words. They are also able to keep track of the descriptions provided in language describing the thoughts and actions of a character in a story (Stine-Morrow & Miller, 1999). Older adults are also able to use strategies effectively to maximize their comprehension of written text (Stine-Morrow, Milinder, Pullara, & Herman, 2001). They also can use their vocabularies and knowledge of context to help overcome deficits in working memory.

Neuroimaging evidence supports the view that older adults use compensatory strategies by activating parts of the frontal cortex while reading to augment their working memory deficiencies (Grossman, Cooke, DeVita, Alsop, Detre, et al., 2002).

Another important compensating factor is the effect of experience on understanding context in language, particularly for those who have developed an extensive vocabulary over their lifetimes (Federmeier, McLennan, De Ochoa, & Kutas, 2002). Older adults have a rich backlog of experiences from which to draw when they listen or read. Even if they cannot hear each word, they can use the context of a situation to draw out the correct meaning. While reading, they can skim for information rather than stop and examine every word or phrase. As will be seen later in the topic of expertise, older adults have well-developed structures of information that allow them to anticipate and organize information that may overwhelm a novice. Even in situations that do not involve expert knowledge of a skill, previous experience can make up for slower processing of new linguistic information. For example, the avid soap opera fan who watches the same program every day can anticipate what the characters will say rather than needing to hear every word that is spoken. In the area of reading articles, the knowledgeable older reader is able to make up for changes in working memory by building more effective structures for retrieving from long-term memory the information from written text, such as a novel or newspaper (Stine-Morrow & Miller, 1999).

Social Aspects of Language

Along with changes in language use and comprehension throughout adulthood are changes in the social aspects of communication (Kemper, 1992). One of these is the tendency of older adults to share with others their reminiscences about the past. Such a change can have very positive outcomes. The ability to tell a good story may improve over adulthood as one develops greater richness and elaboration of linguistic and metaphorical abilities. Reminiscences about the past may also serve a function in solidifying relationships with others from one's own generation. As observed by Kemper (1992), "Elderly adult conversationalists weave together autobiographical details with references to historical events and descriptions of their former lifestyles to establish their own identities and a shared identity" (p. 254). Through such processes, older adults are able to use language to enhance their relationships with others.

With the increased tendency to reminisce, there is also the possibility that an older adult will be perceived negatively by a younger person who finds the older person's speech overly repetitive or too focused on the past (Bieman-Copland & Ryan, 2001). The greater verbosity among older people further complicates intergenerational relationships to the extent that the aging individual focuses on current disabilities or health limitations. Talking

BEHIND THE RESEARCH

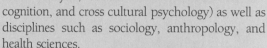

ELLEN RYAN, PROFESSOR OF PSYCHOLOGY, DIVISION OF GERIATRIC PSYCHIATRY, DEPT. OF PSYCHIATRY AND BEHAVIOURAL NEUROSCIENCES, MCMASTER UNIVERSITY

What is most exciting to you about research in this field?

I was originally interested in the communication problems older adults experienced because of age-related losses. However, I soon became fascinated by the excess disability caused by patronizing communication addressed to both healthy older adults and those with impairments. From a practical point of view, we can make a real difference by helping older adults to better manage communication predicaments where they are treated in terms of negative stereotypes. In my workshops with service providers, my goal is to increase their awareness of automatic, but inappropriate reactions in conversations with older clients and to encourage use of their own clinical skills in enhancing their communication. The bottom line can be put this way—the most important principle in talking with older adults is to listen well!

What do you see as the major challenges?

In my opinion, a major challenge for the field is to develop interdisciplinary approaches which combine theory and method from different areas of psychology (e.g., cognitive psychology, discourse analysis, narrative analysis, social cognition, and cross cultural psychology) as well as disciplines such as sociology, anthropology, and health sciences.

Where do you see this field headed in the next decade?

In the next decade, we are likely to develop more understanding of how older adults grow in cognitive and social skills in later life. This will depend on research questions emerging more from the perspective of the older person (e.g., older researchers). We also need to focus on special populations where older adults cope with specific losses, such as hearing, vision, memory. I feel that it is important to develop more comprehensive assessment and treatment plans incorporating strategies of successful aging (selection, optimization, and compensation) as well as enabling environments. Effective communication strategies by and with older adults should play a key role in this endeavor.

extensively about a topic in which the listener has no interest or which makes the listener uncomfortable can have an effect opposite to that intended and possibly isolate the older individual.

The third and possibly the most serious change in communication patterns between young and older adults involves the younger person's incorrect assumption that the elder is frail, cognitively impaired, and handicapped in the ability to speak. The outward physical appearance of a very old person may lead the young adult to make this unfortunate and incorrect assumption about the cognitive abilities of that individual. This incorrect conclusion can lead the younger person to adopt the linguistic pattern known as elderspeak, which is a simplified speech pattern directed at older adults who presumably are unable to understand adult language. According to the **communication predicament model** of aging (see Fig. 7.1), the use of elderspeak constrains the older person from being able to participate fully in conversations with others. Lack of cognitive stimulation due to the adoption of simple speech patterns directed toward the older person can accelerate whatever cognitive declines might otherwise have occurred. Furthermore, the kind of patronizing speech that is involved in elderspeak (e.g., "Can I help you, honey?") forms part of a pattern of over-parenting and failure to encourage independent behaviors in the older person (Ryan, Hummert, & Boich, 1995). Such patterns of speech are most likely to be used by young adults when speaking to a target whom they believe to be infirm (Hummert, Shaner, Garstka, & Henry, 1998). Through this process of infantilization, the older person loses the incentive to attempt to regain self-sufficiency in the basic activities of daily life (Whitbourne, Culgin, & Cassidy, 1995; Whitbourne & Wills, 1993). Moreover, when older adults are treated by younger adults in an infantilizing manner, they are also less likely to want to socialize with each other, potentially leading to social isolation (Salari & Rich, 2001).

FIGURE 7.1

The Communication Predicament Model

EVERYDAY PROBLEM SOLVING

Closely related to the issue of language development in later adulthood is the question of how individuals change over the course of adulthood in their ability to apply their cognitive processes to the problems they encounter in their daily lives. Over the past several decades, researchers have increasingly moved away from investigations of abstract reasoning abilities as applied to academic problems (such as anagrams or puzzles). Instead, current investigations focus on how people tackle the everyday challenges of managing such tasks as personal finances and monitoring diet (Allaire & Marsiske, 2002). Moreover, everyday problem solving can have more serious implications, as in the need for older individuals to monitor and maintain their intake of medications, which is often a complex and challenging task (Park, Hertzog, Kidder, Morrell, & Mayhorn, 1997).

Characteristics of Problem Solving

Psychologists approach the "problem" of problem solving by identifying types of problems and the stages involved in successfully approaching and resolving them. Essentially, **problem solving** involves assessing the current state of a situation, deciding on what is the desired end-state, and finding ways of transforming the current into the desired state. For example, when you are planning your budget for the month, you begin by assessing how much money is in your checkbook (current state). You then decide on how much money to allocate to food, entertainment, and transportation based on your desired end-state (having some money left at the end of the month).

Problems vary tremendously, however, in their structure and complexity. This example of a monthly budget is one that is fairly well structured in that the constraints are clear (there is only so much money in one's checkbook) and a set of steps must be followed. With problems that lack clear goals or when the steps that must be followed are difficult to discern, an increased burden is placed on the individual. Examples of complex problems from the world of technology are shown in Table 7-1.

TABLE 7-1
Everyday Problem Solving in a High-Tech World

Each day, we are required to apply our cognitive abilities to the challenges presented by instructions for using the new toys and tools made possible by technology. The following sample instructions illustrate how difficult this job can be for the average adult.

Item	Instructions
Personal laptop computer	To enter a password, do the following: 1. Type your password. Don't hold down a key too long, because the same character will be entered continuously. 2. Press the Enter key. An X appears if you enter the wrong password. If you fail to enter the correct password in three tries, you must press and hold the power switch for 5 seconds to turn off the computer, wait 5 seconds, and then turn it on again and retry. (From IBM ThinkPad instructions)
Cellular telephone	When you call automated systems, you often have to enter a series of numbers. Instead of entering these numbers by hand, you can store the numbers in your phone book separated by pauses using special characters (P, T). 1. Press Left Soft Key (Menu) 2. Press **2abc Contacts** 3. Press **2abc New Number** 4. Enter the phone number. 5. Press Right Soft Key **Option** to select hard/2-sec pause. 6. Enter additional number(s) 7. Press Left Soft Key **Done**. A confirmation prompt displays. (From LG VX6000 User Guide).
TiVo/DVR	**Troubleshooting: The audio and video are out of sync.** The audio and video may re-sync if you change channels. You can also try restarting your recorder. From TiVo Central, select Messages & Setup, then Restart or Reset System, then Restart the Recorder. On the Restart the Recorder screen press the THUMBS DOWN button three times, then press ENTER. You will see the Welcome screen and the system will restart in about 45 seconds.
Computer program	Problems with page numbering: The document is divided into sections. When you change or delete page numbers, Microsoft Word automatically changes or removes the page numbers throughout the document. However, if the document is divided into sections, and you have broken the connection between them (by clicking Same as Previous on the Header and Footer toolbar), Word changes or removes the page numbers only from the current section. (From Microsoft Word XP help menu)

What makes these problems complex is the fact that they require multiple steps, some of which involve uncertain specifications (such as when to turn the computer on and off) or steps that are contingent on other steps (such as the programming of a TiVo). The items in Table 7-1 are taken from the area of computers and electronics, which is increasingly becoming part of everyday life, much to many people's annoyance. However, complex instructions are present in many "low-tech" areas as well, such as cooking, handcrafts, and work with mechanical objects (such as the infamous vague instructions provided for the assembly of a desk chair or bicycle). Therefore, adults must apply their problem-solving skills to a wide range of situations, many of which are less than ideal.

A Model of Problem Solving in Adulthood

Given the pervasiveness of complex problems in daily life, researchers are naturally interested in determining the factors that influence successful solutions. Sherry Willis and colleagues at Pennsylvania State University working on the **Adult Development and Enrichment Project** (**ADEPT**) are investigating the ability of older adults to solve problems involved in maintaining an independent existence in a house or apartment. Such problems include managing medications, shopping, using the telephone (noncellular, presumably!), taking care of the house, and preparing meals. Using these self-maintenance activities as the content, a model of problem solving was then developed that provides a framework for studying age differences in adulthood. This model is shown in Fig. 7.2 (adapted from Willis, 1996). It provides an excellent framework for discussing the many factors involved in problem solving on a daily basis and how these might change over the adult years.

"What do you think?" | 7-2

Do you think that life has gotten more complex with advances in technology? How?

The instructions for operating a VCR can present a challenge to an adult's everyday problem-solving abilities.

FIGURE 7.2

A Model of Everyday Problem Solving

Antecedents	The Problem	Outcomes
Individual factors: Health Cognition Personality Belief systems	**Problem representation by the individual:** Declarative knowledge Procedural knowledge Beliefs and self-regulation	**Physical well-being:**
Sociocultural factors: Historical period Subcultures	**Task characteristics:** Novelty Complexity Structure	**Psychological well-being:**
	Contextual demands and resources: Social environment Physical environment	

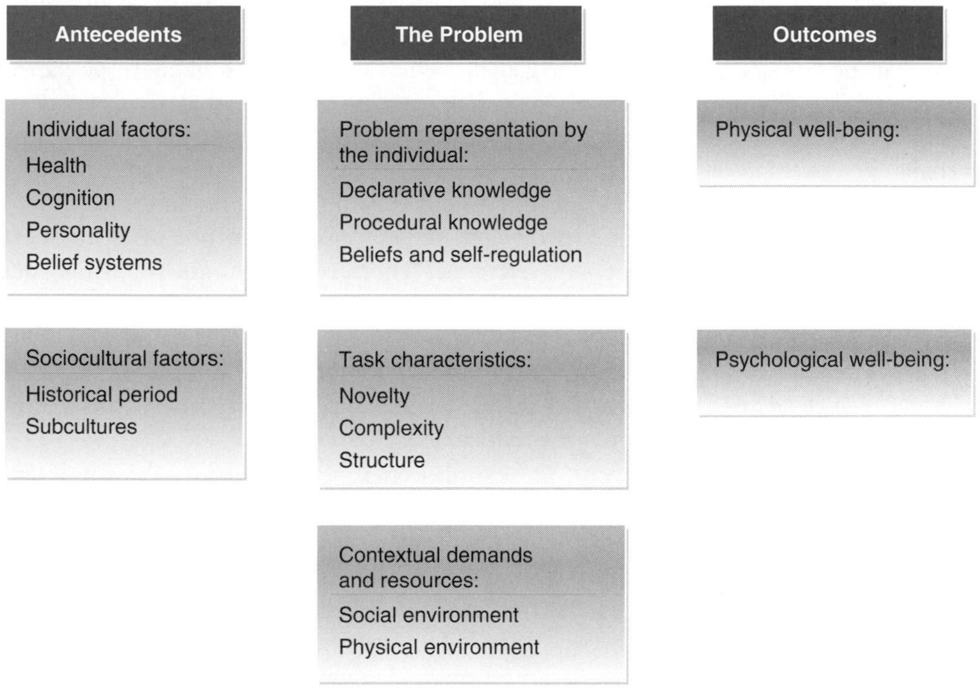

Source: Willis, 1996.

First on the list of individual factors in this model is health status. Adults who are in poor health may have more difficulty with everyday problem solving because they may be physically impaired and therefore less able to handle the demands of a task. Sensory impairments, particularly visual deficits, would seem to present a particular challenge. Imagine reading those complicated VCR instructions when they are typed in tiny print.

Changes in cognitive functioning involved in loss of working memory and speed also play a role in problem solving (Diehl, Willis, & Schaie, 1995). Complex instructions that involve holding one piece of information in memory while addressing another aspect of the problem (as in step 5 of the VCR manual) add to the cognitive demand of the task.

Personality also may play a role in the ability to tackle everyday problems. A personality characteristic mentioned by Willis (1996) is tolerance for ambiguity. People who want fast answers become more frustrated with a nasty computer bug or quirk in a program that requires some imagination to handle satisfactorily. Similarly, it is very difficult for some people to take seriously the notion that some computer problems are best solved by turning the machine off and on (as in step 2 of the laptop instructions). If there is no clear reason for taking such an action, then why do it? If you are one of those people who prefers to jump right into a new computer program without reading the manual, you may be someone who shows high tolerance for ambiguity. Your ability to solve complex problems will benefit from this willingness or preference to settle for some uncertainty and keep an open mind.

Closely related to tolerance for ambiguity is the set of one's belief system about knowledge. People who believe that there is one "right" way to do something may suffer when a complex problem is shown to have several alternative solutions or perhaps no solution at all. An important problem-solving ability is the avoidance of mental set or functional fixedness, in which the individual becomes so focused on one way of doing something that shorter and simpler routes are ignored. For instance, if you can find a shortcut in your word processing program such as using a hot key instead of a series of pull-down menus, you will be more efficient in your ability to write. However, we all know people who refuse to try to learn those shortcuts because they were taught to use the menus and they feel that is the only correct way to proceed.

Sociocultural factors are also important antecedents. Just as historical factors shape many of the daily experiences of the individual, they also shape the problems they confront. Ten years ago, very few adults were struggling with the instructions for a cellular telephone or personal computer. If we go even further back in time to 100 years ago, the problems of daily life become even more distinct from those of today. Instead of computers, the average person faced frustration with the leaking of a fountain pen, and instead of problems figuring out a VCR manual, there would have been problems determining why the backyard well had run dry. Telephones were much less complicated but much less reliable, and the problems in their use might be waiting for a connection. As technology has advanced, so has the level of sophistication needed to cope with these daily annoyances, and this is how historical period influences the nature of problem solving.

Subcultural influences on problem solving also exist, both in terms of the types of problems that present themselves and the types of solutions considered acceptable. Problems with high-tech toys are more likely to occur among people who have the resources to afford such gadgets. They are also more likely to be part of the daily lives of societies that place value on high-speed communications and data processing equipment. Furthermore, cultural variations exist in the types of solutions that a person might provide to problems with social relevance. These could include problems such as how to handle an unwanted pregnancy or a relative who needs full-time nursing care. With no "correct" solution, the choices that people make depend on their religious, social, and political values.

Turning next to the nature of the problem, the first set of factors involves the way individuals represent the problem as they attempt to solve it. One important resource mentioned in this model is declarative knowledge, which is knowledge specific to the domain of the problem. When you are planning an investment strategy, you want to turn to a person with a great deal of knowledge about stocks and mutual funds. Similarly, people will be better able to solve problems if they possess the procedural skills to do so, meaning that they know what steps to take. If you are struggling with a problem figuring out how to program a formula in your computer spreadsheet, there is a good chance that your friend the computer pro has the required procedural knowledge. That person should be able to show you the answer in about two swift keystrokes. Beliefs about one's ability to solve a problem also add to the way that the problem is represented in one's mind. If you feel that you have the ability and experience to work with computerized gadgets, you will be far less intimidated by the 200-page cellular phone manual than someone who shrinks away from anything with a technological bent. Finally, the emotional costs and benefits of a solution also influence the way a problem is conceptualized. Some problems have solutions with high social costs, such as a manager who must cut a budget by firing a long-time valued colleague and friend. Individuals will work hard to avoid having to arrive at such personally upsetting outcomes.

The second set of factors involved in the nature of the problem itself concerns how familiar, complex, and well structured it is. A new problem is generally more difficult to solve than one that has been tackled many times in the past. All other things being equal, it will take longer and the outcome will be less certain when a situation must be confronted for the first time. For example, parents find it much more difficult to set restrictions on the behavior of a first-born teenage child. By the time that child's sibling or siblings are going out on dates, using the car, and making autonomous decisions, the parents feel much more comfortable and confident about their ability to provide the right guidance. Complexity is a second task-relevant factor that influences the solution of everyday problems. It is obviously much harder to make one's way through a Julia Child recipe for beef stew than to defrost a TV dinner! However, structure also plays a role in this process. As mentioned earlier, one notorious problem that contains insufficient structure is the one-page bicycle assembly sheet marked only by vague arrows and poorly drawn diagrams. Solution of this problem will require a great deal more effort on the part of the problem solver and may never really be satisfactorily resolved without expert help.

Third in the set of problem-relevant factors is that of the environment, which includes physical and social components. The social support provided by the environment helps to ease the way toward solving problems, as when people are around and available to provide help. For example, a good solid technical support line can

make the difference between having a product that functions well and one that sits in a closet unused until it is finally discarded. The physical environment also plays a role in solving everyday problems such as, for example, those involving mobility. An older adult who has difficulty walking will be much better able to get around and complete his or her daily tasks in an environment that is handicapped accessible. Ramps, handrails, and obstacle-free pathways will allow for freedom of movement to a person with arthritis or joint problems. Similarly, the quality of signs and lighting of roads and intersections influence the ability of older drivers to handle the demands of maneuvering through city streets.

The outcomes of problem solving in everyday life include physical and psychological well-being. As the above examples illustrate, people's physical well-being is a direct function of how safely they can walk and drive. Similarly, when the problems involve medication or personal care, the outcome can literally be a matter of life or death. These problems can range from needing to figure out the correct series of medications to take to cooking proper meals and dressing appropriately for the weather. Psychological well being is the second possible outcome of problem solving. In addition to the benefits of adapting successfully to situations that may have a bearing on one's physical well-being, the outcome of a successful problem-solving encounter may also be enhanced feelings of competence.

Characteristics of Problem-Solving Abilities in Adulthood

To the framework proposed by Willis, it is also possible to add the interaction between identity and problem solving. Feelings of low self-efficacy about ability to solve problems may arise from overaccommodation to age-related changes in cognitive functioning. As a result of the overwhelming self-doubts that accompany accommodation, the individual finds it more difficult to solve problems that would be well within his or her powers. By contrast, over-assimilation may lead to the denial or minimization of obstacles to successful problem solving, and as a result the individual does not consider all possible routes to achieving a desired goal. At the same time, resolution of a challenging problem can enhance one's identity by reinforcing the feeling that one is a good thinker. Such an awareness would be particularly important to a person who values cognitive functioning and mental agility.

Fortunately, throughout the adult years, individuals acquire greater experience with a variety of problems as well as more depth in their own fields of expertise. These are factors that can enhance both their problem solving performance (Crawford & Channon, 2002) and their feelings of self-efficacy (Artistico, Cervone, & Pezzuti, 2003). At the same time, we know there are changes in cognitive abilities due to alterations in speed of processing and working memory. These factors combine to lead to a set of characteristic changes in the ways that adults approach problems (Willis, 1996).

The acquisition of expertise through years of exposure to certain kinds of problems is a major influence on the way middle-aged and older adults approach familiar everyday situations. They develop an ability to search for the relevant factors in a problem, and this increased selectivity to information allows them to avoid becoming burdened with excess information. Think of the experienced automobile mechanic who, with a single glance at an engine, is able to arrive at an instant diagnosis of the cause of the strange sounds it has been making for the past week. A novice (such as perhaps yourself) might spend hours searching through the car manual, various instruction books, and the

seemingly hundreds of valves and gauges under the hood. By the time you have finished, you may not even remember what you have already checked out. Expert problem solvers are able to avoid this kind of information overload by zeroing in on specific areas that experience has taught them are important to consider. They may also make better choices. In one fascinating study of decision making, older adults were found to avoid the trap that younger people fell into of making "irregular" choices. In this study, decisions were compared when people were given two or three choices. For example, if you say you prefer vanilla ice cream when given the choice of vanilla or chocolate, then you should also say you prefer vanilla when presented with the choice of vanilla, chocolate, or strawberry. Young adults were more likely to make such irregular choices than were older adults, whose decisions were consistent regardless of the alternatives (Tentori, Osherson, Hasher, & May, 2001).

Supporting the notion of improved problem solving among older adults are data from comparisons of younger and older adult pilots. Older pilots (60–84 years of age) did show memory deficits on a task requiring them to read back messages that were read to them. However, there were no age differences when pilots were compared with non-pilots in tasks that required expertise in interpreting information about air routes from charts and messages (Morrow, Menard, Stine-Morrow, Teller, & Bryant, 2001).

Although positive from the standpoint of efficiency, the ability to discount potentially irrelevant factors may have negative consequences. Because experienced problem solvers tend to seek answers to familiar problems by seeking familiar solutions, they may miss something important that is unique to a particular problem. For example, an automobile mechanic who goes directly to the distributor as the source of the problem may not notice a more serious wiring flaw elsewhere. Similarly, a physician who sees certain signs of a frequently encountered diagnosis may not consider a rarer disease that these symptoms may also represent (Sinnott, 1989).

A second advantage that individuals gain through experience with problem solving is an improvement in the way that relevant information from declarative memory is stored. People with experience have well-organized storehouses of knowledge that they can easily access and put to use. The expert on international travel, for example, can quickly tell you the pros and cons of a trip you are planning to a foreign country. Knowledge about the country's hotels, places of interest, and weather patterns is systematically stored in what is essentially a mental file cabinet of major travel destinations. Sports trivia buffs have a similar mastery of large amounts of content matter because it has been organized into systematic units.

Research on the speed of decision making in adults of varying ages confirms that older persons are able to reach an answer more quickly than are younger persons who do not have their knowledge bases as well-sorted or categorized. However, it also appears that older persons make quicker decisions even in areas in which they are not particularly expert. Furthermore, they are less likely to seek additional information once their decision has been made than are young adults (Meyer, Russo, & Talbot, 1995). It is possible that the more rapid problem solving shown by older adults reflects the fact that in many areas of decision-making, their greater experience has given them an edge. Therefore they do not feel as dependent on incoming information as do younger adults.

In addition to having a greater knowledge base that allows older adults to reach a quicker decision, they also possess greater procedural knowledge in areas where they have expertise.

This means that they can work their way more quickly through the sequence of steps needed to reach a solution. Novice problem solvers tend to start with the desired goal of a solution and then develop a strategy as they work their way backward to where they started. By contrast, older adults with experience in an area progress more efficiently through the stages of problem solving without having to pause and contemplate their plan of action. Again, this tendency to work quickly through a series of steps pays off when the problem is a familiar one. However, when there is new information that should be taken into account, the older adult would be less likely to do so.

In cognitive psychology, the terms "top-down" and "bottom-up" are used to differentiate problem solving styles. The **top-down approach** is one in which the individual uses what are called "heuristics" or rules-of-thumb to approach a problem. It is more likely to be used by an expert problem solver. For instance, an experienced cook does not need to measure out precisely the amount of flour needed for baking a pie crust. By contrast, someone using the **bottom-up approach** collects as much data (from the "bottom") as possible before making a decision. When making pie dough for the first time, you would probably measure as precisely as you could the amount of flour to use so that you do not make a mistake.

Although the top-down approach is generally quicker, it can also lead to mistakes, as when the individual makes an incorrect assumption at the beginning stage of problem solving. For example, perhaps you have skipped over Step One of a set of instructions that you thought you "knew" how to follow. Only later did you find out that the instructions were different from what you thought they were, based on your previous experience with similar situations. This kind of mistake comes from too much rather than too little familiarity.

According to Sinnott (1989), this is precisely what happens over the course of adulthood. Older adults use more top-down processing in all situations, young adults use more bottom-up, and middle-aged adults use the more advantageous approach of combining both.

Summarizing these and other analyses of the problem-solving styles of adults of different ages, Willis (1996) suggests that the tendency of older persons to rely on top-down processing and to make quicker decisions with less information may reflect an attempt to conserve cognitive resources. Furthermore, this more rapid decision making may represent an attempt by the older person to minimize the discomfort of ambiguity and to be better prepared to handle threatening situations. By reacting with a faster decision, the older person has more time to prepare to take necessary actions. Thus, if you know it is going to take you longer to cross a street due to a slowing of gait, you may offset this by preparing yourself mentally to make a hastier decision about when to enter the crosswalk.

The notion that older adults are faster at solving problems conflicts with much of the other data on cognition in adulthood. However, the types of measures used in studies of problem solving do not quantify responses in terms of milliseconds, as is true for studies of psychomotor speed. Instead, studies of problem solving involve measures based on the amount of information that is gathered prior to making a decision, and these are not as sensitive to what are effectively fairly small changes in reaction time.

Supporting the findings from studies of aging and cognition are results from neuropsychological testing. For midlife adults, performance on familiar problem-solving tasks appears to be maintained even while the ability to solve new problems may suffer impairments relative to the performance of young adults (Garden, Phillips, & MacPherson, 2001).

In everyday situations involving practical decision making, then, middle-aged and older adults appear to have an advantage when confronted with familiar choices. Their greater experience and expertise in terms of content and process allow them to appraise the problem, come up with a strategy, and then proceed to enact that strategy. However, when a familiar dilemma appears with a new twist, or when a premature decision leads to avoiding important information, older adults are relatively disadvantaged. Young problem solvers may suffer from their lack of familiarity with many situations, but because they can process larger amounts of information in a shorter time, they may avoid some of the traps that befall their elders.

Adult Learners

The literature on problem solving obviously emphasizes the ability to come to a resolution when dealing with a dilemma. However, the ability to "find" problems seems to be an equally compelling aspect of adult cognition. Research and theory on this aspect of adult cognition was stimulated, in part, by Piaget's concept of **formal operations**, the ability of adolescents and adults to use logic and abstract symbols in arriving at solutions to complex problems. Adult developmental researchers have proposed that there is a stage of **post-formal operations**, referring to the way that adults structure their thinking over and beyond that of the adolescent (Commons, Richards, & Armon, 1984; Sinnott, 1998). Post-formal thinking incorporates the tendency of the mature thinker to use logical processes that are specifically geared to the complex nature of adult life. The post-formal thinker is also able to judge when to use formal logic and when, alternatively, to rely on other and simpler modes of representing problems. For example, it is not necessary to use the rules

Adult learners often are more challenging and interested in debate in the classroom.

of formal logic to unplug a stopped drain. Hands-on methods are generally suitable for dealing with many of these practical situations in life involving actions in the physical world.

Related to the post-formal stage of cognitive development is that of **dialectical thinking**, which is an interest in and appreciation for debate, arguments, and counterarguments (Basseches, 1984). Adult thinking involves the recognition that often the truth is not "out there," but that common understandings among people are a negotiated process of give and take. We may not be able to find the ideal solution to many of life's problems, but through the process of people sharing their alternative views with each other, we can at least come to some satisfactory compromises.

The proposition of a post-formal stage of thinking has a great deal of intuitive appeal. Many questions that adults face have no right or wrong answer—just think of some of the cases that are brought to the Supreme Court every year. There are at least as many ambiguities and uncertainties even in the dilemmas that the average person faces in resolving interpersonal conflicts with friends, family, or colleagues. Furthermore, some people seem to seek out and relish the opportunity to engage others in dialogue and intellectual engagement. It would be boring for such individuals to face a world in which all the gray areas were removed from life's "real" problems.

The possibility that adults operate according to post-formal operations leads to a variety of interesting implications about adults as thinkers, problem solvers, and particularly, learners. Adult learners are increasingly becoming part of the concerns of those who teach at the college level; as of 1999, a large percentage of adults were involved in adult education. Over half (51%) of those 35–54, about one-third (37%) of those 55–64, and about one-fifth (19%) of those 65 and older were taking adult education courses. The majority of those under the age of 65 years take courses to help advance on the job (50%–60%). Among those 65 and older, about three quarters (76%) take adult education courses for personal and social development (U.S. Bureau of the Census, 2003).

In the classroom, adult learners may rely more on attaining mastery of the material through using strategies such as taking more copious notes and relying on them more heavily as they are trying to acquire new information (Delgoulet & Marquie, 2002). The adult learner is also more likely to challenge the instructor to go beyond the information and explore alternative dimensions. Such tendencies, though fascinating in the classroom, can lead to problems when it comes to evaluation. For a person who can see all the alternate angles to a standard multiple-choice exam question, it can be very difficult to arrive at the correct answer because more than one has virtues that merit attention. The adult thinker and learner may find it equally fascinating to ponder ambiguities rather than settle on one choice.

Not all adult learners have these characteristics, of course, and the variation from person to person may be related to personality factors, such as willingness to be open to new experiences (which will be discussed in Chapter 8) or tolerance for ambiguity, which was discussed with regard to the ADEPT problem-solving model. However, the emergence of alternative modes of thought, and their continued evolution throughout adulthood, provide an important counterpoint to the findings on the adult's tendency to become more "top-down" and potentially closed-minded with age and experience.

INTELLIGENCE

Psychologists have struggled for decades with defining the specific meaning of the term intelligence beyond the notion that it represents the overall quality of the individual's mental abilities. For nearly as long, psychologists have grappled with the issue of determining the course of development in adulthood for this elusive quality of the human mind.

The potential existence of age effects on intelligence in adulthood has many practical as well as theoretical ramifications. For practical reasons, it is important to find out the relative strengths and weaknesses of younger versus older workers. As indicated in the earlier discussion of problem solving, there appear to be fairly distinct differences in the styles that adults of different ages use when making decisions. Employers in the public and private sectors can make practical use of the analyses generated by psychologists on the more quantified data that emerge from studies using standard intelligence test scores. From a theoretical standpoint, research on intelligence in adulthood has provided new perspectives on the components of thought. This research has also provided insight into the perennial question of how mental processes are affected by "nature versus nurture" as researchers have continued to exploit and explore the application of complex research designs to data on intelligence test scores in adulthood.

Just as one's physical abilities partially define the adult's identity, intelligence serves as an attribute of the person that forms part of one's sense of self. People have a good idea of whether they are "smart" or "dumb," and they carry this self-attribution from grade school well into their later years. Furthermore, for some people, intelligence forms a significant part of identity. Those who value the products of the mind, their ability to solve tough crossword puzzles, and the scores they obtain on board games will be more vigilant for changes in intelligence associated with aging than people whose pride comes from physical competence. In some cases, these changes may be more imagined than real, as people respond to common characterizations of older people as having lost some of their wits. When the changes are present, however, this may prove to be a tough threshold to cross.

Historical Perspectives on Adult Intelligence

Research on intelligence in adulthood emphasizes the description and analysis of individual differences in the years from the 20s and older. The individual differences approach is reflected in the use of standardized intelligence tests as basic data for these studies. In fact, historically, it was the desire to develop age norms across adulthood for tests of intelligence that were originally developed on children that formed the impetus for the first studies on the topic. The first intelligence test, the Stanford-Binet, was designed to evaluate the mental abilities of children. When it became evident that this was not a suitable tool for measuring adult intelligence, the search for appropriate tests and normative standards prompted investigations of the performance of adults of different ages.

> *"What do you think?"* 　　　7-3
>
> Why is it so difficult to define intelligence?

The initial forays into the field of adult intelligence involved cross-sectional and longitudinal comparisons. For example, David Wechsler, who developed the widely used **Wechsler Adult Intelligence Scale** in the 1930s, administered the tests that comprise this instrument to representative samples of adults drawn from each succeeding decade ranging from early adulthood to old age. Standardization data were developed from these scores, but they were also used to describe age-related differences in performance on various facets of intelligence.

Overall, age differences across adulthood followed the "classic aging pattern" (Botwinick, 1977) of an inverted U-shaped pattern, with a peak in early adulthood followed by steady decline. Wechsler scales were divided into "Verbal" and "Performance" (i.e., nonverbal) scales, and older samples were consistently found to maintain their scores on the Verbal scales, particularly vocabulary (Wechsler, 1997). Later, this differential age pattern for verbal and nonverbal abilities was to become the foundation for one of the major theoretical approaches to adult intelligence that is still in use today, the "fluid-crystallized" ability distinction, which will be discussed shortly.

Results from the Wechsler scales, which supported the view that intelligence generally erodes over succeeding decades in adulthood, were in conflict with a smaller but consistent body of evidence from longitudinal studies. When samples of adults were followed through repeated testings using the Wechsler scales or another standardized test, the finding was either no decline or a decline that did not become apparent until very late in life (Cunningham & Owens, 1983).

In the 1950s, K. Warner Schaie began what is now the primary source of data on adult intelligence. Schaie's doctoral dissertation involved a comparison of 500 persons, 50 from each of 10 five-year age intervals, who were part of a prepaid medical plan consisting of 18,000 members in the Seattle, Washington, area. The first set of studies produced the typical cross-sectional age differences, showing negative age effects beginning in the 50s. However, seven years later, Schaie published a followup in which people's scores were compared within age groups between 1956 and 1963. Here were some surprising findings. For most abilities, there was an increase or no change between the first and second testings, even among the oldest age group. The stage was set for what has now become a 40-year plus search for the factors accounting for the aging, or the nonaging, of intelligence. Schaie's foresight in planning a study that would make possible the sophisticated developmental research designs described in Chapter 3 has provided a wealth of information on intelligence in adulthood and the factors that affect its fluctuations.

Theoretical Perspectives on Adult Intelligence

When you think of "intelligence," you probably have some notion that it represents the quality of a person's ability to think. Formal definitions of **intelligence** in psychology come very close to this simple idea of intelligence as an individual's mental ability. However, agreement among opposing theories of intelligence ceases after this point. These theories differ in the number and nature of abilities that are postulated to exist. Fortunately, for our purposes, researchers working in the field of adult development and aging have come to a resolution, in theory if not practice, when characterizing the nature of adult intelligence. Most operate from the assumption that there are two main categories of mental abilities, as indicated above, which correspond roughly to verbal and nonverbal intelligence.

The Concept of "g". As background to the current state of theory in adult intelligence, it is necessary to take one more venture into the history of the field. At the turn of the twentieth century, British psychologist Charles Spearman set about on the ambitious task of formulating a comprehensive theory of intelligence (1904; 1927). He proposed the existence of a "**general factor**" of intelligence, referred to as *g*, which encompasses the ability to infer and apply relationships on the basis of experience. According to Spearman, individuals with high levels of g should be able to receive high scores on various tests that tap into specific mental abilities (each of which is called *s*).

Such tests included the intelligence test devised by Binet, now known as the Stanford-Binet. The concept of a unitary factor in intelligence has emerged again in a large statistical analysis of age-performance relationships among adults 18 to 84 years. Salthouse identified a broad g-type factor associated with age that was also related to age-related deficits in speed and memory (Salthouse, 2001; Salthouse & Ferrer-Caja, 2003).

Primary Mental Abilities. Despite the popularity of intelligence tests based on g, the idea that intelligence is a unitary construct can be criticized for being overly simplistic. Contrasting theories involve proposals of multiple abilities or dimensions of abilities that together comprise intelligence. The multidimensional approach that has proven to be the most productive for understanding adult intelligence was the **primary mental abilities** framework proposed by Thurstone (1938). According to Thurstone, there are seven primary mental abilities: verbal meaning, word fluency (the ability to generate words following a certain lexical rule), number (arithmetic), spatial relations, memory, perceptual speed, and general reasoning. These seven abilities are considered separate and distinct from one another, and together they are thought to cover all possible abilities that characterize intelligence. Five of these abilities form the basis of the majority of current studies on adult intelligence: Verbal Meaning, Space, Reasoning, Number, and Word Fluency.

Fluid-Crystallized Theory. Out of the primary mental ability theory emerged the proposal by theorist Raymond Cattell (1963) that intelligence is composed of two basic sets of abilities: one set based on educational training and one set based on unlearned thought processes. Cattell regarded these abilities as **secondary mental abilities**, a concept based on a statistical method of analysis that attempts to capture the broad constructs that underlie specific abilities. In writing about the broad characteristics of these abilities, Cattell, in conjunction with psychologist John Horn (1966), defined them as "so pervasive relative to other ability structures and so obviously of an intellectual nature that each deserves the name intelligence" (p. 254). The first ability, **fluid intelligence** (also called G_f), is defined as the individual's innate abilities to carry out higher-level cognitive operations involving the integration, analysis, and synthesis of new information, "the sheer perception of complex relations" (Cattell, 1971). Fluid intelligence reflects the quality of biopsychological factors such as the functioning of the nervous system and sensory structures and cannot be trained or taught.

The second broad set of abilities within the Cattell model is **crystallized intelligence** (also called G_c), which represents the acquisition of specific skills and information acquired through familiarity with the language, knowledge, and conventions of one's culture. It involves the learned ability to infer relationships, make judgments, analyze problems, and use problem-solving strategies. Together, fluid and crystallized intelligence form a biopsychosocial definition of intelligence. They incorporate the biological factors related to the integrity of the nervous

FIGURE 7.3

Model of Crystallized-fluid Intelligence

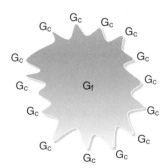

system, the psychological factors involved in cognitive processing, and the social factors derived from education and experience in one's culture. A useful way of imagining and remembering how fluid and crystallized intelligence are related to one another is through a literal translation of the metaphorical labels. Fluid intelligence can be thought of as a free-floating pool of movable resources that can be mobilized in any direction. (see Fig. 7.3). The specific areas into which fluid intelligence becomes channeled and rigidified are the various knowledge areas represented by crystallized intelligence.

Illustrations of the types of tests that make up fluid and crystallized intelligence provide even greater clarification of the definitions of these terms. Examples of the tests of Primary Mental Abilities (PMA Test) used to assess these secondary abilities are shown in Table 7-2. Tests of fluid intelligence measure the ability to develop and infer abstract relationships independently of culture-specific information. The items on these tests either are novel combinations of figures and shapes or are well within the inventory of any individual such as letters and common words. By contrast, tests of crystallized intelligence include items involving language facility and knowledge of moderately advanced mathematics and the rules of formal logic. In keeping with the definition by Cattell and his colleagues of crystallized intelligence as culturally based ability, some of the other tests used in their studies assessed such functions as the use of tools and the ability to solve everyday problems such as computing gasoline mileage or balancing a checkbook.

Definitions and measurement of secondary mental abilities are based on the notion that they are statistically and conceptually independent. However, the two have an intrinsic connection. To acquire the skills and knowledge specific to one's culture and system of education, it is necessary to have the fluid abilities to support the learning of new information. Concept formation and problem solving with culturally specific materials depend on general analytical abilities. Both sets of abilities are also affected by a variety of factors that influence the individual's growth, health, and environmental stimulation. Those who are exposed to optimal conditions such as nutrition, medical care, and education are more likely to develop to their maximal potential in both components of intelligence.

TABLE 7-2
Tests of Primary Mental Abilities

Primary ability	Description	Test	Example	Secondary ability
Verbal Meaning	Recognition and understanding of words	Synonyms	Choose the word that means the same as the one that is underlined: Fracture: complete write *break* forget	Crystallized
Number	Applying numerical concepts	Addition	If apples cost 90 cents a dozen, how much would 4 apples cost? 1. 50 cents (2.) 30 cents 3. 75 cents 4. 60 cents	Crystallized
Word Fluency	Retrieving events from long-term memory	Generate words according to lexical rule	Write in the blanks things that are *always yellow or yellow more often than any other color.*	Fluid
Inductive Reasoning	Identify regularities and infer rules	Complete series	Which letter group does not belong? NOPQ *DEFL* ABCD HIJK UVWX Select the shape to fit the dotted square:	Fluid
Spatial Orientation	Reasoning about geometric forms	Topology Matrices	Choose the figure in which a dot could be placed as in the item on the left: Which figure would fill the empty square:	Fluid

Sources: Letter series, fluency and verbal meaning: French, Ekstrom & Prince, 1963. Figure series and spatial orientation: Cattell, 1971. Letter series: Ekstrom, French, Harman & Dierman, 1976.

The hypothesized life-span course of crystallized and fluid intelligence reflects the combination of factors thought to affect each of the two secondary abilities. Fig. 7.4 depicts the adult course of fluid and crystallized intelligence as observed in an early study (Horn, 1970). The peak of fluid intelligence is hypothesized to be achieved in the years of adolescence, when the integrity of the nervous system and sensory structures are, at least theoretically, at optimum levels. From this point on, the changes associated with aging that reduce the efficiency of these systems lead to a downward trajectory in fluid intelligence. A contrasting age-related trend is proposed for crystallized intelligence, which continues to grow throughout adulthood as the individual acquires experience and culture-specific knowledge.

It makes sense that vocabulary, information about the world, and understanding of why and how things work are all abilities that continue

to evolve in the adult years as people gain more day-to-day exposure to people, places, and things. Consider, for example, what happens every time you solve a new crossword puzzle. The chances are very strong that you will learn at least one new word or fact each time. For example, did you know that the word "topa" means "any one of a variety of fish found in aquaria?" Yet, this was a correct answer to a clue in a recent popular weekly newspaper's puzzle. Assuming you remember this seemingly useless information in the future, you would have increased your crystallized intelligence by coming across this word in the puzzle. As these experiences accumulate over a lifetime, this component of intelligence will continue to grow.

Alternative Views of Intelligence

On the horizon of recent intelligence theories, but not yet applied to adult development and aging, are approaches to intelligence that emphasize knowledge of the world and a variety of other abilities not tapped even by fluid intelligence tests. The **theory of multiple intelligences** by Howard Gardner (1983; 1993) proposes that there are eight independent categories of intelligence, each of which can contribute to an individual's ability to adapt to the world. In addition to the usual abilities included in other theories of intelligence, Gardner's incorporates musical and bodily-kinesthetic (such as athletic ability) intelligence as well as interpersonal (knowledge of others) and intrapersonal (knowledge of self). The latter two abilities correspond closely to Goleman's (1995) notion of **emotional intelligence** described in the Assess Yourself box.

Challenges to traditional views of intelligence were also raised by Robert Sternberg (1985), who based his **triarchic theory of intelligence** on analyses of the strategies used

FIGURE 7.4

Pattern of Adult Age Differences in Fluid and Crystallized Abilities

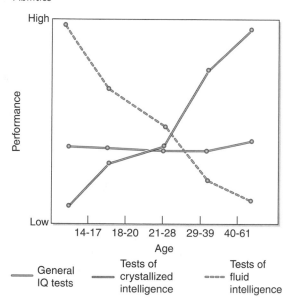

Source: Horn. 1970.

Assess Yourself

Measure Your Emotional IQ

The following items are from a test of "Emotional Intelligence," an alternative to traditional models of intelligence proposed by Daniel Goleman (1995) that focuses on the ability to understand oneself and others. The ability to delay gratification is another aspect of this theory, as can be seen by some of the questions.

A "Y" or "N" indicates that this item would receive a plus score on the test:

1. I am aware of even subtle feelings as I have them. (Y)

2. I find myself using my feelings to help me make decisions in my life. (Y)

3. Bad moods overwhelm me. (N)

4. When I'm angry, I blow my top or fume in silence. (N)

5. I can delay gratification in pursuit of my goals instead of getting carried away by impulses. (Y)

6. When I'm anxious about a challenge, such as a test or public talk, I find it difficult to prepare well. (N)

7. Instead of giving up in the face of setbacks or disappointments I stay hopeful and optimistic. (Y)

8. People don't have to tell me what they feel-I can sense it. (Y)

9. My keen sense of others' feelings makes me compassionate about their plight. (Y)

10. I have trouble handling conflict and emotional upsets in relationships. (N)

11. I can sense the pulse of a group or a relationship and state unspoken feelings. (Y)

12. I can soothe or contain distressing feelings so they don't keep me from doing things I need to do. (Y)

Source: Based on Goleman (1995).

by expert problem solvers. The three aspects of intelligence proposed by Sternberg were componential (the ability to think and analyze), experiential (creativity), and contextual (practical). The contextual aspect of intelligence is perhaps the most interesting in the sense that it corresponds to the kind of "street smarts" needed to handle many of life's dilemmas, but it is not usually tested in a standard intelligence test. The experiential component is relevant as well, corresponding to conceptions of creativity, which will be discussed with regard to aging in Chapter 14.

Sternberg has since moved on and expanded his theory to one of **successful intelligence**, defined as the ability to achieve success in life according to one's personal standards and in the framework of one's sociocultural context

(Sternberg, 1999). Included in successful intelligence are the processing skills identified in the triarchic theory (renamed analytical, creative, and practical). People high in successful intelligence are able to apply these skills to adapt, shape, and select environments, and they are able to capitalize on their strengths, and correct and compensate for their weaknesses.

Although not yet applied directly to the study of adult intelligence, Sternberg's theory seems to have potential to enhance and enrich current formulations. For example, Sternberg's **balance theory of wisdom** (Sternberg, 1998) views wisdom as the ability to balance the various components of intelligence outlined in the theory and to apply them to problems involving the common good or welfare of others. This approach complements the frameworks that are being developed within the tradition of life-span developmental psychology by Baltes and his colleagues. Such formulations greatly expand the notion of intelligence as a quality that goes beyond the ability to receive good test scores.

Empirical Evidence on Adult Intelligence

Empirical studies on adult intelligence follow the more traditional views of intelligence as a set of mental abilities. However, increasingly such studies are beginning to examine personality and other qualities of the individual that can moderate the course of development over the adult years.

Findings on the PMA Scales. Schaie's study of intelligence on the Seattle sample (referred to briefly in Chapter 3) has produced a compelling literature on the complex nature of adult intelligence and the factors that affect its development. The archives of the **Seattle Longitudinal Study** (**SLS**) are now considered to be the major repository of data on intelligence in adulthood; the study is therefore the focus of this next section of the chapter.

The **Primary Mental Abilities test** (**PMA**) developed by Thurstone is the basis for the SLS data. Findings are typically reported separately for each of the five abilities in the PMA. According to Schaie (1996), combinations of PMA scales can be used to understand all the abilities involved in a person's everyday life. The PMA scores can also be interpreted in terms of the fluid-crystallized distinction.

The longitudinal estimates of changes in the five PMA scales are shown in Fig. 7.5. Consistent with the fluid-crystallized theory, scores on Verbal Meaning show an increase from ages 25 to 46, after which they show relative stability until age 60. Scores on this scale remain the highest of all the PMAs until the age of 81 years. Numerical ability shows an early peak and then drops off from the 40s and on, which does not fit the expected pattern for this index of crystallized intelligence. The remaining three PMA scores perform as expected for fluid abilities: All show a leveling off and then a drop by the middle and later years of adulthood.

The overall picture in Fig. 7.5 appears to be one of stability until the 50s or 60s, followed by decline through the oldest age tested. However, there are some cautions that may be helpful to consider (Schaie, 1996). First, although some individuals may show declines in intelligence by the mid-50s, there are not significant losses until the decade of the 70s. A second point is that none of the participants showed general deterioration of functioning, even at the oldest age tested of 88 years. Thus, the age changes in cognitive functioning, though in a negative direction, did not occur significantly across the board (see Fig. 7.6). Third, Schaie concluded that most people are able to retain competent performance of familiar skills, particularly those that are of importance to the individual.

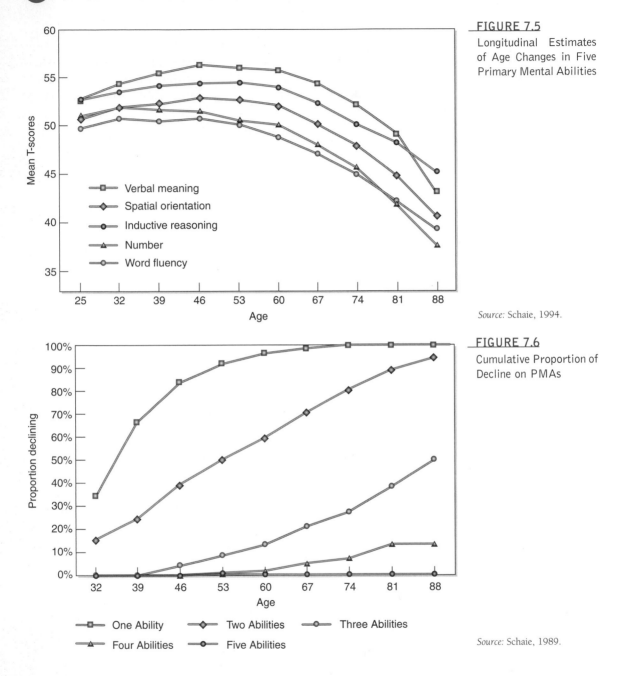

Source: Schaie, 1994.

FIGURE 7.5
Longitudinal Estimates of Age Changes in Five Primary Mental Abilities

FIGURE 7.6
Cumulative Proportion of Decline on PMAs

Source: Schaie, 1989.

Cross-sectional age differences provide another source of information about adult age effects on intelligence, for through the application of sequential designs, Schaie was able to assess the effects of cohort differences on patterns of scores. Fig. 7.7 shows a comparison of cross-sectional differences from data obtained in 1970 and data from 1991. You can see at a glance that the patterns of age differences from these two times of testing are not identical, particularly for certain abilities. This is why it is so dangerous to generalize from a single cross-sectional study to conclusions about overall age patterns. Another way to understand this problem

is by looking at Fig. 7.8, which shows the different patterns of performance on the PMA scales of successive cohorts ranging from those born in 1889 to those born in 1966. There have been clear increases across cohorts in verbal meaning, spatial orientation, and inductive reasoning. By

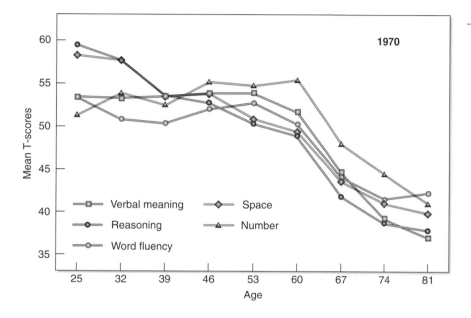

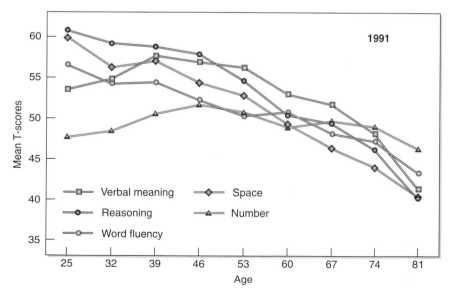

FIGURE 7.7

Cross-sectional Differences from 1970 and 1991

Source: Schaie, 1994.

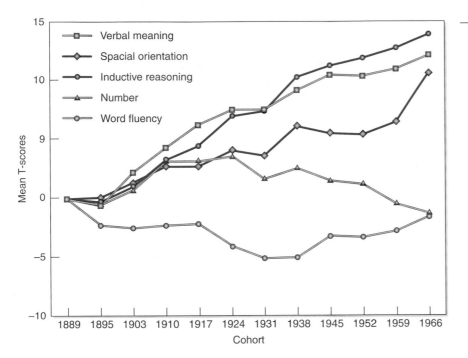

Source: Schaie, 1994.

FIGURE 7.8
Cohort Gradients from 1889 to 1996 on PMA Scales

contrast, numerical ability has shown a downward trend. The only ability that was relatively stable across cohorts was word fluency. Obviously, these differences across cohorts are reflected in the cross-sectional findings, and as can be seen from Fig. 7.7, age difference patterns for word fluency indeed were quite similar in 1970 and 1991.

With these analyses, it is possible to draw some inferences about the effects of aging across adulthood on the five primary mental abilities. Verbal meaning scores appear to reach a peak by the 50s on cross-sectional studies and somewhat later on longitudinal. Approximately 10 years later, these scores start to drop, and by 80 they are about half the level of their highest point. Numerical ability also peaks in middle age, and its drop becomes detectable by the 60s as well. One exception to this age trend appeared in the cross-sectional analysis of 1991. It appears (as many educators have speculated) that some of the basic arithmetic skills are not

as strong in recent cohorts compared to earlier cohorts. This is why, in 1991, older adults were in a relatively favored position compared to their predecessors tested in 1970.

Looking next at the three PMA scales that represent fluid intelligence, we can see that as measured longitudinally, spatial orientation, inductive reasoning, and word fluency remain stable until the late 60s and drop steadily thereafter. Both spatial orientation and inductive reasoning, however, descended downward cross-sectionally from a peak in young adulthood, in both the 1970 and 1991 analyses. Cohort differences on these abilities consistently favored younger cohorts from the 1989 cohort and on. Returning to word fluency, mentioned briefly above, we find that the longitudinal and cross-sectional curves are in fairly good agreement regarding a decrease in this ability after the age of about 60.

Given that both verbal meaning and number are regarded as crystallized abilities, the pattern of findings discussed here may seem to be in conflict with the propositions of crystallized-fluid theory. However, more recent longitudinal data on the fluid-crystallized theory do show declines in crystallized as well as fluid intelligence, although the decline in crystallized is less than in fluid (McArdle, Ferrer-Caja, Hamagami, & Woodcock, 2002). At the same time, fluid intelligence may reflect an individual's knowledge in crystallized domains. An intriguing study of players with varying levels of expertise in the game "Go" revealed that among those with high levels of expertise, the expected decline in memory-based measures of fluid intelligence was not observed (Masunaga & Horn, 2000).

Individual Differences in Patterns of Change. Behind the age trends are individual differences in patterns of gains and losses in adulthood, and the SLS has provided considerable data to help understand these patterns. One obvious factor that would seem to affect intelligence test scores is the individual's health status. As discussed in Chapter 3, retrospective studies showed that people who are fated to die within a period of several years show diminished intellectual functioning. It would make sense that health status would be related to intelligence test performance, and indeed, this has been found in the SLS. Arthritis, cancer, and osteoporosis are health conditions shown to be associated with intelligence test scores (Schaie, 1996). Sensory functioning, particularly vision, is also associated with intelligence test scores (Scialfa, 2000).

The SLS also documented the existence of a relationship between cardiovascular disease and declines in cognitive performance. Independently of such diseases, hypertension in middle adulthood is in itself a risk factor for poorer cognitive performance in the 70s and beyond (Launer, Masaki, Petrovitch, Foley, & Havlik, 1995). Lower limb strength, along with visual sensitivity and reaction time, emerged in one study of women over 60 as related to cognitive

performance (Anstey, Lord, & Williams, 1997). This finding might reflect the fact that women who are physically more active are in better cardiovascular health. Indeed, though small in magnitude, one report has emerged indicating a positive relationship within an older sample between a measure of fluid intelligence and participation in sports (Cerhan, Folsom, Mortimer, Shahar, Knopman, et al., 1998).

Given the theoretical basis of fluid intelligence as reflective of neurological functioning, a relationship between test scores and measures of brain functioning would be expected. Researchers are reporting that fluid intelligence seems to be at least somewhat related to indices of frontal lobe functioning (Bigler, Johnson, Jackson, & Blatter, 1995; Isingrini & Vazou, 1997; Robbins, James, Owen, Sahakian, Lawrence, et al., 1998). Further support for the role of neurological factors comes from longitudinal data on the relationship between psychomotor speed and fluid intelligence. Testing over a 4-year time period on a sample of over 400 older adults showed a considerable degree of overlap between speed and fluid intelligence (Zimprich & Martin, 2002).

Another important source of individual differences is that of gender, and differences between men and women are indeed observed in intelligence test performance in adulthood. Men outperform women on numerical skill, the crystallized ability of knowledge of general information, and one of the fluid ability scales of spatial orientation. However, women receive higher scores on a fluid intelligence measure called Digit Symbol, involving the substitution of symbols for digits in a speeded coding task (Kaufman, Kaufman, McLean, & Reynolds, 1991; Portin, Saarijaervi, Joukamaa, & Salokangas, 1995). In terms of changes over adulthood, women tend to decline earlier on fluid abilities and men show earlier losses on crystallized abilities (Dixon & Hultsch, 1999).

Individual differences in intelligence test scores were also predicted by social and cultural factors as assessed in the SLS. People with higher levels of education are protected somewhat from the negative effects of aging on intelligence, and the same is true of being involved in a complex and stimulating work environment. Being married to a spouse with high levels of education and intelligence is another protective factor, as is exposure to intellectually stimulating environments in general. Retirement has a positive effect on maintenance of intellectual functioning as long as one is leaving a boring and routine job. Those who are engaged in a complex and stimulating occupation show a more pronounced decrement after they retire (Schaie, 1996). Taken together, these qualities add up to higher amounts of what Schaie has called "Life Complexity" (Schaie, 1983). Other researchers have reported similar relationships between intellectual performance and education (Elias, Elias, D'Agostino, Silbershatz, & Wolf, 1997; Plassman, Welsh, Helms, Brandt, Page, et al., 1995; Smits, Smit, van den Heuvel, & Jonker, 1997), lifestyle (Baltes & Lang, 1997; Gold, Andres, Etezadi, Arbuckle, Schwartzman, et al., 1995; Steen, Berg, & Steen, 1998), and socioeconomic status (Aartsen, Smits, van Tilburg, Knipscheer, & Deeg, 2002). Relationships between the intellectual complexity of the environment and intelligence test scores have also been demonstrated in Chinese samples, extending the applicability of the SLS findings (Schaie, Nguyen, Willis, Dutta, & Yue, 2001).

The problem of cause and effect is clearly present in some of this research on lifestyle and intelligence. Do the intellectually more able seek out more stimulating environments, or does involvement in a rich environment lead to greater preservation of mental abilities? Perhaps older people with high levels of intelligence purposefully seek out ways to maximize their abilities. They may also seek out certain complex problems and situations because these fit with their abilities. Another possibility is that people with higher intellectual abilities who have better problem-solving abilities are better able to take advantage of health maintenance and treatment strategies. These are certainly possibilities that are acknowledged by Schaie and his associates. In a study conducted outside the SLS, this interpretation seemed likely. Middle-aged and older adults with higher intelligence test scores were more likely to take advantage of the availability of a memory aid during a decision-making task (Johnson, 1997).

A word of caution is necessary, however. Not all researchers have observed a protective effect of higher education on intelligence test performance. In one five-year longitudinal study, a sample of 69 eminent professors over age 70 were compared with 30 blue-collar workers of the same age as well as with young adult Ph.D. students (Christensen, Henderson, Griffiths, & Levings, 1997). Over the period of the study, it was the blue-collar workers, not the professors, who showed improvement on a measure of verbal reasoning. The professors also suffered relatively greater losses in tests of analogies and reading. In a related study by the same research team (Christensen, Korten, Jorm, & Henderson, 1997), changes over a slightly shorter period were compared in a much larger sample of adults aged 70 years and older. People with a college education and higher were less likely to show declines over the study period than those without a college education in tests involving speed and working memory. However, declines occurred even among the most highly educated group.

Turning to twin studies, which provide a classic method of contrasting genetic with environmental effects, a study of Swedish twin pairs from 41 to 91 years of age provided insight into the relative influence of these effects on levels of ability and changes in ability over time. Although heredity seemed to influence individual variations in ability levels, environmental factors appeared to influence the rate of change over time (Reynolds, Finkel, Gatz, & Pedersen, 2002). Similar findings were obtained in a study of Danish twins, studied using a cohort-sequential design and retested every two years for up to four testings. As with the Swedish study, overall intellectual ability appeared to be a function of genetics; but the rate of change over time was a function of environmental influences (McGue & Christensen, 2002).

Adding perhaps to the complexity of understanding the relationship between lifestyle factors and intellectual changes in adulthood are findings on personality and its relationship to intellectual functioning. Anxiety is one personality factor shown to have a negative relationship to intelligence test performance in that higher anxiety during testing is related to poorer performance on a variety of fluid and crystallized tasks (Wetherell, Reynolds, & Gatz, 2002). The personality variable that Schaie and colleagues found to be most strongly related to aging and intelligence is rigidity-flexibility (Schaie, Dutta, & Willis, 1991). This variable has three components as used in the SLS: psychomotor speed, motor cognitive flexibility, and attitudinal flexibility. In contrast to stereotyped views of older adults as more rigid than younger persons, the results from the SLS on this variable indicate that people are extremely stable in the extent to which they are flexible or rigid. Instead of older people becoming more rigid, it seems that younger and younger cohorts are becoming more flexible. The false appearance that older adults today have somehow changed, becoming more rigid, is simply a cohort effect. Nevertheless, those older adults who are more flexible in their attitudes and personality style appear to have an edge over their more rigid age peers (Schaie et al., 1991). These more flexible individuals are less likely to experience a decline in intellectual functioning. Perhaps like

those with a high tolerance for ambiguity, as discussed earlier, people who are more flexible are willing to play with ideas more and thus maintain greater interest in taking in new information throughout their lives and into old age.

A final personality factor, one that has particular relevance for the identity model, is **intellectual self-efficacy**, or the evaluation of one's own mental abilities. In the SLS, Schaie and his colleagues had a unique opportunity to compare actual changes in intelligence with perceived changes. The data permitted classification of the respondents into three groups: the *realists*, who accurately described their own declines, the *optimists*, who underestimated negative changes in their abilities, and the *pessimists*, who overestimated the losses they had actually experienced. In terms of the identity model, the realists would be said to be balanced, the optimists to be overassimilating (denying the existence of change), and the pessimists to be overaccommodating (becoming overly preoccupied with loss). Who actually declined the most? Surprisingly, it was the optimists. The so-called pessimists increased their scores, or at least showed no changes. Their use of identity accommodation seemed to protect them in some way from suffering losses, perhaps because they were more likely to take protective actions to maintain their intellectual prowess (such as by using memory aids). The optimists protected themselves not from decline but at least from the awareness of decline, which may have at least had beneficial effects on their self-esteem.

Intervention Studies on Adult Intelligence

Training Studies. The documentation of changes in intelligence over the years of adulthood may seem to have somewhat of a down side in that many of the changes are in a negative direction. Furthermore, as you have just seen, the people who are aware of just how much their mental abilities are aging may have somewhat of an advantage in terms of gains and losses. However, at the same time that Schaie and his coworkers attempt to provide an accurate picture of intelligence in adulthood, they just as actively seek methods of intervention. There is a long tradition within the developmental perspective advocated by Schaie, Baltes, and Willis of seeking ways to help preserve people's functioning as strongly as possible for as long as possible.

To put into perspective the findings on training studies, it is necessary to take a few steps backward and present the evolution of the underlying theoretical and philosophical perspective. A quote from the mid-1970s from an influential article by Baltes and Schaie (1976) states this perspective with eloquence: "Our central argument is one for plasticity of intelligence in adulthood and old age as evidenced by large interindividual differences, multidirectionality, multidimensionality, the joint significance of ontogenetic and historical change components, and emerging evidence on modifiability via intervention research" (p. 724). To put it more simply, Baltes and Schaie argued for the need to see intelligence as "plastic" or modifiable. This proposal is based on research we have already seen regarding the existence of individual differences, multiple dimensions of intelligence, and the interaction of aging and cohort effects. Although the research of the 1990s obviously was not available in the 1970s, the basic assumption that adult intelligence is responsive to interventions permeates the later research program of the SLS. According to Baltes and Schaie, if older adults could be taught ways to improve their intelligence test scores, this would serve as a major victory for the plasticity model.

In a handful of early studies conducted in the early 1970s at Penn State University, Baltes,

Willis, and their colleagues demonstrated that, given practice and training in test-taking strategies, older adults could improve their scores on tests of fluid intelligence (Hofland, Willis, & Baltes, 1980; Plemons, Willis, & Baltes, 1978; Willis, Blieszner, & Baltes, 1981). Current studies continue to confirm and expand these findings. For example, training older adults in the strategies used to solve inductive reasoning problems can lead to training gains, particularly for older adults with higher education (Saczynski, Willis, & Schaie, 2002).

Remember that fluid intelligence is theoretically intended to be a "pure" measure of ability, uninfluenced by educational experiences. The Penn State studies, part of the Adult Development and Enrichment Project (ADEPT), involved pre-test post-test designs, with the intervention consisting of five hours of group training in the requisite skills demanded by the fluid ability tests. Similar training methods, but with individual rather than group instruction, were used with members of the SLS sample. The longitudinal nature of the study made it possible to examine additional factors relevant to the effects of training over time. Even after a seven-year period in between training and testing, older adults who were part of the intervention study were able to maintain their advantage over their nontrained age peers (Schaie, 1994). Furthermore, these positive training effects were evident on people who had shown a previous decline in their intellectual functioning in the period prior to training. Booster sessions also proved helpful in maintaining gains in between training and testing. Similar positive effects of training have also been obtained in a German sample (Baltes, 1989; Baltes & Lindenberger, 1988). Furthermore, the gains shown in training studies generalize from one test of a particular ability to another test of that same ability involving different sets of items.

Most recently, the ADEPT findings were expanded in "ACTIVE," a large multisite intervention study described in Chapter 6. Training in the fluid ability of reasoning resulted in significant gains in about three-quarters of the sample. The fact that older adults can be trained in fluid abilities as well as other facets of cognition strongly supports the notion that there is plasticity in abilities well into later life.

THE PSYCHOLOGY OF WISDOM

In moving from training studies to broader conceptualizations of intelligence in adulthood, Baltes has suggested several principles that highlight and extend the notions of variability and modifiability. The principle of **reserve capacity** is that older adults possess abilities that are normally untapped and therefore unproven (Staudinger, Marsiske, & Baltes, 1995). Training studies allow adults the opportunity to express this reserve capacity by making it possible for them to reach their maximum potential. You can think of reserve capacity as your ability to perform to your highest level when you are highly motivated by a teacher, coach, competitor, or friend. You may not have even thought such a strong performance was possible until you completed it successfully.

Following on the principle of reserve capacity is that of **testing the limits**. This is the method developed by Baltes and his coworkers to determine just how much the performance of older adults can be increased through training (Baltes & Kliegl, 1992). By using this method, the amount of reserve capacity that is available can be quantified and compared to that of younger people. The method of testing the limits does not wipe out age differences, in that younger adults still have greater reserve capacity than do older people. Furthermore, when the method of testing the limits is used, not all

older adults are found to have measurable reserve capacities (Baltes, Dittman-Kohli, & Kliegl, 1986).

The concept of reserve capacity also leads to another principle developed by Baltes, that of **selective optimization with compensation** (Baltes & Baltes, 1990). According to this principle, explored earlier with regard to Sternberg's more recent theory, adults attempt to preserve and maximize the abilities that are of central importance and put less effort into maintaining those that are not. Given that resources become increasingly limited as people move into later adulthood, people make conscious decisions regarding how they will spend their time and

The character Dumbledore from "Harry Potter" provided an excellent example of a wise older adult.

effort. Through training, they may be given the incentive and necessary skills to bring an atrophied ability back up to a higher level, but if left to themselves, adults become increasingly likely to pick and choose their battles.

The principle of selective optimization with compensation implies that at some point in adulthood, individuals deliberately begin to reduce their efforts in one area in order to focus more on achieving success in another. It is likely that the areas they choose to focus on are those that are of greater importance and in which the chances of success are higher. Time and health limitations may also be a factor. If someone who has enjoyed weekend tennis games finds the activity too exerting or too hard on the knees, this person may decrease this involvement but compensate by spending more time on the golf course. Similar processes may operate in the area of intellectual functioning. The older individual may exert more effort toward solving word games and puzzles and spend less time on pastimes that involve spatial and speed skills, such as fast-moving computer games. If reading becomes too much of a chore due to fading eyesight, the individual may compensate by switching to books on tape.

We may add some ideas from the identity model into this analysis, specifically, concepts from the multiple threshold model. Individuals may make these choices of what to emphasize based on what aspects of functioning are central to their identities. Those who value the mind will compensate for changes in mental abilities by finding other intellectually demanding activities that they can still perform rather than switching their focus entirely. Furthermore, those who are able to make accommodations to age-related changes without becoming overwhelmed or preoccupied will be able to reestablish a sense of well-being after what may be an initially difficult period.

Ultimately, adults may switch their focus almost entirely away from intellectually challenging activities to activities that involve the successful completion of life tasks. Those of us still in school may find it both enjoyable and relevant to devote our energies to games and activities of the mind, but for many people, cognitive activities hold no compelling interest or attraction. You probably know many people who look forward to college graduation and have no plans to continue anything approaching an academic lifestyle once they are on their own. Baltes refers to this switch from cognitive efforts to involvement in personal enjoyment and relationships as the movement toward the **pragmatics of intelligence**, in which people apply their abilities to the solution of real-life problems. Such problems may involve how to help a troubled granddaughter whose parents have divorced, how to rescue an unsuccessful business venture, or whether to move to a warmer climate after retirement. These abilities become more important to adults than the **mechanics of intelligence**, which involve the cognitive operations of speed, working memory, and fluid intelligence.

Baltes believes that adults become increasingly capable of dealing with higher level conceptual issues that are not tested by conventional intelligence tests. Through his research on the pragmatics of intelligence, he has shown that cognitive development in adulthood involves growth in the ability to provide insight into life's many dilemmas, particularly those that are psychosocial or interpersonal. This is where the quality of wisdom emerges.

According to Baltes and his coworkers, **wisdom** is a form of expert knowledge in the pragmatics of life (see Fig. 7.9) (Staudinger, Smith, & Baltes, 1993). With increasing age in adulthood, through the process of selective optimization with compensation, individuals develop an increasing interest in and capacity to exercise their judgment. The insights that people gain as wisdom develops include awareness of the finitude of life and the role of culture in shaping people's lives and personalities (lifespan contextualism). They become less likely to judge others, and they have a greater appreciation for individual differences in values, life experiences, and beliefs (value relativism).

Another quality is one reminiscent of tolerance of ambiguity, a concept we encountered earlier. This is the ability to recognize and manage uncertainty as a fact of life. Finally, people who are wise also possess a rich base of factual or declarative knowledge and an extensive background of procedural knowledge (Baltes, Staudinger, Maercker, & Smith, 1995).

These conclusions about wisdom were arrived at through studies identifying the characteristics of people nominated by others to be wise and by observing the types of decisions made by these people in real-life dilemmas. Through such research, Baltes and his coworkers have observed that people who are

BIOPSYCHOSOCIAL PERSPECTIVE

EVERY ACTION YOU take involves mental activity, even if it is only the most minimal level of procedural memory such as brushing your teeth. Although most people do not expend a great deal of effort on wondering whether the ability to brush their teeth will change over the course of adulthood, many people do express concern over their memory. For many people in today's society, concern over loss of cognitive functions is synonymous with concern over the aging process in general. The stereotyped view of an older adult with failing mental abilities can cause those who are approaching their middle and later years to fear what the future has in store. According to identity process theory, adults who react to their own perhaps slight memory changes with overaccommodation (i.e., becoming unduly concerned and preoccupied) may be initiating a downward spiral that sets off premature cognitive loss. Their anxiety either interferes with the quality of their thought processes or causes them to give up prematurely and avoid taking preventative actions.

Cultural factors also play a role in this process. People with a strong educational background, which includes college or beyond, may be more highly invested in the life of the mind. Therefore, when they sense (whether correctly or not) that they are losing

this valued function, they are more likely to face the harmful outcomes of identity accommodation. In studies investigating the so-called protective function of education in preventing intellectual changes in middle and later adulthood, failure to find that the college-educated are spared from declines in functioning may reflect in part these identity processes. Apart from these inner dynamics, social factors may be seen as important in that they set the stage for the types of influences that will affect the development of their intellectual functions. People in cognitively more demanding occupations do have a greater chance on a daily basis to exercise their intellectual muscles.

We have moved in these past two chapters from attention to working memory and on into more complex thought processes. By the end of this chapter, we reached a point of focusing less on loss of certain basic functions (speed, resources) and more on gains of broader conceptual abilities. Some of the changes in thought processes identified as occurring in the 50s, 60s, and beyond, such as the ability to see the "big picture," will be reexamined at later points in the book. The productivity of older workers and the creativity among both normal and exceptional older adults will draw on these concepts of wisdom and the pragmatics of intelligence in later adulthood.

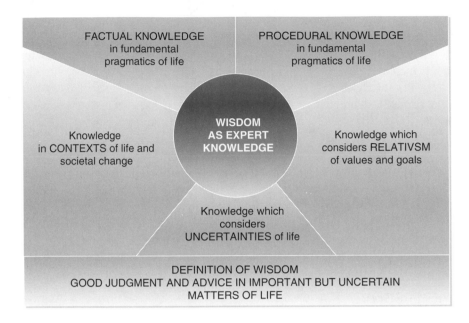

FIGURE 7.9
Model of Components
of Wisdom

Source: Baltes & Staudinger,
1993

"wise" are more likely to be found among the older adult population (Staudinger et al., 1993). However, age alone does not foster wisdom. The development of this mature form of intelligence is brought about through a set of favorable life influences, including a willingness to learn from experience, interest in the welfare of others, training, and mentoring by others. Simply clocking more hours on the planet is not sufficient; the individual must be able to take advantage of what life's lessons (and teachers) have to offer.

SUMMARY

1. The higher cognitive functions include language, problem-solving ability, and intelligence. Changes in memory contribute in part to age-related losses in language such as the ability to derive meaning from spoken or written passages, spell, and find words. As a result, older adults use simpler and less specific language. However, many language abilities are maintained, and older adults are able to use nonlanguage cues to help them derive meanings from language. The social aspects of language include the tendency of older adults to reminisce and tell stories, which can enhance relationships with other older persons but perhaps detract from interactions with the young. The way that younger persons speak to older adults can also be problematic if this involves **elderspeak**, which is patronizing and infantilizing speech directed at an older person. The communication predicament describes the negative effects on cognition and language when older persons are communicated to in this manner.

2. At the ADEPT lab, researchers have developed a model of problem solving in adulthood that incorporates the antecedents, problem structures, and outcomes of problems. Individual and sociocultural factors form the background for problem-solving situations. The way the problem is represented depends on knowledge of the problem

solver, characteristics of the task, and the demands and resources of the social and physical environment. The outcomes of problem-solving influence physical and psychological well-being. As individuals grow older and gain more problem-solving experience, they become more likely to use top-down processes, which leads them to be quicker but potentially less accurate in certain kinds of problems that require considering new information.

3. There are a number of theories of intelligence, but the majority of research on adult intelligence is based on the fluid-crystallized theory. Studies on the primary mental abilities support the theory's proposal that fluid (unlearned, nonverbal) abilities decrease gradually throughout adulthood. By contrast, the crystallized abilities that are acquired through education and training steadily increase through the 60s and show a decrease only after that point. Other conceptions of intelligence, including the theory of multiple intelligences and triarchic theory have not been tested yet on adults of varying ages. The most extensive study of adult intelligence is the Seattle Longitudinal Study (SLS) in which sequential methods have been applied to the Primary Mental Abilities (PMA) test. In addition to providing data on age patterns in intelligence test scores, this study has highlighted relationships with intelligence of health, personality, lifestyle, and sociocultural factors.

4. Intervention studies in which older adults are given training in the abilities tapped by intelligence test scores have yielded support for the notion of plasticity. Even five hours of training can result in improved scores across tests for as long as a seven-year period. Following from these training studies, researchers have proposed establishing the reserve capacity of older adults

not demonstrated in ordinary life by using a method known as testing the limits. According to the principle of selective optimization with compensation, older adults attempt to maximize the abilities that are important to them and do not seek opportunities to expand the abilities that are not of interest or relevance. Many older adults turn to the pragmatics of intelligence, or the practical use of knowledge, and away from the mechanics of intelligence, or the skills typically measured on tests of ability. The quality of wisdom in later life develops as individuals become more interested in developing their abilities in the pragmatics of life.

GLOSSARY

ADEPT (Adult Development and Enrichment Project): research program at Pennsylvania State University working on the ability of older adults to solve problems involved in maintaining an independent existence in a house or apartment.

Balance theory of wisdom: view of wisdom as the ability to balance the various components of intelligence outlined in the theory and apply them to problems involving the common good, or welfare of others.

Bottom-up approach: problem-solving strategy in which the individual collects as much data as possible before making a decision.

Communication predicament model: model in which the use of patronizing speech (elders-peak) constrains the older person from being able to participate fully in conversations with others.

Crystallized intelligence (G_c): the acquisition of specific skills and information acquired through familiarity with the language, knowledge, and conventions of one's culture.

Dialectical thinking: an interest in and appreciation for debate, arguments, and counter-arguments.

Elderspeak: a simplified speech pattern directed at older adults who presumably are unable to understand adult language.

Emotional intelligence: the ability to understand and regulate one's emotions.

Fluid intelligence (G_f): the individual's innate abilities to carry out higher-level cognitive operations involving the integration, analysis, and synthesis of new information.

Formal operations: the ability of adolescents and adults to use logic and abstract symbols in arriving at solutions to complex problems.

General factor (g): the ability to infer and apply relationships on the basis of experience.

Intellectual self-efficacy: the evaluation of one's own mental abilities.

Intelligence: the quality of the individual's mental abilities.

Mechanics of intelligence: cognitive operations of speed, working memory, and fluid intelligence.

Post-formal operations: proposed stage following formal operations referring to the way that adults structure their thinking over and beyond that of the adolescent.

Pragmatics of intelligence: application of a person's abilities to the solution of real-life problems.

Primary mental abilities: factors in intelligence proposed by Thurstone incorporating verbal meaning, word fluency, number, spatial relations, memory, perceptual speed, and general reasoning.

Primary Mental Abilities (PMA) test: test of five primary mental abilities that is the basis for the Seattle Longitudinal Study data.

Problem solving: cognitive process in which the individual assesses the current state of a situation, decides on what is the desired end-state, and finds ways of transforming the current into the desired state.

Reserve capacity: additional abilities possessed by older adults that are normally untapped.

Seattle Longitudinal Study (SLS): major repository of data on intelligence in adulthood.

Secondary mental abilities: the broad constructs that underlie specific abilities.

Selective optimization with compensation: the principle that adults attempt to preserve and maximize the abilities that are of central importance and put less effort into maintaining those that are not.

Successful intelligence: the ability to achieve success in life according to one's personal standards and in the framework of one's socio-cultural context.

Testing the limits: method developed by Baltes and his coworkers to determine how much the performance of older adults can be increased through training.

Theory of multiple intelligences: proposal that there are eight independent categories of intelligence, each of which can contribute to an individual's ability to adapt to the world.

Top-down approach: problem-solving strategy in which the individual uses what are called "heuristics" or rules-of-thumb to approach a problem.

Triarchic theory of intelligence: proposal that there are three aspects to intelligence: componential, experiential, and contextual.

Wechsler Adult Intelligence Scale: test of intelligence with Verbal and Performance scales.

Wisdom: as defined by Baltes, a form of expert knowledge in the pragmatics of life.

Chapter Eight

Personality and Patterns of Coping

"He who is of a calm and happy nature will hardly feel the pressure of age, but to him who is of an opposite disposition, youth and age are equally a burden."

Plato,
427–346 B.C.

The term *personality* has a variety of meanings, ranging from its usage in everyday language to its characterizations in academic psychology. As used in common speech, **personality** refers to an unobservable quality present within the individual that is thought to be responsible for that individual's observable behavior. Someone pays you a compliment because that person is "nice," or "generous," or "friendly." Although within psychology the term has a number of technical definitions, it still is intended to convey the notion that it is an unobservable influence on outward behavior. As was true for intelligence, this somewhat vague and elusive term has a number of alternative meanings, but all the meanings share this emphasis on personality as a force or influence on the individual's actions.

Discussions of personality in adulthood and later life typically revolve around a structure based on traditional theories of personality. Although these theories may be traced back to the time of Hippocrates, who developed the notion that there were four basic temperaments, contemporary approaches generally begin with a discussion of Sigmund Freud's psychodynamic theory.

THE PSYCHODYNAMIC PERSPECTIVE

Freud is credited with having "discovered" the unconscious mind. Although this claim is somewhat of an exaggeration, it is true that Freud was the first to develop a comprehensive theory that incorporated multiple components of personality into an integrated whole. Many current theories of adult development and personality are based on the psychodynamic perspective even if they do not explicitly consider the role of unconscious forces in behavior. However, cognitive processes are increasingly being incorporated into the more traditional focus of psychodynamic approaches.

Although he left a rich body of work that later theorists would subsequently revise and reshape, unfortunately Freud gave relatively little attention to the years of adulthood and old age. According to Freud, the major work of personality development is completed by the age of 5 years, with some additional touches added in adolescence. Furthermore, Freud believed that therapy could not be of much value to individuals over the age of 50, whose personalities were so rigidly set that they could not be radically altered.

Much of personality, Freud theorized, was hidden in the unconscious, with the conscious mind being simply the tip of a large iceberg. The structure in personality most accessible to conscious awareness is the **ego**, which performs the rational, executive functions of mind and organizes the individual's activities so that important goals can be attained. **Defense mechanisms** are intended to protect the conscious mind from knowing the improper urges of the unconscious mind, which include a wide range of socially unacceptable behaviors. Freud believed that unconscious urges drive us not only toward the expression of love and sexuality (*libido*), but also to the destruction of oneself and others. He called this unconscious drive *thanatos*, the death instinct.

The ultimate goal of development, according to Freud, is the ability to "love and work" without experiencing undue conflict. People can never be entirely free from improper desires. However, they can develop defense mechanisms that will allow them to function with a minimum of anxiety. (Some anxiety is, according to Freud, inevitable.) Maturity and healthy use of defense mechanisms are less likely to be found in people who fail to resolve their childhood conflicts. They may spend a large proportion of their adult years involved in unsuccessful efforts to rid themselves of inappropriate sexual attachments to parents or

parent figures. Similarly, people who are not able to regulate their aggressive urges may find themselves ridden with guilt or anxiety about the harm that they have caused or might cause to others.

Ego Psychology

For many psychoanalysts, the most interesting and important component of personality structure is the ego. As mentioned earlier, Freud himself regarded the ego as not having an independent role in personality but merely as serving the desires of the id. However, to other theorists, the ego is equivalent to the conscious mind, performing the functions of integration, analysis, and synthesis of thought. The term **ego psychology** is used to describe the view that the ego plays a central role in actively directing behavior.

Erikson's Ego Development Theory. In Chapter 2, we reviewed the major principles of Erikson's theory of psychosocial development. To recapitulate briefly, the theory proposes that there are eight crisis stages in the maturation of the ego. Each stage represents a point of maximum vulnerability to biological, psychological, and social forces operating on the individual at that particular point in the life span. The outcome of each crisis stage may either be favorable (as in the attainment of identity) or unfavorable (as in the failure to achieve a coherent identity). The resolution of earlier stages forms the basis for resolution of later stages, according to Erikson, and the epigenetic principle lays out the ground plan for the unfolding of psychosocial crises throughout life. Although certain ages are associated with certain stages, earlier issues may arise at a later point in life, and the later stages may move to the forefront in earlier periods if conditions develop that stimulate the individual to confront that issue.

"What do you think?" | 8-1

What factors other than age could account for increases in identity and intimacy from college to early adulthood?

Loevinger's Ego Development Theory. Closely related to Erikson's notion of psychosocial development is that of Jane Loevinger (1976), whose view of the ego incorporates cognition and morality as well as the traditional notion of ego or the self. In some ways, Loevinger's theory can be regarded as a theory that describes development of the old-fashioned notion of "character." Loevinger defines the ego as the structure within personality that attempts to synthesize, master, and interpret experiences. Incorporated into the ego is the individual's ability to regulate impulses, relate to others,

achieve self-understanding, and think about events in the outside world. Its development proceeds in a series of stages that move from lower to higher levels along each of these dimensions. The stages of ego development corresponding to development in adolescence and adulthood according to Loevinger are summarized briefly in Table 8-1.

Individuals in the Conformist stage have only a very basic understanding of self, others, and the reasons for following society's rules. Their views of right and wrong are fairly simple, and they have difficulty conceptualizing the causes for the behaviors and feelings of others. The **Conscientious-Conformist stage** (which is a transitional phase and therefore technically a "level") is the one in which most adults function, according to Loevinger. During this period, individuals begin to gain a conscience, or internal set of rules of right and wrong, and

TABLE 8-1
Stages of Ego Development in Loevinger's Theory

Stage	Description
Conformist Stage	Obeys rules to be accepted by the group and to avoid disapproval. Simple view of emotions. Prone to stereotyping others. Concerned about appearances and reputation.
Conscientious-Conformist Level	The most frequently observed level among adults. Transition between conformist and conscientious stages. Increase in self-awareness of an inner life. Able to see alternatives and exceptions to rules.
Conscientious Stage	Major elements of adult conscience, including long-term personal goals and ideals, sense of responsibility, and internalization of rules. May choose to break the law if it violates personal standards. Complex inner life and ability to understand emotions of self and others.
Individualistic Level	Greater sense of individuality and ability to be emotionally dependent on others. Ability to tolerate uncertainty and contradiction.
Autonomous Stage	Ability to think about and cope with inner conflict, such as conflict between personal needs and duties to others. Sees reality as complex and multidimensional. Recognizes the needs of others for autonomy but cherishes personal ties. Holds to broad, abstract, social ideas.
Integrated Stage	Rarely found in adults. Similar to autonomous stage but in addition has a strong sense of identity and ability to achieve complete expression of the true, inner self.

Source: Loevinger, 1976.

start to gain self-awareness as well as understanding the needs and thoughts of other people. The Conscientious stage involves the development of a true conscience, which is based on a solid appreciation of society's rules and the reasons for those rules. People in the Conscientious stage are also able to comprehend their own emotions and the emotional needs of others. The next stage, the Individualistic, is also a "level" or transition, in which the individual begins to develop an internal set of standards and guidelines for the self. Although still operating in terms of society's standards, the individual is moving toward a point of respecting individuality. In the Autonomous stage, inner standards have become even more clearly articulated. Various personality attributes begin to emerge as the individual's cognitive abilities allow for the recognition of complex causes of the behavior of self and others. Tolerance for ambiguity, an important factor that emerged in Chapter 7 on research on problem solving, intelligence, and wisdom, also becomes more fully developed in people who are in the Autonomous stage. Finally, the Integrated stage, which is reached by relatively few people, is one in which the individual has a clear sense of self, is able to recognize inner conflicts, and highly values individuality. In this stage, the individual is able to achieve the expression of the true "inner self."

Vaillant's Ego Development Theory. A focus on defense mechanisms characterizes the ego development theory proposed by George Vaillant. Like Loevinger, Vaillant considers the ego to be equivalent to the mind's function of integrating and interpreting "inner" (i.e., feelings) and "outer" (i.e., events and experiences) reality. However, Vaillant is more traditionally psychodynamic in that he gives less attention than Loevinger does to the notion of ego as character. As is true for Erikson, Vaillant believes that the ego passes through stages in the years of adulthood, but for Vaillant, these stages are slightly different from those proposed by Erikson.

Vaillant's theory gives particular emphasis to the mechanisms of defense used by the ego as these develop in adulthood (Vaillant, 2000). As in Freudian theory, defense mechanisms are seen by Vaillant as involuntary and unconscious modes of protecting the individual from knowledge about the self and world that would be harmful to one's sense of psychological well-being. The ego serves to interpret, organize, and synthesize the individual's daily experiences. In essence, the ego is the mind. The defense mechanisms are a major function carried out by the ego in its attempts to make sense of the adult's world and experiences. Freud believed that through therapy, individuals would eventually give up their use of defense mechanisms, as they became more aware of their own unconscious impulses. However, for Vaillant, defense mechanisms are present throughout life, even though their form may change. The ego is constantly altering the way that adults perceive various sources of conflict, including their own inner feelings, the actions and feelings of others, and events in the outside world. The use of defense mechanisms allows the individual to reduce the experience of conflict and restore a sense of psychological equilibrium. The result is that the individual feels better, but this may occur at the cost of having altered the perception of reality in some important way. For example, a woman who resents her mother's interference in her life would find it difficult to admit to these negative feelings. Instead of openly expressing her anger, she may distort her view of her mother so that she idealizes her, or she may simply ignore those negative feelings entirely.

Unlike Freud, who proposed that personality is invariant after childhood, Vaillant regards the ego defense mechanisms as evolving throughout the adult years. He regards this evolution as occurring along a dimension of increasing adaptiveness. A maladaptive defense is one that facilitates the individual's adjustment but involves costs in terms of personal happiness and the reactions of other people to the individual. An adaptive defense allows the individual to protect the self from unfavorable self-knowledge or harmful impulses and also helps facilitate the individual's acceptance by others. The listing of defense mechanisms in Table 8-2 provides some concrete examples of how they differ in adaptiveness. The psychotic or immature defense mechanisms lead to problems in daily living for the individual, and the mature defense mechanisms facilitate the individual's adjustment. For example, an individual using the immature defense mechanism of acting out might react to a parking ticket by kicking in the car's bumper. This action may temporarily relieve the individual's anger, but it causes unnecessary physical damage and makes the individual appear to others to be out of control.

Use of a mature defense mechanism such as humor would help the individual feel better and avoid the social and practical cost of a rash action.

Vaillant's second theoretical contribution to ego psychology as applied to adult development is the addition of two stages to Erikson's framework of eight psychosocial crisis stages. According to Vaillant, Identity versus Identity Diffusion is the last psychosocial crisis of childhood, when the individual must establish an identity separate from the family unit. Adulthood is marked by entry into the Intimacy versus Isolation stage. Vaillant regarded the three crucial developmental tasks of adulthood to be the establishment of an intimate relationship, commitment to a career, and the passing of one's wisdom and knowledge on to the next generation. Passage through these stages is the equivalent of completion of developmental tasks. As was suggested earlier, the achievement of a sense of identity is the final piece of development of the "ego." Everything that follows is a function of the individual's identity, as it

TABLE 8-2
Categories of Defenses Identified by Vaillant

Category	Examples
Psychotic	*Delusional projection*—attributing one's own bizarre ideas and feelings to others *Denial*—disclaiming the existence of a feeling, action, or event *Distortion*—significantly exaggerating and altering the reality of feelings and events
Immature	*Projection*—attributing unacceptable ideas and feelings to others *Hypochondriasis*—expressing psychological conflict as exaggerated physical complaints *Acting out*—engaging in destructive behavior that expresses inner conflicts
Neurotic	*Displacement*—transferring unacceptable feelings from the true to a safer object *Repression*—forgetting about a troubling feeling or event *Reaction formation*—expressing the opposite of one's true feelings
Mature	*Altruism*—turning unacceptable feelings into behavior that is helpful to others *Sublimation*—expressing unacceptable feelings in productive activity *Humor*—being able to laugh at an unpleasant or disturbing feeling or situation

Source: Vaillant, 1993.

becomes expressed in the realms of relationships, occupation, and family or the giving of self to the world at large.

To Erikson's scheme of development in adulthood, Vaillant added a Stage 6A, which he labeled Career Consolidation versus Self-Absorption. In this stage, the individual must develop identification with a career (not a job) that is based on the intrinsic features of the work involved in this career. As will be discussed in Chapter 10, many who study occupational commitments regard as more central to identity a job that one enjoys for the sake of the work itself and not the rewards it brings. Similarly, for Vaillant, the development of the ego requires that the individual can become completely immersed in a career on the basis of such intrinsic motivation. The second stage added by Vaillant is Stage 7A, which he called Keeper of the Meaning versus Rigidity. In addition to generativity as conceived by Erikson—the leaving of something behind for future generations—the healthy development of the ego involves a sense of caring and commitment to one's entire community or culture. The "Keeper of the Meaning" is a person who becomes the guardian for a large group or the preserver of a culture. A concrete

example of a person who performs the role of "keeper" is an adult who moves from being an athletic coach of a particular team of children in the town softball league to becoming an administrator of the athletic programs in the entire town. This person is now concerned with the quality of the program as a whole and not just the performance of one team.

The development of ego defenses from less to more maturity occurs in parallel with the adult's movement through the psychosocial stages. The individual is becoming better able to manage and cope with the disappointments, frustrations, and complexities of life through the development of increasingly mature ego defenses. At the same time, the individual gains increasing richness and depth from experiences related to close relationships, work, and community.

Jungian Theory. Another psychodynamic theory with implications for adult development is that of Carl Gustav Jung, who proposed that individuals engage in continuous change throughout adulthood and further, and that maturity is possible only well into the years of midlife. According to Jung, the psyche has four functions: thinking, feeling, sensing, and

A Tibetan Mandala Sand Painting construction from Drepung Loseling Monastery, shown shortly before being destroyed as part of a healing process at Woodward Park in Fresno, California. The Mandala took four days to complete.

intuiting. Thinking is the analytic function, feeling the emotional, sensing the sensual, and intuiting is most easily thought of as responsible for "hunches" or "gut feelings." One function is predominant in young adulthood, and as people reach middle adulthood, they achieve a greater balance so that all four functions become equally represented in the psyche. For example, a young person trained in the sciences may be highly analytical and technical in

BIOPSYCHOSOCIAL PERSPECTIVE

THE POSSIBLE EXISTENCE of a relationship between personality and health in adulthood is a topic of great interest in the fields of health psychology and behavioral medicine. Since the first intriguing data supporting such a relationship were first reported, investigators have sought to determine whether people with certain personality types are more susceptible to chronic or even fatal illnesses such as cardiovascular disease and cancer. Much of the interest in this topic has centered on the "Type A" behavior pattern, a collection of traits thought to increase a person's risk of developing cardiovascular disease (Friedman & Rosenman, 1974). People with Type A personalities are competitive, impatient, feel a strong sense of time urgency, and are highly achievement oriented. They also show unusually high degrees of hostility or anger directed toward others. It is not possible to determine whether the Type A behavior pattern is a cause or a result of whatever cardiovascular problems lead to heightened risk of heart disease. However, there appears to be a relationship between various components of the Type A behavior pattern and cardiovascular disease risk factors, such as high serum cholesterol (the low-density lipoproteins) and the experience of angina pain (Edwards & Baglioni, 1991). In addition, high levels of hostility, part of the Type A pattern, are thought to be independent predictors of mortality (Miller, Smith, Turner, Guijarro, & Hallet, 1996). Type A personality traits may also be part of a larger constellation of cardiovascular risk factors including smoking, body weight, leisure activities, and hormonal levels (Zmuda, Cauley, Kriska, Glynn, Gutai, et al., 1997).

Other data support the existence of a relationship between personality and health. In a study of members of the Terman sample whose mental health was assessed at midlife, the chance of dying over the following 40 years was higher for those who had shown the poorest adjustment at the time of their midlife testing (Martin, Friedman, Tucker, Schwartz, Criqui, Wingard, et al., 1995). However, the relationship between psychological adjustment and health may go even farther back than middle adulthood. Using the data obtained from the Terman sample at childhood, it was possible to determine that those children who were high in the personality trait of conscientiousness had lower death rates than those with low childhood conscientiousness. It was not simply that the conscientious individuals avoided high-risk activities, and therefore accidental death, or that they had better health habits. Instead, these highly conscientious individuals seemed better equipped to cope with life stress, build stable relationships with others, and have high "ego strength" or a "self-healing personality" (Friedman, Tucker, Schwartz, Martin, Tomlinson-Keasey, et al., 1995). Similarly, among women studied longitudinally from college to midlife, a personality trait labeled "Intellectual Efficiency" was positively related to changes in health throughout midlife. In these same studies, personality trait measures of hostility and anxiety were negatively related to health (Adams et al., 1998). Oddly enough, however, the trait of cheerfulness is negatively related to health outcomes, perhaps because people who are high on this trait also tend to be careless about their health (Martin, Friedman, Tucker, Tomlinson-Keasey, Criqui, et al., 2002).

Clearly, personality factors must be considered in a biopsychosocial model of development in adulthood and old age. Traits and behavior patterns that have their origins in inherited predispositions or through early life experiences influence the health of the individual through a variety of direct and indirect pathways.

approaching new situations. However, with increasing experience and maturity, this individual may come to recognize the value of making intuitive decisions. Perhaps this person is a weather forecaster who uses charts, computer projections, and other technical devices to base predictions. As this person spends more time on the job, however, it may become evident that some forecasts are best made without a lot of careful thought but based on "instinct." According to Jung, with greater maturity comes such a tendency to show balance among the psychic functions. Balance also comes with maturity, as in middle age, people become more comfortable acknowledging the aspects of their personalities that lie within the unconscious (Jung, 1968).

Balance between psychic functions and between the conscious and unconscious elements of personality was seen by Jung as the great accomplishment of middle adulthood. Jung used the term **individuation** to describe the psychic integration and potential for full self-expression that emerges during these years. Along with the proposal that humans have an inborn tendency to respond to certain "archetypal" or universal symbols, Jung suggested that there is a fascination in art with a picture depicting a circle within a square (called a mandala). Fine art and even the drawings of children and people from preliterate societies depict this symbol as a universal ideal. From Jung's perspective, the desire to draw a mandala represents the search in all humans for wholeness, integration, and fullest realization of the self.

Studies Based on Ego Psychology

Theories of ego psychology give primary attention to the ego as the organizer of experience. The main concern in studying development is to learn how aging influences the ego's ability to adapt to the conditions and constraints of the outside world and yet manage to achieve expression of the individual's personal needs and interests. Often, but not necessarily, the ego is equated with the self, as in Erikson's use of the term "ego identity" to indicate the individual's self-attribution of personal characteristics. Current studies based on ego psychology are focused on samples in the age range of early to middle adulthood. In large part, this is because interest in adult personality development did not emerge until the late 1960s and early 1970s, and it was then that the major investigations were initiated. These investigations, longitudinal in nature, form the core of knowledge about the ego's growth from the 20s to the 50s. Over the next decade, we can expect more findings to emerge that are pertinent to ego development in later adulthood.

The Rochester Study. The most extensive study based on Erikson's theory is the one conducted by this author and colleagues on a sample of undergraduates and alumni from the University of Rochester. This study began in 1966 when Constantinople (1969) administered a questionnaire measure of psychosocial development to a sample of over 300 students in the classes of 1965–1968. The original sample was followed up 11 years later in 1977 when a new sample of 300 undergraduates was added to allow for sequential analyses (Whitbourne & Waterman, 1979). In the second followup in 1988–1989, yet another undergraduate sample was added. Sequential comparisons could then be made among three cohorts of college students and two cohorts of adults in their early 30s. Longitudinal followup analyses were also made of adults from college up to age 43. Additional data were also collected on other measures of identity and life events at each of the followup testings (Whitbourne & van Manen, 1996; Whitbourne, Zuschlag, Elliot, & Waterman, 1992).

The heart of the findings regarding psychosocial development was the consistency of age changes across two cohorts in the two stages theorized to change the most in college and early adulthood: identity vs. identity diffusion and intimacy vs. isolation. These findings are shown in Figs. 8.1 and 8.2, where high scores represent more favorable psychosocial development. For both cohorts, there were comparable increases in positive scores on Identity versus Identity Diffusion and Intimacy versus Isolation. Identity scores were exactly comparable for Cohorts 1 and 2, but Intimacy scores were higher for Cohort 2. Nevertheless, the similarity of age-related increases supports Erikson's proposition that during these ages this psychosocial issue reaches ascendancy. Analysis of data from another measure given in 1988 to respondents from all three cohorts specifically intended to assess identity development showed convergent support for the notion of continued growth on this dimension during adulthood (Whitbourne & van Manen, 1996).

Psychosocial development scores also were found to be related to life events in a predictive manner. Psychosocial development scores from college were used to predict marital, family (number of children), and career status at the ages of 31 and 42 among the men and women in Cohort 1. The identity scores that these women attained at age 31 (but not in college) predicted their socioeconomic attainments by their early 40s as well as their identity scores at that same age. However, this relationship was in a direction opposite to that of prediction. Women with higher identity scores at age 31 were in *lower*, not higher status occupations at the age of 42. This was because women who were full-time homemakers received the lowest socioeconomic status scores. Women who had strong identities in their early 30s were more likely to remain in the home rather than invest their energies into their careers (Van Manen & Whitbourne, 1997).

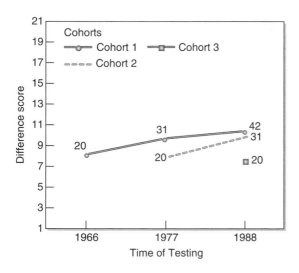

FIGURE 8.1

Identity versus Identity Diffusion Scores between College and Middle Adulthood

Source: Whitbourne et al., 1992.

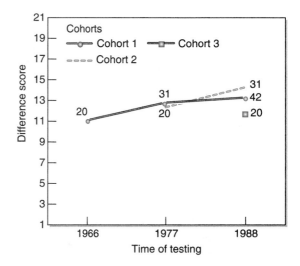

FIGURE 8.2

Intimacy versus Isolation Scores between College and Middle Adulthood

The Mills and Radcliffe Studies. The alumni of two private women's colleges who graduated in the late 1950s and early 1960s form the sample in a series of investigations of midlife personality development. The Mills study began with a sample of almost 150 women who represented two-thirds of the senior classes of 1958 and 1960. The original intention of the study was to investigate the personality characteristics and plans for the future of college women (Helson, 1967). The sample was followed up by mail with personality questionnaires and various life

Mills College women in 1964, a time when they were first tested by Ravenna Helson and her colleagues in what was to become a major longitudinal study of personality development in midlife.

event ratings when the women were, on average, 27, 43, and 52 years of age. The Radcliffe study, first followed up after college, consisted of between 100 and 150 women in the Class of 1964 who were studied at the ages of 18, 31, 37, 43, and 48 years. At each followup, the women were asked to complete standardized personality measures and to provide information about their life events up to that time.

In some reports from this study, data were also available from a sample initially tested when they were in college at the University of Michigan. The Michigan sample consisted of slightly over 100 women who were part of a group of 200 women from the Class of 1967 (Tangri, 1972) followed in 1970, 1981, and 1992. Another sample, consisting of 52 women, were followed from the time they were in medical school at the University of California at San Francisco at age 24 until they were 31 and 46 years old. Their data were combined with those of the Mills and Michigan samples in a study of women's health and personality at midlife (Adams, Cartwright, Ostrove, Stewart, & Wink, 1998). Finally, although the studies focused on women, in one investigation the partners of the Mills women were included in the data collection taking place at ages 27 and 52 years (Wink & Helson, 1993).

The first set of findings concerns overall changes in ego development scores in middle adulthood. These findings come from the data on the Mills sample, who were followed from ages 27 to 43 (Helson & Moane, 1987) and 43 to 52 (Helson & Wink, 1992). Although both studies presented evidence for considerable personality stability, there were increases on the variables of assurance, independence, and self-control, and decreases on a scale of femininity. Overall, these findings were taken to suggest increased personality integration and movement in middle adulthood to becoming a positive contributor to society.

Apart from these overall trends, which again should be thought of in terms of a backdrop of stability, there were individual differences in personality change patterns. The investigators linked these differences to variations in other personality attributes, specifically, level of ego development and identity. One of the questions investigated was whether individuals with higher levels of ego development (in terms of Loevinger's theory) would increase favorably over the course of the study. Several findings confirmed this pattern (Helson & Roberts, 1994; John, Pals, & Westenberg, 1998). Identity also seems to play a role in influencing personality change in women in midlife. Women higher in identity at age 43 were more likely to have achieved higher levels of generativity at age 48 (Vandewater, Ostrove, & Stewart, 1997). Similar findings were obtained in a later analysis in which identity at age 43 was seen to influence the effects of age 21 personality scores in predicting well-being at the age of 60 (Helson & Srivastava, 2001).

Another investigation of the relationship between personality and life patterns was the study of social clock projects and their effects on development (Helson & Moane, 1987). A **social clock project** is the path a woman takes in fulfilling her adult family and work roles. A "feminine social clock" is the traditional pathway of raising a family, and a "masculine occupational clock" is a career in which work comes ahead of family as a life goal. For the slightly less than half of the sample engaged in a social clock project, personality development moved in a more positive direction (Helson & Wink, 1992).

Studies of Defense Mechanisms and Coping.
Vaillant's (1993) Study of Adult Development, which investigated the use of defense mechanisms through middle adulthood, incorporated three very diverse samples. The first was the Harvard Grant Study sample, which was begun at the university's Health Services in 1938 by two physicians who had received a donation from the Grant Foundation to study "healthy" lives. The men in the study were therefore selected based on their excellent physical and psychological conditions. The second group was called the Core City sample, reflecting the fact that they were chosen based on their residence in the inner city. The third sample was composed of 40 women who were first tested when they were young as part of a study on gifted children and then interviewed again when they were in their late 70s.

As can be seen in Table 8-3, there were positive relationships within each of the three samples between maturity of defenses and various indices of adjustment. Subsequent analysis on the Core City men only provided further support for the advantages of mature defenses. Men who used the so-called defenses such as acting out were more likely to experience alcohol problems, unstable marriages, and antisocial behavior (Soldz & Vaillant, 1999). Supporting Vaillant's findings was a 24-year longitudinal study conducted by Cramer (2003) in which over 150 men and women were followed from early to middle adulthood. The use of immature defense mechanisms was related to less favorable scores on personality dimensions representing several facets of adjustment (NEO scores, discussed below).

Age differences in defense mechanisms and related coping processes were the focus of two major cross-sectional investigations (Diehl, Coyle, & Labouvie-Vief, 1996; Labouvie-Vief & Medler, 2002). The direction of these age differences generally was toward the ability of older adults to manage their emotions through the use of mature defense mechanisms that involved controlling negative emotions or trying to put the situation into perspective. In terms of coping, older adults similarly showed less of a

TABLE 8-3
Correlations Between Maturity of Defenses and Measures of Successful Adult Outcome

Variables	Terman Women (n=37)	Harvard Men (n=186)	Core City Men (n=307)
Life satisfaction, age 60–65	.44	.35	n.a.
Mental health rating	.64	.57	.77
Job success, age 47	.53	.34	.45
Marital stability, age 47	.31	.37	.33
Job enjoyment, age 47	.51	.42	.39
% of life employed	.37	n.a.	.39

Source: Vaillant, 1993.

tendency to react in self-destructive or emotional ways. They were more likely to attempt to understand the situation and figure out a way around it, both through problem-focused coping and use of other strategies such as suppressing their negative feelings or channeling those feelings into productive activities. Younger people, including adolescents and young adults, were more likely to react to psychologically demanding situations by acting out against others, projecting their anger onto others, or regressing to more primitive forms of behavior. Consistent with these findings, a longitudinal study of over 2800 adults studied from 1971 to 1994 revealed that aging was associated with a decrease in negative affect (Charles, Reynolds, & Gatz, 2001).

> ## "What do you think?"   8-2
>
> Do you think people's personalities become more "mature" as they get older?

Consistent gender differences have also emerged in studies of defense mechanisms and coping (Diehl et al., 1996; Labouvie-Vief & Medler, 2002). Regardless of age, women were

more likely to avoid unpleasant or stressful situations, to blame themselves when things went wrong, and to seek the support of others. Men were more likely to externalize their feelings and to use reaction formation.

THE TRAIT PERSPECTIVE

When people think of describing someone's personality, they generally begin by coming up with a list of a characteristics or qualities that seem to fit the individual's observable behavior. These characteristics are typically adjectives such as "generous," or "outgoing," or perhaps, "quiet" and "unfriendly." Within trait theories of personality, such adjectives capture the essence of the individual's psychological makeup. The fact that people use these descriptions in everyday life to describe themselves and others agrees with the basic principle of trait theory, namely, that personality is equivalent to a set of stable characteristic attributes.

A **trait**, then, is a stable, enduring attribute that characterizes one element of an individual's personality. The main assumption of trait theories of personality is that the organization of these specific personal dispositions guides behavior. Trait theory is also increasingly coming to be viewed in terms of genetic or constitutional theories of personality. According to these views, there is a constitutional basis for personality that endures throughout life and that is at least partially inherited (Bouchard, 1997; Eaves, Martin, Heath, Schieken, Meyer, et al., 1997).

Assess Yourself

Extraversion-Introversion Test
The (E) or (I) indicates how each item would be scored.

1. I think strangers find me much more approachable than most people. (E)

2. When dealing with people I don't know very well, I feel I am extremely reserved. (I)

3. Small-talk is something I truly enjoy. (E)

4. When I am stuck with someone I don't know in a situation that requires conversation, I feel very uncomfortable. (I)

5. Given a choice, I would prefer to get acquainted with a lot of people without getting involved too intimately. (E)

6. For me, a friend is a person with whom I had a nice conversation in the past. (E)

7. If I had to choose one at the expense of another, I would prefer one or two very intimate friends for life. (E)

8. Alone in a company of people I don't know very well, I am almost always the one who initiates conversation, whatever the circumstances. (E)

9. A new kind of social interaction almost always taxes my nerves/energy. (I)

10. When the phone rings and I am not alone (at home, at work, etc.), I almost always run to get it first. (E)

11. When I am about to make a phone call to someone I don't know very well, I never prepare what I will say. (E)

12. At parties, I never get bored. (E)

13. At parties, I almost always leave as soon as I can without offending the host. (I)

14. At parties, I almost always interact with a few people whom I know. (I)

15. People like myself are, in general, very easy to get to know. (E)

16. When I have some free time, I almost always like to do something with others (go out, visit, call, chat on-line, etc.). (E)

17. When I have a tip or trick which might be useful to others in a given situation, I almost always share it. (E)

18. Other things being equal, I am almost always most efficient when I work alone. (I)

19. Other things being equal, I almost always prefer working in a team. (E)

20. In my environment, there is no one whom I like or dislike. (I)

21. In general, I feel close to people who seem to be very sociable and am usually surrounded by people. (E)

22. When I am alone, I feel very comfortable. (I)

23. When I am alone, I almost always find something interesting to do and never get bored. (I)

24. Given the choice, I would always prefer to be around an intimate friend than someone popular. (I)

25. I would be willing to have a decent and lengthy conversation with almost anybody, including strangers. (E)

26. When someone tells me a story, I am always most interested in knowing who was involved and what happened. (E)

27. When something happens in a social group which I am part of, I am the first one to know. (E)

The Five Factor Model

The predominant trait theory in the field of adult development is based on Costa and McCrae's proposal that there are five major dimensions to personality in adulthood. The **Five Factor Model** (also called the "Big Five") is a theory intended to capture all the essential characteristics of personality described in earlier trait theories. The five personality traits in the Five Factor Model are neuroticism, extraversion, openness to experience, agreeableness, and conscientiousness. Definitions of these terms are shown in Table 8-4. Each of the five traits incorporates six "facets" or subdimensions that as a whole comprise the factor. For example, openness to experience includes openness to fantasy, aesthetics (beauty), feelings, actions, and new ideas. A complete characterization of an individual on the five factors involves providing scores or ratings on the subdimensions.

The chief measure used to assess an individual's personality according to the Five Factor Model is the **NEO Personality Inventory—Revised (NEO-PI-R)**; (Costa & McCrae, 1992). The "NEO" stands for the original three factors in the model, which are neuroticism, extraversion, and openness. Data from the NEO-PI-R are reported in terms of both self-ratings and the ratings by others of the individual. The scores can then be compared to determine whether respondents agree in their self-ratings with the assessments of others. Comparisons can also be made of scores over time in both self- and other ratings.

TABLE 8-4
Five Factor Model

Trait Name	Description	Facets
Neuroticism	Tendency to experience psychological distress, overreactiveness, and instability	Anxiety Hostility Depression Self-consciousness Impulsiveness Vulnerability
Extraversion	Preference for social interaction and lively activity	Warmth Gregariousness Assertiveness Activity Excitement seeking Positive emotions
Openness to experience	Receptiveness to new ideas, approaches, and experiences	Fantasy Aesthetics Feelings Actions Ideas Values
Agreeableness	Selfless concern for others, trust, and generosity	Trust Straightforwardness Altruism Compliance Modesty Tender-mindedness
Conscientiousness	Organization, ambitiousness, and self-discipline	Competence Order Dutifulness Achievement striving Self-discipline Deliberation

Source: Adapted from Costa & McCrae, 1992.

Trait theories regard personality as an entity that reflects constitutional or innate predispositions (McCrae, 2002). According to the Five Factor Model, humans are programmed by these five particular dispositions to be, for example, sociable, warm, intellectually curious, and concerned about others. Supporting the Five Factor Model is an increasing body of evidence suggesting that there are genetic contributions to these particular dispositional characteristics (Bouchard & Loehlin, 2001).

The notion that personality affects the course of an individual's life is an important component of the Five Factor Model (McCrae & Costa, 2003). Intuitively, many people believe that personality development in adulthood is affected by the course of life events. People become cynical after having been betrayed or are less likely to seek out exciting adventures after having become injured in pursuit of such a pastime. However, according to trait theory, experiences rarely cause personality changes. Instead, the shape of people's lives is strongly influenced by the nature of their personalities. Cynical people may be more likely to be betrayed because they themselves are less trusting in the first place. Adventurous people are more likely to place themselves in situations where they are likely to be injured because they are more open to engaging in risk-taking behavior. This principle of trait theory is analogous to the notion of niche-picking described in Chapter 2. People choose situations as a function of their personalities. Once in those

BEHIND THE RESEARCH

PAUL T. COSTA, JR.
CHIEF, LABORATORY OF PERSONALITY & COGNITION, GERONTOLOGY RESEARCH CENTER, NATIONAL INSTITUTE OF AGING

What is most exciting to you about research in this field?
What I find most exciting about the research in the field of personality is the convergence of results, findings, and conceptualizations. It is most gratifying to me, having come from a background in aging and developmental psychology, to see the tremendous impact that longitudinal studies of personality structure have made on the field of personality psychology. It's fair to say that the longitudinal findings played a significant role in the reinvigoration of the whole field of personality. Other exciting aspects are the application of the Five-Factor Model, and our instrument to measure it, the Revised NEO Personality Inventory, being used in a wide spectrum of topics and areas that are too numerous to mention even briefly. To single out just a few that are of personal salience, the cross-cultural and younger developmental age groups are being included in research designs. Also, the search for genetic bases of the facets of the NEO PI-R keeps my engines revved up.

What do you see as major challenges?
Among the major challenges are to explicate or understand how the Five Factor Model as a multivariate trait model articulates with other levels of personality theorizing. For example, Dan McAdams proposes that there are three levels of analysis (of which traits, personal projects, and goals, are at level 2, and identity and life narratives, are at level 3). McCrae and I have begun to articulate a Five Factor Theory of the Person, and the fuller development of that model is a major challenge as I see it.

Where do you see this field headed in the next decade?
In the next decade, I see the field increasingly spreading out to make linkages with other social psychological, applied, and clinical approaches as well as with neurobiological and even molecular genetic levels. A hope, not too unrealistic I trust, is that many of the artificial divisions and barriers that have existed to block a kind of cross-boundary research and theorizing will fade from the scene. In its place will be a truly multidisciplinary and interdisciplinary search for understanding people of all ages and cultures.

situations, people are subject to the force of the events as they unfold.

Another crucial point regarding the Five Factor Model is that it does not necessarily imply that identity remains static throughout the adult years. Personality traits may remain stable, but the individual's awareness of these traits and ability to develop more adaptive behaviors accordingly may shift over time. For example, a parent who is highly conscientious, to the point of perhaps being overly self-disciplined and perfectionistic, may experience conflict with adolescent children who demand greater leniency. The parent may become acutely aware, perhaps for the first time ever, that this conscientiousness is causing trouble. Although the person may not become any less perfectionistic, this new awareness may lead to greater self-understanding and perhaps an attempt to be more sympathetic and patient when teenage children fail to meet the parent's high (and perhaps rigid) standards.

Research Based on the Five Factor Model

The Five Factor Model is an empirically based theory, developed and refined through continued testing of new samples (McCrae, 2002). Beginning in the late 1970s, large data sets on hundreds of people became available involving measures that preceded the NEO-PI-R. These included longitudinal studies conducted at Duke University (Siegler, George, & Okun, 1979), the National Institute of Aging (Baltimore Longitudinal Study) (Douglas & Arenberg, 1978), and the Veterans Administration in Boston (Normative Aging Study) (Costa & McCrae, 1978). Data from Vaillant's study of the development of Harvard undergraduates were also reanalyzed using the NEO framework (Soldz & Vaillant, 1999). The largest data set consisted of a sample of over 10,000 adults

ranging from 35 to 85 years old tested in the National Health and Nutrition Examination Survey I Follow-up Study (NHANES) (Costa & McCrae, 1986).

> **"What do you think?"**   8-3
>
> Is it depressing to think that personality is fixed so early in adulthood? What would you like to change about yourself and do you think you'll be able to do so?

Study after study contains stability (correlational) statistics that are in the neighborhood of .60, .70, and .80 (out of a range from −1.00 to +1.00). Table 8-5 provides a summary of stability coefficients reported for different longitudinal periods on each of the five factors of the model (McCrae & Costa, 2003). The average stability shown in this table is in the .70 range. These figures are consistent with the stability coefficients reported in other studies using trait-based measures (Roberts & DelVecchio, 2000). In line with the high stability coefficients shown for the NEO-PI-R scales, the cross-sectional data from the 30s to the 80s show minimal age differences. Scores on the Neuroticism, Extraversion, and Openness Scales from the NHANES study by decade are shown in Fig. 8.3. Although there were some small differences that reached statistical significance, essentially the curves are flat.

More recent evidence from international studies adds further weight to the already hefty support for stability of adult personality traits (McCrae, Costa, de Lima, Simoes, Ostendorf, et al., 1999). Cross-sectional samples ranging in age from 18 to 84 were obtained from Germany ($n = 3442$), Italy ($n = 690$), Portugal ($n = 1880$), Croatia ($n = 702$), and Korea ($n = 649$). Comparisons were made between late adolescents (18–21) and young (20–29), middle-aged (30–49), and older (50+) adults. The observed differences were consistent with U.S. data in showing slightly but significantly higher scores for the younger age groups on Neuroticism, Extraversion, and Openness, and lower scores on Agreeableness and Conscientiousness. Given the cross-sectional findings appearing in these cross-national samples, which differ vastly in their exposure to cultural influences, a slight reworking of the general theory of stability seemed necessary. In fact, very slow maturational processes may occur after the age of 30, when adults gain in none other than the quality of "psychosocial maturity." These findings fit with observations of shifts in personality traits using the California Personality Inventory on samples of adults tested from their 20s to their mid-70s (Helson, Jones, & Kwan, 2002).

Putting these most recent trait findings together with studies on ego development, we may make the argument that adults do in fact "mellow out" as they grow older. Even though individual differences may remain strong, as a group, older adults become less emotionally volatile and better able to get along with others and to accept responsibility for their actions. Or, as we may also wonder, the volatile ones die younger and only the calm ones remain (McCrae & Costa, 1990).

FIGURE 8.3

Cross-sectional Data from the NHANES-I Study

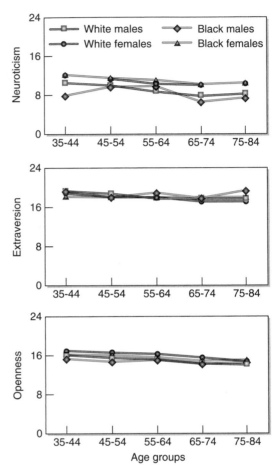

Source: McCrae & Costa, 1990.

TABLE 8-5

Stability of Five Factor Scores

NEO-PI-R Scale	12 Year	10 Year	6 Year	3 Year[a]
Neuroticism	.68–.74	.69	.83	
Extraversion	.75–.80	.84	.82	
Openness	.71		.83	
Agreeableness	.77			.63
Conscientiousness	.71			.79

Source: Adapted from McCrae & Costa, 1990.
[a]3-year data only available for Agreeableness and Conscientiousness.

THE COGNITIVE PERSPECTIVE AND COPING

Cognitive theories emphasize the individual's desire to predict and control experiences as a driving force within personality. Emerging from the cognitive perspective are the **cognitive self theories**, which propose that individuals view the events in their lives from the standpoint of the relevance of these events to the self. These theories also place emphasis on *coping*, or the mechanisms that people use to manage stress.

Because certain tendencies are inherent in the makeup of the self, events may not always be viewed from a realistic perspective. One of these tendencies of the self is to attempt to maintain consistency (Baumeister, 1996, 1997); people prefer to see themselves as stable and predictable. Another basic tendency is for people to view their abilities and personal qualities in a positive light (Baumeister, Bratslavsky, Finkenauer, & Vohs, 2001).

Possible Selves Theory

A variation of the cognitive perspective is the **possible selves** model of Markus and Nurius (1986), which, proposes that the individual's view of the self, or self-schema, guides the choice and pursuit of future endeavors. Possible selves are theorized to serve as psychological resources that can both motivate the individual toward future behavior and serve as a defense of the self in the present. They continue to shift throughout adulthood, and individuals can continue to be future-oriented and hopeful of change until well into later life (Smith & Freund, 2002). A particular variant of the possible self focuses on health (Hooker & Kaus, 1994) and appears to be particularly important for older adults (Frazier, Johnson, Gonzalez, & Kafka, 2002).

When writing about personal experiences in a diary, people may create a "life story" consistent with their current identities.

Individuals are motivated to strive to achieve a hoped-for possible self and will attempt to avoid a dreaded or feared possible self. To the extent that the individual is successful in this process, positive feelings of life satisfaction are theorized to emerge. When the individual is unable to realize a hoped-for possible self or to avoid the dreaded possible self, negative self-evaluations and affect will follow. However, protective mechanisms can come into play at this point and lead to a revision in the possible self to avoid future disappointment and frustration. The revised possible self is more consistent with current experiences.

Coping and Control

Researchers have been interested in the relationship between aging and feelings of control because of the presumably inevitable fact that as people get older, they have less control over what happens to them, both in terms of age-related changes and in terms of changes in the social environment. Coping is a related process, in which individuals attempt to manage stress by changing the environments or themselves to enhance their adaptation to the environment.

The MacArthur Study of Adult Development, a large national survey of almost 3500 adults, showed that despite awareness of increasing constraints in their lives, older adults (over 60) feel that they do have high levels of control in their lives. They are able to view their resources and potential in a positive way rather than focusing on losses (Plaut, Markus, & Lachman, 2003).

"What do you think?" | **8-4**

Do you agree that as people get older they are more likely to change their goals rather than change the environment?

Older adults, according to this theory, face the prospect of encountering more age-related losses and fewer developmental gains. Aging individuals attempt to optimize or maximize the ratios of gains to losses and therefore adjust their desired goals and activities accordingly. A principal mechanism for achieving this optimal balance is through using control processes. There are two basic kinds of control processes on which this theory is based (Rothbaum, Weisz, & Snyder, 1982). In **primary control**, the individual's desires and goals prevail over whatever constraints may be present in the environment. To use a very simple example, consider the situation of walking through the grocery store and seeing the last box of one's favorite cereal at the very top of a tall shelf. In primary control, one might climb up the lower shelves or find something to stand on in order to reach that cereal box. **Secondary control** involves changing the perceptions of one's own goals or desires rather than the environment itself. Thus, instead of finding a way to reach up and grab the box, one would change the goal and settle for a different brand of cereal that lies more closely within reach.

According to the primary and secondary control model (Heckhausen, 1997; Heckhausen & Schulz, 1995), with increasing age in adulthood, individuals attempt to maintain primary control by adopting strategies that offset developmental losses. For the most part, this means that they become increasingly likely to use secondary control. This trajectory reflects loss of the ability to effect changes in the world due to restrictions in mobility and cognitive functioning, and constraints in social opportunities. Through secondary control, aging individuals manage to avoid becoming frustrated when they can no longer achieve primary control over the environment. Instead, they can channel their energies into attainable goals redefined through the process of secondary control.

Another important theoretical principle of the primary and secondary control model is that of selective optimization with compensation (Baltes & Baltes, 1990), discussed in Chapter 7. Both primary and secondary control can be directed toward selectivity or compensation. Individuals can choose to achieve their goals despite age-related losses by becoming more selective or by compensating for them.

In selective primary control, the individual attempts to avoid loss by focusing energy and effort on a more narrow set of objectives. A woman who loves to garden may find that she can no longer care for her entire yard but instead must devote her attention to one beautifully tended bed of roses. In compensatory primary control, the individual attempts to make changes in the environment that will provide help in achieving a desired goal. The woman may hire a gardener so she can maintain the beauty of her entire backyard. Diet and exercise are also seen as forms of compensatory primary control, directed toward age-related changes in physical functioning.

Selective secondary control involves changing one's own approach to personal goals. The individual may choose to make a renewed commitment to an important goal while at the same time reducing commitment to other goals. Were the woman in our example a great cook as well as gardener, she might find that she has to limit her commitment to cooking so that she can pour her energy into gardening (or vice versa, if her family decides they like her cooking better!). Finally, compensatory secondary control involves minimizing the negative effects that failure to achieve a desired goal will have on self-esteem. This strategy is much like *identity assimilation* (see section on Identity Process Theory). The individual may downgrade the desirability of a failed goal or find external causes to blame. If the weeds take over this woman's garden, she may rationalize by claiming that she really did not care that much about the garden after all, or she may regard the cause as due to unusually rainy weather.

According to Heckhausen (1997), the ideal path of development in later life involves achieving a balance among these control strategies according to the opportunities and constraints offered to the individual as the result of the aging process. Older individuals who are able to attribute events in their lives that did not have positive outcomes to forces other than their own abilities or efforts are less likely to experience feelings of regret than they did over the events in their lives that did have positive

outcomes (Wrosch & Heckhausen, 2002). Conversely, those who can attribute their successes to their own abilities are more likely to have a positive sense of well-being (Kunzmann, Little, & Smith, 2001; Lang & Heckhausen, 2001). These findings have interesting implications for identity process theory, as they suggest that people who are well-adjusted in later life tend to use a certain amount of identity assimilation.

Identity Process Theory

In **identity process theory**, the goal of development is optimal adaptation to the environment through establishing a *balance* between maintaining consistency of the self (*identity assimilation*) and changing in response to experiences (*identity accommodation*). Actions upon the environment reflect the individual's attempt to express identity by engaging in preferred activities seen as important and worthwhile. Both identity assimilation and identity accommodation are internal processes in that neither involves a change in the environment. Through identity assimilation, people interpret events in a way that is consistent with their present identities. However, if they experience a threatening experience, identity accommodation comes into play.

According to the identity model, aging involves the potential for experiences that will erode the positive view people have of their identities. However, because identity assimilation outweighs accommodation with increasing age in adulthood, older people are able to maintain their positive self-esteem. The edge that assimilation has over accommodation is theorized to be just enough to maintain this positive view without leading individuals into delusional thinking. That there may be an advantage to identity assimilation in terms of health and mortality was suggested by a fascinating analysis of self-perceptions of aging and longevity (Levy, Slade, Kunkel, & Kasl, 2002). Older adults who managed to avoid adopting negative views of aging (which may be seen as a form of identity assimilation) lived 7.5 years longer than those individuals who did not develop a similar resistance to accommodating society's negative views about aging into their identities.

The **multiple threshold model** predicts that individuals react to specific age-related changes in their physical and psychological functioning in terms of the identity processes. This model was tested out in a study of nearly 250 adults ranging in age from 40 to 95 years old (Whitbourne & Collins, 1998). Individuals who used identity assimilation with regard to these specific changes (i.e., they did not think about these changes or integrate them into their identities) had higher self-esteem than people who used identity accommodation (i.e., became preoccupied with these changes). A certain amount of denial, or at least minimization, seems to be important with regard to changes in the body and identity.

Later studies have examined the relationship between identity and self-esteem more generally and found self-esteem to be higher in people who use both identity balance and identity assimilation (Sneed & Whitbourne, 2001). Identity accommodation, by contrast, is related to lower levels of self-esteem throughout adulthood. However, men and women differ in their use of identity processes in that women use identity accommodation more than do men (Skultety & Whitbourne, in press). In addition, some women who use identity assimilation may claim that they use identity balance to appear as though they are flexible and open to negative feedback, when in reality, they are not comfortable with looking inward and perhaps confronting their flaws (Whitbourne, Sneed, & Skultety, 2002). For both men and women, however, identity assimilation is related to a lower tendency to be self-reflective. Overall, however, identity balance is related to the ability to adapt most flexibly and successfully to age-related changes (Sneed & Whitbourne, 2003).

MIDLIFE CRISIS THEORIES AND FINDINGS

Lying outside the domain of any particular theory is the notion of the **midlife crisis**, which is derived from an age-stage approach to personality in adulthood. Erikson's theory, and to a certain extent Vaillant's, also attempts to divide the years of adulthood into segments based on broad psychosocial issues. The midlife crisis approach emerged from this framework but took it much further by attempting to pinpoint specific psychological events occurring at specific ages. The most well known of these events is the midlife crisis.

Theory of the Midlife Crisis

It is safe to say that every well-educated person in contemporary American society is familiar with the term "midlife crisis." The topic of the midlife crisis has become a permanent addition to popular psychology. A recent search of a popular book Web site revealed over 100 entries on the topic, and there is no sign of diminishing interest in the topic in the foreseeable future. It may therefore surprise you to learn that the concept is largely discounted in academic psychology. Despite the lack of supporting evidence, the midlife crisis is often referred to in common speech and in the media perhaps because it makes such a "good story" (Rosenberg, Rosenberg, & Farrell, 1999). Given its impact on the popular psyche, it is worth exploring the thinking and research that went into its original conceptualization.

"What do you think?" | 8-5

Do you agree that there is a midlife crisis? Have you observed it in people you know?

The term *midlife crisis* originated in the early 1970s as a description of the radical changes in personality that supposedly accompanied entry into the midpoint of life (age 40–45). At this age, it was theorized, the individual is involved in extensive and intensive questioning of goals, priorities, and accomplishments. The prompt for this self-scrutiny, according to theory, was the individual's heightened awareness of the inevitability of death (Jaques, 1965).

The concept of the midlife crisis was first aired in the media when journalist Gail Sheehy (1974) published a best-selling paperback book called *Passages: Predictable Crises of Adult Life*. This book, which was based on a study being conducted at the time by Yale psychologist Daniel Levinson, described the supposed changes that occurred at each decade marker of adulthood. The years of the early 40s, according to this view, were marked by inner turmoil and outer acts of rebellion against the placid, middle-aged lifestyle into which the individual would inevitably slip by the 50s. Shortly after the publication of *Passages*, Levinson published his own best-seller called *Seasons of a Man's Life*, which was the collaborative effort of a team of Yale psychologists, psychiatrists, and sociologists (Levinson, Darrow, Klein, Levinson, & McKee, 1978). This book focused exclusively on the experience of men in midlife through analysis of the interviews of 40 men ranging in age from the mid-30s to mid-40s. The men in the sample were intended to represent men from diverse backgrounds, with 10 from each of the following occupations: business executive, academic biologist, blue-collar worker, and novelist. In addition to these interviews were analyses of the biographies of famous men and the stories of men portrayed in literature.

The core of Levinson's theory of adult development is the **life structure**, defined as "the basic pattern or design of a person's life at a given time" (Levinson et al., 1978, p. 41). To analyze the individual's life structure, it is necessary to analyze the sociocultural world, the conscious and unconscious self, and participation in the world. Both central and peripheral themes can be identified in the life structure. These include family, work, friendship, religion, ethnicity, and leisure. According to Levinson and his colleagues, the life structure evolves through an orderly series of universal stages in adulthood. These stages alternate between periods of tranquility and periods of transition, and each stage has a specific focus. The stages and their associated ages are shown in Fig. 8.4. During periods of stability, the man builds his life structure around the decisions he made in the previous stage. If he chose to pursue a certain career path, he continues in that path throughout the period of stability. However, as the period reaches its close, the man becomes driven by both internal and external factors to question his previous set of commitments. For the next four or five years, during the transitional period that ensues, he explores different alternatives and seeks a new life structure or a modification of the existing one. Levinson believed that these transitional periods are inevitable. Choices are always imperfect, and as the outcome of one set of choices plays itself out, the individual begins to experience regrets and a desire for change. As stated by Levinson (p. 200), "no life structure can permit the living out of all aspects of the self."

The period called the *midlife transition* has a special quality compared to other transitional periods because it involves the most significant shift, from early to middle adulthood. As shown in Fig. 8.4, the period of the midlife transition

FIGURE 8.4
Stages of Adult Development According to Levinson

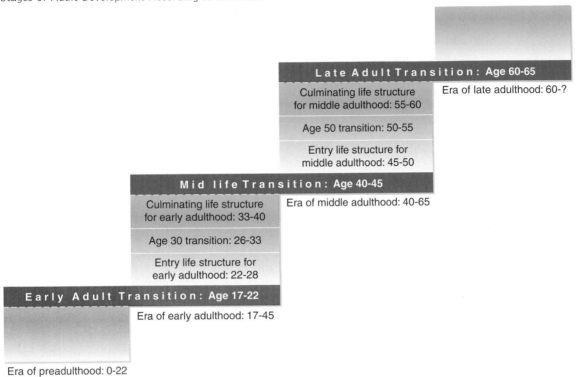

Late Adult Transition: Age 60-65

Culminating life structure for middle adulthood: 55-60

Era of late adulthood: 60-?

Age 50 transition: 50-55

Entry life structure for middle adulthood: 45-50

Mid life Transition: Age 40-45

Culminating life structure for early adulthood: 33-40

Era of middle adulthood: 40-65

Age 30 transition: 26-33

Entry life structure for early adulthood: 22-28

Early Adult Transition: Age 17-22

Era of early adulthood: 17-45

Era of preadulthood: 0-22

Source: Levinson et al., 1978.

("crisis") is targeted as 40–45. As described in the text of the study, however, its beginning can occur anywhere between 38 and 43, and its ending can occur in the years of 44 to 47. This extends the period of the midlife crisis potentially to nine years. This large time span allotted for the midlife crisis is but one of many problems with the theory, as it encompasses nearly the whole of the 40s. Nevertheless, returning to the substance of the midlife crisis, according to Levinson and colleagues, it is oriented around several themes. The first is overcoming disillusionment due to failure to achieve the dreams of youth that inevitably cannot be fully realized. A new set of aspirations, more realistic ones, must be established. The second theme of the midlife

crisis involves making decisions about how to pursue the life structure during middle adulthood. During this time, the man questions his marriage, comes to grips with the maturing of adolescent children, handles promotions or demotions at work, and reflects on the state of the nation and the world. He may begin to establish mentoring relationships with younger persons so that he may pass along the torch of what was handed to him during his early adulthood. Finally, the man must resolve the polarities of his personality involving masculinity and femininity, and feelings about life and death, and find ways of resolving the needs for both autonomy and dependence on others. In Jung's terms, this is the "**individuation**" process.

Some men express their desire to seek radical life changes in midlife by getting a bright red sports car.

Although Levinson's theory predicts that the stage sequences are universal, it does allow for variations in progress through the late 30s that would affect the specific nature of the midlife crisis. In the most frequently observed pattern reported in the sample, the man advanced steadily through a stable life structure but then encountered some form of failure. Usually, this was not a catastrophic loss, such as being fired or thrown out of the house, but it may have been failure to achieve some particular desired goal by a certain age. For instance, he may not have won an award or distinction for which he was striving, for example, the biologist who knows he will never win a Nobel Prize. Most people would not be distraught over such a "failure," particularly if they were generally well-regarded in their profession or community. However, if this goal was part of an individual's "dream," it could lead to serious disappointment and self-questioning. Some men in the sample did in fact realize their dreams, others

failed completely, and still others decided on their own to change their life structures entirely.

The characteristics of the midlife crisis are by now well known through their representation in contemporary literature, theater, movies, and song. For many people, they seem almost synonymous with the particular characteristics of the Baby Boomers, whom current society regards as being obsessed with aging, determined to stay young, and selfishly concerned with their own pleasure. However, as mentioned before, Levinson regarded the midlife crisis to be a virtually universal process that has characterized human existence for at least 10,000 years. In his subsequent publication on women, which was greeted with far less fanfare, Levinson claimed that similar alternations between change and stability characterize adult women (Levinson & Levinson, 1996). Other theories also emerged at about the same time as Levinson's, such as Gould's theory of transformations (Gould, 1978). Vaillant (1977) also temporarily espoused the midlife crisis concept but then renounced this view: "I believe transitions are merely by-products of development...development creates transitions; transitions do not create development" (p. 163). Although Vaillant's view of adult development does depict the growth of the ego as occurring in stages, the midlife crisis is not one of them.

Critiques and Research on the Midlife Crisis

Apart from the original investigation by Levinson and colleagues, little empirical support has been presented for the existence of the midlife crisis as a universal phenomenon. Even before the data were available, however, psychologists in the adult development field expressed considerable skepticism about the concept of the midlife crisis (Brim, 1976; Whitbourne, 1986a).

One of the most significant criticisms of the midlife crisis was the heavy reliance of the Levinson framework on age as a marker of development. On the one hand, Levinson and the other midlife crisis theorists were somewhat vague about exactly when the midlife crisis was supposed to occur. Was it 40–45, 38–47, or, as some had argued, at exactly age 43? The vagueness and fluidity of the age range is one type of weakness. People with any problems in their late 30s to almost 50 can claim that they are having a "midlife crisis" when things are not going their way in life. The specificity of age 43 as the time of the event is another type of weakness in the theory because adults simply do not have such regularly timed events coinciding with a particular birthday. In some ways, the Levinson (and Sheehy) approaches are like horoscopes, providing date-based predictions about personality and events. People like reading their horoscopes because it gives them some basis for being able to predict what will happen to them, but of course, the basis for these predictions is highly flawed. If horoscopes were valid, everyone with the same birth date (day, month, or year) would be the same, and clearly, this is not true.

The Levinson study had other logical and theoretical problems. One was the nature of the original sample. Of the 40 men whose interviews formed the basis for the sample, one-half represented the highly educated and intellectually oriented strata of society. Another one-quarter of the sample consisted of successful business executives. The biased nature of this sample would not have been a problem if Levinson had not tried to generalize to the entire population (now and for all time). However, Levinson did make such extreme claims based on this highly educated, introspective, and financially privileged group of men. Their concerns, such as running companies, publishing novels, and competing for Nobel prizes, are hardly those of the average man or woman.

A second theoretical problem with Levinson's study had to do with the inspiration for the study and its source in the personal life of the investigator. Levinson was very clear in stating his own motivations for beginning the study: "The choice of topic also reflected a personal concern: at 46, I wanted to study the transition into middle age in order to understand what I had been through myself" (p. x). He speculated that perhaps the study's results reflected the "unconscious fantasies and anxieties" (p. 26) of himself and his middle-aged male colleagues.

The third problem with the basis for the study was perhaps more technical. The process of rating the life stages was never clearly explained. The usual standard procedures of establishing agreement among judges for rating interview material were not described. Furthermore, the interview questions were not published, so that the interviews and the ratings were likely biased in the direction of proving the researchers' hypotheses. Given the many weaknesses in the study, it is understandable that other researchers subsequently were unable to replicate Levinson's findings.

One of the first empirical challenges to the midlife crisis concept came from the laboratories of McCrae and Costa, who used their extensive database on personality in adulthood to test predictions based on Levinson's theory (McCrae & Costa, 2003). As you already know, there was remarkable stability on all personality dimensions across the middle years of adulthood (see Table 8-5). However, it seemed worthwhile to test specifically the possibility that a midlife crisis would be revealed with more careful analysis. In short, it was not revealed.

An instructive place to begin in looking at the McCrae and Costa data is the year-by-year plot of scores on the NEO scales, shown in Fig. 8.5. If a midlife crisis existed, it would be revealed as a large increase in Neuroticism scores between ages 40 and 45. However, as is evident, not only were those scores flat, but also they were a very small amount lower in the 43-year-olds. In another attempt to find evidence for the midlife crisis, a Midlife Crisis Scale was created and administered to 350 men ages 30 to 60 years. Items on this scale concerned emotions thought to be related to the midlife crisis such as feelings of meaninglessness, turmoil, and confusion, job and family dissatisfaction, and fear of aging and death. If any questions had detected a midlife crisis, these surely would have. Yet, they did not, either on the initial sample or in a different group of 300 men tested with a slightly shorter version (Costa & McCrae, 1978). The most telling data of all, however, emerged in this second study on the Midlife Crisis Scale. The data had been obtained from men participating in the Boston Normative Aging Study, one of the longitudinal personality investigations that became part of the basis for the Five Factor Model. Men who had received higher scores on the Neuroticism factor 10 years earlier were the

ones who received higher scores on the Midlife Crisis Scale. This finding suggests that those with chronic psychological problems are more likely to experience a phenomenon such as the midlife crisis. However, this experience was by no means universal.

FIGURE 8.5
Scores from McCrae & Costa 1990 for "mid-life crisis" ages.

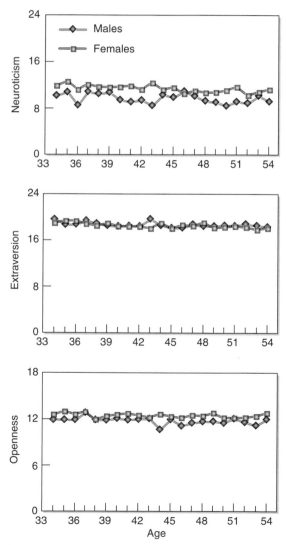

Source: McCrae & Costa, 1990.

So far, all the data reported here contradict the existence of the midlife crisis were derived from the laboratories of McCrae and Costa. There is ample documentation, however, from many other sources. One was the study I conducted on nearly 100 adult men and women between the ages of 24 and 61 (Whitbourne, 1986b). Extensive interview data were collected on identity and life histories. None of the participants, even those in their 40s, fit the criteria for a midlife crisis even when they were asked specifically about the impact of aging on their identities. A second study contradicting the notion of a midlife crisis was conducted on a sample of over 300 men ranging from ages 38 to 48, who completed survey questionnaires and semistructured interviews in the years 1971–1974 (Farrell & Rosenberg, 1981). A smaller group of 20 men participated in a more intensive study involving further questionnaires, interviews, and even family interviews. Once again, however, the midlife crisis failed to appear.

Looking broadly at data spanning early to late adulthood on trait-based personality measures, including those administered in the Mills and Radcliffe studies, continuity rather than change was seen as the dominant theme in midlife (Caspi & Roberts, 2001). Interestingly, in one of the Mills studies on women in midlife, the usual sort of factors that might be expected to trigger a midlife crisis among women did not have any effects on personality. Such potential triggers included menopause, having to care for parents, and concerns about the children leaving the home. Having experienced these events did not lead to negative changes in personality as would be predicted from the midlife crisis theory (Helson & Wink, 1992).

By now the student reading this dissection of the midlife crisis must surely be wondering why the concept continues to remain alive. As mentioned earlier, the idea of a midlife crisis makes a "good story" (Rosenberg et al., 1999). People in their middle years, settled into stable patterns of both personality and social roles, may find it exciting to think about getting that proverbial red sportscar or leaving their jobs behind them and moving to some exotic place. Sensational events such as hurricanes, tornadoes, and other disasters capture the attention of millions of television viewers. Similarly, the idea that personality is subject to major upheavals in the middle years may lead to the persistence of this phenomenon in the public mind far longer than warranted by the data.

SUMMARY

1. Studies of personality in adulthood are based on theories that attempt to define the nature and structure of personality. Within psychodynamic theory, ego psychology focuses on the role of the ego, the structure in personality that is theorized to perform the executive functions of personality. Ego psychologists include Erikson, Loevinger, and Vaillant. Another psychodynamic theory that discusses adult development is that of Jung. Several major longitudinal studies have provided tests of ego psychology theories. Psychosocial development from college to midlife was the focus of the Rochester study, which also examined the relationship of life experiences to personality among men and women. In the Mills and Radcliffe studies, college women were followed using measures testing Erikson's and Loevinger's theories. The interaction of personality and social context was also studied. The Vaillant study examined the use of ego defense mechanisms in three samples of adults. Two large cross-sectional studies also exist in which coping and defense mechanisms were

examined. Together, the findings from this research suggest that through middle age and beyond, individuals become more accepting of themselves, better able to regulate their negative feelings, and more passive in their interactions with the environment. Social context also affects the course of development, and personality in turn affects the way individuals select and react to their experiences.

2. Within the trait perspective, the Five Factor Model has stimulated a large body of longitudinal and cross-sectional studies on personality in men and women throughout the adult age range. Using the NEO-PI-R, researchers have supported the basic assumption of trait theory that personality remains stable across adulthood, particularly after the age of 30. Through the middle adult years, however, personality moves in the direction of increasing psychosocial maturity. Even though individual differences may remain strong, then, older adults become less emotionally volatile and better able to get along with others and accept responsibility for their actions.

3. Cognitive self theories propose that individuals view the events in their lives from the standpoint of the relevance of these events to the self. Identity process theory and the possible selves model fit into this category of theories. Other theories emphasize the individual's attempts to view the self and one's life goals within a consistent framework. Personal control theories regard the motivation to achieve goals as the central organizing theme of personality. These theories include the primary and secondary control model and cognitive control theory. All cognitive theories agree that balance or equilibrium between the self and experiences is the key to achieving a positive sense of well-being.

4. According to the midlife crisis theory, there is a period in middle adulthood during which the individual experiences a radical alteration in personality, well-being, and goals. Midlife crisis theory was developed by Levinson and colleagues through an interview study of 40 adult males and has gained strong support in the popular culture. However, subsequent researchers using a variety of empirical methods have failed to provide support for this theory, and it is generally disregarded within the field of adult development.

GLOSSARY

Cognitive self theories: theories proposing that individuals view the events in their lives from the standpoint of the relevance of these events to the self.

Conscientious-Conformist stage: in Loevinger's theory, period when individuals begin to gain a "conscience," or internal set of rules of right and wrong, and start to gain self-awareness as well as understanding of the needs and thoughts of other people.

Defense mechanisms: in psychodynamic theory, unconscious strategies intended to protect the conscious mind from knowing the improper urges of the unconscious mind, which include a wide range of socially unacceptable behaviors.

Ego: in psychodynamic theory, structure in personality that, according to Freud's theory, is most accessible to conscious awareness, performs the rational, executive functions of mind, and organizes the individual's activities so that important goals can be attained.

Ego psychology: framework of theorists whose conceptualizations of personality revolve around the role of the ego in actively directing behavior.

Five Factor Model (also called "Big Five"): theory intended to capture all the essential characteristics of personality described in other trait theories.

Individuation: in Jung's theory, the psychic integration and potential for full self-expression that emerges during these years.

Life structure: basic pattern or design of an individual's life at a particular point in time.

Midlife crisis: term that originated in the early 1970s as a description of the radical changes in personality that are theorized to accompany entry into the midpoint of life (age 40–45).

NEO Personality Inventory–Revised (NEO-PI-R): chief measure used to assess an individual's personality according to the Five Factor Model.

Personality: an unobservable quality present within the individual thought to be responsible for that individual's observable behavior.

Possible selves: views of the self that guide the choice and pursuit of future endeavors.

Primary control: goal-related behavior in which the individual's desires and goals prevail over whatever constraints may be present in the environment.

Secondary control: goal-related behavior in which individuals change perceptions of their goals or desires rather than the environment itself.

Social clock projects: the path a woman takes in fulfilling her adult family and work roles.

Trait: a stable, enduring attribute that characterizes one element of an individual's personality.

Chapter Nine

Relationships

Relationships with others are essential to everyone's existence. Developmental processes interact at every level throughout life with the ties that we have with our intimate partners, family, friends, and the wider social circles in which we carry out our everyday activities. It is difficult to capture the essential qualities of these many relationships, and it is perhaps even more challenging to study the way these relationships interact with individual developmental processes. As important as we know these relationships are at an intuitive level, it is just as crucial to be able to quantify the nature and impact of social processes in adulthood.

Anyone who reads the newspaper or listens to the evening news is aware that patterns of marriage and family life are changing with each passing year. Fewer people are getting married, and those who do are waiting longer than was true in previous generations. Families are changing in composition as people leave and reenter new long-term relationships, often involving children and extended families as well. In this chapter, these changing family patterns are examined along with attempts by theorists to understand the qualities of close relationships and how they interact with the development of the individual.

MARRIAGE AND INTIMATE RELATIONSHIPS

The marital relationship has come under intense scrutiny in contemporary society. The union between two adults is thought to serve as the foundation of the entire family hierarchy that is passed along from generation to generation. We hear about the death of marriage as an institution; yet, interest in marriage itself never seems to wane in the popular imagination, the media, and the professional literature. The decision to marry involves a legal, social, and, some might say, moral commitment in which two people promise to spend the rest of their lives together. Given the current divorce statistics, we know that many people are not able to maintain the hopeful promises they make to each other in their wedding vows. What factors contribute to a successful marital relationship, and what might lead to its downfall? Social scientists are nowhere near answers to these questions, but there are many, many theories.

Marriage

In 2000, 120 million adults were married, a number that represents 61.5% of males and 57.6% of females in the over-18 population (U.S. Bureau of the Census, 2003a). The percentage of adults who have ever been married is far higher, however. By the age of 55, fully 95% of all men and women in the United States have been married at some point in their lives (National Center for Health Statistics, 2002). The median age of marriage was 26.8 for men and 25.1 for women, a number that has been steadily rising from the early 20s in 1970 (U.S. Bureau of the Census, 2001d).

As a social institution, **marriage** is defined as a legally sanctioned union between a man and a woman. People who are married are expected to pay joint income tax returns and are given virtually automatic privileges to share the rest of their finances, as well as other necessities such as health care and housing. They often share a last name, usually that of the husband's, although some couples create a new, hyphenated last name. Generally, marital partners are entitled to retirement, death, and other insurance benefits, as well as the entire portion of the estate when one partner dies. Although marriages need not legally fit in with the statutes of a religion, they are often performed in a religious context.

Having explained the legal definition of marriage, we can clearly see what is excluded. People who are not legally married are not automatically entitled to the benefits available to those who are. Individuals living within a committed and long-term relationship not sanctioned by the law must seek exceptions to virtually all of the conditions that are set forth for married people. If these individuals are of the same sex and living within a committed homosexual relationship, they face additional barriers to the benefits granted to married persons.

Obviously, the legal definition of marriage includes no mention of the partners' emotional relationship with each other. People can be

Couple getting married in a scenic location

legally married and live apart, both literally and figuratively. Most social scientists distinguish between an intimate and a marital relationship because the two need not exist within the same couple. The legal commitment of marriage adds a dimension to an intimate relationship that is not present in a nonmarital close relationship in that it is technically more difficult to end a marital than a nonmarital relationship. Furthermore, many people view their marriages as moral and spiritual commitments that they cannot or will not violate.

Definitional concerns aside, there is a body of evidence on marriage in adulthood suggesting that adults who are married have many advantages compared to those who are unmarried. These advantages include better health and a healthier life style, greater economic security, and lower mortality (Rogers, 1995; Waite & Gallagher, 2000). These advantages hold true even after controlling for health in young adulthood, as people who get married tend to be in better health than those who do not (Murray, 2000).

There is a substantial sex difference in the percentage of adults 65 and older who are married and living with a spouse, as can be seen in Fig. 9.1. In addition to variations by sex, there are significant variations in marriage rates and age of marriage by race. Among all adults 18 and older, a higher percentage of whites (59%) than blacks (35%) are married (U.S. Bureau of the Census, 2000).

Corresponding to sex differences in marital status among the older adult population are differences in family living situations. As can be seen in Fig. 9.2, men are almost twice as likely to be living with a spouse; by contrast, women are more likely to be living alone or in other situations.

Cohabitation

Living in a stable relationship prior to or instead of marrying is referred to as **cohabitation**. Since the 1960s, there has been a steady increase in the number of couples who choose this lifestyle. In 1960, a total of 439,000 individuals in the

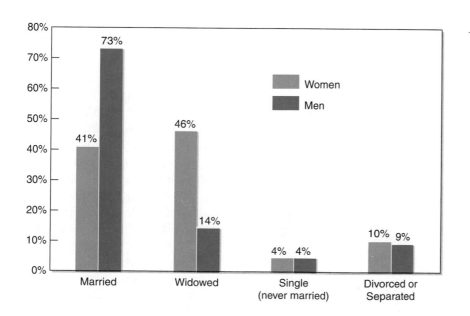

FIGURE 9.1
Marital Status of People 65 and Older

Source: Administration on Aging, 2003.

FIGURE 9.2

Percentage of Adults 65 and Older by Family Living Situation

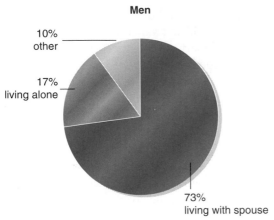

Men

10% other

17% living alone

73% living with spouse

Women

19% other

40% living alone

41% living with spouse

Source: Administration on Aging, 2001.

United States reported that they were cohabitating with a person of the opposite sex. By 2000, this number had risen to 5.5 million (U.S. Bureau of the Census, 2003). At least half of all marriages are now preceded by cohabitation, but there is no evidence that the experience of living together contributes positively to the success of a marriage. In fact, the opposite seems to be true. In contrast to common-sense notions about the advantages of cohabitation before marriage, data on divorce patterns show that there is a greater risk of marital breakup among people who cohabitated. One possible reason is that people who cohabitate are prone to divorce, which is why they did not get married in the first place (Lillard, Brien, & Waite, 1995).

Along with a rise in the overall numbers of couples who cohabitate is a parallel increase in the number of cohabitating adults with children under the age of 15. In 1960, this number amounted to 197,000, but by 2000 it was estimated at over 1.7 million (U.S. Bureau of the Census, 2001e). These numbers translate into 33% of all unmarried-couple households, an increase from about 20% in the late 1980s (Fields & Casper, 2001).

Divorce and Remarriage

The dissolution of a marriage is ordinarily perceived by those involved as a disappointment and a sad event. One or both of the partners may be relieved to see the end of an unsuccessful relationship, but they are nevertheless affected in many ways by the inevitable consequences of the divorce on their daily lives, the lives of children, and the lives of extended family members. A range of practical issues must be resolved, such as changes in housing and financial affairs, but the greatest toll is emotional. For many couples, child custody

---

> **"What do you think?"** | **9-1**
>
> Why are fewer people getting married and why are they waiting longer to enter into marriage for the first time?

arrangements present one of the greatest challenges caused by their altered status as a family.

Earlier, the advantages of marriage were discussed in terms of benefits to health, financial security, and lifestyle. Studies on divorced (compared to married) individuals show that they have lower levels of psychological well-being, poorer health, higher mortality rates, more problems with substance abuse and depression, less satisfying sex lives, and more negative life events (Amato, 2000). Divorced men have a higher risk of suicide than married men (Kposowa, 2000).

Increases in the rate of divorce in the last 30 to 40 years are widely publicized, and the disturbing statistic is often cited that one out of every two marriages will end in divorce. However, the divorce statistics are much more complicated than this simple formula would imply. Those who divorce in a given year are generally not the same people as those who have gotten married, so the number of divorces cannot simply be compared with the number of marriages to determine the odds of divorcing. Furthermore, the divorce rate in any given year includes those people who are divorcing for a second or third time, people who tend to have a higher divorce rate than those who are getting a first divorce, as will be discussed below. Including these individuals in the divorce statistics artificially inflates the divorce rate for all marriages. Another factor influencing the divorce rate is the number of people in the population of marriageable age, which itself is influenced by birth and death rates.

When examined as a rate per 1,000 among the general population, the divorce rate in 2001 was 4.0 (National Center for Health Statistics, 2002). The odds of a current marriage ending in divorce are estimated at 45%, down somewhat from the high of 60% reached in the early 1980s. However, it must be recalled that this percentage is a projection, not a prediction, for it is based on the assumption that marriage and divorce rates will remain constant into the future, an assumption that may not be valid (Popenoe & Whitehead, 1999).

Estimates of the probability of divorce across age groups of adults provide another way of looking at divorce statistics. As can be seen from Fig. 9.3, it is the youngest group of adults whose marriages stand the highest chance of ending in divorce (over 50%). The probability of a first marriage ending in divorce decreases

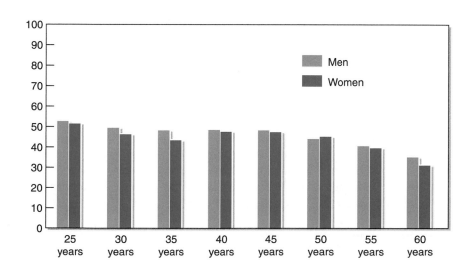

FIGURE 9.3
Lifetime Projected Divorce Rate from First Marriage

Source: Kreider & Fields, 2002.

with each successive age group until it is about 32% averaged across men and women in the 60s.

Although the highest percentages of divorced individuals are found in the 45–59 year age bracket (15%) (U.S. Bureau of the Census, 2000), most divorces occur between the ages of 25 to 29 for women and 30 to 34 for men. Most divorces (63%) occur within the first three years of marriage. Taking into account all marriages that end in divorce, the average length of marriage prior to divorce is about 10 years (Clarke, 1995).

This information about the length of marriage prior to divorce adds more weight to the arguments against the midlife crisis (see Chapter 8). Most divorces do not occur among 40-year-olds but among those who are in early adulthood and are recently married. It seems that if a marriage is not going to work out, difficulties will become apparent early in the relationship, particularly in the first year of marriage (Kurdek, 1993) rather than waiting to surface in middle adulthood. Only 12% of all divorces involve couples who were married 20 years or more (Clarke, 1995).

Divorce statistics also show important variations by race. The divorce rate is 30% higher for black men and 20% higher for black women compared to white men and women. The lowest divorce rates, about half that of blacks, are for people of "other" races, including Hispanic, Asian, and other. The average length of marriage for blacks compared to whites is about one year longer prior to divorce, but this reflects the fact that black couples separate sooner and take longer to divorce. All combinations of interracial marriages end sooner than do those of noninterracial marriages. The shortest marriage (5.3 years) is between a black wife and a man from "another" race (Clarke, 1995). Whites are more likely than blacks to remarry within five years of a divorce by a factor of 2 to 1.

The average duration of a second marriage is about two years less than that of the first marriage, slightly less than eight years for men and women. Third marriages, in turn, last about two years less than second marriages (Clarke, 1995). The rates of redivorcing after remarriage range from 13% of those in their 20s to a high of 36% for those in their late 40s and 35% for those in their early to mid-50s (U.S. Bureau of the Census, 1998). These rates are about double the rates of divorce from first marriages.

Approximately 1 million new children each year are affected by divorce, a figure that has remained constant since 1980 (U.S. Bureau of the Census, 1998). About half (46%) of marriages ending in divorce involve custody arrangements for children. In the majority (72%) of cases, the wife receives custody, compared with only 16% in which joint custody is given and 9% in which custody is given to the husband. There is a greater chance of joint custody being awarded if the couple is between 35 and 44. Men are also more likely to be awarded custody if they are white, are in their late 40s, and are ending their first marriage (Clarke, 1995).

A relatively newly studied phenomenon is that of divorced parents of adult children. Divorced mothers are more likely to have contact on a weekly basis with at least one adult child but for divorced fathers, the opposite is true (Shapiro, 2003).

Widowhood

When a marriage ends in the death of a partner, the survivor is faced with enormous readjustments in every aspect of life. Even when there is time to prepare, adjustment to widowhood is a difficult and painful process. Depressive symptoms may persist for at least several years after the loss (Lichtenstein, Gatz, Pedersen, Berg, & McClearn, 1996; Thompson,

Gallagher-Thompson, Futterman, Gilewski, & Peterson, 1991). Without remarriage, levels of well-being may not return to preexisting levels even for as long as eight years after the loss (Lucas, Clark, Georgellis, & Diener, 2003). Negative effects on health can persist years after death of the spouse (Goldman, Koreman, & Weinstein, 1995). These effects are not limited to people in conventional heterosexual marriages. Gay men who lose partners to AIDS experience depressive symptoms and increased likelihood of engaging in high-risk sexual behaviors (Folkman, Chesney, Collette, Boccellari, & Cooke, 1996; Mayne, Acree, Chesney, & Folkman, 1998).

About 800,000 older adults in the United States become widows each year (HHS, 1999). Women at all ages and among all racial groups are more likely than men to become widows. As was shown in Fig. 9.1, nearly half (46%) of all women over 65 years are widows, which is almost triple the rate for men (14%). The majority (70%) of widows live alone, and it is these widows, rather than those who live with family, who are likely to be impoverished (Dodge, 1995). The chances of becoming a widow increase substantially after the age of 65 years, particularly for black women, of whom 83% are widows.

Psychological Perspectives on Long-Term Relationships

Throughout the vicissitudes of marriage, divorce, remarriage, and widowhood, most adults actively strive to maintain gratifying interactions with others on a day-to-day basis. Furthermore, for many adults, the feeling of being part of a close relationship or network of relationships is the most salient aspect of identity (Whitbourne, 1986). Whether this relationship is called "marriage," "family," "friendship," or "partnership" is not as important as the feeling that one is valued by others and has something to offer to improve the life of other people.

Poets, philosophers, playwrights, and novelists, among others, have attempted for centuries to identify the elusive qualities involved in close relationships. Although they have not been around for as long, psychologists and sociologists have also contributed their share of theories to account for why people develop these relationships and what factors account for their maintenance or dissolution over time. Early theories tended to focus on what now seem like simplistic notions such as whether "opposites attract" or whether, instead, "like attracts like." Explanations of relationship satisfaction across the years of marriage attempted to relate the quality of marital interactions to the presence of children in the home and their ages. As relationships in the real world have seemed to become more complicated, however, so have the theories, and there is now greater recognition of the multiple variations that are possible when adults form close relationships. The emotional factors involved in long-term relationships are also gaining greater attention, as it is realized that some characteristics of human interactions transcend specific age or gender-based boundaries.

Socioemotional Selectivity Theory. The domain of marriage and other close relationships is the focus of **socioemotional selectivity theory**, the proposition that throughout adulthood, individuals reduce the range of their relationships to maximize social and emotional gains and minimize risks (Carstensen, 1987). According to this theory, people change gradually over the years of adulthood and into old age with regard to the functions that interactions with others serve.

Social interactions can have an informational function in that we learn many practical things from other people that help us operate more effectively in the world. Through social

BEHIND THE RESEARCH

LAURA L. CARSTENSEN, PROFESSOR OF
PSYCHOLOGY, STANFORD UNIVERSITY

What is most exciting to you about research in this field?
Much of the early research on aging was descriptive. It was an important first step. It revealed that many of the hunches we had about old age were wrong. In many, many ways, older people are doing better than expected. Now that the descriptive work has been done, the time for major theory building is upon us. Researchers are well-equipped to begin to understand and explain age-related changes. To me, this is the most fun and the most exciting part of science.

What do you see as major challenges?
The greatest challenges in the field, from where I sit, are to formulate questions and interpret findings about aging in an even-handed way. There is such an overwhelming tendency to view aging in a negative light that virtually all age differences are interpreted as age decrements. Consider this example: In the area of social relations, reduced social contact with age was, for years, explained by age-related loss. I am quite convinced at this point that aging people carefully hone their social networks, retaining those social partners who are most important to them and discarding less important ones. Instead of a decrement, this process appears to contribute to the relatively high quality of life in the latter years of life.

Where do you see this field headed in the next decade?
I think that we have begun to see a tide-change. Across the subfields of psychology, researchers are identifying preserved areas of functioning and documenting substantial individual differences in areas. Individual differences are particularly intriguing to social scientists because they argue against inevitability. If many elderly people are healthy and wise, for example, the questions become "why?" and "how?" does this occur. The ultimate question for society at this point in history concerns how to maintain functioning in older people for the benefit of society. Understanding how to optimize the aging process is of course an essential part of the answer.

interactions, we also find long-term partners, for it is through meeting other people and learning about them that we eventually find the one who is "right" for us. Another function of social interaction is to derive a sense of identity. Other people help us see "who" we are, because it is through the feedback of others that we often understand ourselves (a position consistent with the identity process theory). Social interactions also help people regulate emotions.

There is nothing like the shared laughter with a good friend over a distressing situation to help put it behind you. These are the rewards of interactions. However, relationships with others can also have their costs. A certain amount of energy has to be invested into a relationship to make it work out successfully. This fact may be obvious to anyone in a "high-maintenance" relationship, but it is also true of ordinary close relationships in that the partners must make efforts to please each other and provide for each other's emotional needs. Other costs include threats to self-concept: A relationship can make one feel deficient, unloved, or ineffectual.

According to socioemotional selectivity theory, as people grow older, they become more focused on maximizing the emotional rewards of their relationships and less interested in seeking information or knowledge through their interactions with others (see Fig. 9.4). This shift, according to the theory, occurs as people become increasingly sensitive to the inevitable ending of their lives and recognize that they are "running out of time." It is not aging so much as this recognition of less time left to live that triggers the shift in desired goals of interactions. Young adults, when placed either under artificial time constraints through experimental manipulations or under real time constraints, as for those who are HIV positive, show similar preferences toward the emotional functions of social interactions as do older adults (Carstensen, Isaacowitz, & Charles, 1999). According to this theory, endings of any kind bring out strong emotions and cause us to want to spend time with the people who have been closest to us.

According to socioemotional selectivity theory, couples who have been together throughout their adult lives have found ways to maximize the emotional benefits they experience in the relationship.

The desire to maximize emotional rewards leads adults increasingly to prefer spending time in their relationships with people who are familiar to them rather than seeking out new friends and acquaintances. Family and long-time friends are the people who will serve the positive emotional functions of self-validation and affect regulation. Older adults are less interested in

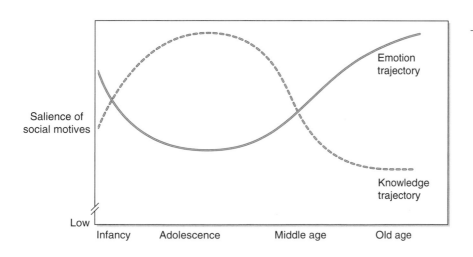

FIGURE 9.4
Socioemotional
Selectivity Theory

Source: Carstenson, Gross, & Fung, 1997.

meeting new people and broadening their social horizons because such individuals do not serve the same emotional functions (Lang & Carstensen, 2002).

Note that the theory does not imply that older people are less capable of showing or feeling emotions or that they are not interested in forming new relationships. The intensity of emotion experienced by an individual does not change over adulthood (Carstensen & Turk-Charles, 1994). However, in keeping with the findings of personality research and aging, emotional understanding appears to improve in the adult years (Labouvie-Vief & Hakim-Larson, 1989). Consequently, older adults may be better able to control the way they express their emotions (Lawton, Kleban, Rajagopal, & Dean, 1992). There is also evidence that older adults have fewer negative emotions, perhaps because they are better able to regulate their affective experiences (Gross, Carstensen, Pasupathi, Tsai, Goetestam Skorpen, & Hsu, 1997). These age differences in emotions form an important cornerstone of socioemotional selectivity theory because they support the notion that emotional experiences are an important part of life for older adults.

In terms of marriage, socioeconomic selectivity theory implies that older adults would prefer to spend time with their marital partner (and other family members) rather than with new people. They should regard the long-term marital relationship as offering perhaps the most potential to serve emotional functions as their experience together over the years has allowed them to understand and respond to each other's needs. Second, if older adults are better able to control their emotions, particularly the negative ones, they should get along better with their partner because each is less likely to irritate the other one. Third, if older adults are nevertheless able to experience strong feelings, their affection for one another should not fade.

The findings of an innovative observational study in which middle-aged and older adult couples were compared in a laboratory communication task support the prediction that the longer-married couples show better regulation of emotions, particularly negative ones (Carstensen, Gottman, & Levenson, 1995). During the discussion of problems in their marriage, the middle-aged couples were more likely to show negative emotions such as anger, disgust, whining, and belligerence, but also more humor, than did the older couples. Although the older couples expressed negative emotions, these were more likely to be intertwined with expressions of positive feelings. The improved abilities in controlling negative emotions appeared to translate into improved strategies between older marital partners for regulating their negative affect toward each other. Moreover, the more happily married of the older couples seemed able to hold off from the pattern shown by unhappy couples of escalating disagreements into outright arguments.

"What do you think?" | **9-2**

Who would you rather spend time with if you knew that you would be moving away within 24 hours, a close friend or a person you have just met?

Attachment Theory. In **attachment theory**, the individual's approach to close relationships in adulthood is seen as originating in the earliest of relationships in life—those with parents (or caregivers). The theory proposes that adults carry remnants of these early patterns into their interactions with close partners. This is an important theory that until recently was applied primarily to the relationships of college students but is now being translated into long-term relationships in adulthood. Increasingly, attachment theory is also being viewed as a theory about the origins of the self through the bonds formed in early childhood (Mikulincer, 1995). In addition, the implications of attachment theory as a theory about couple relationships are beginning to be explored as they affect relationships with children and with the developmental paths taken by children (Mikulincer, Florian, Cowan, & Cowan, 2002).

The basis for attachment theory is the work of British psychoanalyst John Bowlby (1969), whose work with infants and mothers led him to propose that there is an innate drive mechanism (called the attachment behavioral system) that leads infants to seek the attention and protection of caregivers (called attachment figures). When the caregiver provides this attention, the infant feels a sense of security and can explore the environment without fear of abandonment. By contrast, infants become anxious and distressed when they feel the attachment figure is not available or is unresponsive to their calls for attention or help. They seek to reestablish contact if they are left alone, or if they are threatened with the loss of the figure, they become clingy and fearful.

Repeated experiences with the attachment figure lead the child to develop a mental representation of the infant–caregiver relationship, what Bowlby called an internal working model, also called an attachment working model. Over time, the individual begins to see other people and the self in terms of this working model. If the caregiver is reliable and dependable, others are seen as responsive. If the caregiver is unavailable, unconcerned, or perhaps hurtful, others are seen as having the potential to exhibit these uncaring and damaging behaviors. In addition to developing mental representations of others, the infant develops corresponding mental representations of the self. A caregiver who attends to the child's needs enables the child to feel that he or she has favorable attributes. Caregivers who are unresponsive or hurtful to the child plant the seeds for the growth of negative self-conceptions (Bowlby, 1973).

As the individual's attachment working model continues to evolve in the early years of life, it develops into what is called an **attachment style**, or way of thinking about an attachment figure who, in adulthood, is the individual's romantic partner. The attachment to an adult romantic partner is based on emotional commitment rather than physical proximity alone (Sharpsteen & Kirkpatrick, 1997).

Psychologist Mary Ainsworth tested Bowlby's ideas by developing an experimental procedure in which 1-year-old children were temporarily separated from their mothers to assess attachment style (Ainsworth, Blehar, Waters, & Wall, 1978). The child with a **secure attachment style** is not made angry or anxious by the mother's temporary departure and, upon her return, seeks contact with her. The child with **avoidant attachment style** resists contact with the mother, and the child with the **anxious attachment style** appears to want to make contact with the mother but resists her. Because of the mixed behavior of this last group of children, the anxious attachment style is also referred to as the **anxious-ambivalent attachment style**. The majority of children fall into the secure attachment style, and the remaining two types, together considered "insecure," are in the minority.

Attachment style is regarded as a life-long characteristic (Main, 1996). Hazan and Shaver were the first to test out the application of this concept to adult relationships when they applied the original three categories developed by Ainsworth to a self-report measure of adult attachment style (Hazan & Shaver, 1987). Respondents indicate which of three descriptions (secure, avoidant, or anxious-ambivalent) comes closest to their important romantic relationships. Adults with a secure attachment style are involved in more satisfactory and stable long-term relationships (Kirkpatrick & Davis, 1994). Secure partners in marital relationships also show higher quality of communication patterns (Kobak & Hazan, 1991). By contrast, avoidant individuals distance themselves from others, which also causes them to close themselves off from potentially rewarding experiences. Anxiously attached adults also suffer problems in their relationships, as they tend to be overly clinging, nervous about being abandoned, and ruminative about their negative feelings (Mikulincer & Florian, 1998). Insecurity about attachment can also lead them to remain in unhappy marriages (Davila & Bradbury, 2001). Insecurely attached people are also more likely to have strongly averse reactions to the thought of separation from their partners, including a heightening of anxiety about death (Mikulincer, Florian, Birnbaum, & Malishkevich, 2002). Conversely, women with secure attachment have a more positive relationship history in midlife than avoidant women (Klohnen & Bera, 1998).

One significant modification has been made to the adult attachment style model that adds a fourth category. According to Bartholomew and Horowitz (1991), there are two types of avoidant individuals: those who are afraid of closeness with others, and those who place no value on intimacy. The "avoidant" category obscures this important difference. In their categorization system (see Fig. 9.5), the avoidant style is divided into fearful (people who are afraid of closeness) and dismissive (people who do not want to be involved in close relationships).

The largest study on attachment style in adulthood was completed in the context of a national survey of psychopathology among community-dwelling adults, the National Comorbidity Study (NCS) (Kessler, McGonagle, Zhao, Nelson, Hughes, Eshleman, Wittchen, & Kendler, 1994). The nearly 8100 adults in the sample, ranging from 15 to 54 years of age, rated themselves on the three-category Hazan and Shaver attachment style measure (Mickelson, Kessler, & Shaver, 1997). The majority of respondents rated themselves as securely

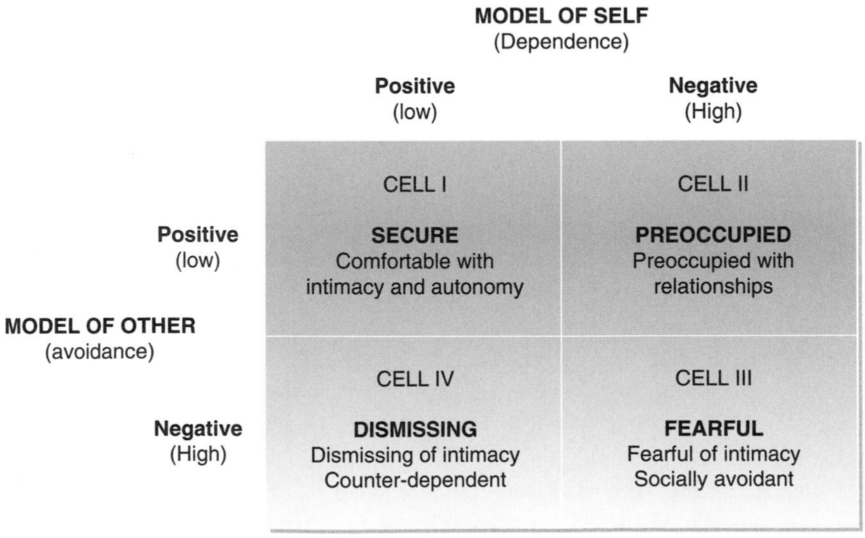

FIGURE 9.5
Model of Attachment Styles

Source: Bartholomew & Horowitz, 1991.

attached, followed in order by avoidant and anxious (see top half of Table 9-1). The main finding of this study was a decrease in the relative percentage of anxiously attached adults in the oldest category (45–54 years).

The other large cross-sectional study on attachment style was conducted as part of the investigation by Diehl and colleagues on age differences in ego defense styles and coping (Diehl, Elnick, Bourbeau, & Labouvie-Vief, 1998). In this investigation, a sample of 304 adults ranging from 20 to 87 years of age rated themselves on the four-category attachment measure. The findings of the Diehl et al. study, shown in the bottom half of Table 9-1, concur with the NCS study in that there was relative stability for the secure attachment style across the three age groups. Preoccupied attachment, corresponding to the anxious attachment style in the NCS study, dropped across age groups to a similar extent. The age differences for the preoccupied and dismissing attachment styles, however, showed a very different pattern from each other and from the avoidant attachment style in the NCS study. The percentage of older adults in the dismissing attachment style was far higher

and the percentage of fearful was far lower than the avoidant style (which combines both) in the NCS study. Diehl and his colleagues concluded that the findings on the dismissing attachment style concur with those on the ego defense and other personality measures from the sample. These findings indicate a tendency for the oldest individuals in the sample to lower their emotional attachments to other people as a way of responding to interpersonal losses.

It is important to remember, however, that the individuals in these cross-sectional studies were just that—individuals. They were not studied in the context of a couple, as was the case in the studies of marital communication conducted by Carstensen and colleagues in tests of socioemotional selectivity theory. It may be that the older adults in the Diehl study gave the appearance of being dismissive because they have learned ways to control their emotional expression and were not overly effusive. Furthermore, this study did not provide a test of the validity of the attachment style ratings to an older sample. Not being "dependent" on someone else, as is part of the definition of the dismissing style, may be an issue that older

TABLE 9-1
Categorizations of Age by Attachment Styles

Study	Age Group	Attachment Style Category (%)			
Mikelson et al., 1997		Secure	Avoidant	Anxious	
	15–24	58.7	19.8	17.4	
	25–34	56.9	27.9	10.7	
	35–44	58.7	28.4	8.6	
	45–54	63.6	23.3	8.0	
Diehl et al., 1998		Secure	Dismissing	Fearful	Preoccupied
	20–39	51.8	15.8	21.9	10.5
	40–59	49.0	22.4	19.4	9.2
	60–88	51.1	40.2	4.3	4.3

Sources: Mickelson, Kessler, & Shaver, 1997; Diehl, Elnick, Bourbeau, & Labouvie-Vief, 1998.

adults are particularly sensitive to, because they do not want to be a burden on others.

When couples are studied with regard to attachment style, a picture more like that from the communication study of Carstensen and colleagues emerges in terms of the outward display of emotions over the course of relationships. In one fascinating naturalistic investigation, couples in an airport lounge were asked to provide attachment-style ratings. Then their behavior was unobtrusively observed while they left the airport lounge to board the airplane (Fraley & Shaver, 1998). The oldest person in this study was 68 years old, and the longest relationship among the couples was 43 years. People who were older and in longer-enduring relationships showed fewer outward displays of affection toward each other when saying goodbye as well as less distress upon separation. Similar findings have been observed, though not in the same context, in men and women in long-term gay and lesbian relationships. With increased time in a relationship, they show a tendency to take each other "for granted" as they feel less of a need to engage in mutual activities (Kurdek, 1995).

Another factor that comes into play in long-term relationships is the extent to which couples adapt to each other's attachment style. According to Bowlby (1973), people assimilate their new experiences in terms of their existing working models. Evidence of infidelity, for example, no matter how minor, would be interpreted by someone with an anxious attachment style as definite proof that the relationship is ending because that experience would be assimilated to the individual's working model. However, over time, the working model comes to be modulated by the effect of repeated interactions through processes of accommodation. In this example, such processes might take place through repeated reassurance by the partner that there is no reason to fear abandonment. In

one of the few studies on attachment style in couples, couples who showed high degrees of agreement about each other's attachment style had higher scores on a problem-solving measure of communication. The relationship between attachment style and marital adjustment was seen as reciprocal. Couples who maintain an accurate view of each other through constant accommodation show healthier communication and adjustment patterns (Davila, Karney, & Bradbury, 1999). When couples were studied over time (the first year of marriage), those who had positive perceptions of their partner's attachment security were more likely to engage in supportive behavior, which ultimately contributed to higher levels of marital satisfaction (Cobb, Davila, & Bradbury, 2001).

Despite changes in the outward expression of attachment over the course of a relationship, there is evidence that the bond formed with a spouse has a unique, irreplaceable role in the emotional life of adults. In a longitudinal study comparing widows and married couples, researchers compared predictions based on attachment theory to those based on stress theory (Stroebe, Stroebe, Abakoumkin, & Schut, 1996). The findings clearly supported predictions based on attachment theory in that those who lost their partners could not find emotional substitutes for their major attachment figures in any other of their existing relationships.

Theories of Relationship Satisfaction and Stability. Attempts by sociologists and social psychologists to understand the dynamics of long-term relationships go back to the 1930s, when interest in marriage and the family had its formal beginnings as a field of inquiry. Some of the questions that researchers working in this tradition ask include the age-old puzzles involved in explaining why some relationships "work" and others do not. Within these traditions, researchers try to account for the factors that cause two people to be attracted to each other. For sociologists, these explanations often involve socioeconomic status or geographic residence. For social psychologists, these explanations involve people's perceptions of themselves and others, as well as their ability to read interpersonal signals in relationships. Explanations of the evolution of long-term relationships revolve around similar factors but, for sociologists, also include the stages of the **family life cycle**, which are stages of marriage based on the ages of children (Duvall, 1977). However, this model does not work well for contemporary marriages, which often do not follow traditional patterns or stages.

Social exchange theory attempts to predict the stability and dissolution of social relationships in terms of rewards and costs of an interaction. Relationships continue when partners perceive that the rewards of remaining in the relationship outweigh the rewards associated with alternatives (Thibaut & Kelley, 1959). The rewards of marriage include emotional security, satisfaction of sexual needs, and social status. When considering a breakup, these rewards are weighed against the barriers presented by legal, financial, social, and religious constraints. The theory predicts that relationships dissolve when the balance shifts so that rewards no longer outweigh the costs (Levinger, 1965). Conversely, increasing levels of intimacy and commitment to a relationship occur over time as the intrinsic rewards of being in the relationship increase and as couples develop increasing levels of dependency. Over time, then, the attractiveness of alternatives tends to fade (Levinger & Huesmann, 1980). Commitment levels to the relationship also grow stronger (Rusbult, 1983).

A variant of social exchange theory is **equity theory**, in which the cost-benefit analysis is extended to a comparison of the benefits that each partner brings to the couple (Walster, Walster, & Berscheid, 1978). Dissatisfaction

with a relationship is theorized to occur when partners perceive that they are overbenefited (the reward-cost ratio is more in favor of them than the partner) or underbenefited (the partner is receiving more than they are). Commitment to the relationship, and hence its stability, decreases as feelings of inequity grow (Sprecher, 1988). Decreased commitment to the relationship in turn decreases the likelihood that couples will remain together (Floyd & Wasner, 1994).

The **behavioral approach to marital interactions** emphasizes the actual behaviors that partners engage in with each other during marital interactions as an influence on marital stability and quality (Karney & Bradbury, 1997). People will be more satisfied in a long-term relationship when their partners engage in positive or rewarding behaviors (such as expressing affection). Punishing or negative behaviors (such as criticism or abuse) decrease satisfaction. This model is useful in examining interaction patterns within the micro-level of a couple's way of resolving conflict, as in the Carstensen et al. (1995) study, which is based on a behavioral analysis of couple interactions. Several specific patterns cause a decrease in the quality of the relationship. These are the husband's rejection of a wife's influence, negative behavior by wives in solving marital problems, and failure of husbands in reducing the negative feelings of their wives (Gottman, Coan, Carrere, & Swanson, 1998). Partners who reject or invalidate the communications of their spouses also experience diminished marital satisfaction over time (Markman & Hahlweg, 1993). Not surprisingly, high levels of hostility expressed by partners are another contributor to unhappy relationships (Matthews, Wickrama, & Conger, 1996).

The use of behavioral observations of marital interactions proved to provide unique insights into predicting who would divorce over the course of a 14-year period in research by Gottman and colleagues. Couples whose marriages were described as "passionless" (showing neither positive nor negative affect) divorced later than couples who were more volatile emotionally during the early married years. Interestingly, one of the most predictive interactions of later divorce was the one in which husbands and wives shared the details of their everyday experiences over the course of an 8-hour period during the day. If these lacked positive affect, the couple was at particular risk for subsequent ending of the relationship. (Gottman & Levenson, 2000, 2002)

As interesting as these results are, such behavioral studies of marital interactions are based on observation of couples in laboratory situations. Therefore, they do not consider the contextual factors in the relationship, such as the actual day-to-day problems that couples face in their lives. Nor do these theories take into account individual differences in personality, the life events that people experience, or socioeconomic status. The role of personality and individual adjustment in marital stability and satisfaction is suggested by several studies relating these individual factors to relationship outcomes. For example, in a 45-year longitudinal study of 300 couples, it was found that the marriages of people in which both partners had high scores on the trait of neuroticism were more likely to be characterized by dissatisfaction and to end in divorce (Kelly & Conley, 1987). Similarly, neuroticism is linked to negative outcomes in long-term gay and lesbian couples (Kurdek, 1997). The possibility that people choose partners who match their own depressive or neurotic characteristics is the basis of the **marital selectivity hypothesis** (Merikangas, Prusoff, & Weissman, 1988).

It seems that both personality and behaviors play a role in long-term marital relationships (Gottman, Swanson, & Murray, 1999). In a longitudinal study of parents studied from the first to fifth year after having their first child, couples

were observed in the home and also provided self-report ratings (Belsky & Hsieh, 1998). Couples that functioned consistently well over the period of the study were high on the trait of agreeableness, and those that functioned consistently poorly were high on neuroticism. However, marital dynamics, specifically conflictual behaviors related to the parenting of the child, were more strongly associated with deterioration of marital quality over time.

Another perspective on long-term relationships is provided by theorists who examine the role of similarity and assumed similarity between partners. According to the **need complementary hypothesis**, people seek and are more satisfied with marital partners who are the opposite of themselves (Winch, 1958). However, the evidence seems to favor the **similarity hypothesis**, which proposes that similarity and perceived similarity predict interpersonal attraction (Byrne, 1971) and satisfaction within long-term relationships (Ferreira & Winter, 1974). Furthermore, over the length of a relationship, partners become more similar to each other (Blankenship, Hnat, Hess, & Brown, 1984). To a certain extent, perceptions of similarity of spouses reflect the tendency that people have to judge an individual's behavior in a relationship on the basis of stereotypes associated with that role, such as what the "typical" husband or wife does (Kenny & Acitelli, 1994). Furthermore, couples who are satisfied in their relationship are more likely to assume that they and their partners are more similar to each other than are partners who are less satisfied in relationships (Acitelli, Douvan, & Veroff, 1993). Projecting one's own feelings and attitudes onto those of the partner can also be viewed as an application of identity assimilation to the intimate relationship (Ebmeyer & Whitbourne, 1990).

Ironically, the tendency to assume that one's partner shares one's own values, attitudes, beliefs, and perceptions can have negative consequences. If one partner assumes what the other partner is thinking or feeling, there may be less of a tendency to want to talk to that partner and check out this perception. Couples who are married longer can become complacent about their relationship and less motivated to resolve disagreements by attempting to understand what their partners are thinking (Thomas, Fletcher, & Lange, 1997). Thus, over time, they actually "read" each other less well, and although they may think that they know how the partner feels, the fact is that they may not.

An unfortunate result of the tendency of longer-married couples to assume they share similarities with the partner can be a loss of intimacy. The ability to share one's feelings and measure these against the partner's response is considered an important contributor to closeness and intimacy within the couple (Reis & Shaver, 1988). As couples share their feelings with each other, this sets up a positive spiral in which each partner becomes more likely to disclose feelings (Laurenceau, Barrett, & Pietromonaco, 1998) leading to further enhancements in intimacy. The decrease in close communication later in a long-term relationship may help to account for the decreases after the first 15 years of marriage in martial adjustment as shown in several longitudinal studies. In a rare glimpse at long-term marriages, Vaillant and Vaillant examined the marital adjustment over 40 years of couples in which the husband had participated in the Harvard Grant Study. Both husbands and wives experienced decreased marital satisfaction between 1 and 15 years after marriage; wives but not husbands continued to show declines in marital adjustment through the full period of the study (Vaillant & Vaillant, 1993). Although not longitudinal, similar findings were obtained in a study of long-married Israeli couples. Marital satisfaction was lower, and feelings of "burnout" were higher, in wives compared to husbands (Kulik, 2002).

Countering the loss of intimacy is the opportunity that couples have to enjoy more leisure-time activities together as a result of retirement and the **empty nest**, or the departure of children from the home (Gagnon, Hersen, Kabacoff, & Van Hasselt, 1999). Interestingly, despite the negative connotations to the empty nest phenomenon, researchers find that rather than being distressed, women are likely to experience mood improvements when their last child moves out of the home. Conversely, when children return home, the quality of a couple's sexual relationship may decline at least in terms of frequency of sexual activities (Dennerstein, Dudley, & Guthrie, 2002).

One interesting variant of theories that attempt to explain marital stability and satisfaction over time is based on studies of remarried adults. The divorce rate for this group, as pointed out earlier, is double that of first-time married people. This finding is somewhat paradoxical in that remarried individuals have similar levels of satisfaction as couples who are married for the first time (Furstenberg & Spanier, 1984; Glenn & Weaver, 1977). This paradox was addressed in a national sample of remarried persons studied longitudinally in the 1980s (Booth & Edwards, 1992). A number of factors were identified that could explain the discrepancy between remarriage divorce rates and marital satisfaction. First, people in remarriages are higher on a factor called **divorce proneness**, meaning that they are more likely to consider divorce as an option when their marriage is not going smoothly. Second, people who are remarried seem to be more critical of the quality of their marriages and more sensitive to some of the inevitable loss of excitement that occurs in the early years of marriage for most people. Third, remarried individuals are more likely to have entered their first marriage while teenagers, perhaps to get away from a troubled home life. They may also have had poorer relationships with in-laws and extended families of their partners, as well as problems with step-children. Finally, though not related to marital instability, people in remarriages come from the lower socioeconomic stratum.

The data on remarriage add another potentially important factor to theories of relationship stability: the tendency of people to be willing to leave a marriage. People with less of a commitment to marriage as a social institution may view the ups and downs of married life with a far more critical eye than those who believe in "til death do us part."

Sexual Behavior in Long-Term Relationships.

The topic of sexuality is clearly an important one for adults regardless of the type of relationship of which they are a part. In Chapter 4 we noted the changes in adulthood in sexual hormones and the reproductive system, but at that time we did not examine the impact of these changes on sexuality and sexual functioning. These changes are better viewed in the present context of intimate relationships.

A starting point for this discussion is contained in data from the National Health and Social Life Survey (NHSLS), a large-scale survey of sexuality in adults that was conducted in the early 1990s and reported in 1999 (Laumann, Paik, & Rosen, 1999). Each person in a nationwide representative sample of over 3100 sexually active adults between the ages of 18 to 59 was given a 90-minute interview, which included responses to questions about the existence of specific sexual dysfunctions. The prevalence of sexual dysfunction in the sample shows a higher rate of difficulties involving low arousal and desire for women compared to men, who in turn have as their most prevalent dysfunction that of premature ejaculation. Overall, the rates of sexual dysfunction were reported as 43% for women and 31% for men. The results when broken down by age indicate that relatively

fewer older women experience difficulties in sexual arousal and desire, but that they are more likely than their younger counterparts to experience pain during intercourse. Problems with erection and low sexual desire were over three times more prevalent in men over 50 than in men in the youngest age group (18 to 29 years). Not surprisingly, these difficulties were more likely to be found in unmarried individuals but, less obviously, sexual problems were less likely to occur in adults with higher levels of education. Race also moderated the findings on sexual dysfunction, with generally the highest rates of difficulties reported by African Americans and the lowest by Hispanic people.

The rates of sexual dysfunction in this sample of adults were moderated somewhat by social status. A deterioration of economic circumstances, as indexed by loss of household income, was related to higher rates of sexual dysfunction in women and erectile dysfunction in men. Sexual functioning was also affected by prior experience of sexual trauma, for both men and women. Men who were perpetrators of sexual assault on women had a threefold increase in risk of erectile dysfunction.

Clearly, in a correlational study such as this one, it is impossible to draw cause and effect conclusions between risk factors and the rates of sexual dysfunction. Nevertheless, the importance of sexual functioning for quality of daily life was indicated by the negative relationship between sexual dysfunction and feelings of personal happiness. This was generally true of women, and it was true of men experiencing erectile dysfunction and low sexual desire. Nevertheless, a minority of individuals with sexual dysfunction reported that they have sought help (10% of men and 20% of women).

These findings on adults ranging from early to middle adulthood point to the existence of a problem that is more widespread than has perhaps been recognized in previous studies of sexuality in adulthood. Unfortunately, the findings do not provide any insights into the sexual experience of older adults, who were not included in the sample. For these we must turn to less extensive and older data based on previous observational, clinical, and survey studies, some of which were not particularly focused on sexuality and sexual functioning.

With regard to women, it is recognized that the physical changes associated with menopause can lead to altered sexual functioning, and that, as reported in the NHSLS, these changes mainly involve increases in the experience of pain during intercourse for postmenopausal women. However, findings from the 1960s to the present suggest that there is no physiological reason for a diminution in a woman's ability to enjoy sexual relations. As was true for the women under 60 studied in the NHSLS, previous researchers considered the main impediment to a woman's ability to experience a rewarding sex life after age 60 to be the unavailability of a partner (Marsiglio & Donnelly, 1991). The changes involved in the aging of the reproductive system for men are far less dramatic than those experienced by women, and an important difference is that men retain the ability to father children into late in life. However, as shown in the NHSLS, sexual functioning, at least with regard to the ability to have an erection, is affected by a number of physiological and psychological factors from middle age onward. Among men over 60, normal age-related changes in sexual functioning involve a slowing down and reduction of intensity in progression through the sexual response cycle. Arousal is slower, orgasm is shorter, and less seminal fluid is ejected. About 50% of the over-60 male population have at least one occasion of erectile difficulty (Starr, 1985). It is estimated that 30 million men, amounting to 5% of men at 40 and 15%–25% of men 65 and over, have erectile dysfunction (Clearinghouse, 2001). Approximately 5% of men 60 and older develop

erectile dysfunction in one year, and the rates are greater for men with lower education and the health problems of diabetes, heart disease, and hypertension (Johannes, Araujo, Feldman, Derby, Kleinman, et al., 2000).

"What do you think?" 9-3

Is it inevitable that older people lose their sexuality?

The changes in functioning experienced by men as they age are subject to a number of moderating factors. Health is a major contributor to the adequacy of erectile functioning in older men (Mazur, Mueller, Krause, & Booth, 2002), particularly disorders involving the cardiovascular and endocrine systems. Psychological factors such as stress, depression, and anxiety also interfere with sexual functioning in men, as can changes in occupational or economic circumstances.

Lack of knowledge about normal sexual changes is another major impediment to the older man's ability to maintain functioning. If a man interprets the normal slowing down in sexual responsivity that occurs as a function of age as a sign of erectile dysfunction, he may be placing himself at risk for **secondary impotence**, which is loss of erectile functioning caused by psychological factors. Another way to think of this phenomenon is as an example of overaccommodation. The man concludes that he is "over the hill" sexually because of a slight alteration or even occasional episode of erectile failure, and this becomes a self-fulfilling prophecy. Unfortunately, because the man's ability to have an erection is the primary determinant of whether a couple can have intercourse, the downward spiral set in motion by overaccommodation in this area affects both partners in a heterosexual relationship. Furthermore, the woman may start to accommodate, in a sense, to the changes in her husband if she starts to believe that she no longer has the ability to excite and arouse him (Starr, 1985).

Attitudes toward sexuality in later adulthood can be another deterrent to the sexual functioning of both men and women. Although attitudes toward sexuality are in general more lenient than they were decades ago, there are still proscriptions against the expression of sexual feelings in older adults, who are looked on as "dirty old men" or "dirty old women." Despite these barriers, the majority of older adults have positive and accepting views about sexuality and feel that it is an important part of their lives. Table 9-2 summarizes a survey of 800 (518 females and 282 men) participants over the age of 60 obtained through community centers. As can be seen from this table, large percentages of respondents endorsed strong positive feelings about the importance of sexuality in their lives (Starr, 1985). At the time of the original publication of this report (Starr & Weiner, 1981), little attention was given to the findings, which in and of itself may indicate the negative attitudes that exist toward sexuality in older adults.

The tide began to change in 1998, however, with the approval by the U.S. Food and Drug Administration of sildenafil citrate (marketed as "Viagra"), a prescription medicine effective in the majority of cases for treating erectile dysfunction. Much greater publicity was given to this condition

TABLE 9-2
Selected Responses from Starr and Weiner's Report on Aging and Sexuality

Topic	Response
Like sex	95% state that they like sex.
Want sex	99% would like to have sex if it were available.
Orgasm	70% regard orgasm as important part of sexual experience. 99% of women are orgasmic at least some of the time.
Masturbation	46% acknowledge masturbating (higher for single, divorced, and widowed women).
Touching and cuddling	93% consider these important.
"Sexy" pictures, books, or movies	62% get aroused by these.
Sexual experimentation	39% would like to try new techniques or experiences.
Nudity	80% felt positive about nudity during lovemaking.
Younger lovers	84% of women and 90% of men endorsed this idea.
Sex and living together without marriage	91% approved of this in principle for older adults.
Homosexuality	64% accept open attitudes toward homosexuality.
Health	76% stated that sex has a positive effect on their health.
Satisfaction	75% state that sex feels the same or better compared with when they were younger. Women are more likely to think of sex as better now (41% women, 27% men).
Sex education	88% received negative or none at all when young.

Source: Starr, 1985

with the introduction of this medication into the market, and its immediate success in the marketplace suggested that it was indeed filling a need. A similar medication known as Vardenafil is being introduced as an effective alternative for men with health conditions that make Viagra an unsafe medication for them to take (Goldstein, Young, Fischer, Bangerter, Segerson, et al., 2003). Of course, this condition often requires more than the provision of a "magic pill." Individuals with erectile dysfunction may need counseling or other treatments in addition to medication. Furthermore, there has been debate about whether a treatment for women would have received as much attention in the media, or even why no comparable treatment has been made available for women. However, the publicity given to the disorder may have the positive result of destigmatizing erectile difficulties in aging men.

Although, as mentioned earlier, being unmarried is related to a higher prevalence of sexual difficulties, there is evidence that older adults engage in sexual relations outside marriage. Estimates of sexual activity in single, divorced, and widowed persons range from 32% (Starr, 1985) to as high as over 50% of women and 75% of men in their 60s and 70s (Brecher, 1984).

PARENTHOOD

The transformation of a marriage into a "family" traditionally is thought to occur when a child enters the couple's life on a permanent basis. Most of the psychological literature on children and families focuses on the children and their adjustment to the various arrangements for living worked out by their parents (Hetherington & Kelly, 2002). However, there is considerable interest in the literature on the period in which a first child is born, the so-called **transition to parenthood**. From a biopsychosocial perspective, this event involves biological changes (when the mother bears the child) as her body adapts to rapid hormonal and other physiological alterations. Psychological changes include both the emotional highs and lows associated with first-time parenthood. In addition, the individual's identity begins to incorporate the concept of being a parent. Social changes involve the new role that adults acquire when they become parents, altering their status with other family members and the community. Clearly, once the transition has been passed, parenthood continues to make a multifaceted impact on the adult's life. Although biological factors recede in importance, psychological effects and social changes continue, in effect, for the rest of the individual's life.

Approximately 4 million babies are born each year in the United States, translating into a birthrate in 2001 of 14.5 per 1000 women of childbearing age (15–44 years). The median age at first birth is 27.1, up from 22.1 in 1970 (Matthews & Hamilton, 2002). Over the past two decades there has been a steady increase in the percentage of women who remain childless, from 10.5% in 1976 to 19% in 2000. In 2000 the percentage of children born to unmarried women was 31%. There is a great disparity between whites and blacks in the proportion of children born to single mothers: 62% of all births to black women in 2000 were to unmarried mothers, compared with 26% for whites (Bachu & O'Connell, 2001).

Family Living Situations

Despite population trends toward more single-parent and cohabiting families, the large majority of households in the United States (69%) consist of people living together as a family. American households are most likely to consist of three-person families, and over half of all families have one or more members under the age of 18. Households with married couples constitute 53% of all households. Less than one-quarter (24.1%)

of all households in the United States consist of married couples with children, the lowest percentage since at least 1970, when 40% of all households were composed of married couples with children (U.S. Bureau of the Census, 2001c). The trends between 1970 and 2000 in households by type are shown in Fig. 9.6. The decline in the proportion of families consisting of married couples with children was accompanied by an increase in nonfamily households, particularly one-person households, the majority of which were headed by a woman.

Another trend in families is an increase in the number of adult sons and daughters (ages 25–34) living with their parents. In 2000 this number was 18.5 million, up from 11.9 million in 1970. The peak year was 1990, when 21.4 million individuals ages 25–34 lived at home with their parents (U.S. Bureau of the Census, 2001a).

Changes in family living situations in recent decades are often discussed in terms of blended families, also known as reconstituted families. Within these family situations, at least one adult is living with a child who is not a biological child of that adult. Often, these family situations develop after a divorce and remarriage (or cohabitation) in which two adults establish a household together. Statistics on **blended families** are difficult to obtain because so many possible variations exist, but some estimates of their frequency can be made from data available on women living with children who were not born to them (National Center for Health Statistics, 1995). For women between the ages of 30 and 34, approximately 11% were living with a nonbiological child. This percentage rises to 17% for women in their 40s. The majority of children in these situations were the son or daughter of a relative, friend, or partner. The dynamics within these relationships, though the subject of many fictional accounts, are only beginning to receive empirical attention as the numbers of blended families rise.

The Transition to Parenthood

Much of the literature on parenthood and its effects on adults developed through studies on the transition to parenthood within traditional two-parent families. The logic behind such research is that the most significant changes occur with the entry of the new member to the family. The original impetus for studies on the

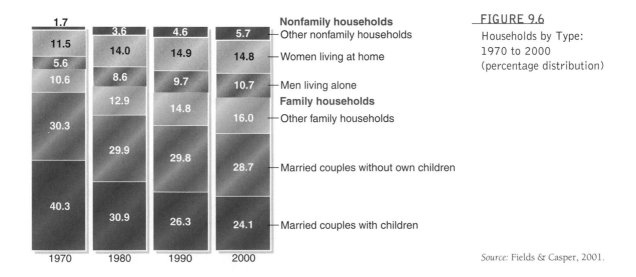

FIGURE 9.6

Households by Type: 1970 to 2000 (percentage distribution)

Source: Fields & Casper, 2001.

transition to parenthood was provided by the findings of several cross-sectional studies of marital satisfaction across the years of adulthood in terms of the family life cycle. These studies pointed to the existence of a U-shaped curve relating number of years married with satisfaction; the low point of the U was associated with the entry into the childbearing years of the family life cycle (Rollins & Galligan, 1978). However, because these studies were cross-sectional, their results are skewed. The upward turn of the U after the childbearing years reflects the disappearance from the population of married couples who were unhappily married but stayed together through the parenting years (Glenn & McLanahan, 1982).

On average, there is a decline in marital satisfaction, particularly pronounced for wives, corresponding to the birth of a child (Belsky & Hsieh, 1998; Cowan & Cowan, 1992). However, there are important variations across couples in the negotiation of this transition (Bradbury, Fincham, & Beach, 2000). Some couples show no changes, and some even show slight improvements when studied longitudinally during the early childbearing years (Belsky & Rovine, 1990).

The major factor accounting for wives' decline in marital satisfaction is the fact that the birth of the child carries with it changes in the allocation of household tasks. The division of labor in the home becomes more traditional after children are born. Working women without children already perform more household duties than men do (Blair & Lichter, 1991), but after becoming mothers, the situation is exacerbated. Mothers assume more of the stereotypically female roles of performing household duties such as laundry, cooking, and cleaning, in addition to child care. Men increase their involvement in paid employment outside the home (Belsky & Pensky, 1988; Kluwer, Heesink, & Van De Vliert, 1997).

"What do you think?" | **9-4**

Why do couples tend to move toward more traditional roles after the birth of the first child?

These lesbian parents, shown with the 6-month-old son of the woman at the right, may be more likely to share parenting and household duties than parents in heterosexual couples, according to research on the transition

Assess Yourself

Sharing of Household Tasks in Male–Female Couples

How do you rate on these questions? Compare yourself to other men and women who filled out this online survey on a major news network Web site (5,849 men and 10,294 women):

* Percentages may not total to 100% for each question due to nonresponses.

1. How many times a week do you wash dishes?

0 times a week	Men: 16%	Women: 4%
1–3 times a week	Men: 42%	Women: 27%
4–6 times a week	Men: 27%	Women: 31%
7+ times a week	Men: 15%	Women: 38%

2. Do you fill the ice trays with water, or do you place the empty tray in the freezer?

   | I fill them, then place them in the freezer. | Men: 93% | Women: 94% |
   | I place the empty tray in the freezer. | Men: 7% | Women: 6% |

3. Who does most of the grocery shopping for the household?

I do the grocery shopping.	Men: 20%	Women: 60%
My spouse does all the grocery shopping.	Men: 31%	Women: 6%
We both do the food shopping.	Men: 49%	Women: 34%

4. Do you make the bed if you are the last person to rise in the morning?

Yes, I make the bed if I am the last to rise.	Men: 34%	Women: 28%
No, I don't make the bed if I'm the last to rise.	Men: 53%	Women: 29%
Regardless of who gets out of the bed last, I still make it.	Men: 13%	Women: 43%

5. How many times a week do you cook meals?

0 times a week	Men: 22%	Women: 4%
1–3 times a week	Men: 48%	Women: 31%
4–6 times a week	Men: 21%	Women: 43%
7+ times a week	Men: 10%	Women: 23%

6. Do you refill the beverage pitcher or do you place the empty pitcher in the refrigerator and wait for someone else to refill it?

   | I fill the beverage pitcher if it's empty. | Men: 89% | Women: 96% |
   | I place the empty pitcher in the refrigerator. | Men: 11% | Women: 4% |

7. Do you leave your clothes on the bathroom floor after taking a shower or do you tidy up when you are finished?

I leave my clothes on the floor.	Men: 15%	Women: 18%
Are you kidding, my spouse would kill me—I tidy up.	Men: 85%	Women: 82%

8. Do you leave used dishes in the sink for your spouse to wash?

Yes, I leave used dishes in the sink.	Men: 40%	Women: 29%
No, I wash the dishes I use.	Men: 60%	Women: 71%

9. Are household chores done by one person, or shared in your household?

All household chores are shared.	Men: 74%	Women: 51%
One person does the housework.	Men: 26%	Women: 49%

10. Does your spouse believe if he or she is the major bread winner or moneymaker, they shouldn't have to do household chores?

Yes, my spouse believes if he/she earns all the money at work, then he/she doesn't have to lift a finger.	Men: 11%	Women: 32%
No, my spouse shares in household responsibilities, regardless of his or her paycheck.	Men: 89%	Women: 68%

11. Have you categorized chores into gender-specific roles? (i.e., men take care of the car and yard work, while women take care of cleaning the house and cooking the meals.)

Yes, there are some things I just can't do.	Men: 42%	Women: 47%
No, there are no gender-specific household chores!	Men: 58%	Women: 53%

Source: MSNBC on-line survey, 1999.

Many investigators see the decrease in marital satisfaction associated with the entry into parenthood as resulting from a shift in household duties. It is especially hard on women who expected greater sharing of child-care and household duties (Cowan, Cowan, & Kerig, 1993; Hackel & Ruble, 1992). When husbands perform more of these roles in the house and there is greater co-parenting, women have higher levels of marital satisfaction (Fish, New, & Van Cleave, 1992). Women who enjoy performing family work, are oriented toward family in terms of their overall life goals, and feel that they are particularly good at it seem to be able to avoid perceiving the unequal division of labor as unfair (Grote, Naylor, & Clark, 2002; Salmela-Aro, Nurmi, Saisto, & Halmesmaeki, 2001).

Attachment style may also play a role in influencing the adjustment that a woman makes to parenthood. Among a sample of 106 couples experiencing this transition, women with ambivalent attachment styles were found to experience a decrease in marital satisfaction if they perceived a loss of support by their husbands. In fact, their perceptions of support from husbands decreased further over time if they entered the transition already having felt that their husbands were not providing them with the support they needed (Simpson & Rholes, 2002). Another contributor to lower marital satisfaction is a decline in the sharing of mutually enjoyable activities, not just the tedious tasks of taking care of the household. All married couples tend to participate in fewer joint activities after the honeymoon is over, but the decline is especially pronounced among those who become parents (Kurdek, 1993). Furthermore, when couples do engage in joint activities, they may be the activities preferred by the wife, leading the husband to feel resentful (Crawford & Huston, 1993).

Fatherhood is increasingly being studied as an aspect of identity in adulthood, reflecting, in part, the increasing role of fathers in the raising of their children (Marsiglio, Amato, Day, & Lamb, 2002). The number of single fathers (sole parents) tripled between the 1980s and 1990s. By 2000 single-father families constituted 5% of all families, and of these, as many as 10% are raising three or more children (Fields & Casper, 2001). The extent to which a single father is able to adjust to the role of sole parent is affected by the characteristics of the children, including their age and gender, and his own characteristics, including his age and educational level. The father's adjustment to this role is also affected by his ability to juggle the roles of parent and worker and to maintain a relationship with his ex-wife or partner, as well as by his original desire to have custody (Greif, 1995).

Countering the trend toward more single fathers is the increase in the number of fathers who have no contact with their children. In 1960 it was estimated that 17% of children lived apart from their biological fathers; by the 1990s this percentage had doubled (Popenoe & Whitehead, 1999). Considerably less is known about stepfathers, another increasing segment of the American population. Changes in marriage, divorce, and remarriage patterns have resulted in a larger number of men who take on the role of father to the children of a wife or partner (Marsiglio, 1992). Men in this role are more highly involved if they have biological children of their own, became stepfathers early in the child's life, have a good relationship with their ex-wife or partner, and have a good relationship with the biological father (Hetherington & Henderson, 1997).

An interesting and important variant on the issue of division of labor and the transition to parenthood among heterosexual couples comes from studies of parenting in lesbian couples. In contrast to heterosexual couples, lesbian couples in general report that they share household duties equally (Kurdek, 1993). Women in lesbian relationships attempt to avoid traditional divisions of household tasks and instead divide household labor according to such personal factors as interest, ability, and time availability. This more egalitarian approach seems to be based on the fact that women in lesbian couples place higher value on equality in their relationships than do heterosexual or gay-male couples (Kurdek, 1993).

It is not clear whether the biological mother in a lesbian relationship takes on more of the traditional roles, while the nonbiological mother becomes more active in paid employment, as is true in a heterosexual couple. Regardless of the actual division of labor, satisfaction with the allocation of duties seems to be an important factor in predicting the functioning of the children of that relationship. This is true for both lesbian and heterosexual couples (Agronick & Duncan, 1998).

Adult Parent–Child Relationships

Past the early childrearing years, little research is available on the relationships between parents and children. Studies on the complexities of intergenerational relationships among older adults and their middle-aged children are, however, beginning to emerge (Allen, Blieszner, & Roberto, 2000). Such research is indicating that these relationships play a vital role in the older adult's well-being. For example, the quality of parent–child relationships is related to mental health outcomes such as loneliness and depression among aging parents (Koropeckyj-Cox, 2002).

As children move through the years of adulthood, there are many facets of relationships with their own parents that can change. For example, as children have their own families, they begin to realize what it was like for their parents. On the one hand, the children may now appreciate what their parents did for them; but on the other hand, they may resent their parents for not having done more. Another changing feature of the relationship stems from the child's increasing concern that parents will require help and support as they grow older. Adult children and their parents may also find that they do not agree on various aspects of life, from an overall philosophy and set of values (such as in the area of politics) to specific habits and behaviors (such as methods of food preparation). Whether parents and their adult children live in the same geographical vicinity and actually see each other must also be added into the equation.

Theoretical Perspectives. Exchange theory provides one approach to viewing the parent–child relationship in adulthood. According to this view, parents and children evaluate their interchange in terms of costs and rewards. In a marital or similar intimate partnership, the result of this evaluation may be that the individuals decide to leave the relationship, but with parents and children, such an outcome is not truly feasible. Of course, parents and children may arrange to discontinue their interactions, but

their formal link is permanent. The parent is always a parent, and the child is always a child.

Another theoretical concept related to exchange theory is the nature of the investment that parents and children have in the relationship. The **developmental stake** principle suggests that parents have a greater investment in their children than children do in their parents (Bengtson & Kuypers, 1971). A child represents a parent's continuity into the future, and parents see themselves in their children as symbols of this continuity. However, children may attempt to separate themselves from their parents in order to feel and appear autonomous. Adding to this difference in perspective may be the tendency of the parent to place higher value on the relationship with a child than vice versa, as theorized by socioemotional selectivity theory (Carstensen, 1992).

Building on the concepts of the developmental stake and socioemotional selectivity theory is the **developmental schism**, which is an emotional gap created between parents and their children (Fingerman, 2001). Because of their differing positions in the life span, members of the two generations are involved in different issues and concerns. One manifestation of the developmental schism is the mother's tendency to regard her daughter as more important than the daughter does the mother and for the daughter to regard the mother as more intrusive than the mother does the daughter. Mothers are also more likely to regard their daughters as confidants than daughters do their mothers. Another possible source of tension is that the daughter still seeks the approval of the mother and feels guilty when she feels that she is not living up to her mother's desires.

Tension or divisions between parents and children may also arise from a related phenomenon—the tendency of parents to see their grown children as reflections of the quality of their parenting (Ryff, Lee, Essex, & Schmutte,

1994). The ability to have produced a successful child may enhance the parent's feeling of being competent in this very crucial life role. However, the child's success is not always considered a reason to rejoice by parents, who may resent the fact that their child has accomplished more than they have.

The term **role reversal** is occasionally encountered in the professional as well as the popular literature on the parents of adult children. According to this view, which is discredited among gerontologists (Brody, 1990), parents and their adult children switch responsibilities. The child must take care of the parent because of physical, cognitive, and social changes in the parent's status. Although the concept is no longer considered valid, the idea that parents become their children's children is unfortunately still prevalent in societal views of aging.

Children do undergo developmental changes that alter their relationships with parents, a concept referred to as **filial maturity** (Blenkner, 1963). During early adulthood, but particularly in the 30s, children begin to relate to their parents in a different way. By taking on the responsibilities and status of an adult (employment, parenthood, involvement in the community), the adult child begins to identify with the parent. The relationship may change as a consequence of this process, as parents and children relate to each other more like equals (Fingerman, 1996).

The idea that one might be forced to take on the role of parent to the parent, however, does create a certain amount of concern and worry in the adult child. This process is referred to as **filial anxiety** (Cicirelli, 1988). This phenomenon may be one that is particularly likely to occur in the United States and other Western industrialized nations. In other cultures, notably Hispanic, Asian, and African American, children have an attitude of **filial obligation** or **filial piety**, meaning that they feel committed to taking care of their parents should this become necessary. There are established traditions within African-American (Wilson, 1986) and Hispanic (Keefe, Padilla, & Carlos, 1979) families of a broader definition of family to include the extended family rather than the nuclear family as the basic family unit. Similarly, the norm in Asian cultures is for parents to live with their children. Even though there has been concern that westernization in these countries will erode that tradition, data from the mid-1990s indicate that this tradition is still strong (Velkoff & Lawson, 1998).

Even in the United States, however, adults and their children are not as distant as is commonly thought. Many maintain high levels of contact (Pillemer & Suitor, 1998). Furthermore, there need not be conflict between parents and their adult children, even when living together. Despite the many possibilities for tension and strain in the relationship, adult children living in the homes of their aging parents experience harmonious relationships rather than conflict (Suitor & Pillemer, 1988). Furthermore, for better or for worse, mothers and their adult daughters not living in the same household seem to prefer avoidance rather than engagement as a means of resolving conflict (Fingerman, 1995). In fact, it is notoriously difficult to demonstrate evidence of conflict in these relationships, as parents prefer not to discuss the problems they have with their adult children with outsiders (Mancini & Blieszner, 1989).

Caregiving. The potential difficulties between adult children and their parents, particularly for women, are thought to rise to the point of crisis when there is the need to provide caregiving to the parent. **Caregiving** consists of providing assistance in carrying out the tasks of everyday life to an infirm older adult. A large body of evidence has accumulated on this topic since the early 1980s (Zarit, Reever, & Bach-Peterson, 1980), most of it cross-sectional. Based on this research, it was considered a foregone conclusion that the caregiving role was a traumatic one for the adult child. The daughters in this situation, referred to as "women in the middle" (Brody, 1981) or the **sandwich generation** (sandwiched between her mother and her children), were thought to be victims of extreme stress due to their "caregiver burden." However, longitudinal studies have since provided evidence of ameliorating factors in the caregiving situation and even the possibility that the daughters in these situations experience some benefits.

One factor that appears to play a role in ameliorating caregiving burden is that, consistent with exchange theory, daughters see themselves as gaining in monetary rewards (inheritance) as a result of their taking care of aging parents (Caputo, 2002). The extent to which parents provided children with financial support when the children were younger also has an effect on later social support provided as parents grow older (Silverstein, Conroy, Wang, Giarrusso, & Bengtson, 2002). Equity theory may apply to the way that siblings share the burden of care of the parents in that there is a tendency to try to equalize the sense of shared responsibility, if not in reality then in the way that the situation is perceived (Ingersoll-Dayton, Neal, Ha, & Hammer, 2003). The third factor that reduces caregiving stress is the provision by others in the family of help with the parent's care. Despite the belief that one child (the daughter) has sole responsibility for caregiving, close to two-thirds of caregivers have significant assistance from someone else, either a sibling or spouse. Support from the husband, in particular, may increase a woman's feelings of mastery in her performance of the roles of wife and caregiver (Martire, Stephens, & Townsend,

1998). The way the daughter copes with the challenges of providing care is another important moderator of stress. Caregivers who use emotion-focused coping, such as wishing the situation would change, are more likely to become depressed than those who use problem-focused coping, in which they tackle the daily dilemmas of their situation directly. Daughters with higher levels of education are more likely to use problem-focused coping, adding education to the list of factors that influence caregiver outcome.

Rather than being a universally negative experience, then, caregiving may not present as traumatic a situation for middle-aged daughters as is often portrayed in the media. Although women in this age group face many demands on their time, they are also likely to have a wider range of resources, particularly if they have received the benefits of higher levels of education.

Intergenerational Solidarity Model. A model incorporating the various dimensions present in the adult child–parent relationship is the **intergenerational solidarity model** (Bengtson & Schrader, 1982). According to this model, six dimensions characterize the cohesiveness of these relationships. These include factors such as distance apart, frequency of interaction, feelings of emotional closeness, agreement in areas such as values and lifestyles, exchanges of help, and feelings of obligation. This model was tested on a nationally representative sample of 971 adults ages 18–90, focusing on adults who did not live with their parents. From the adult children's responses to the questions pertaining to each of the dimensions, a five-category typology was formed of adult child–parent relationships (Silverstein & Bengtson, 1997). These are summarized in Table 9-3. The frequency of parent–child relationships varied considerably according the gender of the parent. The most common type of mother–child relationship was tight-knit, but the most common father–child relationship was characterized as detached. Altogether, the results add up to a picture of greater intergenerational solidarity between mothers and adult children than between fathers and their children.

A number of other characteristics of parents and children were related to the strength of the relationship. Daughters were more likely to have tight-knit relations with their mothers, and sons to have obligatory relationships. However, daughters and sons did not differ with regard to their relationships to their fathers: The majority of both daughters and sons were in the detached category. Children were less likely to have close relations with their parents when the parents had divorced or were widowed, an effect that was far more pronounced for fathers than for mothers. The age of the child also influenced the nature of the relationship with the parent. Young adults had stronger ties than did middle-aged adults to both mothers and fathers, in part, because they were still dependent on social, emotional, and tangible support from them. However, the adult children past middle age (whose parents were in advanced old age) were again as likely to be close to their parents, including their fathers. It is possible that at this point, children had reconciled their differences with their fathers in an attempt to reestablish close intimate ties, an interpretation consistent with socioemotional selectivity theory.

TABLE 9-3
Typology of Adult Child–Parent Relations

Type	Definition	Percent of Mothers	Percent of Fathers
Tight-knit	Adult children are engaged with their parents based on all six indicators of solidarity.	31%	20%
Sociable	Adult children are engaged with their parents based on geographic proximity, frequency of contact, closeness, and similarity of opinions but *not* based on providing assistance and receiving assistance.	28%	23%
Obligatory	Adult children are engaged with their parents based on geographic proximity, and frequency of contact but *not* based on emotional closeness and similarity of opinions. While only about one-third of children in this class are engaged in providing and receiving assistance, this proportion is slightly higher than that for the sample as a whole.	16%	16%
Intimate but distant	Adult children are engaged with their parents on emotional closeness and similarity of opinions but *not* based on geographic proximity, frequency of contact, providing assistance, and receiving assistance.	19%	14%
Detached	Adult children are *not* engaged with their parents based on any of the six indicators of solidarity.	7%	27%

Source: Adapted from Silverstein & Bengtson, 1997.

BIOPSYCHOSOCIAL PERSPECTIVE

A MODEL THAT provides a biopsychosocial perspective on relationships in adulthood is that of the **social convoy**, which proposes that people have a network of close relationships that "carries" them or provides social support throughout their lives (Kahn & Antonucci, 1980). Although the convoy may change in structure, it maintains continuity in terms of size (5 to 10 close social ties) and the exchange of support that takes place between the individual and others in his or her social network. The convoy can be thought of as a concentric set of circles, with the closest family members in the innermost circles and more distant relationships extending outward (Antonucci & Akiyama, 1987; Chatters, Taylor, & Jackson, 1985).

According to the social convoy model, support is exchanged in both directions from and to others in the convoy. However, as people get older, they feel they are more likely to receive rather than provide support to others, perhaps because they feel that they provided more support in the past. Nevertheless, exchange relationships remain reciprocal throughout adulthood (Antonucci & Akiyama, 1987) and in areas such as emotional support, older parents continue to serve as an important resource for middle-aged women (Townsend & Franks, 1995). In contrast to younger generations, who include more friends in their innermost circle, older adults are more likely to include family members, particularly among Hispanics (Levitt, Weber, & Guacci, 1993). A preference for fewer rather than more friends begins to emerge relatively early in adulthood, by the 30s (Lansford, Sherman, & Antonucci, 1998).

Thus, social relationships continue to maintain importance throughout life, and people remain highly involved in a network of close interactions well into later adulthood. There is a predominant tendency for people to feel satisfied with the number of people within their closest circle of the convoy, and the extent to which they do is a factor in predicting their psychological well-being (Antonucci, Fuhrer, & Dartigues, 1997).

This approach to social support and relationships in adulthood has extensive implications for a biopsychosocial model. In the first place, biological factors are at the core of many of the transitions in relationships that people experience in adulthood, ranging from physical changes associated with the normal aging process to the increased susceptibility to chronic diseases that occurs in later adulthood. The physiological changes associated with pregnancy and childbirth may also be seen as contributing to the experience of the transition to parenthood. However, the relationship between social changes in adulthood and physical functioning may also operate in the other direction. The extent to which an individual experiences satisfaction with the social network may contribute to improved physical functioning and health in the cardiovascular, endocrine, and immune systems (Uchino, Cacioppo, & Kiecolt-Glaser, 1996).

Clearly, much of what occurs during adulthood and in later life takes place against a backdrop of intricate interpersonal relationships. Looking within the individual at biological, cognitive, and personality changes is important, but the ever-present perspective provided by others in one's social network remains a dominant force in adult development.

Race and ethnicity were also related to the strength of adult child–parent relationships. Obligatory relationships were more common in whites compared to blacks and Hispanics, and whites were more likely than blacks to have detached relations with their mothers. Tight-knit relationships between mothers and adult children were more common in low-income families. Although minority status was not related to relationships with fathers, income was. Children in higher-income families were most likely to be intimate but distant.

In addition to providing considerable detail about the nature of adult child–parent relationships, these findings point to the importance of looking at these relations in a multidimensional manner. The existence of types in which parents and children were emotionally but not

The nature of relationships in extended families show important variations by race and ethnicity.

functionally close, and in contrast, functionally but not emotionally close, indicates that a simple measure of solidarity fails to capture the complexity of contemporary intergenerational relationships. Furthermore, it is clear from this study that, even for fathers, only a minority of adult children perceive themselves as both emotionally and socially distant from their parents.

SIBLINGS

Although not a heavily investigated area, those who study the sibling relationship in adulthood point to its many unique features within the constellation of family interactions (Cicirelli, 1995). Those who are siblings by birth share a genetic background, and those who have been raised together share many experiences dating to early childhood. By the time siblings reach later adulthood, it is quite possible that they are the only remaining members of their original family and that they have known each other longer than anyone else they have known in their entire lives. As is true for adult child–parent relationships, the sibling relationship is not one of choice, and, to be sure, many people

allow their connections with brothers and sisters to fall by the wayside (Gold, 1989). However, four out of five older adults have at least one surviving sibling with whom they have contact (Brody, Hoffman, Kleban, & Schoonover, 1989). Even if they do not stay in frequent contact, they may still maintain the relationship and tend to value it in a positive manner (Bedford, Volling, & Avioli, 2000).

The potential exists for this relationship to be the deepest and closest of an adult's life, and to bring with that closeness both shared joy and shared pain. For the most part, it appears that sibling relationships are positive in middle and later adulthood. The large majority (about 90%) report that they neither argue nor are competitive with their siblings (Cicirelli, 1982), and conversely, only 10% fall into a sibling category with the self-evident label of "hostile" (Gold, 1989). However, these data are based on self-report, and when adult siblings are observed in actual discussion situations, the presence of "sibling rivalry" is significantly higher, nearing 45% (Ross & Milgram, 1982).

In one of the few systematic investigations of sibling relationships in adulthood (unfortunately, conducted only on young adults), three dimensions were identified: warmth, conflict, and rivalry (Stocker, Lanthier, & Furman, 1997). Examples from the questionnaire used in this study that illustrate each of these dimensions are shown in Table 9-4.

The warmth dimension, though identified in this study in a sample of young adults, has also emerged in studies of middle-aged and older adults. Amount of contact appears to be a factor that is related to closeness or warmth (Lee, Mancini, & Maxwell, 1987), and although it would make sense that siblings who live near each other feel closer, this need not necessarily be the case.

It was somewhat surprising in the Stocker et al. study to see that young adults, who were

TABLE 9-4
Items from the Adult Sibling Relationship Questionnaire

Scale	Question
Warmth	How much do you and this sibling have in common?
	How close do you feel to this sibling?
	How much does this sibling try to cheer you up when you are feeling down?
	How much does this sibling give you practical advice?
	How much do you and this sibling think alike?
	How much does this sibling think that you have accomplished a great deal in life?
Conflict	How much do you irritate this sibling?
	How much do you dominate this sibling?
	How much do you and this sibling argue with each other?
Rivalry	Do you think your mother favors you or this sibling more?
	Does this sibling think your father is closer to him/her or you?
	Do you think your father supports you or this sibling more?

Source: Stocker, Lanthier, & Furman, 1997.

no longer living at home, still experienced conflict and rivalry, dimensions that have also been identified in the studies on older siblings. Interestingly, however, feelings of conflict and rivalry were only minimally related to warmth, reflecting the ambivalence that adult siblings may feel toward each other. In child sibling pairs, warmth and conflict are negatively related to each other. Another difference from childhood sibling relationships was that a power or dominance dimension did not emerge from the analyses. Apparently, by adulthood, siblings view themselves as equal and differences based on age disappear, similar to the phenomenon that occurs as adult children begin to perceive themselves as peers of their parents. However, one aspect of childhood family experience that did carry over into these adult sibling relationships was the size of the family. Siblings from large families experienced less closeness in adulthood.

The sibling relationship is one that, though quite likely influenced by early experiences and patterns established in childhood, does fluctuate throughout adulthood. Increased closeness between siblings is associated with a number of significant life events, such as marriage, the birth of children, divorce and widowhood, and the development of health problems or death of a family member (Connidis, 1992). Sibling ties seem to be particularly sensitive to these events. Such events give siblings greater shared experiences, understanding of each other, and insight into the dynamics of their relationship.

GRANDPARENTS

For many older adults, the rewards of family life begin to grow much richer when they reach the status of grandparents. At this point, they are in a position to be able to enjoy the benefits of expressing their generativity through interacting with the youngest generation. However, they can avoid the more arduous tasks of parenthood. As we saw earlier, one of the most challenging aspects of life for the older person, particularly the woman over 85, is loss of a spouse. The opportunity to be a grandparent can offset some of this loss.

Unfortunately, not all grandparents are able to enjoy the benefits of their status, nor do all grandparents want to assume this role. Furthermore, grandparents are increasingly being asked to substitute for a parent who is not present in the home, or whose job has extensive time commitments.

Many people still think of grandparents as the warm, generous, older adults who have ample time to spend with their families and want to do so. However, variations in patterns of grandparenting, along with a rapidly increasing growth in the number of grandparents in the population, may require that this image be changed.

There are no definitive population statistics on the percentage of older adults who are grandparents. Estimates are that 94% of the older adult population with children are grandparents, and close to 50% are great-grandparents (Hooyman & Kiyak, 1991). Along with changing family patterns in the United States, it is also quite likely that many more individuals become grandparents or acquire additional grandchildren through the remarriage of children and the gaining of step-grandchildren.

Grandparents Raising Grandchildren

Although general population statistics are not available on grandparents in the general population, data have become available over the last 10 years on a phenomenon that is rapidly growing in scope. This is the existence of **grandparents raising grandchildren**, in which the grandparent takes the primary responsibility as caregiver for the grandchild. The first data on this phenomenon became available in the 1990 U.S. Census, and updates throughout the 1990s continued to track this growing trend. Figure 9.7 demonstrates the growth in percentages from 1970 to 1997. As of 2000, there were 3.8 million children living in homes maintained by their grandparents, which amounted to 5.3% of

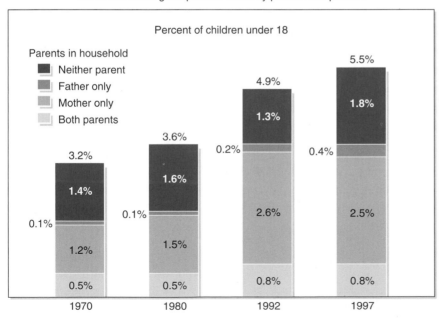

Grandchildren in grandparents' home by presence of parents

FIGURE 9.7

Grandchildren Raised in Grandparents' Home

Source: Bryson & Casper, 1999.

all children under the age of 18 years. There were 1.4 million children living with grandparents and no parents present (U.S. Bureau of the Census, 2001b). This situation, referred to as a **skip generation family** (Bryson & Casper, 1999), may occur for a variety of reasons, including substance abuse by parents, child abuse or neglect, teenage pregnancy or failure of parents to handle children, unemployment, divorce, AIDS, and incarceration of parents (Pinson-Millburn, Fabian, Schlossberg, & Pyle, 1996).

The ramifications of the skip generation family are both positive and negative. On the positive side, only a small percentage (15% of grandmothers and 21% of grandfathers) of these grandparents are over the age of 65 years, and over one-third of them rate their health as "excellent" or "very good."

In addition, the role of surrogate parent can contribute positively to the grandparent's sense of identity, particularly for African-American grandmothers (Pruchno & McKenney, 2002).

However, on the negative side, these women are at risk for experiencing severe economic hardship (Fuller-Thomson, Minkler, & Driver, 1997). Grandfathers as primary caregivers are more likely to be white, employed, own their homes, and in general live in better economic circumstances (Casper & Bryson, 1998). However, only 6% of skip generation families are headed by grandfathers (Bryson & Casper, 1999).

Another phenomenon that is beginning to receive attention is the role of great-grandparents in the family and the potential that this is an increasing possibility in families with short intergenerational time spans (less than 20–23 years). According to Bengston, relationships across more than two generations are taking on increasing importance in the United States and will continue to do so into the foreseeable future (Bengston, 2001).

"What do you think?" | **9-5**

What types of grandparents do you have? How would you rate them on the grandparent style types?

Patterns of Grandparenting

The majority of studies of grandparenting have been primarily descriptive, pointing to several varieties or types of grandparenting styles observed in various samples but lacking an appreciation of the multidimensionality of this role and relationship. Other studies have delineated various functions of grandparenting, but again, at a primarily descriptive level and often from the point of view of the grandparent rather than other family members (Roberto, 1990). The classic study of grandparenting conducted by Neugarten and Weinstein (1964) identified five types of grandparents. The *formal* grandparent follows what are believed to be the appropriate guidelines for the grandparenting role, which includes providing occasional services and maintaining an interest in the grandchild, but not becoming overly involved. The *fun seeker* emphasizes the leisure aspects of the role and provides primarily entertainment for the grandchild. The *surrogate parent*, as the name implies, takes over the caretaking role with the child. The *reservoir of family wisdom*, which is usually a grandfather, is the head of the family who dispenses advice and resources but also controls the parent generation. Finally, the *distant figure* is the grandparent who has infrequent contact with the grandchildren, appearing only on holidays and other special occasions.

Other attempts to characterize or delineate styles or categories of grandparenting have followed a similar pattern, with distinctions typically being made among the highly involved,

There are a variety of patterns of grandparenting; clearly, the grandmother and grandchild shown here have a close and positive relationship.

friendly, and remote or formal types of grandparents (Mueller, Wilhelm, & Elder, 2002). The "remote-involved" dimension is one that seems to resonate in the attitudes that grandchildren have toward their grandparents as well (Roberto & Stroes, 1992). The symbolic value of the grandparent in the family lineage, or the "family watchdog" (Troll, 1985), is another central component identified in several classifications.

Researchers have also attempted to understand the meaning that grandparenthood has to older adults. Based on an investigation of over 300 grandparents, Kivnick (1982) identified five dimensions: *Centrality* refers to the extent to which being a grandparent becomes more important than other activities, the extent to which being a grandparent is a part of the individual's identity, and the extent to which grandparenthood weighs in the individual's definition of the meaning of life. The dimension of *valued elder* applies to the extent to which grandparents see themselves as resources and the amount of concern they have over how they are remembered by their grandchildren. Related to this dimension is *immortality through clan*, which is a sense of responsibility for the family ("clan"), identification with grandchildren, and

the immortality of the family. In the dimension of *reinvolvement with personal past*, grandparenthood is seen in terms of reliving past experiences and thinking about the individual's own grandparents. Finally, the *spoil* dimension involves the extent to which grandparents indulge the desires of their grandchildren. Although conceptualized differently from the grandparenting typologies, the dimensional approach also identifies the themes of formality of role, closeness to grandchild, and entertainment. The meaning of grandparenting, which is not specified in the other typologies, however, is unique to this examination of the personal meaning of this family position.

Although these variations may exist in patterns of grandparenting, it is safe to say that the role of grandparent is an important one for the older adult. As is true for parenting, there can also be a developmental stake between grandparents and grandchildren, such that grandparents feel a stronger sense of connection to the younger generation than grandchildren feel toward them (Crosnoe & Elder, 2002). Moreover, grandparents who are unable to maintain contact with their grandchildren due to parental divorce or disagreements within the family are likely to suffer a variety of negative consequences, including poor mental and physical health, depression, feelings of grief, and poorer quality of life (Drew & Smith, 2002).

FRIENDSHIPS

Of the areas of relationships examined in this chapter, friendship has probably received the least attention regarding its function, meaning, and changes over the course of adulthood. Yet, as the college-age reader would almost certainly agree, friends are a crucial aspect of life. It is not clear why the social life of middle-aged and older adults is generally disregarded in favor of

Joe Torchio and Lou Fried, the nursing home room-mates whose late-life friendship was chronicled by author Tracy Kidder.

studies of family life, but fortunately some emerging frameworks may guide further research in this area.

Qualitative evidence for the importance of friends in adulthood abounds, however, as any glance through literature, drama, or certainly the movies would attest. Friendships in old age are perhaps given the least attention in the arts and popular culture. One stunning exception was provided by author Tracy Kidder. His nonfiction account of two male residents of a Massachusetts nursing home called *Old Friends* (Kidder, 1993) presented a moving portrayal of a newly formed relationship emerging between two unlikely friends in an unlikely environment.

Theoretical Perspectives

Socioemotional selectivity theory provides some perspective on the role of friendships in later adulthood, suggesting that older people prefer family to friends, but they also prefer that time spent with friends is indeed with "old friends" (Lang & Carstensen, 1994). Interestingly, the men in the Kidder book had *not* known each

other prior to becoming friends, but their friendship was based on very intense shared experiences that would seem to fit the theory's predictions. Nevertheless, the friendships that should matter the most to older people, according to theory, should be the ones that stretch back at least several decades.

Taking a life course perspective, Hartup and Stevens (1997) suggested that the major dimension that underlies close friendships is reciprocity, or a sense of mutuality. The fundamental characteristic of reciprocity is that there is a giving and taking within the relationship at a deep, emotional level involving intimacy, support, sharing, and companionship. At the behavioral level, reciprocity is expressed in such actions as exchanging favors, gifts, and advice. Close friends in adulthood confide in each other, help each other in times of trouble, and attempt to enhance each other's sense of well-being. Although there may be developmental differences across the life span in the expression of reciprocity, the essence of all friendships remains this sense of deep mutuality. According to Hartup, another important function of friendships is socializing, or helping each other through life transitions in other spheres, such as changes in health, marital relationships, residence, and work. In this theory the men in Kidder's book would be explained in terms of the mutual help they provided to each other in adapting to the nursing home environment.

Patterns of Friendships

Friendship patterns at any age may be seen as following a developmental trajectory from formation to dissolution (Adams & Blieszner, 1994). The stage of *friendship formation* involves moving from being strangers to acquaintances to friends. The *maintenance* phase encompasses what is usually thought of as "friendship," during which friends sustain an active interest and involvement with each other. They may evaluate the quality of the friendship periodically during this phase, deciding to increase or decrease their level of involvement. In terms of Hartup's framework, it would be during the maintenance phase that levels of reciprocity are highest. Friendships may remain in the maintenance phase for many decades at varying levels of closeness. The end of a friendship, which occurs during the *dissolution* phase, may be hard to identify. A friendship may end gradually over a period of years as feelings of reciprocity diminish and the relationship essentially falls by the wayside. Friendships may also end through a conscious decision based on insurmountable disagreements and conflict.

"What do you think?" | **9-6**

What types of friends do you have? How many people would you count as close friends?

Friendships in adulthood may also be distinguished in terms of the closeness of the relationship, which may or may not change over time. People may maintain **peripheral ties**, which are not characterized by a high degree of closeness, for many years (Fingerman & Griffiths, 1999). Peripheral ties include people such as neighbors, coworkers, professional contacts, or the parents of one's children's friends. These relationships may be amicable and cordial but never progress beyond this level. Other peripheral ties may be those that are in the friendship formation stage and will later progress to close friendships. A third type of peripheral tie is a tie that was formerly a close friendship and has now moved to the dissolution/disinterest stage.

There may also be variations in friendship patterns in adulthood based on individual differences in approaches toward friends, called **friendship styles** (Matthews, 1986). *Independent* individuals may enjoy friendly, satisfying, and cordial relationships with people but never form close or intimate friendships. *Discerning* individuals are extremely selective in their choice of friends, retaining a small number of very close friends throughout their lives. Finally, *acquisitive* people are readily able to make and retain close friendships throughout their lives and therefore have a large social network.

The majority of middle-aged adults (93–94%) state that they have friends, although the number diminishes after the age of 65 to 88% of women and 78% of men (Fischer & Phillips, 1982). The amount of time spent with friends ranges from 7% in middle age to 9% after the age of 65, with variations according to gender and marital status. Women spend more time with friends than men do, and widowed individuals of both genders spend more time interacting with friends than do those who are married (Hartup & Stevens, 1997). People tend to choose as friends other adults who are similar in gender, socioeconomic status, and ethnicity (Adams & Blieszner, 1995; Matthews et al., 1996). Throughout adulthood, close social ties serve as a buffer against stress and are related to higher levels of well-being and self-esteem. Relationships with friends may even be more predictive of high levels of self-esteem than even income or marital status (Siebert, Mutran, & Reitzes, 2002). In cases where family members are not available, friendships serve as an important substitute for keeping an individual socially connected (Lang & Carstensen, 1994).

As important as friendships are, it is important to keep in mind the finding that emerged earlier in the discussion of widowhood. People who have become widows in the middle and later adult years feel that friendships cannot replace the emotional rewards of marriage (Stroebe et al., 1996). Social support is vital in protecting an individual from experiencing extreme amounts of stress in response to difficult life circumstances, but even close friends cannot meet the unique functions of the spouse.

SUMMARY

1. Close relationships form an important component of adult life, and although these patterns are changing in the United States, development in adulthood and later life interacts in important ways with the ties that people have with others. The large majority of adults get married, and although marriage rates are decreasing and people are waiting longer to get married than in previous decades, the majority of adults are living in a marital relationship. In increasingly older age groups, the proportion of men who are married becomes higher than the proportion of women. The majority of people living with a partner (not married) are between 25 and 34 years of age. Men are more likely to marry after divorce and widowhood than are women. Whites are more likely to marry than blacks. Cohabitation rates have been increasing in recent decades, and there are more single mothers today than there were in 1960. Divorce rates have increased since 1960 but were lower in 1998 than in 1980. The likelihood of a marriage ending in divorce is 43%, down from 60% in the early 1980s. Divorces are most likely to occur within three years of marriage, and the average length of marriage prior to divorce is about 10 years. Divorce rates are higher among blacks than whites. About half of all marriages ending in divorce involve custody of children. More women than men are widows, and the rate of widowhood is highest in the population among black women over the age of 65.

2. Socioemotional selectivity theory proposes that, over the course of adulthood, individuals select social interactions that will maximize the emotional rewards of relationships, so that older adults prefer to spend time with spouses and family rather than acquaintances. Older adults in a long-term relationship have more favorable interactions because they have learned how to regulate their negative affect. Attachment theory proposes that adults relate to partners on the basis of attachment style and the mental representations that individuals have about relationships. Studies on adult age differences in attachment style show that older adults are less likely to be anxiously attached and more likely to be dismissive compared to younger adults. However, the majority of adults are securely attached. Theories of relationship satisfaction include social exchange theory, equity theory, and behavioral theory. The need complementarity and similarity hypotheses attempt to explain how adults become attracted to each other. The concept of divorce proneness may account for the higher rates of divorced among remarried individuals, who feel less committed to the institution of marriage.

3. Sexual behavior in long-term relationships undergoes changes due to alterations with aging in sexual responsivity. Both men and women move through the sexual response cycle at a slower rate. A survey of adult sexual behavior indicates a sexual dysfunction rate of 43% for women and 31% for men, particularly for those in poor economic circumstances. Health and psychological factors such as stress and anxiety influence the sexual functioning of older adults, and these conditions can lead to secondary impotence, a psychologically caused form of erectile dysfunction. Although physical changes may occur in sexual responsivity, older adults

express strong interests in maintaining sexual relationships, including sexual relations outside of marriage for those who are single, widowed, or divorced.

4. Birth rates have decreased over the past 20 years, and women are having children at later ages. Most women, however, have their first child before the age of 30. Women who have a child after they are 30 are more highly educated and have higher incomes, but they also have a higher risk of encountering medical complications. Men with higher education and occupation are more involved in raising their children but spend less time in providing care. The number of single fathers is increasing, but there are also more fathers who have no contact with children.

5. Despite population trends toward more single-parent and cohabiting families, the large majority of households in the United States (69%) consist of people living together as a family. American households are most likely to consist of three-person families, and over half of all families have one or more members under the age of 18. Households with married couples constitute 53% of all households. Less than one-quarter (24.1%) of all households in the United States consist of married couples with children, the lowest percentage since at least 1970, when 40% of all households were composed of married couples with children. Studies of the transition to parenthood indicate that decreases in marital satisfaction are especially likely to occur when the division of labor assumes more traditional lines in the household. More egalitarian relationships are found among lesbian couples who enter parenthood. The study of adult child–parent relationships reveals a number of important phenomena related to their changes in roles and altered views of each other. Although caregiving is usually thought of in negative terms, there is some evidence of positive outcomes when daughters use problem-focused coping strategies and have higher levels of education. The intergenerational solidarity model proposes six dimensions to characterize the cohesiveness of these relationships. Siblings are another important family tie in adulthood, and closeness between siblings varies over the adult years along with other family and life events. The majority of older adults are grandparents, a relationship that tends to be positive, but there is a trend toward grandparents raising grandchildren in a *skip generation* (no parents present) household. Theoretical explanations of grandparenting focus on the remote-involved dimension, and various categorization schemes are based on this concept.

6. Friendships are another source of important close relationships in adulthood, and even if individuals are not involved in tight-knit friendships, they may have many important peripheral ties.

GLOSSARY

Anxious attachment style (also called **anxious-ambivalent attachment style**): mixed approach to attachment figure.

Attachment style: way of thinking about an attachment figure.

Attachment theory: proposal that the individual's approach to close relationships in adulthood originates in the infant's relationships with caregivers.

Avoidant attachment style: resistant approach to attachment figures.

Behavioral approach to marital interactions: approach that emphasizes the actual behaviors that partners engage in with each other during marital interactions as an influence on marital stability and quality.

Blended families (also called **reconstituted families**): families in which the parents were not originally married to each other in which there are children and stepchildren of one or both parents.

Caregiving: the provision of aid in daily living activities to an infirm older adult, often a relative.

Cohabitation: living in a stable relationship prior to or instead of marrying.

Developmental schism: an emotional gap created between parents and their children.

Developmental stake: principle that suggests parents have a greater investment in their children than children do in their parents.

Divorce proneness: characteristic of divorced people to be more likely to consider divorce as an option when their marriage is not going smoothly.

Empty nest: the departure of children from the home.

Equity theory: proposal that relationships continue when the partners feel they are contributing equal benefits.

Family life cycle: stages of marriage based on the ages of children.

Filial anxiety: the idea that one might be forced to take on the role of parent to the parent.

Filial maturity: the identification of the adult child with the parent.

Filial obligation (or **filial piety**): the feeling that one is obligated to take care of aging parents should this become necessary.

Friendship styles: friendship patterns in adulthood based on individual differences in approaches toward friends.

Grandparents raising grandchildren: family situation in which the grandparent takes the primary responsibility as caregiver for the grandchild.

Intergenerational solidarity model: model proposing six dimensions that characterize the cohesiveness of adult child–parent relationships.

Marital selectivity hypothesis: the proposal that people choose partners who match their own depressive or neurotic characteristics.

Marriage: legally sanctioned union between a man and a woman.

Need complementary hypothesis: the proposal that people seek and are more satisfied with marital partners who are the opposite of themselves.

Peripheral ties: friendships that persist but are not characterized by a high degree of closeness.

Role reversal: discredited belief that parents and their adult children switch responsibilities.

Sandwich generation: popular term used to refer to women with aging parents needing help and children living in the home.

Secondary impotence: loss of erectile functioning caused by psychological factors.

Secure attachment style: healthy approach to attachment figures.

Similarity hypothesis: the proposal that similarity and perceived similarity predict interpersonal attraction.

Skip generation family: family in which children are living with grandparents and no parents are present.

Social convoy: proposal that people have a network of close relationships that "carries" them or provides social support throughout their lives.

Social exchange theory: proposal that relationships continue when partners perceive that the rewards of remaining in the relationship outweigh the rewards associated with alternatives.

Socioemotional selectivity theory: the proposition that, throughout adulthood, individuals reduce the range of their relationships to maximize social and emotional gains and minimize risks.

Transition to parenthood: the period in which a first child is born to a married couple.

Chapter Ten

Work, Retirement, and Leisure Patterns

"Old age hath yet his honour and his toil."

Alfred Lord Tennyson
1809–1892

The majority of adults are involved in productive activities in some form of paid employment. For some individuals, the experience of work is positive, fulfilling, and expressive of their personal interests and abilities. Others are not so fortunate, and for them, work is a means to an end of supplying income that can be used toward fulfilling activities in the realms of leisure, recreation, or family. Regardless of the enjoyment that work provides, however, it is the primary focus of life among people from the 20s and onward until they retire. Furthermore, the nature of their work, the amount of income it provides, and the conditions in which their work is conducted carry over to virtually every other area of their lives. Finally, identity is defined in important ways in terms of job title, prestige, security, and status.

Given the importance of work in adulthood, what is the impact of retirement? Researchers, theorists, and counselors have been intrigued with this question, and as you will learn, there are no easy answers. Although the thought of

retirement may seem very far away to the average college-age student, it must be planned for much sooner than you might think!

WORK PATTERNS IN ADULTHOOD

The work experiences of adults are best understood by first looking at the context in which employment occurs. The **labor force** includes all civilians in the over-16 population who are living outside of institutions (prisons, nursing homes, residential treatment centers) and who have or are actively seeking employment. In 2003, the total civilian noninstitutionalized population over the age of 16 amounted to 220 million people, and of these, two-thirds were in the labor force. Almost all (94%) of these individuals were employed, meaning that 63% of all available workers in the United States are employed (http://www.bls.gov/news.release/ empsit.t01.htm).

The distribution of age groups in the labor force is shown in Fig. 10.1 from 1950 to projections for 2006. As can be seen from this figure, the labor force age dynamics have shifted over this period and are expected to continue to shift over the next five years. These dynamics reflect the movement of the so-called baby boom generation through the population such that beginning in the 1970s, when they entered the workforce, the relative proportions of older workers diminished and younger workers increased.

Although whites, blacks, and Hispanics have similar labor force participation rates, the unemployment rates are higher for blacks and Hispanics than for whites. (U.S. Bureau of the Census, 2003a, Table 593). The labor force

participation rate of men has always been greater than that of women; however, there has been a dramatic rise since 1960 of married women in the workforce. Among married women, those with young children have been entering the labor force at a steadily increasing rate since 1960. This increase was particularly steep for women with children under the age of 6, whose labor participation rate increased from 19% in 1960 to 63% in 2001 (U.S. Bureau of the Census, 2003a). The relative proportion of women in the labor force is expected to continue to increase through 2010 (Fullerton & Toossi, 2001).

Occupational Level

The **occupational level** of a job refers to its position on the hierarchy of jobs in terms of amount of required training, prestige, and income. The majority of occupations in the United States are in the top two levels of the occupational hierarchy. The top level includes managerial and professional workers, and the next highest level includes jobs that are technical, sales-oriented, or administrative. Together, these (Kerby & Ragan, 2002) make

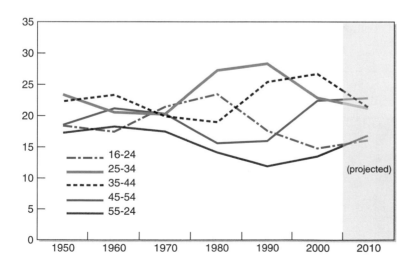

FIGURE 10.1
Percentage Distribution of the Labor Force by Age

Source: Bureau of Labor Statistics, 2003.

up almost 60% of the U.S. labor force. The **managerial and professional level jobs** include executives, managers, and professionals such as physicians, architects, engineers, computer scientists, teachers, counselors, social workers, and lawyers. The technical, sales, and administrative level jobs include laboratory and health technicians, airplane pilots, sales representatives, secretaries, clerical workers, mail carriers, clerks, bank tellers, and teachers' aides. The next largest category of occupations are those at the **service level**, which includes people who provide assistance to others such as private household workers, child-care workers, food workers, and hairdressers. These occupations are sometimes referred to as **pink-collar jobs**. Also included in service occupations are the protective service occupations, including police officers and firefighters. Traditional **blue-collar jobs** include machine operators, fabricators, laborers, truck drivers, and farm workers. A second category of blue-collar workers are those in the precision production, craft, and repair occupations, which include mechanics, repairers, and construction workers.

Management and professional level jobs reach their peak in the 45–54 age bracket. There are relatively few individuals over the age of 55 in the technical occupations, which includes the projected growth industry of computer programming. In contrast, sales-level jobs are relatively more frequent and increase for men and women after the age of 55. Workers over 55 also are more likely to be employed in service jobs (Bureau of Labor Statistics, 1999).

Income levels vary considerably with age, as can be seen in Fig. 10.2. The highest median income is earned by those in the 45–54 age bracket. This fact is consistent with the data on age by occupational level. The highest percentages of people in the managerial and professional levels, which are also the highest paying occupations, are within this age bracket.

There are wide disparities in income across occupational levels, and in general, men earn more than do women. (See Fig. 10.3) In part, this discrepancy between men and women may be accounted for by the fact that women are more likely to have part-time jobs, which by definition provide a lower income. In addition, women are more likely to be in the lower-paid service occupations. However, even for full-time sales workers, women earn only 60% of the salary of men. Female executives earn two-thirds the salaries of males (among full-time workers). Across all occupational levels, women earn about three-quarters the salaries of men (Bureau of Labor Statistics, 1999). Age plays somewhat of a role in influencing the relationship between gender and income.

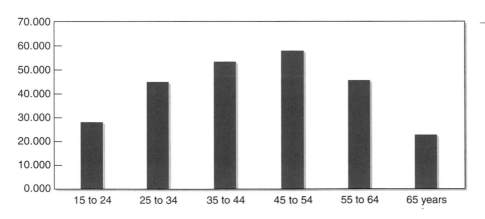

FIGURE 10.2
Median Income by Age

Source: DeNavas-Walt & Cleveland, 2002.

Educational Level

An important contributor to occupational level and ultimately income is an individual's level of education. There is a steady rise in income with each level of education, although those with a professional degree (M.D., D.D.S., J.D.) earn more than those with a doctorate in an academic field (Ph.D. or Ed.D.). Nevertheless, at all educational levels, women earn less than men (see Fig. 10.3). Over their work lives, men with professional degrees earn $2 million more than do women. There are also disparities in earnings by race. Among those with bachelor's degrees, white non-Hispanics have a projected lifetime earning of $2.2 million compared to $1.7 million for blacks and Hispanics (Day & Newberger, 2002). There is a negative relationship between age and amount of education. The 45–59 age groups contain the highest percentage of all age groups with a postcollege degree.

Corresponding to differences in occupational levels, the income levels of both black and Hispanic workers are also lower than those of whites. The disparity is particularly pronounced among men. Although whites are more likely to have achieved a college education than are blacks or Hispanics, these differences in education do not account entirely for differences in employment rates, occupational level, and income. For example, in 2001, among men with a doctorate degree, whites earned an average of $99,238; Hispanics, $70,103; and blacks, $58,276 (U.S. Bureau of the Census, 2003b).

> ### "What do you think?" | 10-1
>
> What might be the impact on lifestyle and health of differences in occupational level by race?

Black males with a college education have relatively lower income than their white male counterparts in part because they are less likely to be employed in the higher-paying managerial and technical occupational levels. More white male college graduates are employed at these levels than are black male college graduates. Furthermore, black male college graduates are twice as likely to be working in blue-collar jobs than whites who have a college education (U.S. Bureau of the Census, 1998c). The term **glass ceiling**, which is typically applied to females in managerial level jobs who are unable to rise to executive levels, also applies to highly educated nonwhite men (Hogan, Kim, & Perrucci, 1997).

In general, people over the age of 65 have lower levels of education than do those between the ages of 25 and 64. The breakdown in education by age is shown in Fig. 10.4. As can be seen, people over 65 are less likely to have a college education than people under 65. In addition to what is shown in this figure, in the over-65 group, males are more likely than females to have a college education, a sex difference not evident among

FIGURE 10.3

Lifetime Earnings Estimates by Age and Educational Attainment

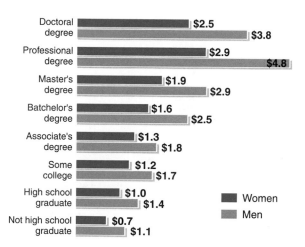

	Women	Men
Doctoral degree	$2.5	$3.8
Professional degree	$2.9	$4.8
Master's degree	$1.9	$2.9
Batchelor's degree	$1.6	$2.5
Associate's degree	$1.3	$1.8
Some college	$1.2	$1.7
High school graduate	$1.0	$1.4
Not high school graduate	$0.7	$1.1

Source: U.S. Bureau of the Census, 2000a.

FIGURE 10.4

Percentage of College Graduates by Age

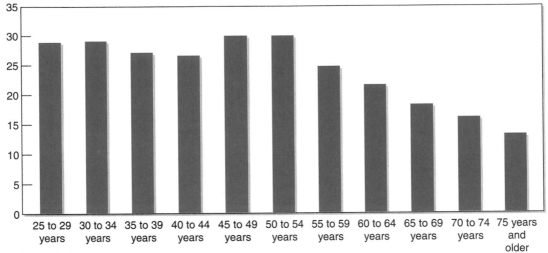

Source: Day & Newberger, 2002.

those in the 25–64 age bracket. In fact, there is a slight tendency for women in the younger age groups to be more highly educated than men. However, even white women over the age of 65 are more likely to have a college education than either group of minority males in this age group.

Another statistic not shown in Fig. 10.3 is the percentage of people who report having had no formal education at all. Although this percentage is relatively low for blacks and whites in all age groups, about one-tenth of Hispanic males and females over 65 have not received any formal schooling.

In the 1990s, women became increasingly likely to hold jobs at the managerial and executive levels, but their salaries still lagged behind those of men.

VOCATIONAL DEVELOPMENT

Education, race, gender, and age are some of the social factors that influence an individual's position within the world of work. These social factors remain important throughout adulthood and into retirement in regard to people's patterns of work involvement. However, the individual's choice of an occupation, or **vocation**, as it is also called, reflects that individual's personal preferences and interests. You are in college based on your desire to enter a given field. You may be majoring in psychology, consumer studies, nursing, education, chemistry, or music. How did you choose this major? Assuming the process was not randomly made, your choice reflects your personality, skills, and experience. These are the factors that vocational development theories take into account when attempting to explain the career choices that individuals make and to determine their happiness and productivity once they have acted on those choices. Starting from a career-counseling orientation, vocational development theorists and researchers are beginning to incorporate concepts from developmental science such as the importance of context and relationships (Savikas, 2002).

Holland's Vocational Development Theory

According to **Holland's vocational development theory**, vocational aspirations and interests are the expression of an individual's personality. The theory proposes that there are six types of vocational interests, competencies, and behaviors, each of which is identified by its initial letter: Realistic (R), Investigative (I), Artistic (A), Social (S), Enterprising (E), and Conventional (C). Based on the letters that describe the six types (also called codes), the theory is also referred to as the **RIASEC** model (see Fig. 10.5). Vocational environments (occupations) can also be described

in terms of the same six codes. These are the settings that elicit, develop, and reward the specific interests, competencies, and behaviors associated with each of the types (Gottfredson, 1999). According to Holland, occupations reflect particular patterns of job requirements and rewards that are characteristic of their environments. Social occupations involve work with people, and Realistic occupations involve work with one's hands.

The rating of interests and occupations using Holland's framework involves applying a two- or three-letter code that is a combination of RIASEC code ratings. The first letter reflects the primary type into which the interest or occupation falls ("S" for Social, for example). The second and third letters allow for a more accurate and differentiated picture of the individual or occupation. Both a construction worker and a corrections officer are R code occupations, and both have the RE code designation. They differ in their third code, which is C for the construction worker and S for the corrections officer.

In addition to the theorized vocational and occupational descriptions, personality descriptions are thought to characterize each of the six types, based on correspondence between the Holland codes and scores on the NEO-PI-R. These have developed over the years as personality tests have been administered to large samples of workers, and scores on the five factors have been contrasted according to their primary RIASEC codes (Barrick, Mount, & Gupta, 2003; Larson, Rottinghaus, & Borgen, 2002).

The six RIASEC types are theorized to be organized within the individual in a hexagonal structure, as shown in Fig. 10.5. This structure implies that the types have a relationship to each other based on their distance from each other on the structure. Types that are most similar (such as R and C) are closest, and those that are the most dissimilar (such as C and A) are furthest away from each other.

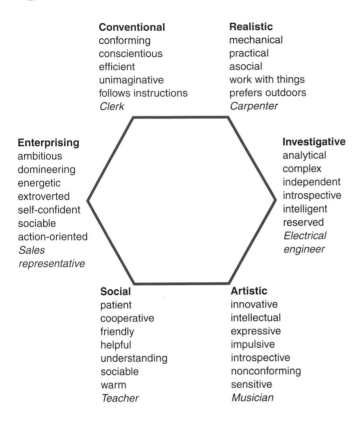

Conventional
conforming
conscientious
efficient
unimaginative
follows instructions
Clerk

Realistic
mechanical
practical
asocial
work with things
prefers outdoors
Carpenter

Enterprising
ambitious
domineering
energetic
extroverted
self-confident
sociable
action-oriented
Sales representative

Investigative
analytical
complex
independent
introspective
intelligent
reserved
Electrical engineer

Social
patient
cooperative
friendly
helpful
understanding
sociable
warm
Teacher

Artistic
innovative
intellectual
expressive
impulsive
introspective
nonconforming
sensitive
Musician

FIGURE 10.5

Holland's RIASEC model

Source: Holland, 1997. Adapted and reproduced by special permission of the Publish, Psychological Assessment Resources, Inc., Odessa, FL 33556, from the Self-Directed Search Assessment Booklet by John L. Holland, Ph.D. Copyright 1970, 1977, 1990, 1994 by PAR, Inc. Further reproduction is prohibited without permission from PAR, Inc.

According to Holland, workers seek an occupation in which there is **congruence** or "fit" between their RIASEC type and that of the occupation. Workers will also be most productive, according to the theory, when their interests and job are congruent. Unfortunately, people cannot always find jobs congruent with their interests. In these situations, Holland's theory predicts that individuals will experience low job satisfaction and a high degree of instability as they continue to seek more fulfilling work environments.

Assessment of Vocational Interests. The RIASEC theory is empirically derived from the responses of individuals expressing their vocational interests on paper-and-pencil measures. Two major assessment instruments are used to describe the profile of an individual's vocational interests. The **Strong Vocational Interest Inventory (SVII)** (Harmon, Hansen, Borgen, & Hammer, 1994) consists of items in which respondents indicate their preferences for occupations, topics of study, activities, and types of people. The Holland scales provide the major organizational framework of the scales. The SVII is administered by a professional counselor and must be scored through a testing service. Holland also developed the **Self-Directed Search (SDS)**, a self-administered and self-scored test, that provides immediate feedback to clients involved in vocational or career guidance (Holland, 1994). In addition to providing assessment along the RIASEC dimensions, the SDS provides a sense of the individual's aspirations as well as abilities (Gottfredson, 2002).

College graduation is a time when young adults assess their talents and interests and try to find an ideal match in the world of work.

Assessment of Environments and Occupations. Work environments are assessed by rating the work activities and institutional characteristics of occupations and work environments according to standard criteria. The product of this effort is the **Holland Dictionary of Occupational Titles** (Gottfredson & Holland, 1989). The Holland codes now have become fully integrated into **O*NET**, the **Occupational Information Network**, an on-line interactive national database of occupations that is intended for purposes of job classification, training, and vocational counseling (Peterson, Mumford, Borman, Jeanneret, & Fleishman, 1999). Individuals who are trying to find a job that will fit their interests, training, and experience can be greatly aided by this system. O*NET provides a comprehensive and searchable database of occupations, along with important data such as salary and expected growth in the next 10 years.

Criticisms and Alternatives. Empirical tests of Holland's theory have focused on the validity of the hexagonal model and predictions concerning the relationship between stability, change, and congruence (Holland, 1996). Large-scale analysis of the RIASEC structure on numerous populations have provided considerable support for the typology and arrangement of types into the circular or hexagonal shape. However, questions have arisen about the size of the observed relationships (often in the range of .30 or less), the value of the congruence concept, and the applicability of the model to diverse populations (Chartrand & Walsh, 1999). Given what we know about the marketplace, as well as the variations in education, income, employment rates, and occupational levels according to race and gender, these problems may come as no surprise.

The fundamental theoretical difficulty with this or any vocational interest model is the assumption that people are infinitely free to express their true personalities and interests in the world of work. This assumption clearly does not apply to people who come from disadvantaged backgrounds and face limited educational opportunities or outright discrimination (Brown, 1995; Fitzgerald & Betz, 1994). Recall the college-educated black men who are working in blue-collar occupations rather than in the white-collar occupations for which they were trained. They are not able to express their vocational interests with the same freedom as white men with college educations.

Other difficulties in extending the RIASEC model to the population at large pertain to the age of people who have served as participants in the studies conducted by Holland and others testing the RIASEC model. In some cases, these have included high school and college-age students who are not facing the actual constraints of the workplace. Other studies have involved people changing careers, and these individuals similarly may represent a select portion of the population. Furthermore, the adult working populations in these studies were primarily white male American men employed in jobs for which they were trained (Lattimore & Borgen,

1999). It may be inappropriate to generalize from the findings with these populations to those of other gender, racial, or socioeconomic backgrounds. Furthermore, cultural factors or differences in experiences within the workplace or school may lead people of different backgrounds to have different interpretations of the same interest scale item (Rounds & Tracey, 1996).

The RIASEC Model and I/O Psychology. Because of its widespread incorporation into occupational interest inventories and classification schemes, the RIASEC model is likely to be prominent for some time to come. Vocational counselors have adopted the RIASEC model as an easily interpretable and user-friendly system. Assessment tools for both people and jobs are readily available and inexpensive, and there is adequate (if not perfect) empirical support for it from large-scale studies (McDaniel & Snell, 1999). Finally, from the standpoint of linking vocational development with personality theory and the larger framework of adult development, Holland's attempts to articulate the vocational types as personality types are positive signs.

Within the field of industrial-organizational (I/O) psychology, congruence is now considered to be a major focus of matching people and jobs. However, at the same time, human resource specialists are beginning to recognize the importance of determining the fit or match among individuals working together as a team (Muchinsky, 1999). Does an RCE type get along better with another RCE, or would their similar styles lead to narrow thinking and lack of productivity among members of a work unit? Perhaps the RCE should be working alongside an SAI, who will complement the "thing"-oriented approach of the Realistic individual.

Finally, as Holland himself has somewhat wistfully observed (Holland, 1996), the workplace of the future will have less stability than the workplace of the past. In the future, there will be greater mobility and transience and less stability than was true of the large "big brother" corporations. Furthermore, workers may experience fewer opportunities to find congruent work environments, particularly in occupations within the Realistic and Conventional codes as the workplace becomes increasingly technological. Instead of finding congruence at work, such individuals may need to seek their self-expression through the domain of leisure.

"What do you think?" **10-2**

What are your vocational daydreams? Do you think you have the abilities to fulfill these daydreams? How would you find out if you did?

Super's Self-Concept Theory

The desire to achieve full realization of the individual's potential is at the heart of **Super's self-concept theory**. According to Super (1957, 1990), career development is a process driven by the individual's desire to achieve full self-concept realization through work. If you see yourself as an artist, then you will desire work in which you can express the view of yourself as an artist. In contrast to Holland's theory, which emphasizes vocational preferences (that you might prefer artistic work), Super's theory places the focus on the occupation that a person sees as most "true" to the inner self. Super's theory also takes into account the fact that because of the constraints of the marketplace people are not always able to achieve full realization of their self-concepts. In a society with relatively little demand for artists, the person with the artistic self-concept will seek self-expression in a job that allows for a certain degree of creativity and yet will bring in a paycheck. Such an individual may seek a career in computer graphic design, for example, because that is a more viable occupation than that of dancer or oil painter.

BEHIND THE RESEARCH

John L. Holland, President, RIASEC International

What is most exciting to you about research in this field?

Unexpectedly, I am most excited about the testing and extension of my theory of careers from 1959 to the present. With each decade researchers have usually supported the main ideas in this typology of persons and environments and have extended it to many populations here and abroad. This work has led to some useful revisions about every 12 to 13 years. I was surprised that the typology works well in many other countries; my goal was only to create something that would work most of the time in the United States.

The recent work by the Gottfredsons (Gottfredson & Gottfredson, 2000) exemplifies the theory's continuing development. Gottfredson included the Environmental Identity scale in a national study of delinquency prevention. This brief scale, assembled by Gottfredson and myself, proved to be a reliable measure of environment. More important, it contributes to a tentative explanation of organizational outcomes. In a sentence, secondary schools with a clear focus (the school is perceived as organized and has well-defined rules) have desirable outcomes (morale, safety); unfocused or disorganized schools have undesirable outcomes.

What do you see as major challenges?

Different theories face different problems. For my theory, it is how to sustain a focused and strong research effort. Specifically, I hope others will explore the neglected topics. These include studies of the environmental constructs, the recent theoretical revisions (Holland, 1997), applying the classification to work histories in the 90s and beyond, and my favorite topic, the study of vocational aspirations. The congruence hypotheses need more high-quality research; there is too little. The recent inventories, the Position Classification Inventory (Gottfredson & Holland, 1991) and the Career Attitudes and Strategies Inventory (Holland & Gottfredson, 1994), require validation by others. The developmental research was positive, but more research is required.

Super's developmental speculations face other challenges. For instance, one of Super's disciples needs to step up and integrate his theoretical fragments into a coherent account. His pioneering work might also benefit from a comprehensive summary of the evidence so that his speculations may be evaluated.

Where do you see this field headed in the next decade?

I don't know, but a likely scenario is the continuation of some of the current trends.

The self-efficacy boom may continue to flower and have useful outcomes.

The effort devoted to traditional research topics (interests, abilities, job demands, performance, persistence, and satisfaction) will continue to decline as advocacy groups push for research on a diverse set of topics.

The influence of traditional training and of scientific research will continue to decline as practitioners and gurus acquire more status.

The Internet will become a major force with a wide range of desirable and undesirable influences. The desirable influences we know now. It's a grand source of occupational information including the O*NET. It also offers a vast collection of unstudied career aids, devices, and ideas, both original and stolen. It is a threat to career and personality inventories where there is no influential regulation.

I expect my work to gradually become background for career practice and research, or perhaps someone will assimilate it into a new and more useful formulation. Who knows?

According to Super, the expression of a person's self-concept through work occurs in a series of stages that span the years from adolescence to retirement. The first stage, the **exploration stage**, is associated with adolescence to the mid-20s. During this time, individuals are exploring career alternatives and selecting a vocation that they will find to be expressive of their self-concept. Within the next stage, called **establishment**, individuals in their mid-20s to mid-40s are focused on achieving stability, meaning that they will attempt to remain within the same occupation. Having explored alternatives in the previous stage, individuals now attempt to preserve their focus within the occupation. At the same time, however, they seek to advance to higher occupational levels. The person working as a computer graphics designer in a large software company may feel satisfied with this particular occupation but attempt to gain a higher managerial position. In the **maintenance** stage, which incorporates the mid-40s to mid-50s, individuals attempt to hold onto their positions rather than to seek further advancement. Finally, in the **disengagement stage**, from the mid-50s to mid-60s, workers begin to prepare for retirement, perhaps looking for satisfactory leisure activities that will replace their work-role involvement.

An important clarification of Super's theory regards his use of age to demarcate the stages. Although ages are used in definitions of the stages, people are not literally seen as moving from stage to stage like clockwork. Instead, personality and life circumstances set the pace of movement through the career development stages. The ages provide an expectable set of markers but are by no means fixed. In fact, it is becoming evident that at any point during adulthood workers may undergo a maintenance-like period called **plateauing** (Ettington, 1998), a term that refers to the attainment of a point in one's career where further hierarchical advancement is unlikely. People may reach their plateau at a young age if they enter a so-called dead-end job, or if their

One of the most dramatic examples of a midlife career changer is that of actor Arnold Schwarzenegger, who became governor of California in 2003.

moves within or between companies involve lateral changes rather than vertical advancement.

Furthermore, it is possible for individuals to experience **recycling**, in which they change their main field of career activity part way into occupational life and reexperience the early career development stages. A stimulus for the recycling process is likely to be technological or social change that results in the phasing out of certain occupations or the downsizing of a corporation for economic reasons. Recycling may also be stimulated by a desire to engage in a new occupational search for voluntary reasons. In either case, the individual who recycles through the career development stages has the opportunity to gain enhanced maturity, coping power, and creative productivity (Smart & Peterson, 1997).

VOCATIONAL SATISFACTION

Implied in the vocational development theories of Holland and Super is the assumption that people seek to maximize their level of satisfaction in their day-to-day work. Although not everyone can achieve full self-realization in their work, people may come to find sources of satisfaction either within the work itself or in the rewards it provides. On the other hand, a job may possess neither source of fulfillment but instead remain a daily grind that must be endured to maintain self and family. Theories and research on **vocational satisfaction** deal with these questions of how people find enjoyment in the work that they do or, conversely, of what factors limit their ability to achieve an optimal vocational situation.

Factors Related to Vocational Satisfaction

Vocational satisfaction is the extent to which the worker has positive views of the job or aspects of a job (Dawis, 1996). Because of its presumed importance in determining both how productive and committed the worker is within the job, it is one of the most heavily researched areas in vocational psychology. Although it may be relatively simple to define vocational satisfaction in these general terms, it is surprisingly difficult to identify its components or, more importantly, determinants.

Intrinsic and Extrinsic Factors. A basic distinction that seems to cut across the various theories of vocational satisfaction is the difference between factors endogenous or inherent in the work itself and those that are exogenous or unrelated to the particular work involved in the job. The factors inherent in the work itself are referred to as **intrinsic factors** and include the physical and mental actions that the individual must perform in order to carry out the job. For example, sculpting involves the intrinsic physical activities of molding clay or stone, and accounting involves the intrinsic mental activities of manipulating numbers. Obviously, sculpting involves mental work, as the artist plans the piece before and during its completion. Conversely, intrinsic to

accounting is the manipulation of keys on the keyboard or the writing of numbers on the page with a pencil. However, these are secondary activities compared to the nature of the work itself. The central defining feature of an intrinsic factor is that it cannot be found in precisely the same fashion in a different type of job. Molding materials is intrinsic to sculpting, and computing numbers is intrinsic to accounting.

Intrinsic factors can also be characterized as involving or engaging the individual's sense of identity in that the work directly pertains to one's sense of competence, autonomy, and stimulation of personal growth. Work that is intrinsically rewarding allows the individual to feel truly "connected" to both the activities and purpose of the job and to experience a positive sense of competence and self-esteem (Mutran, Reitzes, & Fernandez, 1997). The individual's ability to express autonomy and self-direction in the daily running of the job are also part of the intrinsic aspects of work because these factors are directly tied to the individual's sense of self (Kalleberg, 1977). Furthermore, the engagement of intrinsic motivation in work that is cognitively challenging and self-directed maintains a constant stimulus for cognitive activity and may serve to enhance intellectual functioning over time (Schooler, Mulatu, & Oates, 1999).

The opposite of intrinsic factors in work are the **extrinsic factors**, which are the features that accompany the job but may also be found in other jobs with very different intrinsic characteristics. The easiest extrinsic factor to understand is salary. People may earn the same salary whether they harvest grain or provide care to preschool children. Paychecks are issued for work performed, and although some jobs earn more than others, the same salary can be earned in many alternative ways. A professional athlete may earn such a vast salary that it appears to be an inherent part of the job, but an oil magnate may earn the same amount of money for a very different set of job activities. Therefore, salary is not intrinsic to work.

Assess Yourself

Quiz for Mid-Life Career Change Assessment

Increasingly, middle-aged workers are being advised to look into job alternatives. The following assessment device was published by the American Association of Retired Persons to help individuals evaluate their current positions. There are no "right" or "wrong" answers.

Is It Time to Change Jobs?

Does your job offer you few challenges? Has your company hinted at possible job layoffs? Do you like your work but not your working conditions? This assessment piece can help you determine if it might be time to look for a new job.

   To begin assessing the gains of staying put or the rewards of moving on, answer the following nine questions. Most questions will have further probing and clarifying questions to help you in this process.

1. Is Your Industry in Trouble?
   - Are layoffs, mergers, or acquisitions commonplace in your industry?
   - Are there government initiatives underway that might affect your industry adversely?
   - Demographically, is your industry's customer base leveling off or declining?
   - Has the level of competition in your industry escalated?

2. Is Your Company Competitive?
   - Have profits in your company been small or nonexistent in recent years?
   - Is your company's market share small or contracting compared to that of its competitors?
   - Does your company depend on business from other organizations that are going through cutbacks?
   - Is more than 20% of company earnings going to repay debts?

3. Has Your Company Downsized Once Already?
   - Has your organization offered an early retirement program or tried other cost-cutting measures?

4. Is Your Job Type at Risk?
   - Has the particular product or service with which you are most closely connected done poorly in recent years?
   - Could the kind of work you do be outsourced to a contractor, consultant, or even to another department?
   - Is your main responsibility to filter or compile information?
   - Do you monitor, check, or inspect?
   - Are you a manager who manages managers?

Assess Yourself

- Would you have a hard time substantiating your direct contribution to the bottom line?
- Is there someone else with a lower salary who could do your job?
- Does your job lack visibility?
- Are you pounding away in your corporate cubicle or on the road so much that you are "invisible"?
- Have you been in the same job for more than six years?

5. Is Your Geographical Region Going Downhill?
   - In the city and region where your headquarters and key business units are located, is the economy in trouble?
   - Are key units of your company being affected by local or regional layoffs in other industries?

6. Have Your Opportunities to Learn Disappeared?
   - Are you in a "no stretch" job?

7. Are Your Skills Too Narrow?
   - Has your career specialty narrowed so much that if the technology becomes obsolete or the organization's priorities change, you'll be trapped?

8. Are You Trapped in a Track?
   - Do you sometimes say "I hate this work!" or "What am I doing with my life?" or "I can't face one more Monday morning?"

9. Has Your Life Situation Changed?
   - Have your family responsibilities been expanded or decreased?
   - Has your health changed?

If you have answered yes to a number of these questions, you might want to begin exploring other career options.

Source: AARP, 1999.

Other extrinsic factors relate to the conditions of work such as the comfort of the environment, demands for travel, convenience of work hours, friendliness of coworkers, amount of status associated with the job, and adequacy of the company's supervision and employment policies. These aspects of work do not directly engage the individual's sense of personal identity and competence. Although a high salary may certainly reinforce an individual's sense of worth (particularly in Western society), as pointed out earlier, high salaries may be earned in many ways that are not necessarily tied to one's true vocational passions.

Even if you have never thought about the intrinsic–extrinsic distinction, it is relatively

---

easy to conceptualize. The same distinction may apply to coursework. You know when you are in a course that you truly love because the topic sparks your deepest intellectual curiosity, hence your intrinsic motivation is strong. Conversely, when looking at a course for extrinsic purposes, you are trying to find one that will fit your schedule, or one in which an "A" is almost guaranteed. Extending to work situations, you may or may not have had a job yet in which you felt involvement at an intrinsic level. However, you may be able to think of people you know whose work has intrinsic meaning to them. Perhaps you have encountered a sales or service person who seemed genuinely interested in helping you find a necessary item or solve a problem and was willing to work with you until you found the satisfactory solution. This may have been an employee who found the job to be intrinsically rewarding, feelings that were expressed in the apparent pride that he or she took in helping you with your situation.

Many vocational psychologists propose that intrinsic and extrinsic factors possess motivational properties (Katzell & Thompson, 1990). When workers are motivated for intrinsic reasons, they are thought to be doing so for the purpose of seeking personal expression, autonomy, and challenge. Conversely, extrinsic motivation is the desire to work to seek the benefits of pay, good job conditions, friendly coworkers, and an employer with fair and equitable policies. When considering these two forms of motivation, theorists have argued about which is more important or even whether the two are mutually exclusive.

One of the earliest theories about work motivation is the **two-factor theory** developed by Herzberg and colleagues in the late 1950s (Herzberg, Mausner, & Snyderman, 1959). According to this theory, intrinsic factors are motivators whose fulfillment allows the worker to achieve self-actualization. The extrinsic

aspects of work are hygiene factors that either enhance or detract from an environment in which workers can realize their aspirations. The central hypothesis of the two-factor theory is that job motivators are more powerful than hygiene factors in leading to vocational satisfaction. Favorable hygiene factors could only prevent the development of job dissatisfaction, but they could not promote it.

Another perspective on the intrinsic–extrinsic dimension comes from research on the effects of reinforcements or incentives on performance quality and job motivation (Katzell & Thompson, 1990). Reinforcement theory proposes that people are motivated to perform well when their good performance is followed by positive consequences provided by the employer. Incentive theory also focuses on the factors that will motivate workers to perform better. Salary is both reinforcement and incentive. The question that has emerged in research on job motivation is whether the provision of financial incentives and reinforcements raises extrinsic motivation at the cost of lowering intrinsic motivation. According to **cognitive evaluation theory**, financial incentives cause employees to feel less self-determination and psychological investment in their jobs. Consequently, their performance suffers (Deci & Ryan, 1985; Kohn, 1993). Not only is money not a motivator, as in two-factor theory, but it is actually theorized to detract from the quality of performance when it is used as an incentive.

Most theories concerning extrinsic motivation, however, predict that tying salary into job performance increases the desire to work and that extrinsic rewards do not decrease intrinsic motivation (Eisenberger & Cameron, 1996). Statistical estimates derived from laboratory experiments, field experiments, and experimental simulations of the relationship between financial incentives and the quality of performance are all positive, ranging from .24 to .56, with an average effect size of .34 (on a scale of 0 to 1) (Jenkins, Mitra, Gupta, & Shaw, 1998). The majority of evidence, then, seems to support the importance of extrinsic rewards as motivators for working adults. Furthermore, the majority of job incentive programs are based on this principle (Katzell & Thompson, 1990).

Occupational Reinforcement Patterns. Another influential theory of vocational satisfaction focuses on **occupational reinforcement patterns (ORPs)**, which are the work values and needs likely to be reinforced or satisfied by a particular occupation. According to the theory of work adjustment proposed by Dawis and Lofquist (1984), vocational satisfaction is directly related to the extent to which a worker feels that the environment fulfills his or her work-related needs, also called worker values. There are six fairly self-explanatory categories into which worker values fall: achievement, job security and working conditions, recognition, social relationships, support from management, and independence. Each occupation has an ORP based on its potential to reinforce or satisfy one or more of the six worker values. Furthermore, associated with each value are specific work needs. For example, the achievement work value is associated with the specific work needs of ability utilization and feelings of accomplishment.

Personality. Holland's theory of vocational development indirectly implicates personality as a factor that affects job satisfaction. Several theories focus more specifically on personality traits that may have a direct influence on vocational satisfaction. One of these traits is **dispositional affectivity**, which is the general dimension of a person's affective responding. A person may have the favorable trait of positive affectivity, meaning that he or she tends to look at the "bright" side of a situation. The converse, negative affectivity, refers to a state of being

predisposed to experience negative mood states (Lease, 1998). Research on this dimension of personality has found a relationship between affectivity and satisfaction, commitment, and intention to leave one's job (Cropanzano, Rupp, & Byrne, 2003). People with positive affectivity are more likely than those high on negative affectivity to be satisfied in their job, committed to it, and unlikely to leave when faced with problems or difficulties. Conversely, people with negative affect are more likely to feel emotionally exhausted by work (Houkes, Janssen, de Jonge, & Bakker, 2003), which as shown earlier, can presumably lead to lower levels of satisfaction. Looking at the intrinsic–extrinsic dimension, people with high neuroticism scores are less likely to feel that their jobs are intrinsically rewarding (Boudreau, Boswell, & Judge, 2001). Perhaps for this reason, neuroticism is negatively related to job satisfaction; by contrast, extraversion and job satisfaction are positively related (Judge, Heller, & Mount, 2002; Seibert & Kraimer, 2001).

People with high levels of positive affectivity tend to be optimistic about their prospects of future success and promotion. They may retain this hopeful outlook for many years. In an intensive 20-year study of managerial level employees at American Telegraph and Telephone (AT&T), Howard and Bray found that the well-adjusted men in the sample retained an optimistic approach to their prospects for promotion over a very long period. (Howard & Bray, 1988). However, there is a downside to this process. Eventually, dreams of advancement may not only fade but lead to great disillusionment. When it was clear that job prospects would not improve, the men with the generally optimistic outlook on their work were prone to developing physical symptoms, refusing to work to their maximum ability, or even sabotaging the work of their company (Duffy, Ganster, & Shaw, 1998).

Personality traits other than affectivity also have a relationship to development in the job. In one longitudinal study of adolescents (18-year-olds), personality traits such as sociability, desire for achievement, and aggressiveness were predictive of the nature of the characteristics of the jobs they sought. Eight years later, experiences on the job in turn predicted changes in personality traits (Roberts, Avsholom, & Moffitt, 2003). These findings are consistent with studies based on the Five Factor Model described in Chapter 8, suggesting that personality change is most likely to occur in young adulthood. Work experiences, then, appear to provide a significant context in which that change occurs.

Attachment Style. It may seem odd to view attachment style, known to be a factor in interpersonal relationships, as a predictor of job satisfaction. Yet, researchers working within the attachment model have found surprisingly strong relationships between various indicators of vocational satisfaction and the personality variable of attachment style. According to the theoretical model of attachment, adults are psychologically more capable of engaging in satisfying work activity if they have a secure attachment style. In this framework, the work behavior of the well-adjusted adult is equated with the ability of the securely attached young infant to explore the environment without fear of abandonment. In both cases, the individual is able to achieve a balance between attachment to others and healthy exploration. Just as children derive a sense of competence from play and exploration, adults derive feelings of worth from the ability to engage successfully in work activities.

This conceptual model derived from attachment theory was supported in a study of working adults in which attachment style was found to be related to work attitudes and satisfaction (Hazan & Shaver, 1990). Securely

attached individuals showed the best work adjustment and satisfaction. They were not overly concerned about failure, did not let work interfere with their friendships or health, and were able to take enjoyable vacations from work without feeling guilty. By contrast, anxious/ambivalent subjects showed undue concern about their work performance, felt they were not appreciated by others, and feared they would be fired for poor performance. Their work performance actually did suffer because they were not self-motivated, were easily distractible, and were unable to complete projects. Their incomes were lower than those of people in the other two attachment styles. Consistent with their attitudes toward romantic relationships, avoidant subjects had a strong preference for working alone, substituted work life for their social life, and did not wish to take vacations from work.

"What do you think?" | **10-3**

How would a person with an insecure attachment style handle rejection at work? Why?

Conflict between Work and Family. The interaction between life at home and life on the job is a topic of considerable research on involvement in family roles and how it affects or is affected by job satisfaction. Adults divide their time, energy, and role involvement in many areas of life, but the two that carry the most weight are the areas of occupation and family life. Both areas of involvement carry major obligations and responsibility, and both contribute heavily to the individual's sense of identity.

There are three basic models of work–family interrelations. According to the **spillover model**, attitudes and behaviors associated with one domain have an effect on attitudes and behavior carried out in the other domain (Grzywacz & Marks, 2000). The negative spillover model proposes that unhappiness at work leads the individual to experience unhappiness at home, and vice versa. The positive variant of the spillover model proposes that there is role enhancement such that a supportive spouse can lessen the daily tension created by an unsatisfying job. The role strain model proposes that work and family involvement are inversely related, so that the higher the person's involvement in his or her work role, the lower the individual's involvement in the family. The workaholic, according to this view, has little energy or time for family relationships. Conversely, high involvement with family should preclude total commitment to the job. Finally, the **segmentation model** is based on the assumption that individuals can compartmentalize their lives, so that they manage to keep their attitudes and behavior at work separate from those that are associated with life at home.

The majority of current studies on the work–family interaction favor the spillover hypothesis. Involvement in work and family roles is seen as inherently in conflict. According to most theorists, the demands of work have a negative impact on the quality of family life. Moreover, the extent to which conflict is experienced between work and family demands is related to absenteeism, job satisfaction, life satisfaction, self-esteem, and a greater likelihood of seeking another job (Ernst Kossek & Ozeki, 1998). Work–family conflict also takes its toll on the individual's physical and mental health, causing emotional strain, fatigue, perception of overload, and stress associated with feeling that one needs to be in two places at once. There are variations in the extent and impact of work–family conflict, however, and it is not experienced equally by all workers. Conflict is most likely to occur among mothers of young children, dual-career couples, and those who are highly involved with their jobs. However, there are individual differences in personality and family structure, so that not all individuals who fit this description experience the same degree of stress.

Jobs with flexible hours help reduce conflict by providing workers with the opportunity to meet more of their obligations at home within a broader time frame than the traditional work hours of 9 to 5 (Scandura & Lankau, 1997). Supportive supervisors, who recognize the inevitable commitments of family obligations and their possible impact on work performance, can also help ameliorate the experience of conflict (Schirmer & Lopez, 2001).

Age and Vocational Satisfaction

One of the most puzzling questions in the vocational literature concerns the issue of whether age is related to job satisfaction. Early studies on the relationship between age and job satisfaction provided evidence that older workers are more satisfied with their jobs than younger workers. However, even this general conclusion was clouded by the question of whether the relationship was linear, U-shaped, or nonexistent (Bernal, Snyder, & McDaniel, 1998). A counterpart to job satisfaction is job turnover, as dissatisfied employees are more likely to leave their jobs. As is true for job satisfaction, job turnover is not related to age (Healy, Lehman, & McDaniel, 1995). There are also interactions with cohort differences among generations of workers who have different values and attitudes toward work. Job **tenure** (length of time in the job), gender, level of employment, and salary also interact with age differences in job satisfaction (Riordan, Griffith, & Weatherly, 2003). Individuals who reach a plateau in their career are likely to experience a drop in job satisfaction (Boudreau et al., 2001). Finally, emotional exhaustion is now being looked at as another factor that must be considered when examining the relationship between age and job satisfaction. In a study of over 200 employees and their supervisors, employees who felt emotionally exhausted, regardless of age, had lower commitment to their jobs and, hence, lower scores on a variety of performance and satisfaction indices (Cropanzano et al., 2003). For the moment, then, it is best to set aside the issue of whether aging generally relates to job satisfaction and move on to the components of job satisfaction as they may change in relation to age.

The first component of job satisfaction of relevance to the age–job satisfaction puzzle is the extent to which job involvement is intrinsically or extrinsically motivated. The most comprehensive examination of aging and its relation to the intrinsic–extrinsic dimension of work satisfaction was conducted on two national samples of employees in the late 1970s (Kalleberg & Loscoco, 1983). Overall, in this study, job satisfaction increased from the 20s to the late 40s, leveled off until the late 50s, and then continued to increase until the 60s. However, this overall finding was less interesting than the results of analyses conducted on the intrinsic–extrinsic components of job satisfaction. Younger workers placed higher value on the intrinsic rewards of challenge, meaning, and fulfillment in their jobs. By contrast, older workers placed higher value on the financial rewards of work and tended to see work as a means to an end, that is, as a way of finding satisfaction in the nonwork domains of life such as leisure and family. Some workers did not fit this general pattern. Those who regarded work as a salient aspect of their identities experienced a period of readjustment in their middle career years that was associated with lower job satisfaction, perhaps as they shifted their work-related priorities.

Among the many qualifications of the age–job satisfaction relationship that emerged in this study was the importance of work in general to an individual's identity and the importance of particular aspects of work. In addition, gender interacted with the age–job satisfaction relationship, with women showing an entirely different pattern of age-related differences than men. Only the women who identified strongly with their jobs showed a linear positive relationship between age and job satisfaction, and those women who did not value their jobs showed no relationship between age and their satisfaction from work. Furthermore, there were different patterns of findings across the three waves of testing in the study (1969, 1973, and 1977), indicating time of measurement effects on overall job satisfaction and on the interaction between age and gender. Women in the later testings were more likely to identify with their jobs, reflecting increasing employment rates of women in this period of history.

Findings from other investigations echo some of the important themes of the Kalleberg and Loscoco (1983) study, the employment data from the beginning of the chapter, and the vocational development theory of Super. Adults appear to reach a peak in their job level and salary by the time they reach their late 40s to early 50s. They are financially more secure than younger workers, and many have had the opportunity to move into jobs that reflect their vocational preferences and identity. At this point, they do not see a particular need to devote their entire energy to their career. Their job may have lost its psychological meaning, but they remain in the company to continue to accumulate retirement or pension benefits.

At the same time as the individual reaches the mid- to late-career point, identity processes may come into play as a way of coping with plateauing or failing to reach previously aspired-to career goals. People who have reached their own peak, but perhaps not the one they hoped to reach when younger, begin to focus on the positive aspects of their work accomplishments rather than their inability to meet earlier career goals. This process may also increase the tendency to focus on family and nonwork commitments as a source of feelings of competence. Identity assimilation with regard to work may also be part of a larger tendency to focus on positive aspects of life in general, a tendency reflected in higher life satisfaction scores among older adults (Warr, 1994). The reality of the situation is that most individuals will be retiring within the next 10 to 15 years, and they may be starting to make the mental shift toward the upcoming phase of life. Another factor that may affect the older worker's commitment and involvement in the job is exposure to age discrimination in the workplace. Although older workers are protected by federal law prohibiting discrimination (see below), negative stereotypes about the abilities and suitabilities of older persons in the workplace persist (Sterns & Gray, 1999). Even worse, if an older worker is forced to find a new job, the job search takes longer and requires more interviews (Simon, 1995). Older workers may begin to disengage mentally when they feel that they are subject to these age stereotypes, pressures to retire in the form of downsizing, and the message that their skills are becoming obsolete (Lease, 1998). As will be seen later, these pressures can lead older workers to be less likely to engage in the career development activities that would enhance their ability to remain on the job or find a new one if their job is eliminated due to downsizing.

This general picture by no means applies to all workers. As already indicated, gender plays a major role in this process, particularly as women's roles in the workplace have shifted radically since the time of some of the early studies. Furthermore, discrimination prohibits even the college-educated minority male from achieving his maximum employment potential, and therefore may keep him from reaching a point of perceived financial security in his late 40s and early 50s. Level of occupation is yet another factor, as a person in a managerial position who is earning a high salary has the resources to invest time and energy in nonwork options. Of course, with a higher level of employment may go higher daily job demands, leading to less time for leisure pursuits. However, as found in the AT&T study, relative success within the company seems to be related to overall satisfaction, such that the more successful are also the more satisfied (Bray & Howard, 1983).

Individual differences in the extent to which an adult believes in the "work ethic" may also interact with the age–job satisfaction relationship. The work commitment of individuals with strong work ethic values may never taper off, even if it does not mean higher financial rewards. Personality can also influence work commitment. The AT&T study found that people with higher ratings of overall adjustment had higher work commitment throughout their careers. They became more interested in their work as time progressed and developed higher internal standards of excellence (Howard & Bray, 1988).

Vocational satisfaction in later adulthood may also be affected by the extent to which the worker is experiencing age-related changes in physical and cognitive functioning that interfere with ability to perform the job satisfactorily. The aging process may alter the degree of person-environment fit between the individual and the job in important ways and indirectly have an impact on feelings of satisfaction and fulfillment.

AGE AND VOCATIONAL PERFORMANCE

As with the relationship between age and vocational satisfaction, the age–performance relationship is muddied by a host of individual difference factors and potentially confounding variables. These variables include the quality of the measures of performance, the fact that younger cohorts are more highly educated, and the existence of variations within cohorts in health, cognitive functioning, and previous job experience. There is also a tendency for workers who cannot perform the job to leave it, and for those who remain in the job to reach a level of expertise that outweighs the negative effects of aging on speed, strength, or cognitive demands. The strength of the individual's commitment to the job also affects performance and satisfaction (Wright & Bonett, 2002). The combined effect of these many factors is to produce no consistent overall trends in the job performance of older workers (Warr, 1994).

Significant individual differences both in abilities and in attitudes toward work also affect job performance. Some older workers are focused on maintaining their current status and planning how to finish out the end of their careers without jeopardizing this status. Others may have already experienced some disability and are in the process of attempting to compensate for their losses while still maintaining their position at work. Yet others have not and will not suffer apparent losses of functioning at work and can therefore maintain their high levels of performance until they retire (Hansson, DeKoekkoek, Neece, & Patterson, 1997).

Initial interest in the quality of job performance among older workers can be traced to the early 1940s, when it appeared that population shifts were leading to a rising proportion of older, and possibly less productive, workers. Following World War II and the subsequent baby boom, these concerns were temporarily allayed, as the shifts then moved in the reverse direction toward a younger workforce. However, with the aging of the Baby Boomers, concern is once again emerging about the characteristics and abilities of older workers and how their performance will affect the country's overall

productivity. Obviously, society has moved in an increasingly technological direction since the 1940s, so concerns about older workers are less about physical functioning and more about their cognitive abilities. Will the aging Baby Boomers be able to keep up their productivity in an increasingly technical marketplace?

Research on cognitive functioning in later life has provided insights on the potential tradeoff experienced by older persons in speed and capacity versus accumulated skill and experience. Warr (1994) proposed a two-dimensional model of aging and job performance that takes these factors into account and balances them against the demands of a job (see Table 10-1). Jobs may be classified according to the dimension of basic capacity (cognitive or physical demands) and the dimension of experience (familiarity). Jobs will show age-related losses if their demands are negatively affected by aging and they do not have benefits associated with experience. For example, jobs that require crystallized intelligence (which does not decrease until well past retirement) and depend on experience should theoretically show improved performance in later adulthood. By contrast, if the job is highly dependent on strength, speed, or working memory, and experience on the job is not an advantage, the individual's performance will suffer. Performance on jobs that are dependent on skills that are affected negatively by aging but allow for compensation through experience can be maintained in later adulthood. For example, experienced typists learn to anticipate the words further ahead on the page than do younger typists. The strategy of the older typists effectively compensates for age-related reductions in typing speed (Salthouse & Saults, 1987).

With this framework in mind, it is instructive to examine several areas of job performance that have been studied with regard to age. One area is that of shift work in which the individual's

TABLE 10-1
Expected Relationship between Age and Performance

Basic Capacities Are Exceeded with Increasing Age	Performance Is Enhanced by Experience	Expected Relationship with Age
No	Yes	Positive
No	No	Zero
Yes	Yes	Zero
Yes	No	Negative

Source: Warr, 1994.

work hours change from the ordinary daytime hours to evenings or nights. Although these changing schedules present a challenge for workers of all ages, it is particularly hard on older workers (Harma, 1996). This is a good example of a job in which age effects are decidedly negative (sleep patterns), and there is no benefit of experience because a person cannot improve over time in a shiftwork job on this aspect of performance.

Absentee rates are another important factor in examining worker productivity and aging. Voluntary absences, which are those in which an employee decides not to report for work, are more frequent among younger workers by a factor of two to three. Thus, older workers are more reliable in this respect. On the other hand, it might be thought that older workers have higher rates of involuntary absenteeism, in which they are unable to work because of illness. However, this fact has not been established, and even so, when all rates of absenteeism are combined, older workers still have lower rates than younger workers (Warr, 1994).

Injuries are another area of investigation in analyzing the relationship between age and job performance. Here again, it might be thought that because of age-related limitations in physical or cognitive functioning, older workers are more subject to loss of productivity due to accidents on the job. Older workers do appear to be more careful, however. For example, they have a lower rate of injury within the construction industry, which has the highest percentage of fatalities of all industries. Yet, when older workers experience an injury, it is more likely to cause permanent disability or a fatality (Agnew & Suruda, 1993; Kisner & Fosbroke, 1994). Overall, workers over the age of 55 are one-third as likely to suffer an injury as those who are under 35 years of age, but when older workers are injured, they typically require twice the length of time (10 days) to recover (Bureau of Labor Statistics, 2002).

With regard to overall physical fitness, decreases in physical strength and agility can certainly have a negative influence on job performance in some areas of employment, particularly when manual labor is involved. However, workers of any age can suffer from conditions that impair their performance, such as a cold or muscle ache. Furthermore, as pointed out by Warr (1994), every worker has restrictions in the kind of work that he or she can perform. The fact that older workers may have some limitations due to physical aging changes does not mean that they cannot achieve adequate performance on all types of jobs. People learn to cope with their limitations and gravitate to jobs they are able to perform (Daly & Bound, 1996). If they become disabled enough, they will leave the job market altogether.

Passage of the **Age Discrimination in Employment Act (ADEA)** in 1967 provided protection against the firing or nonhiring of workers on the basis of their age. This legislation was intended to provide protection for older workers (over 40) from discrimination by employers who would otherwise seek to replace them with younger, cheaper, and presumably more productive employees. However, the ADEA did not protect workers in occupations where age had a presumed effect on the performance of critical job tasks in these occupations. In the 1970s, gerontologists became interested in the question of whether restrictions on the basis of age in these occupations could be justified based on the job performance of older workers (Hansson et al., 1997). For example, this law does not cover workers in the protective service occupations of police officers and firefighters on the grounds that their occupations demand that they be able to engage in highly demanding physical activity. However, there are variations in the physical abilities of older workers in these occupations, just as there are in the general population. Aerobic capacity is considered a key indicator of the ability to perform adequately in these occupations because emergencies such as running after a criminal or fighting a fire demand strength and exertion. Variations in these abilities are a function of the degree of exercise in which the worker participates outside the job, as has been demonstrated within the protective service occupations (Franke & Anderson, 1994; Sothmann, Landy, & Saupe, 1992). Aerobic exercise training is an excellent way for individuals in these occupations maintain their fitness levels (Harrell, Johnston, Griggs, Schaefer, Carr, et al., 1996).

Airline pilots are another group not protected by the ADEA, as they face mandatory retirement at age 60. However, studies of airplane accident rates show a decline in those caused by pilot error until the mid-40s, followed by a leveling off throughout the remaining years of active work involvement (Kay, Harris, Voros, Hillman, Hyland, et al., 1994). Gerontologists have suggested that the mandatory retirement laws as applied to airline pilots should be changed to take into account actual job performance rather than predictions based on age or even performance on laboratory tasks (Birren & Fisher, 1995). Obviously, the airline industry takes a very conservative stance on this issue, for even a single instance of pilot error can have enormous consequences. However, young and inexperienced pilots may be just as, if not more, vulnerable to accidents caused by pilot error.

These findings on age and job performance, like those in the area of vocational satisfaction, point to the importance of applying knowledge about adult development and aging in general to specific questions relating to older workers. Sterns and Miklos (1995) have advocated the application of a life-span developmental orientation to work and career choices in later adulthood. According to this model, human resource policies and systems of selection, training, and performance appraisal could benefit from knowledge of normative age-related changes, cohort differences, and the influence of nonnormative factors on the development of individuals in the context of the workplace.

One example of the application of this framework to helping older workers remain productive is in the area of job training and development. Such training can be an important intervention to help older workers remain productive and up to date with the latest technology. Willingness to engage in job training to develop new skills is crucial in the rapidly changing workplace, even for managers and executives (Hall & Mirvis, 1995). Unfortunately, older workers must battle against ageist stereotypes, held by both employers and the workers themselves, causing them to feel that they cannot improve their skills through training. Belief in these stereotypes can lead older workers to doubt their self-efficacy; in terms of the identity model, they overaccommodate the view that aging causes a loss of essential job skills. As a result, a self-fulfilling prophecy develops, and they become, in fact, less able to keep up with new technologies. According to a model proposed by Maurer (2001), there are a set of factors that contribute to feelings of self-efficacy, including direct or vicarious (watching others) learning, persuasion, and changes in physiological functioning and health. Self-efficacy, in turn, influences attitudes toward training and development activities. Intervention at the point of raising self-efficacy can, then, give the older worker the confidence needed to engage in these important development activities so they can retain their job skills.

RETIREMENT

Traditionally, **retirement** is the end of an individual's work career. Many people think of retirement as an event that is marked by a ceremony such as the proverbial "gold watch" given to the retiree as a thanks for years of loyal service. This traditional image of retirement is rapidly vanishing. In fact, even though it is a popular view, it may have applied only to a minority of workers—men in the middle and upper middle social classes with organized or regular careers. Furthermore, compared to other celebratory rituals in adulthood, such as college graduation, marriage, and the birth of children, retirement is more likely to carry with it ambivalent associations.

Just as labor force participation affects and is affected by the health of the economy, the opportunities for financial security available to retirees are heavily dependent on forces such as interest rates, tax policies, inflation, and the overall growth of the economy. Debates over retirement benefits such as Social Security are at the tip of the iceberg when it comes to the factors that affect the fate of the millions of retired persons in the United States. In this chapter, the focus is on psychological factors involved in the retirement decision and adjustment to retirement, but it is important to be aware of the larger context in which these personal decisions and outcomes occur.

Definitions of Retirement

Retirement is defined simply as the withdrawal of an individual in later life from the labor force (Moen, 1996). Rather than being a discrete event (as the gold watch ceremony would imply), most workers experience retirement as a gradual process. The retirement process includes at least five phases (Sterns & Gray, 1999): an anticipatory period that may last for decades, the decision itself, the act of retirement, continual adjustment following the actual event, and further decisions regarding the structuring of the individual's life and activity patterns. However, there are variations in these phases in the mid- to late 60s, as indicated in one large study of retirees (Mutchler, Burr, Pienta, & Massagli, 1997). Only about 10% of retirees showed the "crisp" pattern of leaving the workplace in a single, unreversed, clear-cut exit. Another 15% experienced a "blurred" exit in which they exited and reentered the workplace. They may have retired from a long-term job to accept **bridge employment** (Feldman, 1994), such as an insurance agent who retires from the insurance business but works as a crossing guard or server at a fast-food restaurant. Another one-third of workers never retired at all, and the remainder retired early or were otherwise unemployed. Ultimately, the criteria for retirement are met when the individual is collecting government benefits or a pension, considers himself or herself "retired," and does not spend time during the week at work (Talaga & Beehr, 1995).

This definition of retirement does not encompass a form of retirement that receives a great deal of media attention, namely, the departure of professional athletes from their respective sports. Gymnasts may "retire" at the age of 18, as was true for Mary Lou Retton, and occasionally, a football or baseball player will retire at the relatively "advanced" age of 37 or 40. President Bill Clinton is "retiring" from the presidency in his early 50s. All these individuals are not retired in the traditional sense of the word. because even though they left their primary field of endeavor, they have not left the labor force. In fact, many go on to another career or develop financial interests that are at least as lucrative as their previous occupations.

Facts about Retirement

The number of retired people is difficult to estimate because of the lack of a firm definition of retirement. However, estimates can be made based on labor force and income statistics. As of 2001, there were 4.3 million Americans 65 and older (13.1% of all those 65 and older) in the labor force, meaning that they were working or actively seeking work. This included 2.5 million men (17.7%) and 1.8 million women (9.7%). They constituted 3.0% of the U.S. labor force (Administration on Aging, 2003). Approximately 10.5 million people were receiving pension benefits other than Social Security, and 29.1 million retired workers over the age of 65 were receiving Social Security benefits (U.S. Bureau of the Census, 2003a).

Earnings make up 23% of the income of older adults. However, the largest proportion of income for older adults comes from payments from Social Security (38%) and pensions (18%).

The remaining share of income (18%) comes from assets (see Fig. 10.6). (http://www.aging-stats.gov/tables%202001/tables-economics.html# Indicator%208). The average Social Security benefit for an individual was $844, and for a couple $1420 (U.S. Bureau of the Census, 2003a).

Retirement is in many ways a twentieth-century phenomenon (Sterns & Gray, 1999). Throughout the 1700s and mid-1800s very few people retired, and by 1900 about 70% of all men over 65 years were still in the labor force. The jobs held by older workers often held high status and prestige. Their wisdom and experience were valued, and it was considered a benefit to society to have their contributions to the workplace. However, pressures on the economy in combination with the growth of unions led, by the early 1930s, to the first instance in the United States of compulsory retirement (in the railroad industry). Because older workers were forced to retire but did not receive retirement benefits, they lived in poverty. The passage of the **Social Security Act** in 1935 provided much-needed financial relief for the older population. By 1940, the percentage of older workers in the

FIGURE 10.6

Income of People 65 and Older

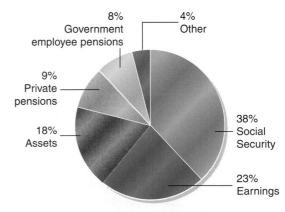

Source: Social Security Administration, 2002.

labor force had dropped to slightly over 40%, and the numbers have continued to decrease.

Attitudes toward retirement were largely negative until the mid-1960s because lack of employment was associated with poverty. However, with increases in earnings and Social Security benefits, retirement began to gain more acceptance. Changes in federal policy toward older workers were also occurring. As mentioned earlier, the passage of the ADEA in 1967 meant that workers in the 40–65 age range were protected from age discrimination. An amendment to the ADEA in 1978 eliminated mandatory retirement before age 70, and in 1986, mandatory retirement was eliminated from most occupations (Sterns & Gray, 1999). With these changes in retirement laws, it has also become easier for workers to continue in the jobs they have held throughout their lives or to find new employment even while they earn retirement benefits from their previous occupations. These changes in age discrimination and retirement laws have eased the potential stress of the transition, so that retired individuals no longer necessarily experience the poor health, low income, and loss of status that was associated with exit from the labor force earlier in the 1900s.

Furthermore, workers in the industrialized nations in Europe are increasingly looking favorably on retirement, and the trend over the previous three decades was toward earlier retirement ages (Gendell & Siegel, 1996). Although this situation helps to give retirement a more positive image, it creates another problem by placing greater strain on pension plans, including Social Security in the United States (Binstock, 1999). In 2002, the benefits paid to retired workers amounted to $388.1 billion dollars (http://www.ssa.gov/OACT/STATS/table4a4.html). In the future, to reduce this pressure on retirement benefits, it may be necessary to entice older workers to remain in the labor force rather than retire. Given that current

Baby Boomers are less likely to save for retirement, however (Glass & Kilpatrick, 1998), there may be more financial incentives for them to remain in the labor market.

The Effects of Retirement on the Individual

Among sociological theories on the effect of aging on social roles, questions about the impact of retirement have consistently assumed a primary role. Does loss of the work role cause changes in mental and physical health? Do age-related losses in functioning precede retirement? Or is there no clear-cut relationship between changes in work patterns and health in later life? The answers to these questions have implications for both the health and well-being of millions of older Americans, as well as potential importance for employers and retirement counselors.

There are three predominant theoretical perspectives on the effect of retirement on the individual (Hansson et al., 1997; Moen, 1996). Given the vagueness of the definition of retirement, it may seem impossible to develop a rational theoretical perspective that would account for the many variations in the work patterns of older adults. To make sense out of these theories, it is necessary to assume that the individual being theorized about is in fact retired (i.e., no longer in the labor force). Furthermore, given the nature of the gender distribution in the workforce, at least until relatively recently, these theories primarily concern men. Later, the impact of retirement on women will be examined based on some of the more recent research on this topic.

The predominant view of retirement for many years was based on **role theory**. According to this perspective, the individual's roles, or normative expectations for behavior, provide a major source of fulfillment because they integrate the individual with society. The more roles

Retired individuals may become heavily involved in volunteer activity, as is true for these men working in a Habitat program in Coahoma, Mississippi.

the individual fills (worker, family member, friend, community member), the higher the individual's physical and psychological well-being. Among all the roles that adults may hold, the work role is one of the most important because it defines the individual's daily activities, status, and social group. According to role theory, as older workers lose their social roles, they lose their integration with society (Rosow, 1967). Loss of the work role through retirement in particular leads a person to feel adrift, unimportant, depressed, anxious, and isolated. These negative effects can translate into poor health and ultimately a higher risk of mortality (House, Landis, & Umberson, 1988). Individuals who have had a strong psychological investment in their jobs are particularly likely to suffer after loss of their work role through retirement.

Countering the role theory is the **continuity theory of retirement** (Atchley, 1989), which proposes that retirement does not lead to serious disruptions in the individual's sense of identity, social connections, or feelings of productivity. According to this perspective, the changes in work patterns associated with retirement do not constitute a significant loss of self-definition. Retirees maintain their previous goals, patterns of activities, and relationships, even though they are no longer reporting on a daily basis for work. Older adults view retirement as another stage of their careers, one that they have planned for and positively anticipated. The fact that many individuals maintain some form of employment after they have officially retired is further evidence in favor of continuity theory, suggesting that individuals may move into and out of the labor force with relative ease. Retirement does not constitute a crisis but another and different level of work involvement than that of the pre-retirement years.

The life course perspective views retirement as a normative stage of vocational development. Changes that are associated with this period of life are seen as logical outgrowths of earlier life events. The factors that shaped the individual's prior vocational development will have a persisting influence throughout retirement. For example, women's work lives are shaped by different factors than those of men, and these factors will continue to play out in the way that they experience retirement (Kim & Moen, 2001). The life course perspective also emphasizes the normative timing of events. According to this view, retirement will be stressful and create difficulties when its timing is unexpected. An individual who is forced to retire earlier than planned due to corporate layoffs will experience a higher degree of stress and disruption than an employee who is retiring "on time."

Retirement and Health. Implied in the role theory of retirement is the belief that loss of the work role leads to a general deterioration of the individual's well-being, both physical and mental. For many years, retirement researchers were convinced that the lack of focus and sense of importance in life was the direct stimulus for a downturn in the retiree's health, with an associated increase in mortality. In other words, the retiree, without a purpose in life, soon became ill and died. In the extreme version of this scenario, the retiree commits suicide due to a general sense of uselessness and irrelevance.

However, it is now recognized that this dismal view of retirement is a myth (Bosse, 1998). Older individuals are in fact more likely to develop ill health and die, but this is due to changes related to aging and chronic disease, which are more prevalent in the older population. Another flaw in the myth of retirement and health is related to the fact that individuals who are in poor health or suffering psychological symptoms are more likely to retire voluntarily. Their subsequent deterioration is not caused by retirement but constituted the cause for retirement (Henretta, Chan, & O'Rand, 1992). Charles Schultz, creator of the comic strip, *Peanuts*, died in February 2000 on the day he retired (when his last strip was printed). However, he had a terminal illness that led to his original decision to retire.

"What do you think?" | **10-4**

Why might health decline after retirement? Why might it improve?

Some individuals may experience improvement in their health status and feelings of well-being after retirement as they are now freed from the stress of the job. Their health-related behaviors may also improve because they may be able to spend more time in health-promoting activities such as exercise and avoid unhealthy habits such as smoking and consumption of alcohol and caffeine (Midanik, Soghikian, Ransom, & Tekawa, 1995). In terms of psychological health, there is evidence that retirement does not have deleterious effects on self-esteem or depression and may actually have a positive impact on feelings of well-being, a lowering of stress, and a reduction of anxiety and stress (Drentea, 2002).

Factors That Influence Adjustment to Retirement. Although retirement alone does not appear to be the direct cause of poor health in later life, perhaps as many as one-third of retired individuals do experience the loss of the work role as a stressful life event (Bosse, Aldwin, Levenson, & Workman-Daniels, 1991). Individuals vary in their patterns of adjustment to retirement. However, several common factors appear to put an individual at greater risk for negative consequences of exiting the work role. Retiring early, before the age of 62, is considered one significant risk factor (Palmore, Fillenbaum, & George, 1984). Although individuals who retire earlier than expected because of poor health may regret the need to leave their work role, they may be better off than they would if they were forced to keep working. Those who retire early for health problems may experience an improvement in their health after being released from the pressures of their job (Moen, 1996).

From a life course perspective, the exiting of the work role in an "off-time" or premature fashion is seen as more stressful or disruptive than going through the transition in an "on-time" or expectable fashion (Stallings, Dunham, Gatz, Baker, & Bengtson, 1997). Furthermore, those who are able to maintain their preferred level of participation in the labor force appear to experience advantages in terms of physical and psychological functioning (Herzog, House, & Morgan, 1991). Men with a strong commitment to work, good health, and a desire not to retire may well continue to maintain employment into their 70s and early 80s (Parnes & Sommers, 1994).

Related to the timing of retirement is the reason for retiring. When early retirement suddenly becomes mandatory because of downsizing, individuals lose control over the timing of their retirement and suffer negative consequences in terms of well-being (Armstrong-Stassen, 2001; Kalimo, Taris, & Schaufeli, 2003). Voluntary retirement is far less stressful and is seen as a positive event, as the individual is now free to pursue personal interests and avocations (Floyd, Haynes, Doll, Winemiller, Lemsky, et al., 1992). The amount of time allowed for retiring is another related factor. A minimum of two years planning prior to early retirement is related to a positive retirement experience compared to a decision made six months or less prior to retirement (Hardy & Quadagno, 1995). For men at least, the amount of planning for retirement may be one of the most important predictors of satisfaction (Dorfman, 1989).

Socioeconomic level has a complex relationship to retirement satisfaction. People of higher socioeconomic levels are less likely to retire, and they retire at later ages. Intrinsic satisfaction associated with work is more likely to be found in individuals in the higher occupational levels of professionals, executives, and managers, causing them to be less likely to engage in retirement planning (Kosloski, Ekerdt, &

DeViney, 2001). The extent to which an individual believes in the work ethic—that it is important to be productive and contribute to society (the economy)—is another factor related to retirement stress. On the positive side, having a higher level of education has advantages that promote retirement adjustment (Szinovacz & Washo, 1992). Higher socioeconomic status allows the individual to take advantage of the opportunities that retirement offers for productive and enjoyable leisure activities, such as involvement in retirement learning communities and the chance to travel. Individuals with higher levels of education and previous experience in managerial or professional positions may be better able to find part-time employment after retirement if they desire it. Past experience in community organizations and activities may also make it easier for such individuals to find rewarding opportunities for unpaid volunteer work and participation in clubs, organizations, and informal networks.

The continuity of an individual's work career is thought to be a further influence on the impact of retirement, at least for men. Those in **orderly careers** spend the majority of their employed years in related occupations. The higher the extent of orderliness in people's careers, the higher their attachments to their communities, friends, and social activities. The social integration these individuals maintain during their careers eases their retirement transition and means that they are likely to be in better physical and psychological health. Individuals with more continuous work histories also have higher socioeconomic status and income than those in disorderly careers, and these are factors generally related to greater satisfaction with retirement. However, on the negative side, such workers may be more attached to their jobs and are less satisfied with retirement (Gee & Baillie, 1999).

Apart from these factors that are in many ways related to occupational level, the loss of

BIOPSYCHOSOCIAL PERSPECTIVE

AN INDIVIDUAL'S VOCATIONAL opportunities and decisions made in early adulthood have a continuing impact not only on financial security and status but also on health and mortality well into the later years (Hayward, Friedman, & Chen, 1996). Unfortunately, for many people, factors outside their control, such as race and ethnicity, limit these choices. For individuals whose vocational situations are affected by such constraints, the role of identity and the possibility for realizing one's true vocational interests are far less significant than the reality of these sociocultural factors.

In addition to the effects of social constraints on job opportunities are potential effects on health. A study of Finnish workers yielded evidence that those with lower control over their hours, particularly women, had poorer health than those who were able to control their hours of work. These health problems included problems both in physical and mental health, measured as absences due to sickness and as psychological distress (Ala-Mursula, Vahtera, Kivimaki, Kevin, & Pentti, 2002). Since people in jobs at the lower levels of the socioeconomic spectrum tend to have less autonomy in determining their hours at work, this appears to be

another indirect mechanism through which health is affected by levels of education and income.

In later adulthood, the relationship between social class and health persists. Although Social Security coverage has helped close the income gap for individuals over the age of 65, the toll taken by years of poorer health habits, access to health care, and exposure to injury and disease still exists after retirement. Moreover, these factors contribute to the incidence of chronic diseases starting in the 40s and 50s. The income gradient is less steep for those over 65, but there still is an inverse relationship between income and risk of dying from cardiovascular disease. Furthermore, quality of life and health assessments appear to be related to income among all adults over the age of 18 (Pamuk, Makuc, Heck, Reuben, & Lochner, 1998). Race is another factor to consider in this equation. Retired black men have less positive retirement experiences, both due to disproportionately lower earnings and to a greater likelihood of health problems (Hayward et al., 1996). The inequities in earnings potential and opportunity to work in white collar jobs that affect black men thus continue into the retirement years.

income associated with retirement contributes to a difficult retirement transition (Bosse, Spiro, & Kressin, 1996), particularly for blacks (Fernandez, Mutran, Reitzes, & Sudha, 1998). Racial inequalities in income that exist throughout the employment years persist and are worsened in retirement (Hogan et al., 1997). In general, the relationship between income and health that applies to adults of working age also applies to adults who are retired. Those with ample financial resources are better able to afford both health care and the amenities of life that are associated with a better lifestyle in retirement.

Personality has not been given a great deal of attention in the retirement literature, and to

the extent that it has, the results are not at all conclusive. However, some investigators have examined the impact of people's views of themselves as retirees, which may be seen as linked in some ways to identity and are predictive of the quality of the retirement transition. For example, individuals with a high degree of **retirement self-efficacy**—that is, who believe themselves able to make a smooth and satisfactory adjustment to retirement—actually experience lower levels of anxiety associated with retirement (Carter & Cook, 1995). According to this notion, retirees evaluate themselves on the extent to which they see themselves as retiring successfully, and this self-appraisal influences their degree of retirement planning. Similarly, individuals with an internal locus of control, meaning that they see themselves as active agents in their own adjustment, have higher satisfaction in retirement (Gall, Evans, & Howard, 1997). High self-esteem and the perception of oneself as a competent worker are additional psychological factors related to retirement quality (Mutran et al., 1997).

There has been somewhat of a debate in the literature concerning the effect of retirement on a married couple's relationship. According to one school of thought, the "spouse underfoot syndrome," which traditionally applied to the husband, meant that partners were more likely to experience conflict now that they were in each other's presence for most of the daytime as well as nighttime hours. However, the contrasting view is of retirement as a second honeymoon, in which couples are now free to enjoy each other's company on a full-time basis without the constraints presented by the need to leave home for eight or more hours a day. The transition itself from work to retirement seems to takes a toll on marital satisfaction due to an increase in the level of conflict. The greatest conflict is observed when one partner is working while the other has retired. Eventually, however, these problems seem to subside, and after about two years of retirement for both partners, levels of marital satisfaction once again rise (Moen, Kim, & Hofmeister, 2001).

Events in the context of the family, such as widowhood or problems with grandchildren, can also add to difficulties in adjusting to retirement (Bosse et al., 1996). In one longitudinal study of almost 900 workers, older adults with financial responsibilities for family members were less likely to retire, particularly if they were helping to support their children. However, a desire to spend time with family members also served to motivate some of these workers to retire at an earlier age (Szinovacz, DeViney, & Davey, 2002).

Gender Differences in the Retirement Experience

Given the differential rate of participation in the labor force for previous cohorts of men and women, the majority of research on retirement has been conducted on male samples. In the earliest research on retirement in women, conducted in the 1970s, the findings suggested that women had more positive attitudes toward retirement than did men (Atchley, 1982). However, it is quite likely that the labor force experience of women who retired at this time was very different from the experience of current cohorts of women. The women who were studied in the 1970s had a less consistent work history than later cohorts of women, and most were employed for financial reasons rather than because they were committed to their jobs. By the 1980s, researchers reported significantly lower retirement satisfaction for women than men as well as more initial stress immediately following women's exit from the workforce (Seccombe & Lee, 1986). Difficulties in adjusting to retirement are particularly likely to occur among women holding lower status jobs (Richardson & Kilty, 1991). For women in the 1980s, when employment was beginning to increase, it appears that retirement came at a time before they were ready to stop working.

One of the largest-scale studies of the retirement experience of women in the 1990s was the Cornell Retirement and Well-Being Study, conducted in the mid-1990s on a sample of over 750 retired individuals between the ages of 50 and 72 years. The women in this study, whose work lives spanned the mid-1940s to the 1990s, had less continuous work histories than men. They spent fewer years in the labor force, took more breaks from employment, and spent a larger proportion of time working part-time than did men. Unlike the men in the sample, who experienced lower retirement satisfaction the longer they had worked, women who had spent more time in the labor force (fewer gaps and part-time employment) had higher satisfaction during their retirement years than women who had less continuous work histories. These differences remained even after other relevant factors were controlled, such as income, health, the nature of the job, and the reason for and timing of retirement. One exception to this overall finding was that women with more year-long gaps in employment had higher retirement satisfaction, perhaps because they had developed alternative activities and interests on which they could fall back after retirement. Unlike men, for whom the extent of advance planning predicted degree of satisfaction with retirement, women's retirement satisfaction was predicted by the timing of their work patterns (Quick & Moen, 1998).

There are other differences between men and women in the retirement experience. Women are more likely to spend time with relatives and become involved in organization work than are men, who socialize more with their pre-retirement friends (Dorfman, 1995). The retirement of women is more likely to be affected by the poor health of their spouse or other family members. The need to retire for family reasons rather than personal reasons may in turn lead to lower retirement satisfaction in women (Szinovacz, 1987). Even if family members are not in poor health, women are more likely to retire for family reasons (Ruhm, 1996). If they are caring for their husbands, they are five times more likely to retire than if they do not have this responsibility (Dentinger & Clarkberg, 2002). In contrast, for men, the decision to retire is more likely to be based on personal rather than family reasons (Martin Matthews & Brown, 1988). However, if a spouse is in poor health, it is more likely that a man will continue to work so that he can provide financial support (Talaga & Beehr, 1995).

In summary, work and retirement are broad and fascinating areas of study in the field of adult development and aging. Research from a developmental perspective has been somewhat slow to get off the ground. However, the increasing study of the topics of vocational satisfaction, performance, retirement adjustment, personality, and social structural factors is providing greater clarification regarding this significant component of adult life.

LEISURE PURSUITS IN LATER ADULTHOOD

Throughout adulthood, individuals express themselves not only in their work lives but in their hobbies and interests. Occupational psychologists and academics studying the relationship between job characteristics and satisfaction often neglect the fact that, for many adults, it is the off-duty hours rather than the on-duty hours that contribute the most to identity and personal satisfaction. However, marketers are being to recognize the value of developing promotional campaigns that appeal to older adults who potentially have resources to spend on leisure pursuits (Sterns & Gray, 1999). People over 50 control over three-quarters of all financial assets in the United States and account for approximately 40% of all consumer demand. They own over half of the credit cards in the United States and have more discretionary income than any other age group, meaning that they have more money to spend on leisure and other personal pursuits ("Selling to seniors," 1999). This phenomenon is not limited to the United States; for example, Australia is beginning to recognize the consumer power of the aging market (http://www.abc.net.au/rn/talks/lm/stories/s20606.htm).

As individuals move through adulthood and into retirement, it becomes more important to develop leisure interests so that they will have activities to provide their lives with a focus and meaning. In addition, leisure pursuits can serve important functions in helping people to maintain their health through physical activity and their cognitive functioning through intellectual stimulation. The social functions of leisure are also of potential significance, particularly for people who have become widowed or have had to relocate because of finances, a desire for more comfortable climates, or health. Some forms of leisure may even become part of a therapy program for an older adult who is trying to regain lost functions, such as mobility, coordination, or control over movements of the hands.

This woman's involvement in the creative and leisure pursuit of pottery may help her maintain her cognitive skills, health, and psychological well-being.

> ### *"What do you think?"*   10-5
>
> Do you think people choose their leisure activities on the basis of the same or the opposite type that they express in the workplace?

Researchers who study leisure time activities in later adulthood find strong evidence linking leisure participation to improvement in feelings of well-being, particularly among those who are trying to overcome deficits in physical functioning or social networks (Silverstein & Parker, 2002). Furthermore, cognitively challenging leisure activities can have the same effect as cognitively challenging work of helping individuals maintain their intellectual functioning over time (Schooler & Mulatu, 2001). The effects of leisure on physical health can also be striking. In one particularly impressive study, a sample of 799 men ages 39 to 86 were divided into groups on the basis of whether they were bereaved. Involvement in social activities was found to moderate the negative effects of stress on the physical functioning of the bereaved men (Fitzpatrick, Avron, Kressin, Greene, & Bosse, 2001). Being involved in volunteer work can also contribute to improved physical health. As was shown in a study of the oldest-old, involvement of over 100 hours a year in either paid or volunteer work was predictive of lower rates of illness and death (Luoh & Herzog, 2002).

As was shown in Chapter 5, older adults are less likely than younger people to engage in physical activities as leisure time pursuits. There is evidence that over time older adults become even less likely to participate in leisure pursuits that involve some type of activity. Researchers following a sample of 380 older adults living in Manitoba, Canada, found that over an eight-year period, there was a decrease in leisure activities involving travel or going out to theater, movies, sporting events. At the same time, the amount of time spent television watching and reading remained constant (Strain, Grabusic, Searle, & Dunn, 2002).

It is one thing to be able to document the favorable effects of leisure activities on health and well-being and another to be able to help individuals select appropriate activities in which to become involved. Although it might be beneficial to become involved in highly social activities, for example, not everyone is going to seek out this type of experience. Similarly, not everyone will desire leisure activities that involve a high degree of cognitive stimulation. Based on this reasoning, researchers have found that the Holland RIASEC model can be applied to leisure activities in older adults (Kerby & Ragan, 2002). Just as individuals can be counseled to seek a person–environment fit for vocations, they might also be advised to find the leisure pursuit that will keep them motivated and, hence, active in a pursuit that will ultimately have value in maximizing their functional abilities.

SUMMARY

1. Work is a major focus of adult life from the 20s until retirement and beyond. Labor force age dynamics have shifted in the past 50 years with movement of the baby boom generation and the aging of the labor force. There are gender and race variations in labor force participation and employment rates. Men are more likely to be in the labor force than women. Whites have lower unemployment rates than blacks or Hispanics. More married women are entering the labor force, especially those with young children. Occupational levels vary by age, sex, and race. Management and professional level jobs peak in the 45–54 age bracket. People over 55 are less likely to be employed in technical

occupations. Sales and service jobs have higher rates among the over-55 workers. Men earn larger salaries than women, even within the same occupational level. Highest earnings are achieved in the 45–54 age group. Higher educational levels are associated with higher income. The majority of women, but only 25% of men, are employed in the service industry. Within the service industry there are gender differences in specific areas such as computers, education, health, and social services. Many differences exist within the white, black, and Hispanic portion of the population that pervade all factors related to occupational attainment, including occupational level, education, and income. A glass ceiling appears to apply to women in managerial-level jobs who are prevented from advancing to professional and executive jobs; a similar barrier exists for college-educated black males.

2. Contemporary vocational psychology is oriented primarily around Holland's RIASEC theory of vocational development, which is the basis for O*NET, the most recent system developed by the U.S. government for cataloging occupational interests and types. The RIASEC model proposed by this theory is a hexagon that describes people and jobs. The highest level of worker satisfaction and productivity is theorized to occur when there is congruence. Tests are available that counselors and workers can use to identify their ideal occupations. Although the Holland model is accepted within I/O psychology, changes in the workplace may lead to assessment of individuals within teams and to application of the model to interests outside of work. Super's self-concept theory proposes that individuals move through several stages of career development in which they attempt to maximize the expression of their self-concept in their work. Rather than proceed

straight through these stages, however, individuals may plateau at the maintenance stage or recycle through earlier stages after a career change.

3. Theories and research on vocational satisfaction attempt to determine the relative influence of intrinsic and extrinsic factors on worker's happiness and productivity in a job. Occupational reinforcement patterns are the work values and needs that are likely to be satisfied in a job, and if these are present, the individual will be more satisfied. Personality and attachment style also appear to affect vocational satisfaction. Conflict between work and family is a source of potential vocational dissatisfaction, and several models are proposed that describe the nature of this relationship. Researchers have not established whether age is related to vocational satisfaction because the influence of job tenure must also be taken into account. Younger workers appear to value intrinsic factors, and older workers appear to move toward greater emphasis on extrinsic factors as they begin to plan for retirement. Identity processes may also play a role in this process.

4. The question of whether older workers are as productive as younger workers is another focus of occupational research. The model proposed by Warr suggests that older workers are relatively advantaged in jobs that rely on experience and perform more poorly in jobs that demand speed. Older workers have lower injury and absentee rates; however, when they are injured on the job they require more time to recover. Passage of the ADEA in 1967 offered protection to workers over 40 from discrimination by employers, although several occupations are excluded from this legislation.

5. Retirement is defined as the individual's withdrawal from the labor force in later life. Rather than being a discrete event, however, for most people it spans a process that may last for years. The phenomenon of retirement is a relatively recent occurrence, and over the twentieth century it became increasingly associated with positive attitudes as worker benefits increased. Theories attempting to understand the impact of retirement include role theory, continuity theory, and the life course perspective. Most retired people do not suffer a loss of health, either mental or physical, but some do experience the transition as stressful. Factors that put individuals at risk are retiring early (before age 62), unexpectedly, and as the result of outside forces. Socioeconomic status has a complex relationship to retirement satisfaction, as higher income leads to more resources in retirement but also makes it more difficult to leave the job. A high degree of retirement self-efficacy seems to promote healthy adjustment. Family events and relationships can present other complicating factors. Most of the retirement research is on males, but studies of women indicate that the timing of career events and the health of family members are important for retirement satisfaction in ways that are different than for men.

6. Leisure activities can serve a variety of important functions for adults throughout their working lives, but particularly in later adulthood after retirement. Researchers have identified positive effects of leisure involvement on physical functioning, well-being, and, ultimately, mortality.

GLOSSARY

Age Discrimination in Employment Act (ADEA): federal law initially passed in 1967 to prohibit discrimination against workers on the basis of age. Later expanded to prohibit mandatory retirement except in selected occupations.

Blue-collar jobs: occupations involving physical labor.

Bridge employment: employment in one job while officially retired from another job.

Cognitive evaluation theory: the view that financial incentives cause employees to feel less self-determination and psychological investment in their jobs.

Congruence: "fit" between a person's RIASEC type and that of the occupation within Holland's vocational development theory.

Continuity theory of retirement: proposal that retirement does not lead to serious disruptions in the individual's sense of identity, social connections, or feelings of productivity.

Disengagement stage: stage in Super's self-concept theory in which workers begin to prepare for retirement.

Dispositional affectivity: the general dimension of a person's affective responding.

Establishment stage: stage in Super's self-concept theory in which individuals in their mid-20s to mid-40s are focused on achieving stability.

Exploration stage: stage in Super's self-concept theory associated with the years from adolescence to the mid-20s.

Extrinsic factors: features that accompany a job that may also be found in other jobs.

Glass ceiling: the invisible barrier that prohibits women and minorities from being able to rise to executive levels, although they possess the skills and experience.

Holland Dictionary of Occupational Titles: catalog of occupations based on RIASEC code ratings.

Holland's vocational development theory: proposal by Holland that vocational aspirations and interests are the expression of an individual's personality.

Intrinsic factors: aspects of a job inherent in the work itself.

Labor force: all civilians in the over-16 population who are living outside of institutions and who have or are actively seeking employment.

Maintenance stage: stage in Super's self-concept theory in which individuals attempt to hold onto their positions rather than seek further advancement.

Managerial and professional level jobs: occupations at the level of executives, managers, and professionals.

Occupational Information Network (O*NET): on-line interactive national database of occupations intended for purposes of job classification, training, and vocational counseling.

Occupational level: position of a job on the hierarchy of jobs in terms of amount of required training, prestige, and income.

Occupational reinforcement patterns (ORPs): the work values and needs likely to be reinforced or satisfied by a particular occupation.

Orderly careers: occupations held by an individual that are logically connected.

Pink-collar jobs: occupations at the service level.

Plateauing: the attainment of a point in one's career where further hierarchical advancement is unlikely.

Recycling: process in which workers change their main field of career activity part way into occupational life and reexperience the early career development stages.

Retirement: the withdrawal of an individual in later life from the labor force.

Retirement self-efficacy: a person's belief that he or she will be able to make a smooth and satisfactory adjustment to retirement.

RIASEC model: Holland's vocational development theory which proposes that there are six facets of vocational interests and enviroments— Realistic (R), Investigative (I), Artistic (A), Social (S), Enterprising (E), and Conventional (C).

Role theory: proposal that normative expectations for behavior provide a major source of fulfillment because they integrate the individual with society.

Segmentation model: proposal that individuals can compartmentalize their lives with regard to work and family roles.

Self-Directed Search (SDS): self-administered and self-scored test based on Holland's vocational development theory.

Service level: occupation level that includes people who provide assistance to others.

Social Security Act: law passed by Congress in 1935 that provided retirement income for older adults.

Spillover model: proposal regarding work and family roles that attitudes and behaviors from one role carry over into the other.

Strong Vocational Interest Inventory (SVII): test in which respondents indicate their preferences for occupations, topics of study, activities, and types of people.

Super's self-concept theory: proposal that career development is a process driven by the individual's desire to achieve full realization of his or her self-concept in work that will allow the self-concept to be expressed.

Tenure: length of time in the job.

Two-factor theory: theory of work motivation developed by Herzberg proposing that the intrinsic features of a job are motivators and the extrinsic features of a job are hygiene factors.

Vocation: another term for occupation.

Vocational satisfaction: the extent to which the worker has positive views of the job or aspects of a job.

White-collar jobs: occupations at the managerial, professional, and technical level.

Chapter Eleven

Mental Health Issues and Treatment

U p until now, the processes discussed with regard to psychological development in the middle and later years have covered "normal" behavior. Personality and social processes as applied to the individual's adaptation to life have focused on stability and change within the parameters of the average or expectable life. The people who have participated in studies discussed had no documented psychological disorders, and they lived in community settings, most likely their own homes. Although many generalities can be made from within the framework of normal development, the characteristics and developmental processes of individuals who fall outside that framework will not be given proper attention. In this chapter, the developmental processes in adulthood of people with diagnosable psychological disorders will be presented. In addition, this chapter will discuss treatment sites for adults who are unable to live on their own, because of either physical or psychological disabilities.

PSYCHOLOGICAL DISORDERS IN ADULTHOOD

The field of **psychopathology** focuses on the scientific study of psychological disorders. Within this field, researchers and theorists attempt to provide an understanding of the causes of abnormal behavior as well as an understanding of how best to diagnose and treat people who are experiencing disorders. A **psychological disorder** is a set of behaviors that lie outside the range of ordinary human experience.

The criteria used to judge behavior as "abnormal" include feeling personal or subjective distress, being impaired in everyday life, causing a risk to the self or other people, and engaging in behavior that is socially or culturally unacceptable (Halgin & Whitbourne, 2003). People who have a hobby of collecting coins would not be considered abnormal, for example, because they are engaging in a behavior that does not cause them harm and is culturally acceptable. By contrast, consider people who collect old newspapers, magazines, and cereal boxes until there is no room left in their house for anything else and they are living in squalor. These individuals might very well be considered to have a psychological disorder. These so-called *hoarders* are not only engaging in behavior that is outside the norm but may be putting themselves at risk for fire and other harm due to the filth and debris that have accumulated in their home.

Diagnosis of Psychological Disorders

Specific sets of behaviors that meet the conditions of abnormality are given a diagnosis according to the criteria set forth in the psychiatric manual known as the **Diagnostic and Statistical Manual**, the most recent of which is the Fourth Edition Text Revision known as the **DSM-IV-TR** (American Psychiatric Association, 2000). The first version of this diagnostic system was developed by the American Psychiatric Association in 1952 as an attempt to systematize the approaches used by mental health workers in working with clients who exhibited signs of psychological disturbance. The current version is based on hundreds of field studies in which researchers specializing in particular disorders have attempted to establish a reliable and valid diagnostic system. Unfortunately, the DSM-IV-TR was not developed with consideration of how the diagnostic categories for psychological

disorders might change over the adult years. Given some of the distinctive characteristics of these disorders in later life, as will be discussed in this chapter, this creates problems in applying diagnoses to older adults.

In the DSM-IV-TR, a disorder is diagnosed by matching a client's symptoms to the description of symptoms in the manual. For a specific diagnosis to be given based on the client's symptoms, the client must meet the minimum criteria for that diagnosis, and not show symptoms of another diagnosis that would better account for those symptoms. The clinician can then move on to develop a treatment plan based on methods that have been established as effective for people with that particular diagnosis. Although the DSM-IV-TR is based on the so-called medical model, in which a set of behaviors is labeled a disorder, it is intended to be atheoretical, meaning that it is not based on any particular theoretical orientation.

The DSM-IV-TR has five axes, or dimensions, along which a clinician rates a client who is brought in for possible treatment. Axis I includes clinical syndromes or disorders. These are collections of symptoms that together form a recognizable pattern of disturbance. Included in Axis I are mood disorders, dementia, anxiety disorders, substance-related disorders, schizophrenia, sexual disorders, eating disorders, sleep disorders, and disorders first evident in infancy, childhood, and adolescence. On Axis II are personality disorders, which are disorders thought to reflect a disturbance within the basic personality structure of the individual. Mental retardation and disorders in the individual's ability to carry out the tasks of daily living are also included on Axis II. An individual may have both an Axis I disorder (such as major depression) and an Axis II disorder (such as paranoid personality disorder). The ratings on Axis III are of medical conditions that, although not a primary focus of treatment, have a bearing on the client's psychological condition. For example, an individual with diabetes may be faced with medical problems that have a bearing on his or her symptoms of depression or anxiety. Ratings of psychosocial stressors and environmental problems are made on Axis IV, which allows the clinician to take into account any particular contextual conditions that have a bearing on the psychological disorder. Finally, on Axis V, the clinician provides an overall rating of the client's general level of functioning, which may range from suicidal (ratings of 1–20) to superior (91–100).

Major Axis I Disorders in Adulthood

The disorders on Axis I cause severe disturbances in the lives of afflicted adults. These conditions may persist for many years, and even if their symptoms dissipate over time, the individual may be on more or less constant alert for a renewed outbreak. Fortunately, a minority of adults experience these disorders, but those who do face struggles in their family relationships, work lives, and ability to live independently in the community. Table 11-1 lists the major Axis I disorders that focused on in this chapter, with a description of how the symptoms are manifest in adults over age 65 (discussed within each disorder).

TABLE 11-1

Descriptions of Selected Axis I Disorders of the DSM-IV-TR as Observed in Older Adults

Category	Description	Examples of Specific Disorders	Variations in Older Adults
Mood disorders	Disturbance in mood	Major depressive disorder Bipolar disorder	Depression may appear as cognitive impairments, social isolation. Bipolar disorder may appear with hostility, irritability, and paranoia.
Anxiety disorders	Intense anxiety, worry, or apprehension	Generalized anxiety disorder Panic disorder Specific phobia Obsessive-compulsive disorder Post-traumatic stress disorder	Changes in health and physical symptoms interact with symptoms of anxiety.
Schizophrenia and other psychotic disorders	Psychotic symptoms such as distortion of reality and serious impairment in thinking, behavior, affect, and motivation	Schizophrenia Schizoaffective disorder Delusional disorder	Shift from positive to negative symptoms in older adults; depressive symptoms may coexist with symptoms of schizophrenia; poorer cognitive functioning than would be expected on the basis of age.
Substance-related disorders	Use or abuse of psychoactive substances	Substance dependence Substance abuse Substance intoxication	Older adults at higher risk than may be thought for these disorders.

Epidemiology. Statistics on psychological disorders are given in terms of prevalence and incidence. Prevalence refers to the number of people with the disorder over a specified period. A frequently used statistic is **lifetime prevalence**, which is the number or percentage of people who ever develop the disorder in their lifetimes. **One month prevalence** refers to individuals who report having had the symptoms of the disorder within the past 30 days. **Incidence** refers to the number of new cases that emerge within a given period such as a month or a year.

Two major epidemiological studies have been conducted as a basis for estimating such statistics in the years of adulthood. The National Institute of Health Epidemiological Catchment Area (ECA) study was conducted on samples of over 20,000 adults in five U.S. communities (Robins & Regier, 1991). Interviews were used to assess psychological symptoms across several major Axis I disorder categories. Subsequently, the National Comorbidity Study (NCS) (Kessler, McGonagle, Zhao, Nelson, Hughes, et al., 1994) was conducted on a national sample of 8000 adults living across the United States. The purpose of this study was to investigate both the prevalence of the major psychological disorders and their comorbidity. Assessment of **comorbidity** involves determining the extent to which individuals suffer from more than one disorder at the same time. A third epidemiological study, funded by the National Institute of Aging, is the multisite Established Population for Epidemiological Studies of the Elderly (EPESE) database. This study provided specific information on populations over the age of 65 from four representative areas in the United States—East Boston, New Haven, Iowa, and North Carolina (Cornoni-Huntley, Blazer, Lafferty, Everett, Brock, et al., 1990). In addition, data from the National Health Interview Survey (NHIS) are used to estimate the prevalence of psychological distress among adults of all ages. Results from the 2002 NHIS on the extent to which adults report psychological distress by age are shown in Fig. 11.1 (Centers for Disease Control and Prevention, 2003). As can be seen in Fig. 11.1, serious a minority of adults report that they experience psychological distress. Also evident is the fact that such distress is least likely to be reported by men and women ages 65 and older.

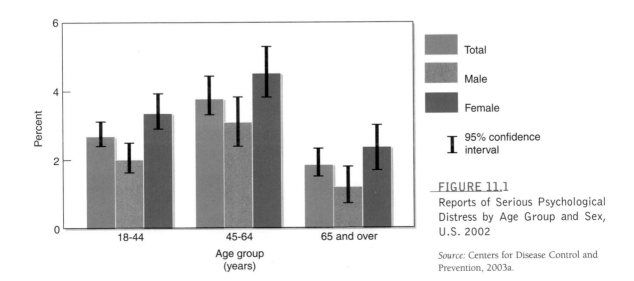

FIGURE 11.1

Reports of Serious Psychological Distress by Age Group and Sex, U.S. 2002

Source: Centers for Disease Control and Prevention, 2003a.

Both the ECA and NCS studies found that alcohol and drug-related disorders were the most common ones affecting the general adult population. However, the two studies differed sharply in their estimates of the lifetime prevalence of these and other psychological disorders. In the ECA study, this number was estimated to be 32% of the population, and in the NCS, it was estimated at a far higher 54%. Drug and alcohol problems were found to affect 14% in the ECA study but 27% in the NCS. The disparity between studies may be accounted for in part by the difference in assessment instruments used and in part by the nature of the samples. The NCS was carried out somewhat later than the ECA study, but this does not seem to be a sufficient basis for the difference in findings.

One major contribution of the NCS was the finding of high rates of comorbid conditions among adults with psychological disorders. Nearly 60% of those individuals were found to have at least one other diagnosis at some point in their lives. Often, the disorders that were comorbid involved some form of substance abuse (Kessler, 1997). The high rates of psychological disorders estimated from the NCS emphasize the importance of looking at development in adulthood and later life in terms of normal as well as abnormal behaviors. Combining the findings from both studies leads to estimates of from one-third to one-half of adults who at any point in their lives experience significant psychological symptoms. Most studies of adult development and aging conducted outside the framework of psychopathology fail to take these statistics into account. However, it is important to keep in mind that the odds are fairly high that respondents in studies of so-called normal cognition, personality, and social processes are experiencing at least one form of psychological disturbance.

An overall picture of the prevalence rates of Axis I disorders is presented in Table 11-2,

which summarizes one-year prevalence data from the ECA study for adults over age 55. Some of the exact numbers may not agree with data presented in specific sections of this chapter due to variations in the ages of samples and the basis for prevalence statistics (e.g., one month versus one year or lifetime). However,

TABLE 11-2

Best Estimate 1-Year Prevalence Rates of Axis I Disorders Based on Epidemiologic Catchment Area, Age 55+

	Prevalence (%)
Any Anxiety Disorder	11.4
Simple Phobia	7.3
Social Phobia	1.0
Agoraphobia	4.1
Panic Disorder	0.5
Obsessive-Compulsive Disorder	1.5
Any Mood Disorder	4.4
Major Depressive Episode	3.8
Unipolar Major Depression	3.7
Dysthymia	1.6
Bipolar I	0.2
Bipolar II	0.1
Schizophrenia	0.6
Somatization	0.3
Antisocial Personality Disorder	0.0
Anorexia Nervosa	0.0
Severe Cognitive Impairment	6.6
Any Disorder	19.8

Source: Department of Health and Human Services, 1999.

Note: Generalized anxiety disorder was not included in the ECA diagnostic criteria.

these numbers provide a good overview of the relative rates of the major disorders that potentially can affect older adults. At any given time, however, a much smaller percentage say that they have serious psychological symptoms. As noted in Fig. 11.1, estimates from the NHIS place the incidence of significant distress at about 3% among all noninstitutionalized adults.

Mood Disorders. Disturbances of mood, known as mood disorders, involve abnormalities in the individual's experience of emotion. There are four major categories of mood disorders: depressive disorders, bipolar disorders, mood disorders due to a general medical condition, and substance-induced mood disorders.

Depressive disorders are characterized by periods of dysphoria (sad mood), lasting varying amounts of time and involving varying degrees of severity. The experience of what is called a **manic episode** is one of the features of **bipolar disorder** (formerly known as manic-depression). In a manic episode, an individual feels unusually "high," meaning elated, grandiose, expansive, and highly energetic. Mood disorders due to a general medical condition involve the presence of a medical condition that causes psychological symptoms mimicking those of a mood disorder. In the case of major depression, these conditions include multiple sclerosis, Cushing's disease, Parkinson's disease, Huntington's disease, Addison's disease, cerebrovascular disease, hypothyroidism, and COPD. Nutritional problems, such as B12 deficiency, can also cause lethargy and fatigue such as that seen in major depression. Clinicians regard a general medical condition as a likely cause of manic episodes in older adults who have no prior history of mood disorder. Such conditions can include tumors, cerebrovascular disease, neurological disorders, and head trauma. Finally, substance-induced mood disorders may develop as the result of the use of narcotics and alcohol, medication, and/or exposure to an environmental toxin.

"What do you think?" | **11-1**

For what reasons might older adults express symptoms of mood disorders differently than do younger adults?

Over the course of adulthood, the prevalence of major depressive disorder, according to the NCS, is estimated to be 16.6% (Kessler, Berglund, Demler, Jin, Koretz, et al., 2003). Therefore, a large percentage of individuals are affected by this disturbance of mood at some point in their lives. At any given time, about 1 to 5% of adults in the United States meet the diagnostic criteria for major depression or dysthymia. At all ages, the rates of major depressive disorder and dysthymia in women are about double the rates of men. However, persons over the age of 65 are less likely to experience these disorders than are people under the age of 65. Among persons over the age of 65, the prevalence is estimated to be 1% for major depressive disorder and 2% for dysthymia (Abeles, Cooley, Deitch, Harper, Hinrichsen, et al., 1997). These percentages appear to hold across African Americans and whites (Blazer, Landerman, Hays, Simonsick, & Saunders, 1998). There are, however, gender differences in the experience of depression in later life. Although women are more likely to suffer from depressive symptoms earlier in life, men seem to be more likely to develop depressive symptoms over the course of later adulthood (Barefoot, Mortensen, Helms, Avlund, & Schroll, 2001).

Although the prevalence of a diagnosable mood disorder is lower in older adults, many report symptoms of depressive disorders. From 8% to 20% of older adults living in the community experience depressive symptoms, with almost double that percentage (17% to 35%) in primary care settings (Gurland, Cross, & Katz, 1996). Even though older adults may not meet the diagnostic criteria for these disorders, they may nevertheless be troubled by significant depressive symptoms that do not improve over time (Beekman, Geerlings, Deeg, Smit, Schoevers, et al., 2002).

Older adults are less likely to report some of the traditionally recognized symptoms of depression such as dysphoria, guilt, low self-esteem, and suicidal thoughts. They are more likely to seek treatment for somatic complaints such as constipation, abdominal cramps, weight loss, or aches and pains. They may also seek treatment for other psychological symptoms that do not appear to be those of depression, such as anxiety, abnormalities in psychomotor functioning, cognitive dysfunction, suicidal behavior, and delusions that there is something wrong with their bodies or that they are being persecuted (King & Markus, 2000). The term **depletion syndrome** describes the feelings of enervation, social withdrawal, loss of interest, sense of hopelessness, and a loss of appetite that may be observed in older adults who do not display outright symptoms of depression (Newmann, Engel, & Jensen, 1991).

Many older adults with treatable depression are reluctant to report symptoms or seek therapy.

A related phenomenon is **late-onset depression**, which is mild or moderate depression that first appears after the age of 60. Risk factors for late-onset depression include becoming a widow, having had less than a high school education, experiencing impairments in physical functioning, and being a heavy alcohol drinker (U.S. Department of Health and Human Services, 1999). Late onset depression is more likely to be accompanied by psychotic symptoms (Gournellis, Lykouras, Fortos, Oulis, Roumbos, et al., 2001). These psychotic symptoms include hypochondriacal delusions and nihilistic delusions, or the belief that the self, others, or the world have ceased to exist. Depression may also occur in conjunction with dementia, particularly in the early stages as individuals begin to come to grips with the implications of the disease for their future (Harwood, Sultzer, & Wheatley, 2000).

Age differences in rates of depressive disorders may reflect personality and emotional changes associated with aging, as described in Chapter 8. Conversely, the experience of depression in middle adulthood can have a negative impact on quality of life in later adulthood. In Vaillant's study on the Core City men (described in Chapter 8), depression at age 50 had a positive predictive effect on subjective well-being at age 70 (Vaillant & Western, 2001). Physical disability, such as that associated with arthritis, can also contribute to the development of depressive disorders in later adulthood (Oslin, Datto, Kallan, Katz, Edell, et al., 2002).

Researchers are attempting to sort out the relationship between depression and hormonal status in older adults. Women with Alzheimer's disease who are not taking estrogen seem especially vulnerable to the symptoms of depression. (Carlson, Sherwin, & Chertkow, 2000); however, estrogen replacement alone does not seem to be sufficient to benefit women with moderate to severe depression (Robinson, 2001) nor is it recommended for other health reasons (Hays, Ockene, Brunner, Kotchen, Manson, et al., 2003). For men, hormone levels may have clearer relationships to the experience of dysthymia. Testosterone levels are lower among men with this more chronic but less severe form of depression than among men with no depressive disorder or with major depressive disorder (Seidman, Araujo, Roose, Devanand, Xie, et al., 2002).

Health care professionals are not well trained in recognizing the signs of depression in their older clients. In part, this is because, as mentioned earlier, older adults do not necessarily report their symptoms in a manner that allows for accurate diagnosis. In addition, however, health care providers are not attuned to diagnosing psychological disorders in their older clients. Physicians spend less time per visit with an older patient than a younger patient. Furthermore, insurance companies reimburse for mental health diagnosis and intervention at a lower rate. Some health care providers may assume that depression is a natural consequence of aging and therefore pay less attention to its symptoms. Alternatively, a health care worker may wish to avoid stigmatizing older clients by diagnosing them with a psychological disorder (Duberstein & Conwell, 2000). Another possibility is that practitioners are unaware of the potential benefits of treatment, or they are uncertain about how to proceed with treatment of older people (Morris, Cyrus, Orazem, Mas, & Bieber, 1991). Misdiagnosis may also occur because the symptoms of mood disorders may occur in conjunction with a medical condition, leading either to failure to detect the mood disorder or misattribution of the symptoms.

One important factor associated with higher risk for depression in older adults is the presence of sensory disorders. Older adults with hearing impairments, visual impairments, or both are more likely to experience depressive symptoms (Lupsakko, Mantyjarvi, Kautiainen, & Sulkava, 2002). Psychosocial issues such as bereavement, loneliness, and stressful life events are a second source of risk factors for depressive disorders in later adulthood (Bruce, 2002). Medical disorders are a third risk factor (Alexopoulos, Buckwalter, Olin, Martinez, Wainscott, et al., 2002). The prevalence of depressive symptoms and disorders is higher among older adults being treated in medical settings such as clinics, hospitals, and long-term care institutions. Prevalence rates in clinics and hospitals are estimated to range from 12% to 20% (Blazer, 1999). These figures rise to as high as 30% among older individuals living in long-term care settings (King & Markus, 2000). Unfortunately, older adults seen in medical settings are not adequately diagnosed or treated (Charlson & Peterson, 2002).

Over the long term, without receiving appropriate treatment in the form of medication or psychotherapy, these untreated older adults are at greater risk of impairments in physical and cognitive functioning, failure to care for themselves, psychological distress, and death (Abrams, Lachs, McAvay, Keohane, & Bruce, 2002; Cooper, Harris, & McGready, 2002; Han, 2002). Those with more severe symptoms of depression and those whose depression is unremitting are more likely to suffer in terms of higher rates of mortality over time (Geerlings, Beekman, Deeg, Twisk, & Van Tilburg, 2002). One mechanism thought to account for the relationship between depression and higher morbidity is dysfunction in the immune system. Depression may activate cytokines that eventually lead to cardiovascular disease, osteoporosis, arthritis, type 2 diabetes, cancers, periodontal disease, frailty, and functional decline (Kiecolt-Glaser & Glaser, 2002).

The prevalence of bipolar affective disorder is far lower than major depressive disorder, with an estimated rate of 1.6% of the adult U.S. population (Kessler et al., 1994). Rates of bipolar disorder are lower in older adults (0.1%) than in the younger population (1.4%) (Robins & Regier, 1991). The likelihood of an individual experiencing a manic episode for the first time in old age is relatively low. The onset of a bipolar illness typically is in late adolescence or early adulthood.

Anxiety Disorders. In the category of disorders known as anxiety disorders, the major symptom is that of excessive anxiety, a state in which an individual is more tense, apprehensive, and uneasy about the future than is warranted by objective circumstances. For example, it would be appropriate to be worried about the prospect of a hurricane destroying a person's house if in fact there was a hurricane watch for the vicinity. However, if a person was constantly worrying about hurricanes even when the likelihood of occurrence was very small, this might be considered a symptom of an anxiety disorder. The individual becomes preoccupied by the belief that something terrible is about to happen and nothing can be done to stop it. The experience of anxiety also involves a focusing inward on the unpleasant feelings that accompany anxiety such as a pounding heart or shortness of breath. Often, these feelings may become a major focus of the individual's symptoms.

Approximately 12% of the adult population are diagnosed with an anxiety disorder each year (Robins & Regier, 1991). Women at all ages have about twice the rate of anxiety disorders as men, and these disorders are more common in the under-65 population than among older adults (Beekman, Bremmer, Deeg, van Balkom, Smit, et al., 1998).

As was true for mood disorders, clinicians who work with older adults are concerned that anxiety disorders fail to be recognized in clients within this age group. The major reason is the difficulty in arriving at an accurate diagnosis of anxiety disorders in older adults (Scogin, Floyd, & Forde, 2000). At any age, the symptoms of an anxiety disorder may be produced by or at least exist alongside a medical condition, including Alzheimer's disease. However, because such chronic diseases as cancer and cardiovascular disease are more likely to be present in older adults, these conditions can complicate the process of diagnosis. The older adult may attribute anxiety symptoms to these medical conditions rather than see them as treatable. Health practitioners themselves may not be attuned to diagnosing psychological symptoms in an older individual with physical health problems. As a result, the presence of an anxiety disorder may be missed along with an opportunity for intervention.

"What do you think?"   11-2

How can mental health professionals be better trained to diagnose anxiety disorders in older adults?

There are six categories of anxiety disorder. In generalized anxiety disorder, a person feels an overall sense of uneasiness and concern but without having a particular focus. The primary symptom of this disorder is worry, especially over minor problems. Other symptoms are a general sense of restlessness, difficulty concentrating, fatigue, irritability, muscle tension, and sleep disturbance. In later adulthood, generalized anxiety disorder may be triggered by stress, and concerns about health play a prominent role (Scogin et al., 2000). About 5% of adults have this disorder (Wittchen, Zhao, Kessler, & Eaton, 1994). Among older adults, the six-month prevalence (those who reported symptoms in the past six months) is 2%, and the lifetime prevalence is estimated at 4.6% (Blazer, George, & Hughes, 1991). However, a higher percentage of older adults experience symptoms of generalized anxiety (Graham & Vidal-Zeballos, 1998), and some findings suggest that there is a more common "subsyndromal" version of generalized anxiety disorder among older adults whose symptoms are not severe enough to warrant a diagnosis of the disorder itself (Diefenbach, Hopko, Feigon, Stanley, Novy, et al., 2003).

The form of anxiety disorder known as **panic disorder** involves the experience of panic attacks, which are episodes in which the individual experiences physical symptoms involving extreme shortness of breath, a pounding heart, and the belief that death is imminent. People who suffer from panic disorder may have these episodes at unpredictable times, and eventually they may also develop **agoraphobia**, which is the fear of being trapped or stranded during a panic attack. To avoid this frightening and embarrassing situation, the individual then begins to stay at home and to avoid places such as elevators, shopping malls, or public transportation, where escape during an attack would be difficult. Estimates are that approximately 1.5 to just under 3% of adults have panic disorder, although as many as 15% may have experienced a panic attack at least once in life (Weissman, Bland, Canino, Faravelli, Greenwald, et al., 1997).

The prevalence of agoraphobia is estimated to be much higher than panic disorder, affecting perhaps 5% of the adult U.S. population (Kessler et al., 1994). Panic disorder is rare among older adults, but agoraphobia is more common, developing after an illness, a fear-provoking event, or in relation to a medical condition. For example, an older adult may be too anxious to leave the home after having been mugged on the street. Another scenario is that an older adult is afraid of embarrassment related to concerns about urinary incontinence. Unlike younger adults, who may develop agoraphobia following a panic attack, it is more likely that this condition in older adults is related to fear of harm or embarrassment (Scogin et al., 2000).

People with a **specific phobia** have an irrational fear of a particular object or situation. There are many types of specific phobias ranging from fear of snakes to fear of enclosed places. A common form of specific phobia is blood-injury phobia, which is fear of seeing blood or seeing a surgical procedure. Although from a psychodynamic perspective, the fear of certain objects (such as knives) may have unconscious meaning (the knife is a phallic symbol), many psychologists account for the acquisition of specific phobias as occurring through a classical conditioning process. Cognitive-behavioral psychologists would maintain, moreover, that a significant aspect of the phobia is the person's unrealistic view of being unable to handle the feared situation or object. This disorder was the most commonly observed form of anxiety disorder in older adults identified in the ECA study (referred to in Table 11-2 as "simple" phobia).

People with **social phobia** have a form of anxiety disorder that applies to situations in which they must perform some action in front of others. In addition to the obvious scenarios that create distress for such individuals, including giving a public musical performance or speaking to a large group, ordinary situations such as eating in the presence of others can create high degrees of anxiety. Severe symptoms of social phobia are present in about 3% of adults, and less extreme symptoms are present in up to 13% of the population. Women are more likely to suffer from this disorder than are men (Kessler et al., 1994). A specific form of social phobia that applies only to public speaking also occurs, in which the individual can manage without distress as long as such situations can be avoided (Kessler, Stein, & Berglund, 1998).

Obsessive-compulsive disorder is a form of anxiety disorder in which individuals suffer from obsessions, or repetitive thoughts (such as the belief that one's child will be harmed), and compulsions, which are repetitive behaviors (such as handwashing). The obsessions and compulsions are unrelenting, irrational, and distracting. This disorder is not the same as obsessive-compulsive personality disorder, in which an individual has the personality traits of being excessively rigid and perfectionistic. People with the anxiety disorder have unrelenting feelings of anxiety that are partially relieved only by performing compulsive rituals or thinking certain thoughts. The lifetime prevalence of obsessive-compulsive disorder is about 2% of the adult population (Sasson, Zohar, Chopra, Lustig, Iancu, et al., 1997). The one-month prevalence among older adults is estimated at 0.8%, making this a relatively rare disorder in this age group.

In the anxiety disorder known as **post-traumatic stress disorder (PTSD)**, an individual suffers prolonged effects of exposure to a traumatic experience, an event that is distressing, if not disastrous. Examples of traumatic experiences include earthquakes, fires, physical assault, and war. Although many people who are exposed to these types of experiences suffer from an acute stress disorder for a period of time, a certain percentage develop symptoms that persist for months or even years. People with PTSD may find themselves incapacitated by flashbacks or reminders of the event, intrusions of thoughts about the disaster, hypersensitivity to events similar to the trauma, and attempts to avoid these disturbing images and reminders. The individual may also become detached from other people and the ordinary events of daily life. In addition to type of disasters or trauma that adults may face is the physical or sexual abuse that might be experienced by a child.

Exposure to trauma in the form of combat during war is a major source of PTSD among the current over-65 population, of whom about one million served in World War II and the Korean War. Within this population, those exposed to combat are at heightened risk for PTSD (Spiro, Schnurr, & Aldwin, 1994). However, some characteristics of an individual seem to predispose certain individuals to be more likely to experience combat. In one study of Vietnam veterans, it was found that men from lower socioeconomic status had a greater chance of being directly exposed to high-exposure combat situations, as they were more likely to serve on the front line (Green, Grace, Lindy, Gleser, & Leonard, 1990). Furthermore, those men with a history of mood disorders and **substance abuse** were more likely to become involved in combat situations in which they witnessed grotesque injuries, such as those that were inflicted on Vietnam citizens. Upon their return home, these were also the men who were less likely to seek social support or treatment.

Another investigation of precombat influences on the development of PTSD was conducted in the context of the Harvard Grant Study, described in Chapter 8. In this study on World War II veterans (Lee, Vaillant, Torrey, & Elder, 1995), the men with greater economic resources were more rather than less likely to be exposed to combat. They were more athletically active and more eager to become involved in the fighting. Although they experienced symptoms of PTSD, these symptoms did not interfere with their ability to achieve satisfactory postwar adjustment in terms of both family and work lives. Later on in life, however, the combat survivors also suffered more chronic illness and were more likely to die before the age of 65 than those men who were not involved in heavy combat. Contrasting these two studies on the veterans of two different wars points to the importance of the social context as well as an

Exposure to combat in their youth increased the risk of chronic illness and mortality among World War II veterans.

individual's personal experiences in setting the stage for the later development of PTSD symptoms. Citizens in the United States were far more supportive of the country's efforts in World War II than in the Vietnam War.

Some clinicians expect that the incidence of PTSD among the older adult population will grow in future years due to the aging of Vietnam veterans. Estimates are that at the age of 19, the prevalence of PTSD among Vietnam soldiers was 15%. Since PTSD can arise many years after exposure to trauma, these numbers may well continue to increase (U.S. Department of Health and Human Services, 1999). Exposure to the terrorist attacks in the United States of September 11, 2001, may also increase the rate of PTSD among older adults, even those not directly exposed to the attacks themselves (van Zelst, de Beurs, & Smit, 2003).

Anxiety may occur in conjunction with depression, a disorder being considered for inclusion in future DSMs that would have the name **mixed anxiety-depressive disorder**. In this disorder, the individual experiences recurrent or persistent dysphoria for at least one month along with at least four symptoms of anxiety disorders such as worry, dread of the future, irritability, and sleep disturbance along with other symptoms of depressive disorder such as low self-esteem and hopelessness. These symptoms, when present in older adults, can significantly lower their ability to carry out everyday activities. Furthermore, people with mixed anxiety-depressive disorder tend to be less responsive to treatment (Flint & Rifat, 1997).

Schizophrenia and Other Psychotic Disorders. The psychological disorder known as **schizophrenia** is perhaps the one that most mystifies students of psychopathology, because of its long association with the notion of "mental illness." A person with schizophrenia has a wide range of unusual symptoms, ranging from hallucinations (false perceptions) to delusions (false beliefs), which are known as *positive* symptoms. However, there may also be *negative* symptoms of apathy, withdrawal, and lack of emotional expression. Often, a person's speech may be disordered, and motor behavior may be extremely altered. There are variations in type of schizophrenia, but all share the common feature of involving a severe disturbance in the person's ability to remain in touch with reality.

The DSM-IV-TR has three sets of criteria (A, B, and C) that must be present in order for schizophrenia to be diagnosed. Criterion A involves the presence of delusions, hallucinations, disorganized speech, extremely disorganized behavior, or negative symptoms. Two or more of these must be present for schizophrenia to be diagnosed, although only one must be present if the delusions are bizarre or the hallucinations involve voices that comment on the person's activities. For Criterion B to be satisfied, the individual must show significant impairment in at least one area of daily life, such as functioning at work, in school, in social relationships, or in self-care. Criterion C involves the duration of symptoms. The diagnosis of schizophrenia is given only if symptoms are present for at least six months, of which one month involved active symptoms from Criterion A. Although all diagnoses in the DSM-IV-TR involve **differential diagnosis** (ruling out other diagnoses), for schizophrenia, these are specified as exclusionary criteria. Such conditions that must be ruled out include **mood disorders**, medical diagnoses, substance use, and a lifelong disorder such as autism, which is a significant disturbance in communication and interpersonal functioning present from childhood.

Once the diagnosis for schizophrenia is established, a classification must be made of the course of the disorder within the particular individual. The diagnosis of the course of the disorder is based on the fact that people with this disorder show a variety of patterns over their lives of symptom exacerbation and remission, as will be discussed below. In addition to the course of the disorder, a diagnosis also includes which of the five major types of schizophrenia described in DSM-IV-TR are displayed within the individual. The *catatonic* type involves bizarre motor behaviors such as rigid posturing or excessive activity. In *paranoid* schizophrenia, the individual is preoccupied with delusions or hallucinations that involve the theme of being persecuted or followed. People with *undifferentiated* schizophrenia have a variety of symptoms such as delusions or hallucinations, but they do not have a consistent theme or pattern to these symptoms. Disorganized schizophrenia involves the presence of flat or inappropriate affect, disorganized speech, and disorganized behavior. For individuals who no longer meet the full diagnostic criteria for schizophrenia but still show some symptoms, there is a final category called the *residual* type.

It is estimated that schizophrenia has a lifetime prevalence of about 1% (American Psychiatric Association, 2000), with a peak prevalence at 1.5% for the 30–44 age group and 0.2% in people older than 65 (Keith, Regier, & Rae,

1991). In part, the apparent decrease in older age groups reflects the higher risk of mortality for people with this disorder. In the large majority of people who develop this disorder, the onset is before age 40, although the onset in women is about five years later than that of men. Also, reflecting the higher life expectancy of women, there is a crossover in the gender distribution of the disorder, with a higher prevalence of schizophrenia among older women than older adult men (Meeks, 2000).

The first systematic definition of schizophrenia as "premature dementia" (*dementia praecox*) was developed by the German psychiatrist Emil Kraepelin, and for many years it was thought of as a permanently disabling condition. However, it is now known that the long-term outcome of the disorder is highly variable. Approximately 20% to 25% of people who develop the disorder improve to the point of complete remission, and at the other end of the spectrum, 10% remain chronically impaired. Among the remaining 50% to 70%, the disorder shows a varying course with gradual improvements in social functioning and a reduction of psychotic symptoms (Meeks, 2000). Some individuals can achieve very significant recovery after many years of being chronically impaired, including being able to work, drive a car, and live independently in their own home (Palmer, Heaton, Gladsjo, Evans, Patterson, et al., 2002).

Despite the favorable outcomes achieved by some who suffer from schizophrenia, there are serious ramifications of having had the disorder at some point in life. The nature of this disturbance and its association with other illnesses, suicide, or substance abuse mean that a person with this diagnosis faces serious threats to health and mortality throughout the adult years (Ruschena, Mullen, Burgess, Cordner, Barry-Walsh, et al., 1998). Furthermore, although negative symptoms may become more prominent than positive symptoms, people who have this disorder in later adulthood continue to exhibit significant impairment. Depression, poorer cognitive functioning, and social isolation are other complications that can be experienced by older adults with schizophrenia (Graham, Arthur, & Howard, 2002). Furthermore, the symptoms of schizophrenia themselves can lead to significant disruptions in everyday life as well as greater likelihood of negative life events (Patterson, Shaw, Semple, Moscona, Harris, et al., 1997).

On the positive side, older adults who have suffered from schizophrenia for many years develop a wide range of coping skills (Solano & Whitbourne, 2001). Those naturally developing mechanisms can be augmented with clinical interventions that focus on skills for coping with everyday life problems. Emotional support is another important component of treatment for older individuals with a long history of this disorder (Semple, Patterson, Shaw, Grant, Moscona, et al., 1999).

Although not in DSM-IV-TR, another apparent form of schizophrenia known as **late-onset schizophrenia** can occur among adults over the age of 45 years (Jeste, Symonds, Harris, Paulsen, Palmer, et al., 1997), a condition also referred to as *paraphrenia*. In contrast to early-onset schizophrenia, the late-onset variety is more likely to involve paranoid symptoms, show less severe cognitive impairment, and be subject to better response to antipsychotic medications. Individuals with the late-onset form of schizophrenia appear to function at a higher level in their youth than do people who develop the more common form of early-onset schizophrenia. It is possible that individuals with the late-onset form of the disorder share the same genetic vulnerability thought to be involved in other forms of schizophrenia (Lohr, Alder, Flynn, Harris, & McAdams, 1997). For some reason, however, they were protected or had other advantages that prevented the emergence of symptoms (Meeks, 2000). The disorder may be triggered in later adulthood in connection with sensory losses such as changes in vision and hearing, which make it more difficult for the individual to perceive accurately the actions and speech of other people (Zarit & Zarit, 1998).

Another form of psychotic disorder is called **brief psychotic disorder**, which is a period in which an individual shows a burst of psychotic symptoms such as delusions, bizarre behavior, and disorganized thought. Such an episode might follow a stressful event or period such as a disaster, personal trauma, or possibly a seemingly normal event such as the birth of a child. The symptoms subside, however, within a period of a month. There is also a psychotic disorder involving abnormalities in mood. **Schizoaffective disorder** is a diagnosis given to people who have a depressive, manic, or mixed episode at the same time as they are experiencing symptoms of schizophrenia.

Delusional disorders form another diagnostic category within the psychotic disorders. In a delusional disorder, the individual develops a delusional belief around a particular theme or idea. One example is the form of delusional disorder known as *erotomania*, in which people believe (falsely) that they are loved by another person, often one who is famous. Another is *persecutory* delusional disorder, in which people believe (again falsely) that others are plotting against them. Finally, **shared psychotic disorder** occurs when two or more people develop a joint delusional system. These people may be involved in a close, perhaps unusually dependent, relationship. One person is usually the dominant one, who convinces the other to follow along with the delusional system of ideas. The dependent partner follows along in order to gain the approval, love, and security offered by the dominant partner. Frequently, the two people involved in this type of relationship are sisters, but the disorder may also be found in parent–child and husband–wife combinations.

Delirium, Dementia, and Amnestic Disorders. Disorders involving significant loss of cognitive functioning as the result of neurological dysfunction or medical illness form the category in DSM-IV-TR known as **delirium, dementia, and amnestic disorders.** These disorders in previous versions of the DSM were called "organic" or "cognitive" disorders, indicating that they have different causes and characteristics than the other psychological disorders included in the diagnostic system. However, the terminology has moved toward the current descriptive one (that simply summarizes the disorders in this category) because it is becoming increasingly difficult to distinguish disorders that have a neurological or physiological basis from those that do not.

"What do you think?" | **11-3**

How can clinicians avoid making errors in diagnosing disorders that look like dementia?

The disorder known as Alzheimer's disease is technically regarded within DSM-IV-TR as a cause of dementia. The term *dementia* is used to apply to a change in cognitive functioning that occurs progressively over time. The symptoms include loss of memory and of the ability to use language (*aphasia*), to carry out coordinated bodily movements (*apraxia*), to recognize familiar objects, and to make rational judgments. As discussed in Chapter 5, Alzheimer's disease is one cause of dementia, but there can be others, such as long-term substance abuse, vascular disease, and Parkinson's disease, to name a few.

In contrast to the long-term changes that occur in dementia, the condition known as **delirium** is an acute state in which the individual experiences a disturbance in consciousness and attention. There may also be cognitive changes, including memory loss, disorientation, and inability to use language. The cause of delirium is a change in the brain's functioning due to substance use, improper medications, head injury, high fever, or vitamin deficiency. Most cases of delirium subside within days, but the condition may persist as long as a month. During this time, unfortunately, the individual may be misdiagnosed with dementia, and an opportunity for intervention will have been lost or at least made more complicated.

People who suffer from **amnesia** have as their main symptom profound memory loss. Their amnesia may involve an inability to learn or remember new information (*anterograde*) or the inability to recall information into the past (*retrograde*). An amnestic disorder may be due to chronic use of substances such as medications, psychoactive substances, or exposure to environmental toxins. However, amnesia may also be caused by head trauma, loss of oxygen supply to the brain, and the sexually transmitted disease of herpes simplex.

Substance-Related Disorders. As just indicated, the chronic use of psychoactive substances can cause one or more disorders of cognitive functioning. DSM-IV-TR includes a set of disorders that involve disturbances in the pattern of use of a variety of substances, ranging from caffeine to heroin. Within this framework, two concepts are of central importance in determining whether an individual has a substance-related disorder. Substance abuse involves maladaptive patterns of use of a substance that involve failure to meet social obligations, using the substance in situations that can be physically hazardous or lead to arrest, and creating interpersonal conflicts. People who suffer from **substance dependence** show a cluster of symptoms that include a set of physiological, cognitive, and behavioral changes related to use of the substance over a prolonged period. Often, the symptoms of substance dependence include **tolerance**, which is the need to take in a larger and larger dose to achieve the desired effect, and **withdrawal**, which is the physical and psychological reaction to the substance's removal from the body. In some cases, the symptoms of withdrawal can be extreme and frightening, such as violent bodily tremors, cold sweat, and high levels of anxiety.

Assess Yourself

See how much you know about Alzheimer's disease and its treatment.

Question 1
The annual financial burden of Alzheimer's, including the cost of care and lost productivity, is estimated at:
- A. $100 million worldwide.
- B. $100 million in the United States alone.
- C. $100 billion worldwide.
- D. $100 billion in the United States alone.

Question 2
Which of the following statements is TRUE?
- A. Alzheimer's is one cause of dementia.
- B. Dementia is a form of Alzheimer's.
- C. Dementia is an early stage of Alzheimer's, but not a later stage.
- D. None of the above.

Question 3
Besides Alzheimer's, which of the following also can cause dementia?
- A. Strokes.
- B. Medications.
- C. Infections.
- D. All of the above.

Question 4
On average, Alzheimer's disease is diagnosed at the age of:
- A. 65 years
- B. 70 years
- C. 75 years
- D. 80 years

Question 5
Which of the following statements is TRUE?
- A. Heredity plays no role in Alzheimer's.
- B. Heredity is the sole determining factor in who develops Alzheimer's.
- C. Even in families in which several people have had Alzheimer's, most members do not develop the disease.
- D. None of the above.

Assess Yourself *(continued)*

Question 6
Which of the following statements is TRUE?
 A. Many people age without any significant deterioration of mental function.
 B. Changes in mental capabilities in part depend on the amount of mental stimulation you maintain.
 C. A lot of people become more forgetful as they age.
 D. All of the above are true.

Question 7
Which of the following statements is FALSE?
 A. People with severe dementia need constant supervision.
 B. People with severe dementia need new challenges every day to sustain mental function.
 C. People with severe dementia often lose the ability to perform routine tasks such as buckling a belt.
 D. All of the above are true.

Question 8
Unlike other diseases, there is little benefit to early diagnosis of Alzheimer's.
 A. True
 B. False

Answers: 1 D, 2 A, 3 D, 4 D, 5 C, 6 D, 7 D, 8 B.

In 2001, illicit drugs were used by an estimated 28 million persons 12 years and older, representing 13% of the population (Substance Abuse and Mental Health Services Administration, 2002). Based on estimates from this sample, 7% of the U.S. population over 12 used at least one drug such as marijuana, LSD, cocaine, or heroin within the past year. As can be seen in Fig. 11.2, the majority of adults who abuse or are dependent on alcohol or illicit drugs are in their late teens and early 20s. Very small percentages of adults 40 and older reported abusing or being dependent on either illicit drugs or alcohol. However, approximately 16% of those 65 and older are estimated to have alcohol use disorders (Menninger, 2002).

Older adults are particularly at risk for abuse of prescription drugs, as 25% of the medications used in the United States are taken by adults over the age of 65 years. Sleeping pills and tranquilizers present a particular risk for this age group (Abeles et al., 1997). As mentioned in Chapter 4, another danger in the use of these drugs is the longer time they take to clear the excretory system due to changes in the kidney, leading to the potential of an overdose even when the individual takes the prescribed amounts.

Attention has only recently been drawn to the problems of older drinkers. In part, this is because there is selective survival of people who do not use alcohol. The people who used alcohol to excess are no longer in the population by the time they reach their 60s and 70s. Estimates are that 2 to 5% of men and 1% of women over 65 abuse substances (Abeles et al., 1997), and that 1 to 2% of men and 0.3% of women over 65 are alcohol abusers (Grant, Harford, Dawson, Chou, Dufour, et al., 1995). In contrast to the under-65 population, among those over 65 the prevalence rates of alcohol abuse are higher for African Americans. Hispanic females over 65 have the lowest rates of alcohol abuse. In the future, it is estimated that rates of alcohol abuse will increase significantly with the aging of the current cohort of Baby Boomers, who have higher rates of alcohol consumption than previous generations (U.S. Department of Health and Human Services, 1999).

FIGURE 11.2

Percentages of Persons Aged 12 or Older Reporting Past Year Abuse or Dependence for Alcohol or Any Illicit Drug,* by Detailed Age Categories: 2001

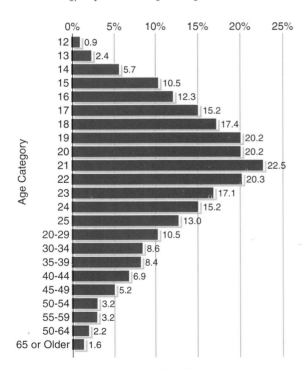

Source: Substance Abuse and Mental Health Services Administration, 2002.

Symptoms of alcohol dependence are thought to be present in as many as 14% of older adults who receive medical attention in hospitals and emergency rooms. It is also estimated that alcohol use is relatively prevalent in settings in which only older adults live, such as nursing homes and retirement communities. The risks of alcohol abuse among this population are considerable, ranging from cirrhosis of the liver (a terminal condition) to heightened rate of injury through hip fractures and motor vehicle accidents. Alcohol may also interact with the effects of prescription medications, potentially limiting their effectiveness. Even without a change in drinking patterns, an older person may experience difficulties associated with physiological changes that affect tolerance. Long-term alcohol use may also lead to changes in the frontal lobes and cerebellum, exacerbating the effects of normal aging on cognitive and motor functioning (National Institute on Alcohol Abuse and Alcoholism, 1998) In severe and prolonged alcohol abuse, dementia can develop, leading to permanent memory loss and early death (see Chapter 5).

Axis II Disorders

The **personality disorders** on Axis II of the DSM-IV-TR fall into three groups or clusters. Cluster A includes paranoid, schizoid, and schizotypal personality disorders, which are characterized by odd and eccentric personality traits and behavior patterns. People in Cluster B have antisocial, borderline, narcissistic, and histrionic personality disorders. These disorders share the quality of being overdramatic, emotional, and unpredictable. Finally, Cluster C comprises avoidant, dependent, and obsessive-compulsive personality disorders, which share the qualities of anxious and fearful traits and behaviors.

The concept of personality disorder may seem to be one that is not particularly developmental in that it applies to long-standing dispositions which by definition are inflexible. Once adulthood is reached, it would seem that the stage is set for the manifestation of the disorder and its pervasive influence on the individual's life. However, there is a way to think of the personality disorders as developmental in the sense that they require adaptation. As with the personality trait model, which assumes personality stability, it is also assumed that over the course of adulthood individuals learn to adjust to the limitations or idiosyncrasies caused by their personality disorder. The individual with obsessive-compulsive disorder, for example, is extremely rigid, moralistic, and preoccupied with detail. The traits associated with the disorder are difficult to live with on a daily basis. Yet, over time, the individual may gain insight if not into the disorder than at least into the limitations it presents. Such an individual will be unhappy when placed in situations where events or objects are in disarray. To avoid the distress caused by such situations, the individual can learn to avoid them or at least learn how to tolerate them. A second developmental issue concerns the question of whether the nature or degree of personality disorder symptoms changes over adulthood.

The prevalence of personality disorders in the general population is estimated to be 9% (Samuels, Eaton, Bienvenu, Brown, Costa, et al., 2002), a prevalence that is fairly steady across adulthood (Abrams & Horowitz, 1999). However, there are variations in the rates of specific personality disorders by age. Because of its relevance to the criminal justice system, antisocial personality disorder has received perhaps the most attention of all the Axis II disorders. Based on the ECA, the lifetime prevalence of antisocial personality disorder is estimated to be 4.5% of adult males and 0.8% of adult females (Robins & Regier, 1991).

The DSM-IV-TR diagnosis of antisocial personality disorder is characterized by **psychopathy**, a set of traits that are thought to lie at the core of the disorder. There are two dimensions or factors to psychopathy as measured by the Psychopathy Check List (Hare, 1997). Factor 1 is a cluster of traits that represent disturbances in the capacity to experience emotions such as empathy, guilt, and remorse. This cluster also includes manipulativeness, egocentricity, and callousness. Factor 2 incorporates the unstable and impulsive behaviors that contribute to the socially deviant lifestyle of the individual with this disorder.

Studies of the relationship between age and antisocial personality disorder provide support for the notion that the maladaptive personality traits that constitute the essence of personality disorders are extremely stable over time (Harpur, Hart, & Hare, 2002). The results of one large-scale study of psychopathy, conducted on nearly 900 male prisoners between the ages of 18 and 89, are shown in Fig. 11.3. Scores on Factor 1, which represent the "personality" contribution to the disorder, do not show evidence of age differences. By contrast, scores on the items that reflect socially deviant and impulsive behaviors show a dramatic decrease across age groups. This picture drawn from Factor 2 of the PCL scores corresponds closely to data on the numbers of prisoners by age reported by the U.S. Department of Justice. In 1997, the large majority of federal (89.5%) and state (87%) prisoners were 55 or older (Justice, 2003).

Changes over adulthood in the impulsive and antisocial element of psychopathy may reflect a number of factors other than changes in the personality disorder itself. The apparent decrease in antisocial behavior may reflect the fact that people who were high on Factor 2 of psychopathy are no longer alive. In addition to having been killed in violent crime or as the

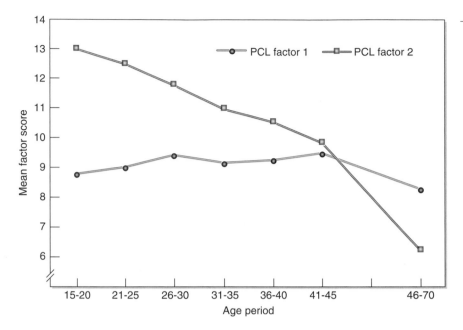

Source: Harpur & Hare, 1994.

FIGURE 11.3

Scores on the Psychopathy Checklist Factors by Age

result of drug abuse, such individuals also have a higher than expected mortality rate due to higher rates of alcohol abuse and poor health habits (Laub & Vaillant, 2000). At the same time, the relative stability of Factor 1, which reflects the personality traits at the heart of psychopathy, attests to the insensitivity of this dimension to the effects of age or experience on people with this disorder. Along with the personality data presented in Chapter 8, one interpretation of these findings is that even older criminals (or at least those with antisocial personality disorder) learn to avoid incarceration, or else are motivated for other reasons to reduce their involvement in activities that will land them in prison.

Other personality disorders also change in prevalence over adulthood (Segal, Coolidge, & Rosowsky, 2000) There are lower rates for histrionic and borderline personality disorders. By contrast, the prevalence is higher for obsessive-compulsive and schizoid personality disorders, as well as dependent personality disorder. These patterns fit the **maturation hypothesis**, which suggests that the Cluster B or "immature" personality types (borderline, histrionic, narcissistic, and antisocial) improve or at least are more treatable in older adults. By contrast, the "mature" types (obsessive-compulsive, schizoid, and paranoid) become worse. To a certain extent, there is stability of the underlying personality dimensions, as in psychopathy. However, the expression of these dimensions in outward behavior may change. Possible explanations for such changes include brain injury, disease, and life stresses. Prior adaptation and the individual's social support network are additional factors that can influence the severity of personality disorders in later adulthood. For example, older adults with long-standing personality disorders become better at coping with their symptoms (Segal, Hook, & Coolidge, 2001). Specific features of each personality disorder may interact differentially with changes associated with the normal aging process. An outline of these hypothesized changes is presented in Table 11-3.

TABLE 11-3
Theorized Patterns in Later Life of Axis II Disorders of the DSM-IV-TR

Disorder	Theorized Patterns in Later Life
Antisocial personality disorder	Age may have little effect on underlying traits of psychopathy, although outward deviant behaviors may diminish.
Borderline personality disorder	This disorder may or may not decrease with age; lower prevalence rates in some studies may reflect early mortality due to risky behaviors and suicide.
Histrionic personality disorder	Subjects are intolerant of physical changes associated with aging that signify to them a loss of attractiveness and sexuality.
Narcissistic personality disorder	"Narcissistic injuries" due to loss of power and prestige and general ageism in society may exacerbate symptoms of the disorder.
Paranoid personality disorder	Sensory deficits and cognitive changes may lead to isolation due to the belief that others are threatening or talking about them in negative ways.
Schizoid personality disorder	The need to depend on others for care will be stressful due to lifelong patterns of social isolation.
Schizotypal personality disorder	No particular predictions with regard to aging are possible; however, in the absence of dementia, an older person who exhibits odd and disorganized behavior may be suffering from this disorder.
Avoidant personality disorder	Clients are unwilling to apply for and receive needed social and supportive services; can become lonely, anxious, and frightened.
Dependent personality disorder	Widowhood will be extremely difficult for this person, who will become helpless, lost, and vulnerable, and may turn to children to replace the spouse.
Obsessive-compulsive personality disorder	This disorder may be exacerbated by aging due to heightened need for control in the face of physical, cognitive, and social losses.

Source: Based on Segal et al., 2000.

To summarize, the major feature of personality disorders in later life is that they decrease in intensity and frequency. However, they may also take a modified form that makes them relatively more difficult for clinicians to manage.

> ### "What do you think?"   11-4
> How does the maturation hypothesis relate to changes in normal personality in middle and later life?

ELDER ABUSE

A condition that may become one of serious clinical concern is the abuse of an older adult through the actions of another person, or through self-neglect that leads to significant loss of functioning. The term **elder abuse** is used to refer to a large category of actions taken directly against older adults through inflicting physical or psychological harm.

Elder abuse is a notoriously difficult behavior to document, as it is surrounded by guilt, shame, fear, and the risk of criminal prosecution.

Victims are afraid to report abuse because of concern over retribution, and the perpetrators obviously do not wish to reveal that they are engaging in this heinous activity. Estimates of the prevalence of elder abuse first became available in the 1980s when the issue received national attention after it was brought before the Select Committee on Aging in 1981. At that time, it was suggested that 4% of the 65 and older population were victims of moderate to severe abuse. By 2003, it was estimated that between 1 and 2 million adults 65 and older were the victims of abuse or mistreatment by someone on whom they depended for care (Committee on National Statistics, 2003).

The most comprehensive information on elder abuse came from the National Elder Abuse Incidence Study (NEAIS) conducted by the National Center on Elder Abuse at the American Public Human Services Association (National Center on Elder Abuse at the American Public Human Services Association, 1998), based on data from a representative sample of 20 counties from across the United States. The NEAIS was unusual in that data were obtained not only from local officials designated to investigate reports of elder abuse but also from "sentinels" or professionals working in the community who were specifically trained to look for signs of elder abuse in cases that would not have been officially reported.

NEIAS identified several major categories of elder abuse. Physical abuse is the use of physical force that may lead to bodily injury, pain, or loss of functioning. Acts of violence such as hitting and kicking fall in this category, as do the unwarranted use of medications and physical restraints to limit an older person's ability to move. Sexual abuse includes any nonconsensual sexual contact with an older adult and all types of sexual assault or battery. Those who inflict emotional or psychological abuse on an older adult cause them to suffer emotional pain, humiliation, and distress. Treating an older person like an infant or isolating the individual from others or from social interaction would also be included as psychological abuse. Neglect is the failure to take care of an older person for whom one has responsibility, such as not providing food, water, clothing, shelter, personal care, or medication. Abandonment is one step further than neglect, in that the older person is actually deserted. Financial or material exploitation involves the illegal or improper use of an older person's funds or property, such as misusing or stealing an older person's money, home, or possessions.

The underlying theory for NEAIS was the **iceberg model of elder abuse** (Fig. 11.4), which proposes that the majority of elder (and child) abuse cases are undetected and do not become counted in official statistics. As a result, the reported prevalence of elder abuse is a serious underestimate of the true number of cases. The use of sentinels was intended to overcome this limitation by increasing the likelihood of cases being detected. As predicted by the iceberg model, a minority of abuse cases detected in NEAIS had been reported to official social services agencies. The large majority (84%) were never reported to official agencies but were detected by the sentinels who were enlisted to work for the study. With regard to specific forms of abuse, as can be seen from the

FIGURE 11.4
Iceberg Model of Elder Abuse

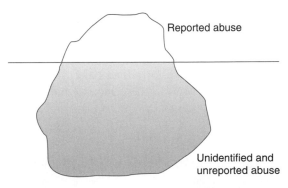

Reported abuse

Unidentified and unreported abuse

Source: National Center on Elder Abuse at the Public Human Services Association, 1998.

breakdown of the results by age in Fig. 11.5, the prevalence of all forms of abuse was increasingly higher in each older five-year age group, with the highest rates for abandonment in the 75–80 category. Women were more likely to be abuse victims than men. Further analyses by race, not shown in Fig. 11.5, revealed that blacks were more likely to be abandoned, and whites were more likely to be more actively abused through physical or verbal assaults. The largest percentage of alleged abusers, across all groups, comprised the victims' children (47%).

Clearly, the problem of elder abuse is a serious social and mental health issue. People who are victims of abuse, not surprisingly, have a higher mortality rate than their age peers, even controlling for medical conditions (Lachs, Williams, O'Brien, Pillemer, & Charlson, 1998). They are more vulnerable to psychological distress (Yan & So-kum, 2001). The high risk that the oldest-old experience with regard to abuse is of particular concern, as this is a rapidly growing segment of the population. Studies such as NEAIS, in addition to providing much-needed information, can become the basis for further planning and interventions to reduce the frequency of this tragic situation.

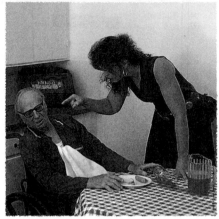

BREAK THE SILENCE
ON ELDER ABUSE, NEGLECT AND EXPLOITATION

FAMILY VIOLENCE IS AGELESS

CALL ADULT PROTECTIVE SERVICES
1 800 371 7897
ALL CALLS ARE CONFIDENTIAL

Six County RSVP Senior Sentinel Program • Utah State Adult Protective Services • National Center on Elder Abuse

Posters such as this one attempt to bring to public attention the problem of elder abuse.

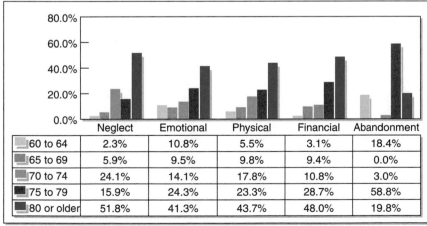

	Neglect	Emotional	Physical	Financial	Abandonment
60 to 64	2.3%	10.8%	5.5%	3.1%	18.4%
65 to 69	5.9%	9.5%	9.8%	9.4%	0.0%
70 to 74	24.1%	14.1%	17.8%	10.8%	3.0%
75 to 79	15.9%	24.3%	23.3%	28.7%	58.8%
80 or older	51.8%	41.3%	43.7%	48.0%	19.8%
Percent of victims experiencing abuse	48.7%	35.4%	25.7%	29.9%	2.9%

FIGURE 11.5
Reports of Elder Abuse by Age of Victim and Type of Abuse

Source: National Center on Elder Abuse at the American Public Services Association, 1998.

BIOPSYCHOSOCIAL PERSPECTIVE

Despite the presence of chronic physical health conditions in adulthood, the majority of adults are able to retain a positive sense of subjective health. If we look at the ratings that people give of their health status, we also see a striking pattern of relatively positive appraisals. Figure 11.6 shows the percentage of respondents who indicate that their health is "good to excellent." Overall, about 70% of those over 75 rate their health positively. Even among African-American respondents over age 65, who have the lowest percentages in almost all the age groups, the majority nevertheless give themselves a positive health appraisal.

There are important lessons in these numbers, in terms of both identity process theory and the biopsychosocial perspective. In terms of identity process theory, older individuals are apparently able to minimize the perceived effect of potentially disabling health conditions through identity assimilation. These positive ratings occur even in the face of osteoporosis and osteoarthritis, conditions that cause pain,

restriction of movement, and increased vulnerability to accidental injury. The majority of older adults are able to separate whatever discomfort and disability are associated with these conditions from their overall feelings about their abilities and their health. Truly, these "survivors" have found ways to reduce their daily preoccupations with conditions that might daunt the coping mechanisms of a 20-year-old.

There may be limits placed on the ability to use identity assimilation, however, with regard to chronic and disabling conditions. Environmental factors can accentuate the physical disabilities associated with certain diseases through the restriction of health care options. This causes individuals to be more vulnerable to some disabling conditions and less able to take advantage of the benefits associated with exercise. Anxiety over health care coverage can further contribute to the perception of health problems, adding the "psychological" component to this biopsychosocial approach to health in older adults.

FIGURE 11.6

Percentage of Persons Age 65 or Older Who Reported Having Good to Excellent Health by Age Group, Sex, and Race, 1994–1996

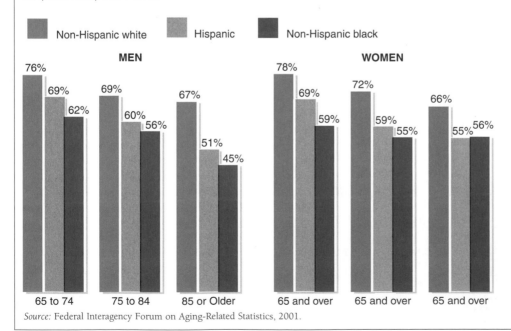

Source: Federal Interagency Forum on Aging-Related Statistics, 2001.

SUICIDE

The suicide rate in the United States of all age, race, and sex groups is highest for white males aged 85 and older (see Chapter 13). In this section, we will explore the medical and psychiatric risk factors for suicide in older adults, focusing specifically on this group with the highest rate.

Close to 90% of adults who complete suicide have a diagnosable psychiatric disorder. The most frequent diagnoses are major depressive disorder, alcohol abuse or dependence, and schizophrenia. Among suicide victims ages 65 years and above, rates of psychiatric disorders are nearly as high as in the general population, ranging from 71% to over 90%. A single episode of major depression of mild to moderate severity without any other form of psychopathology is the greatest risk factor for suicide in this age group. Symptoms of anxiety, but not anxiety disorder, also are present in older adults who commit suicide. Individuals who have a history of substance abuse, including alcohol abuse, are also at higher risk. The fact that mild to moderate symptoms of depression are observed in older adults before they commit suicide means that suicides are much more difficult to detect by health care workers (Duberstein & Conwell, 2000).

Certain personality disorders are more likely to be associated with completed suicide in older adults. These include avoidant personality disorder and schizoid personality disorder, which are characterized by withdrawal and social isolation (Duberstein & Conwell, 1997). Suicide risk is also heightened in individuals who find it difficult to adapt to age-related changes in their physical functioning, health, and social roles (Duberstein, 1995). Those who are anxious, rigid, and obsessional also are at heightened risk due, at least in part, to an inability to discuss their thoughts and feelings with others (Conwell,

Duberstein, & Caine, 2002; Turvey, Conwell, Jones, Phillips, Simonsick, et al., 2002).

The presence of a physical disease is another potential risk factor for suicide among older adults (Conwell et al., 2002). Impairments associated with cancer and cardiovascular disease in particular seem to be related to suicide risk. Given the difficulty of diagnosing depression among older adults, as discussed earlier, it would seem particularly important for health care providers to be aware of these risk factors when working with older adults who have these diseases. Sadly, it is estimated that from 43% to 76% of all suicide victims had seen a health care provider within a month of their death (Duberstein & Conwell, 2000). Greater sensitivity to symptoms of mood disorders in conjunction with evaluation of the additional psychological and medical risk factors could potentially increase the chances that these health care providers would have been able to intervene.

TREATMENT ISSUES IN MENTAL HEALTH CARE

The issue of health care, for both medical and psychiatric conditions, became a major problem in the United States at the turn of the twenty-first century. Changes in the composition of the population, occurring with the well-publicized increases in the baby boom generation, are of particular concern. As this population ages, it will undoubtedly put strains on an already over-extended mental health care system, which is struggling to meet the needs of the current generation of older adults. Clearly, more training will be needed both for practitioners currently in the field and those who will be entering the ranks of therapists and other mental health care workers (Qualls, Segal, Norman, & Gallagher-Thompson, 2002).

Treatment for Psychological Disorders

The psychological disorders discussed in this chapter involve a variety of potential causes and, therefore, may be treatable by a variety of approaches. Psychological treatment involves the planning for and implementation of treatment by a clinician, a professionally trained individual such as a clinical psychologist, psychiatrist, or social worker. Most clinicians who work with adult populations differentiate the approaches they take to young and middle-aged adults from the approaches they take to older adults (Zarit & Zarit, 1998). With the adoption in 2003 by the American Psychological Association of Guidelines for Psychological Practice with Older Adults (American Psychological Association, 2003), it will now be clearer exactly how clinicians need to adapt their approaches to older clients (see Table 11-4).

In addition to potentially different etiologies for disorders at different points in adulthood, clinicians must take into account the potential effects of chronic medical conditions, as well as normal age-related changes in physical, cognitive, and social functioning (Hinrichsen & Dick-Siskin, 2000). Finally, variations by ethnic and minority status must be recognized by clinicians. It is essential that clinicians become competent in assessing and treating individuals from a range of backgrounds (Ferraro, 2002; Lau & Gallagher-Thompson, 2002).

Within the professional realm of psychology, specialists are increasingly emerging who have received training in **geropsychology**, applications of the field of gerontology to the psychological treatment of older adults. Geropsychologists, for example, may specialize in assessment of cognitive disorders, such as dementia, that are found in the older population. Another term that may be used to describe professionals with this training is **clinical geropsychology**, which emphasizes the fact that this specialty is used primarily in applied settings such as hospitals, clinics, and long-term institutions.

Assessment

Clinicians begin their treatment of a client's psychological disorder by conducting a multifaceted clinical assessment. The **assessment** procedure involves evaluation of the psychological, physiological, and social factors that are potentially affecting the individual's current state of functioning. Most psychological assessments are intended to provide a diagnosis (according to the DSM-IV-TR) and lay the groundwork for a treatment plan. In some cases, assessments may be used for special purposes, as in making legal determinations of mental competence or in evaluating an individual's appropriateness for a particular occupation. When used in the context of treatment, however, psychological assessments focus on providing the most accurate reading possible of a client's specific disorder on which treatment can then be based.

All clinical assessment involves differential diagnosis, the process of ruling out alternative diagnoses. In the case of older adults, this process involves establishing whether the symptoms that appear to be due to psychological disorder could be better accounted for by a medical condition (Bartels & Mueser, 1999). Current and past substance abuse should be included in this evaluation.

Another important determination that must be made in assessment is between dementia and other psychological disorders, such as depression, which can cause memory loss and difficulties in concentration. There are several significant differences in the symptom pattern of individuals with these disorders. In depression, the symptoms of **dysphoria** are more severe, and the individual is likely to exaggerate the extent to which he or she is experiencing memory loss. People who have dementia tend, in contrast, to be overconfident about their cognitive abilities. Recognition memory (stating whether an item was presented) tends to be satisfactory in people who are depressed, but they perform more

TABLE 11-4
Summary of APA Guidelines for Psychological Practice with Older Adults

In 2003, the American Psychological Association (APA) approved a set of guidelines containing recommendations for clinical work with older adults. These highlights from the guidelines describe specific ways in which psychologists are encouraged to

Work with older adults within their scope of competence and seek consultation or make appropriate referrals when indicated.

Recognize how their attitudes and beliefs about aging and about older individuals may be relevant to their assessment and treatment of older adults.

Gain knowledge about theory and research in aging.

Understand diversity in the aging process, particularly how sociocultural factors such as gender, ethnicity, socioeconomic status, sexual orientation, disability status, and urban versus rural residence may influence the experience and expression of health and of psychological problems in later life.

Be knowledgeable about psychopathology within the aging population and aware of the prevalence and nature of that psychopathology when providing services to older adults.

Be familiar with the theory, research, and practice of various methods of assessment with older adults, and knowledgeable of assessment instruments that are psychometrically suitable for use with them.

Develop skill in tailoring assessments to accommodate older adults' specific characteristics and contexts.

Develop skill at recognizing cognitive changes in older adults, and conduct and interpret cognitive screening and functional ability evaluations.

Be familiar with the theory, research, and practice of various methods of intervention with older adults.

Be familiar with and develop skill in applying specific psychotherapeutic interventions and environmental modifications with older adults and their families.

Understand the issues pertaining to the provision of services in the specific settings in which older adults are typically located or encountered.

Recognize issues related to the provision of prevention and health promotion services with older adults.

Understand the special ethical and/or legal issues entailed in providing services to older adults.

Increase their knowledge, understanding and skills with respect to working with older adults through continuing education, training, supervision and consultation.

Source: American Psychological Association, 2003

poorly on tests of free recall, where they have to state verbally the items that were presented. People with dementia have memory problems on tests of both recall and recognition. Finally, people with depression report their memory loss as starting suddenly, and their mental status varies from test to test. People with dementia show a progressive loss of cognitive abilities. These differences are important for clinicians to note in their assessment of older adults because, as was pointed out in Chapter 5, if the depression is caught in time there is a good chance of successful treatment.

Assessment should also be tailored to the particular physical and cognitive needs of the individual, particularly for older adults. They should be made to feel comfortable and relaxed, and should be given sufficient time to ask questions about the procedure, which may be unfamiliar and even frightening to them. Some of the practical concerns of clients should be attended to, such as making sure they have the correct eyeglasses and a hearing aid if necessary. A person who has difficulty writing due to arthritis, for instance, will be unable to complete paper-and-pencil measures. Rest periods may be necessary during a lengthy testing session, or the session may have to be divided into shorter units. The clinician should also be aware of the changes in sensory abilities, motor functions, and cognitive processes that may hamper the client's understanding of problems or questions given during the assessment process. For example, materials should be presented in large print to visually impaired clients. Even something seemingly insignificant, such as the hum of office equipment in the background, may compromise an older adult's performance (Edelstein, Martin, & McKee, 2000) It is also important to be sensitive to cultural or language differences between clinician and client, regardless of the age of the client (Halgin & Whitbourne, 2003).

Clinical Interview. In a **clinical interview**, the clinician asks questions of the client to establish insight into the client's psychological processes. The clinician can also use the opportunity to interact face-to-face with the client to observe the client's behavior. This interview may take the form of an unstructured interview, which involves a series of open-ended questions, or it may follow a structured format. An example of a structured clinical interview is the Composite International Diagnostic Interview (CIDI) developed by the World Health Organization to obtain international comparisons of psychological disorders (World Health Organization, 1997). A form of the CIDI was used in the National Comorbidity Study discussed earlier. The Structured Clinical Interview for DSM-IV-TR (SCID) was a similar tool used in the development and validation of the DSM-IV-TR (First, Spitzer, Gibbon, & Williams, 1997). These instruments are extremely important for establishing the prevalence of psychiatric disorders and are useful for individual diagnostic purposes. Increasingly, these are being tested for their applicability to adults of varying ages (Segal, Kabacoff, Hersen, Van Hasselt, & Ryan, 1995). In some cases, however, it may be more appropriate or productive to use an interview that has less structure. Questions can be rephrased if they are unclear, and topic areas can be explored that may be of particular relevance to the client. An unstructured interview can also be beneficial in assessing older adults with cognitive difficulties who find it difficult to concentrate or need help in maintaining their focus (Edelstein et al., 2000).

Mini-Mental State Exam. An assessment instrument used extensively in the diagnostic process for older adults is the mental status examination, discussed in Chapter 5 as a tool in the psychological assessment of dementia. The most well known of these instruments is the Mini-Mental State Exam (Folstein, Folstein, & McHugh, 1975). (See Table 11-5.) Although it is quick and relatively easy to administer and is useful for charting changes in dementing symptoms over time, it is not particularly specific to dementia and does not allow for precise measurement of cognitive functioning (Edelstein et al., 2000). It is primarily a screening tool, and it should be followed with more thorough testing procedures. Another problem with the MMSE is that it is not effective for detecting dementia in African Americans (Mast, Fitzgerald, Steinberg, MacNeill, & Lichtenberg, 2001). Given these and other problems with the MMSE, clinicians are increasingly turning to more sophisticated cognitive and neuropsychological testing methods that examine a broader range of abilities (Mast, MacNeill, & Lichtenberg, 2002).

TABLE 11-5
Mini-Mental State Exam

MINIMENTAL LLC

NAME OF SUBJECT _____ Age _____

NAME OF EXAMINER _____ Years of School Completed _____

Approach the patient with respect and encouragement.

Ask: Do you have any trouble with your memory? ☐ Yes ☐ No   Date of Examination _____

May I ask you some questions about your memory? ☐ Yes ☐ No

SCORE	ITEM
5 ( )	**TIME ORIENTATION** Ask: What is the year _____ (1), season _____ (1), month of the year _____ (1), date _____ (1), day of the week _____ (1)?
5 ( )	**PLACE ORIENTATION** Ask: Where are we now? What's the state _____ (1), city _____ (1), part of the city _____ (1), building _____ (1), floor of the building _____ (1)?
3 ( )	**REGISTRATION OF THREE WORDS** Say: Listen carefully. I am going to say three words. You say them back after I stop. Ready? Here they are. PONY (wait 1 second), QUARTER (wait 1 second), ORANGE (wait 1 second). What were those words? _____ (1) _____ (1) _____ (1) Give 1 point for each correct answer, then repeat them until the patient learns all three.
5 ( )	**SERIAL 7s AS A TEST OF ATTENTION AND CALCULATION** Ask: Subtract 7 from 100 and continue to subtract 7 from each subsequent remainder until I tell you to stop. What is 100 take away 7? _____ (1) Say: Keep Going _____ (1) _____ (1) _____ (1) _____ (1)

(continued)

TABLE 11-5 (continued)
Mini-Mental State Exam

3 (　) RECALL OF THREE WORDS

Ask:

What were those three words I asked you to remember?

Give one point for each correct answer. _____ (1)

_____ (1) _____ (1)

2 (　) NAMING

Ask:

What is this? (show pencil) _____ (1) What is this? (show watch)

_____ (1)

1 (　) REPETITION

Say:

Now I am going to ask you to repeat what I say. Ready? No ifs, ands, or buts.

Now you say that _____ (1)

3 (　) COMPREHENSION

Say:

Listen carefully because I am going to ask you to do something.

Take this paper in your left hand (1), fold it in half (1), and put it on the floor. (1)

1 (　) READING

Say:

Please read the following and do what it says, but do not say it aloud. (1)

Close your eyes

1 (　) WRITING

Say:

Please write a sentence. If patient does not respond, say: Write about the weather. (1)

_____

_____

1 (　) DRAWING

Say: Please copy this design.

(continued)

TABLE 11-5 *(continued)*
Mini-Mental State Exam

TOTAL SCORE _____ Assess level of consciousness along a continuum

	Alert	Drowsy	Stupor	Coma

YES NO   YES NO FUNCTION BY PROXY

Cooperative: ☐ ☐   Deterioration from   Please record date when patient was
Depressed: ☐ ☐   previous level of   last able to perform the following tasks.
Anxious: ☐ ☐   functioning: ☐ ☐   Ask caregiver if patient independently
Poor Vision: ☐ ☐   Family History of   handles:
Poor Hearing: ☐ ☐   Dementia: ☐ ☐   YES NO DATE
Native Language: Head Trauma: ☐ ☐   Money/Bills: ☐ ☐ ____
_____   Stroke: ☐ ☐   Medication: ☐ ☐ ____
                        Alcohol Abuse: ☐ ☐   Transporation: ☐ ☐ ____
                        Thyroid Disease: ☐ ☐ Telephone: ☐ ☐ ____

Interview Measures for Specific Disorders. Several interview-based measures exist for the assessment of specific symptoms. The Geriatric Depression Scale (GDS) includes a true–false set of questions about depressive symptoms, that excludes somatic disturbances likely to be endorsed by older adults regardless of their level of depression (such as changes in energy level or sleep) (Yesavage, Brink, Rose, Lum, Huang, et al., 1983). The Anxiety Disorders Interview Schedule (ADIS-R) (DiNardo & Barlow, 1988) is useful in assessing older adults, as it has been found to provide ratings in agreement with clinical diagnoses of social phobia, GAD, simple phobia, and panic disorder (Scogin et al., 2000). The Hamilton Rating Scale of Depression (Hamilton, 1967) and the Hamilton Anxiety Rating Scale (Hamilton, 1959) have also been tested with older adults and are useful in evaluating both severity and number of the individual's symptoms.

Self-Report Clinical Inventories. Easier to administer but at the cost of placing greater burden on the test-taker are self-report clinical inventories in which the client answers a set of questions concerning the experience of particular symptoms related to a diagnostic category. Many of these tests were developed for young or middle-aged adults, and therefore their applicability to older adults is either unknown or low. Unlike interviews, the clinician cannot adjust the administration of these measures to the needs or background of the client. Older adults and people from various cultural backgrounds may not interpret the questions as the authors of the test had intended, leading to results that do not provide a valid indication of the client's psychological status.

Nevertheless, research is accumulating on the validity and utility of self-report inventories designed to be sensitive to specific groups of disorders. The Beck Depression Inventory-II (Beck, Steer, & Brown, 1996), an update of the original measure published in 1961, is one of the most widely used clinical inventories, and evidence is accumulating in favor of its use on both older and younger adult populations. On the negative side, this measure includes items on bodily functioning that may lead to confusing results when used with older persons. A widely used self-report measure of anxiety administered to adults of all ages is the Spielberger State-Trait Anxiety Inventory (Speilberger, Gorsuch, & Lushene, 1970). The major disadvantage of self-report scales in which clients indicate whether they have specific symptoms is that these measures are, in fact, self-report. Individuals may provide inaccurate answers either because they want to present a certain picture of themselves or because they are unable to make accurate judgments. Older adults with severe cognitive impairments may be unable to answer the questions or may have a distorted view of their abilities, denying the extent of their memory loss and other symptoms. Under certain conditions, however, self-reports can be reliable and accurate, particularly when used for older adults who do not have cognitive impairments. The main point is that they should not be used as the only source of information about a client, particularly in cases of severe cognitive deficits (Edelstein et al., 2000).

Personality and Diagnostic Assessments. Psychological tests also include personality and diagnostic assessments, used to provide a broad picture of the individual's thoughts, dispositions, and behaviors. The most well-known self-report diagnostic personality measure is the Minnesota Multiphasic Personality Inventory-2 (MMPI-2) (Hathaway & McKinley, 1989), which contains 567 true–false items organized into 10 clinical scales and 3 validity scales. The profile of scale scores is used to provide an indication of the individual's personality and possible psychological disorders. The NEO-PI-R (Costa & McCrae, 1992) (described in Chapter 8) is another self-report personality test increasingly being used in clinical settings. A third self-report test is the Millon Clinical Multiaxial Inventory (MCMI-III) (Millon, 1994), designed to assist clinicians in diagnosing personality disorders.

Projective tests, the second major category of personality assessment, include the Rorschach Inkblot Test and the Thematic Apperception Test (TAT) (Morgan & Murray, 1935). In these tests, the individual is presented with ambiguous stimuli, such as an inkblot (for the Rorschach) or a black-and-white drawing of people in a variety of situations (the TAT). The themes, content, and language used by the test-taker are then evaluated for the presence of particular issues, eccentricities, or presumed underlying conflicts. Because projective measures are more subjectively interpreted than the self-report tests such as the MMPI or NEO-PI-R, empirically oriented psychologists regard them with skepticism. However, many clinicians from the psychodynamic tradition regard the projective tools as invaluable aids to providing a comprehensive look at an individual's personality.

Behavioral assessments may also be included in a personality assessment when clinicians wish to determine the frequency of particular problematic behaviors. In a behavioral assessment, the frequency of the behavior is recorded along with its antecedents (conditions that are present before the behavior occurs) and its consequences (conditions that follow the behavior). For example, an older adult with dementia who engages in wandering may be given a behavioral assessment in which the frequency of wandering is tabulated per hour. At the same time, the assessment would include antecedents, such as whether visitors are present, and consequences, such as whether the wandering is followed by increased staff attention. Cognitive behavioral assessments involve having the individual record thoughts that were present at the time that particular events occurred or prior to carrying out specific behaviors. A depressed individual may be told to keep track of instances of depressive thoughts, along with any possible situations or other thoughts that seem to provoke them.

BEHIND THE RESEARCH

MARGARET GATZ, PH.D., PROFESSOR OF PSYCHOLOGY,
UNIVERSITY OF SOUTHERN CALIFORNIA

What is most exciting to you about research in this field?

Older adults, contrary to many people's image, are not more vulnerable to mental disorder than younger adults. In fact, rates of depression and anxiety disorders appear to be lower in older adults than in middle aged individuals and young adults. One intriguing question is why there are not more older adults with mental disorder, given ageism in society, increased frequency of physical health problems with age, deaths of family and friends, and all of the other difficulties to which older people are subjected. At least some of the answer is probably that people generally do improve with age with respect to their abilities to manage stress.

Among older adults who have a mental disorder, some proportion had psychological problems earlier in their lives that have continued into old age. Others had no previous psychological problems. Among those with no past history of mental disorder, often there are biological explanations for the first appearance of symptoms in old age. For example, depression can be a side effect of certain medications, anxiety can accompany certain physical illnesses, and dementia reflects the existence of important neurological changes.

Clinical psychologists can be useful with respect to differential diagnosis, sometimes identifying reversible sources of cognitive change, and suggesting strategies for managing nonreversible changes. Older adults with depression and anxiety often are not treated at all or are treated with medications. There is a great deal of room for improving referral to psychotherapy, which is just as effective at any age.

What do you see as major challenges?

It is immensely challenging to sort out the various roles of various risk factors (e.g., genetic risk, physical health correlates, environmental stressors) and protective factors (e.g., social supports, good problem solving and stress management skills) in explaining mental health and mental illness in old age. This knowledge ultimately has implications for prevention. What can we recommend, based on research, that will lead to an old age with fewer emotional and cognitive problems?

Where do you see this field headed in the next decade?

Unquestionably the next decade will continue to have a major emphasis on genes. The past decade has brought explosive advances in knowledge of genetics. Those advances touch centrally on aging and mental disorder, insofar as many of the discoveries concern dementia, other age-related diseases, or longevity itself. We can expect that people's genetic profile will increasingly be taken into account in health care decision making, for example, how often to screen for a particular disease or which treatments to recommend for particular illnesses. I predict that the increased genetic knowledge may have a paradoxical effect in focusing people's attention on factors that they can control, such as their own health habits. The past 10 years were the Decade of the Brain; the next 10 years will be the Decade of Behavior. Clinical psychologists can play a role in helping people to interpret genetic risk correctly, encouraging an appreciation for the fundamental importance of behavioral factors in illness, designing health promotion programs in ways that aid adherence to good habits, and evaluating those interventions.

Brain Scans. Finally, physiological assessments such as brain scans (EEG, MRI, CAT, PET) and lab tests may be given to an individual when abnormalities are suspected in some aspect of physical functioning thought to have an impact on behavior. Many of these abnormalities were discussed in Chapter 5 in the context of tests for Alzheimer's disease and other forms of dementia. However, they may also be of value in assessment of depression, for abnormalities in CT and MRI scans have been observed in older depressed individuals (King & Markus, 2000). Tests of the cardiovascular or gastrointestinal system may also be included in a psychological assessment to determine the presence of stress-related diseases. Neuropsychological tests would also be included in a complete assessment to determine the possible presence of functional abnormalities not reflected in brain imaging scans.

Therapy

The processes of assessment and diagnosis are the basis for the clinician's development of a treatment plan. First, the clinician must establish goals of treatment, which may include the short-term need to resolve an immediate crisis, as well as long-term goals toward resolution of symptoms through changes in the individual's personality or relationships. Next, the clinician must establish the site at which treatment will take place, which will be discussed below. Third, the clinician determines which theoretical perspective will best apply for this individual's case. The range of perspectives may include somatic (biological) treatments, psychological treatment including psychotherapy, and treatments based on sociocultural models, such as family or **group therapy**. Finally, the clinician must take into account not only the client's diagnosis but also the client's age, for developmental issues are important factors in

considering the appropriateness of treatment strategies.

Somatic Therapy. A variety of somatic therapies increasingly are being used in the treatment of psychological disorders. Several of the somatic treatments currently in use were developed prior to the discovery of psychotherapeutic medications (in the 1950s) as methods of managing severe psychological disturbance. They remain in use because medical researchers have found them effective in treatment disorders that are resistant to more conventional forms of therapy.

Psychosurgery, which involves performing a surgical intervention on the brain, was introduced in the 1930s as a method of controlling the symptoms of psychotic disorders such as schizophrenia. This form of psychosurgery involved severing the connections between the frontal lobes and the rest of the brain, a procedure that reduced aggressive symptoms but also caused significant personality and motivational impairments. Currently, a form of psychosurgery known as *cingulotomy* is being used in the treatment of severe cases of obsessive-compulsive disorder. This procedure involves destruction of the cingulate bundle, an area of the brain thought to be involved in anxiety. This method is effective for approximately half of individuals whose symptoms cannot be relieved by medication (Kim, Chang, Koo, Kim, Suh, et al., 2003).

A second somatic treatment, which also has its roots in the mid-twentieth century, is **electroconvulsive therapy (ECT)**. In this treatment, an electric current is applied through electrodes attached across the head. The individual suffers seizure-like symptoms (which can be controlled through muscle relaxants), but the main effect of the treatment is thought to result from the passage of electrical current through the brain. When this method was developed in the 1930s by an Italian neurologist for use in treating epilepsy, it was thought to be most useful for treating schizophrenia. The method fell into disfavor both because of its popular characterization in the media (Ken Kesey's *One Flew Over the Cuckoo's Nest*) and its replacement by psychotherapeutic medications. Renewed interest in ECT began to develop in the 1980s when it was found to be an effective method of relief for very severe depression (Manning, 2003) and more recently, for bipolar disorder as well (Malhi, Mitchell, & Salim, 2003). ECT also appears to be an effective alternative for individuals over age 60 who have not responded to other forms of treatment (Niederehe & Schneider, 1998).

"What do you think?"	11-5

Why might the current generation of older adults be reluctant to become involved in therapy?

By far, the most common method of somatic treatment involves **psychotherapeutic medications**, substances that by their chemical nature alter the individual's brain structure or function. A list of the most common psychotherapeutic medications, their mechanisms of operation, and the disorders for which they are prescribed is shown in Table 11-6. These medications may be prescribed to adults of any age; however, when administered to older adults, clinicians must take precautions to avoid adverse drug reactions. As mentioned previously, medications take longer to clear the excretory system of the kidneys, so unless they are prescribed in lower doses for older adults, there is a risk of toxic accumulations in the blood. Another risk is that of **polypharmacy**, in which individuals receive multiple prescription medications. In addition to having potent effects of their own, psychotherapeutic medications can also interact with other prescription medications. Certain foods, such as cheese and chocolate, may also interact with certain medications, such as MAOIs. Clinicians must take care to avoid these potentially lethal interactions.

Despite potential drawbacks and side effects, psychotherapeutic medications have proven highly effective (50% to 70%) for older adults in the treatment of depression (Flint & Rifat, 2000; Niederehe & Schneider, 1998). Antidepressants can be helpful in alleviating depression even in the oldest-old (Gildengers, Houck, Mulsant, Pollock, Mazumdar, et al., 2002). Lithium carbonate is an effective medication for the treatment of bipolar disorder. To prevent recurrence of manic episodes, the individual must take lithium on a continuous basis. SSRIs are particularly useful for older adults because they lack the side effects of MAOIs and TCAs (Klysner, Bent-Hansen, Hansen, Lunde, Pleidrup, et al., 2002; Mottram, Wilson, Ashworth, & Abou-Saleh, 2002). Unfortunately, failure to diagnose depression correctly in older adults may lead to either undertreatment of depressive symptoms or treatment with the wrong medication, such as antianxiety medications rather than antidepressants (Sonnenberg, Beekman, Deeg, & Van Tilburg, 2003).

The combination of psychotherapy and psychotherapeutic medication is the recommended strategy for treating major depression in older adults in order to target both the psychological and biological components of the disorder (Thompson, Coon, Gallagher-Thompson, Sommer, & Koin, 2001). Similarly, treatment of schizophrenia in later life seems to benefit from this two-pronged approach involving both psychotherapy and medication (Sable & Jeste, 2002).

TABLE 11-6
Common Psychotherapeutic Medications for Specific Disorders

Substance (trade name)	Method of Action	Disorder
Selective Serotonin Reuptake Inhibitors— Fluoxetine (Prozac) Sertraline (Zoloft) Fluvoxamine (Luvox) Buproprion (Wellbutrin) Paroxetine (Paxil)	Block serotonin reuptake mechanism, resulting in increased levels of serotonin	Depression, anxiety disorders including obsessive-compulsive disorder, eating disorders, may be used to control symptoms of borderline personality disorder.
Clozapine (Clozaril) Resperidone (Risperdal)	Block serotonin receptors as well as dopamine receptors (to a lesser extent) in the limbic system	Schizophrenia as well as symptoms of Alzheimer's disease
Benzodiazepines— Chlordiazepoxide (Librium) Diazepam (Valium) Alprazolam (Xanax)	Bind to receptor sites of GABA neurons that inhibit brain sites involved in producing symptoms of anxiety such as panic attacks	Anxiety disorders
Buspirone (BuSpar)	Mimics the effect of serotonin, stimulating the serotonin receptors	Anxiety disorder, particularly generalized anxiety disorder
Lithium carbonate (Lithium)	Decrease catecholamines levels	Bipolar disorder
Tricyclic antidepressants— Amitriptyline (Elavil, Endep) Nortriptyline (Pamelor) Imipramine (Tofranil)	Block reuptake of norepinephrine and serotonin, increasing their excitatory effect on the postsynaptic neurons	Depression
Monoamine Oxidase Inhibitors (MAOI's)— Phenelzine (Nardil) Tranylcypromine (Parnate)	Inhibit the monoamine oxidase enzyme which converts norepinephrine and serotonin into inert substances	Depression
Neuroleptics—Low-potency (require large doses): Chlorpromazine (Thorazine) Thioridazine (Mellaril) Middle-potency (require moderate doses): Trifluoperazine (Stelazine) Thiothixine (Navane) High-potency (require low doses): Haloperidol (Haldol) Fluphenazine (Prolixin)	Block dopamine receptors, reducing the frequency of psychotic symptoms but also interfering with movement and endocrine function	Schizophrenia and also used in treatment of symptoms of Alzheimer's disease
Disulfiram (Antabuse)	Inhibits aldehyde deydrogenase, an enzyme that helps to metabolize alcohol	Alcohol dependence
Methadone	Synthetic opioid that mimics the effects of heroin	Heroin dependence

As indicated in Table 11-6, a number of psychotherapeutic medications are available for the treatment of **anxiety disorders** in adults. Benzodiazepines, which are the most frequently prescribed antianxiety medications, are highly addictive. They require higher and higher doses to obtain their intended effects, and they are likely to lead to significant withdrawal symptoms, so that the person's symptoms increase after treatment is discontinued. Older adults are particularly vulnerable to these effects and, furthermore, may experience a number of potentially dangerous side effects such as unsteadiness, daytime sleepiness, impaired cognitive functioning, and slowed reaction time (Paterniti, Dufouil, & Alperovitch, 2002). The medication buspirone has fewer of these side effects and would therefore seem to be a safe alternative to benzodiazepines; unfortunately, however, little research has been done on the effectiveness of buspirone with older adults. Furthermore, it must be taken for six to eight weeks before it reduces anxiety, so that it is not helpful for treating acute symptoms of anxiety.

Other medications useful in treating anxiety in older adults are the beta-blockers, which reduce sympathetic nervous system activity

Although older adults may be reluctant to seek therapy, when they do, the odds are high that their treatment will be successful.

(Sadavoy & LeClair, 1997). Older adults with certain chronic diseases cannot use this medication, however, because it affects other systems such as the cardiovascular system. SSRIs are another category of medications that are useful in treating people with anxiety disorders, particularly when they also have depressive symptoms. They are also effective in treating obsessive-compulsive disorder, panic disorder, and social phobias. Other antidepressants, such as tricyclics, tend to be useful in treating obsessive-compulsive and panic disorders.

Medications for the treatment of schizophrenia include the antipsychotic medications known as **neuroleptics**. These medications alter dopamine activity and are effective in reducing delusions and thought disorder and lowering the chance of an individual's experiencing a relapse. People with early-onset schizophrenia are maintained on these medications for many years, allowing them to live independently in the community. Older adults who develop late-life schizophrenia also seem to respond to neuroleptics. However, they should be given smaller doses, and greater care must be taken with regard to side effects than is true for younger persons (Salzman, 1992). These side effects include confusion and agitation, dizziness, and motor disturbances. Some of these motor disturbances can resemble those of Parkinson's disease. The most serious side effect of neuroleptic medication is tardive dyskinesia, which involves involuntary, repetitive movements, particularly in the muscles of the face. These movements include chewing, moving the jaw from side to side, and rolling the tongue. Other abnormal movements of the body can also occur. Older adults are more likely than younger adults to experience tardive dyskinesia, even after treatment is discontinued (Jeste, Lohr, Eastham, Rockwell, & Caligiuri, 1998). Medications that alter serotonin functioning used for treatment of schizophrenia (clozapine and resperidone) do not produce these effects on motor functioning. However, clozapine can have fatal side effects and must be carefully monitored, particularly in older adults (Meeks, 2000).

Psychotherapy. The process of **psychotherapy** involves the delivery of treatment to an individual through the application of psychological methods. Psychotherapy might involve one or a combination of theoretical perspectives ranging from psychoanalysis to behaviorism (see Table 11-7). The feature shared by all methods of psychotherapy is a focus on an attempt to bring about change within the individual through a deliberate intervention. In most approaches to psychotherapy, the clinician meets regularly with the individual (referred to as the "client") in sessions of a fixed length that target a particular set of concerns.

In **psychoanalytic or psychodynamic psychotherapy**, the clinician focuses on unconscious processes, such as conflicts, defense mechanisms, dreams, and issues based on early relationships with parents. The goal of therapy is to rework unconscious conflicts and through this process reduce so-called neurotic symptoms such as anxiety and self-defeating behavior. Therapy based on psychodynamic theory also attempts to strengthen or build the individual's sense of self, enabling the individual to develop clearer boundaries between the self and others. Although psychoanalysis in the classical or traditional sense was intended to be carried out intensively and over a period of many years, current applications within managed care systems (which limit the number of sessions a client may have) involve briefer and more focused therapy aimed at resolving specific issues.

Methods of **humanistic or client-centered therapy** form a second set of approaches to therapy. The emphasis in these methods is on helping the individual gain greater self-acceptance and ultimately achieve fuller expression of the true or underlying self. An important goal of humanistic psychotherapy is to free the individual from anxiety about being rejected or regarded as deficient by others who are important in that person's life. Clients are helped to communicate their needs and perspectives more clearly to others and in the process, to improve to their relationships and their ability to express the true self.

TABLE 11-7
Methods of Psychotherapy

Method	Focus of Change
Psychoanalytic	Unconscious processes, such as conflicts, defense mechanisms, dreams, and issues based on early relationships with parents
Humanistic	Greater self-expression and self-acceptance; improved communication and relationships with others
Behavioral	Particular behaviors that client seeks to reduce or change
Cognitive	Dysfunctional and illogical thought processes that contribute to negative emotions
Cognitive-behavioral	Specific maladaptive behaviors and thoughts that contribute to negative emotions
Interpersonal (IPT)	Deficient social skills and problems in interpersonal relationships (intended specifically for treatment of major depressive disorder)

Behavioral approaches to therapy take specific aim at particular problematic behaviors that the client seeks to change. Treatment of depression is based on the view that depressive symptoms result from lack of pleasant or positively reinforcing events in the individual's life. Clients are given "homework" assignments in which they are instructed to increase the number of pleasant events in their daily lives. Other behavioral methods involve procedures such as **systematic desensitization**, in which a client is taught to replace an unwanted response (such as fear) with a desirable response (such as relaxation). For an individual who is afraid of flying, for example, therapy might involve teaching the individual to relax rather than tense up in various situations that lead up to but do not include flying in an airplane. Another application of behavioral therapy is **contingency management**, in which a specific desirable outcome is made dependent (or "contingent") upon the performance of a specific behavior. An individual who is trying to stop smoking would receive a reward for every period of time during which no cigarettes were smoked. In behavioral therapies that take advantage of the social learning or social cognitive tradition, the client may be shown a successful "model" of the desired behavior. The **social-cognitive** approach to therapy attempts to raise a client's sense of self-efficacy by enabling the client to have step-like increments in success at completing a previously unattainable goal.

In cognitive therapy, the clinician attempts to change the client's maladaptive emotions and ways of coping with difficult situations by changing the client's thoughts (hence the term *cognitive*). A client with depression, whose depression is related to feelings of low self-esteem, would be taught to avoid certain mental traps that lead to convictions of worthlessness and failure. For example, a person who is

convinced that any sort of failure is a negative reflection on one's worth as a human being would obviously be very depressed following an experience in which a desired goal was not attained. Clinicians working from the framework of cognitive therapy use a method known as **cognitive restructuring**. The individual is encouraged to develop greater **tolerance** toward negative experiences and not make sweeping overgeneralizations such as one failure is equivalent to total failure as a person (Ellis, 1998). The cognitive variant of behavioral treatment, known as cognitive-behavioral treatment, involves encouraging the client to develop new behaviors and constructive ways of thinking about the self. For example, the depressed individual would be rewarded for spending more time in positive activities (behavioral) and would be trained to view failures from a more favorable perspective.

Behavioral interventions in the form of reinforcement and providing structure may also be useful for older adults experiencing memory loss. These can be particularly helpful if accompanied by changes in the physical or social environment that make it possible for the individual to engage in independent activities rather than having to depend on others. Memory training and **cognitive therapy** that increase a person's sense of self-efficacy (see Chapter 6) can also help increase cognitive functioning (Abeles et al., 1997). Behavioral treatments can also help alleviate insomnia in older adults, which, in turn, can help reduce the risk of depression (Rybarczyk, Lopez, Benson, Alsten, & Stepanski, 2002).

Finally, **interpersonal therapy** integrates cognitive methods with a focus on social factors that contribute to psychological disturbance. This method was developed for treatment of depression, where it has been extensively tested and refined. Interpersonal therapy involves a combination of methods, but the main focus is on training in social skills, interpersonal relationships, and methods of conflict resolution.

Options other than individual psychotherapy based on sociocultural approaches involve treatment of the client within a social context. In **family therapy**, the individual's symptoms are regarded as the expression of problems within the entire system of relationships within the family. The involvement of clients who share the perspective and problems of the client in treatment is used as a therapeutic tool in group therapy. With the therapist as facilitator, members of the group openly share their problems, receive feedback from peers, and work to develop more effective interpersonal skills. Such an approach has proven to be effective in the treatment of alcohol dependence, particularly when such groups provide social support (Barrick & Connors, 2002). **Milieu therapy** is an intervention most often used in a therapeutic setting such as a rehabilitation facility, psychiatric hospital, or treatment facility within the community. All health professionals working within the environment work as a team to provide consistently constructive and therapeutic interactions with the client.

The theorists and clinicians who developed contemporary methods of psychotherapy and sociocultural therapy were not particularly sensitive to developmental issues or to the need to alter their approach based on the age of the client. Apart from Freud's admonition that psychotherapy should not be attempted on anyone over the age of 50, there is little specific guidance in the literature about how and whether to adapt these methods to adults of different ages. However, clinicians working within clinical geropsychology are formulating such guidelines that take into account the specific concerns of older adults (Zarit & Knight, 1996).

A number of complicating factors can influence the provision of treatment to individuals seeking psychotherapy in the later adult years.

These involve factors that alter both the nature of psychological difficulties experienced by older adults and the nature of the therapeutic process (Hinrichsen & Dick-Siskin, 2000). The nature of psychological difficulties experienced by older adults may vary by virtue of the fact that there is a greater probability of physical health impairments among older adult clients, particularly those over age 75. Changes in identity associated with these impairments can themselves stimulate the need for psychotherapy. In addition, the pain and physical discomfort caused by physical health problems can interact with psychological disorders, such as depression. Psychosocial issues may also confront an older adult and should be taken into account in the provision of psychotherapy involving relationships with family. Death of family and friends, changes in relationships with children and spouses, and the need to provide care to a spouse or parent are additional problems faced by older adult clients.

Clinicians have proposed treatments geared specifically to older adults. In a variant of traditional psychodynamic therapy, **life review therapy** (Butler, 1974) involves helping the older adult rework past experiences with the goal of gaining greater acceptance of previous life events. The purpose of this process is to facilitate the natural reminiscence process that accompanies the ego integrity versus despair psychosocial issue, as described by Erikson (see Chapter 8). There is some evidence that life review therapy is beneficial to older adults with mild symptoms of depression, but for people with severe symptoms, the evoking of painful memories from the past can have negative effects (King & Markus, 2000). Interpersonal therapy also appears to be effective in relieving recurrent major depression in older adults, particularly when combined with antidepressant medication. In a controlled study of the effects of monthly interpersonal therapy (*maintenance*) combined with a tricyclic antidepressant, 80% remained free of symptoms for the three-year period during which they were followed. Even individuals in the over-70 group showed significant and lasting benefits from this combined treatment (Reynolds, Frank, Perel, Imber, Cornes, et al., 1999).

Behavioral treatment that focuses on increasing the number of positive reinforcements in the individual's life is another beneficial treatment of depression in older adults (Teri, 1994). Such an approach is based on the notion that older adults may be experiencing depressive symptoms owing to decreases in pleasant events associated with physical changes, loss of friends, and loss of rewarding social roles. Cognitive-behavioral therapy appears to have considerable relevance to work with older depressed clients, particularly for those who have a tendency to focus excessively on age-related changes in physical functioning, memory, and health. The elements of **cognitive-behavioral treatment** for older adults with depression include instructing clients to keep track of their pleasant and unpleasant events, helping them understand the relationship between their mood and these behaviors, looking for changes that can be made in daily life, increasing their social skills, and teaching them to be alert to and try to change their negative thoughts about the self (Gallagher-Thompson & Thompson, 1996). Learning how to manage their health by taking an active role in their own treatment is another cognitive-behavioral intervention that can reduce the experience of depressive symptoms (Wrosch, Schulz, & Heckhausen, 2002).

For these elements of therapy to succeed, older adult clients may need to be given help in learning to view therapy as a collaborative process in which they have an active role (King & Markus, 2000). This approach is more likely to have success with clients who have more

education and are comfortable with the idea of receiving homework. On the other hand, some clients who are seeking to gain greater insight into the nature of their symptoms may feel that cognitive-behavioral therapy does not delve deeply enough into underlying psychological processes (Zeiss & Steffan, 1996).

Cognitive-behavioral therapy is also being applied to the treatment of **generalized anxiety disorders**. Findings of its effects are mixed, with some researchers reporting a reduction in symptoms (Stanley, Beck, Novy, Averill, Swann, et al., 2003), and others reporting no measurable effect when compared to a control group (Wetherell, Gatz, & Craske, 2003). One crucial factor appears to be the provision of memory aids such as homework reminders during treatment so that the treatment will have maximum possible impact (Mohlman, Gorenstein, Kleber, de Jesus, Gorman, et al., 2003). Social skills can also be taught through cognitive-behavioral methods to older adults suffering from schizophrenia, allowing them to have more satisfactory interactions with others in their environment (Patterson, McKibbin, Taylor, Goldman, Davila-Fraga, et al., 2003).

In contrast to treatment approaches focusing on one specific form of treatment, clinicians are also recommending that integration occur across models. In an integrative approach, the clinician working within one framework would select therapeutic methods based on other models that meet the client's specific needs and situations (Hillman & Stricker, 2002). For example, a psychodynamically oriented clinician working with a depressed older adult woman may incorporate behavioral methods, psychotherapeutic medication, and the involvement of family and other health care providers.

Generational differences between current cohorts of older adults and the middle-aged individuals more commonly seen in psychotherapy must be taken into account by clinicians working with this age group. Older adults may be skeptical about the therapy process, having been less socialized than younger cohorts to accept the need for psychological interventions. Part of therapy may involve educating older adult clients to feel less embarrassed or stigmatized by the process. An additional factor that can alter the nature of therapy for older adults is the existence of sensory and cognitive impairments, which affect the nature of communication between clinician and client. Finally, when the therapist is younger than the client, there is the possibility that the client sees the therapist as a "child" and therefore reacts differently than would be the case if the age differences were reversed. It is also possible that the therapist brings to the situation negative attitudes and stereotypes about aging that complicate the therapeutic relationship with the older adult client.

Despite the many challenges that face therapists working with older adult clients, it appears that treatment can lead to positive outcomes. Although individual models of therapy have been discussed here, many studies have shown positive effects of group interventions (Gatz, Fiske, Fox, Kaskie, Kasl-Godley, McCallum, & Wetherell, 1998). These interventions have the additional advantage of allowing older adults to feel more comfortable about the therapeutic process because they are able to interact with and learn from their peers.

SUMMARY

1. Psychological disorders and treatment issues incorporate a broad range of topics that are of great importance to the functioning of adults and older persons in the United States. Included in psychological disorders are behaviors that lie outside the range of ordinary human experience. The DSM-IV-TR contains descriptions of the disorders that can affect children and adults; unfortunately, it was not specifically written with the concerns of older adults in mind. In many cases, there are differences between the over-65 and under-65 populations of adults in the way that these disorders are manifested in behavior. Axis I disorders include clinical syndromes (organized patterns of disturbances), and Axis II includes personality disorders and mental retardation.

2. Epidemiological surveys place the prevalence of psychological disorders at between one-third to one-half of the adult population. There is a lower prevalence of all disorders among adults over the age of 65 years. Depressive symptoms are more likely to be found in the over-65 population than depressive disorders. Older adults are more likely to experience physical symptoms of depression and are less likely to express emotional disturbances such as guilt or suicidality. Depletion syndrome and late-onset depression are two variants of depressive disorders found in the over-65 population. Health care professionals may not be attuned to diagnosing depressive symptoms in older adults. Anxiety is also a relatively common disorder in the older adult population, and like mood disorders, estimates of anxiety symptoms are higher than estimates of the prevalence of anxiety disorders. It is thought that PTSD prevalence in the over-65 population will increase as Vietnam veterans become older. The majority of cases of schizophrenia emerge before the age of 40; cases that originate late in adulthood are referred to as late-onset schizophrenia. Delirium, dementia, and cognitive disorders form another category of Axis I disorders. Substance-related disorders are more likely to occur in younger adults. However, alcohol abuse and dependence are becoming an area of concern for the over-65

population, as are disorders related to the use of prescription medications.

3. The personality disorders found in Axis II are grouped into three clusters: those involving odd or eccentric behaviors, a second group of disorders that involve highly dramatic and "immature" symptoms, and a third group involving anxious and fearful traits. According to the maturation hypothesis, adults with personality disorders in the immature category experience fewer symptoms in later life. This hypothesis is consistent with data on a reduction in the traits and behaviors associated with psychopathy (antisocial personality disorder) among older adults.

4. Two additional topics of concern in the area of mental health and aging are elder abuse and suicide. According to a nationwide survey, the incidence of elder abuse is approximately 1% of older adults who are victimized each year. However, the large majority of cases normally escape detection. Adult children are most likely to be perpetrators of abuse. White men over the age of 85 have the highest risk of suicide in the population of the United States. The problem of suicide in older adults is exacerbated by the fact that older persons who are experiencing suicidal thoughts are unlikely to communicate these thoughts to health practitioners.

5. The field of clinical geropsychology involves the provision of psychological services to older adults. Treatment begins with thorough assessment. A number of tools are available that can be applied specifically to persons in later life. These tools range from clinical interviews to structured self-report inventories. Assessment of people within this age group requires that the clinician adapt the test materials and the testing situation to the specific needs and cognitive or sensory limitations of the older adult. Therapy methods range from somatic treatments such as ECT and medications to psychotherapy. Cognitive and interpersonal therapy methods appear to hold considerable promise for treatment of older adults.

GLOSSARY

Agoraphobia: the fear of being trapped or stranded during a panic attack.

Amnesia: profound memory loss.

Anxiety disorders: psychological disorders in which the major symptom is that of excessive anxiety.

Assessment: evaluation of the psychological, physiological, and social factors that are potentially affecting the individual's current state of functioning.

Bipolar disorder: Mood disorder characterized by the experience of manic episodes.

Brief psychotic disorder: a period in which an individual shows a burst of psychotic symptoms such as delusions, bizarre behavior, and disorganized thought.

Clinical geropsychology: specialty used primarily in applied settings such as hospitals, clinics, and long-term institutions.

Clinical interview: assessment method in which the clinician asks questions of the client to establish insight into the client's psychological processes.

Clinician: a professionally trained individual such as a clinical psychologist, psychiatrist, or social worker.

Cognitive restructuring: form of cognitive therapy in which the individual is encouraged to develop greater tolerance toward negative experiences and not make sweeping overgeneralizations.

Cognitive therapy: form of psychotherapy in which the clinician attempts to change the client's maladaptive emotions and ways of coping with difficult situations by changing the client's thoughts.

Cognitive-behavioral treatment: form of psychotherapy in which the client is encouraged to develop new behaviors and constructive ways of thinking about the self.

Comorbidity: situation in which an individual suffers from more than one disorder at the same time.

Contingency management: form of behavioral treatment in which a specific desirable outcome is made dependent (or "contingent" upon) the performance of a specific behavior.

Delirium: an acute state in which the individual experiences a disturbance in consciousness and attention.

Delirium, dementia, and amnestic disorders: disorders involving significant loss of cognitive functioning as the result of neurological dysfunction or medical illness.

Dementia: a change in cognitive functioning that occurs progressively over time.

Delusional disorders: psychotic disorder involving delusional belief around a particular theme or idea.

Depletion syndrome: the feelings of enervation, social withdrawal, loss of interest, sense of hopelessness, and a loss of appetite that may be observed in older adults who do not display outright symptoms of depression.

Depressive disorders: mood disorders characterized primarily by periods of intense sadness.

Diagnostic and Statistical Manual, Fourth Edition, Text Revision or DSM-IV-TR: psychiatric manual published by the American Psychiatric Association.

Differential diagnosis: the process of ruling out alternative diagnoses.

Dysphoria: sad mood.

Elder abuse: actions taken directly against an older adult through the inflicting of physical or psychological harm.

Electroconvulsive therapy (ECT): somatic treatment in which an electric current is applied through electrodes attached across the head.

Family therapy: form of therapy in which the individual's symptoms are regarded as the expression of problems within the entire system of relationships within the family.

Generalized anxiety disorder: Anxiety disorder in which a person feels an overall sense of uneasiness and concern but without having a particular focus.

Geropsychology: applications of the field of gerontology to the psychological treatment of older adults.

Group therapy: form of therapy in which the involvement of clients who share the perspective and problems of the client in treatment is used as a therapeutic tool.

Humanistic or client-centered therapy: form of psychotherapy in which the emphasis is on helping the individual gain greater self-acceptance and ultimately achieve fuller expression of the true or underlying self.

Iceberg model: proposal that the majority of elder (and child) abuse cases are undetected and do not become counted in official statistics.

Incidence: the number of new cases of a disorder that emerge within a given period such as a month or a year.

Interpersonal therapy: form of psychotherapy integrating cognitive methods with a focus on social factors that contribute to psychological disturbance.

Late-onset depression: mild or moderate depression that first appears after the age of 60.

Late-onset schizophrenia: form of schizophrenia that can occur among adults over the age of 45 years.

Life review therapy: psychological intervention intended to help an older adult rework past experiences with the goal of gaining greater acceptance of previous life events.

Lifetime prevalence: the number or percentage of people who ever develop a given disorder in their lifetimes.

Manic episode: period during which an individual feels unduly elated, grandiose, expansive, and energetic.

Maturation hypothesis: proposal that the Cluster B or "immature" personality types (borderline, histrionic, narcissistic, and antisocial) improve or at least are more treatable in older adults.

Medicaid: a federal and state matching entitlement program that pays for medical assistance for certain individuals and families with low incomes and resources.

Milieu therapy: intervention most often used in a therapeutic setting such as a rehabilitation facility, psychiatric hospital, or treatment facility within the community in which all health professionals in the environment work as a team to provide consistently constructive and therapeutic interactions with the client.

Mixed anxiety-depressive disorder: disorder in which the individual experiences recurrent or persistent dysphoria along with at least four symptoms of anxiety disorders.

Mood disorders: psychological disorders involving abnormalities in the individual's experience of emotion.

Neuroleptics: medications intended to reduce psychotic symptoms by altering dopamine activity.

Obsessive-compulsive disorder: a form of anxiety disorder in which individuals suffer from obsessions (repetitive thoughts) and compulsions (repetitive behaviors).

One month prevalence: the number or percentage of people who report having had symptoms of a disorder within the past 30 days.

Panic disorder: anxiety disorder involving the experience of panic attacks.

Personality disorders: disorders thought to reflect a disturbance within the basic personality structure of the individual.

Polypharmacy: circumstance in which individuals receive multiple prescription medications.

Post-traumatic stress disorder (PTSD): anxiety disorder in which an individual suffers prolonged effects of exposure to a traumatic experience.

Psychoanalytic or psychodynamic psychotherapy: form of psychotherapy in which the clinician focuses on unconscious processes, such as conflicts, defense mechanisms, dreams, and issues based on early relationships with parents.

Psychological disorder: a set of behaviors that lie outside the range of ordinary human experience.

Psychopathology: the scientific study of psychological disorders.

Psychopathy: a set of traits thought to lie at the core of the disorder.

Psychosurgery: somatic intervention that involves performing a surgical intervention on the brain.

Psychotherapeutic medications: substances that by their chemical nature alter the individual's brain structure or function.

Psychotherapy: the delivery of treatment to an individual through the application of psychological methods.

Schizoaffective disorder: a diagnosis given to people who have a depressive, manic, or mixed episode of symptoms at the same time as they are experiencing symptoms of schizophrenia.

Schizophrenia: severe form of psychopathology involving a wide range of unusual symptoms affecting thought, language, motivation, and the expression of emotion.

Shared psychotic disorder: psychotic disorder that occurs when two or more people develop a joint delusional system.

Social phobia: a form of anxiety disorder that applies to situations in which people must perform some action in front of others.

Social-cognitive: form of psychotherapy involving attempts to raise a client's sense of self-efficacy by enabling the client to have steplike increments in success at completing a previously unattainable goal.

Specific phobia: an irrational fear of a particular object or situation.

Substance abuse: maladaptive patterns of use of a substance that involves failure to meet social obligations, use of the substance in situations that can be physically hazardous or lead to arrest, and creation of interpersonal conflicts.

Substance dependence: a cluster of symptoms that include a set of physiological, cognitive, and behavioral changes related to use of the substance over a prolonged period.

Systematic desensitization: form of behavioral treatment in which a client is taught to replace an unwanted response (such as fear) with a desirable response (such as relaxation).

Tolerance: the need to take in a larger and larger dose to achieve the desired effect.

Withdrawal: the physical and psychological reaction to the substance's removal from the body.

Chapter Twelve

Treatment Sites for Chronic Disorders in Adulthood

When individuals are faced with physical or psychological disabilities that make it impossible for them to care for themselves, some form of institutional or community care is necessary. Most people prefer to live on their own, independently, in their own homes. Consequently, the decision to move to a long-term facility for care of a chronic disease or to be placed in the hands of others for care at home is can be a difficult and emotionally painful experience.

An institutional facility is one that provides individuals with medical or psychiatric care along with programs intended to restore lost functioning. Hospitals are short-term institutional facilities to which people are admitted with the understanding that they will be discharged when they no longer need round-the-clock treatment. At the other end of the spectrum are residential facilities into which an individual moves more or less permanently after no longer being able to live in an independent home setting.

Closely related to the issues of treatment for health care is that of funding, which is also covered in this chapter. Individuals in later life who must be hospitalized for physical and psychological problems are increasingly confronting the rising cost of health care as a barrier to effective resolution of their difficulties. In addition to the problems that result from failure to receive proper treatment, this situation creates considerable stress and anguish for the older individual. Coverage of this topic includes a number of facts and figures about current health insurance programs for long-term care within institutions and the community. It is important for students of adult development and aging to become familiar with the current situation. It is just as important to keep abreast of the rapidly changing issues in this area that occur almost on a month-to-month basis in the current U.S. health care scene.

INSTITUTIONAL FACILITIES FOR LONG-TERM CARE

Individuals with chronic disabilities, cognitive disorders, or physical infirmities that keep them from living independently may receive treatment in one of a variety of institutional long-term care settings. These institutions range from hospital-like facilities to residential living situations with minimal food and services.

Nursing Homes

For individuals whose illness or disability requires daily nursing care as well as other support services, nursing homes provide comprehensive care in a single setting. A **nursing home** is a residence that provides a room, meals, skilled nursing and rehabilitative care, medical services, and protective supervision. The care provided in nursing homes includes treating problems that residents have in the areas of cognition, communication, hearing, vision, physical functioning, continence (regulation of the elimination of urine and feces), psychosocial functioning, mood and behavior, nutrition, oral and dental care, skin condition, and medications. Residents may receive urinary training programs, assistance with feeding and mobility, rehabilitative activities, and social services.

Typically, nursing homes are thought of as permanent residences for the older adults who enter them, but about 30% of residents are discharged and able to move back into the community. About one-quarter of people admitted to nursing homes die there, and another 36% move to another facility (Sahyoun, Pratt, Lentzner, Dey, & Robinson, 2001).

> **"What do you think?"** | **12-1**
>
> Would you consider placing a chronically ill relative in a nursing home? Why or why not? What would you look for in a nursing home?

Nursing homes are certified by state and federal governmental agencies to provide services at one or more levels of care. **Skilled nursing facilities** provide the most intensive nursing care available outside of a hospital. The nursing services provided at this level of care include applying dressings or bandages, providing bowel and bladder retraining, catheterization, enemas, full bed baths, injections, irrigation, nasal feeding, oxygen therapy, and measurement of temperature, pulse, respiration, and blood pressure. In an **intermediate care facility,** health-related services are provided to individuals who do not require hospital or skilled nursing facility care but do require institutional care above the level of room and board. There are also intermediate care facilities specifically designated for people who have mental retardation and are unable to live on their own in the community.

Over half (56%) of the nursing homes in the United States are owned or leased by multifacility organizations or chains, a phenomenon that grew throughout the 1990s. The remainder consists of privately owned independent facilities or special units based in hospitals (Harrington,

Residents of a nursing home engaging in a lively conversation

Carrillo, Wellin, & Shemirani, 2002). Nursing home services have become big business in the United States. In 2000, nursing home expenditures were estimated to be $55.9 billion, or about 10% of the total health care expenditures in the United States and 3% of the total U.S. expenditures. As of 2000, there were nearly 17,000

nursing homes, with a total of over 1.8 million beds (U.S. Bureau of the Census, 2003). Nursing homes have become larger over the past 30 years, as can be seen in Fig. 12.1. The majority house between 50 and 199 beds, with the smaller homes (less than 50 beds) diminishing to a small percentage as compared with the early 1970s.

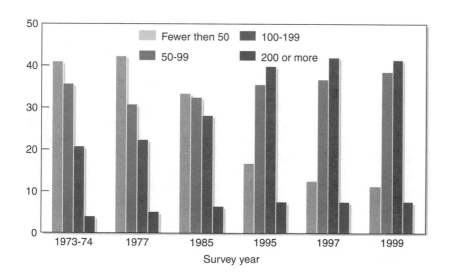

FIGURE 12.1

Percentage Distribution of Nursing Homes by Bed Size: United States, Selected Years

Source: National Center for Health Statistics, 2004.

Residential Care Facilities

An alternative to a nursing home is a **residential care facility**, which provides 24-hour supportive care services and supervision to individuals who do not require skilled nursing care. The services they provide include meals, housekeeping, and assistance with personal care such as bating and grooming. Some may provide other services such as management of medications and social and recreational activities.

Board and Care Homes. Board and care homes are group living arrangements that are designed to meet the needs of people who cannot live on their own in the community but who also need some nursing services. Typically, they provide help with activities of daily living such as bathing, dressing, and toileting. Although it would seem as though these homes provide a "homelike" setting, this is apparently not the case. A survey conducted by the Institute of Medicine determined that the services provided in these facilities do not adjust the care they provide to the specific needs of the residents. They are typically understaffed, and the staff who do work in these settings are not required to receive training (Wunderlich, Kohler, & Committee on Improving Quality in Long-Term Care, 2001).

Group Homes. Group homes provide independent, private living in a house shared by several older individuals. Residents split the cost of rent, housekeeping services, utilities, and meals.

Assisted Living Facilities. **Assisted living** facilities are housing complexes in which older persons live independently in their own apartments. The residents pay a regular monthly rent that usually includes meal service in communal dining rooms, transportation for shopping and appointments, social activities, and housekeeping service. Some facilities have health services available on location. These facilities are professionally managed and licensed and may be one of several levels of care within the same housing community. The cost for living in an assisted living facility may range from hundreds to thousands of dollars a month. In some states, funds may be available for those who cannot afford to live in these facilities on their own through government support programs. However, most residents pay the rental and other fees out of their own funds.

The philosophy of assisted living is that private, residentially oriented buildings are combined with high levels of service that allow for "aging in place" so that residents can live within the same environment even if they undergo changes in their health or physical and cognitive functioning. However, many facilities do not achieve these goals. Moreover, they are too expensive for the moderate- and low-income older adults, and those that are affordable do not offer high levels of service or privacy (Wunderlich et al., 2001).

Adult Foster Care. An older adult may receive adult foster care, in which a family provides care in their their home. The services provided in these settings include meals, housekeeping and help with dressing, eating, bathing, and other personal care. These settings offer some advantages because of their homelike feeling, but they are small and rely on a live-in caregiver for help with personal care, cooking, housekeeping, and activities, so the caregiver's resources may be spread thin. If one resident becomes ill and must receive more nursing care, other residents may suffer from lack of attention. Another possible disadvantage is that residents may feel that they have less privacy than in a residential care setting (Wunderlich et al., 2001).

BEHIND THE RESEARCH

CHARLENE HARRINGTON, PH.D., R.N., F.A.A.N.,
PROFESSOR OF SOCIOLOGY AND NURSING, DEPARTMENT OF
SOCIAL AND BEHAVIORAL SCIENCES, UNIVERSITY OF CALIFORNIA,
SAN FRANCISCO

What is most exciting about research in this field?

Nursing home research is my major passion, and my primary focus has been on improving the quality of nursing home care. After over 25 years of working in this area, I find that not a great deal of progress has been made improving nursing home quality. The nation still has between 25 and 33% of its nursing homes that are operating with poor quality that jeopardizes the health and safety of its residents. With over 1.6 million frail and vulnerable residents living in the nation's nursing homes at any point in time, poor quality is a major scandal that deserves the highest level of research, regulatory, and policy attention. The exciting part of research on nursing homes, and long-term care more generally, is its complexity and the fact that quality is intricately related to the organization, delivery, and financing of care. All of the inter-related issues need to be addressed if progress is going to be made. The greatest challenge is to consider what research would have a policy impact that could change the system of care.

What are the major challenges?

The caregiving workforce in nursing homes is the major challenge. The vast majority of facilities have inadequate numbers of registered nurses, licensed vocational nurses, and nursing assistants to carry out the basic care for the residents. As a result, many residents do not receive adequate assistance with eating, toileting, transferring, walking, dressing, and bathing. Many are left in bed or wheelchairs most of the day, put in diapers, and physically and socially neglected so that pressure ulcers, incontinence, contractures, weight loss, depression, and pain develop that could otherwise be prevented. Not only are

residents at risk, but the nursing staff in many facilities have a low morale, high injury rates, and high turnover rates (with three out of four nurses leaving their jobs every year). The latest research shows that at least 1 direct care giver is needed for every seven or eight residents, and one registered nurse is needed for every 18 residents or a minimum of 4.1 total nursing hours per resident day. Without improved staffing ratios, wages and benefits, education and training, work environments, and other changes in care management, quality of care cannot be expected to improve. Since government pays for about 60% of all nursing home care, government needs to take the initiative to pay for and demand increases in staffing and wage/benefits rates to make these essential improvements.

Where is the field headed in the next decade?

At a time when the economy is poor and political efforts are being proposed to cut back government spending on health and welfare services, nursing homes are facing a financial catastrophe. The positive hope is that policymakers, whose own parents and grandparents often need long-term care, will begin to focus on making improvements in the financing and the accountability of the nursing home and long-term care industry. As the Baby Boomers begin to age, they will demand a higher quality of care and demand options to live at home or in the community. Perhaps then the country will consider alternative financing such as public long-term care insurance and a system of care that ensure high quality and appropriate services. Nurses are critical to making changes in the quality of care as well to making political changes that will guarantee that every nursing home resident has the best possible care.

COMMUNITY-BASED SERVICES AND FACILITIES

There are a variety of support services designed to allow older adults, even those with some form of disability, to live on their own in the community. Some of these services are offered by volunteer groups at no cost to the individual. Others are fee-based, but may be paid for by Medicare.

Home Health Services

An increasing number of older adults who are ill or disabled are able to maintain an independent life in the community by using **home health services**. A variety of services are available within this broad category of care. Such services include "Meals on Wheels," the provision of a hot meal once a day; so-called friendly visiting, in which someone comes to the home for a social visit; and assistance with shopping. Other home-based services can include laundry, cooking, and cleaning.

Researchers have found that home health care that simulates the types of restorative services provided in nursing homes such as physical therapy, speech therapy, occupational therapy, rehabilitation, and interventions targeted at particular areas of functional decline can help to maintain the older person in the home longer and reduce the need for institutionalization and emergency room care (Tinetti, Baker, Gallo, Nanda, Charpentier, et al., 2002).

"What do you think?"   **12-2**

What would you think about living in an assisted living or continuing care retirement community when you become older? What might be the advantages and disadvantages of such an arrangement?

In 2000, nearly 1 million persons 65 years of age and over were home health care patients. The

Meals on Wheels programs are often a part of home health services, which allow older adults to remain in their homes rather than requiring institutionalization. Volunteer Dr. Sheldon Ekland-Olson (left), Provost of the University of Texas, is shown here providing a packaged lunch to a participant in the Austin Meals on Wheels and More Program.

majority are women, and over half are 75 and older (Centers for Disease Control and Prevention, 2002). Almost all live in private homes, and half live with family members (Munson, 1999) In 2001, a total of $33.2 billion was spent by the U.S. government on home health care (http://cms.hhs.gov/statistics/nhe/historical/t3.asp).

Geriatric Partial Hospital

In a **geriatric partial hospital**, daily outpatient therapy is provided with intensive, structured multidisciplinary services to older persons who have recently been discharged from a psychiatric hospital. The partial hospital may also serve as an alternative to hospitalization. Therapists in this setting focus on medication management and compliance, social functioning, discharge planning, and relapse prevention. A less intense program than the geriatric partial hospital program is **geriatric continuing day treatment**, in which clients attend a day treatment program three days a week but are encouraged to live independently during the remaining days of the week. **Day care centers** are another form of community treatment in which individuals receive supervised meals and activities on a daily basis.

Accessory Dwelling Units

An older adult may be housed in a separate apartment in a relative's home. An accessory dwelling unit, also known as an "in-law apartment," is a second living space in the home that allows the older adult to have independent living quarters, cooking space, and a bathroom.

Subsidized Housing

Other alternatives in community care involve the provision of housing in addition to specialized services that can maintain the person in an independent living situation. **Subsidized senior housing** is provided for individuals with low to moderate incomes. People using subsidized housing live in low-rent apartment complexes and have access to help with routine tasks such as housekeeping, shopping and laundry.

Continuing Care Retirement Community (CCRC)

A more comprehensive community living setting is a **continuing care retirement community (CCRC),** which is a housing community that provides different levels of care based on the residents' needs. The levels of care provided range from independent living apartments to skilled nursing care in an affiliated nursing home. Within the same CCRC, there may be individual homes or apartments where residents can live independently, an assisted living facility, and a nursing home. Residents move from one setting to another based on their needs, but they continue to remain part of their CCRC community. Many CCRCs require a large payment prior to admission and also charge monthly fees. Some communities are beginning to allow residents to rent rather than buy into the facility.

Residents moving into CCRCs typically sign a contract that specifies the conditions under which they will receive long-term care. One option provides unlimited nursing care for a small increase in monthly payments. A second type of contract includes a predetermined amount of long-term nursing care; beyond this, the resident is responsible for additional payments. In the third option, the resident pays fees for service, which means full daily rates for all long-term nursing care.

There are advantages to living in CCRCs. In addition to the relative ease of moving from one level of care to another, CCRCs provide social activities, access to community facilities, transportation services, companionship, access to health care, housekeeping, and maintenance. Residents may travel, take vacations, and be involved in activities outside the community itself.

CCRCs are accredited by a commission sponsored by the American Association of Homes and Services for the Aging. To be accredited, a CCRC must pass a two-and-a-half-day test that evaluates the facility's governance and administration, resident life and services, finance, and health care.

LEGISLATIVE ISSUES IN CARE OF OLDER ADULTS

The regulation of nursing homes and community-based services for older adults and the disabled is a major focus of health policy and legislation in the United States. This is in large part because funding of these services is provided by federal and state agencies.

1987 Omnibus Budget Reconciliation Act of 1987 (OBRA 1987)

The current laws governing the operation of these facilities have their origins in a report to the U.S. Congress in 1986 by the Institute of Medicine called "Improving the Quality of Care in Nursing Homes." This report recommended major changes in the quality and nature of services provided to nursing home residents. The result of the report was the Omnibus Budget Reconciliation Act of 1987, which included the **Nursing Home Reform Act** ("Reconciliation" in this context means an expedited process in the U.S. Congress that applies to government spending programs as a way of expediting the budgetary process in these cases). OBRA 1987 mandated that facilities must meet physical standards, provide adequate professional staffing and services, and maintain policies governing the administrative and medical procedures of the nursing facility. A significant component of this legislation was the provision

of safeguards to assure quality of care and protection of residents' rights. The bottom line was that each resident must be provided with services and activities to attain or maintain the highest practicable physical, mental, and psychosocial well-being. Facilities are required to care for residents in a manner and an environment that promotes, maintains, or enhances quality of life.

The conditions of the Nursing Home Reform Act specify that nursing homes must be licensed in accordance with state and local laws, including all applicable laws pertaining to staff, licensing, and registration, fire, safety, and communicable diseases. They must have a governing body legally responsible for policies and the appointment of a qualified administrator. One or more physicians must be on call at all times to cover an emergency, and there must be 24-hour nursing care services, including at least one full-time registered nurse. The facility must admit eligible patients regardless of race, color, or national origin.

The specific services that are required in addition to availability of physicians and nurses are specialized rehabilitation, social services, pharmaceutical services, dietary services, dental services, and an ongoing activities program. The goal of the activities program should be to encourage self-care and the individual's return to normal life in the community through social, religious, and recreational activities, and by visits with relatives and friends. Nursing homes are required to maintain confidential records, employ appropriate methods for obtaining and dispensing medications, and have arrangements for obtaining required clinical, laboratory, X-ray, and other diagnostic services.

The series of resident rights developed as part of the Nursing Home Reform Act include choice of physician and treatment, freedom from physical and mental abuse, the right to privacy and treatment with respect and dignity, the right to confidential records, and the right to have needs and preferences met. In addition, residents have the right to refuse medications and treatments, voice their grievances, and transfer or leave the facility when appropriate. They are also required to be informed in writing about services and fees before entering the nursing home, the right to manage their own money (or choose someone to do so), and to keep personal belongings and property to the extent that these do not interfere with the rights, health, or safety of others.

The legislation also established procedures to ensure that all conditions are met for maintaining compliance with the law. These procedures include monitoring of the performance of facilities by outside survey agencies to determine whether they comply with the federal conditions of participation.

1997 Balanced Budget Act

Changes to the nursing home rates for post-hospital care were incorporated into the Balanced Budget Act of 1997 and implemented in March 2000. These changes involved moving to a prospective payment system in which rates paid to **skilled nursing facilities** cover the costs of furnishing most covered nursing home services, excluding payment for physicians and certain other practitioner services. Under the prospective payment system, each facility receives a fixed amount for treating patients diagnosed with a given illness, regardless of the length of stay or type of care received. Prior to this system, nursing homes filed bills to Medicare based on a fee-for-service schedule. The intention of the change in payments was to curb the rapidly rising costs of Medicare as well as to adjust the payments to the specific needs of the patient. By paying more for the patients whose medical expenses are legitimately higher than those who have less expensive medical needs, nursing homes can provide better health care, adjusted for the needs of the individual resident.

1998 Nursing Home Initiative

Ten years after the Nursing Home Reform Act was put into place, a series of investigations and U.S. Senate hearings called attention to weaknesses in federal and state survey and enforcement activities that constituted serious threats to the well-being of residents (http://research.aarp.org/health/fs83_reform.html). In 1997, the U.S. Senate Committee on Aging received reports that documented inadequate care in California nursing homes that led to widespread death and suffering of residents. These reports triggered a hearing in 1998 by the Committee on California Nursing Homes. At this hearing, a General Accounting Office (GAO) report revealed that there was weak enforcement of the NHRA, putting many residents at risk of inadequate care. Fully 98% of nursing homes were found to have more than minimal (35%), substandard (33%), or serious (30%) deficiencies. Particularly troubling was the fact that even when serious problems were identified, there was no enforcement of actions that would ensure that the deficiencies were corrected and did not recur.

These shocking reports about nursing homes abuse made it clear that NHRA enforcement procedures were not working. In response to these findings, the Clinton Administration announced the 1998 Nursing Home Initiative. This initiative proposed a series of steps designed to improve enforcement of nursing home quality standards, which were then adopted by HCFA. These included altering the timing of nursing home inspections to include both weekends and evenings as well as weekdays, providing more frequent inspectors of previous violators, imposing immediate sanctions on nursing homes found guilty of a second offense involving violations that harm residents, allowing states to impose monetary penalties on violators, and not lifting sanctions against offenders until an on-site visit verified that they were complying with federal regulations. The result of these efforts was increased federal spending to ensure that states provide adequate survey and certification, raising the amount budgeted for these activities from $290 million in 1998 to 359 million in 2000.

Congressional Hearings on Nursing Home Abuse

Following the California study and the announcement of the 1998 Nursing Home Initiative, GAO and HCFA conducted additional research that included nursing homes nationwide. By September 2000, the U.S. Senate Committee on Aging held a hearing on the outcomes of the Nursing Home Initiatives revealed that the initiatives had resulted in improvements to state survey and federal oversight procedures, including increases in the number of surveyors, improved tracking of complaints, new methods to detect serious deficiencies, and improved organization of nursing home oversight activities (http://research.aarp.org/health/fs83_reform .html). However, additional hearings on nursing home quality held by the U.S. Senate Committee on Aging in 1999 and 2000 revealed that nursing home abuse remained a serious problem. These hearings revealed that nationwide 27% of nursing homes were cited with violations causing actual harm to residents or placing them at risk of death or serious injury; another 43% were cited for violations that created a potential for more than minimal harm. These hearings also revealed flaws in the surveys; significant problems were often missed, such as pressure sores, malnutrition, and dehydration. In some cases, the nursing homes were cited because a member of the nursing staff committed acts of abuse against residents including beatings, sexual abuse, and verbal abuse. The findings of these hearings are in the report, "Abuse of Residents Is a Major Problem in U.S. Nursing Homes", prepared for Representative Henry A. Waxman Minority Staff Special Investigations Division, Committee on Government Reform, U.S. House of Representatives, July 30, 2001. http://www.house.gov/reform/ min/pdfs/pdf_inves/pdf_nursing_abuse_rep.pdf

The Senate committee found that if residents or family members made formal complaints, these were uninvestigated for weeks or months; the filing of complains was also discouraged by the states. Even if serious deficiencies were found, there was inadequate enforcement, so the nursing homes involved did not correct the problems. Finally, the majority (54%) of nursing homes were understaffed, putting residents at increased risk of hospitalization for avoidable causes, pressure sores, and significant weight loss.

2002 Nursing Home Quality Initiative

In November 2002, the federal government initiated the National Nursing Home Quality Initiative, a program intended to help consumers find the highest quality nursing homes. The initiative combined new information for consumers about the quality of care provided in individual nursing homes with resources available to nursing homes to improve the quality of care in their facilities (see the Assess Yourself box). The initiative consists of continuing efforts to regulate and enforce standards of care in nursing homes, provide improved consumer information on the quality of care in each nursing home, make available community-based quality improvement programs, and collaborate with nursing homes to help them improve their quality. Assistance is provided by Quality Improvement Organizations (QIOs), government contractors offering improvement assistance to skilled nursing facilities. The initiative also includes the training of volunteers to serve as ombudspersons to help families and residents find nursing homes that provide the highest possible quality of care and give consumers tools they need to make an informed, educated decision on selecting a nursing home.

Rating a Nursing Home

The ratings of nursing homes on the Medicare Web site provide vital information for older adults and their families about what they can expect from their local institutions. The table below shows the results for a fictitious nursing home as described on this Web site. How would your potential nursing home compare to this one?

SUNNY REST NURSING HOME

As of 11/19/2003:

134 Certified Beds
132 Residents in certified beds
99% of certified beds occupied
Medicare certified
Medicaid certified
Type of ownership: For-profit corporation
Not located in a hospital
Not a Multinursing home (chain) ownership
Both resident and family councils

Quality Measures	Percentage for SUNNY REST NURSING HOME	State Average	National Average
The Percentage of Residents with Loss of Ability in Basic Daily Tasks	13%	17%	155
The Percentage of Residents with Pressure Sores	5%	9%	8%
The Percentage of Residents with Pain	1%	8%	10%
The Percentage of Residents in Physical Restraints	0%	7%	10%
The Percentage of Residents with Infections	13%	18%	NA

Inspection Results
Range of health deficiencies in this state: 0–38
Average number of health deficiencies in this state: 6
Average number of health deficiencies in the United States: 7

Assess Yourself *(continued)*

Date of last inspection: 11/19/2002

Complaint investigations during: 10/01/2001 – 12/31/2002

Total number of health deficiencies for this nursing home: 6

Mistreatment Deficiencies

Inspectors determined that the nursing home failed to:	Date of Correction	Level of Harm	Residents Affected (Few, Some, or Many)
1. Write and use policies that forbid mistreatment, neglect and abuse of residents and theft of residents' property. (11/19/2002)		2 = Minimal harm or potential for actual harm Least → Most 1 **2** 3 4	Few

Quality Care Deficiencies

Inspectors determined that the nursing home failed to:	Date of Correction	Level of Harm	Residents Affected (Few, Some, or Many)
2. Make sure each resident is being watched and has assistance devices when needed, to prevent accidents. (02/13/2002)		3 = Actual harm Least → Most 1 2 **3** 4	Few

Nursing Home Staffing
Number of Nursing Staff Hours per Resident per Day

	Number of Residents	RN Hours per Resident per Day*	LPN/LVN Hours per Resident per Day*	CNA Hours per Resident per Day*	Total Number of Nursing Staff Hours per Resident per Day*
Average in the United States	88.5	0.7	0.8	2.4	3.9
Average in the State of Massachusetts	97.1	0.9	0.7	2.3	3.9
SUNNY REST NURSING HOME	132	0.85	0.49	2.52	3.86

* Hours per resident per day is the average daily work (in hours) given by the entire group of nurses or nursing assistants divided by total number of residents. The amount of care given to each resident varies.

Please use our **Nursing Home Checklist** for help with narrowing your nursing homes choices. The checklist provides questions and observations that are important to keep in mind as you visit nursing homes and will help you make a good choice for you or your relative.

http://www.medicare.gov/NHCompare/Search/NursingHomeResults.asp

CHARACTERISTICS AND NEEDS OF NURSING HOMES AND THEIR RESIDENTS

Although there is a relatively small percentage overall of people 65 and older living in nursing homes (1.56 million, or 4.5% in 2000), the percentage of older adults who are institutionalized increases dramatically with age, rising from 1.1% for people ages 65–74 to 4.7% for people ages 75–84, and 18.2% for people 85+ (Administration on Aging, 2003).

Information about nursing homes and nursing home residents comes from two nationally based sources of information about nursing homes and the nature and quality of care they provide. The most complete is the On-line Survey, Certification, and Reporting system (OSCAR). The OSCAR system has information from the state surveys of all certified nursing facilities in the United States, which are entered into a uniform database. The state surveyors assess both the process and the outcomes of nursing home care in 15 major areas. Each of these areas has specific regulations, which state surveyors review to determine whether or not facilities have met the standards. Where a facility fails to meet a standard, a deficiency or citation is given. The deficiencies are given for problems that can result in a negative effect on the health and safety of residents.

The second source of information is the National Nursing Home Survey (NNHS) carried out by the Centers for Disease Control and Prevention (CDC) in the years 1973–74, 1977, 1985, 1995, 1997, and 1999. The NNHS includes samples of about 1500 facilities that provide data from both staff and residents in the form of interviews and questionnaires.

Home health agencies are required to submit data on their effectiveness using the Outcomes Assessment and Information Set (OASIS), mandated for use by Medicare-certified home health agencies.

Characteristics of Residents

The most common primary diagnosis of nursing home residents upon admission is cardiovascular disease. However, the greatest form of disability is loss of cognitive skills associated with Alzheimer's disease (Schultz, Ellingrod, Moser, Kutschner, Turvey, et al., 2002). Given that Alzheimer's disease is found in nearly half of all nursing home residents (43% in 2001), this means that difficulties in carrying out daily living skills are a significant problem among nursing home residents. In fact, over 50% of nursing home residents are chairbound, meaning that they are restricted to a wheelchair. Despite the large number of residents with Alzheimer's disease, only 5.4% of nursing homes have special care units devoted specifically to their care (Harrington et al., 2002).

Mood and anxiety disorders are present in nearly 20% of all older adults living in these settings (Sahyoun et al., 2001). Over half (54.7%) receive psychotropic medications, which includes antidepressants, antianxiety drugs, sedatives, hypnotics, and antipsychotics (Harrington et al., 2002). Although these medications have the potential to be abused if they are given to control and sedate residents, there is no evidence that this is the case (Wunderlich et al., 2001). In fact, some regard this as a positive sign, indicating that health care staff are becoming more sensitive to the need to treat psychological symptoms, such as depression, in residents.

Medicare, Medicaid, and other forms of health insurance will be discussed later as the financing of long-term care is related to the quality of health care that older adults receive. Basically, Medicare and Medicaid are government-based programs that pay for certain long-term care costs. As of 2001, about two-thirds (67%) of residents have their nursing home expenses paid for by Medicaid, about one-quarter (23.3%) pay for nursing homes themselves through their own funds or other forms of insurance, and the remainder (9.8%) have their nursing home expenses paid for by Medicare (Harrington et al., 2002).

Characteristics of Nursing Homes

The size of nursing homes is on the increase. Between 1995 and 2001, the average number of beds per facility increased from 99 to 106. At the same time, however, the occupancy rate (how many beds are filled) dropped from 90 to 83%. A lower occupancy rate translates into greater availability of beds for residents who must rely on some form of government subsidy to pay for their care. The majority (65.0%) of nursing homes in the United States fall into the category of "for-profit" facilities, meaning that their revenue must exceed their expenses. Nonprofit facilities, which include primarily those run by religious organizations, constitute the second largest group (28.6%), and government-owned facilities, primarily those run by the Veterans Administration, compose the remainder (6.4%). Therefore, most nursing homes are run like businesses with the goal of making a profit. Related to this issue is the payment mode of residents. When nursing homes have more private-pay patients, they are able to provide better care because the rates for these patients are higher than the reimbursement rates that the facilities receive from governmental subsidies.

As the U.S. government attempts to improve the quality of care provided to nursing homes, monitoring continues on a yearly basis through the listing of deficiencies as reported to OSCAR. In the years between 1997 and 2001, there was a gradual increase in the average number of deficiencies (Harrington et al., 2002). In 2001, the average number of deficiencies varied substantially across states from a low of 2.8 per facility in Vermont to 11.5 in California and the District of Columbia. The percentage of facilities reporting no deficiencies in the United States increased from 15.2 percent in 1995 to 21.6 percent in 1997, only to decline again to 13.7 percent in 2001. On this indication of quality, the percentage of facilities with no deficiencies varied by state with the District of Columbia and Nevada having the poorest record (0% having no deficiencies) to Virginia with the best record (33.9%).

Deficiencies that cause harm or immediate jeopardy to residents are considered the most serious of all. Nursing homes are cited when they have one or more of these as determined by OSCAR. After a peak in 1999 (30.6% of facilities), the records improved in 2001 (down to 21.1%). However, this still means that one out of every five nursing homes has at least one serious deficiency.

The Top 10 Deficiencies in 2001 are shown in Fig. 12.2. As can be seen from this figure, the five categories with the highest number of deficiencies were failure to ensure sanitary food (31.9%), ensure quality of care (23.7%), remove accident hazards in the environment (22.1%), meet professional standards in conducting resident assessments (18.8 %), and prevent accidents (18.6%).

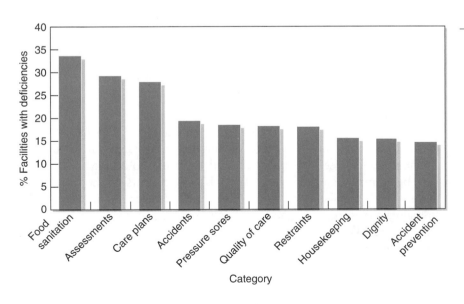

FIGURE 12.2

Top 10 Deficiencies in Nursing Homes in 2001

Source: Harrington et al., 2002.

Food Sanitation. Proper sanitation must be ensured in storing, preparing, distributing, and serving food to prevent the spread of food-borne illnesses. Nursing homes that fail to provide proper sanitation of food place residents at risk of food poisoning and the spread of disease and infection. Because poor sanitation was the most frequently occurring deficiency in 2001, found in nearly one-third of nursing homes, there are clear ramifications for the health and well-being of residents. Nearly two-thirds of the nursing homes in Arkansas (61.6%) had this deficiency; Virginia with 4% had the best record.

Restraints. Restraints are defined as mechanical devices, materials, or equipment that restricts freedom of movement or normal access to one's body. A deficiency is listed if restraints are used for the purposes of discipline or convenience and not required to treat the resident's medical symptoms. Restraints are criticized because their use on a regular basis can cause decreased muscle tone and increased likelihood of falls, incontinence, pressure ulcers, depression, confusion, and mental deterioration. In the years between 1995 and 2001, the percentage of facilities with deficiencies in this area declined from 17.3% to 11.0% in the United States. However, the improper use of restraints varied considerably by state, from a high of 37% in Hawaii to 3.2% in Iowa.

Dignity, Respect, and Privacy. Nursing homes are rated for deficiencies in the area of dignity and respect if they fail to provide care that treats residents as individuals, allowing them to feel that their particular needs are being met. Care that is provided with dignity and respect includes helping residents to maintain their personal hygiene, dress properly, and eat without needing to be fed. Residents should be given privacy, listened to, and communicated with in a respectful manner.

A physical therapist assists this woman in regaining her mobility. Being treated with dignity and respect is an important contributor to a nursing home resident's satisfaction with care.

In 2001, 17.3% of all facilities were rated as deficient in this area, up from 13.2% in 1997. The state of Arizona had the highest percentage of facilities with deficiencies in the area of dignity and respect (45%); New Hampshire (1.4%) had the lowest.

A related issue is privacy and confidentiality. Residents have the right to privacy in the realm of their personal belongings, and what they talk about with others through mail, telephone, or personal conversations. Residents should also be able to lock away their personal possessions in their rooms. Very few nursing homes were cited for deficiencies in these areas in 2001.

Housekeeping. Maintenance of a safe and clean environment is a basic job of nursing homes, as a way of preventing residents from disease, infection, and harm due to accidents. In 2001, there were 16.9% of nursing homes in the United States with deficiencies in the area of housekeeping. Arizona's record (44.6%) was the poorest; and Hawaii's (0%), the best.

Nursing Staff, Services, and Programs. Facilities must have sufficient nursing staff to provide nursing and related services to attain or maintain the highest practicable physical, mental, and psychosocial well-being of residents. In 2001, few facilities met this requirement. Over the period of 1995 to 2001, total nursing hours provided by registered nurses, licensed practical nurses, and nurses aides averaged 3.3 hours per resident per day in 2001, or 70 minutes per 8-hour shift.

An area related to nursing services is that of the provision of activities that meet the interests and needs of the residents in terms of their physical, emotional, and social well-being. Nursing homes nationwide received fairly good scores on this count, with only 7.9% being rated for deficiencies in 2001. However, two states had nearly 20% deficiency rates, including Wyoming (20.6%) and Nevada (19.6%).

Incontinence. An area in which more efforts are needed for intervention involves incontinence. Nearly one-half (49.2%) of all nursing home residents have urinary incontinence; that is, they are unable to control the elimination of urine. However, only 6% of residents were involved in bladder-training programs, which are behavioral methods designed to assist residents to gain and maintain bladder control (pelvic exercises and frequent toileting). Bowel incontinence, which involves lack of ability to control the elimination of feces at least once a week, had a rate of 41.8% among 2001 nursing home residents. Training programs exist that are designed to assist residents to gain and maintain control through use of diet, fluids, and regular schedules. However, these were available to only 3.8% of residents in 2001 (Harrington et al., 2002). Clearly, the socially appropriate regulation of one's bodily functions is an important need that, if unmet, can detract from the quality of an individual's life as well as the quality of the life of the staff.

In 2001, 10.4% of facilities had deficiencies for this standard (Harrington et al., 2002). The

Institute of Medicine study concluded that because this problem is reversible in many cases, high prevalence of incontinence suggests poor care (Wunderlich et al., 2001).

FINANCING OF LONG-TERM CARE

It is difficult to open the newspaper or turn on the television without hearing a discussion of the urgent need in the United States to address the economic issues involved in health care. These discussions often occur in the context of other issues affecting adults using a wide range of health care services, from outpatient medical care to private psychotherapy. Changes in health maintenance organizations (HMOs) have created havoc in many sectors of the health care industry, causing great anxiety among the public, politicians, and health care professionals. In many ways, the health care financing crisis is a function of the huge expenses associated with the long-term care of older adults. Insecurity over the financing of health care can constitute a crisis for adults of any age, but particularly for older persons who have limited financial resources. The ability to receive proper treatment for long-term disorders is therefore both a social and an individual issue.

As noted above, the majority of nursing home residents have their health care paid for by Medicaid, a government program. The expenses for nursing homes run high; as of 1999, the average cost of nursing home care was $3609 per month (Centers for Disease Control and Prevention, 2002). In 2001, total U.S. expenditure on nursing homes was 98.9 billion, which is 7% of all national health care expenditures (http://cms.hhs.gov/statistics/nhe/historical/t3.asp).

Nursing homes and other facilities in which older adults receive treatment are subject to strict federal and state requirements to ensure that they comply with the standards set forth in the legislation that created the funding programs. The

President Lyndon B. Johnson signing the Medicare bill into effect on July 30, 1965.

intimate connection between financing and regulation of these long-term care facilities has provided the incentive for nursing homes to raise their level of care so that they can qualify for this support.

Long-term health care financing has a history dating back to the early 1900s and the nation's first attempts to devise government health insurance programs. In the ensuing century, as these programs began to be established, their benefits structure and financing grew increasingly complex and diversified. Throughout this process, the developers of these plans, which involve state and federal agencies along with private insurance companies, have attempted to respond to the rapidly changing needs of the population and the even more rapidly changing nature of the U.S. economy.

Medicare

After considering and debating a variety of long-term health care plans for older adults, the U.S. Congress passed legislation as part of the Social Security Amendments of 1965 establishing the Medicare and the Medicaid programs. Title XVIII, known as **Medicare**, is entitled Health Insurance for the Aged and Disabled. The Medicare legislation established a health insurance program for older adults to complement the insurance provided by Title II of the Social Security Act to retirees, survivors, and disabled persons. Since its enactment, Medicare has been subject to numerous legislative and administrative changes designed to improve health care services to older adults, the disabled, and the poor. In 1973, the program was expanded to broaden eligibility to those already receiving Social Security benefits, people over 65 who qualify for Social Security benefits, and individuals with end-stage renal disease requiring continuous dialysis or kidney transplant. The Department of Health and Human Services (DHHS) has the overall responsibility for administration of the Medicare program, with the assistance of the Social Security Administration (SSA). In 1977, the Health Care Financing Administration (HCFA) was established under the DHHS to administer Medicare and Medicaid; it was replaced in July 2001 by the Centers for Medicare and Medicaid Services (CMS) as part of a large-scale reform of services to beneficiaries. CMS has responsibility for formulation of policy and guidelines, oversight and operation of contracts, maintenance and review of records, and general financing. State agencies also play a role in the regulation and administration of the Medicare program in consultation with CMS.

In late 2003, the U.S. government enacted the 2003 Medicare Modernization Act. The intent of this law was to provide people with Medicare improved health care coverage and a wider range of benefits. Most significant of the changes is the inclusion of coverage for prescription drugs. Starting in 2004, discount cards allowed Medicare recipients to be eligible for savings on prescription drugs, with savings estimated to be 10–25% or more on many drugs. Individuals earning less than about $12,000 a year or married couples whose incomes are less than about $16,000 may qualify for a subsidy of $600 to help pay for prescription drugs. Beginning in 2006, a full prescription drug benefit will be added to Medicare by allowing recipients to enroll in insurance plans that cover prescription drugs. The monthly premium will be about $35 a month and there will be a $250 deductible per year. With this plan, Medicare will pay 75% of drug costs between the deductible and $2250. Between $2250 and $5100 per year, beneficiaries will pay all drug costs. However, when drug costs exceed $5100 per year, Medicare will pay 95%. Additional preventive benefits will also go into effect as a result of the new law, including one physical exam and screening for heart disease and diabetes.

Critics of the new legislation argue that these prescription privileges do not go far enough. In addition to the large deductible when costs are between $2250 and $5100, older adults who sign up for this plan are no longer eligible to receive prescription benefits through private insurance companies. Skyrocketing prescription drug costs exacerbate the problem. Of the 50 drugs most commonly used by older adults, the average annual cost per prescription is $1000 or more. Hence, the new prescription privileges will still leave many older adults with significant out-of-pocket expenses for medications required to maintain them in good health.

"What do you think?"	12-3

Do you think that Medicare's coverage of prescription drugs is sufficient? Why or why not?

There are two primary parts to Medicare: Hospital Insurance (HI), also known as Part A, and Supplementary Medical insurance (SMI), also known as Part B. Part A covers intensive medical and psychiatric services. A third part of Medicare, which is optional, is called Part C, also called Medicare+Choice. A summary of each of these parts is provided in Table 12-1.

A **benefit period** is the time frame used to determine benefits. A benefit period begins when the patient is admitted to the hospital and ends when there has been a break of at least 60 consecutive days since inpatient hospital or skilled nursing care was provided. A new benefit period begins with the next hospital admission.

Medicare Part A (Hospital Insurance or HI) coverage includes the cost of a semiprivate hospital room, meals, regular nursing services, operating and recovery room, intensive care, inpatient prescription drugs, laboratory tests, X-rays, psychiatric hospital, and inpatient rehabilitation. All other medically necessary services and supplies provided in the hospital are also completely covered. Luxury items, cosmetic surgery, vision care, private nursing, private rooms (unless necessary for medical reasons), and rentals of television and telephone are not included in coverage.

Coverage in a skilled nursing facility includes rehabilitation services and appliances (walkers, wheelchairs) in addition to those services normally covered for inpatient hospitalization. Home health services are also included in Part A of Medicare. Although there is no charge for these services, patients must pay 20% of the costs of all durable medical equipment. Finally, hospice care is covered by Medicare Part A. The respite periods covered for hospice care are meant to allow a break for the patient's caregiver.

Medicare Part B, also known as **Supplementary Medical Insurance (SMI)**, provides benefits available to individuals ages 65 and over with payment of a monthly premium. Part B (SMI) can be considered coverage for physician services provided in both hospital and nonhospital settings. Certain other nonphysician services are also provided, however, including tests, supplies, medications, and other medical costs not covered by HI (see Table 12-1). To be covered, all services must be either medically necessary or one of the prescribed preventive benefits.

TABLE 12-1
Structure of Medicare

Medicare Program	What It Covers	Conditions
PART A (HOSPITAL INSURANCE)	Inpatient hospitalization Insurance)	First 60 days free (after deductible) for each benefit period. Days 61–90 require copayment. 60 lifetime reserve days for medical hospital patients and 190 lifetime reserve dates for those requiring psychiatric hospitalization.
	Skilled nursing care	Follows within 30 days of hospitalization of 3 or more days and is medically necessary. First 20 days of benefit period are free, followed by a copayment for days 21–100 of each benefit period.
	Home health care	Up to 100 visits within 14 days of hospitalization. Patient must be homebound and require services on an intermittent or part-time basis.
	Hospice care	Two 90-day periods, an unlimited number of 60-day periods, and 5-day respite periods. Prescription coverage also included with copayments. Expectation is that patient will die within six months of beginning hospice care.
PART B (SUPPLEMENTAL MEDICAL INSURANCE)	Physicians' services	80% of the approved charge for most reasonable and necessary doctors' services, except routine checkups.
	Home health services	100% of the cost for up to 35 hours per week of skilled nursing and home health aide services. Skilled therapy services for the homebound who require skilled nursing or skilled therapy on a part-time or intermittent basis.
	Preventive services	Influenza and pneumonia shots, mammograms, pap smears, bone density measurement, colorectal cancer screening, and diabetes self-management.
	Durable medical equipment	80% of the approved charge for most reasonable and necessary medical equipment bought from Medicare-certified suppliers.
	Outpatient hospital services	80% of the actual charge, which is typically higher than the approved Medicare charge.
	Physical therapy services	80% of the approved charge for services provided by Medicare-certified independent physical therapists, up to a total of $1500 a year.
	Laboratory tests and X-rays	100% of the approved charge for many reasonable and necessary laboratory tests, and 80% of the approved charge for X-rays required for medical diagnosis.
	Mental health services	50% of the approved charge for most outpatient mental health services.
	Ambulance services	80% of the approved charge.
	Blood	80% of the approved charge for any additional blood after patient pays for the first three pints.
PART C	Medicare+Choice	Additional insurance through health maintenance organizations, preferred provider organizations, private fee-for-service plans, and a government-sponsored insurance plan.

A third part of Medicare, sometimes known as **Part C**, is the **Medicare+Choice program**, which was established by the Balanced Budget Act of 1997 (Public Law 105-33) and put into effect in 1998. Medicare beneficiaries who have both Part A and Part B can choose to get their benefits through a variety of risk-based plans including Health Maintenance Organizations (HMDs), Preferred Provider Organizations (PPOs), private fee-for-service plans, and a health insurance policy administered by the federal government. In 2004, this will change to Medicare Advantage with further changes in 2006. In addition to Medicare, supplemental insurance called **Medigap** or **Medicare SELECT** can be purchased through individual insurance plans or HMOs. These plans will also change in 2006.

Currently, many private insurance companies sell Medicare supplemental insurance policies, and similar coverage may be available to retirees through an employer- or union-provided group health plan. Other alternative supplemental insurance plans are available, associated in part with the Balanced Budget Act of 1997. These plans are intended for beneficiaries who need a comprehensive medical and social service delivery system. One of these, known as Programs of All-inclusive Care for the Elderly (PACE), provides an alternative to institutional care for persons 55 and over who require a nursing facility level of care and who meet the eligibility requirements for the program within each state. A Social HMO (S/HMO) is another option intended to provide comprehensive health benefits beyond those provided by Medicare, such as care coordination, prescription drug benefits, chronic care benefits covering short-term nursing home care, and a full range of home- and community-based services. Eyeglasses, hearing aids, and dental benefits may also be provided. Both of these programs are small but are expected to change as a result of the 2003 legislation.

Medicare has grown enormously since its inception. In 1966, Medicare covered 19.1 million people, a number that rose to over 40 million by 2001 (the large majority of whom were 65 and older). The total benefits paid out by Medicare totaled nearly $234.5 billion in 2001, or 12% of the total U.S. budget, (http://w3.access.gpo.gov/usbudget/fy2001/guide02. html) (http://cms.hhs.gov/statistics/nhe/historical/t4.asp). Nursing homes received $11.6 billion dollars from Medicare in 2001 (http://cms. hhs.gov/statistics/nhe/historical/t7.asp) (CMS, 2003). As can be seen in Fig. 12.3, the percentage of the gross national product spent on Medicare is projected roughly to triple during the next 70 years.

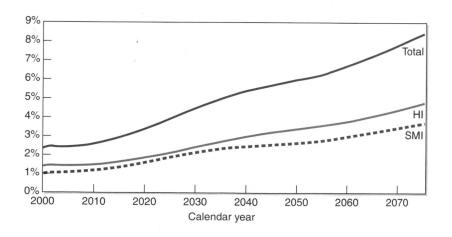

FIGURE 12.3

Percentage of Gross National Product Spending on Medicare, 2000–2070

Source: Centers for Medicare & Medicaid Services, 2003.

Medicaid

Title XIX of the Social Security Act of 1965, known as **Medicaid**, is a federal and state matching entitlement program that pays for medical assistance for certain individuals and families with low incomes and resources. Initially, Medicaid was formulated as a medical care extension of federally funded programs providing income assistance for the poor, with an emphasis on dependent children and their mothers, the disabled, and the over-65 population. Eligibility for Medicaid has expanded, however, and now is available to a larger number of low-income pregnant women, poor children, and some Medicare beneficiaries who are not eligible for any cash assistance program. Changes in legislation have also focused on increased access, better quality of care, specific benefits, enhanced outreach programs, and fewer limits on services. Another change is the addition of managed care as an alternative means of providing health services (Waid, 1998).

Medicaid provides assistance for a wide range of medical services for those who fall in the category for their state of residence of being in need. For older adults, these services include inpatient and outpatient hospital services, physician services, nursing facility services, home health care for persons eligible for skilled nursing services, laboratory and X-ray services, prescribed drugs and prosthetic devices, optometrist services and eyeglasses, rehabilitation and physical therapy services, and home and community-based care to cover certain chronic impairments.

Individuals covered by Medicare who are not otherwise "poor" may nevertheless require Medicaid when their benefits have run out and they cannot afford to pay their medical expenses. Many states have a "medically needy" program for such individuals, who have too much income to qualify as categorically needy. This program allows them to "spend down" to the point at which they are eligible for Medicaid by paying medical expenses to offset their excess income. Medicaid then pays the remaining portion of their medical bills by providing services and supplies that are available under their state's Medicaid program. Services that are covered by both programs will be paid first by Medicare and the difference by Medicaid, up to the state's payment limit. Medicaid also covers additional services (e.g., nursing facility care beyond the 100-day limit covered by Medicare, prescription drugs, eyeglasses, and hearing aids).

Medicaid is the largest source of funding for medical and health-related services for the poor. In 2001, it provided health care assistance to more than 34 million people, at a cost of $228 billion. Nursing homes received $47 billion from Medicaid in 2001 (http://cms.hhs.gov/statistics/nhe/historical/t7.asp). Together, Medicare and Medicaid financed $443 billion in health care services in 2001, which was 36% of the nation's total health care bill (private and public funding combined) and 83% of all public spending on health care (http://cms.hhs.gov/statistics/nhe/historical/t4.asp).

PSYCHOLOGICAL ISSUES IN LONG-TERM CARE

For many years, researchers in the area of institutionalization and aging have denounced the practices of nursing home administrators for their lack of attention to the psychosocial needs of residents, including needs for autonomy and self-determination. In the late 1980s, evidence from studies examining the effects of simple interventions pointed to the physical and mental health benefits associated with even a small amount of personal control over the institutional environment (Rodin, 1986) In one of the classic studies in the field, it was found that giving residents a houseplant to care for significantly improved functioning on a variety of measures, including morbidity and mortality (Langer & Rodin, 1976).

With OBRA 1987, and the subsequent investigations of the quality of nursing home care, attention turned once again to the psychosocial needs of residents and strategies that can be implemented to enhance the quality of life in nursing homes. Unfortunately, change is slow to come about, and by the mid-1990s, researchers concluded that nursing homes in the United States had not made significant changes in the freedom of choice afforded to residents on a day-to-day basis (Kane, Caplan, Urv-Wong, Freeman, Aroskar, et al., 1997). In terms of the rhythm of life in the average nursing home, although deficiencies in activities were cited by only 8% of nursing homes, there still remains a good deal of room for improvement. A study of the daily life of residents conducted in 2002 revealed that, as was the case in the 1960s, residents spend almost two-thirds of the time in their rooms doing nothing (Ice, 2002). For many residents, there is simply not enough to do in the average nursing home (Martin, Hancock, Richardson, Simmons, Katona, et al., 2002).

Models of Adaptation

Theoretical models attempting to provide insight into the adaptation of the individual to the institutional environment of a long-term care facility began to develop in the 1970s with the increasing attention in gerontology on ecological approaches to the aging process. Of particular concern in an applied sense are the avoidable disturbances in behavior that can be prevented by appropriate attention to the needs of the individual within the particular setting.

A seemingly irresolvable problem, however, in the provision of institutional care is that it is necessary to attempt to satisfy the needs of the "average" resident, and as is true for many averages, the average resident is a hypothetical construct. To put this in very concrete terms, consider the issue of temperature control. For some residents, an ambient temperature of 68 degrees is extremely pleasant, but for others, 76 is the ideal place to set the thermostat. An institution must regulate the temperature of the entire building, however. In attempting to please the average resident, the administrator would need to adjust the temperature to the mean of these two numbers, which would be 72. Neither resident will find this temperature to be a comfortable one, yet on the "average" it is the correct level. Researchers are continuing to test new ways of quantifying the physical environment, a process that ultimately may translate into more effective ways to maximize the comfort levels of residents (Sloane, Mitchell, Weisman, Zimmerman, Foley, et al., 2002).

Clearly, it is unrealistic to expect any single model to integrate these multiple and complex factors. Perhaps for this reason, empirical interest in the institutionalization process has dwindled somewhat from the 1970s, when several teams of researchers were actively investigating environmental models and aging. However, one of these models offers some useful concepts for predicting how well people will adapt to an institutional setting. This model, the **competence-press model** (Lawton & Nahemow, 1973), predicts an optimal level of adjustment that institutionalized persons will experience on the basis of their levels of competence (physical and psychological) compared to the demands or "press" of the environment. As shown in Fig. 12.4, there is a funnel-shaped relationship between competence and press according to this model. In the middle of the funnel is optimal adjustment, which occurs

BIOPSYCHOSOCIAL PERSPECTIVE

The issue of developing a treatment setting that will meet the needs of individuals while at the same time reaching the hypothetical "average" is one that is appropriately viewed from a biopsychosocial perspective. From a biological point of view, it is necessary to consider differences in physiological aging processes that contribute to the temperature preferences just in this chapter. Perhaps more serious, in terms of health implications, are physiological factors that affect mobility, resistance to infection, cognitive functioning, and the host of processes that contribute to overall levels of physical functioning. People within a single institution, although they are infirm to a certain degree, will differ in the exact degree of infirmity they have, which affects their ability to carry out daily living tasks and adapt to new situations. Furthermore, and of great importance to many people, there are huge differences in food taste preferences based, in part, on physical factors and in part on cultural background.

From a psychological point of view, individuals living under the same roof of an institutional setting vary in their ability to interact with others; their levels of depression, anxiety, and clarity of thinking; and personal dispositions. They also vary in the way they prefer to be treated by staff and in whether they resent or demand a certain degree of autonomy and independence. Some like to be called "honey," and some become infuriated by what they regard as patronizing treatment. The extent to which they have experienced institutional life will to a certain extent affect their attitudes toward the present setting. Long-term residents of psychiatric facilities, for example, may have learned to turn a blind eye to certain kinds of treatment simply because they have unfortunately become immune to it. There are also, of course, large variations in cognitive abilities among residents of the same institution, ranging from people with advanced cases of Alzheimer's disease to those whose illnesses are primarily physical.

In the area of social processes, differences among residents may be vast, contributing to significant adjustment difficulties. First, cultural differences may exist between staff and residents. Apart from the fact that these groups represent different subcultures within the institution, differences in social class, ethnicity, age, and experiences in the world outside the institution can interfere with their ability to establish a common ground as a basis for positive relationships. Differences may also exist among residents of varying cultural backgrounds. The social world of the family constitutes yet another important group in a long-term care facility. Family members have their own history of relationships with the patients and their own expectations about what should happen in the nursing home to facilitate the adjustment of their relatives. Finally, social factors in a larger sense may affect all members of the institutional environment. Residents, staff, and the administrators of long-term care settings are influenced in important ways by changes made at the level of federal and state governments that affect funding.

when there is an approximate match between an individual's abilities and the environment's demands. A small degree of discrepancy is acceptable, but when the mismatch goes outside this range, the individual will experience negative affect and develop maladaptive behaviors. For example, the intellectually competent older resident (high competence) will do well in a setting in which autonomous decisions are expected (high press), but a person with a significant cognitive impairment will adapt maximally when the environment is very structured (low press).

By considering the interaction between the individual and the environment of the institution, the competence-press model avoids making sweeping generalizations about whether institutions should attempt to provide either high levels or low levels of stimulation and demands. The model also allows room for multiple dimensions

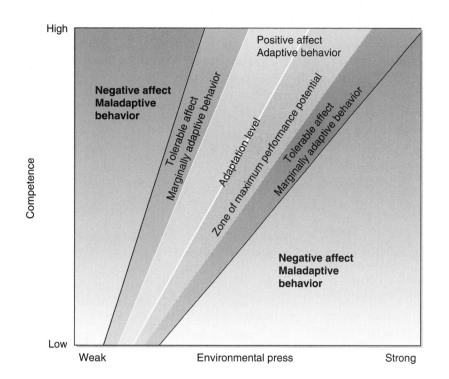

High

Low

Weak   Environmental press   Strong

Competence

Negative affect
Maladaptive
behavior

Tolerable affect
Marginally adaptive behavior

Adaptation level

Positive affect
Adaptive behavior

Zone of maximum performance potential

Tolerable affect
Marginally adaptive behavior

Negative affect
Maladaptive
behavior

<u>FIGURE 12.4</u>

Competence-Press Model of Environmental Adaptation

Source: Lawton & Nahemow, 1973.

of competence and press to be considered when evaluating older adults (Lichtenburg, MacNeill, Lysack, Adam, & Neufeld, 2003). Competence may be defined in terms of physiological or psychological characteristics. The social factors in this model, namely, the level of press in the environment, may also be conceptualized among multiple dimensions, ranging from the extent to which the individual is expected to make adaptations to a different cultural milieu within the institution. Financial pressure may also be seen as a form of press, as individuals with fewer economic resources have fewer alternatives when they are not satisfied with their placement.

"What do you think?"	**12-4**

How does the competence-press model respond to individual differences among residents?

Suggestions for Improving Institutional Care

The implications of the competence-press model are that the needs of individuals should be met to the extent possible within the institutional setting. Innovations in nursing home care are being developed with this as a goal. For example, bathing, a situation that can be distressing when conducted in a way that embarrasses or exposes the resident, can be treated in a more individualized manner, making it a less aversive experience (Camp, Cohen-Mansfield, & Capezuti, 2002). Nurses' aides, who manage many of the daily living activities of residents, can be taught to use behavioral methods to help residents maintain self-care and, hence, independence (Burgio, Stevens, Burgio, Roth, Paul, et al., 2002). Such interventions can also benefit staff–resident relationships. Since satisfaction with treatment by staff is such a significant component of satisfaction with the institution (Chou, Boldy, & Lee, 2002), any intervention that maximizes positive interactions between staff and residents is bound to have a favorable impact on the sense of well-being experienced by residents (Chou et al., 2002).

New models for nursing home design attempt to break up the monotony of most settings to create more of a feel of a community or neighborhood. Nursing stations are removed from view, allowing residents and staff to share lounges. Hallways have alcoves that can store medicine carts and nursing stations. Other models of change stress new ways of allocating staff to meeting the care needs of residents. For example, rather than basing staff assignments on the completion of specific tasks for all residents (bathing, changing dressings, administering medications), staff are assigned to meet all the needs of a particular group of residents. Although such a system increases the staffing requirements, institutions using this system reduced their overall expenses because of reductions in the areas of restraints and antipsychotic medications. Hospitalization rates, staff turnover, and success in rehabilitation also improved, as did the satisfaction that residents expressed about their care (IOM). Another improvement involves the use of a team approach to providing mental health services. When staff work as a multidisciplinary team, residents receive better services; at the same time, staff are more informed and perform more effectively in their jobs (Bartels, Moak, & Dums, 2002).

The concerns of institutionalized older adults, particularly those with psychological disorders, are of great importance within the fields of gerontology, clinical geropsychology, and geriatric psychiatry. The dignity and self-respect of the resident, which is fortunately now being regulated by state and federal certification standards, can best be addressed by multidimensional approaches that take into account personal and contextual factors. Interventions based on these approaches will ultimately lead to a higher quality of life for those who must spend their last days or months in the care of another.

SUMMARY

1. A wide range of treatment sites are available that are specifically designed for older adults such as nursing homes and residential care facilities. The percentage of older adults in these treatment sites with cognitive deficits is relatively high. Increasing attention is being given to home health care. Other residential sites include special housing that is designed for older adults. The rights of nursing home residents became protected with passage of the Nursing Home Reform Act in 1987. Since passage of this legislation, complaints about nursing home care have decreased. However, care in nursing homes is an area that still needs continued monitoring, as was evident by the findings obtained in the 2002 General Accounting Office report on nursing home abuse.

2. Medicare is designed to provide hospital insurance and supplemental medical insurance. Other forms of insurance attached to Medicare are becoming increasingly available to older adults. Medicaid is intended to reduce the burden of health care costs among those who are in need of help in payment for medical services, but individuals receiving this assistance must "spend down" to eliminate their assets. The cost of health care assistance through these programs amounted to $443 billion in health care services in 2001. This amount was more than one-third of the nation's total health care bill and almost three-quarters of all public spending on health care.

3. Psychological issues in long-term care focus on the provision of an adequate environment that will maximally meet the needs of residents. The competence-press model proposes an ideal relationship between how demanding an environment is and the abilities of the resident to meet those demands.

GLOSSARY

Assisted living: living arrangement in which older persons live independently in their own apartment within an assisted living complex.

Benefit period: time frame within Medicare used to determine benefits.

Competence-press model: proposal that there is an optimal level of adjustment which institutionalized persons will experience on the basis of their levels of competence compared to the demands or "press" of the environment.

Continuing care retirement community (CCRC): a housing community that provides different levels of care based on the residents' needs.

Day care centers: form of community treatment in which individuals receive supervised meals and activities on a daily basis.

Geriatric continuing day treatment: program in which clients attend a day treatment program three days a week but are encouraged to live independently during the remaining days of the week.

Geriatric partial hospital: treatment site in which daily outpatient therapy is provided with intensive, structured multidisciplinary services to older persons who have recently been discharged from a psychiatric hospital.

Home health services: services provided to older adults who are ill or disabled but are able to maintain an independent life in the community.

Intermediate care facility: treatment site in which health-related services are provided to individuals who do not require hospital or skilled nursing facility care but do require institutional care above the level of room and board.

Medicaid: a federal and state matching entitlement program that pays for medical assistance for certain individuals and families with low incomes and resources.

Medicare: Title XVIII of the Social Security Act, entitled Health Insurance for the Aged and Disabled.

Medicare Part A (Hospital Insurance or HI): coverage of inpatient hospitalization and related services.

Medicare Part B (Supplementary Medical Insurance (SMI): provision of medical benefits to individuals age 65 and over with payment of a monthly premium.

Medicare Part C (Medicare+Choice program): additional medical insurance available for purchase through Medicare.

Medigap or Medicare SELECT: supplemental insurance that can be purchased through individual insurance plans or HMOs.

Nursing home: a residence that provides a room, meals, skilled nursing and rehabilitative care, medical services, and protective supervision.

Nursing Home Reform Act: U.S. federal legislation passed in 1987, which mandated that facilities must meet physical standards, provide adequate professional staffing and services, and maintain policies governing the administrative and medical procedures of the nursing facility.

Residential care facility: treatment site that provides 24-hour supportive care services and supervision to individuals not requiring skilled nursing care.

Skilled nursing facility: treatment site that provides the most intensive nursing care available outside of a hospital.

Subsidized senior housing: form of housing provided for individuals with low to moderate incomes.

Chapter Thirteen

Death and Dying

> *"Because I could not stop for death—He kindly stopped for me."*
> Emily Dickinson
> 1830–1886

For many people, the concept of death is as fascinating as it is frightening. By definition, it remains the great unknown; even those individuals who have had so-called near-death experiences cannot claim with certainty that what happened to them is an accurate prediction of what is to come in the future.

Younger people may not give their own death much thought, as long as they are in good health. However, those who live until the years of later adulthood may find themselves prone to consider their mortality on a more frequent basis. Even if they do not give attention to the existential questions of their own mortality, they are faced with the need to make practical arrangements such as planning the funeral or finalizing the will. Perhaps what most people wish for is to live as long as possible in as healthy a state as possible and to experience a death that will be quick and relatively painless. This concept is one we will return to at several points in this and the next chapter. Another theme relating to death is the desire to leave something of oneself behind and to have made an impact on other people's lives.

As we shall see many times throughout this chapter, death has a social meaning as well as a personal meaning to the individual. For example, after a person's death, the meaning of that death shifts from something that was thought about by the individual to something that is thought about by others. When a person dies prematurely, for example, for many years to come the person may be thought of in terms of that early death, particularly when the death is due to sudden illness or an accident. The meaning that death gives to the life that was lived is another dimension to an already very complicated and multifaceted process.

Kurt Cobain, lead singer of the revolutionary rock band of the early 1990s, Nirvana. Tragically, Cobain died of a self-inflicted gunshot wound in 1994. Although he will be remembered for his music, he is also remembered for the tragic way in which he died.

TECHNICAL PERSPECTIVES ON DEATH

From a medical and legal perspective, the term **death** is defined as the point when there is irreversible cessation of circulatory and respiratory functions, or when all structures of the brain have ceased to function (President's Commission for Study of Ethical Problems in Medicine and Biomedical and Behavioral Research, 1981).

Determination of the point of death has become more complicated over the course of the past three decades, however, since the advent of intensive care. It is possible to keep a person "alive" almost indefinitely on life support systems such as artificial respirators and heart pumps. The term **dying** refers to the period during which the organism loses its vitality.

The popular term "brain dead" refers to individuals who are in a so-called **persistent vegetative state**. The subcortical areas of the brain remain intact and therefore are able to regulate basic bodily functions, including sleep–wake cycles, but the individual lacks conscious awareness. One problem with the 1981 definition of death is that it does not include people with intact brain stem functioning whose organs may be suitable for transplantation (Keogh & Akhtar, 1999; Price, 1997). Therefore, an alternative definition was proposed to suggest that death is not a single event but a chain of events or processes in which different aspects of brain functioning cease at different times (Halevy & Brody, 1993). Taking this point of view into account, however, physicians would still prefer that for practical purposes death be viewed as meeting a single set of social, legal, and scientifically acceptable criteria (Field, Cassel, & Committee on Care at the End of Life, 1997).

Medical Aspects of Death

Although the death experience varies from person to person, there are some commonalities in the physical changes shown by a person who will die within a few hours or days. The symptoms that death is imminent include being asleep most of the time, being disoriented, breathing irregularly, and having visual and auditory hallucinations, decreased ability to see, diminished production of urine, mottled skin, cool hands and feet, an overly warm trunk, and excessive secretions of bodily fluids (Gavrin &

Chapman, 1995). An older adult who is close to death is likely to be unable to walk or eat, have difficulty recognizing family members, be in constant pain, and feel that breathing is difficult. A common syndrome observed at the end of life is the **anorexia-cachexia syndrome**, which involves a loss of appetite (anorexia) and atrophy of muscle mass (cachexia). The majority of cancer patients experience cachexia, and it is also found commonly in patients who have AIDS and dementia. In addition to the symptoms already mentioned, patients who are dying are likely to experience nausea, difficulty swallowing, bowel problems, dry mouth, and the accumulation of liquid in the abdomen, which leads to bloating. Anxiety, depression, confusion, and dementia are also common psychological symptoms experienced at the end of life (Field et al., 1997).

Obviously, the symptoms experienced by dying individuals involve pain and suffering, not only for the patients themselves but also indirectly for their family members. However, those who work with the dying observe that against this backdrop, the final period of life can also involve emotional and spiritual growth (Field et al., 1997). As will be seen later, the notion of "acceptance" as the final stage of dying implies an ability to transcend these painful physical symptoms.

The cause of an individual's death must be verified by a coroner or medical examiner, who must code the cause or causes of death, either through external examination or an autopsy. The cause of death information must then be recorded on a death certificate. The coding system in use throughout the world is the World Health Organization International Classification of Diseases, Tenth Revision (ICD-10), which replaced the ICD-9 in 1999.

In many cases, the cause of death may be established on the basis of the individual's symptoms prior to death, particularly if the

death occurred while the individual was under medical supervision. However, in other cases, the cause of death can only be performed by autopsy, a medical procedure in which the body is opened and the internal organs and structures are examined. Laboratory tests may also be performed to determine the conditions present in the body prior to death. An autopsy may be performed for research or educational purposes if the pathologist wishes to relate specific symptoms present in life to conditions that can only be determined after death. Death from Alzheimer's disease is one case in which an autopsy may be performed for this reason. Permission of the next of kin is needed both to perform the autopsy and to determine what materials, if any, are to be retained from the body. Variants of these procedures may need to be employed if the death occurred due to an accident involving multiple fatalities or if there was a disaster involving hundreds or thousands of deaths.

A special type of autopsy, known as the medicolegal autopsy, is conducted under conditions such as when the death was due to homicide, suicide, or accident. This type of autopsy may also be used when a person in previously good health has died suddenly with no apparent cause, or in cases of poisoning, employment-related causes, or adverse medical treatment. Such autopsies are also conducted when the deceased was a public official or when the body is to be cremated or buried at sea (Randall, Fierro, & Froede, 1998). In a medicolegal autopsy, special procedures are used to evaluate assault or trauma on the deceased prior to death (such as rape) and fatal injury through gunshot wounds or insect bites.

Mortality Facts and Figures

Although based on statistics derived from death, **mortality data** provide a fascinating picture of the factors that influence the course of human life from birth through advanced old age. In some ways, mortality can be regarded as the ultimate dependent variable in the study of physical and behavioral aspects of health. Mortality data include both death rates and causes of death, and they are often broken down according to age, sex, race, and geographic area. In the majority of cases, death statistics provide clear numbers that indicate the outcomes of particular environmental conditions or disease processes. However, mortality data are not always 100% clear. There may be some question about the validity of cause of death information as well as debate about the point at which death occurs, as in the case of people who have been on life support machines for prolonged periods.

Mortality rates are calculated based on deaths per 100,000 estimated population in a specified group of people. **Age-specific death rates**, then, are the number of deaths per 100,000 of the particular age group (such as 25–34). **Age-adjusted death rates** are used to compare relative mortality risk across groups and over time. Because death rates are higher in increasingly older groups, this factor must be taken into account when describing deaths due to particular diseases or overall death rates for given years. The age-adjusted death rate is calculated by obtaining the weighted averages of the **age-specific death rates**, with the weights reflecting the proportion of individuals in that age group in the population. In this way, the average age-adjusted death rate has taken into account the fact that, although older groups have higher death rates, they are also less prevalent in the population. For example, in 2001 the death rate for individuals 85 years and older was 15,133.8 per 100,000 in the population (nearly three times the rate for those 75–84). However, people in the 85 and older age group are only 1.5% of the U.S. population. By correcting the high death rate in the over-85 age

group for their small representation in the population, death rates for the entire population will not be overestimated.

Improvements in public health are measured in terms of age-adjusted mortality rates, such that the lower this rate, the healthier is the population. Within this context, it is considered desirable that not only will people live to be older before they die, but that they will experience less disability prior to their death. This concept, referred to as **compression of morbidity**, appears to be occurring within the U.S. population as a whole (Manton, Corder, & Stallard, 1997). Consistent with the preventive theme of this book, healthy lifestyles were found in one 12-year longitudinal study to be related to a shorter period of disability prior to death. At the start of the study, participants were divided into three groups on the basis of their lifestyles. The risk-factor–free group (no smoking, high physical activity, normal weight) maintained close to zero disability scores near zero for over a decade prior to their death. The groups with two or more unhealthy factors had higher levels of disability, with large increases in the year and a half before their death. Those with moderate risk were able to remain relatively healthy until just three months prior to their death (Hubert, Bloch, Oehlert, & Fries, 2002).

Along similar lines as the compression of morbidity notion, it would be considered a measure of a population's health to have relatively low age-specific death rates until the point is reached which represents the limit to the human life span, now thought of as about age 120 years. It would also be desirable for these rates to be consistent across race, sex, and socioeconomic groups. To the extent that there are variations according to these factors, a population would be considered to have inequities in conditions that foster adequate disease prevention and health care.

BIOPSYCHOSOCIAL PERSPECTIVE

There is a well-established relationship between social status and mortality (Adler, Boyce, Chesney, Cohen, Folkman, et al., 1994). It has been known since the mid-nineteenth century that men in laboring and trade occupations have higher death rates than those of the professional class (Macintyre, 1997). People in lower socioeconomic classes are also more likely to suffer from communicable diseases, exposure to lead, and work-related injuries (Pamuk, Makuc, Heck, Reuben, & Lochner, 1998). Not only the level of occupation but the pattern of jobs held throughout adulthood is related to mortality rates. The risk of mortality is lower in men who move up from manual to professional or managerial level occupations (House, Kessler, Herzog, & Mero, 1990; Moore & Hayward, 1990). Furthermore, men who hold a string of unrelated jobs have higher rates of early mortality than those with stable career progressions (Pavalko, Elder, & Clipp, 1993).

Although at one time the disparity in death rates was considered to be due to poorer sanitation, nutrition, and housing, current explanations focus on psychosocial factors as well. Stress is an important part of this equation. Workers in jobs who lack control over the pace and direction of what they do with their time (as is true in an assembly-line or migrant farming job) are at higher risk of dying from cardiovascular disease. In a 25-year followup study of over 12,500 male workers (aged 25 to 74), it was found that even being exposed to five years of assembly-line work increased the risk of dying from heart disease. Workers who participated in this type of work for the full period of the study had an 83% higher mortality risk than would be expected on the basis of their age (Johnson, Stewart, Hall, Fredlund, & Theorell, 1996).

Income is also related to mortality throughout adulthood. For example, 45-year-olds with the highest incomes can expect to live three to seven years longer than those with the lowest incomes. An eight-year followup of over 3600 adults showed that people from the low- and moderate-income levels had a higher rate of mortality than those from the more affluent sectors of society. This finding held even when controlling for differences among the income groups in health risk behaviors as well as age, sex, race, urbanicity, and education (Lantz, House, Lepkowski, Williams, Mero, et al., 1998). It is known that income is related to cigarette smoking prevalence. Adults with incomes below the poverty level are almost twice as likely to smoke as are men in the highest income groups (Schoenborn, Vickerie, & Barnes, 2003).

However, differences between income groups in health risk behaviors are not sufficient to explain differences in mortality rates. As observed in the Lantz et al. study, adults in the lowest income category were more than three times as likely to die during the followup period of the study than those in the highest income group. Rather than look toward explanations of social class and income differences in mortality as a function of personal choices made by individuals to control their health, these researchers suggest that the influences are far more pervasive, relating to lifelong exposure to social inequality. Such inequality incorporates a host of factors including exposure to environmental health hazards, inequalities in health care, lack of social support, loss of a sense of mastery and control, chronic exposure to discrimination, and an impoverished childhood. Rather than focus on changing behaviors at the level of the individual, more widespread changes are necessary to reduce inequities in the social structure.

In 2001, there were 2,416,425 deaths in the United States, which is translated into a crude death rate of 848.5 per 100,000 population. This number is substantially lower than the death rate in 1900, which was about 1720 per 100,000 (Arias, Anderson, Kung, Murphy, & Kochanek, 2003). As shown in Fig. 13.1, since 1930 age-adjusted mortality has dropped to a rate that is about 16% lower than that of 1980. Although death rates are decreasing, discrepancies exist within specific subgroups. In the case of gender, women have lower mortality rates than men. The age-adjusted mortality rate in 2001 was 1029.1 for males and 8721.8 for females. There are also disparities in mortality rates between whites (836.5) and blacks (1101.2), which translates into a mortality rate that is 1.3 times higher for blacks, meaning that the average risk for the black population is 33% higher than for whites.

There are significant variations in death rates by marital status and education, with marriage and higher levels of education serving a protective function (Cooper, Harris, & McGready, 2002). Marital status is related to mortality rate such that those who are never married have nearly twice the age-adjusted rate of death compared to those who were ever married. This disparity between the never married and those who have been married is greater in males than in females. Educational status is also related to mortality rate, as can be seen in Fig. 13.2. At all age groups, those with a college education or better have lower mortality rates.

Mortality rates throughout the world declined steadily throughout the twentieth century, beginning in European countries and eventually spreading to other continents. Improvements in nutrition, sanitation, and water supply associated with higher income levels are regarded as major reasons for the decline in mortality rates, but improvements in health care are also significant factors. Exceptions to this trend may be found in the parts of Africa affected by AIDS and among adult males in central and eastern Europe. In general, however, over 4 out of 10 deaths in developing countries are due to infectious diseases. In developed countries, almost half the deaths that occur are due to diseases of the circulatory system (American Heart Association, 2003). Mortality rates are disproportionately high among the poor in countries throughout the world as well as within the United States. Across all countries studied by the World Health Organization, the poor are over four times more likely to die between the ages of 15 and 59 as the nonpoor.

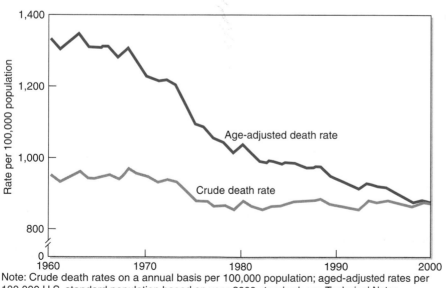

FIGURE 13.1

Crude and Age-Adjusted Death Rates: United States, 1960–2000

Note: Crude death rates on a annual basis per 100,000 population; aged-adjusted rates per 100,000 U.S. standard population based on year 2000 standard; see Technical Notes.

Source: Minino et al., 2002.

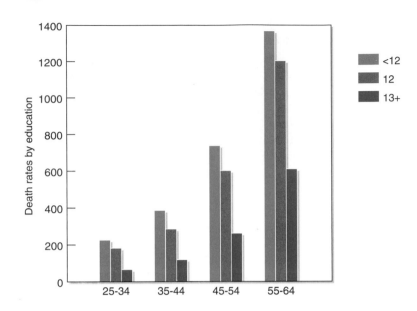

Source: Minino et al., 2002.

FIGURE 13.2
Death Rates by Education

CULTURAL PERSPECTIVES

From the biological and medical perspectives, death is an event that can be defined entirely by a set of physical changes within the body's cells. By contrast, from a sociocultural perspective, the important features of death are the interpretations that a society or culture places on the processes through which life ends. Awareness of the end of life is a uniquely (so we think) human characteristic, as is the ability to endow this event with meaning. That meaning, in turn, is seen as a social creation that reflects the prevailing philosophy, economics, and family structure of a culture. According to the sociocultural perspective, people learn the social meaning of death from the language, arts, and death-related rituals of their cultures. A culture's **death ethos**, or prevailing philosophy of death, can be inferred from funeral rituals, treatment of those who are dying, belief in the presence of ghosts, belief in an afterlife, the extent to which death topics are taboo, the language used to describe death (through euphemisms such as "passed away"), and the representation of death in the arts. Death may be viewed as sacred or profane, as an unwanted extinction of life or a welcome release from worldly existence (Atchley, 2000).

Throughout the course of Western history, remarkable alterations in cultural meanings and rituals have been attached to the process of death and to the disposition of dead bodies. Perhaps the most well known of all death rituals were those practiced by the ancient Egyptians. They believed that a new, eternal life awaited the dead and that the body had to be preserved through mummification in order to make it the permanent home for the spirit of the deceased. The mummies were buried in elaborate tombs, where they were decorated and surrounded by valued possessions. Family members would visit the tombs to bring offers of food that would sustain the dead in the afterlife. It was once thought that only the kings and wealthy nobles were mummified, but it is now known that even ordinary people preserved their dead, though in a humbler manner than was true of nobility. Furthermore, although the Egyptian mummies are the most well-known, they were by no means the only ones to exist, as was found in an investigation of the mummies in the Andean mountains of Peru.

Cultural views within Western society toward death and the dead have undergone many shifts from ancient times to the present (Aries, 1974, 1981). For many centuries until the early Middle Ages, death was considered "tame," accepted as a natural part of life, and neither to be avoided nor exalted. Beginning in the Middle Ages, however, death began to be viewed as an end to the self, as people examined its personal meaning. The view of death as a time of final reckoning with God began to evolve, and people began to attach significance to personal tombs and epitaphs. The rise of scientific thinking and models led, in the 1700s, to a view of death as remote, as a punishment

or break with life, to be avoided or denied. By the 1800s, as part of the rise of romanticism, death became glorified, and it was considered noble to die for a cause (the "beautiful death"), as many people had in the revolutions in America and Europe. However, entry into the twentieth century brought the period known as "invisible death," involving the denial of death and medicalization of the dying process. People put their faith in science, which in turn took control over the dying individual. Rather than being a shared experience with others, death and mourning became private. In the large scheme of the universe of scientific discoveries, the death of an individual began to be seen as inconsequential.

Contemporary American attitudes toward death reflect this history but are also shaped by and reflect a complex mixture of media images, religious and cultural traditions, and health care practices. The media treatment of death is often sensationalistic, as shown in cases when many people die at once in a bombing, mass murder,

Although mummies are associated with death rites of ancient Egypt, they exist in other parts of the world. This is the frozen mummy known as the "Ice Princess," found in Peru in 1995. Hundreds of other mummies were discovered buried in stone in the Andean highlands dating back over 500 years.

plane crash, or earthquake. In some cases, treatment of news stories involving massive loss of life, as occurred with the deaths due to the terrorist attacks on the World Trade Center on September 11, 2001, attempts to bring the losses to human proportions by focusing on the families of those who died. Similarly, the death of one famous person in a fatal accident may preoccupy the American or European media for weeks, as was the case in the deaths of Princess Diana and John F. Kennedy, Jr. Horror stories may also be presented in the media coverage of people with terminal illness. These include news items or fictional portrayals of people who live in a comatose state for years on life support. Others are of people whose terminal care brings a family to the brink of poverty because their health insurance does not cover hospital costs. Death may also be presented in sentimentalized ways as when a loving wife and mother is depicted as being torn from her husband and children or when two young lovers are parted in an untimely way. These images represent the worst fears that people have about their own death—that it will come tragically and prematurely or that it will follow a long, agonizing, painful, and expensive process.

The religious background of many Americans provides some comfort in the face of these frightening images, through teachings that emphasize the existence of an afterlife and the belief that human events occur because of some higher purpose. The loss of a loved one, particularly when it occurs "prematurely" (i.e., before old age), may be seen as a test of one's faith. The grieving comfort themselves with the knowledge that they will be reunited in heaven with the deceased where they will spend eternity together. Bereaved individuals may also seek solace in the belief or perception that they can sense the presence of departed loved ones. Another belief in which people may find comfort is that death is a blessed relief from a world

of trouble and pain. As the bereaved or terminally ill attempt to come to grips with the ending of a life, they rely on these beliefs to make sense out of the death or achieve some kind of understanding of its meaning.

Changes in health care interact with these cultural images, both in terms of how and where death occurs. Because the age of dying has increased from 1900 to the present, death has increasingly become associated with later life. At the same time, death has become institutionalized and "invisible" (Aries, 1974) as it has moved from the home to the hospital. People no longer are witness to the physical death of another, and therefore it is not as much a part of daily life as in years past (DeSpelder & Strickland, 1999). As death has become removed from the everyday world, it has acquired more fear and mystery. Furthermore, instead of developing their own personal meanings, people are at the mercy of whatever images of death are presented in the media.

Fear of death and dying within contemporary Western society is thought to be linked not only to changes in the timing and location of death but also to fear of aging and growing old. The desire to stop or slow the aging process is evident throughout advertisements of everything from wrinkle creams to exercise machines, and America is often thought of as a youth-oriented culture, despite the aging of the Baby Boomers. Cultural depictions of death seem inextricably linked to fear of loss of capacity, attractiveness, and social relevance. Both reflect an unwillingness, which is perhaps part of the American tradition, to accept the limits imposed by the biological facts of aging and death (Field et al., 1997). Individuals also fear the process of **social death**, through which they are treated as nonpersons by family or health care workers as they are left to spend their final months or years in the hospital or nursing home. Another perspective on fear of death is based on Terror Management Theory (Solomon, Greenberg, & Pyszcynski, 1991). According to this social-psychological perspective, people regard with panic and dread the thought of the finitude of their lives. They engage in defensive mechanisms to protect themselves from the anxiety and threats to self-esteem that this awareness produces.

Assess Yourself

Top Ten Funeral Tips

Are you aware of these suggestions regarding funeral costs? Assess your knowledge of funeral planning.

1. Talk about funerals with family members ahead of time.
   At the time of death, survivors may be vulnerable to the subtle ploys of the mortician to spend, spend, spend—"to show how much you care." If your plans are mentioned only in a will, the will may not be read until long after other arrangements have been made. Make sure your family knows what your wishes are.

2. Price shop by phone or in person.
   There are at least twice as many funeral homes in this country as can be supported by the death rate. Therefore, many fees include the waiting-around-until-you-die time . . . part-time work for full-time pay. That's not always the case, however, and price-shopping can save you thousands of dollars.
   To see if you'd be getting a reasonable deal, mentally calculate the actual time you think each funeral option takes. Then add an hour or two for behind-the-scenes work for each one. (Remember, too, that funeral homes have large property tax bills, 24-hour phone coverage, and expensive Yellow Pages ads.) Carefully total the cost for everything and then ask, "Will there be any other charges?" If you will be paying more than $100 per hour, you've got a high-priced mortuary. If the cost for services seems reasonable, be sure to check the cost for caskets (see next item). In the past, many mortuaries depended on a high markup for their profit.

3. Make a simple wood casket.
   As of July 19, 1994, it is illegal for a mortuary to charge a "handling fee" for bringing in an outside casket. Or choose a "minimum container" from the mortuary and drape it with attractive material of your own taste. If a funeral home charges much more than $400–$500 for a modest casket, it's a good bet it's taking a 300%, 400%, or 500% markup. That thought alone might be enough to decide on a simple but dignified "plain pine box."

4. Take a friend or clergy with you.
   Having someone who will help you resist subtle pressures to spend more than you want can be very supportive when you are faced with subtle manipulation.

5. Consider cremation.

   It costs a great deal less to ship cremated remains from one state to another. Cemetery space will probably cost less than the space needed for body burial. Or remains can be buried/scattered wherever you choose.

6. Plan a memorial service without the body present.

   In that case, there would be no need for embalming, a fancy casket, or expensive transporting of the body back and forth. Private family visitation and "good-byes" can occur in the hospital or home, before you call a funeral director. Use a church, park, or community center for the memorial service without attending funeral home staff. You can then comfortably consider using a low-cost funeral director from another community to transport the body directly to a crematory or cemetery, if the local prices are too high.

7. Consider body donation to a medical school.

   In some areas, there may be no cost to the family whatsoever. In other circumstances, the cost of transporting the body may be the only cost. Often—if you ask—cremated remains will be returned to the family after scientific study, usually within a year or two.

8. Remember that it is just a box-for-the-box.

   If you prefer body burial, ask for a "grave liner"—rather than a "coffin vault"—at a portion of the price. And again, be sure to shop around. The "outer burial container"—as the trade now refers to it—is quickly becoming a new way for morticians to increase their income and is an added burden on your funeral finances. With prices as much or more than caskets, remember that it will get quickly covered by the cemetery lawn.

9. Handle all arrangements without using a funeral director.

   This is permitted in 42 states, and families that have done so have found it loving and therapeutic. The book, *Caring for Your Own Dead*, tells what permits are required in each state, where and when to file them, plus a great deal of other practical information for families or church groups choosing this meaningful way to say goodby (see our online bookstore).

10. Join a memorial society.

    Many people have a contract with local mortuaries for discount services. Or some of the price-shopping may have been done for you already. There are reciprocal benefits if you move to or die in another state. Supporting a memorial society will help to keep this consumer information available for future generations, and the membership fee is modest.

The development of increasingly sophisticated medical technology has in many ways complicated these already complex issues. Physicians can now keep people alive under far less tenable circumstances than in the past, and they can restore life to a person who has, temporarily, died. Issues of organ and tissue transplants further cloud the boundary between life and death. Related trends in attitudes toward death emphasize the quality of the death experience and the fear of enduring a prolonged period of terminal decline. **Death with dignity**, the idea that death should not involve extreme physical dependency or loss of control of bodily functions, emerged from the desire of patients and their families to avoid a lengthy and protracted dying process (Humphrey, 1991). The next seemingly logical step to follow, initiated by Dr. Jack Kevorkian (Kevorkian, 1991), was to make it possible for a terminally ill patient to complete suicide, a process referred to as **physician-assisted suicide**. Similar in intent is euthanasia, which involves the direct killing of a patient by a physician who administers a lethal injection. Social movements that advocated these measures were instrumental in stimulating the medical community to establish guidelines and practices for the care of the terminally ill at the end of life (see below). However, in terms of cultural attitudes, they reflect the dread that many in our society feel about losing their ability to control this most important aspect of life.

THE DYING PROCESS

Death is an event that marks the end of the process of dying, the period during which an organism loses its viability. During the period of dying, the individual is thought to be likely to die within a few days to several months. People with terminal illnesses that last for years may not be thought of as "dying" because their deaths are not as predictable. Most discussions of dying refer to individuals whose deaths are expected to occur within a period of days to months, although individuals with life-threatening illnesses would also be considered in a sense as "dying" (Field et al., 1997).

FIGURE 13.3
Dying Trajectories

A. Sudden death from an unexpected cause

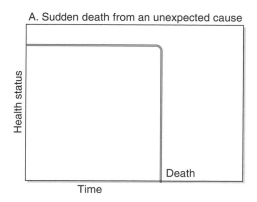

B. Steady decline from a progressive disease with a "terminal" phase

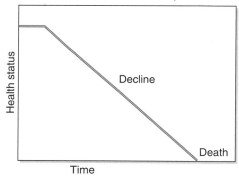

C. Advanced illness marked by slow decline with periodic crisis and "sudden" death

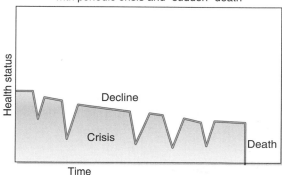

Source: Field & Cassel, and the Committee on Care at the End of Life, 1997.

There are many variations in the dying process, a concept captured by the term **dying trajectory**, or the rate of decline in functioning prior to death (Glaser & Strauss, 1968). There are two major features of a dying trajectory: duration and shape. Fig. 13.3 shows three possible such trajectories. Those who die suddenly are depicted by curve A, an unexpected and quick trajectory. These would be people with no prior knowledge of illness, as in a victim of sudden cardiac failure, or people who die in accidents. The second and third trajectories include individuals who have advance warning of a terminal illness and who experience a lingering period of loss of function. The steady downward trajectory shown in curve B would apply to people whose disease causes them to undergo a steady and predictable decline. This curve would apply to many people who die of cancer. In curve C are people whose trajectory takes a generally downward course that is marked by a series of crises. Eventually, their death occurs during a crisis related to their illness or to another fatal cause.

Other individuals may be at increased risk of dying, though technically they do not have a terminal disease. One set consists of individuals in their 80s or older who are in good health but have limited physical reserves. They may die from complications associated with an acute condition such as influenza or a broken hip due to a fall. In other cases, people whose organ systems are gradually deteriorating may slowly lose the ability to care for themselves while at the same time developing an illness such as renal failure or pneumonia that eventually causes them to die. The immediate cause of death may be the illness, but it has occurred against a backdrop of general loss of function.

Stages of Dying

Amid the growing institutionalization of death and the attempts by the medical establishment to prolong life, a small book published in 1969 was to alter permanently Western attitudes toward and treatment of the dying. This book, by Elisabeth Kübler-Ross (1969), called *On Death and Dying*, described five **stages of dying** considered to occur universally among terminally ill patients. These stages of dying have since become part of the cultural mystique surrounding the dying process, even as professionals critique both the specific stages and the notion of stages at all.

The five stages of dying, according to Kübler-Ross, are as follows. The first stage, *denial*, describes the patient's reaction to having been informed that he or she has a terminal illness. The individual simply refuses to accept the diagnosis. The second stage, *anger*, is the reaction the patient has to the news, which is now no longer denied. The individual feels cheated or robbed of the opportunity to live and is furious with the powers that are causing this to happen. In *bargaining*, the third stage, the patient attempts to strike a deal with God or whatever force is seen as responsible for the disease. Examples of bargaining would be offering to attend religious services on a regular basis if given the chance to live longer, if not recover. People in this stage may "ask" to be allowed to live until an important upcoming event such as the marriage of a child. Fourth comes *depression* and sense of loss, as the inevitability of the disease's progress is acknowledged. Finally, the individual reaches the fifth stage, *acceptance*, during which the finality of the disease is no longer fought or regretted. As death approaches, it is regarded as a natural end state and perhaps even a release from pain and suffering.

The critical point that Kübler-Ross attempted to make in her writing is that to reach acceptance of a fatal illness, the dying person must be allowed to talk openly with family members and health care workers. Rather than hide the diagnosis or pretend that

ROBERT KASTENBAUM, PROFESSOR EMERITUS,
HUGH DOWNS SCHOOL OF HUMAN COMMUNICATION,
ARIZONA STATE UNIVERSITY

What is most compelling to you about research in this field?

Why were we born to die? What meaning and comfort can we find in the dying process? How can we go on after a person at the center of our life has died? Why should we choose life over death when everything seems hopeless? These are questions that take us to the very edge of human understanding and confront us with some of the most difficult moments in our lives. It is a compelling experience to walk with the aged, the dying, the grieving, and the suicidal to that edge and perhaps learn a little that might prove useful to us all.

What do you see as the major challenges?

There are four persistent challenges: (a) trying to understand other people's realities without imposing our own hopes, fears, and assumptions; (b) making accurate and useful observations without violating privacy or having an undue influence on what is happening; (c) overcoming strongly entrenched barriers to communication about the personal side of death-related issues; (d) finding a balance between objectivity and compassion, and between individual experience and societal response. Researchers who have not faced their own mortality and grief are likely to suffer both in their person and in the quality of their work.

Where do you see this field headed in the next decade?

End-of-life decisions often have been made by professionals and health care systems. There is now an encouraging trend for individuals and families to have their say. Further research is needed to improve communication among patients, families, health care professionals, clergy, attorneys, and agency managers to provide the opportunity for informed choices and a realistic array of options. Studies are also starting to provide knowledge that can improve our theoretical understanding of the related processes of dying and grieving. A decade from now perhaps we will have relinquished unfounded assumptions and have more mature conceptual models to guide our understanding.

everything will be all right, those who interact with the dying individual need to give that person a chance to express the many emotions that surface, ranging from anger to depression. Recall that this book was written at the height of the death as "invisible" period, during which it was just as likely as not that a physician would not share the diagnosis of cancer with a patient and family.

Unfortunately, the original views of Kübler-Ross became distorted as the book's popularity grew. The five stages began to be interpreted as a series of steps that must be followed with each dying patient. If a patient refused to engage in *bargaining*, for instance, then it must mean something was wrong with the way that person was working through the stages. Critics of this approach pointed out that there could be many variations in the dying process that the five-stage model ignored. For example, not everyone would either live long enough or have the ability to reach acceptance. Furthermore, people could fluctuate in the order through which they progressed through the stages. Another point is that Kübler-Ross was writing about relatively young patients, and denial may very well have been a natural reaction to the news of their impending death. For older individuals, denial may not be the first reaction, or it may not occur at all. The Kübler-Ross formulation also ignores other emotions that dying individuals may experience, such as curiosity, hope, relief, and apathy. As with many events that take place during life, the dying process is highly individualized and may take many different forms depending on the individual's personality, life history, cultural background, age, and specific nature of the illness. Finally, and perhaps most crucial, is the fact that researchers were unable to establish the existence of the stages among dying individuals.

Psychological Perspectives on the Dying Process

Rather than proposing that dying individuals go through specific stages as they prepare for their final moments, others have suggested that as the end of life approaches, people attempt to make sense out of the past patterns of their lives. According to Marshall (1980), people engage in these processes when they begin to understand that their life is finite. Such an understanding might be arrived at when a person is diagnosed as having a terminal illness. Another process that occurs more generally, however, is the **awareness of finitude**, which is reached when an individual passes the age when parents or, perhaps, siblings, have died. For example, if a person's father died at the age of 66, when this individual reaches that age, a kind of counting-down process begins. The individual anticipates the end of life and understands that life really will end.

Having passed the age of awareness of finitude, individuals then embark on a process called **legitimization of biography** in which they attempt to gain perspective on their past life events. They attempt to see what they have done as having meaning, and they prepare the "story" of their lives by which they will be remembered in the minds of others. Some individuals may put their memoirs in writing, while others achieve an internal reckoning in which they evaluate their contributions as well as their shortcomings.

Personality also plays a role in influencing feelings about death and dying. In a study of older adults ranging from 60 to 100 years of age, it was those people who believed in fate, chance, or luck as determining what happens to them who had higher self-esteem. As predicted by Terror Management Theory, people with higher self-esteem, in turn, were less likely to fear death as an end to the self (Cicirelli, 2002)

The notion that the end of life, or awareness of life's end, triggers an intense period of self-evaluation is also an important component of Erikson's concept of ego integrity, as described in Chapter 8. Erikson emphasized that during this period of life, individuals deal with mortality and questions related to the ending of their existence by attempting to place their lives into perspective. Butler (1974) specifically referred to this process as the **life review**, a time of taking stock through reminiscence or a mental reliving of events from the long-ago past. Presumably, this process may occur at any age, as the dying individual attempts to achieve a peaceful resolution with past mistakes and events that can no longer be made up for or changed. As pointed out in Chapter 11, life review therapy may be useful for older adults who might not spontaneously engage in this potentially important process.

ISSUES IN END-OF-LIFE CARE

Improvements in medical technology along with changes in attitudes toward death and dying have led, within the past two decades, to radical alterations in the approach to the terminally ill. On the one hand, clinicians have become far more sensitive to the emotional and physical needs of dying patients, leading to an examination and reworking of some of the standard approaches to end-of-life care. On the other hand, legislation and social movements that advocate for the rights of dying patients have argued for greater autonomy and decision making. These efforts attempt to establish as part of medical treatment a role for patients to participate actively not only in the course of their care, but also its ending. Many of these issues involve legal and ethical considerations as well as those that are strictly medical.

Advance Directives and the Patient Self-Determination Act

In 1991, a federal bill known as the **Patient Self-Determination Act (PSDA)** (passed one year earlier) went into effect in all organizations receiving Medicare or Medicaid (House of Representatives, Omnibus Reconciliation Act of 1990, *Congressional Record—House*, October 26, 1990, Section 4260, 4751). This legislation guarantees the right of all competent adults to write a **living will or advance directive (AD)** to state their wishes should they require medical or surgical treatment to prolong their lives. The PSDA was passed in response to growing recognition of the burden placed on the dying and their families by advances in medical technology that make it possible to prolong life through artificial means. Prior to becoming ill, an individual could now put in writing his or her wishes regarding end-of-life treatment. Furthermore, the PSDA mandated that health care

professionals receive education themselves as well as provide information to patients about ADs upon their admission to the hospital. It was mandated that the existence of an AD be documented in the medical record. Each state was permitted to establish and define its own legislation concerning advance directives, but the basic federal requirements had to be met in all Medicare- and Medicaid-funded facilities.

In an AD or living will, individuals are asked to consider a number of issues. These include what their preferences would be for medical interventions, whether they would trust another person ("proxy") to act on their behalf, and whether they have a specific desire for (or opposition to) any particular medical interventions. They are also encouraged to discuss their desires with family, their physicians, and other health care providers. Having considered these issues, individuals can then make legally binding arrangements which state that they shall not be sustained by artificial life support if they are no longer able to make that decision themselves. Protection against abuse of the process is provided by various safeguards such as requirements for witnesses and the determination of a terminal condition by more than one physician. (These may vary by state.) In addition to documenting the patient's wishes, the PSDA was intended to ensure more active involvement in planning and treatment by patients and to uphold the principles of respect for their dignity and autonomy.

Research on the End of Life

Until relatively recently, little empirical data were available on the experience of dying among those with terminal illnesses or debilitating conditions. A wealth of information has emerged from the collaborative study among five major medical centers around the country, the **Study to Understand Prognoses and**

Preferences for Outcomes and Risks of Treatments (SUPPORT). It provided data both on the final days of dying patients and on the impact of attempts to improve treatment of dying patients through education of health personnel. For two separate two-year periods (1989–1991 and 1992–1994), SUPPORT enrolled all patients who met the study-entry criteria of being in the advanced stages of one of the following conditions: coma, acute respiratory failure, multiple organ system failure with sepsis or a malignant condition, chronic obstructive pulmonary disease, congestive heart failure, cirrhosis, colon cancer, or non-small-cell lung cancer. It was expected that about half of the people who enrolled in the study would die within a six-month period after entry (Lynn, Teno, Phillips, Wu, Desbiens, et al., 1997). Along with SUPPORT, another sample ("HELP") was enrolled of persons 80 years of age and older who were hospitalized in one of four of the centers. This sample was included to make it possible to study the experience of hospitalized persons at advanced ages.

The first set of findings from the SUPPORT and HELP samples concerned the proportion of deaths that occurred in hospitals, nursing homes, hospices, and homes. The majority of patients in SUPPORT stated that they preferred to die at home; nonetheless, most of the deaths occurred in the hospital (Pritchard, Fisher, Teno, Sharp, Reding, et al., 1998). Furthermore, the percentage of SUPPORT patients who died in the hospital varied by more than double across the five hospitals in the study (from 29% to 66%). The primary factor that accounted for the probability of a patient dying in the hospital rather than at home was becoming terminally ill in regions of the country that had a higher availability of hospital beds. The probability of dying at home was lower in regions that had more nursing homes and hospices. Patient preferences, clinical condition, and socioeconomic status did not predict place of death. Interestingly, in the Canadian Study of Health and Aging, a large-scale investigation of predictors of mortality, institutionalization was associated with a higher risk of dying within the next five years, even after accounting for other relevant factors (Østbye, Steenhuis, Wolfson, Walton, & Hill, 1999).

Second, SUPPORT documented the physical and psychological characteristics of dying persons. These data were obtained through interviews with family members, who reported on the experiences of their dying relatives. As mentioned earlier, pain is a major feature of the dying experience, and this was clearly shown in SUPPORT. During the last three days of life, approximately 40% of patients who were conscious were reported to have been in severe pain. More than half of those who died from a serious illness had great difficulty breathing (dyspnea), and about one-quarter were severely confused. Nausea was not as prevalent, but fatigue was found to affect nearly 80% of all patients. As might be imagined, these physical symptoms caused great discomfort, as was reported by almost three-quarters of the family members of dying patients (Lynn et al., 1997). Even more distressing, however, was the fact that the patients suffering the most severe pain and psychological symptoms (confusion, depression, and anxiety) were most dissatisfied with the level of pain control provided to them. Dissatisfaction with the level of pain control also varied by hospital, physician specialty, and income, with those having lower incomes reporting the most dissatisfaction (Desbiens, Wu, Broste, Wenger, Connors, et al., 1996). Sadly, even after training designed to provide patients, families, physicians, and nurses with information about pain management strategies, no improvements were noted in the experience of pain control among those patients who participated in this intervention (Desbiens et al.,

1996). Apparently, aggressive pain management is needed far earlier in the process than within the last few months or days of life (Field et al., 1997).

The next set of findings from this study concerns the type of care provided to dying patients and whether it was consistent with their preferences. Here the distinction was between aggressive measures taken to prolong life in contrast with **palliative care**, which provides comfort care through measures such as pain control. The provision of aggressive care in cases where patients express a preference for comfort only is referred to in the end-of-life literature as **overtreatment** (Field et al., 1997). The majority of patients in SUPPORT preferred to receive palliative rather than aggressive care, but from 3% to 17% (depending on diagnosis) were given life-sustaining treatments regardless of their preferences. These life-sustaining treatments included resuscitation attempts, being placed on a ventilator, or having a feeding tube inserted into the stomach. Overall, over half of the patients had one of these life-sustaining treatments within the three days before they died (Lynn et al., 1997). Furthermore, in contrast to aggressive life-sustaining procedures, no clear guidelines were provided for those who received palliative care (Goodlin, Winzelberg, Teno, Whedon, & Lynn, 1998).

In the case of patients with colorectal cancer specifically (who tended to be in the most pain), it appeared that physicians and patients had difficulty communicating with each other about prognosis and treatment preferences (Haidet, Hamel, Davis, Wenger, Reding, et al., 1998). Related studies were conducted under the auspices of SUPPORT on patients hospitalized with exacerbation of severe heart failure. As in the larger study, physicians in the majority of cases did not accurately perceive the preferences of their patients for resuscitation (Krumholz, Phillips, Hamel, Teno, Bellamy, et al., 1998).

The final and in some ways the most critical aspect of SUPPORT was investigation of the effectiveness of the PSDA, the legislation that created the requirement of advance directives, or ADs. The two periods of testing (1989–1991 and 1992–1994) coincided with the two years before and the two years immediately after implementation of PSDA. Of the 9105 patients in the study, 4301 were enrolled in the early period and 4804 in the second period. The patients studied in the second period were divided into two groups: an intervention group (2652 patients) and a control group (2152 patients) (Teno, Lynn, Connors, Wenger, Phillips, et al., 1997). The intervention consisted of communication by nurses of detailed information on the prognoses and preferences of patients, which was intended to promote discussions about the course of their care. However, the intervention failed to lead to changes in the frequency of discussions about treatment preferences between physicians and patients. The intervention had no effects on other aspects of end-of-life care, including those identified as most important in the experience of dying patients, such as pain control and overtreatment.

Another aspect of SUPPORT was investigation of the **do not resuscitate (DNR) order**, a document placed in a patient's chart specifying the individual's desire not to be resuscitated if he or she should suffer a cardiac or respiratory arrest (a DNR may be part of an AD). The physician places this order with the consent of the patient or patient surrogate. In SUPPORT, investigators conducted an analysis of patients' preferences for cardiopulmonary resuscitation, severity of illness, and time to the first DNR order. Although DNR orders were issued sooner for patients who had requested a DNR order, only about one-half of the patients who preferred not to be resuscitated actually had DNR orders written. Furthermore, DNR orders were more likely to be issued for patients with poorer prognoses. However, the age of the patient also appeared to play a role in the determination of when an order was placed. Those who were over age 75 were more likely to have a DNR written for them regardless of their prognosis (Hakim, Teno, Harrell, Knaus, Wenger, et al., 1996).

In a subsequent investigation within SUPPORT, the methods of resuscitation examined were expanded to include withholding of ventilator support, surgery, and dialysis according to age, prognosis, and patient preferences. Again, age was associated with the decision to withhold life-sustaining treatment. In addition, physicians were more likely to underestimate the preferences for life-sustaining care among older patients (Hamel, Phillips, Teno, Lynn, Galanos, et al., 1996). Misunderstandings about patient preferences are more likely to arise when the patients are older because physicians assume that they would prefer not to be revived. It is also possible that physicians are less willing to invest the resources that would keep their older patients alive. The presence of a health care proxy, however, someone who is able to monitor and speak for the patient, can increase the chances that the dying individual's wishes will be respected (Fins, Miller, Acres, Bacchetta, Huzzard, et al., 1999). However, this proxy must be carefully chosen as one who will in fact represent the patient's wishes accurately (Fowler, Coppola, & Teno, 1999; Tsevat, Dawson, Wu, Lynn, Soukup, et al., 1998).

The findings of SUPPORT continue to be confirmed by other researchers, who document further the lack of coordination among health care providers, poor communication with dying patients, and failure to alleviate pain in terminally ill individuals. Even when advance directives are written, their language is often vague and inconsistent (Happ, Capezuti, Strumpf, Wagner, Cunningham, et al., 2002). Further

adding to the problems identified by SUPPORT is the lack of action being taken by the U.S. Congress to address the concerns of patients in need of end-of-life care (Goldstein & Lynn, 2002).

The prevalence of chronic pain is estimated to occur in 45% to 80% of nursing home residents (Wunderlich, Kohler, & Committee on Improving Quality in Long-Term Care, 2001). Yet, adequate pain medication is not provided. A study of patients living in nursing homes in the state of Oregon found that of the residents suffering from pain, 39% were inadequately treated (Wagner, Goodwin, Campbell, Eskro, Frank, et al., 1997). Untreated pain was also identified in a study of nursing home residents suffering from cancer; about one-quarter received no pain medication even though they experienced pain on a continual basis (Bernabei, Murphy, Frijters, DuPaquier, & Gardent, 1997). Other researchers have identified racial disparities in the presence of DNRs and living wills, with African Americans and Hispanics less likely to have advance care plan documents in their medical files (Degenholtz, Arnold, Meisel, & Lave, 2002). Similar cultural barriers were identified in studies on HIV-infected adults; physicians were less likely to communicate with African-American and Latino patients about end-of-life issues compared with white patients (Wenger, Kanouse, Collins, Liu, Schuster, et al., 2001).

Physician-Assisted Suicide and Euthanasia

Requesting an order for DNR and writing a living will are steps patients take to avoid prolonging life in the event that their bodily functions spontaneously cease to operate. These measures are taken as protection against the likelihood that the individual loses the capacity to make a conscious decision about allowing life to end naturally. In physician-assisted suicide, individuals make the conscious decision, while they are still able to do so, that they want their lives to end before dying becomes a protracted process. Similarly, in **euthanasia**, although the physician's action causes death, the intent is to prevent the suffering associated with a prolonged ending of life.

A strongly vocal proponent of physician-assisted suicide was Dr. Jack Kevorkian. In 1956, he was dubbed "Dr. Death," not because he assisted a patient's suicide, but because he published a journal article in which he discussed his efforts to photograph the eyes of dying patients. Throughout the 1980s, he published numerous articles on euthanasia, and by 1989 he had built a "suicide machine" which he then used in 1990 on his first patient, a 54-year-old woman with Alzheimer's disease. Throughout the 1990s, he conducted a series of over 100 assisted suicides. In a highly controversial *60 Minutes* segment aired in November, 1998, Kevorkian ended the life of a 52-year old man suffering from a terminal neurological disease. In this case, Kevorkian administered the lethal dose, so the death was technically euthanasia,

not assisted suicide. This action led to Kevorkian's arrest and subsequent conviction on second-degree murder charges.

In the state of Michigan, where Kevorkian was tried and convicted, physician-assisted suicide is illegal. However, other states have different approaches to physician-assisted suicide. Two lawsuits in New York and Washington challenged the constitutionality of laws that prohibit physician-assisted suicide and were brought to the Supreme Court in early 1997 (*Vacco v. Quill*, No. 95-1858 and *State of Washington v. Glucksberg*, No. 96-110). These lawsuits followed popular referendums in both California and Washington in 1990 and 1991 defeating proposals to legalize physician-assisted suicide. However, Oregon voters approved a similar proposal in 1994. The Oregon Death with Dignity Act (ODDA) specifies that a physician may prescribe lethal medication to hasten death for competent, terminally ill persons who voluntarily request it (Oregon Death with Dignity Act, 2 Ore. Rev. Stat. §§ 127.800—127.897).

To put this into context, directives specifying the withholding or withdrawal of life-extending medical treatment represent voluntary passive euthanasia. This procedure is legal in all states, whereas physician-assisted suicide is legal only in Oregon. Voluntary active euthanasia, which is a request for the physician to end the life of terminally ill patients, is legal in European countries such as the Netherlands and Belgium.

Those who favor physician-assisted suicide (or active euthanasia) and who support measures such as the Oregon Death with Dignity Law regard as essential the individual's right to make the decision, the need to relieve suffering, and fears that life can be extended beyond the point when it has meaning (Latimer, 1991). Those who oppose physician-assisted suicide regard as primary the physician's ethical code to

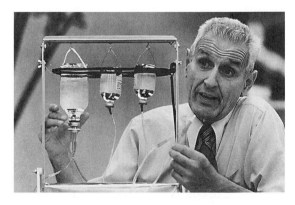

Dr. Jack Kervorkian with the "Thanatron," the machine he invented in which, under his supervision, a patient can self-administer a combination of drugs that puts the patient to sleep and then causes a heart attack.

"do no harm" (Jennings, 1991). Opponents also are concerned with abuse or misuse and the belief that life-and-death decisions fall in the province of religion (O'Rourke, 1991). Furthermore, the status of being "terminally ill" may be unclear because the definition of what is terminal cannot be supported reliably by data (Lynn, 1996). Other arguments against assisted suicide are that personal growth may occur even in the last stages of dying (Byock, 1993).

Surveys conducted to determine the extent to which measures such as the ODDA are seen favorably show some variations in attitudes toward physician-assistance. In Oregon, the large majority of psychologists were in favor of the ODDA, both in terms of supporting its enactment (78%) and in terms of stating that they would consider physician-assisted suicide for themselves (Fenn & Ganzini, 1999). Physicians (31%), however, are far less likely to support the enactment of such legislation (Duberstein et al., 1995). Although the ODDA raises an important ethical question, practically speaking, there has been little in the way of change in Oregon in response to this law because only a small number of terminally ill patients have chosen to end their lives in this manner (Hedberg, Hopkins, & Kohn, 2003).

One of the strongest arguments against physician-assisted suicide is based on evidence that the decision by the terminally ill individual to end life may be based on lack of appropriate care of dying individuals. Those dying patients who are suicidal may have treatable psychological symptoms that, when addressed properly, lead them to regain the will to live. There is tremendous variation even on a day-to-day basis in feelings about assisted suicide (Pacheco, Hershberger, Markert, & Kumar, 2003). People who make this decision may be suicidal because they are depressed, anxious, or in pain. When the source of their symptoms is identified and treatment is attempted, the desire to die wanes

(Bascom & Tolle, 2002), and the individual may be grateful for having additional time to live (Hendin, 1999).

Suggestions for End-of-Life Care

Clearly, those who are dying wish to have their preferences respected with regard to the way they wish to end their lives. Because there is no one scenario that best describes the type of ending that they envision, individuals must be given the opportunity to make the choice that best fits their values and desires (Vig, Davenport, & Pearlman, 2002). Unfortunately, this is generally not the case, in part because dying patients are often not able to express their wishes. One suggestion to overcome this obstacle to respecting the individual's autonomy is to reconstruct the patient's wishes from documents or relatives (Sullivan, 2002). There may also be problems stemming from differences in cultural values between health care workers and patients. Interviews with Chinese older adults living in Canada revealed a lack of acceptance of advance directives due to differences in values between Confucianist, Buddhist, and Taoist religions and those of Western medicine (Bowman & Singer, 2001). It is therefore necessary to understand the patient's cultural background when providing end-of-life care (Crawley, Marshall, Lo, & Koenig, 2002). For this reason, it is crucial to discuss options for care with family members (Haley, Allen, Reynolds, Chen, Burton, et al., 2002; Hickman, 2002).

Another problem is the lack of coordination within long-term care facilities in the decision-making process used to initiate end-of-life care. Nursing home staff often have not developed procedures to communicate either among themselves or with patients to determine at what point in the resident's illness palliative care should begin (Travis, Bernard, Dixon, McAuley, Loving, et al., 2002). As with the provision of good nursing home care, an interdisciplinary approach can help to overcome the problems of lack of coordination and communication among health care workers (Connor, Egan, Kwilosz, Larson, & Reese, 2002).

Increasingly, the provision of end-of-life care designed to meet the needs of the individual patient is the domain of a facility known as a **hospice** (Ganzini, Nelson, Lee, Kraemer, Schmidt, et al., 2001). The term hospice is ordinarily used to refer to a site or program that provides medical and supportive services for dying patients and their families and friends (Field et al., 1997). Within the hospice environment, the needs of dying patients are attended to with regard to their needs for physical comfort, psychological and social support, and the opportunity to express and have met their spiritual needs. The care is palliative, focusing on controlling pain and other symptoms, and it is likely to take place within the home. Hospice care was introduced in the 1960s, with the goal of alleviating the pain, nausea, confusion, and sleep disturbances experienced by cancer patients within their last months of life (Kastenbaum, 1999). The first well-known hospice was St. Christopher's in London, which opened in 1967. The hospice movement spread to the United States in the 1970s and was recognized by Congress in 1982. At that point, hospice benefits were made available to persons on Medicare who had a life expectancy of less than six months.

When asked to provide their perspectives on the desired aspects of end-of-life care, patients describe concerns very similar to those that are addressed within the hospice framework. These needs include obtaining adequate pain control and symptom management, avoiding an extended period of dying, achieving a sense of personal control, relieving the burden they place on others, and strengthening ties with those who are close to them (Kelly, Burnett,

Pelusi, Badger, Varghese, et al., 2002). For African Americans in particular, management of pain appears to be a particularly important issue. Within nursing home settings, African-American patients are less likely to receive adequate pain control (Engle, Fox-Hill, & Graney, 1998).

In 1997, the American Medical Association approved a set of guidelines to establish quality care for individuals at the end of life. These included providing patients with the opportunity to discuss and plan for end-of-life care, assurance that attempts will be made to provide comfort and respect the patient's end-of-life wishes, assurance of dignity, and attention to the individual's goals. These rights also include minimizing the burden to the family and assisting the bereaved through the stages of mourning and adjustment. There is some indication that efforts such as this are improving the quality of care provided to terminally ill patients. A 1996 survey of over 1000 physicians studied 20 years earlier reported an increase in the willingness of these physicians to discuss issues related to prognosis end-of-life care (Dickinson, Tournier, & Still, 1999). Moreover, medical schools are increasingly incorporating palliative care into their curriculums (Dickinson, 2002).

The report of the Committee on the Care at the End of Life sponsored by the Institute of Medicine recommended attending to the practical needs of patients as a crucial component of care (Field et al., 1997). This includes assisting the patient and family in obtaining home health services, making changes in the home to accommodate the patient, and providing help with routine daily tasks such as shopping. Attending to these practical needs may also involve a variety of other people in the patient's social network. Neighbors can provide help with daily tasks, employers can allow for flexible work schedules of caregivers, and groceries and pharmacies can provide delivery services. In general, the community can be supportive in alleviating some of the stress encountered by caregivers in adjusting to the need to care for a terminally ill relative. Furthermore, the comfort provided to the patient can carry over to meeting other psychological needs. In the course of providing for the concerns of everyday life, the patient is also felt to be cared for in a larger sense.

BEREAVEMENT

Bereavement is the process during which an individual attempts to overcome the death of another person with whom there was a relationship. The bereavement process may occur at any point in an individual's life. However, it is more likely to take place in later adulthood when people have an increased risk of losing spouse, siblings, friends, colleagues, and other peers.

The physical and psychological symptoms associated with bereavement are particularly severe in the first year following the loss. The physical symptoms can include shortness of breath, frequent sighing, tightness in chest, feelings of emptiness, loss of energy and strength, and upset stomach. In some cases, the individual may be vulnerable to physical illness due to the reduced effectiveness of the immune system, which is sensitive to psychological disturbances. The emotional reactions to bereavement include anger, depression, anxiety, sleep disturbances, and preoccupation with thoughts of the deceased. Other problems associated with bereavement include impairments in attention and memory, a desire to withdraw from social activities, and increased risk of accidents. The symptoms of bereavement, as difficult as they are, nevertheless appear to subside greatly in most people after a period of one year (Lindstrom, 1995a).

As this woman mourns the loss of her husband, she may experience a host of physical and psychological reactions ranging from anger and depression to physical illness.

Death of a Spouse

The death of a spouse is regarded as one of the most stressful events of life, and for many older adults, widowhood involves the loss of a relationship that may have lasted as long as 50 years or more. Among the many ramifications of widowhood are loss of an attachment figure, interruption of the plans and hopes invested in the relationship, and construction of a new identity in accordance with the reality of being single (Field, Nichols, Holen, & Horowitz, 1999). People who are widowed are more likely to be lonely for years following their loss, even if they live with other people (Lichtenstein, Gatz, Pedersen, Berg, & McClearn, 1996). They may experience symptoms such as sensing the presence, dreaming about, and having hallucinations or illusions of seeing or hearing the deceased (Lindstrom, 1995b; LoConto, 1998). These feelings of grief over the loss of the spouse may persist for as long as two and a half years (Ott & Lueger, 2002).

A number of factors may affect the extent to which an individual experiences adverse effects of widowhood. One set of factors has to do with the bereaved individual's personality. A major prospective study of over 200 individuals who were tested before they became widowed, and for 18 months after they became widowed, identified five patterns of bereavement: common grief, chronic grief, chronic depression, improvement during bereavement, and resilience (Bonanno, Wortman, Lehman, Tweed, Haring, et al., 2002). In *common grief*, the individual experiences an initial increase in depression, which diminishes over time. This pattern is actually relatively infrequent. More likely to occur is *resilient grief*, in which the bereaved person shows little or no distress following the loss. Two additional patterns distinguish grief from depression. In *chronic grief*, the individual experiences high levels of both depression and grief within six months after the loss, and the grief does not subside over time. In *chronic depression*, the bereaved person suffers from high levels of depression prior to and after the loss. In improvement during bereavement, depression and grief subside. These patterns are shown in Fig. 13.4. In addition to measuring marital conflict, investigators examined the coping resources, interpersonal dependency, personality traits (based on the Five Factor Model), religiosity, world views, and social support. People with high levels of interpersonal dependency (including dependence on their spouses) were most likely to show the chronic grief pattern. Those who showed the pattern of *resilience* were most accepting of death and were more likely to agree with the notion that the world is just (i.e., that "people get what they deserve"). Studies such as these underscore the notion that bereavement is not a unitary process and that there are multiple factors influencing reactions to the loss of a spouse.

Age is another individual difference factor predicting reactions to widowhood. It is well established by now that younger widows suffer more negative consequences of widowhood, including more severe deterioration of health

and higher mortality rates (Stroebe, Stroebe, Gergen, & Gergen, 1981; Stroebe & Stroebe, 1987). One reason for the differing effects of widowhood on younger and older spouses may be the expectedness of the death. Older spouses are more prepared for the death of the partner, a fact that is particularly true for women, who are likely to be younger than their husbands. However, being able to anticipate the death is not necessarily the key factor in accounting for the age difference in reactions to widowhood.

Anticipatory grief may heighten rather than reduce the grief that follows the spouse's death (Gilliland & Fleming, 1998). For older individuals, being caregivers of a spouse during a protracted period of decline is physically and emotionally taxing, counteracting any potentially protective effects of being able to prepare psychologically for the death. In fact, after the death of their spouses, these individuals may experience improved health behaviors (Schulz, Beach, Lind, Martire, Zdaniuk, et al., 2001). Younger widows may benefit somewhat more

FIGURE 13.4

Patterns of Grief in Widowhood

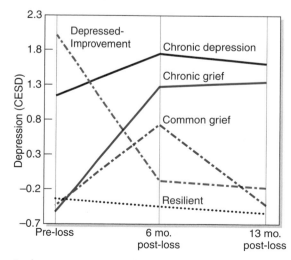

Source: Bonanno, Wortman, Lehman, Tweed, & Haring, et al., 2002.

from the forewarning given to them by an anticipated death because they may be better able to withstand the caregiving process. Complicating the issue is the fact that the bereaved spouse feels some relief when the caregiving burden is removed, and this reaction may in turn lead to guilt and self-blame. Difficult emotional responses may also follow the death of a spouse due to illnesses such as cancer and Alzheimer's disease that involved marked physical and mental deterioration (McKiernan, 1996).

Men appear to experience greater stress following the death of their wives than women upon the death of their husbands (Stroebe, 2001). Widowers are at greater mortality risk within the first six months after bereavement than are widows, with a mortality rate estimated in one study to be 12 times higher for men than women for those over 75 years of age (Gallagher-Thompson, Futterman, Farberow, Thompson, & Peterson, 1993). This sex difference in reactions to bereavement does not appear to be due to the greater social support that women experience as widows (Stroebe, Stroebe, & Abakoumkin, 1999). Men are more likely to remarry, but women are more likely to form new friendships, particularly with neighbors (Lamme, Dykstra, & Broese Van Groenou, 1996). It is possible that social support plays a greater role in the adaptation of women to widowhood, but for men (particularly current cohorts) a more relevant factor is the availability of practical support in performing household tasks (Gass, 1989).

A **dual-process model** of stress and coping has been proposed to account for the multiple changes that occur following the loss of a spouse (Stroebe & Schut, 1999). According to this model, the stress experienced following the loss of a partner can be divided into two broad categories. The emotional category includes the sadness directly associated with the loss of the loved one as attachment figure. The second category includes the set of life changes that accompany

the loss, including moving from an identity as being a part of a couple to the identity of being a single person. For example, becoming a widow can lead to social isolation when a woman's friends were all friends of the couple. According to this model, the bereaved must deal with both components of loss. If they focus on one to the exclusion or neglect of the other, they will have a much more difficult and lengthy period of readjustment The model postulates that dealing with both the direct emotional consequences of loss and concurrently occurring life changes is essential for adjustment to loss and that preoccupation with one of these aspects, to the neglect of the other, slows down this process.

The dual processes involved in coping with the stress of bereavement are known as the *loss* and *restoration* dimensions. The loss dimension involves coping with the emotional pain of not having the attachment figure present. Coping with the secondary stress of changes in daily life and identity is the restoration dimension. Health adjustment is promoted by alternating between the two forms of coping. At times, it is best to confront the emotional loss of the partner; at other times, it is most advantageous to avoid confronting these emotions and instead attempting to manage the secondary consequences of loss (Stroebe, 2001).

Death of Other Family Members

The loss of an adult child is perhaps the most distressing and devastating of all forms of bereavement. The grief an older adult experiences over an adult child's death is highly intense and is associated with increased risk of depression, guilt, and health complaints. The distress of a parent who loses a child may also be associated with feelings of helplessness, insecurity, and isolation. In addition, the individual experiences a loss of identity as a parent and the very practical loss of a central supportive figure in the older person's life (McKiernan, 1996). Loss of an adult child also violates the individual's normative expectations that a parent dies before the children. Consequently, the depression and deterioration of health experienced after an adult child's death may persist unabated for a decade, if not longer (de Vries, Davis, Wortman, & Lehman, 1997). Although these feelings may never be completely overcome, bereaved parents seem to be able to find a sense of meaning and purpose in life, particularly through connections with other people and the feeling of connection with the lost child (Wheeler, 2001).

In the death of a grandchild, the emotional pain of the older individual is intensified by that shared with the child's parents. Feelings of guilt over being alive while one's grandchild is not may accompany the emotional devastation over the child's loss (Fry, 1997). The suffering of grandparents may be especially pronounced when they were involved in raising the child, as was documented for grandmothers of children killed in the Oklahoma City bombing of 1995. However, at least for these grandmothers, a sense of community and having each other for support helped to foster resilience even in the face of this profound loss (Allen, Whittlesey, Pfefferbaum, & Ondersma, 1999).

Compared with the death of a child or grandchild, the death of a parent is a far more normative event of adult life. Nevertheless, this experience can cause psychological distress and a deterioration of health status (Umberson & Chen, 1994). The death of a parent can also lead to increased marital conflict, particularly when the loss is of a father (Umberson, 1995). In general, daughters are more negatively affected by parental death than are sons who, in turn, tend to be more accepting of the loss (Moss, Resch, & Moss, 1997).

Although somewhat normative as well, the deaths of siblings and friends are also sources of distress in later adulthood. The death of a brother in particular may bring not only emotional pain but increased financial hardship (Hays, Gold, & Peiper, 1997). For those who suffer the loss of friends, in addition to feelings of grief there may be an increased incentive to develop new relationships, including closer relations with other friends and relatives (Roberto & Stanis, 1994).

Certain losses that occur in adulthood fall outside the category of family and friends but may be painful nevertheless. Individuals whose job places them in situations where they work with dying persons may experience severe anxiety symptoms that interfere with their daily lives and ability to perform their jobs. For example, not only the survivors but also the recovery workers in the 1995 Oklahoma City bombing were found to experience lingering symptoms of trauma that proved resistant to treatment (Tucker, Pfefferbaum, Nixon, & Foy, 1999).

Theories of Bereavement

Until relatively recently, conventional and professional wisdom regarding bereavement was based on the assumption that the survivor must "work through" the death of the deceased. According to this view, the individual must experience a period of mourning, but after that, it is time to move on and seek new relationships and attachments. In part, this view was based on the assumption within psychodynamic theory that to resolve grief normally, emotional bonds to the loved one must be severed (Bowlby, 1980). However, a new view of bereavement is taking shape. It is recognized that expressions of continuing attachment are potentially adaptive in providing the individual with a sense of continuity in the face of loss (Kastenbaum, 1999). This view, which is held within contemporary non-Western cultures such as the Japanese and Egyptian Muslim cultures, was also strongly maintained by nineteenth-century romanticists. Furthermore, and though not advocated by the professional community, continued attachment to the deceased remains a part of the experience of bereaved individuals (Stroebe, Gergen, Gergen, & Stroebe, 1992).

Feelings of continued attachment to the deceased may be expressed in several of the behaviors noted earlier as "symptoms" of bereavement. For example, the sense of the spouse's presence helps maintain the feeling that the spouse is watching over or guiding the individual. Another form of attachment is to maintain the spouse's possessions because of their symbolic value. Comfort may also come from keeping alive the memories of the deceased spouse. Rather than abandoning all these forms of attachment to the spouse, part of successful adaptation seems to involve moving away from the concrete reminders of the deceased (possessions) to the more abstract ties that involve thoughts and memories (Field, Gal-Oz, & Bonanno, 2003). Such forms of coping may help the individual acknowledge and accept the death while making the transition to a new, single identity. Mastery over the loss may then occur, even as the deceased spouse remains an active mental presence. According to this view, the normal response to grief involves living with rather than "getting over it."

It may be the ability to move ahead without losing memory for the departed individuals in one's life that long-lived individuals possess and makes it possible for them to survive repeated losses in later adulthood. These individuals have developed ways of integrating the pain of multiple losses into their lives and can take their lives in positive new directions (Kastenbaum, 1999). In the future, this process may be made that much less painful by the understanding among mental health professionals of the need to retain rather than abandon the emotional ties of attachment.

SUMMARY

1. The concept of death holds a great deal of fascination because it is a complex, multifaceted and, for many people, frightening issue. Death is defined as the point of irreversible loss of bodily functions, although this state may be difficult to determine as a result of the advent of life support systems which can keep people in a persistent vegetative state. At the end of life, individuals experience a number of physical changes, many of which are physically uncomfortable in addition to involving a great deal of pain. Autopsies may be performed after death to classify the cause of death or if legal factors are involved in the death itself.

2. Mortality data provide insight into the variations by age, sex, and race in the causes of death. Younger adults are more likely to die from accidents and older adults from heart disease. HIV-related deaths appear to be on the decline; however, AIDS is still the number-one killer of blacks in the 25–44 age bracket. Variations exist, however, within age, race, and sex groups reflecting sociocultural factors in lifestyles and risk factors. Mortality rates are decreasing around the world, primarily because of a decrease in infant mortality. However, mortality reductions vary according to the level of a country's economic development. The poor are disproportionately more likely to die in all countries around the world, particularly where there is inadequate health care.

3. A culture's death ethos is reflected in the traditions established by that culture in funeral rituals, belief in the afterlife, and the language used to describe death. Western attitudes toward death have undergone major shifts throughout history. Contemporary American attitudes regard death in a sensationalistic way, but there is a predominant tendency to

institutionalize death and make it "invisible." The death with dignity movement has attempted to promote the idea that the individual should have control over the conditions of death. Associated phenomena in the United States are physician-assisted suicide and euthanasia.

4. The dying process may occur through one of several dying trajectories, or rate of decline in functioning prior to death. The landmark book by Kübler-Ross described five stages of dying. Researchers and clinicians do not necessarily adhere to this stage model, but there is value in the notion of encouraging the dying patient to be able to talk about his or her experience. Sociologists suggest that awareness of finitude triggers a recognition of one's mortality, leading to legitimization of biography. The life review is a process that older adults may engage in to develop an integrated perspective on the self prior to death.

5. Issues in end-of-life care focus on the extent to which dying patients can exert control over their medical care. As a result of the Patient Self-Determination Act, individuals can establish advance directives that indicate whether they wish to extend their lives through artificial means prior to needing to make this decision. The SUPPORT study on end-of-life care revealed a number of serious weaknesses in the medical care of dying patients in the United States. Many were in pain, felt their preference for palliative care was not respected, and did not believe that they had an adequate opportunity to discuss their preferences with their health care providers. Physician-assisted suicide is a controversial issue that is now legal in the state of Oregon. Arguments against this practice are that individuals requesting this end to their lives are depressed and would not desire suicide if their mood disorder were properly addressed. Hospices are settings that provide medical and supportive services for dying patients, allowing them to receive personal attention and maintain contact with family. Guidelines for end-of-life care are being instituted by the American Medical Association.

6. Bereavement is the process of mourning the loss of a close person. The death of a spouse is the most severe loss an individual can experience, but the death of other family members, especially children, causes extreme and long-lasting distress. In the past, theories of grief resolution focused on the need to "work through" a bereavement. Current views are emphasizing an alternative in which the bereaved are more accepting of the sad feelings accompanying the loss.

GLOSSARY

Age-specific death rates: the number of deaths per 100,000 of the particular age group.

Age-adjusted death rates: mortality statistic calculated by obtaining the weighted averages of the age-specific death rates, with the weights reflecting the proportion of individuals in that age group in the population.

Age-specific death rates: the number of deaths per 100,000 of the particular age group.

Anorexia-cachexia syndrome: condition at the end of life which involves a loss of appetite (anorexia) and atrophy of muscle mass (cachexia).

Autopsy: a medical procedure in which the body is opened and the internal organs and structures are examined.

Awareness of finitude: point at which an individual passes the age when parents or, perhaps, siblings, have died.

Bereavement: the process in which an individual attempts to overcome the death of another person with whom there was a relationship.

Compression of morbidity: concept referring to the desirable state in which people live to be older before they die and also experience less disability prior to their death.

Death: the point when there is irreversible cessation of circulatory and respiratory functions, or when all structures of the brain have ceased to function.

Death ethos: a culture's prevailing philosophy of death.

Death with dignity: the idea that death should not involve extreme physical dependency or loss of control of bodily functions.

Do not resuscitate (DNR) order: a document placed in a patient's hospital chart specifying the individual's desire not to be resuscitated if he or she should suffer a cardiac or respiratory arrest.

Dual-process model: a model of bereavement proposing that there are two processes involved in bereavement: the first with regard to loss of the attachment figure, and the second with regard to loss of role and identity.

Dying: the period during which an organism loses its viability.

Dying trajectory: the rate of decline in functioning prior to death.

Euthanasia: the direct killing of a patient by a physician who administers a lethal injection.

Hospice: a site or program that provides medical and supportive services for dying patients and their families and friends.

Legitimization of biography: process in which older or dying individuals attempt to gain perspective on the events in their past lives.

Life review: a time of taking stock through reminiscence or a mental reliving of events from the long-ago past.

Living will or advance directive (AD): written statement by an individual concerning preferred treatment should he or she require medical or surgical treatment to prolong life.

Medicolegal autopsy: a special type of autopsy conducted under conditions such as when the death was due to homicide, suicide, or accident.

Mortality data: statistics derived from death.

Overtreatment: the provision of aggressive care in cases where terminally ill patients express a preference for comfort only.

Palliative care: comfort care to dying individuals through measures such as pain control.

Patient Self-Determination Act (PSDA): legislation affecting all organizations receiving Medicare or Medicaid guaranteeing the right of all competent adults to write a living will or advance directive (AD).

Persistent vegetative state: condition in which the subcortical areas of the brain remain intact and therefore are able to regulate basic bodily functions, including sleep–wake cycles, but the individual lacks conscious awareness.

Physician-assisted suicide: situation in which a physician provides the means for a terminally ill patient to complete suicide.

Social death: situation in which the dying are treated as nonpersons by family or health care workers as they are left to spend their final months or years in the hospital or nursing home.

Stages of dying: denial, anger, bargaining, depression, and acceptance.

Study to Understand Prognoses and Preferences for Outcomes and Risks of Treatments (SUPPORT): large investigation providing data on the final days of dying patients and on the impact of attempts to improve treatment of dying patients through education of health personnel.

Terror Management Theory: social-psychological perspective proposing that people regard the thought of the finitude of their lives with panic and dread.

Chapter Fourteen

Successful Aging and Creativity

"Grow old along with me! The best is yet to be."

Robert Browning
1812–1889

Many theorists and researchers have proposed that because of the personal and social losses experienced by the average older person, there is an inevitable deterioration of well-being and adjustment. Yet, survival into the later years of adulthood requires that, in fact, the individual can negotiate the many threats presented to living a long life. These include the threats of dying from accident, illness, and violent acts. Because they have managed to avoid these threats to their existence and personal happiness, there may be some special quality about increasingly older individuals that can account, in part, for their having reached advanced old age.

In this final chapter, we will have the opportunity to explore the topics of psychological growth and creativity in the later adult years. The concept of "survival" as applied to old age fails to capture the additional element present in the lives of successful agers—namely, the ability to achieve heightened levels of personal expression and happiness. As we look at **successful aging**, it is these inspirational qualities that can guide and sustain our own optimism and hope about our future adult years.

THEORETICAL PERSPECTIVES ON SUCCESSFUL AGING

The study of successful aging is, in part, an attempt by theorists and researchers to identify and understand the factors that contribute to the ability of the older individual to survive. However, as noted above, the study of successful aging goes beyond the question of survival. Successful aging involves the additional quality of enhancing the healthy spirit and sense of joy in life seen in older adults who seem to transcend physical limitations. In many ways, successful aging is synonymous with "mental health" in that the qualities thought to be desirable for optimal adaptation, such as a positive outlook and greater self-understanding, are also part of the criteria for successful aging. The fact that these qualities are achieved in later adulthood, thought to be a time of loss and perhaps a diminution of energy, is regarded as placing this type of mental health into a special category of adaptive phenomena.

"What do you think?"   14-1

Do you know people who exemplify successful aging? What are their characteristics?

A model of successful aging based on a major research effort in the United States known as the MacArthur Foundation Study of Aging in America, incorporates three interactive components (Rowe & Kahn, 1998). The absence of disease and the disability associated with disease is the first component, which includes not being ill but also not having the risk factors that will increase the chances of disease and disability. The second component is maintaining high cognitive and physical function, which gives the individual the potential to be active and competent. The third component, called "engagement with life," refers to involvement in productive activity and involvement with other people. Notice that successful aging, according to this definition, does not mean that the individual manages somehow to avoid growing old. To age "successfully" still means to "age."

When discussing successful aging, people have a tendency to view the happy and productive older person as an anomaly. This productive older person has managed to avoid the expected state of gloom and despair that is thought to be a normal accompaniment to the aging process. The implicit assumption is that

aging inevitably brings about depression and despair, so when people do not show these qualities, they must be truly special. However, as we have seen elsewhere in this book, most older people do not become depressed, and personality development in middle and later adulthood appears to be in the positive direction of greater adaptiveness. Furthermore, based on Erikson's theory, older adults are theoretically able to achieve a fuller or more complete level of development than are those who are younger and whose egos have not been as thoroughly tested by time and events.

One reason that the successful ager is thought of as the miraculous exception rather than the rule is that many theorists, researchers, and laypeople believe in the **social indicator model** (Mroczek & Kolarz, 1998). According to this model, demographic and social structural variables, such as age, gender, marital status, and income, account for individual differences in levels of well-being. Because by demographic standards older individuals are in a disadvantaged position on indices such as income, health, education, and marital status, they should therefore have lower feelings of happiness. When an individual is able to avoid becoming depressed by the potentially disturbing circumstances of poor health, widowhood, and low income, then that person seems deserving of some kind of special recognition.

As judged solely by the standards of being able to avoid the despair brought about by lower status on important social indicators, however, there would in fact be many successful agers. The majority of older adults maintain relatively high levels of well-being, a phenomenon referred to as the paradox of well-being (Mroczek & Kolarz, 1998). Despite their objective difficulties, people in later life feel good about themselves and their situations. Successful aging, then, appears to be the norm rather than the exception. As can be seen from Fig. 14.1, which summarizes data from over 32,000 Americans studied from 1972 to 1994, the large majority of individuals in the later adult years rate themselves as "very" or "pretty" happy (Mroczek & Kolarz, 1998). Findings from countries around the world support this positive image of aging as a time of increased feelings of satisfaction (Diener & Suh, 1998). Regardless of age, most people report having a positive evaluation of themselves and their lives (Diener, 1998). This fact is certainly consistent with the identity process model as well, which predicts that most people view themselves and their circumstances in a positive light.

Clearly, however, individuals of all ages vary in their levels of happiness and well-being, and not everyone can be equally optimistic about their life situations. It is for this reason that research within the successful aging framework has focused on refining the concept of well-being and studying in depth its correlates in middle and later adulthood.

SUBJECTIVE WELL-BEING

The variable studied within the psychology of adult development and aging most closely related to the notion of successful aging is **subjective well-being**. In a general sense, subjective well-being refers to an individual's overall sense of happiness. For research purposes, however, the concept is divided into three components: positive affect, negative affect, and **life satisfaction**, or the cognitive evaluation of one's life circumstances (Diener, 1998).

Perhaps the most extensive recent investigation of the factors contributing to subjective well-being in middle adulthood was the Midlife in the United States Survey (MIDUS) carried out within the context of the MacArthur Study of Successful Midlife Development. The MIDUS study has recently begun to release published reports of its findings, including a detailed analysis of the correlates of subjective well-being (Mroczek & Kolarz, 1998). The MIDUS sample was made up of over 2700 participants, who were asked to complete mail and phone surveys

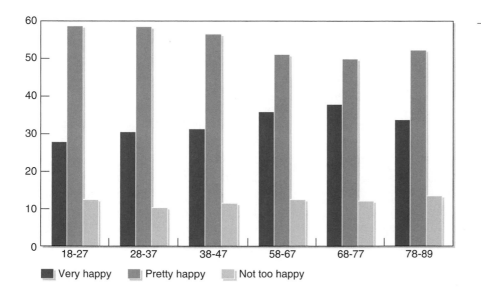

FIGURE 14.1
Ratings of Happiness by Age Decade

Source: Mroczek & Kolarz, 1998.

focusing on issues of middle and later adulthood. The surveys were completed in 1995 through early 1996. The ages of the participants ranged from 25 to 74 years, with an average of 46, placing the sample squarely within midlife.

In the MIDUS study, the relationship between subjective well-being and age was found to vary as a function of gender, personality, and marital status. Furthermore, the results differed according to which component of subjective well-being was investigated. Positive affect was higher in the older age groups, and particularly so for women. For men, personality interacted with age in ratings of positive affect. Higher positive affect scores were found only in the older group of introverted men. Men who were extraverts had high positive affect scores throughout the adult age range tested. Only the married men showed a relationship between age and ratings of negative affect. The older groups of married men had lower scores than the younger married men in the sample.

The findings of the MIDUS study were consistent in many ways with earlier data in that the older adults in the sample emerged as successful agers, at least as judged in terms of their ratings of affect. However, the data also indicated the contributing roles of personality, context, and, by inference, motivational and coping strategies used to maintain high levels of well-being in middle and later adulthood. The only anomaly of the MIDUS study related to marital status and satisfaction in men, a finding generally not observed in the well-being literature. In fact, when studied longitudinally as a predictor of adjustment, marital status appears to have more of a favorable influence on well-being in later life. Research on the Terman sample, a sample of gifted men and women studied since the 1930s, showed that over the course of adulthood, men who focused on their marriages and family tended to have more positive levels of adjustment than those who focused on their careers (Crosnoe & Elder, 2002).

With regard to personality, the existence of higher scores for extraverted men throughout adulthood in the MIDUS study points to the importance of considering longstanding dispositional factors as influences on well-being throughout life. Some researchers maintain that there is a hereditary component to well-being (McCrae, 2002), possibly involving having the E2 allele of the ApoE gene (Zubenko, Stiffler, Hughes, Fatigati, & Zubenko, 2002). The majority of individuals may be biologically programmed to experience high levels of well-being, with slight individual variations within this range (Diener & Diener, 1996). The notion that well-being reflects personality traits is known as the **set point perspective** (Mroczek & Kolarz, 1998). According to this view, biologically determined temperament sets the boundaries for the levels of well-being an individual experiences throughout life. Extraverts have an advantage over introverts according to this viewpoint, for people high on the trait of extraversion tend to view the world in a more positive light, regardless of actual circumstances. Furthermore, it is possible that extraverted people, because of their sunny natures, have more success in their dealings with others and, therefore, a stronger objective basis for their optimism.

The **paradox of well-being** can be explained in part by the existence of personality traits, particularly to the extent that they influence the interpretations that people place on their experiences. However, of greater interest to researchers are the psychological mechanisms that people use to reach higher levels of well-being than their objective circumstances would warrant. Simple **adaptation** or habituation is one of these theorized psychological mechanisms that individuals may use to maintain high well-being in the face of objectively negative circumstances. Through adaptation, people learn to live at a certain level of health, income, or discomfort in their situations as they adjust their daily lives to fit the constraints presented to them. The kind of negative life events that people may experience within the course of ordinary life (deaths of relatives, divorce of self or parents, loss of job) may even be adapted to through a kind of habituation process within a surprisingly short time in some cases, perhaps within a period of months (Suh, Diener, & Fujita, 1996).

> ### "What do you think?" 14-2
>
> Are people who feel good about themselves despite objective limitations better off than people who are realists? Why or why not?

The extent to which experiences are consistent with goals provides another source of the basis for subjective well-being (Austin & Vancouver, 1996). If people are able to achieve or make progress toward reaching their goals, they will feel better about themselves and their experiences. Furthermore, they will be more satisfied with their objective situations in life if they see these as potentially contributing to the achievement of their goals (Diener & Fujita, 1995). For example, an individual may live in a cramped and uncomfortable student apartment while in graduate school if this is seen as facilitating a long-term educational goal of obtaining an advanced degree. There are life-span components to goal setting as well. Longitudinal data from the Terman study of gifted individuals revealed that individuals who set high goals for themselves in midlife were the most likely to have high goals in later adulthood, particularly if they valued having a rich cultural life and contributing to society (Holahan & Chapman, 2002).

On a more active level, individuals may alter their views of their life circumstances through coping mechanisms, which can include problem-focused and emotion-focused strategies. Although the objective nature of life circumstances must be taken into account (Diener, Oishi, & Lucas, 2003), coping accounts for the way that individuals interpret these circumstances. For example, Folkman (1997) reported that caregivers of men with HIV were able to maintain a positive outlook on their very stressful situations through such coping strategies as positive reappraisal, problem-focused coping, and reliance on spiritual beliefs. Religion also plays a role in adapting to difficult life circumstances, serving as another important coping resource for many older adults (Van Ness & Larson, 2002). Finally, cultures and nations vary in their norms or expectations for experiencing emotions. For example, people in China have the lowest frequency and intensity of both positive and negative emotions compared to people living in the United States, Australia, and even Taiwan (Eid & Diener, 2001).

Another active adaptational process is **social comparison**, through which individuals look at the situations of others who are more unfortunate than they are, and comfort themselves with the thought that things could be worse (Michalos, 1985). In the face of threat, such as death from cancer, individuals manage to maintain a positive outlook by regarding themselves as having adjusted better than have others to the disease (Helgeson & Taylor, 1993). Similarly, older individuals may use social comparison to help negotiate potentially stressful transitions, such as having to relocate their place of residence (Kwan, Love, Ryff, & Essex, 2003). Regulation of affect, through processes described in socioemotional selectivity theory, is another mechanism that individuals may use to maintain a positive outlook on life, particularly in later adulthood. Changes in the ability to regulate affect and alterations in the nature of the individual's relationships may provide a concrete basis for improved feelings of well-being (Mroczek & Kolarz, 1998). It is not simply a change in perspective, but a change in the focus of one's emotional investment, that accounts for the ability of older adults to experience high levels of well-being.

Positive relationships with others also contribute to well-being. Older adults who feel that they have high levels of social support are higher in feelings of subjective well-being and quality of life (Bowling, Banister, Sutton, Evans, & Windsor, 2002). Possible mechanisms through which social support can lead to well-being have been found to include enhanced sense of self-esteem, which in turn has positive effects on subjective health, which in turn enhances well-being. Interestingly, even physical performance factors, such as measures of gait (walking), may be improved by the individual's enhanced sense of self that follows from social support (Kim & Nesselroade, 2002). The specific aspect of self-esteem involved in these processes is the sense that one is valued by others (Bailis & Chipperfield, 2002). Older adults who value social participation tend to maintain a consistent level of activity over time, as long as their health permits, and they tend to become involved in a variety of activities, including political participation (Bukov, Maas, & Lampert, 2002).

At a less empirical level, Erikson captured some of the creative qualities of the process of successful aging in the book *Vital Involvement in Old Age* (Erikson, Erikson, & Kivnick, 1986). The book analyzes interviews conducted on 29 participants in the Berkeley Growth Study, who had been studied from birth and were in their 80s at the time of the interviews. Erikson and his collaborators identified people who had risen above the infirmities and limitations of aging. For example, one woman, an "inveterate reader," had become blind. Rather than give up her goal of reading, she switched to books on tape. This woman also felt free to "act on impulse" in the area of cooking: "If I want to bake a cake during the day, I just do it" (Erikson et al., 1986, p. 193). The story of this woman, like that of others in the sample, demonstrated that "although impairment and a certain degree of disability may be inevitable in old age, handicap and its deleterious effects on psychosocial well-being need not necessarily follow" (Erikson et al., 1986, p. 194). Not all the people in the sample shared this determination to overcome adversity. The key factor seemed to be an ability to define oneself independently of age- or illness-based limitations.

Finally, identity processes may provide a means of maintaining high levels of well-being in the face of less than satisfactory circumstances. Through identity assimilation, individuals may place a positive interpretation on what might otherwise cause them to feel that they are not accomplishing desired objectives. The process of the **life story**, through which individuals develop a narrative view of their lives that emphasizes the positive, is an example of identity assimilation as it alters the way that people interpret events that might otherwise detract from their self-esteem (Whitbourne, Sneed, & Skultety, 2002). For instance, older psychiatric patients in one study were found to minimize or even deny the fact that they had spent a significant part of their lives within the hospital (Whitbourne & Sherry, 1991). The sense of subjective well-being is maintained as individuals manage to portray their identity in a positive light, even when their actual experiences would support less favorable interpretations.

PRODUCTIVITY AND CREATIVITY

Although many strategies people use to enhance their well-being involve an active process of reinterpreting their experiences, there is still a reactive focus to the subjective well-being literature. Within this framework, individuals are seen as finding ways to adjust their experiences or their views of their experiences so that they are able to maintain a positive overall outlook. However, this literature does not necessarily address the extent to which individuals seek out new experiences and encounters that will move them beyond their current levels of well-being and accomplishments. Successful aging must surely involve more than maintaining a positive outlook on life, even as that life becomes potentially more stressful. To tackle this issue, it is necessary to go beyond some of the traditional social psychological literature on aging and move into the areas of productivity and creativity in adulthood.

The Relationship between Age and Creativity: Early Studies

Creativity is conventionally thought of as the ability to produce a notable or extraordinary piece of work. It is judged by a group of experts relative to a particular time period as being novel, useful to society, having an impact on society, and having an element of surprise. For almost two centuries, researchers and theorists have been interested in the question of whether aging is associated with changes in creativity as measured by the production of creative works. Examples of illustrious creative figures who continued to remain productive in old age, such as Michelangelo (1475–1564), challenge the stereotyped notion that youth is prime time for the expression of genius. The first empirical investigation of this question was conducted by Quetelet (1835/1968), who attempted to determine the quality of plays written by French playwrights over the course of the adult years.

The most extensive early investigation into the question of age and productivity was conducted by Lehman in his 1953 book *Age and Achievement* (Lehman, 1953). Lehman analyzed the production by age of creative works in all fields from the sciences to the arts. His analysis included both the number of works produced and their quality, but his major focus was on works that had significant impact in their fields. The major conclusion to emerge from Lehman's study was that the peak of productivity in the adult years tends to occur prior to the age of 40, and often between 30 and 35. However, the age period corresponding to a creative peak, in terms of quality and quantity, varies by the discipline of enterprise, as illustrated in Fig. 14.2. In these graphs, the vertical axis represents the percentage of total works completed by an individual in the five-year intervals shown on the horizontal axis. In other words, the graph shows the percentage of an individual's total works completed within each five-year age span. A peak corresponds to the five-year period when the majority of a person's works were completed. The curves represent averages for all individuals whose works were analyzed by age.

Lehman concluded from data such as that presented in Fig. 14.2 by discipline that earlier peaks are reached in the sciences and in fields in which success was dependent on intellectual imagination and physical ability. Increasingly later peaks are reached in fields that rely on experience and diplomacy. The writing of "best books" by authors falls in between these extremes, for success in literature involves imagination, discipline, and the philosophical perspectives gained from experience. A more detailed portrayal of the age peaks in various disciplines showing these relationships more clearly is given in Table 14-1. Although in general the ages increase in moving from the top to the bottom of the table, there is an exception for movie actresses, who have an earlier peak age than actors, a fact that is almost certainly still true today.

FIGURE 14.2
Age and Production in Three Disciplines

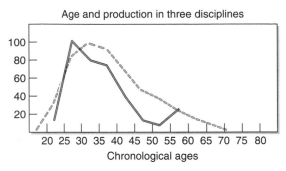

(a) Age versus production in chemistry. Solid line – 52 of the greatest chemical discoveries by 46 men now deceased. Broken line – 903 contributions of lesser average merit by 244 chemists now deceased.

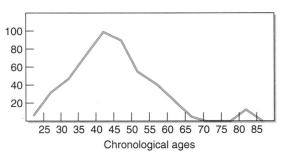

(b) Age versus production of 224 "best books" by 101 authors.

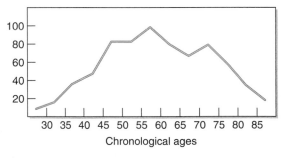

(c) Ages of chief ministers of England from 930 to 1950.

Source: Lehman, 1953.

TABLE 14-1
Peak Ages within Disciplines

Field	Peak Age
Athletics (tennis, baseball)	25–29
Chemistry	26–30
Mathematics	30–34
Physics	30–34
Practical inventions	30–34
Orchestral music	35–39
Psychology	30–39
Chess championships	29–33
Philosophy	35–39
Music	35–39
Art (oil paintings)	32–36
Best books	40–44
Movie actors (best paid)	30–34
Movie actresses (best paid)	23–27
College presidents	50–54
U.S. presidents	55–59
Foreign ambassadors	60–64
Senators	60–64
Supreme Court justices	70–74
Speakers of the House	70–74
Popes	82–92

Source: Lehman, 1953

The next major investigation conducted on age and creativity was conducted by Dennis (1966), who examined the total output, regardless of the quality of work, by contributors to seven domains within the arts and sciences. A summary of his findings is shown in Fig. 14.3. As can be seen from this figure, although there is a rather steep decline after the peak age in the arts, and somewhat less so in the sciences, productivity in terms of scholarship is maintained at a steady rate throughout later adulthood, with even a slight peak in the 60s. Dennis attempted to compensate for the differential ages lived by creators, which would obviously cut down on productivity in the later years, by limiting his sample to people who lived to be at least 80 years old. Furthermore, unlike Lehman, who factored the impact of a work into his age curves, Dennis did not attempt to evaluate the quality of a contribution. Instead, Dennis relied entirely on counts of published or produced works.

This original group of studies can be summarized as showing a rapid increase in creative output that reaches a career peak in the late 30s or early 40s, after which a steady decline begins. The peak and rate of decline vary by discipline, but the decline occurs nevertheless (Simonton, 1988). Based on this research, one would have to argue that creative productivity is unlikely to be a component of successful aging. Fortunately, the pessimistic interpretation of the early literature may not tell the whole story. As pointed out by Lehman (1953), "older thinkers" produced many great achievements. Fig. 14.4, for example, shows the production of great works of art, and as is evident, there is an

upturn in the 70s for "best" paintings. This apparent increase is in part a function of the fact that fewer individuals are alive at these ages. Those who are producing works of art represent a select portion of the population of artists who probably always were productive, a point that we will return to later. Although the tip of the peak is not as pronounced as in the earlier years, it nevertheless represents the work of some exceptionally talented older artists.

Similar late-life upturns can also be found in other disciplines within Lehman's investigation, including mathematics, physics, astronomy, medicine, philosophy, music, and poetry. A summary of some of the major contributors in this compilation is shown in Table 14-2. What might seem to be a striking omission is Ludwig van Beethoven, who produced some of his greatest work at the end of his life, including his renowned late string quartets. However, because he died at the age of 56, his late-career accomplishments would not be considered within discussions of late-life productivity. Similarly, the amazingly prolific Wolfgang Mozart died at the age of 35. These examples also illustrate some of the problems of conducting this type of research as important figures who die at a younger age but who might have remained productive had they lived longer are not counted.

FIGURE 14.3

Age and Productivity by Discipline

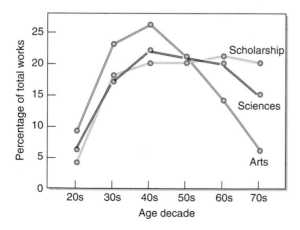

Source: Simonton, 1990 based on data from Dennis, 1966.

FIGURE 14.4

Production of Works of Art by Age ("best paintings")

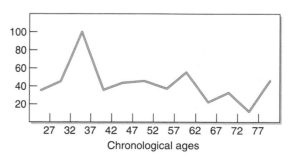

Source: Lehman, 1953

TABLE 14-2
Well-known Late-Life Creative Artists

Name	Field	Age at Contribution	Contribution
Giovanni Bellini, 1430–1516	Art	83	Altarpiece in San Giovanni Cristostomo, Venice
Anton Bruckner, 1824–1896	Music	70	Ninth Symphony
Michelangelo Buonaroti, 1475–1564	Art	89	Pieta Rondanini
Miguel de Cervantes, 1547–1616	Literature	68	Don Quixote (2nd part)
Benjamin Franklin, 1706–1790	Invention	78	Bifocals
Sir John Floyer, 1649–1734	Medicine	75	First medical text on geriatrics
Galileo Galilei, 1564–1642	Mechanics	74	Dialogues on mechanics
Johann Wolfgang von Goethe, 1749–1832	Literature	80	Faust (2nd part)
Thomas Hardy, 1840–1928	Poetry	88	Winter Words (posthumous)
Victor Hugo (1802–1885)	Poetry	75	The Art of Being a Grandfather
Alexander Humboldt, 1769–1859	Cosmology	78	Cosmos
Samuel Johnson, 1709–1784	Biography	72	Lives of the English Poets
Andrea Mantegna, 1431–1506	Painting	70	Parnassus
Gioacchino Rossini, 1792–1868	Music	72	Petite Messe solennelle
Herbert Spencer, 1820–1903	Philosophy	76	System of Philosophy
John Stephens, 1749–1838	Invention	76	First American built locomotive
Alfred Tennyson, 1809–1892	Literature	80	Crossing the Bar
Giuseppe Verde, 1813–1901	Music	80	Falstaff
Wilhelm Wundt, 1832–1920	Psychology	82–88	Social Psychology (2nd Edition)

Note: Warr, 1994.

A related problem with the simple counts or percentages of creative works as a function of age is that the works of all individuals lose their distinctness when curves representing the average are drawn. This problem is called the **compositional fallacy** and refers to the fact that when the average productivity rates per time period are averaged across the careers of several individuals, the summary curve that results does not describe the productivity of any of the individuals in that group (Simonton, 1997). Beethoven was productive up until his death at age 56, but another composer may have stopped producing new works at the age of 35 or 40. When the two productivity rates are averaged for the age of 50, for example, Beethoven's productivity will be underestimated and the other composer's will be overestimated. Furthermore, the fact that Beethoven died before reaching his sixtieth birthday means that a highly productive individual will have been removed from the population of composers and so his personal creativity will not be reflected in statistics on creativity in later life. The averaging of productive achievements across individuals results in a loss of information on the careers of individuals who themselves may vary in their ability to produce creative works. Clearly, Beethoven was a highly productive individual whose abilities even in midlife are obscured when his work is collapsed with those of others.

"What do you think?" | **14-3**

What is the difference between evaluating a person's creativity by number of works produced vs. quality of works produced?

Simonton's Model of Age and Creative Productivity. The types of problems just described in research on age and creative achievement led one of the more recent researchers on this topic to develop a model of late-life productivity that would be relatively insensitive to these methodological problems. Simonton (1997) originated a mathematical model relating age to creative productivity that controls for individual differences in **creative potential** and the nature of an individual's field of endeavor (Fig. 14.5). He developed this model through mathematical analyses of the previous data collected by Lehman, Dennis, and others.

There are three basic assumptions of Simonton's model of creative productivity (Simonton, 1998b). First of all, individuals vary in what he calls the initial creative potential, which is a hypothetical count of the total number of works that an individual would be able to produce in a life span with no upper limits. It can also be thought of as the number of original ideas that a given individual could ever theoretically produce. The second assumption is that the individual's creative potential is translated into concrete products (e.g., compositions, scientific articles) through a two-step process. One component of this process is **ideation**, the production of ideas for new products. The second component of the process is **elaboration**, which is the laborious process of transforming ideas into actual products. The productivity of an individual as a function of time is a function of m, a, and b, where m = creative potential, a = ideation rate, and b = elaboration rate.

A key aspect of Simonton's model is that the productivity of an individual is defined on the basis of **career age**, which is the age at which an individual begins to embark on his or her career (Simonton, 1988). Other researchers based their theories on chronological age and

FIGURE 14.5

Factors in Simonton's Theoretical Model of Creative Productivity

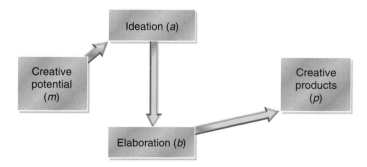

BEHIND THE RESEARCH

**DEAN KEITH SIMONTON, PROFESSOR OF PSYCHOLOGY
UNIVERSITY OF CALIFORNIA, DAVIS.**

What is most exciting to you about research in this field?
"When the age is in, the wit is out," said Shakespeare, echoing a recurrent and commonplace belief about intellectual development in the latter part of life. For a long time, the notion of age decrements dominated the literature on the relation between age and creativity as well. To me, the most exciting ideas to emerge from recent research is that creativity does not necessarily have to display an inexorable decline with age. Instead, the degree and nature of any age decrement is contingent on a host of extraneous factors, some of which are under personal control. These results have become especially exciting for me after I entered the latter half of my own life!

What do you see as the major challenges?
The study of the relationship between age and creativity is perhaps the oldest research subject in the behavioral sciences. The first objective and quantitative inquiry was published by Quetelet back in 1835. Since that time, a huge number of additional empirical investigations have been published, so that we now possess a vast amount of knowledge about how creativity changes across the life span. What is more elusive, however, is a comprehensive theoretical understanding for all of these findings. Although I have tried to put forward a theoretical model, I am the first to confess that it represents no more than a first step toward a complete and precise account.

Where do you see this field headed in the next decade?
Currently, there is a movement afoot to develop a truly positive psychology. Positive psychology concentrates on human assets and strengths rather than deficits and weaknesses. As an obvious source of personal strength and even societal benefit, creativity has become among the core topics of this movement. At the same time, a large cohort of individuals throughout the world-the baby boom generation-is headed toward the more mature years of life. This trend makes it all the more urgent to comprehend what kinds of creative assets human beings can expect in their concluding years.

as a result did not take into account the fact that people begin their careers at different ages. In calculating peak age of productivity, the age at which a person embarks on a career must be accounted for to control for the fact that some people may be past their prime when others are just beginning theirs in terms of their chronological age.

The final model that results from combining creative potential, ideation, and elaboration rate as a function of career age (not chronological age) is shown in Fig. 14.6 (Simonton, 1984). In this figure, career age is represented as t, and the annual production of creative ideas is represented as p. The peak age and the rate of decline are based on equations derived from differential calculus, and the values of a, b, and m were estimated from the published data on career productivity across a variety of fields of endeavor.

FIGURE 14.6
Simonton's Model Relating Productivity and Career Age

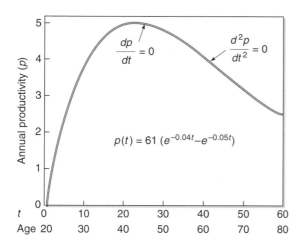

$$p(t) = 61\ (e^{-0.04t} - e^{-0.05t})$$

Source: Simonton, 1984, p. 86

Within this general model, variations are predicted to occur in the relationship between career age and productivity when the values of a and b vary, which they do across creative disciplines. For example, in fields such as poetry and pure mathematics, the values are those shown in Figure 14.6, (0.04 and 0.05). However, in other fields, these numbers may be lower, reflecting the fact that in certain areas, people take longer to produce ideas and to turn their ideas into creative works. The differences may show that ideas in poetry and mathematics have faster rates of information processing because they are based on simpler, more abstract, and finite concepts compared to history and geology. Therefore, the numbers for a and b in history and geology are smaller, (estimated at 0.02 and 0.03). Although these seem to be small differences, when put into the equation, the result is a career curve with a lower peak and a longer or more slowly diminishing tail.

Variations may also occur in the extent of an individual's creative potential. Even within the same domain of creative activity, people vary in their ability to produce creative works (again, think of Beethoven). A very productive individual will have a different career trajectory than one who is more limited in the ability to produce novel ideas. For this part of the model, Simonton attempted to specify three points in the career of a creative individual which, in very straightforward terms, are the first, best, and last significant contributions. The age of first contribution corresponds to the age at which the first work of high quality is produced. This is the point that signifies the beginning of the individual's career. The age of best contribution defines the peak of the career, when a work is produced that most enhances the individual's reputation. Finally, the age of last contribution corresponds to the end of the individual's career, and although there may be further productions, they will not have any noteworthy value. The ages of first, best, and last creative productions are predicted within Simonton's model on the basis of age of career onset and degree of creative potential. A sample of four curves based on variations in these factors is shown in Fig. 14.7. In these curves, t = career age and Age = actual age.

The top graphs in this figure show people who have an early career onset age, meaning that they have their first significant production at the actual age of 20. A person with high creative potential will show a rapid growth in productivity to the age of best contribution and will maintain relatively high productivity until late in both career and actual ages. The bottom two graphs are of individuals with a late onset career, with a first contribution at age 30. These individuals will peak later and continue to produce until a later actual age than those with an early onset. Individuals who begin early, then, peak early and achieve their last significant production at an earlier age than those who begin later. Furthermore,

FIGURE 14.7

Typology of Career Trajectories

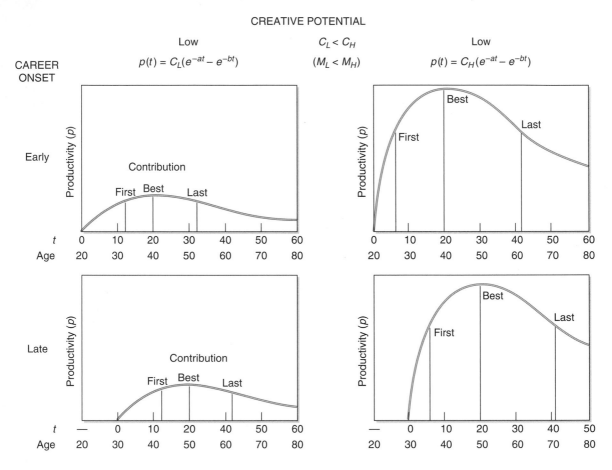

Source: Simonton, 1997.

those with higher creative potential will remain more productive throughout their careers than will those with lower potential, regardless of when they produce their first important work. However, those with higher creative potential will also achieve a significant production relatively earlier in their careers than those with lower potential. Those with higher creative potential also achieve their last important creative landmark at a later age than do those with lower potential.

A question that might seem important is whether quality of creative productivity has any connection to quantity. According to the **equal odds rule**, there is a positive relationship between quality and quantity of work. Those who produce more output are more likely to score a "hit" or success than are those who produce fewer works. An implication of this principle is the notion that people are most likely to produce their best work during their peak period of productivity on the basis of probability alone.

Returning to the question of the relationship between age and creative output, Simonton's model places the greatest emphasis not on actual age but on career age. Productivity in later life will be higher among people who began their careers at a later age and so will the age of best work. However, people with high creative potential are more likely to have a high rate of productivity both early and late in their careers. There will be as long as a 20-year span between best and last work for highly creative people compared to the 10-year span for the less creative. Some individuals with very low creative potential may produce only one significant work, which is their first, best, and last contribution (a "one-hit wonder," in today's terms).

Even though later life may be associated with a drop from the time of peak productivity, Simonton's model allows for the possibility of highly productive and creative older individuals. Some of the individuals in Table 14-2 began their careers at relatively late ages. Anton Bruckner, for example, wrote his first symphony at the age of 42 and his first masterpiece at the age of 50. A late career peak would also be reached by an individual who changed fields in midcareer, which resets the career clock back to zero. Other individuals excelled in later life in fields with relatively late peaks such as history and philosophy. Individuals with a high degree of creative potential also have longer careers than do those who have less potential. Verdi composed his first operatic masterpiece at the age of 29 and his last at the age of 80. Highly productive older individuals, according to the equal odds rule, have a relatively high probability of creating a masterwork. In addition, as discussed below, there may be a resurgence in creativity that occurs within the last years of life leading to a secondary peak, much as in Fig. 14.4 (Simonton, 1998b).

Characteristics of Last Works. Apart from their frequency or overall impact, the creative products of older artists, composers, writers, and scientists have been observed to possess special qualities not observed in the work of younger persons. One of these is the **old age style** (Lindauer, 1998), an approach to one's art that eliminates the fine details and instead presents the essence of the work's intended meaning. The work becomes less objective and focused on formal perfection and instead more subjective. In a painting, for example, the artist may simplify the image by eliminating details closely tied to accurate renditions of objects and people. A sculptor may concentrate more on the form and underlying emotion of the piece rather than on representing each and every detail. Henri Matisse referred to this change in his style as a "distillation of form. I now keep only the sign which suffices, necessary for its existence in its own form, for the composition as I conceive it" (Brill, 1967, p.40).

A good example of the old age style is provided by the work of Michelangelo, whose two pietas, produced in youth and old age, contrast sharply in their style and emotional tone. The old age style may also be seen in a writer's work, as it becomes more reflective, introspective, and subjective (Lubart & Sternberg, 1998). Characters in literature may be portrayed more realistically but also with greater empathy, and they come to take on greater complexity and a sense of timelessness (Adams-Price, 1998).

The emergence of an old age style can be seen in the works of many artists in addition to Michelangelo, including Rembrandt, Renoir, Matisse, Degas, Georgia O'Keeffe, and Picasso. Large brushstrokes may take the place of painstakingly crafted renderings, and as a result, the work is more intense. As in the case of the pietas, the artist may choose to focus on themes related to aging or death. This is not to say that the work has become depressing, but that it

BIOPSYCHOSOCIAL PERSPECTIVE

MODELS OF SUCCESSFUL aging and creativity are useful and inspiring, but an important shortcoming is that they fail to take sufficient account of sociocultural context. Socioeconomically and racially disadvantaged individuals have a much lower chance of ever reaching old age, much less "successful" old age, as traditionally defined within psychology. Certain sectors of the population, particularly minorities from low-income backgrounds, do not have the opportunity to achieve good health and full expression of their innate abilities. The emphasis on religion in the lives of older African Americans provides an important coping mechanism for surviving discrimination, poor living conditions, and demoralization (Taylor & Chatters, 1991). However, this does not negate the fact that education and income remain lower among blacks in the United States and that even men with a college education are likely to suffer career discrimination, as noted in Chapter 10.

A second critical fact in analyses of successful aging regards the definition of eminence as used in studies of aging and creativity. Women are far less likely than would be expected on the basis of chance to appear in lists of the creative and productive at any age. However, it is only within the area of children's literature that Lehman (1953) listed women as constituting anywhere near 50% of the notable contributors. A total of only 20 women were listed in the Lehman work as "worthy of mention" (p. 91). The second group who receives little, if any, mention is African Americans. Simonton (1998a) explored the question of whether assessments of creative output among historical figures would show evidence of bias against this group. He examined whether African Americans who had achieved recognition within reference works specific to black scholarship would also be mentioned in reference works of the white majority culture.

Although there was considerable convergence between the minority and majority reference works, one-fifth of African Americans who had achieved eminence in the minority reference works were not mentioned in any of the majority indices of eminence. Furthermore, certain areas of accomplishment within black culture were not recognized within the majority reference works, including law, education, religion, classical music, and the sciences. White reference works gave higher ratings to African Americans in the fields of athletics, and jazz and blues music, but African American sources gave greater recognition to those who achieved eminence in the civil rights movement.

These differential patterns of recognition, though against a backdrop of closer than expected similarities between minority and white reference works, point to differential opportunities that affect an individual's ability to achieve career recognition, if not personal fulfillment. Clearly, differences in educational opportunities as well as cultural values play a role in determining the ultimate achievements of people from nonmajority backgrounds. And those who do manage to break through cultural barriers are likely to receive considerable recognition within their own as well as the majority culture. Some examples are Jackie Robinson, who was the first African American to play major league baseball, Booker T. Washington, the first black to receive an honorary degree from Harvard, and William Grant Still, the first black to conduct a major symphony orchestra and to have his own composition performed by a major American orchestra. These "famous firsts" seem particularly important within African American reference works of eminence because they attest to the ability of highly talented and persistent individuals to overcome the effects of discrimination. That their work has until recently been overlooked in studies of aging and creativity limits the generalizability of current models of successful aging.

presents the reality of the artist's life and impending death in a manner that may have particular clarity and a strong impact on the viewer. These features of old age style are by no means universal, however, for some artists may continue to paint with the attention to detail and refinement shown in their earlier work. Furthermore, as was true for Marc Chagall and Henri Matisse, the colors and themes may remain bright and rich.

The "old age style" in Michelangelo's (1475–1564) work can be seen in these two pietas. The St. Peter's Pieta (left) is carefully crafted, lavish in detail, and serene; the Rondanini Pieta (right) is roughly carved and portrays a far less peaceful image. In fact, the Rondanini is a fragment, destroyed partly by Michelangelo's own hand shortly before he died. Art historians suggest that he intended it for his own tomb.

Related to old-age style is the **swan song phenomenon**, a brief renewal of creativity that can stimulate the creation of new works and a new style of work (Simonton, 1989). Musical compositions that reflect the swan song phenomenon are characterized by shorter main themes and simpler melodies than the prior works of the composer. An example of the swan song is *Lachrymosa*, from Mozart's last work, the Requiem in D minor, written while he was dying (this is the music in the funeral scene of the movie, *Amadeus*). As in Mozart's case, the resurgence of creativity that stimulates the swan song may come about with the composer's awareness of increased closeness to death. With the approach of their death, composers may strip away some of their professional and personal ties and focus with renewed vigor on their music. These works often become some of the most successful that the composers produce, and thus in many ways may grant the composer a certain immortality. The swan song phenomenon is perhaps a special case of the old age style because it also implies a certain simplicity and paring away of distractions and details.

A third feature of the old age style is observed primarily among scientists and academicians. The focus of the work moves from innovation and discovery toward integration and synthesis of existing knowledge. The individual may

This Picasso painting ("The Young Painter," 1972) provides a vivid illustration of the old age style. Note the simplicity of line and form.

he became more expressive and less bound by conventional forms. Blindness forced changes in the painting of a number of well-known older artists, including Georgia O'Keeffe, Mary Cassatt, Edgar Degas, and Claude Monet. Henri Matisse suffered from stomach cancer and was confined to a wheelchair at the end of his life. Despite these severe limitations, these artists continued to produce great works until or nearly until their last years of life. In the case of the artist Monet, cataracts caused changes not only in the clarity of his vision but in his ability to see colors. As he painted his beloved water lilies, he was literally unable to see the colors on the canvas that he knew appeared in nature. Even special glasses (colored yellow) could not correct this defect, and it was not until he was successfully treated with cataract surgery at the age of 85 that his color vision was restored. His final work, an enormous series of water lilies, was installed in a Paris museum after his death. The colors in these final paintings were as vibrant as they had been in his earlier work. Similarly,

become more involved in the writing of texts and integrative reviews. In some cases, the subject matter shifts to studies of aging, as was true for B. F. Skinner toward the end of his life (Skinner & Vaughan, 1983) and apparently for Sir John Floyer, who wrote the first geriatrics text in the early 1700s when he was 75 years old. A shift to age-related concerns may also be apparent in a person's research or practical inventions, as was the case for Benjamin Franklin, who invented bifocals when he himself was 78 years old.

The old age style may be stimulated by proximity to death, a desire to leave behind a legacy, or perhaps as a reaction to age-related changes or health problems. Beethoven became deaf in his later years, and his musical style also changed. For example, in his late string quartets,

Wolfgang Amadeus Mozart on his deathbed. During his final weeks of life, he composed "Requiem in D Minor," a masterful work that contained Lachrymose, one of the most haunting examples of the swan song. In the movie "Amadeus," Lachrymose is played during the funeral scene.

unable to paint, Matisse changed his medium to paper sculptures, which have since become some of the classic instances of this master's life contributions (the book's cover features a prime example). In another creative medium, the poet William Carlos Williams suffered a stroke in his 60s, after which he became severely depressed. Following treatment for depression, he went on to produce some of his greatest works, including the Pulitzer Prize-winning Pictures from Bruegel, published when he was 79 (Cohen, 1998).

The limitations caused by physical and sensory age-related changes suffered by some of these artists were not necessarily met with equanimity. Michelangelo, for example, attempted to destroy his last pieta, and it was saved only through the efforts of his apprentices. Similarly, Monet destroyed many of the canvases he produced during the years he suffered from cataracts. Picasso's final self-portrait "facing death" portrays the face of a man who refuses to accept his own physical aging. Georgia O'Keeffe, who

lived to the age of 98, was similarly frustrated with her inability to see in her last decade of life and her need to change mediums to sculpture and pottery. Nevertheless, all of these individuals lived very long lives, and despite their personal frustrations, they managed to express their creative potential right up until the very end.

SUCCESSFUL AGING: FINAL PERSPECTIVES

Individuals in later life appear not only to manage to feel satisfied with their lives but also to be able to achieve new forms of creative expression. Many scientists, artists, writers, and political leaders have produced notable contributions in their later adult years. The accomplishments of these unusual individuals adds to the literature on subjective well-being as well as the framework proposed by Erikson and colleagues of "vital involvement" to add support to the concept of successful aging.

Assess Yourself

"Draw Your Life"

Thinking back on your life and projecting into the future, complete on a separate sheet of paper the "Draw Your Life" activity. Turn the page so that it is horizontal, and draw a line at the bottom labeled "Age and/or Year." Now sketch out the events in your life, marking off any major periods or eras, from the past through the present and into the future. After you have finished, look to see how the curve corresponds to some of the productivity curves shown in this chapter. Second, look at your sense of time perspective. Is your drawing primarily future-, present-, or past-oriented? Third, what areas of accomplishment are important to you? Did you include events from your work and school life, your family, or the outside world? Compare your drawing to those of other students and see how they differ. Keep this drawing with your notes from this class and look back on it in the future to see if the events you predicted would happen have in fact occurred.

As was shown in the analysis of Simonton's model of creative productivity, people who begin their careers with a high degree of creative potential are likely to maintain higher creative output well into their 60s, 70s, and beyond. Where does this creative potential come from? In part, the level of talent needed to sustain such a long and productive career appears to have a genetic basis. Unusually gifted people, whether in the arts, politics, or athletics, have, to a certain extent, inherited innate physical, social, and intellectual abilities that form the basis for their ultimate success (Bouchard, 1994; Eysenck, 1995). These abilities are most likely not unitary traits, but a constellation of inherited tendencies that together produce the unique attributes needed for success in the chosen field of endeavor (Lykken, 1998). Of course, for these abilities to be expressed requires sustenance through the environment, in the form of training, opportunities, and provision of incentives (Simonton, 1999). Furthermore, through the principle of niche-picking, people with certain inherited predispositions will seek the opportunities they need to express and further develop their talent (Scarr & McCartney, 1983).

"What do you think?" **14-4**

How is productivity measured in "ordinary" people at the end of life?

Moving beyond the unusual contributions of highly creative individuals, we can see creativity as a process that characterizes ordinary people as well. Creativity can be thought of as a process of personality development in which the individual develops a completely open mind to new experiences and is able to enjoy and appreciate the finer nuances of life. Ordinary people can create creative products that are novel, useful,

and personally satisfying in forms ranging from a flower arrangement to a pleasing snapshot. Life transformations such as retirement can also be approached creatively as a liberating experience (Cohen, 1999).

For the ordinary individual who does not achieve lasting fame, then, the process of successful aging may involve an equally creative process of constructing a personal narrative or life story (Luborsky, 1998). This narrative will involve a complex negotiation of cultural (Luborsky & McMullen, 1999) and personal forces (Whitbourne, 1985). Cultural forces shape the parameters individuals use to evaluate themselves and by which they are evaluated by others. Furthermore, these forces set the parameters for the opportunities that individuals have to achieve their goals. Part of a "successful" life narrative may involve coming to grips with the recognition of how cultural constraints have affected the individual's ability to realize the hopes and dreams of youth. Yet, the individual must also strive to transcend these constrictions and arrive at a personal sense of meaning in life that rises above the boundaries of culture and time.

SUMMARY

1. The process of successful aging involves being able to overcome the threats to physical and psychological well-being presented by the aging process. However, in addition to "survival," successful aging involves the ability to become engaged with life in terms of both relationships and productive activity. Subjective well-being, a component of successful aging, is higher in older adults, a phenomenon referred to as the paradox of well-being. There are several possible mechanisms through which higher subjective well-being is achieved, including adaptation, goal achievement, coping mechanisms,

social comparison, and the use of identity assimilation in forming a life story.

2. Research on productivity and creativity has involved attempts to determine whether older individuals are more or less able to maintain the quality and quantity of works produced when younger. Variations by discipline were observed in early studies in which peak ages were reached earlier for areas in which imagination and physical ability are required. However, the findings of various authors indicated overall declines after peaks reached in young adulthood. In some cases, upturns were noted in the productivity of individuals living until the 70s and beyond among exceptionally talented older persons. Many achievements have also been produced by people in advanced old age. This area of research is hampered by the fact that some individuals who may have maintained their productivity do not live until old age. Furthermore, average productivity rates do not take into account the individual variations shown in the quality and quantity of works. Simonton's model of creative productivity describes the relationship between age and production of creative works using a mathematical formula that incorporates creative potential, ideation, and elaboration based on the career age of an individual rather than chronological age. In this model, highly productive individuals begin early and maintain a high production rate long into their careers. Those who are more productive are also more likely to produce works of high quality.

3. The old age style characterizes the works of older artists and musicians. One component of the old age style is simplification of detail and increasing subjectivity. The swan song phenomenon is a related phenomenon, referring to the tendency of composers to produce very simple themes in their last works. Among scientists and academicians, the old age style refers to a tendency to synthesize, producing works such as texts and reviews that integrate existing knowledge. The old age style may be a reaction to increasing proximity to death or to the presence of age-related changes or health problems.

4. For individuals who do not achieve lasting fame through their work, the expression of creativity may come about through the construction of a personal narrative. In this process, the individual comes to grips with the accomplishments and failures of his or her life and arrives at a personal sense of meaning.

GLOSSARY

Adaptation: psychological mechanisms that individuals may use to maintain high well-being in the face of objectively negative circumstances.

Career age: the age at which an individual begins to embark on his or her career.

Compositional fallacy: the fact that when the productivity rates per time period are averaged across the careers of several individuals, the summary curve that results does not describe the productivity of any of the individuals in that group.

Creativity: the ability to produce a notable or extraordinary piece of work.

Creative potential: hypothetical count of the total number of works that an individual would be able to produce in a life span with no upper limits.

Elaboration: the laborious process of transforming ideas into products.

Equal odds rule: the fact that there is a positive relationship between quality and quantity of work.

Ideation: the production of ideas for new products.

Life satisfaction: the cognitive evaluation of one's life circumstances.

Life story: process through which individuals develop a narrative view of their lives that emphasizes the positive.

Old age style: an approach to one's art that eliminates the fine details and instead presents the essence of the work's intended meaning.

Paradox of well-being: proposal that despite their objective difficulties, people in later life feel good about themselves and their situations.

Set point perspective: proposal that biologically determined temperament sets the boundaries for the levels of well-being an individual experiences throughout life.

Social comparison: process through which individuals look at the situations of others who are more unfortunate than they are and comfort themselves with the thought that things could be worse.

Social indicator model: proposal that demographic and social structural variables account for individual differences in levels of well-being.

Subjective well-being: psychological state composed of positive affect, negative affect, and life satisfaction.

Successful aging: term used to reflect the ability of an older person to adapt to the aging process.

Swan song phenomenon: a brief renewal of creativity that can stimulate the creation of new works and a new style of work.

References

A typology. *International Journal of Aging and Human Development, 28*, 37–51.

Aartsen, M. J., Smits, C. H., van Tilburg, T., Knipscheer, K. C., & Deeg, D. J. (2002). Activity in older adults: Cause or consequence of cognitive functioning? A longitudinal study on everyday activities and cognitive performance in older adults. *Journals of Gerontology Series B: Psychological Sciences and Social Sciences, 57*, P153–162.

Abe, M., Nakura, J., Yamamoto, M., Jin, J. J., Wu, Z., Tabara, Y., Yamamoto, Y., Igase, M., Kohara, K., & Miki, T. (2002). Association of GNAS1 gene variant with hypertension depending on smoking status. *Hypertension, 40*, 261–265.

Abeles, N., Cooley, S., Deitch, I., Harper, M. S., Hinrichsen, G., Lopez, M., & Molinari, V. (1997). *What practitioners should know about working with older adults.* Washington, DC: American Psychological Association.

Abrams, R. C., & Horowitz, S. V. (1999). Personality disorders after age 50: A meta-analytic review of the literature. In E. Rosowsky, R. C. Abrams & R. A. Zweig (Eds.), *Personality disorders in older adults: Emerging issues in diagnosis and treatment* (pp. 55–68). Mahweh, NJ: Erlbaum.

Abrams, R. C., Lachs, M., McAvay, G., Keohane, D. J., & Bruce, M. L. (2002). Predictors of self-neglect in community-dwelling elders. *American Journal of Psychiatry, 159*, 1724–1730.

Achenbaum, W. A. (1978). *Old age in the new land The American experience since 1970.* Baltimore: Johns Hopkins University Press.

Acitelli, L. K., Douvan, E., & Veroff, J. (1993). Perceptions of conflict in the first year of marriage: How important are similarity and understanding? *Journal of Social and Personal Relationships, 10*, 5–19.

Adams, R. G., & Blieszner, R. (1994). An integrative conceptual framework for friendship research. *Journal of Social and Personal Relationships, 11*, 163–184.

Adams, R. G., & Blieszner, R. (1995). Midlife friendship patterns. In N. Vanzetti & S. Duck (Eds.), *A lifetime of relationships* (pp. 336–363). San Francisco: Brooks/Cole.

Adams, S. H., Cartwright, L. K., Ostrove, J. M., Stewart, A. J., & Wink, P. (1998). Psychological predictors of good health in three longitudinal samples of educated midlife women. *Health Psychology, 17*, 412–420.

Adams-Price, C. (1998). Aging, writing, and creativity. In C. Adams-Price (Ed.), *Creativity and successful aging: Theoretical and empirical approaches* (pp. 289–310). New York: Springer.

Adler, N. E., Boyce, T., Chesney, M. A., Cohen, S., Folkman, S., Kahn, R. L., & Syme, S. L. (1994). Socioeconomic status and health: The challenge of the gradient. *American Psychologist, 49*, 15–24.

Administration on Aging (2001a). *A Profile of Older Americans: 2001.* Washington, DC: http://www.aoa.gov/aoa/stats/profile/2001/6.html

Administration on Aging (2002). *The Many Faces of Aging: Resources to Effectively Serve Minority Older Persons.* Washington, DC.

Administration on Aging (2003). *A Profile of Older Americans.* http://www.aoa.gov/prof/Statistics/profile/2002profile.pdf, accessed 12/11/03.

Administration on Aging (2004). *A Profile of Older Americans 2003:* http://www.aoa.gov/prof/Statistics/profile/2003/2003 profile.pdf, accessed 1/20/04.

Agency for Health Care Policy and Research (AHCPR). (1996). *Urinary Incontinence in Adults: Acute and Chronic Management. Clinical Practice Guideline No. 2.* Rockville, MD: AHCPR publication 96–0682.

Agnew, J., & Suruda, A. J. (1993). Age and fatal work-related falls. *Human Factors, 35,* 731–736.

Agronick, G. S., & Duncan, L. E. (1998). Personality and social change: Individual differences, life path, and importance attributed to the women's movement: A longitudinal analysis. *Journal of Personality and Social Psychology, 74,* 1545–1555.

Ainsworth, M., Blehar, M., Waters, E., & Wall, S. (1978). *Patterns of attachment: A psychological study of the strange situation.* Hillsdale, NJ: Erlbaum.

Aisen, P. S., & Pasinetti, G. M. (1998). Glucocorticoids in Alzheimer's disease. The story so far. *Drugs and Aging, 12,* 1–6.

Akima, H., Kano, Y., Enomoto, Y., Ishizu, M., Okada, M., Oishi, Y., Katsuta, S., & Kuno, S. (2001). Muscle function in 164 men and women aged 20–84 yr. *Medicine and Science in Sports and Exercise, 33,* 220–226.

Alam, M., Arndt, K. A., & Dover, J. S. (2002). Severe, intractable headache after injection with botulinum a exotoxin: Report of 5 cases. *Journal of the American Academy of Dermatology, 46,* 62–65.

Ala-Mursula, L., Vahtera, J., Kivimaki, M., Kevin, M. V., & Pentti, J. (2002). Employee control over working times: associations with subjective health and sickness absences. *Journal of Epidemiology and Community Health, 56,* 272–278.

Aldwin, C. M., & Gilmer, D. F. (1999). Health and optimal aging. In J. C. Cavanaugh & S. K. Whitbourne (Eds.), *Gerontology: Interdisciplinary perspectives* (pp. 123–154). New York: Oxford University Press.

Alexopoulos, G. S., Buckwalter, K., Olin, J., Martinez, R., Wainscott, C., & Krishnan, K. R. (2002). Comorbidity of late life depression: an opportunity for research on mechanisms and treatment. *Biological Psychiatry, 52,* 543–558.

Alfredsson, L., Hammar, N., Fransson, E., de Faire, U., Hallqvist, J., Knutsson, A., Nilsson, T., Theorell, T., & Westerholm, P. (2002). Job strain and major risk factors for coronary heart disease among employed males and females in a Swedish study on work, lipids and fibrinogen. *Scandinavian Journal of Work, Environment & Health, 28,* 238–248.

Allaire, J. C., & Marsiske, M. (2002). Well- and ill-defined measures of everyday cognition: Relationship to older adults' intellectual ability and functional status. *Psychology and Aging, 17,* 101–115.

Allen, J. R., Whittlesey, S., Pfefferbaum, B., & Ondersma, M. L. (1999). Community and coping of mothers and grandmothers of children killed in a human-caused disaster. *Psychiatric Annals, 29,* 85–91.

Allen, K. R., & Walker, A. J. (2000). Qualitative research. In C. Hendrick & S. S. Hendrick (Eds.), *Close relationships* (pp. 19–30). Thousand Oaks, CA: Sage Publications.

Allen, K. R., Blieszner, R., & Roberto, K. A. (2000). Families in the middle and later years: A review and critique of research in the 1990s. *Journal of Marriage and the Family, 62,* 911–926.

Allolio, B., & Arlt, W. (2002). DHEA treatment: myth or reality? *Trends in Endocrinology and Metabolism, 13,* 288–294.

Aloia, J. F., Vaswani, A., Feuerman, M., Mikhail, M., & Ma, R. (2000). Differences in skeletal and muscle mass with aging in black and white women. *American Journal of Physiology—Endocrinology & Metabolism, 278,* E1153–1157.

Altman, D. F. (1990). Changes in gastrointestinal, pancreatic, biliary, and hepatic function with aging. *Gastroenterology Clinics of North America, 19,* 227–234.

Amato, P. R. (2000). The consequences of divorce for adults and children. *Journal of Marriage and the Family, 62,* 511–521.

American Cancer Society (2002). Cancer facts and figures 2001. http://www.cancer.org/docroot/STT/stt_0_2001.asp?sitearea=STT&level=1F&F2001.pdf. Accessed 1/23/04.

American College of Sports Medicine (1998). American College of Sports Medicine Position Stand. Exercise and physical activity for older adults. *Medicine and Science in Sports and Exercise, 30,* 992–1008.

American Heart Association (2003). *International Cardiovascular Disease Statistics.*

American Psychiatric Association (2000). *(DSM-IV-TR) Diagnostic and Statistical Manual of Mental Disorders,* (4th ed.), *Text Revision.* Washington, DC: American Psychiatric Association.

American Psychiatric Association (2000). *DSM-IV: Diagnostic and Statistical Manual of Mental Disorders Text Revision.* Washington DC: American Psychiatric Association.

American Psychological Association (2003). *Ethical Principles of Psychologists and Code of Conduct.* Retrieved August 2003, from http://www.apa.org/ethics/code2002.html#8_02

American Psychological Association, (2003). *Guidelines for psychological practice with older adults.* Washington, D.C.: American Psychological Association.

Aminoff, T., Smolander, J., Korhonen, O., & Louhevaara, V. (1996). Physical work capacity in dynamic exercise with differing muscle masses in healthy young and older men. *European Journal of Applied Physiology and Occupational Physiology, 73,* 180–185.

Ancoli-Israel, S. (1997). Sleep problems in older adults: Putting myths to bed. *Geriatrics, 52,* 20–30.

Anderson, R. N. (2002). *Deaths: Leading causes for 2000* (Vol. 50, No. 16). Hyattsville MD: National Center for Health Statistics.

Anschutz, L., Camp, C. J., Markley, R. P., & Kramer, J. J. (1985). Maintenance and generalization of mnemonics for grocery shopping by older adults. *Experimental Aging Research, 11,* 157–160.

Anschutz, L., Camp, C. J., Markley, R. P., & Kramer, J. J. (1987). Remembering mnemonics: A three-year follow-up on the effects of mnemonics training in elderly adults. *Experimental Aging Research, 13,* 141–143.

Anstey, K. J., Lord, S. R., & Williams, P. (1997). Strength in the lower limbs, visual contrast sensitivity, and simple reaction time predict cognition in older women. *Psychology and Aging, 12,* 137–144.

Antonucci, T. C., & Akiyama, H. (1987). Social networks in adult life and a preliminary examination of the convoy model. *Journal of Gerontology, 42,* 519–527.

Antonucci, T. C., Fuhrer, R., & Dartigues, J. (1997). Social relations and depressive symptomatology in a sample of community-dwelling French older adults. *Psychology and Aging, 12,* 189–195.

Arias, E., & Smith, B. L. (2003). *Deaths: Preliminary data for 2001.* Hyattsville, MD: National Center for Health Statistics.

Arias, E., Anderson, R. N., Kung, H.-C., Murphy, S. L., & Kochanek, K. D. (2003). Deaths: Final data for 2001. *National Vital Statistics Report, 52, No. 3.*

Aries, P. (1974). *Western attitudes toward death: From the middle ages to the present.* Baltimore, MD: Johns Hopkins University Press.

Aries, P. (1981). *The hour of our death.* New York: Knopf.

Armstrong-Stassen, M. (2001). Reactions of older employees to organizational downsizing: The role of gender, job level, and time. *Journals of Gerontology: Series B: Psychological Sciences and Social Sciences, 56,* P234–P243.

Artistico, D., Cervone, D., & Pezzuti, L. (2003). Perceived self-efficacy and everyday problem solving among young and older adults. *Psychology & Aging, 18,* 68–79.

Asanuma, M., Nishibayashi-Asanuma, S., Miyazaki, I., Kohno, M., & Ogawa, N. (2001). Neuroprotective effects of nonsteroidal anti-inflammatory drugs by direct scavenging of nitric oxide radicals. *Journal of Neurochemistry, 76,* 1895–1904.

Ashford, J. W., & Mortimer, J. A. (2002). Non-familial Alzheimer's disease is mainly due to genetic factors. *Journal of Alzheimer's Disease, 4,* 169–177.

Aspinall, R., & Andrew, D. (2000). Thymic involution in aging. *Journal of Clinical Immunology, 20,* 250–256.

Atchley, R. C. (1982). The process of retirement: Comparing women and men. In M. Szinovacz (Ed.), *Women's retirement: Policy implications of current research* (pp. 153–168). Beverly Hills, CA: Sage.

Atchley, R. C. (1989). A continuity theory of normal aging. *The Gerontologist, 29,* 183–190.

Atchley, R. C. (2000). *Social forces and aging* (9th ed.). Belmont, CA: Wadsworth Thomson Learning.

Austin, J. T., & Vancouver, J. F. (1996). Goal constructs in psychology: Structure, process, and content. *Psychological Bulletin, 120,* 338–375.

Babb, T. G., & Rodarte, J. R. (2000). Mechanism of reduced maximal expiratory flow with aging. *Journal of Applied Physiology, 89,* 505–511.

Bachu, A., & O'Connell, M. (2001). *Fertility of American women: June 2000. Current Population Reports, P20-543RV.* Washington, DC: U.S. Census Bureau.

Baddeley, A. D. (1986). *Working memory.* London: Oxford University Press.

Baddeley, A., Chincotta, D., & Adlam, A. (2001). Working memory and the control of action: Evidence from task switching. *Journal of Experimental Psychology: General, 130,* 641–657.

Bailis, D. S., & Chipperfield, J. G. (2002). Compensating for losses in perceived personal control over health: a role for collective self-esteem in healthy aging. *Journals of Gerontology: Series B: Psychological Sciences and Social Sciences, 57,* P531–539.

Ball, K., Berch, D. B., Helmers, K. F., Jobe, J. B., Leveck, M. D., Marsiske, M., Morris, J. N., Rebok, G. W., Smith, D. M., Tennstedt, S. L., Unverzagt, F. W., & Willis, S. L. (2002). Effects of cognitive training interventions with older adults: A randomized controlled trial. *Journal of the American Medical Association, 288,* 2271–2281.

Baltes, M. M., & Lang, F. R. (1997). Everyday functioning and successful aging: The impact of resources. *Psychology and Aging, 12,* 433–443.

Baltes, P. B. (1968). Longitudinal and cross-sectional sequences in the study of age and generation effects. *Human Development, 11,* 145–171.

Baltes, P. B. (1979). Life-span developmental psychology: Some converging observations on history and theory. In P. B. Baltes & J. O. G. Brim (Eds.), *Life-span development and behavior* (Vol. 2, pp. 255–279). New York: Academic Press.

Baltes, P. B. (1989). Cognitive training research on fluid intelligence in old age: What can older adults achieve by themselves? *Psychology and Aging, 4,* 217–221.

Baltes, P. B., & Baltes, M. M. (1990). Psychological perspectives on successful aging: A model of selective optimization with compensation. In P. B. Baltes & M. M. Baltes (Eds.), *Successful aging: Perspectives from the behavioral sciences* (pp. 1–34). New York: Cambridge University Press.

Baltes, P. B., & Baltes, M. M. (1990). Psychological perspectives on successful aging: A model of selective optimization with compensation. In P. B. Baltes & M. M. Baltes (Eds.), *Successful aging: Perspectives from the behavioral sciences* (pp. 1–34). New York: Cambridge University Press.

Baltes, P. B., & Graf, P. (1996). Psychological aspects of aging: Facts and frontiers. In D. Magnusson (Ed.), *The lifespan development of individuals: Behavioral, neurobiological, and psychosocial perspectives* (pp. 427–460). New York: Cambridge University Press.

Baltes, P. B., & Kliegl, R. (1992). Further testing of limits of cognitive plasticity: Negative age differences in a mnemonic skill are robust. *Developmental Psychology, 28,* 121–125.

Baltes, P. B., & Lindenberger, U. (1988). On the range of cognitive plasticity in old age as a function of experience: 15 years of intervention research. *Behavior Therapy, 19,* 283–300.

Baltes, P. B., & Schaie, K. W. (1976). On the plasticity of intelligence in adulthood and old age: Where Horn and Donaldson fail. *American Psychologist, 31,* 720–725.

Baltes, P. B., & Staudinger, U. M. (1993). The search for a psychological wisdom. *Current Directions in Psychological Science, 2,* 75-80.

Baltes, P. B., Dittman-Kohli, F., & Kliegl, R. (1986). Reserve capacity of the elderly in aging-sensitive tests of fluid intelligence: replication and extension. *Psychology and Aging, 1,* 172–177.

Baltes, P. B., Staudinger, U. M., Maercker, A., & Smith, J. (1995). People nominated as wise: A comparative study of wisdom-related knowledge. *Psychology and Aging, 10,* 155–166.

Barbar, S. I., Enright, P. L., Boyle, P., Foley, D., Sharp, D. S., Petrovitch, H., & Quan, S. (2000). Sleep disturbances and their correlates in elderly Japanese American men residing in Hawaii. *Journals of Gerontology: Biological Sciences, 55,* M406–411.

Barbaste, M., Berke, B., Dumas, M., Soulet, S., Delaunay, J. C., Castagnino, C., Arnaudinaud, V., Cheze, C., & Vercauteren, J. (2002). Dietary antioxidants, peroxidation and cardiovascular risks. *Journal of Nutrition Health and Aging, 6,* 209–223.

Barefoot, J. C., Mortensen, E. L., Helms, M. J., Avlund, K., & Schroll, M. (2001). A longitudinal study of gender differences in depressive symptoms from age 50 to 80. *Psychology and Aging, 16,* 342–345.

Barja, G. (2002). Endogenous oxidative stress: Relationship to aging, longevity and caloric restriction. *Ageing Research Reviews, 1,* 397–411.

Barner, E. L., & Gray, S. L. (1998). Donepezil use in Alzheimer disease. *Annals of Pharmacotherapy, 32,* 70–77.

Barrick, C., & Connors, G. J. (2002). Relapse prevention and maintaining abstinence in older adults with alcohol-use disorders. *Drugs and Aging, 19,* 583–594.

Barrick, M. R., Mount, M. K., & Gupta, R. (2003). Meta-analysis of the relationship between the five-factor model of personality and Holland's occupational types. *Personnel Psychology, 56,* 45–74.

Bartels, S. J., & Mueser, K. T. (1999). Severe mental illness in older adults: Schizophrenia and other late-life psychoses. In M. A. Smyer & S. H. Qualls (Eds.), *Aging and Mental Health* (pp. 182–207). Malden, MA: Blackwell.

Bartels, S. J., Moak, G. S., & Dums, A. R. (2002). Mental health services in nursing homes: Models of mental health services in nursing homes: A review of the literature. *Psychiatric Services, 53,* 1390–1396.

Bartholomew, K., & Horowitz, L. M. (1991). Attachment styles among young adults: A test of a four-category model. *Journal of Personality and Social Psychology, 61,* 226–244.

Bascom, P. B., & Tolle, S. W. (2002). Responding to requests for physician-assisted suicide: "These are uncharted waters for both of us …" *Journal of the American Medical Association, 288,* 91–98.

Basseches, M. (1984). *Dialectical thinking and adult development.* Norwood NJ: Ablex.

Baulieu, E. E., Thomas, G., Legrain, S., Lahlou, N., Roger, M., Debuire, B., Faucounau, V., Girard, L., Hervy, M. P., Latour, F., Leaud, M. C., Mokrane, A., Pitti-Ferrandi, H., Trivalle, C., de Lacharriere, O., Nouveau, S., Rakoto-Arison, B., Souberbielle, J. C., Raison, J., Le Bouc, Y., Raynaud, A., Girerd, X., & Forette, F., (2000). Dehydroepiandrosterone (DHEA), DHEA sulfate, and aging: Contribution of the DHEAge Study to a sociobiomedical issue. *Proceedings of the National Academy of Science USA, 97,* 4279–4284.

Baumeister, R. F. (1996). Self-regulation and ego threat: Motivated cognition, self deception, and destructive goal setting. In P. M. Gollwitzer & J. A. Bargh (Eds.), *The psychology of action: Linking cognition and motivation to behavior* (pp. 27–47). New York: Guilford Press.

Baumeister, R. F. (1997). Identity, self-concept, and self-esteem: The self lost and found. In R. Hogan, J. A. Johnson & S. R. Briggs (Eds.), *Handbook of personality psychology* (pp. 681–710). San Diego, CA: Academic Press.

Baumeister, R. F., Bratslavsky, E., Finkenauer, C., & Vohs, K. D. (2001). Bad is stronger than good. *Review of General Psychology, 54,* 323–370.

Baumgartner, R. N., Heymsfield, S. B., & Roche, A. F. (1995). Human body composition and the epidemiology of chronic disease. *Obesity Research, 3,* 73–95.

Baur, J. A., Zou, Y., Shay, J. W., & Wright, W. E. (2001). Telomere position effect in human cells. *Science, 292,* 2075–2077.

Beck, A. T., Steer, R. A., & Brown, G. K. (1996). *Beck Depression Inventory-II.* San Antonio, TX: Psychological Corporation.

Bedford, V. H., Volling, B. L., & Avioli, P. S. (2000). Positive consequences of sibling conflict in childhood and adulthood. *International Journal of Aging and Human Development, 51,* 53–69.

Beekman, A. T., Bremmer, M. A., Deeg, D. J., van Balkom, A. J., Smit, J. H., de Beurs, E., van Dyck, R., & van Tilburg, W. (1998). Anxiety disorders in later life: a report from the Longitudinal Aging Study Amsterdam. *International Journal of Geriatric Psychiatry, 13,* 717–726.

Beekman, A. T., Geerlings, S. W., Deeg, D. J., Smit, J. H., Schoevers, R. S., de Beurs, E., Braam, A. W., Penninx, B. W., & van Tilburg, W. (2002). The natural history of late-life depression: a 6-year prospective study in the community. *Archives of General Psychiatry, 59*, 605–611.

Belkin, V., Livshits, G., Otremski, I., & Kobyliansky, E. (1998). Aging bone score and climatic factors. *American Journal of Physical Anthropology, 106*, 349–359.

Bellipanni, G., Bianchi, P., Pierpaoli, W., Bulian, D., & Ilyia, E. (2001). Effects of melatonin in perimenopausal and menopausal women: A randomized and placebo controlled study. *Experimental Gerontology, 36*, 297–310.

Belsky, J., & Hsieh, K.-H. (1998). Patterns of marital change during the early childhood years: Parent personality, coparenting, and division-of-labor correlates. *Journal of Family Psychology, 12*, 511–528.

Belsky, J., & Pensky, E. (1988). Marital change across the transition to parenthood. *Marriage and Family Review, 12*, 133–156.

Belsky, J., & Rovine, M. (1990). Patterns of marital change across the transition to parenthood: Pregnancy to three years postpartum. *Journal of Marriage and the Family, 52*, 5–20.

Bemben, M. G., Massey, B. H., Bemben, D. A., Misner, J. E., & Boileau, R. A. (1996). Isometric intermittent endurance of four muscle groups in men aged 20–74 yr. *Medicine and Science in Sports and Exercise, 28*, 145–154.

Bengston, V. L. (2001). Beyond the nuclear family: The increasing importance of multigenerational bonds. *Journal of Marriage and the Family, 63*, 1–16.

Bengtson, V. L., & Kuypers, J. A. (1971). Generational difference and the developmental stake. *Aging and Human Development, 2*, 249–260.

Bengtson, V. L., & Schrader, S. S. (1982). Parent-child relations. In D. J. Mangen & W. A. Peterson (Eds.), *Research instruments in social gerontology: Vol 2.* (pp. 115–185). Minneapolis: University of Minnesota Press.

Benjamin, A. S., & Craik, F. I. (2001). Parallel effects of aging and time pressure on memory for source: Evidence from the spacing effect. *Memory and Cognition, 29*, 691–697.

Bergendahl, M., Iranmanesh, A., Mulligan, T., & Veldhuis, J. D. (2000). Impact of age on cortisol secretory dynamics basally and as driven by nutrient-withdrawal stress. *Journal of Clinical Endocrinology and Metabolism, 85*, 2203–2214.

Bergin, P. S., Bronstein, A. M., Murray, N. M. F., Sancovic, S., & Zeppenfeld, D. K. (1995). Body sway and vibration perception thresholds in normal aging and in patients with polyneuropathy. *Journal of Neurology, Neurosurgery and Psychiatry, 58*, 335–340.

Bernabei, R., Murphy, K., Frijters, D., DuPaquier, J. N., & Gardent, H. (1997). Variation in training programmes for Resident Assessment Instrument implementation. *Age and Ageing, 26 (Suppl 2)*, 31–35.

Bernal, D., Snyder, D., & McDaniel, M. (1998). The age and job satisfaction relationship: Does its shape and strength still evade us? *Journal of Gerontology: Psychological Sciences, 53B*, P287–P293.

Berntsen, D., & Rubin, D. C. (2002). Emotionally charged autobiography memories across the life span: The recall of happy, sad, traumatic and involuntary memories. *Psychology & Aging, 17*, 636–652.

Berr, C., Lafont, S., Debuire, B., Dartigues, J. F., & Baulieu, E. E. (1996). Relationships of dehydroepiandrosterone sulfate in the elderly with functional, psychological, and mental status, and short-term mortality: a French community-based study. *Proceedings of the National Academy of Sciences USA, 93*, 13410–13415.

Bharucha, A. E., & Camilleri, M. (2001). Functional abdominal pain in the elderly. *Gastroenterological Clinics of North America, 30*, 517–529.

Bieman-Copland, S., & Charness, N. (1994). Memory knowledge and memory monitoring in adulthood. *Psychology and Aging, 9*, 287–302.

Bieman-Copland, S., & Ryan, E. B. (1998). Age-biased interpretation of memory successes and failures in adulthood. *Journal of Gerontology: Psychological Sciences, 53B*, P105–P111.

Bieman-Copland, S., & Ryan, E. B. (2001). Social perceptions of failures in memory monitoring. *Psychology and Aging, 16*, 357–361.

Biesalski, H. K. (2002). Free radical theory of aging. *Current Opinion in Clinical Nutrition and Metabolic Care, 5*, 5–10.

Bigler, E. D., Johnson, S. C., Jackson, C., & Blatter, D. D. (1995). Aging, brain size, and IQ. *Intelligence, 21*, 109–119.

Bilato, C., & Crow, M. T. (1996). Atherosclerosis and the vascular biology of aging. *Aging, 8*, 221–234.

Binder, E. F., Schechtman, K. B., Birge, S. J., Williams, D. B., & Kohrt, W. M. (2001). Effects of hormone replacement therapy on cognitive performance in elderly women. *Maturitas, 38*, 137–146.

Binstock, R. H. (1999). Public policy issues. In J. C. Cavanaugh & S. K. Whitbourne (Eds.), *Gerontology: Interdisciplinary perspectives* (pp. 414–447). New York: Oxford University Press.

Birch, M. P., Messenger, J. F., & Messenger, A. G. (2001). Hair density, hair diameter and the prevalence of female pattern hair loss. *British Journal of Dermatology, 144*, 297–304.

Birren, J. E. (1974). Translations in gerontology—from lab to life: Psychophysiology and speed of response. *American Psychologist, 29,* 808–815.

Birren, J. E., & Fisher, L. M. (1995). Rules and reason in the forced retirement of commercial airline pilots at age 60. *Ergonomics, 38,* 518–525.

Bjorntorp, P. (1995). Neuroendocrine ageing. *Journal of Internal Medicine, 238,* 401–404.

Bjorntorp, P. (1996). The regulation of adipose tissue distribution in humans. *International Journal of Obesity and Related Metabolic Disorders, 20,* 291–302.

Blackman, M. R., Sorkin, J. D., Munzer, T., Bellantoni, M. F., Busby-Whitehead, J., Stevens, T. E., Jayme, J., O'Connor, K. G., Christmas, C., Tobin, J. D., Stewart, K. J., Cottrell, E., St Clair, C., Pabst, K. M. & Harman, S. M. (2002). Growth hormone and sex steroid administration in healthy aged women and men: A randomized controlled trial. *Journal of the American Medical Association, 288,* 2282–2292.

Blair, S. L., & Lichter, D. T. (1991). Measuring the division of household labor: Gender segregation of housework among American couples. *Journal of Family Issues, 12,* 91–113.

Blankenship, V., Hnat, S. M., Hess, T. G., & Brown, D. R. (1984). Reciprocal interaction and similarity of personality attributes. *Journal of Social and Personal Relationships, 1,* 415–432.

Blanpied, P., & Smidt, G. L. (1993). The difference in stiffness of the active plantarflexors between young and elderly human females. *Journal of Gerontology: Medical Sciences, 48,* M58–63.

Blazer, D. G. (1999). Depression. In W. R. Hazzard, J. P. Blass, J. W.H. Ettinger, D. B. Halter & J. G. Ouslander (Eds.), *Principles of geriatric medicine and gerontology* (4th ed., pp. 1331–1339). New York: McGraw-Hill.

Blazer, D. G., Landerman, L. R., Hays, J. C., Simonsick, E. M., & Saunders, W. B. (1998). Symptoms of depression among community-dwelling elderly African-American and white older adults. *Psychological Medicine, 28,* 1311–1320.

Blazer, D., George, L. K., & Hughes, D. (1991). The epidemiology of anxiety disorders: An age comparison. In C. Salzman & B. D. Lebowitz (Eds.), *Anxiety in the Elderly: Treatment and Research* (pp. 17–30). Berlin: Springer-Verlag.

Blenkner, M. (1963). Social work and family relations in later life with some thoughts on filial maturity. In E. Shanas & G. F. Streib (Eds.), *Social structure and the family: Generational relations* (pp. 46–59). Englewood Cliffs, NJ: Prentice Hall.

Bliwise, N. G. (1992). Factors related to sleep quality in healthy elderly women. *Psychology and Aging, 7,* 83–88.

Bohannon, R. W. (1997). Comfortable and maximum walking speed of adults aged 20–79 years: Reference values and determinants. *Age and Ageing, 26,* 15–19.

Boisnic, S., Branchet-Gumila, M. C., Le Charpentier, Y., & Segard, C. (1999). Repair of UVA-induced elastic fiber and collagen damage by 0.05% retinaldehyde cream in an ex vivo human skin model. *Dermatology, 199 Suppl 1,* 43–48.

Bonanno, G. A., Wortman, C. B., Lehman, D. R., Tweed, R. G., Haring, M., Sonnega, J., Carr, D., & Nesse, R. M. (2002). Resilience to loss and chronic grief: A prospective study from preloss to 18-months postloss. *Journal of Personality & Social Psychology, 83,* 1150–1164.

Boonen, S., Lesaffre, E., Dequeker, J., Aerssens, J., Nijs, J., Pelemans, W., & Bouillon, R. (1996). Relationship between baseline insulin-like growth factor-I (IGF-I) and femoral bone density in women aged over 70 years: Potential implications for the prevention of age-related bone loss. *Journal of the American Geriatrics Society, 44,* 1301–1306.

Booth, A., & Edwards, J. N. (1992). Starting over: Why remarriages are more unstable. *Journal of Family Issues, 13,* 179–194.

Born, J., Uthgenannt, D., Dodt, C., Nunninghoff, D., Ringvolt, E., Wagner, T., & Fehm, H. L. (1995). Cytokine production and lymphocyte subpopulations in aged humans. An assessment during nocturnal sleep. *Mechanisms of Ageing and Development, 84,* 113–126.

Bosse, R. (1998). Retirement and retirement planning in old age. In I. H. Nordhus, G. R. VandenBos, S. Berg & P. Fromhold (Eds.), *Clinical geropsychology* (pp. 155–159). Washington, DC: American Psychological Association.

Bosse, R., Aldwin, C. M., Levenson, M. R., & Workman-Daniels, K. (1991). How stressful is retirement? Findings from the Normative Aging Study. *Journal of Gerontology: Psychological Sciences, 46,* P9–P14.

Bosse, R., Spiro, A., III, & Kressin, N. R. (1996). The psychology of retirement. In R. T. Woods (Ed.), *Handbook of the clinical psychology of ageing* (pp. 141–157). Chichester, UK: Wiley.

Botwinick, J. (1977). Intellectual abilities. In J. E. Birren & K. W. Schaie (Eds.), *Handbook of the psychology of aging* (pp. 580–605). New York: Van Nostrand Reinhold.

Bouchard, T. J. J., & Loehlin, J. C. (2001). Genes, evolution, and personality. *Behavior Genetics, 31,* 243–273.

Bouchard, T. J., Jr. (1997). The genetics of personality. In K. Blum & E. P. Noble (Eds.), *Handbook of psychiatric genetics* (pp. 273–296). Boca Raton, FL: CRC Press.

Bouchard, T. J., June. *Science, 264,* 1700–1701. (1994). Genes, environment, and personality. *Science, 264,* 1700–1701.

Boudreau, J. W., Boswell, W. R., & Judge, T. A. (2001). Effects of personality on executive career success in the United States and Europe. *Journal of Vocational Behavior, 58,* 53–81.

Bowlby, J. (1969). *Attachment and loss: Attachment.* New York: Basic Books.

Bowlby, J. (1973). *Attachment and loss: Separation, anxiety and anger.* New York: Basic Books.

Bowlby, J. (1980). *Attachment and loss:* Vol. 3. *Loss: Sadness and depression.* London: Hogarth.

Bowling, A., Banister, D., Sutton, S., Evans, O., & Windsor, J. (2002). A multidimensional model of the quality of life in older age. *Aging and Mental Health, 6,* 355–371.

Bowman, K. W., & Singer, P. A. (2001). Chinese seniors' perspectives on end-of-life decisions. *Social Science and Medicine, 53,* 455–464.

Bradbury, T. N., Fincham, F. D., & Beach, S. R. H. (2000). Research on the nature and determinants of marital satisfaction: A decade in review. *Journal of Marriage and the Family, 62,* 964–980.

Brattberg, G., Parker, M. G., & Thorslund, M. (1997). A longitudinal study of pain: Reported pain from middle age to old age. *Clinical Journal of Pain, 13,* 144–149.

Braver, T. S., Barch, D. M., Keys, B. A., Carter, C. S., Cohen, J. D., Kaye, J. A., Janowsky, J. S., Taylor, S. F., Yesavage, J. A., Mumenthaler, M. S., Jagust, W. J., & Reed, B. R. (2001). Context processing in older adults: Evidence for a theory relating cognitive control to neurobiology in healthy aging. *Journal of Experimental Psychology: General, 130,* 746–763.

Bray, D. W., & Howard, A. (1983). The AT&T longitudinal studies of managers. In K. W. Schaie (Ed.), *Longitudinal studies of adult development* (pp. 266–312). New York: Guilford.

Brecher, E. (1984), *Love, sex, and aging.* Boston: Little, Brown.

Breteler, M. M. (2000). Vascular risk factors for Alzheimer's disease: an epidemiologic perspective. *Neurobiology of Aging, 21,* 153–160.

Brill, F. (1967). *Matisse.* London: Paul Hamlyn.

Brim, O. G., Jr. (1976). Theories of the male mid-life crisis. *The Counseling Psychologist, 6,* 2–9.

Brincat, M. P. (2000). Hormone replacement therapy and the skin. *Maturitas, 35,* 107–117.

Brink, J. M., & McDowd, J. M. (1999). Aging and selective attention: An issue of complexity or multiple mechanisms? *Journal of Gerontology: Psychological Sciences, 54B,* P30–P33.

Broadbent, D. E. (1958). *Peception and communication.* London: Pergamon Press.

Brody, E. M. (1981). "Women in the middle" and family help to older people. *The Gerontologist, 21,* 471–479.

Brody, E. M. (1990). Role reversal: An inaccurate and destructive concept. *Journal of Gerontological Social Work, 15,* 15–23.

Brody, E. M., Hoffman, C., Kleban, M. H., & Schoonover, C. B. (1989). Caregiving daughters and their local siblings: Perceptions, strains, and interactions. *The Gerontologist, 29,* 529–538.

Bronfenbrenner, U. (1979). *The ecology of human development.* Cambridge, MA: Harvard University Press.

Bronfenbrenner, U. (1995). Developmental ecology through space and time: A future perspective. In P. Moen, G. H. J. Elder & K. Luscher (Eds.), *Examining lives in context: Perspectives on the ecology of human development* (pp. 619–647). Washington DC: American Psychological Association.

Bronfenbrenner, U. (2001). Human development, bioecological theory of. In N. J. Smelser & P. B. Baltes (Eds.), *International encyclopedia of the social and behavioral sciences* (pp. 6963–6970). New York: Elsevier.

Bronfenbrenner, U., & Ceci, S. J. (1994). Nature-nurture reconceptualized in developmental perspective: A bioecological model. *Psychological Review, 101,* 568–586.

Brookmeyer, R., & Kawas, C. (1998). Projections of Alzheimer's Disease in the United States and the public health impact of delaying disease onset. *American Journal of Public Health, 88,* 1337–1342.

Brookmeyer, R., Corrada, M. M., Curriero, F. C., & Kawas, C. (2002). Survival following a diagnosis of Alzheimer disease. *Archives Neurology, 59,* 1764–1767.

Brower, K. J., & Hall, J. M. (2001). Effects of age and alcoholism on sleep: A controlled study. *Journal of Studies on Alcohol, 62,* 335–343.

Brown, L. A., Gage, W. H., Polych, M. A., Sleik, R. J., & Winder, T. R. (2002). Central set influences on gait. Age-dependent effects of postural threat. *Experimental Brain Research, 145,* 286–296.

Brown, M. T. (1995). The career development of African Americans: Theoretical and empirical issues. In F. T. L. Leong (Ed.), *Career development and vocational behavior in racial and ethnic minorities* (pp. 7–36). Hillsdale, NJ: Erlbaum.

Bruce, M. L. (2002). Psychosocial risk factors for depressive disorders in late life. *Biological Psychiatry, 52,* 175–184.

Bruunsgaard, H., & Pedersen, B. K. (2000). Effects of exercise on the immune system in the elderly population. *Immunology and Cell Biology, 28,* 523–531.

Bryson, K., & Casper, L. M. (1999). *Coresident grandparents and grandchildren* (No. P23-198). Washington, DC: U.S. Bureau of the Census.

Bukov, A., Maas, I., & Lampert, T. (2002). Social participation in very old age: cross-sectional and longitudinal findings from BASE. Berlin Aging Study. *Journals of Gerontology: Series B: Psychological Sciences and Social Sciences., 57,* P510–517.

Bureau of Labor Statistics (1999). *What women earned in 1998* (No. Summary 99-5). Washington, DC: Bureau of Labor Statistics.

Bureau of Labor Statistics (2002). *Lost worktime injuries and illnesses: Characteristics and resulting time away from work, 2000* (No. USDL 02-196).

Burgio, K. L., Locher, J. L., & Goode, P. S. (2000). Combined behavioral and drug therapy for urge incontinence in older women. *Journal of the American Geriatrics Society, 48*, 370–374.

Burgio, L. D., Stevens, A., Burgio, K. L., Roth, D. L., Paul, P., & Gerstle, J. (2002). Teaching and maintaining behavior management skills in the nursing home. *Gerontologist, 42*, 487–496.

Burke, D. M. (1997). Language, aging, and inhibitory deficits: Evaluation of a theory. *Journal of Gerontology. Series B: Psychological Sciences and Social Sciences, 52B*, P254–264.

Burke, D. M., & Mackay, D. G. (1997). Memory, language, and aging. *Philosophical Transactions of the Royal Society of London—Series B: Biological Sciences, 352*, 1845–1856.

Burke, D. M., MacKay, D., Worthley, J., & Wade, E. (1991). On the tip of the tongue: What causes word finding failures in young and old adults? *Journal of Memory and Language, 30*, 542–579.

Butler, R. (1974). Successful aging and the role of life review. *Journal of the American Geriatrics Society, 22*, 529–535.

Byock, I. R. (1993). Consciously walking the fine line: Thoughts on a hospice response to assisted suicide and euthanasia. *Journal of Palliative Care, 9*, 25–28.

Byrne, D. (1971). *The attraction paradigm.* San Diego, CA: Academic Press.

Cabeza, R., Grady, C. L., Nyberg, L., McIntosh, A. R., Tulving, E., Kapur, S., Jennings, J. M., Houle, S., & Craik, F. I. (1997). Age-related differences in neural activity during memory encoding and retrieval: A positron emission tomography study. *Journal of Neuroscience, 17*, 391–400.

Calle, E. E., Rodriguez, C., Walker-Thurmond, K., & Thun, M. J. (2003). Overweight, obesity, and mortality from cancer in a prospectively studied cohort of U.S. adults. *New England Journal of Medicine, 348*, 1625–1638.

Calvaresi, E., & Bryan, J. (2001). B vitamins, cognition, and aging: A review. *Journals of Gerontology Series B: Psychological Sciences and Social Sciences, 56*, P327–P339.

Cameron, J. D., Rajkumar, C., Kingwell, B. A., Jennings, G. L., & Dart, A. M. (1999). Higher systemic arterial compliance is associated with greater exercise time and lower blood pressure in a young older population. *Journal of the American Geriatrics Society, 47*, 653–656.

Camp, C. J., Cohen-Mansfield, J., & Capezuti, E. A. (2002). Use of nonpharmacologic interventions among nursing home residents with dementia. *Psychiatric Services, 53*, 1397–1404.

Caprio-Prevette, M. D., & Fry, P. S. (1996). Memory enhancement program for community-based older adults: Development and evaluation. *Experimental Aging Research, 22*, 281–303.

Caputo, R. K. (2002). Adult daughters as parental caregivers: Rational actors versus rational agents. *Journal of Family and Economic Issues, 23*, 27–50.

Carlson, L. E., Sherwin, B. B., & Chertkow, H. M. (2000). Relationships between mood and estradiol (E2) levels in Alzheimer's disease (AD) patients. *Journals of Gerontology: Psychological Sciences, 55*, P47–53.

Carson, P. J., Nichol, K. L., O'Brien, J., Hilo, P., & Janoff, E. N. (2000). Immune function and vaccine responses in healthy advanced elderly patients. *Archives of Internal Medicine, 160*, 2017–2024.

Carstensen, L. L. (1987). Age-related changes in social activity. In L. L. Carstensen & B. A. Edelstein (Eds.), *Handbook of clinical gerontology* (pp. 222–237). Elmsford, NY: Pergamon Press.

Carstensen, L. L. (1992). Social and emotional patterns in adulthood: Support for socioemotional selectivity theory. *Psychology and Aging, 7*, 331–338.

Carstensen, L. L., & Turk-Charles, S. (1994). The salience of emotion across the adult life span. *Psychology and Aging, 9*, 259–264.

Carstensen, L. L., Gottman, J. M., & Levenson, R. W. (1995). Emotional behavior in long-term marriage. *Psychology and Aging, 10*, 140–149.

Carstensen, L. L., Gross, J. J., & Fung, H. H. (1997). The social context of emotion. *Annual Review of Gerontology and Geriatrics, 17*, 325–352.

Carstensen, L. L., Isaacowitz, D. M., & Charles, S. T. (1999). Taking time seriously: A theory of socioemotional selectivity. *American Psychologist, 54*, 165–181.

Carter, M. A. T., & Cook, K. (1995). Adaptation to retirement: Role changes and psychological resources. *Career Development Quarterly, 44*, 67–82.

Cash, T. F. (1990). The psychology of physical appearance: Aesthetics, attributes, and images. In T. F. Cash & T. Pruzinsky (Eds.), *Body images: Development, deviance, and change* (pp. 51–79). New York: Guilford Press.

Casper, L. M., & Bryson, K. R. (1998). *Co-resident grandparents and their grandchildren: Grandparent maintained families. Working Paper No. 26.* Washington, DC: Population Division, U.S. Bureau of the Census.

Casper, L. M., Barnett, E., Williams, Jr., G. I., Halverson, J. A., Braham, V. E., Greenlung, K. J. Atlas of Stroke Mortality: Racial, Ethnic, and Geographic Disparities in the United States. Atlanta, GA: Department of Health and Human Services, Centers for Disease Control and Prevention; January 2003.

Caspi, A., & Roberts, B. W. (2001). Target article: Personality development across the life course: The argument for change and continuity. *Psychological Inquiry, 12*, 49–66.

Castaneda, C., Charnley, J. M., Evans, W. J., & Crim, M. C. (1995). Elderly women accommodate to a low-protein diet with losses of body cell mass, muscle function, and immune response. *American Journal of Clinical Nutrition, 62*, 30–39.

Cattell, R. B. (1963). Theory of fluid and crystallized intelligence: A critical experiment. *Journal of Educational Psychology, 54*, 1–22.

Cattell, R. B. (1971). *Abilities: Their structure, growth, and action.* Boston: Houghton Mifflin.

Cavan, R. S., Burgess, E. W., Havighurst, R. J., & Goldhamer, H. (1949). *Personal adjustment in old age.* Chicago: Science Research Associates.

Cavanaugh, J. C. (1989). The importance of awareness in memory aging. In L. W. Poon, D. C. Rubin & B. A. Wilson (Eds.), *Everyday cognition in adulthood and late life* (pp. 416–436). Cambridge: Cambridge University Press.

Cavanaugh, J. C. (1999). Theories of aging in the biological, behavioral, and social sciences. In J. C. Cavanaugh & S. K. Whitbourne (Eds.), *Gerontology: Interdisciplinary perspectives* (pp. 1–32). New York: Oxford University Press.

Cavanaugh, J. C., & Green, E. E. (1990). I believe, therefore I can: Self-efficacy beliefs in memory aging. In E. A. Lovelace (Ed.), *Aging and cognition: Mental processes, self-awareness, and interventions* (pp. 189–230). Amsterdam: North Holland.

Cavanaugh, J. C., & Murphy, N. Z. (1986). Personality and metamemory correlates of memory performance in younger and older adults. *Educational Gerontology, 12*, 385–394.

Cawthon, R. M., Smith, K. R., O'Brien, E., Sivatchenko, A., & Kerber, R. A. (2003). Association between telomere length in blood and mortality in people aged 60 years or older. *Lancet, 361*, 394–395.

Centers for Disease Control and Prevention (1998). AIDS among persons aged greater than or equal to 50 Years—United States, 1991–1996. *MMWR Weekly, 47*(02), 21–27.

Centers for Disease Control and Prevention (2000). Age-specific excess deaths associated with stroke among racial/ethnic minority populations—United States, 1997. *Morbidity and Mortality Weekly Reports, 49*(05), 94–97.

Centers for Disease Control and Prevention (2002). *Health United States 2002*, Washington, DC.

Centers for Disease Control and Prevention (2002a). Health United States 2002.

Centers for Disease Control and Prevention (2002b). Hypothermia-Related Deaths — Utah, 2000, United States, 1979-1998. *Morbidity and Mortality Weekly Report, 51* (04), 76–78.

Centers for Disease Control and Prevention (2002c). *National Diabetes Fact Sheet.* Retrieved August 2003, from http://www.cdc.gov/diabetes/pubs/estimates.htm#prev

Centers for Disease Control and Prevention (2003). Diabetes: Deadly, disabling, and on the rise.

Centers for Disease Control and Prevention (2003a). Physical activity and good nutrition: Essential elements to prevent chronic diseases and obesity. http://www.cdc.gov/nccdphp/aag/aag_dnpa.htm. Accessed 1/23/04.

Centers for Disease Control and Prevention (2003b). *Early Release of Selected Estimates Based on Data From the January–September 2002 National Health Interview Survey,* Released March 19 2003.

Centers for Disease Control and Prevention (2003c). HIV and AIDS cases reported through December 2002. Accessed Nov. 2003, www.cdc.gov/hiv/stats/hasr/402.htm

Centers for Medicare & Medicaid Services (2003). 2003 Annual Report of the Board of Trustees of the Federal Hospital Insurance and Federal Supplementary Medical Insurance Trust Funds. http://cms.hhs.gov/publications/trusteesreport/2003/default.asp. Accessed 1/23/04.

Cerella, J., Poon, L. W., & Williams, D. M. (1980). Age and the complexity hypothesis. In L. W. Poon (Ed.), *Aging in the 1980s* (pp. 332–340). Washington DC: American Psychological Association.

Cerhan, J. R., Folsom, A. R., Mortimer, J. A., Shahar, E., Knopman, D. S., McGovern, P. G., Hays, M. A., Crum, L. D., & Heiss, G. (1998). Correlates of cognitive function in middle-aged adults. *Gerontology, 44*, 95–105.

Chandra, R. K. (2001). Effect of vitamin and trace-element supplementation on cognitive function in elderly subjects. *Nutrition, 17*, 709–712.

Charles, S. T., Reynolds, C. A., & Gatz, M. (2001). Age-related differences and change in positive and negative affect over 23 years. *Journal of Personality and Social Psychology, 80*, 136–151.

Charlson, M., & Peterson, J. C. (2002). Medical comorbidity and late life depression: What is known and what are the unmet needs? *Biological Psychiatry, 52*, 226–235.

Charness, N. (1989). Age and expertise: Responding to Talland's challenge. In L. W. Poon, D. C. Rubin & B. A. Wilson (Eds.), *Everyday cognition in adulthood and late life* (pp. 437–456). Cambridge, England: Cambridge University Press.

Chartrand, J., & Walsh, W. B. (1999). What should we expect from congruence? *Journal of Vocational Behavior, 55*, 136–146.

Chatters, L. M., Taylor, R. J., & Jackson, J. S. (1985). Size and composition of the informal helper networks of elderly blacks. *Journal of Gerontology, 40*, 605–614.

Cherry, K. E., & LeCompte, D. C. (1999). Age and individual differences influence prospective memory. *Psychology and Aging, 14*, 60–76.

Cherry, K. E., Martin, R. C., Simmons-D'Gerolamo, S. S., Pinkston, J. B., Griffing, A., & Gouvier, W. D. (2001). Prospective remembering in younger and older adults: Role of the prospective cue. *Memory, 9*, 177–193.

Cho, E., Stampfer, M. J., Seddon, J. M., Hung, S., Spiegelman, D., Rimm, E. B., Willett, W. C. & Hankinson, S. E. (2001). Prospective study of zinc intake and the risk of age-related macular degeneration. *Annals of Epidemiology, 11*, 328–336.

Chou, S. C., Boldy, D. P., & Lee, A. H. (2002). Resident satisfaction and its components in residential aged care. *Gerontologist, 42*, 188–198.

Christensen, H., Henderson, A. S., Griffiths, K., & Levings, C. (1997). Does ageing inevitably lead to declines in cognitive performance? A longitudinal study of elite academics. *Personality and Individual Differences, 23*, 67–78.

Christensen, H., Korten, A. E., Jorm, A. F., & Henderson, A. S. (1997). Education and decline in cognitive performance: Compensatory but not protective. *International Journal of Geriatric Psychiatry, 12*, 323–330.

Cicirelli, V. C. (1982). Sibling influence throughout the lifespan. In M. E. Lamb & B. Sutton-Smith (Eds.), *Sibling relationships: Their nature and significance across the lifespan* (pp. 267–284). Hillsdale, NJ: Erlbaum.

Cicirelli, V. G. (1988). A measure of filial anxiety regarding anticipated care of elderly parents. *Gerontologist, 28*, 478–482. December 2001.

Cicirelli, V. G. (1995). *Sibling relationships across the life span.* New York: Plenum.

Cicirelli, V. G. (2002). Fear of death in older adults: predictions from terror management theory. *Journals of Gerontology: Series B: Psychological Sciences and Social Sciences, 57*, P358–366.

Cipolli, C., Neri, M., De Vreese, L. P., & Pinelli, M. (1996). The influence of depression on memory and metamemory in the elderly. *Archives of Gerontology and Geriatrics, 23*, 111–127.

Clark, R., Anderson, N. B., Clark, V. R., & Williams, D. R. (1999). Racism as a stressor for African Americans: A biopsychosocial model. *American Psychologist, 54*, 805–816.

Clarke, S. (1995). *Advance report of final divorce statistics, 1989 and 1990* (Vol. 43, No. 9, Suppl.). Hyattsville, MD: National Center for Health Statistics.

Clearinghouse, N. K. a. U. D. (2001). Kidney and Urologic Diseases of the United States (Vol. 2003).

Cobb, R. J., Davila, J., & Bradbury, T. N. (2001). Attachment security and marital satisfaction: The role of positive perceptions and social support. *Personality and Social Psychology Bulletin, 27*, 1131–1143.

Coffey, C. E., Lucke, J. F., Saxton, J. A., Ratcliff, G., Unitas, L. J., Billig, B., & Bryan, R. N. (1998). Sex differences in brain aging: A quantitative magnetic resonance imaging study. *Archives of Neurology, 55*, 169–179.

Coffey, C. E., Ratcliff, G., Saxton, J. A., Bryan, R. N., Fried, L. P., & Lucke, J. F. (2001). Cognitive correlates of human brain aging: a quantitative magnetic resonance imaging investigation. *Journal of Neuropsychiatry and Clinical Neuroscience, 13*, 471–485.

Coffey, C. E., Wilkinson, W. E., Parashos, I. A., Soady, S. A., Sullivan, R. J., Patterson, L. J., Figiel, G. S., Webb, M. C., Spritzer, C. E. & Djang, W. T. (1992). Quantitative cerebral anatomy of the aging human brain: A cross-sectional study using magnetic resonance imaging. *Neurology, 42*, 527–536.

Cohen, G. (1996). Memory and learning in normal aging. In R. T. Woods (Ed.), *Handbook of the Clinical Psychology of Ageing* (pp. 43–58). London: Wiley.

Cohen, G. (1998). The effects of aging on autobiographical memory. In P. Thompson & D. J. Herrmann (Eds.), *Autobiographical memory: Theoretical and applied perspectives* (pp. 105–123). Mahwah NJ: Lawrence Erlbaum.

Cohen, G. D. (1998). Creativity and aging: Ramifications for research, practice, and policy. *Geriatrics, 53* (Suppl. 1), S4–S8.

Cohen, G. D. (1999). Human potential phases in the second half of life: Mental health theory development. *American Journal of Geriatric Psychiatry, 7*, 1–7.

Cohen, G. D. (2000). *The creative age: Awakening human potential in the second half of life.* New York: AVON Books.

Coleman, P. D., & Flood, D. G. (1987). Neuron numbers and dendritic extent in normal aging and Alzheimer's disease. *Neurobiology of Aging, 8*, 521–545.

Commenges, D., Scotet, V., Renaud, S., Jacqmin-Gadda, H., Barberger-Gateau, P., & Dartigues, J. F. (2000). Intake of flavonoids and risk of dementia. *European Journal of Epidemiology, 16*, 357–363.

Committee on National Statistics (2003). *Elder mistreatment: Abuse, neglect, and exploitation in an Aging America.* Washington, DC: National Academies Press.

Commons, M., Richards, F., & Armon, C. (Eds.). (1984). *Beyond formal operations: Late adolescent and adult cognitive development.* New York: Praeger.

Connell, B. R. (1996). Role of the environment in falls prevention. *Clinics in Geriatric Medicine, 12*, 859–880.

Connidis, I. A. (1992). Life transitions and the adult sibling tie: A qualitative study. *Journal of Marriage and the Family, 54*, 972–982.

Connor, L. T., Dunlosky, J., & Hertzog, C. (1997). Age-related differences in absolute but not relative metamemory accuracy. *Psychology and Aging, 12*, 50–71.

Connor, S. R., Egan, K. A., Kwilosz, D. M., Larson, D. G., & Reese, D. J. (2002). Interdisciplinary approaches to assisting with end-of-life care and decision making. *American Behavioral Scientist, 46*, 340–356.

Consedine, N. S., Magai, C., Cohen, C. I., & Gillespie, M. (2002). Ethnic variation in the impact of negative affect and emotion inhibition on the health of older adults. *Journals of Gerontology Series B: Psychological Sciences and Social Sciences, 57*, P396–408.

Constantinople, A. (1969). An Eriksonian measure of personality development in college students. *Developmental Psychology, 1*, 357–372.

Conwell, Y., Duberstein, P. R., & Caine, E. D. (2002). Risk factors for suicide in later life. *Biological Psychiatry, 52*, 193–204.

Cooper, J. K., Harris, Y., & McGready, J. (2002). Sadness predicts death in older people. *Journal of Aging & Health, 14*, 509–526.

Cooper, J. K., Harris, Y., & McGready, J. (2002). Sadness predicts death in older people. *Journal of Aging and Health, 14*, 509–526.

Cooper, R. S., Rotimi, C. N., & Ward, R. (1999). The puzzle of hypertension in African-Americans. *Scientific American, 280*, 56–63.

Cornoni-Huntley, J., Blazer, D. B., Lafferty, M. E., Everett, D. F., Brock, D. B., & Farmer, M. E. (1990). *Established populations for epidemiologic studies of the elderly. Vol. 2: Resource data book*, pp. 90–495. Washington, DC: National Institute on Aging.

Corwin, J., Loury, M., & Gilbert, A. N. (1995). Workplace, age, and sex as mediators of olfactory function: Data from the National Geographic Smell Survey. *Journal of Gerontology: Psychological Sciences, 50*, P179–186.

Costa, P. T. J., & McCrae, R. R. (1978). Objective personality assessment. In M. Storandt, I. C. Siegler & M. F. Elias (Eds.), *The clinical psychology of aging* (pp. 119–143). New York: Plenum.

Costa, P. T., & McCrae, R. R. (1986). Cross-sectional studies of personality in a national sample: I. Development and validation of survey measures. *Psychology and Aging, 1*, 140–143.

Costa, P. T., Jr., & McCrae, R. R. (1992). *Revised NEO Personality Inventory (NEO-PI-R) and NEO Five-Factor Inventory (NEO-FFI) professional manual*. Odessa FL: Psychological Assessment Resources.

Cotman, C. W., & Berchtold, N. C. (2002). Exercise: A behavioral intervention to enhance brain health and plasticity. *Trends in Neuroscience, 25*, 295–301.

Courtney, A. C., Hayes, W. C., & Gibson, L. J. (1996). Age-related differences in post-yield damage in human cortical bone. Experiment and model. *Journal of Biomechanics, 29*, 1463–1471.

Cowan, C. P., & Cowan, P. A. (1992). *When partners become parents*. New York: Basic Books.

Cowan, P. A., Cowan, C. P., & Kerig, P. K. (1993). Mothers, fathers, sons, and daughters: Gender differences in family formation and parenting style. In P. A. Cowan, D. Field, D. A. Hansen, A. Skolnick & G. E. Swanson (Eds.), *Family, self and society: Toward a new agenda for family research* (pp. 165–195). Hillsdale, NJ: Erlbaum.

Cowell, P. E., Turetsky, B. I., Gur, R. C., Grossman, R. I., Shtasel, D. L., & Gur, R. E. (1994). Sex differences in aging of the human frontal and temporal lobes. *Journal of Neuroscience, 14*, 4748–4755.

Cowgill, D. O., & Holmes, L. D. (1972). *Aging and modernization*. New York: Appleton-Century-Crofts.

Cowie, C. C., Harris, M. I., Stern, M. P., Boyko, E. J., Reiber, G. E., & Bennett, M. B. (1995). *Diabetes in America* (2nd ed. NIH Publication No. 95-1468). Bethesda MD: National Institute of Diabetes and Digestive and Kidney Diseases.

Craik, F. I. M. (1994). Memory changes in normal aging. *Current Directions in Psychological Science, 3*, 155–158.

Craik, F. I. M., & Jennings, J. M. (1992). Human memory. In F. I. M. Craik & T. A. Salthouse (Eds.), *The handbook of aging and cognition* (pp. 51–110). Hillsdale NJ: Erlbaum.

Cramer, P. (2003). Personality change in later adulthood is predicted by defense mechanism use in early adulthood. *Journal of Research in Personality, 37*, 76–104.

Crawford, D. W., & Huston, T. L. (1993). The impact of the transition to parenthood on marital leisure. *Personality and Social Psychology Bulletin, 19*, 39–46.

Crawford, S., & Channon, S. (2002). Dissociation between performance on abstract tests of executive function and problem solving in real-life-type situations in normal aging. *Aging and Mental Health, 6*, 12–21.

Crawley, L. M., Marshall, P. A., Lo, B., & Koenig, B. A. (2002). Strategies for culturally effective end-of-life care. *Annals of Internal Medicine, 136*, 673–679.

Cropanzano, R., Rupp, D. E., & Byrne, Z. S. (2003). The relationship of emotional exhaustion to work attitudes, job performance, and organizational citizenship behaviors. *Journal of Applied Psychology, 88*, 160–169.

Crosnoe, R., & Elder, G. H., Jr. (2002). Life course transitions, the generational stake, and grandparent–grandchild relationships. *Journal of Marriage and the Family, 64*, 1089–1096.

Crosnoe, R., & Elder, G. H., Jr. (2002). Successful adaptation in the later years: A life course approach to aging. *Social Psychology Quarterly, 65*, 309–328.

Cuce, L. C., Bertino, M. C., Scattone, L., & Birkenhauer, M. C. (2001). Tretinoin peeling. *Dermatologica Surgery, 27*, 12–14.

Cumming, E., & Henry, W. E. (1961). *Growing old: The process of disengagement*. New York: Basic Books.

Cunningham, W. R., & Owens, W. A. J. (1983). The Iowa State Study of adult development and abilities. In K. W. Schaie (Ed.), *Longitudinal studies of adult psychological development* (pp. 20–39). New York: Guilford.

Daly, M. C., & Bound, J. (1996). Worker adaptation and employer accommodation following the onset of a health impairment. *Journal of Gerontology: Social Sciences, 51*, S53–60.

Damush, T. M., Stump, T. E., & Clark, D. O. (2002). Body-mass index and 4-year change in health-related quality of life. *Journal of Aging & Health, 14*, 195–210.

Davies, D. F., & Shock, N. W. (1950). Age changes in glomerular filtration rate, effective renal plasma flow, and tubular excretory capacity in adult males. *Journal of Clinical Investigation, 29*, 496–507.

Davila, J., & Bradbury, T. N. (2001). Attachment insecurity and the distinction between unhappy spouses who do and do not divorce. *Journal of Family Psychology, 15*, 371–393.

Davila, J., Karney, B. R., & Bradbury, T. N. (1999). Attachment change processes in the early years of marriage. *Journal of Personality and Social Psychology, 76*, 783–802.

Davis, H. P., Trussell, L. H., & Klebe, K. J. (2001). A ten-year longitudinal examination of repetition priming, incidental recall, free recall, and recognition in young and elderly. *Brain and Cognition, 46*, 99–104.

Dawis, R. V. (1996). Vocational psychology, vocational adjustment, and the workforce: Some familiar and unanticipated consequences. *Psychology, Public Policy, and Law, 2*, 229–248.

Dawis, R. V., & Lofquist, L. H. (1984). *A psychological theory of work adjustment.* Minneapolis: University of Minnesota Press.

Dawson-Hughes, B., Harris, S. S., Krall, E. A., & Dallal, G. E. (2000). Effect of withdrawal of calcium and vitamin D supplements on bone mass in elderly men and women. *American Journal of Clinical Nutrition, 72*, 745–750.

Day, J. C., & Newberger, E. C. (2002). *The big payoff: Educational attainment and synthetic estimates of work-life earnings.* Current Population Reports, P23-210. Washington, DC: U.S. Census Bureau.

de Groot, C. P., Perdigao, A. L., & Deurenberg, P. (1996). Longitudinal changes in anthropometric characteristics of elderly Europeans. SENECA Investigators. *European Journal of Clinical Nutrition, 50*, 2954–3007.

de Leon, M. J., George, A. E., Golomb, J., Tarshish, C., Convit, A., Kluger, A., De Santi, S., McRae, T., Ferris, S. H., Reisberg, B., Ince, C., Rusinek, H., Bobinski, M., Quinn, B., Miller, D. C., & Wisniewski, H. M. (1997). Frequency of hippocampal formation atrophy in normal aging and Alzheimer's disease. *Neurobiology of Aging, 18*, 1–11.

de Lignieres, B. (1993). Transdermal dihydrotestosterone treatment of "andropause". *Annals of Medicine, 25*, 235–241.

De Santi, S., de Leon, M. J., Convit, A., Tarshish, C., Rusinek, H., Tsui, W. H., Sinaiko, E., Wang, G. J., Barlet, E., & Volkow, N. (1995). Age-related changes in brain: II. Positron emission tomography of frontal and temporal lobe glucose metabolism in normal subjects. *Psychiatric Quarterly, 66*, 357–370.

de Vries, B., Davis, C. G., Wortman, C. B., & Lehman, D. R. (1997). Long-term psychological and somatic consequences of later life parental bereavement. *Omega—Journal of Death and Dying, 35*, 1997.

Dealberto, M. J., Pajot, N., Courbon, D., & Alperovitch, A. (1996). Breathing disorders during sleep and cognitive performance in an older community sample: The EVA study. *Journal of the American Geriatrics Society, 44*, 1287–1294.

DeCarli, C., Murphy, D. G., Gillette, J. A., Haxby, J. V., Teichberg, D., Schapiro, M. B., & Horwitz, B. (1994). Lack of age-related differences in temporal lobe volume of very healthy adults. *American Journal of Neuroradiology, 15*, 689–696.

Deci, E. L., & Ryan, R. M. (1985). *Intrinsic motivation and self-determination in human behavior.* New York: Plenum.

Degenholtz, H. B., Arnold, R. A., Meisel, A., & Lave, J. R. (2002). Persistence of racial disparities in advance care plan documents among nursing home residents. *Journal of the American Geriatrics Society, 50*, 378–381.

Deigner, H. P., Haberkorn, U., & Kinscherf, R. (2000). Apoptosis modulators in the therapy of neurodegenerative diseases. *Expert Opinions on Investigative Drugs, 9*, 747–764.

Delgoulet, C., & Marquie, J. C. (2002). Age differences in learning maintenance skills: A field study. *Experimental Aging Research, 28*, 25–37.

DeLorey, D. S., & Babb, T. G. (1999). Progressive mechanical ventilatory constraints with aging. *American Journal of Respiratory and Critical Care Medicine, 160*, 169–177.

DeNavas-Walt, C., & Cleveland, R. W. (2002). U.S. Census Bureau, Current Population Reports, P60–218, Money Income in the United States: 2001. Washington D.C.: U.S. Government Printing Office

Dennerstein, L., Dudley, E., & Guthrie, J. (2002). Empty nest or revolving door? A prospective study of women's quality of life in midlife during the phase of children leaving and re-entering the home. *Psychological Medicine, 32*, 545–550.

Dennis, W. (1966). Creative productivity between the ages of 20 and 80 years. *Journal of Gerontology, 21*, 1–8.

Denti, L., Pasolini, G., Sanfelici, L., Ablondi, F., Freddi, M., Benedetti, R., & Valenti, G. (1997). Effects of aging on dehydroepiandrosterone sulfate in relation to fasting insulin levels and body composition assessed by bioimpedance analysis. *Metabolism: Clinical and Experimental, 46*, 826–832.

Dentinger, E., & Clarkberg, M. (2002). Informal caregiving and retirement timing among men and women: Gender and caregiving relationships in late midlife. *Journal of Family Issues, 23*, 857–879.

Department of Health and Human Services (1999). Mental health: A report of the Surgeon General. Bethesda, MD: U.S. Public Health Service.

Desai, M. M., Zhang, P., & Hennessy, C. H. (1999). Surveillance for morbidity and mortality among older adults—United States, 1995–1996. *Morbidity and Mortality Weekly Reports, 48(SS08)*, 7–25.

Desai, P. P., Hendrie, H. C., Evans, R. M., Murrell, J. R., DeKosky, S. T., & Kamboh, M. I. (2003). Genetic variation in apolipoprotein D affects the risk of Alzheimer disease in African-Americans. *American Journal of Medical Genetics, 116*, 98–101.

Desbiens, N. A., Wu, A. W., Broste, S. K., Wenger, N. S., Connors, A. F., Jr., Lynn, J., Yasui, Y., Phillips, R. S., & Fulkerson, W. (1996). Pain and satisfaction with pain control in seriously ill hospitalized adults: Findings from the SUPPORT research investigations. For the SUPPORT investigators. Study to Understand Prognoses and Preferences for Outcomes and Risks of Treatmentm. *Critical Care Medicine, 24*, 1953–1961.

DeSpelder, L. A., & Strickland, A. L. (1999). *The last dance: Encountering death and dying* (5th ed.). Mountain View, CA: Mayfield.

Dickinson, G. E. (2002). A quarter century of end-of-life issues in U.S. medical schools. *Death Studies, 26*, 635–646.

Dickinson, G. E., Tournier, R. E., & Still, B. J. (1999). Twenty years beyond medical school: Physicians' attitudes toward death and terminally ill patients. *Archives of Internal Medicine, 159*, 1741–1744.

Diefenbach, G. J., Hopko, D. R., Feigon, S., Stanley, M. A., Novy, D. M., Beck, J. G., & Averill, P. M. (2003). 'Minor GAD': Characteristics of subsyndromal GAD in older adults. *Behaviour Research & Therapy, 41*, 481–487.

Diehl, M., Coyle, N., & Labouvie-Vief, G. (1996). Age and sex differences in coping and defense across the life span. *Psychology and Aging, 11*, 127–139.

Diehl, M., Elnick, A. B., Bourbeau, L. S., & Labouvie-Vief, G. (1998). Adult attachment styles: Their relations to family context and personality. *Journal of Personality and Social Psychology, 74*, 1656–1669.

Diehl, M., Willis, S. L., & Schaie, K. W. (1995). Everyday problem solving in older adults: Observational assessment and cognitive correlates. *Psychology and Aging, 10*, 478–491.

Diener, E. (1998). Subjective well-being: Three decades of progress. *Psychological Bulletin, 125*, 276–302.

Diener, E., & Diener, C. (1996). Most people are happy. *Psychological Science, 7*, 181–185.

Diener, E., & Fujita, F. (1995). Resources, personal strivings, and subjective well-being: A nomothetic and idiographic approach. *Journal of Personality and Social Psychology, 68*, 926–935.

Diener, E., & Suh, E. (1998). Age and subjective well-being: An international analysis. In K. W. Schaie & M. P. Lawton (Eds.), *Annual review of gerontology and geriatrics. Vol. 17: Focus on emotion and adult development* (Vol. 17, pp. 304–324). New York: Springer.

Diener, E., Oishi, S., & Lucas, R. E. (2003). Personality, culture, and subjective well-being: Emotional and cognitive evaluations of life. *Annual Review of Psychology, 54*, 403–425.

Dijk, D. J., Duffy, J. F., Riel, E., Shanahan, T. L., & Czeisler, C. A. (1999). Ageing and the circadian and homeostatic regulation of human sleep during forced desynchrony of rest, melatonin and temperature rhythms. *Journal of Physiology (London), 516 (Pt. 2)*, 611–627.

DiNardo, P. A., & Barlow, D. H. (1988). *Anxiety Disorders Interview Schedule-Revised (ADIS-R)*. Albany, NY: Graywind Publications.

Dixon, R. A., & Hultsch, D. F. (1983). Structure and development of metamemory in adulthood. *Journal of Gerontology, 38*, 682–689.

Dixon, R. A., & Hultsch, D. F. (1999). Intelligence and cognitive potential in late life. In J. C. Cavanaugh & S. K. Whitbourne (Eds.), *Gerontology: Interdisciplinary perspectives* (pp. 213–237). New York: Oxford University Press.

Dobbs, A. R., & Rule, B. G. (1987). Prospective memory and self-reports of memory abilities in older adults. *Canadian Journal of Psychology, 41*, 209–222.

Dodge, H. H. (1995). Movements out of poverty among elderly widows. *Journal of Gerontology: Social Sciences, 50*, S240–249.

Doll, R., Peto, R., Boreham, J., & Sutherland, I. (2000). Smoking and dementia in male British doctors: Prospective study. *British Medical Journal, 320*, 1097–1102.

Dorfman, L. T. (1989). Retirement preparation and retirement satisfaction in the rural elderly. *The Journal of Applied Gerontology, 8*, 432–450.

Dorfman, L. T. (1995). Health, financial status, and social participation of retired men and women: Implications for educational intervention. *Educational Gerontology, 21*, 653–669.

Douglas, K., & Arenberg, D. (1978). Age changes, cohort differences, and cultural change on the Guilford-Zimmerman Temperament Survey. *Journal of Gerontology, 33*, 737–747.

Dreher, F., & Maibach, H. (2001). Protective effects of topical antioxidants in humans. *Current Problems in Dermatology, 29*, 157–164.

Drentea, P. (2002). Retirement and mental health. *Journal of Aging and Health, 14*, 167–194.

Drew, L. M., & Smith, P. K. (2002). Implications for grandparents when they lose contact with their grandchildren: Divorce, family feud, and geographical separation. *Journal of Mental Health & Aging, 8*, 95–119.

Duberstein, P. R. (1995). Openness to experience and completed suicide across the second half of life. *International Psychogeriatrics, 7*, 183–198.

Duberstein, P. R., & Conwell, Y. (1997). Personality disorders and completed suicide: A methodological and conceptual review. *Clinical Psychology: Science and Practice, 4*, 359–376.

Duberstein, P. R., & Conwell, Y. (2000). Suicide. In S. K. Whitbourne (Ed.), *Psychopathology in later life* (pp. 245–276). New York: Wiley.

Duberstein, P. R., Conwell, Y., Cox, C., Podgorski, C. A., Glazer, R. S., & Caine, E. D. (1995). Attitudes toward self-determined death: A survey of primary care physicians. *Journal of the American Geriatrics Society, 43*, 395–400.

Duffy, J. F., Dijk, D. J., Hall, E. F., & Czeisler, C. A. (1999). Relationship of endogenous circadian melatonin and temperature rhythms to self-reported preference for morning or evening activity in young and older people. *Journal of Investigative Medicine, 47*, 141–150.

Duffy, J. F., Zeitzer, J. M., Rimmer, D. W., Klerman, E. B., Dijk, D. J., & Czeisler, C. A. (2002). Peak of circadian melatonin rhythm occurs later within the sleep of older subjects. *American Journal of Physiology: Endocrinology and Metabolism, 282*, E297–303.

Duffy, M. K., Ganster, D. C., & Shaw, J. D. (1998). Positive affectivity and negative outcomes: The role of tenure and job satisfaction. *Journal of Applied Psychology, 83*, 950–959.

Dugan, E., Roberts, C. P., Cohen, S. J., Preisser, J. S., Davis, C. C., Bland, D. R., & Albertson, E. (2001). Why older community-dwelling adults do not discuss urinary incontinence with their primary care physicians. *Journal of the American Geriatrics Society, 49*, 462–465.

Dunlosky, J., & Connor, L. T. (1997). Age differences in the allocation of study time account for age differences in memory performance. *Memory and Cognition, 25*, 691–700.

Duvall, E. M. (1977). *Family development* (5th ed.). Philadelphia: Lippincott.

Eaves, L., Martin, N., Heath, A., Schieken, R., Meyer, J., Silberg, J., Neale, M., & Corey, L. (1997). Age changes in the causes of individual differences in conservatism. *Behavior Genetics, 27*, 121–124.

Ebmeyer, J. B., & Whitbourne, S. K. (1990). *Identity and intimacy in marriage: A study of couples.* New York: Springer-Verlag.

Edelstein, B., Martin, R. R., & McKee, D. R. (2000). Assessment of older adult psychopathology. In S. K. Whitbourne (Ed.), *Psychopathology in later life* (pp. 61–88). New York: Wiley.

Edelstein, S. L., & Barrett-Connor, E. (1993). Relation between body size and bone mineral density in elderly men and women. *American Journal of Epidemiology, 138*, 160–169.

Edwards, J. R., & Baglioni, A. J. (1991). Relationship between Type A behavior pattern and mental and physical symptoms: A comparison of global and component measures. *Journal of Applied Psychology, 76*, 276–290.

Eid, M., & Diener, E. (2001). Norms for experiencing emotions in different cultures: Inter- and intranational differences. *Journal of Personality and Social Psychology, 81*, 869–885.

Einstein, G. O., McDaniel, M. A., Manzi, M., Cochran, B., & Baker, M. (2000). Prospective memory and aging: Forgetting intentions over short delays. *Psychology and Aging, 15*, 671–683.

Einstein, G. O., McDaniel, M. A., Smith, R., & Shaw, P. (1998). Habitual prospective memory and aging: Remembering instructions and forgetting actions. *Psychological Science, 9*, 284–288.

Eisen, A., Entezari-Taher, M., & Stewart, H. (1996). Cortical projections to spinal motoneurons: changes with aging and amyotrophic lateral sclerosis. *Neurology, 46*, 1396–1404.

Eisenberger, R., & Cameron, J. (1996). Detrimental effects of rewards: Reality or myth? *American Psychologist, 51*, 1153–1166.

Elder, G. H., Jr., Shanahan, M., & Clipp, E. C. (1994). When war comes to men's lives: Life course patterns in family, work, and health. *Psychology and Aging, 9*, 5–16.

Elias, M. F., Elias, P. K., D'Agostino, R. B., Silbershatz, H., & Wolf, P. A. (1997). Role of age, education, and gender on cognitive performance in the Framingham Heart Study: Community-based norms. *Experimental Aging Research, 23*, 201–235.

Ellis, A. (1998). Flora: A case of severe depression and treatment with rational emotive behavior therapy. In R. P. Halgin & S. K. Whitbourne (Eds.), *A casebook in abnormal psychology: From the files of experts* (pp. 166–181). New York: Oxford University Press.

Engle, V. F., Fox-Hill, E., & Graney, M. J. (1998). The experience of living-dying in a nursing home: Self-reports of Black and White older adults. *Journal of the American Geriatrics Society, 46*, 1091–1096.

Enserink, M. (1998). First Alzheimer's disease confirmed. *Science, 279*, 2037.

Epstein, M. (1996). Aging and the kidney. *Journal of the American Society of Nephrology, 7*, 1106–1122.

Era, P., Schroll, M., Ytting, H., Gause-Nilsson, I., Heikkinen, E., & Steen, B. (1996). Postural balance and its sensory-motor correlates in 75-year-old men and women: A cross-national comparative study. *Journal of Gerontology: Medical Sciences, 51*, M53–63.

Erfurth, E. M., & Hagmar, L. E. (1995). Decreased serum testosterone and free triiodothyronine levels in healthy middle-aged men indicate an age effect at the pituitary level. *European Journal of Endocrinology, 132*, 663–667.

Erikson, E. H. (1959). Identity and the life cycle: Selected papers. *Psychological Issues Monograph, 1*, 1–177.

Erikson, E. H. (1963). *Childhood and society* (2nd ed.). New York: Norton.

Erikson, E. H., Erikson, J. M., & Kivnick, H. Q. (1986). *Vital involvement in old age.* New York: W.W. Norton.

Ernst Kossek, E., & Ozeki, C. (1998). Work–family conflict, policies, and the job–life satisfaction relationship: A review and directions for organizational behavior-human resources research. *Journal of Applied Psychology, 83*, 139–149.

Escalante, A., Lichtenstein, M. J., & Hazuda, H. P. (1999). Determinants of shoulder and elbow flexion range: results from the San Antonio Longitudinal Study of Aging. *Arthritis Care Research, 12*, 277–286.

Escalante, A., Lichtenstein, M. J., Dhanda, R., Cornell, J. E., & Hazuda, H. P. (1999). Determinants of hip and knee flexion range: results from the San Antonio Longitudinal Study of Aging. *Arthritis Care Research, 12*, 8–18.

Ettington, D. R. (1998). Successful career plateauing. *Journal of Vocational Behavior, 52*, 72–88.

Evans, D. A., Scherr, P. A., Cook, N. R., Albert, M. S., Funkenstein, H. H., Smith, L. A., Hebert, L. E., Wetle, T. T., Branch, L. G., Chown, M., Hennekens, C. H., & Taylor, J. O. (1990). Estimated prevalence of Alzheimer's Disease in the United States. *Milbank Quarterly, 68*, 267–289.

Evans, W. J. (1995). What is sarcopenia? *Journal of Gerontology: Biological Sciences, 50*, 5–8.

Evrard, M. (2002). Ageing and lexical access to common and proper names in picture naming. *Brain and Language, 81*, 174–179.

Eysenck, H. J. (1995). *Genius: The natural history of creativity.* Cambridge, UK: Cambridge University Press.

Farlow, M. R., Hake, A., Messina, J., Hartman, R., Veach, J., & Anand, R. (2001). Response of patients with Alzheimer disease to rivastigmine treatment is predicted by the rate of disease progression. *Archives of Neurology, 58*, 417–422.

Farrell, M. P., & Rosenberg, S. D. (1981). *Men at midlife.* Boston: Auburn House.

Featherman, D. L., & Stevens, G. (1982). A revised socioeconomic index of occupational status: Application in analysis of sex differences in attainment. In R. M. Hauser, D. Mechanic, A. O. Holler & T. Hauser (Eds.), *Social structure and behavior* (pp. 141–181). San Diego: Academic Press.

Federal Interagency Forum on Aging-Related Statistics (2001). Older Americans: Key indicators of well-being. Hyattsville, MD.

Federmeier, K. D., McLennan, D. B., De Ochoa, E., & Kutas, M. (2002). The impact of semantic memory organization and sentence context information on spoken language processing by younger and older adults: An ERP study. *Psychophysiology, 39*, 133–146.

Fedok, F. G. (1996). The aging face. *Facial Plastic Surgery, 12*, 107–115.

Feldman, D. C. (1994). The decision to retire early: A review and conceptualization. *Academy of Management Review, 19*, 285–311.

Feldman, H. A., Johannes, C. B., Araujo, A. B., Mohr, B. A., Longcope, C., & McKinlay, J. B. (2001). Low dehydroepiandrosterone and ischemic heart disease in middle-aged men: Prospective results from the Massachusetts Male Aging Study. *American Journal of Epidemiology, 153*, 79–89.

Fenn, D. S., & Ganzini, L. (1999). Attitudes of Oregon psychologists toward physician-assisted suicide and the Oregon Death With Dignity Act. *Professional Psychology: Research and Practice, 30*, 235–244.

Fernandez, M. E., Mutran, E. J., Reitzes, D. C., & Sudha, S. (1998). Ethnicity, gender, and depressive symptoms in older workers. *Gerontologist, 38*, 71–79.

Ferrari, E., Cravello, L., Muzzoni, B., Casarotti, D., Paltro, M., Solerte, S. B., Fioravanti, M., Cuzzoni, G., Pontiggia, B., & Magri, F. (2001). Age-related changes of the hypothalamic-pituitary-adrenal axis: Pathophysiological correlates. *European Journal of Endocrinology, 144*, 319–329.

Ferraro, F. R. (2002). *Minority and cross-cultural aspects of neuropsychological assessment.* Bristol, PA: Swets and Zeitlinger.

Ferraro, K. F., & Farmer, M. M. (1996). Double jeopardy, aging as leveler, or persistent health inequality? A longitudinal analysis of white and black Americans. *Journal of Gerontology: Social Sciences, 51*, S319–328.

Ferreira, A. J., & Winter, W. D. (1974). On the nature of marital relationships: Measurable differences in spontaneous agreement. *Family Process, 13*, 355–370.

Field, A. E., Colditz, G. A., Willett, W. C., Longcope, C., & McKinlay, J. B. (1994). The relation of smoking, age, relative weight, and dietary intake to serum adrenal steroids, sex hormones, and sex hormone-binding globulin in middle-aged men. *Journal of Clinical Endocrinology and Metabolism, 79*, 1310–1316.

Field, M. J., Cassel, C. K., & Committee on Care at the End of Life, (1997). *Approaching death: Improving care at the end of life, Institute of Medicine, Division of Health Care Services.* Washington, DC: National Academy Press.

Field, N. P., Gal-Oz, E., & Bonanno, G. A. (2003). Continuing bonds and adjustment at 5 years after the death of a spouse. *Journal of Consulting and Clinical Psychology, 71*, 110–117.

Field, N. P., Nichols, C., Holen, A., & Horowitz, M. J. (1999). The relation of continuing attachment to adjustment in conjugal bereavement. *Journal of Consulting and Clinical Psychology, 67*, 212–218.

Fields, J., & Casper, L. M. (2001). *America's family and living arrangements: Population characteristics March 2000. Current Population Reports,* P20-537. Washington, DC: U.S. Census Bureau.

Fillenbaum, G. G., Hanlon, J. T., Landerman, L. R., & Schmader, K. E. (2001). Impact of estrogen use on decline in cognitive function in a representative sample of older community-resident women. *American Journal of Epidemiology, 153*, 137–144.

Fingerman, K. L. (1995). Aging mothers' and their adult daughters' perceptions of conflict behaviors. *Psychology and Aging, 10*, 639–649.

Fingerman, K. L. (1996). Sources of tension in the aging mother and adult daughter relationship. *Psychology and Aging, 11*, 591–606.

Fingerman, K. L. (2001). *Aging mothers and their adult daughters: A study in mixed emotions.* New York: Springer.

Fingerman, K. L., & Griffiths, P. C. (1999). Seasons greetings: Adults' social contacts at the holiday season. *Psychology and Aging, 14*, 192–205.

Fins, J. J., Miller, F. G., Acres, C. A., Bacchetta, M. D., Huzzard, L. L., & Rapkin, B. D. (1999). End-of-life decision-making in the hospital: Current practice and future prospects. *Journal of Pain and Symptom Management, 17*, 6–15.

First, M. B., Spitzer, R. L., Gibbon, M., & Williams, J. B. W. (1997). *SCID-I/P (for DSM-IV) Patient Edition Structured Clinical Interview for DSM-IV Axis I Disorders, Research Version, Patient/Non-patient Edition. (SCID-I/P).* New York: Biometrics Research, New York State Psychiatric Institute.

Fischer, C. S., & Phillips, S. L. (1982). Who is alone? Social characteristics of people with small networks. In L. A. Peplau & D. Perlman (Eds.), *Loneliness: A sourcebook of current theory, research, and therapy* (pp. 21–39). New York: Wiley Interscience.

Fish, L. S., New, R. S., & Van Cleave, N. J. (1992). Shared parenting in dual-income families. *American Journal of Orthopsychiatry, 62*, 83–92.

Fitzgerald, J. M. (2000). Younger and older jurors: The influence of environmental supports on memory performance and decision making in complex trials. *Journals of Gerontology Series B: Psychological Sciences and Social Sciences, 55*, P323–331.

Fitzgerald, L. F., & Betz, N. E. (1994). Cultural development in cultural context: The role of gender, race, class, and sexual orientation. In M. Savikas & R. Lent (Eds.), *Convergence in theories of career development* (pp. 103–117). Hillsdale, NJ: Erlbaum.

Fitzgerald, M. D., Tanaka, H., Tran, Z. V., & Seals, D. R. (1997). Age-related declines in maximal aerobic capacity in regularly exercising vs sedentary women: A meta-analysis. *Journal of Applied Physiology, 83*, 160–165.

Fitzpatrick, T. R., Spiro, A., Kressin, N. R., Greene, E., & Bosse, R. (2001). Leisure activities, stress, and health among bereaved and non-bereaved elderly men: The Normative Aging Study. *Omega: Journal of Death and Dying, 43*, 217–245.

Fletcher, G. F., Balady, G., Blair, S. N., Blumenthal, J., Caspersen, C., Chaitman, B., Epstein, S., Sivarajan Froelicher, E. S. Froelicher, V. F., Pina, I. L. & Pollock, M. L. (1996). Statement on exercise: benefits and recommendations for physical activity programs for all Americans. A statement for health professionals by the Committee on Exercise and Cardiac Rehabilitation of the Council on Clinical Cardiology, American Heart Association. *Circulation, 94*, 857–862.

Flint, A. J., & Rifat, S. L. (1997). Anxious depression in elderly patients. Response to antidepressant treatment. *American Journal of Geriatric Psychiatry, 5*, 107–115.

Flint, A. J., & Rifat, S. L. (2000). Maintenance treatment for recurrent depression in late life. A four-year outcome study. *American Journal of Geriatric Psychiatry, 8*, 112–116.

Fliser, D., Franek, E., Joest, M., Block, S., Mutschler, E., & Ritz, E. (1997). Renal function in the elderly: Impact of hypertension and cardiac function. *Kidney International, 51*, 1196–1204.

Floyd, F. J., & Wasner, G. H. (1994). Social exchange, equity, and commitment: Structural equation modeling of dating relationships. *Journal of Family Psychology, 8*, 55–73.

Floyd, F. J., Haynes, S. N., Doll, E. R., Winemiller, D., Lemsky, C., Burgy, T. M., Werle, M., & Heilman, N. (1992). Assessing retirement satisfaction and perceptions of retirement experiences. *Psychology and Aging, 7*, 609–621.

Folkman, S. (1997). Positive psychological states and coping with severe stress. *Social Science and Medicine, 45*, 1207–1221.

Folkman, S., Chesney, M., Collette, L., Boccellari, A., & Cooke, M. (1996). Postbereavement depressive mood and its prebereavement predictors in HIV+ and HIV– gay men. *Journal of Personality and Social Psychology, 70*, 336–348.

Folstein, M. F., Folstein, S. E., & McHugh, P. R. (1975). Mini-Mental State: A practical method for grading the cognitive state of patients for the clinician. *Journal of Psychiatric Research, 12*, 189–198.

Fontaine, K. R., Redden, D. T., Wang, C., Westfall, A. O., & Allison, D. B. (2003). Years of life lost due to obesity. *Journal of the American Medical Association, 289*, 187–193.

Foos, P. W. (1989). Age differences in memory for two common objects. *Journal of Gerontology: Psychological Sciences, 44*, P178–P180.

Ford, D. H., & Lerner, R. M. (Eds.). (1992). *Developmental systems theory: An integrative approach*. Newbury Park, CA: Sage.

Forde, C. G., Cantau, B., Delahunty, C. M., & Elsner, R. J. (2002). Interactions between texture and trigeminal stimulus in a liquid food system: Effects on elderly consumers preferences. *Journal of Nutrition Health and Aging, 6*, 130–133.

Fowler, F. J., Jr., Coppola, K. M., & Teno, J. M. (1999). Methodological challenges for measuring quality of care at the end of life. *Journal of Pain and Symptom Management, 17*, 114–119.

Fraley, R. C., & Shaver, P. R. (1998). Airport separations: A naturalistic study of adult attachment dynamics in separating couples. *Journal of Personality and Social Psychology, 75*, 1198–1212.

Franke, W. D., & Anderson, D. F. (1994). Relationship between physical activity and risk factors for cardiovascular disease among law enforcement officers. *Journal of Occupational Medicine, 36*, 1127–1132.

Franks, M. M., Herzog, A. R., Holmberg, D., & Markus, H. R. (1999). Educational attainment and self-making in later life. In C. D. Ryff & V. W. Marshall (Eds.), *The self and society in aging processes* (pp. 223–246). New York: Springer.

Fratiglioni, L., & Wang, H. X. (2000). Smoking and Parkinson's and Alzheimer's disease: Review of the epidemiological studies. *Behavior and Brain Research, 113*, 117–120.

Frazier, L. D., Johnson, P. M., Gonzalez, G. K., & Kafka, C. L. (2002). Psychosocial influences on possible selves: A comparison of three cohorts of older adults. *International Journal of Behavioral Development, 26*, 308–317.

Frette, C., Barrett-Connor, E., & Clausen, J. L. (1996). Effect of active and passive smoking on ventilatory function in elderly men and women. *American Journal of Epidemiology, 143*, 757–765.

Friedman, H. S., Tucker, J. S., Schwartz, J. E., Martin, L. R., Tomlinson-Keasey, C., Wingard, D. L., & Criqui, M. H. (1995). Childhood conscientiousness and longevity: Health behaviors and cause of death. *Journal of Personality and Social Psychology, 68*, 696–703.

Friedman, M., & Rosenman, R. H. (1974). *Type A behavior and your heart*. New York: Knopf.

Frontera, W. R., Hughes, V. A., Fielding, R. A., Fiatarone, M. A., Evans, W. J., & Roubenoff, R. (2000). Aging of skeletal muscle: A 12-yr longitudinal study. *Journal of Applied Physiology, 88*, 1321–1326.

Fry, P. S. (1997). Grandparent's reactions to the death of a grandchild: An exploratory factor analytic study. *Omega—Journal of Death and Dying, 35*, 1997.

Fuiano, G., Sund, S., Mazza, G., Rosa, M., Caglioti, A., Gallo, G., Natale, G., Andreucci, M., Memoli, B., De Nicola, L., & Conte, G. (2001). Renal hemodynamic response to maximal vasodilating stimulus in healthy older subjects. *Kidney International, 59*, 1052–1058.

Fuller-Thomson, E., M., Minkler, M., & Driver, D. (1997). A profile of grandparents raising grandchildren in the United States. *The Gerontologist, 37*, 406–411.

Fullerton, H. N., & Toossi, M. (2001). Labor force projections to 2010: steady growth and changing composition. *Monthly Labor Review Online, 124, No. 11*.

Furstenberg, F., & Spanier, G. (1984). *Recycling the family: Remarriage after divorce*. Beverly Hills, CA: Sage.

Gaeta, H., Friedman, D., Ritter, W., & Cheng, J. (2001). An event-related potential evaluation of involuntary attentional shifts in young and older adults. *Psychology and Aging, 16*, 55–68.

Gagliese, L., & Melzack, R. (1997). Chronic pain in elderly people. *Pain, 70*, 3–14.

Gagnon, M., Hersen, M., Kabacoff, R. L., & Van Hasselt, V. B. (1999). Interpersonal and psychological correlates of marital dissatisfaction in late life: A review. *Clinical Psychology Review, 19*, 359–378.

Galasko, D., Edland, S. D., Morris, J. C., Clark, C., Mohs, R., & Koss, E. (1995). The consortium to establish a registry for Alzheimer's disease (CERAD): XI. Clinical milestones in patients with Alzheimer's disease followed over 3 yrs. *Neurology, 45*, 1451–1455.

Gall, T. L., Evans, D. R., & Howard, J. (1997). The retirement adjustment process: Changes in the well-being of male retirees across time. *Journal of Gerontology: Psychological Sciences, 52B*, P110–P117.

Gallagher, D., Ruts, E., Visser, M., Heshka, S., Baumgartner, R. N., Wang, J., Pierson, R. N., Pi-Sunyer, F. X., & Heymsfield, S. B. (2000). Weight stability masks sarcopenia in elderly men and women. *American Journal of Physiology—Endocrinology & Metabolism, 279*, E366–375.

Gallagher-Thompson, D., & Thompson, L. W. (1996). Applying cognitive-behavioral therapy to the psychological problems of later life. In S. H. Zarit & B. G. Knight (Eds.), *A guide to psychotherapy and aging* (pp. 61–82). Washington, DC: American Psychological Association.

Gallagher-Thompson, D., Futterman, A., Farberow, N., Thompson, L. W., & Peterson, J. (1993). The impact of spousal bereavement on older widows and widowers. In M. S. Stroebe, W. Stroebe & R. O. Hansson (Eds.), *Handbook of bereavement*. Cambridge: Cambridge University Press.

Gallo, L. C., & Matthews, K. A. (2003). Understanding the association between socioeconomic status and physical health: Do negative emotions play a role? *Psychological Bulletin, 129*, 10–51.

Gamboz, N., Russo, R., & Fox, E. (2002). Age differences and the identity negative priming effect: An updated meta-analysis. *Psychology and Aging, 17*, 525–531.

Ganzini, L., Nelson, H. D., Lee, M. A., Kraemer, D. F., Schmidt, T. A., & Delorit, M. A. (2001). Oregon physicians' attitudes about and experiences with end-of-life care since passage of the Oregon Death with Dignity Act. *Journal of the American Medical Association, 285*, 2363–2369.

Garden, S. E., Phillips, L. H., & MacPherson, S. E. (2001). Midlife aging, open-ended planning, and laboratory measures of executive function. *Neuropsychology, 15*, 472–482.

Gardner, H. (1983). *Frames of mind: The theory of multiple intelligences.* New York: Basic Books.

Gardner, H. (1993). *Multiple intelligences: The theory in practice.* New York: Basic Books.

Garnero, P., Sornay Rendu, E., Chapuy, M. C., & Delmas, P. D. (1996). Increased bone turnover in late postmenopausal women is a major determinant of osteoporosis. *Journal of Bone and Mineral Research, 11*, 337–349.

Gass, K. A. (1989). Appraisal, coping, and resources: Markers associated with the health of aged widows and widowers. In D. A. Lund (Ed.), *Older bereaved spouses: Research and practical applications* (pp. 79–94). New York: Hemisphere.

Gatz, M., Fiske, A., Fox, L. S., Kaskie, B., Kasl-Godley, J. E., McCallum, T. J., & Wetherell, J. L. (1998). Empirically validated treatments for older adults. *Journal of Mental Health and Aging, 4*, 9–26.

Gatz, M., Pedersen, N. L., Berg, S., Johansson, B., Johansson, K., Mortimer, J. A., et al. (1997). Heritability for Alzheimer's disease: The study of dementia in Swedish twins. *Journal of Gerontology: Medical Sciences, 52*, M117–125.

Gavrin, J., & Chapman, C. R. (1995). Clinical management of dying patients. *Western Journal of Medicine, 163*, 268–277.

Gearing, M., Mirra, S. S., Hedreen, J. C., Sumi, S. M., Hansen, L. A., & Heyman, A. (1995). The Consortium to Establish a Registry for Alzheimer's Disease (CERAD). Part X. Neuropathology confirmation of the clinical diagnosis of Alzheimer's disease. *Neurology, 45*, 461–466.

Gee, S., & Baillie, J. (1999). Happily ever after? An exploration of retirement expectations. *Educational Gerontology, 25*, 109–128.

Geerlings, S. W., Beekman, A. T., Deeg, D. J., Twisk, J. W., & Van Tilburg, W. (2002). Duration and severity of depression predict mortality in older adults in the community. *Psychological Medicine, 32*, 609–618.

Gendell, M., & Siegel, J. S. (1996). Trends in retirement age in the United States, 1955-1993, by sex and race. *Journal of Gerontology: Social Sciences, 51*, S132–139.

George, L. K. (2000). Well-being and sense of self: What we know and what we need to know. In K. W. Schaie & J. Hendricks (Eds.), *Societal impact on the aging self.* New York: Springer.

Gescheider, G. A., Beiles, E. J., Checkosky, C. M., Bolanowski, S. J., & Verrillo, R. T. (1994). The effects of aging on information-processing channels in the sense of touch: II. Temporal summation in the P channel. *Somatosensory and Motor Research, 11*, 359–365.

Gildengers, A. G., Houck, P. R., Mulsant, B. H., Pollock, B. G., Mazumdar, S., Miller, M. D., Dew, M. A., Frank, E., Kupfer, D. J., & Reynolds, C. F., 3rd. (2002). Course and rate of antidepressant response in the very old. *Journal of Affective Disorders, 69*, 177–184.

Gilliland, G., & Fleming, S. (1998). A comparison of spousal anticipatory grief and conventional grief. *Death Studies, 22*, 541–569.

Glaser, B. G., & Strauss, A. L. (1968). *Time for dying.* Chicago: Aldine.

Glass, J. C., Jr., & Kilpatrick, B. B. (1998). Gender comparisons of baby boomers and financial preparation for retirement. *Educational Gerontology, 24*, 719–745.

Glenn, N. D., & McLanahan, S. (1982). Children and marital happiness: A further specification of the relationship. *Journal of Marriage and the Family, 44*, 63–72.

Glenn, N., & Weaver, C. (1977). The marital happiness of remarried divorced persons. *Journal of Marriage and the Family, 39*, 331–337.

Gold, D. P., Andres, D., Etezadi, J., Arbuckle, T., Schwartzman, A., & Chaikelson, J. (1995). Structural equation model of intellectual change and continuity and predictors of intelligence in older men. *Psychology and Aging, 10*, 294–303.

Gold, D. T. (1989). Sibling relationships in old age:

Goldman, N., Koreman, S., & Weinstein, R. (1995). Marital status and health among the elderly. *Social Science and Medicine, 40*, 1717–1730.

Goldstein, I., Young, J. M., Fischer, J., Bangerter, K., Segerson, T., & Taylor, T. (2003). Vardenafil, a new phosphodiesterase type 5 Inhibitor, in the treatment of erectile dysfunction in men with diabetes: A multicenter double-blind placebo-controlled fixed-dose study. *Diabetes Care, 26*, 777–783.

Goldstein, N. E., & Lynn, J. (2002). The 107th Congress's legislative proposals concerning end-of-life care. *Journal of Palliative Medicine, 5*, 819–827.

Goleman, D. (1995). *Emotional intelligence.* New York: Bantam Books.

Golomb, J., Kluger, A., de Leon, M. J., Ferris, S. H., Mittelman, M., Cohen, J., & George, A. E. (1996). Hippocampal formation size predicts declining memory performance in normal aging. *Neurology, 47*, 810–813.

Goodlin, S. J., Winzelberg, G. S., Teno, J. M., Whedon, M., & Lynn, J. (1998). Death in the hospital. *Archives of Internal Medicine, 158*, 1570–1572.

Goodpaster, B. H., Carlson, C. L., Visser, M., Kelley, D. E., Scherzinger, A., Harris, T. B., Stamm, E., & Newman, A. B. (2001). Attenuation of skeletal muscle and strength in the elderly: The health ABC study. *Journal of Applied Physiology, 90*, 2157–2165.

Gottfredson, G. D. (2002). Interests, aspirations, self-estimates, and the Self-Directed Search. *Journal of Career Assessment, 10*, 200–208.

Gottfredson, G. D., & Gottfredson, D. C. (2000). *The National Study of Delinquency Prevention in Schools (Final Report to the National Institute of Justice)*. Ellicott City, MD: Gottfredson Associates, Inc.

Gottfredson, G. D., & Holland, J. L. (1989). *Dictionary of Holland occupational codes* (2nd ed.). Odessa, FL: Psychological Assessment Resources.

Gottfredson, G. D., & Holland, J. L. (1991). *The Position Classification Inventory: Professional manual*. Odessa, FL: Psychological Assessment Resources.

Gottfredson, L. S. (1999). The meaning and measurement of environments in Holland's theory. *Journal of Vocational Behavior, 55*, 57–53.

Gotthardt, U., Schweiger, U., Fahrenberg, J., Lauer, C. J., Holsboer, F., & Heuser, I. (1995). Cortisol, ACTH, and cardiovascular response to a cognitive challenge paradigm in aging and depression. *American Journal of Physiology, 268*, R865–873.

Gottman, J. M., & Levenson, R. W. (2000). The timing of divorce: Predicting when a couple will divorce over a 14-year period. *Journal of Marriage and the Family, 62*, 737–745.

Gottman, J. M., & Levenson, R. W. (2002). A two-factor model for predicting when a couple will divorce: Exploratory analyses using 14-year longitudinal data. *Family Process, 41*, 83–96.

Gottman, J., Coan, J., Carrere, S., & Swanson, C. (1998). Predicting marital happiness and stability from newlywed interactions. *Journal of Marriage and the Family, 60*, 5–22.

Gottman, J., Swanson, C., & Murray, J. (1999). The mathematics of marital conflict: Dynamic mathematical nonlinear modeling of newlywed marital interaction. *Journal of Family Psychology, 13*, 3–19.

Gould, R. L. (1978). *Transformations: Growth and change in adult life*. New York: Simon and Schuster.

Gournellis, R., Lykouras, L., Fortos, A., Oulis, P., Roumbos, V., & Christodoulou, G. N. (2001). Psychotic (delusional) major depression in late life: A clinical study. *International Journal of Geriatric Psychiatry, 16*, 1085–1091.

Graham, C., Arthur, A., & Howard, R. (2002). The social functioning of older adults with schizophrenia. *Aging and Mental Health, 6*, 149–152.

Graham, K., & Vidal-Zeballos, D. (1998). Analyses of use of tranquilizers and sleeping pills across five surveys of the same population (1985–1991): The relationship with gender, age and use of other substances. *Social Science and Medicine, 46*, 381–395.

Grant, B. S., Harford, T. C., Dawson, D. A., Chou, P., Dufour, M., & Pickering, R. (1995). Prevalence of DSM-IV alcohol abuse and dependence, United States, 1992. *Alcohol Health and Research World, 18*, 243–248.

Gratzinger, P., Sheikh, J. L., Friedman, L., & Yesavage, J. A. (1990). Cognitive interventions to improve face-name recall: The role of personality trait differences. *Developmental Psychology, 26*, 889–893.

Green, B. L., Grace, M. C., Lindy, J. D., Gleser, G. C., & Leonard, A. (1990). Risk factors for PTSD and other diagnoses in a general sample of Vietnam veterans. *American Journal of Psychiatry, 147*, 729–733.

Greendale, G. A., Kritz-Silverstein, D., Seeman, T., & Barrett-Connor, E. (2000). Higher basal cortisol predicts verbal memory loss in postmenopausal women: Rancho Bernardo Study. *Journal of the American Geriatrics Society, 48*, 1655–1658.

Greif, G. L. (1995). Single fathers with custody following separation and divorce. *Marriage and Family Review, 20*, 213–231.

Griffin, W. S., Sheng, J. G., Royston, M. C., Gentleman, S. M., McKenzie, J. E., Graham, D. I., Roberts, G. W., & Mrak, R. E. (1998). Glial-neuronal interactions in Alzheimer's disease: The potential role of a "cytokine cycle" in disease progression. *Brain Pathology, 8*, 65–72.

Griffiths, C. E. (1999). Drug treatment of photoaged skin. *Drugs & Aging, 14*, 289–301.

Grimby, A., & Wiklund, I. (1994). Health-related quality of life in old age. A study among 76-year-old Swedish urban citizens. *Scandinavian Journal of Social Medicine, 22*, 7–14.

Gross, J. J., Carstensen, L. L., Pasupathi, M., Tsai, J., Goetestam Skorpen, C., & Hsu, A. Y. C. (1997). Emotion and aging: Experience, expression, and control. *Psychology and Aging, 12*, 590–599.

Grossberg, G., & Desai, A. (2001). Review of rivastigmine and its clinical applications in Alzheimer's disease and related disorders. *Expert Opinions in Pharmacotherapy, 2*, 653–666.

Grossman, M., Cooke, A., DeVita, C., Alsop, D., Detre, J., Chen, W., & Gee, J. (2002). Age-related changes in working memory during sentence comprehension: an fMRI study. *Neuroimage, 15*, 302–317.

Grote, N. K., Naylor, K. E., & Clark, M. S. (2002). Perceiving the division of family work to be unfair: Do social comparisons, enjoyment, and competence matter? *Journal of Family Psychology, 16,* 510–522.

Grzywacz, J. G., & Marks, N. F. (2000). Reconceptualizing the work-family interface: An ecological perspective on the correlates of positive and negative spillover between work and family. *Journal of Occupational Health Psychology, 5,* 111–126.

Guinot, C., Malvy, D. J., Ambroisine, L., Latreille, J., Mauger, E., Tenenhaus, M., Morizot, F., Lopez, S., Le Fur, I., & Tschachler, E. (2002). Relative contribution of intrinsic vs. extrinsic factors to skin aging as determined by a validated skin age score. *Archives of Dermatology, 138,* 1454–1160.

Gupta, M. A. (1995). Concerns about aging and a drive for thinness: A factor in the biopsychosocial model of eating disorders? *International Journal of Eating Disorders, 18,* 351–357.

Gurland, B. J., Cross, P. S., & Katz, S. (1996). Epidemiological perspectives on opportunities for treatment of depression. *American Journal of Geriatric Psychiatry, 4 (Suppl. 1),* S7–S13.

Haapanen, N., Miilunpalo, S., Vuori, I., Oja, P., & Pasanen, M. (1996). Characteristics of leisure time physical activity associated with decreased risk of premature all-cause and cardiovascular disease mortality in middle-aged men. *American Journal of Epidemiology, 143,* 870–880.

Hackel, L. S., & Ruble, D. N. (1992). Changes in the marital relationship after the first baby is born: Predicting the impact of expectancy disconfirmation. *Journal of Personality and Social Psychology, 62,* 944–957.

Hagestad, G. O., & Neugarten, B. L. (1985). Age and the life course. In R. H. Binstock & E. Shanas (Eds.), *Handbook of aging and the social sciences* (pp. 35–61). New York: Van Nostrand Reinhold.

Haidet, P., Hamel, M. B., Davis, R. B., Wenger, N., Reding, D., Kussin, P. S., Connors, A. F., Jr., Lynn, J., Weeks, J. C., & Phillips, R. S. (1998). Outcomes, preferences for resuscitation, and physician–patient communication among patients with metastatic colorectal cancer. SUPPORT Investigators. Study to Understand Prognoses and Preferences for Outcomes and Risks of Treatments. *American Journal of Medicine, 105,* 222–229.

Hakim, R. B., Teno, J. M., Harrell, F. E., Jr., Knaus, W. A., Wenger, N., Phillips, R. S., Layde, P., Califf, R., Connors, A. F., Jr., & Lynn, J. (1996). Factors associated with do-not-resuscitate orders: patients' preferences, prognoses, and physicians' judgments. SUPPORT Investigators. Study to Understand Prognoses and Preferences for Outcomes and Risks of Treatment. *Annals of Internal Medicine, 125,* 284–293.

Hakkinen, K., & Pakarinen, A. (1995). Acute hormonal responses to heavy resistance exercise in men and women at different ages. *International Journal of Sports Medicine, 16,* 507–513.

Halevy, A., & Brody, B. (1993). Brain death: Reconciling definitions, criteria, and tests. *Annals of Internal Medicine, 119,* 519–525.

Haley, W. E., Allen, R. S., Reynolds, S., Chen, H., Burton, A., & Gallagher-Thompson, D. (2002). Family issues in end-of-life decision making and end-of-life care. *American Behavioral Scientist, 46,* 284–298.

Halgin, R. P., & Whitbourne, S. K. (2003). *Abnormal psychology: Clinical perspectives on psychological disorders* (4th ed.). New York: McGraw-Hill.

Hall, D., & Mirvis, P. (1995). The new career contract: developing the whole person at midlife and beyond. *Journal of Vocational Behavior, 47,* 269–289.

Hamel, M. B., Phillips, R. S., Teno, J. M., Lynn, J., Galanos, A. N., Davis, R. B., Connors, A. F., Jr., Oye, R. K., Desbiens, N., Reding, D. J., & Goldman, L. (1996). Seriously ill hospitalized adults: do we spend less on older patients? Support Investigators. Study to Understand Prognoses and Preference for Outcomes and Risks of Treatments. *Journal of the American Geriatric Society, 44,* 1043–1048.

Hamilton, M. (1959). The assessment of anxiety states by rating. *British Journal of Medical Psychology, 32,* 50–55.

Hamilton, M. (1967). Development of a rating scale for primary depressive illness. *British Journal of Social and Clinical Psychology, 6,* 278–296.

Han, B. (2002). Depressive symptoms and self-rated health in community-dwelling older adults: A longitudinal study. *Journal of the American Geriatrics Society, 50,* 1549–1556.

Hansson, R. O., DeKoekkoek, P. D., Neece, W. M., & Patterson, D. W. (1997). Successful aging at work: Annual review, 1992–1996: The older worker and transitions to retirement. *Journal of Vocational Behavior, 51,* 202–233.

Happ, M. B., Capezuti, E., Strumpf, N. E., Wagner, L., Cunningham, S., Evans, L., & Maislin, G. (2002). Advance care planning and end-of-life care for hospitalized nursing home residents. *Journal of the American Geriatrics Society, 50,* 829–835.

Hardy, J., & Selkoe, D. J. (2002). The amyloid hypothesis of Alzheimer's disease: Progress and problems on the road to therapeutics. *Science, 297,* 353–356.

Hardy, M. A., & Quadagno, J. (1995). Satisfaction with early retirement: Making choices in the auto industry. *Journal of Gerontology: Social Sciences, 50B,* S217–S228.

Hare, R. D. (1997). *Hare Psychopathy Checklist-Revised (PCL-R).* Odessa FL: Personality Assessment Resources.

Harkins, S. W., Davis, M. D., Bush, F. M., & Kasberger, J. (1996). Suppression of first pain and slow temporal summation of second pain in relation to age. *Journal of Gerontology: Medical Sciences, 51,* M260–265.

Harma, M. (1996). Ageing, physical fitness and shiftwork tolerance. *Applied Ergonomics, 27*, 25–29.

Harman, S. M., Metter, E. J., Tobin, J. D., Pearson, J., & Blackman, M. R. (2001). Longitudinal effects of aging on serum total and free testosterone levels in healthy men. Baltimore Longitudinal Study of Aging. *Journal of Clinical Endocrinology and Metabolism, 86*, 724–731.

Harmon, L. W., Hansen, J. C., Borgen, F. H., & Hammer, A. L. (1994). *Strong Interest Inventory applications and technical guide.* Palo Alto, CA: Consulting Psychologists Press.

Harpur, T. J., Hart, S. D., & Hare, R. D. (2002). Personality of the psychopath. In P. T. J. Costa & T. A. Widiger (Eds.), *Personality disorders and the five-factor model of personality* (2nd ed., pp. 299–324). Washington, DC: American Psychological Association.

Harrell, J. S., Johnston, L. F., Griggs, T. R., Schaefer, P., Carr, E. G., Jr., McMurray, R. G., Meibohm, A. R., Munoz, S., Raines, B. N., & Williams, O. D. (1996). An occupation based physical activity intervention program: improving fitness and decreasing obesity. *American Association of Occupational Health Nurses Journal, 44*, 377–384.

Harrington, C., Carrillo, H., Wellin, V., & Shemirani, B. B. (2002). Nursing facilities, staffing, residents, and facility deficiencies, 1995 through 2001. San Francisco, CA: Department of Social and Behavioral Sciences University of California.

Harris, M. B. (1994). Growing old gracefully: Age concealment and gender. *Journal of Gerontology: Psychological Sciences, 49*, P149–158.

Hart, C. L., Hole, D. J., & Smith, G. D. (2000). The contribution of risk factors to stroke differentials, by socioeconomic position in adulthood: The Renfrew/Paisley Study. *American Journal of Public Health, 90*, 1788–1791.

Hartley, A. A. (1992). Attention. In F. I. M. Craik & T. A. Salthouse (Eds.), *The handbook of aging and cognition* (pp. 3–50). Hillsdale NJ: Erlbaum.

Hartup, W. W., & Stevens, N. (1997). Friendships and adaptation in the life course. *Psychological Bulletin, 121*, 355–370.

Harwood, D. G., Sultzer, D. L., & Wheatley, M. V. (2000). Impaired insight in Alzheimer disease: association with cognitive deficits, psychiatric symptoms, and behavioral disturbances. *Neuropsychiatry, Neuropsychology, and Behavioral Neurology, 13*, 83–88.

Hasher, L., & Zacks, R. T. (1988). Working memory, comprehension, and aging: A review and a new view. In G. H. Bower (Ed.), *The psychology of learning and motivation* (Vol. 22, pp. 193–225). New York: Academic.

Hasher, L., Chung, C., May, C. P., & Foong, N. (2002). Age, time of testing, and proactive interference. *Canadian Journal of Experimental Psychology, 56*, 200–207.

Hasher, L., Zacks, R. T., & May, C. P. (1999). Inhibitory control, circadian arousal, and age. In D. Gopher & A..Koriat (Eds.), *Attention and performance, XVII, Cognitive regulation of performance: Interaction of theory and application* (pp. 653–675). Cambridge, MA: MIT Press.

Hashimoto, Y., Niikura, T., Ito, Y., Kita, Y., Terashita, K., & Nishimoto, I. (2002). Neurotoxic mechanisms by Alzheimer's disease-linked N141I mutant presenilin 2. *Journal of Pharmacology and Experimental Therapeutics, 300*, 736–745.

Hathaway, S. R., & McKinley, J. C. (1989). *The Minnesota Multiphasic Personality Inventory-2.* Minneapolis: University of Minnesota Press.

Hattori, M., Fujiyama, A., Taylor, T. D., Watanabe, H., Yada, T., Park, H.-S., Toyoda, A., Ishii, K., Totoki, J., Choi, D.-K., Soeda, E., Ohki, M., Takagi, T., Sakaki, Y., Taudien, S., Blechschmidt, K., (2000). The DNA sequence of human chromosome 21. *Nature, 405*, 311–319.

Havighurst, R. J. (1972). *Developmental tasks and education.* New York: McKay.

Hayflick, L. (1994). *How and why we age.* New York: Ballantine Books.

Hayflick, L., & Moorhead, P. S. (1961). The serial cultivation of human diploid cell strains. *Experimental Cell Research, 25*, 585–621.

Hays, J. C., Gold, D. T., & Peiper, C. F. (1997). Sibling bereavement in late life. *Omega—Journal of Death and Dying, 35*, 1997.

Hays, J., Ockene, J. K., Brunner, R. L., Kotchen, J. M., Manson, J. E., Patterson, R. E., Aragaki, A. K., Shumaker, S. A., Brzyski, R. G., LaCroix, A. Z., Granek, I. A., Valanis, B. G., & the Women's Health Initiative Investigators (2003). Effects of estrogen plus progestin on health-related quality of life. *New England Journal of Medicine*, 1839–1854.

Hays, M. T., & Nielsen, K. R. (1994). Human thyroxine absorption: Age effects and methodological analyses. *Thyroid, 4*, 55–64.

Hayward, M. D., Friedman, S., & Chen, H. (1996). Race inequities in men's retirement. *Journal of Gerontology: Social Sciences, 51*, S1–10.

Hazan, C., & Shaver, P. (1987). Romantic love conceptualized as an attachment process. *Journal of Personality and Social Psychology, 52*, 511–524.

Hazan, C., & Shaver, P. R. (1990). Love and work: An attachment-theoretical perspective. *Journal of Personality and Social Psychology, 59*, 270–280.

He, W., & Schachter, J. P. (2003). *Internal migration of the older population: 1995 to 2000*. Washington, DC: U.S. Bureau of the Census.

Healy, M. C., Lehman, M., & McDaniel, M. A. (1995). Age and voluntary turnover: A quantitative review. *Personnel Psychology, 48*, 335–345.

Heaton, J. P., & Morales, A. (2001). Andropause—A multi-system disease. *Canadian Journal of Urology, 8*, 1213–1222.

Heckhausen, J. (1997). Developmental regulation across adulthood: Primary and secondary control of age-related challenges. *Developmental Psychology, 33*, 176–187.

Heckhausen, J., & Schulz, R. (1995). A life-span theory of control. *Psychological Review, 102*, 284–304.

Hedberg, K., Hopkins, D., & Kohn, M. (2003). Five years of legal physician-assisted suicide in Oregon. *New England Journal of Medicine, 348*, 961–964.

Hedden, T., & Park, D. (2001). Aging and interference in verbal working memory. *Psychology and Aging, 16*, 666–681.

Hedden, T., & Park, D. C. (2003). Contributions of source and inhibitory mechanisms to age-related retroactive interference in verbal working memory. *Journal of Experimental Psychology: General, 132*, 93–112.

Heft, M. W., Cooper, B. Y., O'Brien, K. K., Hemp, E., & O'Brien, R. (1996). Aging effects on the perception of noxious and non-noxious thermal stimuli applied to the face. *Aging, 8*, 35–41.

Helgeson, V. S., & Taylor, S. E. (1993). Social comparisons and adjustment among cardiac patients. *Journal of Applied Social Psychology,, 23*, 1171–1195.

Helson, R. (1967). Personality characteristics and developmental history of creative college women. *Genetic Psychology Monographs, 76*, 205–256.

Helson, R., & Moane, G. (1987). Personality change in women from college to midlife. *Journal of Personality and Social Psychology, 53*, 176–186.

Helson, R., & Roberts, B. W. (1994). Ego development and personality change in adulthood. *Journal of Personality and Social Psychology, 66*, 911–920.

Helson, R., & Srivastava, S. (2001). Three paths of adult development: Conservers, seekers, and achievers. *Journal of Personality and Social Psychology, 80*, 995–1010.

Helson, R., & Wink, P. (1992). Personality change in women from the early 40s to the early 50s. *Psychology and Aging, 7*, 46–55.

Helson, R., Jones, C., & Kwan, V. S. Y. (2002). Personality change over 40 years of adulthood: Hierarchical linear modeling analyses of two longitudinal samples. *Journal of Personality and Social Psychology, 83*, 752–766.

Hendin, H. (1999). Suicide, assisted suicide, and medical illness. *Journal of Clinical Psychiatry, 60*, 2.

Henkel, L. A., Johnson, M. K., & De Leonardis, D. M. (1998). Aging and source monitoring: Cognitive processes and neuro-psychological correlates. *Journal of Experimental Psychology: General, 127*, 251–268.

Henretta, J. C., Chan, C. G., & O'Rand, A. M. (1992). Retirement reason versus retirement process: Examining the reasons for retirement typology. *Journal of Gerontology: Social Sciences, 47*, S1–S7.

Hermann, M., & Berger, P. (2001). Hormonal changes in aging men: A therapeutic indication? *Experimental Gerontology, 36*, 1075–1082.

Hernandez-Perez, E., Khawaja, H. A., & Alvarez, T. Y. (2000). Oral isotretinoin as part of the treatment of cutaneous aging. *Dermatologic Surgery, 26*, 649–652.

Herskind, A. M., McGue, M., Holm, N. V., Sorensen, T. I., Harvald, B., & Vaupel, J. W. (1996). The heritability of human longevity: a population-based study of 2872 Danish twin pairs born 1870–1900. *Human Genetics, 97*, 319–323.

Herskind, A. M., McGue, M., Iachine, I. A., Holm, N., Sorensen, T. I., Harvald, B., & Vaupel, J. W. (1996). Untangling genetic influences on smoking, body mass index and longevity: A multivariate study of 2464 Danish twins followed for 28 years. *Human Genetics, 98*, 467–475.

Herzberg, F., Mausner, B., & Snyderman, B. B. (1959). *The motivation to work*. New York: Wiley.

Herzog, A. R., House, J. S., & Morgan, J. N. (1991). Relation of work and retirement to health and well-being in older age. *Psychology and Aging, 6*, 202–211.

Hess, T. M., Auman, C., Colcombe, S. J., & Rahhal, T. A. (2003). The impact of stereotype threat on age differences in memory performance. *Journals of Gerontology Series B: Psychological Sciences, 58*, P3–11.

Hetherington, E. M., & Kelly, J. (2002). *For better or for worse: Divorce reconsidered*. New York: Norton.

Hetherington, M., & Henderson, S. H. (1997). Fathers in step families. In *The role of the father in child development* (pp. 212–226). New York: Wiley.

HHS (Department of Health and Human Services) (1999). *Mental health: A report of the Surgeon General*. Bethesda, MD: U.S. Public Health Service.

Hibberd, C., Yau, J. L., & Seckl, J. R. (2000). Glucocorticoids and the ageing hippocampus. *Journal of Anatomy, 197* Pt 4, 553–562.

Hickman, S. E. (2002). Improving communication near the end of life. *American Behavioral Scientist, 46*, 252–267.

Hillman, J., & Stricker, G. (2002). A call for psychotherapy integration in work with older adult patients. *Journal of Psychotherapy Integration, 12*, 395–405.

Hinrichsen, G. A., & Dick-Siskin, L. P. (2000). Psychotherapy with older adults. In S. K. Whitbourne (Ed.), *Psychopathology in later life* (pp. 323–353). New York: Wiley.

Ho, G., & Scialfa, C. T. (2002). Age, skill transfer, and conjunction search. *Journals of Gerontology Series B: Psychological Sciences and Social Sciences, 57*, P277–287.

Hofland, B. F., Willis, S. L., & Baltes, P. B. (1980). Fluid performance in the elderly: Intraindividual variability and conditions of assessment. *Journal of Educational Psychology, 73*, 573–586.

Hogan, R., Kim, M., & Perrucci, C. C. (1997). Racial inequality in men's employment and retirement earnings. *Sociological Quarterly, 38*, 431–438.

Hogervorst, E., Williams, J., Budge, M., Riedel, W., & Jolles, J. (2000). The nature of the effect of female gonadal hormone replacement therapy on cognitive function in post-menopausal women: A meta-analysis. *Neuroscience, 101*, 485–512.

Holahan, C. K., & Chapman, J. R. (2002). Longitudinal predictors of proactive goals and activity participation at age 80. *Journals of Gerontology Series B Psychological Sciences and Social Sciences, 57*, P418–425.

Holland, J. L. (1994). *The Self-Directed Search*. Odessa, FL: Psychological Assessment Resources.

Holland, J. L. (1996). Exploring careers with a typology: What we have learned and some new directions. *American Psychologist, 51*, 397–406.

Holland, J. L. (1997). *Making vocational choices: A theory of vocational personalities and work environments (3rd ed.)*. Odessa, LF: Psychological Assessment Resources.

Holland, J. L., & Gottfredson, G. D. (1994). *Career Attitudes and Strategies Inventory: An inventory for understanding adult careers*. Odessa, FL: Psychological Assessment Resources. http://www.bls.gov/opub/mir/2001/11/art2abs.htm

Hooker, K., & Kaus, C. R. (1994). Health-related possible selves in young and middle adulthood. *Psychology and Aging, 9*, 126–133.

Hooyman, N., & Kiyak, H. A. (1991). *Social gerontology: A multidisciplinary perspective*. Boston: Allyn & Bacon.

Horber, F. F., Kohler, S. A., Lippuner, K., & Jaeger, P. (1996). Effect of regular physical training on age-associated alteration of body composition in men. *European Journal of Clinical Investigation, 26*, 279–285.

Horn, J. L. (1970). Organization of data on life-span development of human abilities. In L. R. Goulet & P. B. Baltes (Eds.), *Life-span developmental psychology: Theory and research* (Vol. 1, pp. 211–256). New York: Academic Press.

Horn, J. L., & Cattell, R. B. (1966). Refinement and test of the theory of fluid and crystallized intelligence. *Journal of Educational Psychology, 57*, 253–270.

Horstmann, T., Maschmann, J., Mayer, F., Heitkamp, H. C., Handel, M., & Dickhuth, H. H. (1999). The influence of age on isokinetic torque of the upper and lower leg musculature in sedentary men. *International Journal of Sports Medicine, 20*, 362–367.

Hortobagyi, T., Zheng, D., Weidner, M., Lambert, N. J., Westbrook, S., & Houmard, J. A. (1995). The influence of aging on muscle strength and muscle fiber characteristics with special reference to eccentric strength. *Journal of Gerontology: Biological Sciences, 50B*, B399–406.

Houkes, I., Janssen, P. P. M., de Jonge, J., & Bakker, A. B. (2003). Personality, work characteristics and employee well-being: A longitudinal analysis of additive and moderating effects. *Journal of Occupational Health Psychology, 8*, 20–38.

House, J. S., Kessler, R. C., Herzog, A. R., & Mero, R. P. (1990). Age, socioeconomic status, and health. *Milbank Quarterly, 68*, 383–411.

House, J. S., Landis, K. R., & Umberson, D. (1988). Social relationships and health. *Science, 241*, 540–545.

Howard, A., & Bray, D. W. (1988). *Managerial lives in transition: Advancing age and changing times*. New York: Guilford.

Hoyle, R. H. (Ed.). (1995). *Structural equation modeling: Concepts, issues, and applications*. Thousand Oaks, CA: Sage.

Hubert, H. B., Bloch, D. A., Oehlert, J. W., & Fries, J. F. (2002). Lifestyle habits and compression of morbidity. *Journals of Gerontology: Series A: Biological Sciences and Medical Sciences, 57*, M347–351.

Hughes, V. A., Frontera, W. R., Wood, M., Evans, W. J., Dallal, G. E., Roubenoff, R., & Fiatarone Singh, M. A. (2001). Longitudinal muscle strength changes in older adults: Influence of muscle mass, physical activity, and health. *Journals of Gerontology: Biological Sciences, 56*, B209–217.

Hulette, C., Nochlin, D., McKeel, D., & Morris, J. C. (1997). Clinical-neuropathologic findings in multi-infarct dementia: A report of six autopsied cases. *Neurology, 48*, 668–672.

Hultsch, D. F., Hertzog, C., & Dixon, R. A. (1987). Age differences in metamemory: Resolving the inconsistencies. *Canadian Journal of Psychology, 41*, 193–208.

Hummert, M. L., Garstka, T. A., Shaner, J. L., & Strahm, S. (1994). Stereotypes of the elderly held by young, middle-aged, and elderly adults. *Journal of Gerontology: Psychological Sciences, 49*, P240–P249.

Hummert, M. L., Shaner, J. L., Garstka, T. A., & Henry, C. (1998). Communication with older adults: The influence of age stereotypes, context and communicator age. *Human Communication Research, 25*, 124–151.

Humphrey, D. (1991). *Final exit: The practicalities of self-deliverance and assisted suicide for the dying*. Eugene Oregon: Hemlock Society.

Hunter, G. R., Wetzstein, C. J., Fields, D. A., Brown, A., & Bamman, M. M. (2000). Resistance training increases total energy expenditure and free-living physical activity in older adults. *Journal of Applied Physiology, 89*, 977–984.

Hurley, B. F. (1995). Age, gender, and muscular strength. Journal of Gerontology Series A: *Biological Sciences and Medical Sciences, 50A*, 41–44.

Huttenlocher, P. (1979). Synaptic density in human frontal cortex—Developmental changes and effects of aging. *Brain Research, 163*, 195–205.

Hy, L. X., & Keller, D. M. (2000). Prevalence of AD among whites: A summary by levels of severity. *Neurology, 55*, 198–204.

Ice, G. H. (2002). Daily life in a nursing home: Has it changed in 25 years? *Journal of Aging Studies, 16*, 345–359.

in't Veld, B. A., Ruitenberg, A., Hofman, A., Stricker, B. H., & Breteler, M. M. (2001). Antihypertensive drugs and incidence of dementia: The Rotterdam Study. *Neurobiology of Aging, 22*, 407–412.

Ingersoll-Dayton, B., Neal, M. B., Ha, J.-H., & Hammer, L. B. (2003). Redressing inequity in parent care among siblings. *Journal of Marriage and the Family, 65*, 201–212.

Inoue, Y. (1996). Longitudinal effects of age on heat-activated sweat gland density and output in healthy active older men. *European Journal of Applied Physiology and Occupational Physiology, 74*, 72–77.

Inoue, Y., Nakao, M., Araki, T., & Ueda, H. (1992). Thermoregulatory responses of young and older men to cold exposure. *European Journal of Applied Physiology, 65*, 492–498.

Intons-Peterson, M. J., Rocchi, P., West, T., McLellan, K., & Hackney, A. (1998). Aging, optimal testing times, and negative priming. *Journal of Experimental Psychology: Learning, Memory, and Cognition, 24*, 362–376.

Insurance Institute for Highway Safety (2000). Safety facts on the elderly. http://www.hwysafety.org/srpdfs/sr3208.pdf. Accessed 1/23/04.

Iqbal, P., & Castleden, C. M. (1997). Management of urinary incontinence in the elderly. *Gerontology, 43*, 151–157.

Ishida, K., Sato, Y., Katayama, K., & Miyamura, M. (2000). Initial ventilatory and circulatory responses to dynamic exercise are slowed in the elderly. *Journal of Applied Physiology, 89*, 1771–1777.

Isingrini, M., & Vazou, F. (1997). Relation between fluid intelligence and frontal lobe functioning in older adults. *International Journal of Aging and Human Development, 45*, 99–109.

Jacoby, L. L. (1999). Ironic effects of repetition: Measuring age-related differences in memory. *Journal of Experimental Psychology: Learning, Memory, & Cognition, 25*, 3–22.

Jacoby, L. L., Debner, J. A., & Hay, J. F. (2001). Proactive interference, accessibility bias, and process dissociations: Valid subjective reports of memory. *Journal of Experimental Psychology: Learning, Memory, and Cognition, 27*, 686–700.

James, K., Premchand, N., Skibinska, A., Skibinski, G., Nicol, M., & Mason, J. I. (1997). IL-6, DHEA and the ageing process. *Mechanisms of Ageing and Development, 93*, 15–24.

Janowsky, J. S., Chavez, B., & Orwoll, E. (2000). Sex steroids modify working memory. *Journal of Cognitive Neuroscience, 12*, 407–414.

Jaques, E. (1965). Death and the mid-life crisis. *International Journal of Psychoanalysis, 46*, 502–514.

Jazwinski, S. M. (2000). Aging and longevity genes. *Acta Biochimica Polonica, 47*, 269–279.

Jenkins, G. D., Jr., Mitra, A., Gupta, N., & Shaw, J. D. (1998). Are financial incentives related to performance? A meta-analytic review of empirical research. *Journal of Applied Psychology, 83*, 777–787.

Jennings, B. (1991). Active euthanasia and forgoing life-sustaining treatment: Can we hold the line? *Journal of Pain and Symptom Management, 6*, 312–316.

Jeste, D. V., Lohr, J. B., Eastham, J. H., Rockwell, E., & Caligiuri, M. P. (1998). Adverse neurobiological effects of long-term use of neuroleptics: Human and animal studies. *Journal of Psychiatric Research, 32*, 201–214.

Jeste, D. V., Symonds, L. L., Harris, M. J., Paulsen, J. S., Palmer, B. W., & Heaton, R. K. (1997). Nondementia nonpraecox dementia praecox? Late onset schizophrenia. *American Journal of Geriatric Psychiatry, 5*, 302–317.

Jick, H., Zornberg, G. L., Jick, S. S., Seshadri, S., & Drachman, D. A. (2000). Statins and the risk of dementia. *Lancet, 356*, 1627–1631.

Jin, Y.-S., Ryan, E. B., & Anas, A. P. (2001). Korean beliefs about everyday memory and aging for self and others. *International Journal of Aging & Human Development, 52*, 103–113.

Johannes, C. B., Araujo, A. B., Feldman, H. A., Derby, C. A., Kleinman, K. P., & McKinlay, J. B. (2000). Incidence of erectile dysfunction in men 40 to 69 years old: longitudinal results from the Massachusetts male aging study. *Journal of Urology, 163*, 460–463.

Johansson, B., Allen-Burge, R., & Zarit, S. H. (1997). Self-reports on memory functioning in a longitudinal study of the oldest old: Relation to current, prospective, and retrospective performance. *Journal of Gerontology: Psychological Sciences, 52*, 139–146.

John, O. P., Pals, J. L., & Westenberg, P. M. (1998). Personality prototypes and ego development: Conceptual similarities and relations in adult women. *Journal of Personality and Social Psychology, 74*, 1093–1108.

Johnson, J., Stewart, W., Hall, E., Fredlund, P., & Theorell, T. (1996). Long-term psychosocial work environment and cardiovascular mortality among Swedish men. *American Journal of Public Health, 86,* 324–331.

Johnson, M. D., Bebb, R. A., & Sirrs, S. M. (2002). Uses of DHEA in aging and other disease states. *Ageing Research Reviews, 1,* 29–41.

Johnson, M. M. S. (1997). Individual differences in the voluntary use of a memory aid during decision making. *Experimental Aging Research, 23,* 33–43.

Johnson, T. M., 2nd, Kincade, J. E., Bernard, S. L., Busby-Whitehead, J., & DeFriese, G. H. (2000). Self-care practices used by older men and women to manage urinary incontinence: Results from the national follow-up survey on self-care and aging. *Journal of the American Geriatrics Society, 48,* 894–902.

Jonker, C., Launer, L. J., Hooijer, C., & Lindeboom, J. (1996). Memory complaints and memory impairment in older individuals. *Journal of the American Geriatrics Society, 44,* 44–49.

Judge, T. A., Heller, D., & Mount, M. K. (2002). Five-factor model of personality and job satisfaction: A meta-analysis. *Journal of Applied Psychology, 87,* 530–541.

Jung, C. G. (1968). *Analytical psychology: Its theory and practice.* New York: Vintage Books.

Just, M. A., & Carpenter, P. A. (1992). A capacity theory of comprehension: Individual differences in working memory. *Psychological Review, 99,* 122–149.

Justice, D. o. (2003). *Sourcebook of criminal justice statistics.*

Kahn, R. L., & Antonucci, T. C. (1980). Convoys over the life course: Attachment, roles, and social support. In P. B. Baltes & O. G. Brim (Eds.), *Life span development and behavior* (Vol. 3, pp. 253–286). San Diego, CA: Academic Press.

Kahneman, D. (1973). *Attention and effort.* Englewood Cliffs, NJ: Prentice Hall.

Kalimo, R., Taris, T. W., & Schaufeli, W. B. (2003). The effects of past and anticipated future downsizing on survivor well-being: An Equity perspective. *Journal of Occupational Health Psychology, 8,* 91–109.

Kalleberg, A. (1977). Work values and job rewards: A theory of job satisfaction. *American Sociological Review, 42,* 124–143.

Kalleberg, A. L., & Loscoco, K. A. (1983). Aging, values and rewards: Explaining age differences in job satisfaction. *American Sociological Review, 48,* 78–90.

Kane, R. A., Caplan, A. L., Urv-Wong, E. K., Freeman, I. C., Aroskar, M. A., & Finch, M. (1997). Everyday matters in the lives of nursing home residents: Wish for and perception of choice and control. *Journal of the American Geriatrics Society, 45,* 1086–1093.

Karani, R., McLaughlin, M. A., & Cassel, C. K. (2001). Exercise in the healthy older adult. *American Journal of Geriatric Cardiology, 10,* 269–273.

Karney, B., & Bradbury, T. (1997). Neuroticism, marital interaction, and the trajectory of marital satisfaction. *Journal of Personality and Social Psychology, 72,* 1075–1092.

Kasch, F. W., Boyer, J. L., Schmidt, P. K., Wells, R. H., Wallace, J. P., Verity, L. S., Guy, H., & Schneider, D. (1999). Ageing of the cardiovascular system during 33 years of aerobic exercise. *Age and Ageing, 28,* 531–536.

Kastenbaum, R. (1999). Dying and bereavement. In John C. Cavanaugh & S. K. Whitbourne (Eds.), *Gerontology: An interdisciplinary perspective* (pp. 155–185). New York: Oxford.

Katzell, R. A., & Thompson, D. E. (1990). Work motivation: Theory and practice. *American Psychologist, 45,* 144–153.

Katzman, R., Zhang, M. Y., Chen, P. J., Gu, N., Jiang, S., Saitoh, T., Chen, X., Klauber, M., Thomas, R. G., Liu, W. T., & Yu, E. S. (1997). Effects of apolipoprotein E on dementia and aging in the Shanghai Survey of Dementia. *Neurology, 49,* 779–785.

Kaufman, A. S., Kaufman, J. L., McLean, J. E., & Reynolds, C. R. (1991). Is the pattern of intellectual growth and decline across the adult life span different for men and women? *Journal of Clinical Psychology, 47,* 801–812.

Kawas, C., Gray, S., Brookmeyer, R., Fozard, J., & Zonderman, A. (2000). Age-specific incidence rates of Alzheimer's disease: The Baltimore Longitudinal Study of Aging. *Neurology, 54,* 2072–2077.

Kay, E. J., Harris, R. M., Voros, R. S., Hillman, D. J., Hyland, D. T., & Deimler, J. D. (1994). *Age 60 study, part III: Consolidated database experiments final report.* Washington, DC: Federal Aviation Administration (NTIS No. DOT/FAA/AM-94/22).

Kaye, J. A., Swihart, T., Howieson, D., Dame, A., Moore, M. M., Karnos, T., Camicioli, R., Ball, M., Okn, B., & Sexton, G. (1997). Volume loss of the hippocampus and temporal lobe in healthy elderly persons destined to develop dementia. *Neurology, 48,* 1297–1304.

Keefe, S. E., Padilla, A. M., & Carlos, M. L. (1979). The Mexican-American extended family as an emotional support system. *Human Organization, 38,* 144–152.

Keith, S. J., Regier, D. A., & Rae, D. S. (1991). Schizophrenic disorders. In L. N. Robins & D. A. Regier (Eds.), *Psychiatric disorders in America* (pp. 33–52). New York: Free Press.

Kelley, G. A., & Sharpe Kelley, K. (2001). Aerobic exercise and resting blood pressure in older adults: A meta-analytic review of randomized controlled trials. *Journals of Gerontology Series A: Medical Sciences, 56,* M298–303.

Kelly, B., Burnett, P., Pelusi, D., Badger, S., Varghese, F., & Robertson, M. (2002). Terminally ill cancer patients' wish to hasten death. *Palliative Medicine, 16,* 339–345.

Kelly, E. L., & Conley, J. J. (1987). Personality and compatibility: A prospective analysis of marital stability and marital satisfaction. *Journal of Personality and Social Psychology, 52*, 27–40.

Kelly, K. S., & Hayslip, B., Jr. (2000). Gains in fluid ability performance and their relationship to cortisol. *Experimental Aging Research, 26*, 153–157.

Kemper, S. (1992). Language and aging. In F. I. M. Craik & T. A. Salthouse (Eds.), *The handbook of aging and cognition* (pp. 213–270). Hillsdale, NJ: Erlbaum.

Kemper, S. (1992). Language and aging. In F. I. M. Craik & T. A. Salthouse (Eds.), *The handbook of aging and cognition* (pp. 213–270). Hillsdale NJ: Erlbaum.

Kemper, S., & Sumner, A. (2001). The structure of verbal abilities in young and older adults. *Psychology and Aging, 16*, 312–322.

Kemper, S., Greiner, L. H., Marquis, J. G., Prenovost, K., & Mitzner, T. L. (2001). Language decline across the life span: Findings from the Nun Study. *Psychology and Aging, 16*, 227–239.

Kemper, S., Marquis, J., & Thompson, M. (2001). Longitudinal change in language production: Effects of aging and dementia on grammatical complexity and propositional content. *Psychology and Aging, 16*, 600–614.

Kenny, D. A., & Acitelli, L. K. (1994). Measuring similarity in couples. *Journal of Family Psychology, 8*, 417–431.

Keogh, A. T., & Akhtar, T. M. (1999). Diagnosing brain death: the importance of documenting clinical test results. *Anaesthesia, 54*, 81–85.

Kerby, D. S., & Ragan, K. M. (2002). Activity interests and Holland's RIASEC system in older adults. *International Journal of Aging and Human Development, 55*, 117–139.

Kern, W., Dodt, C., Born, J., & Fehm, H. L. (1996). Changes in cortisol and growth hormone secretion during nocturnal sleep in the course of aging. *Journal of Gerontology: Medical Sciences, 51A*, M3–9.

Kessler, R. C. (1997). The prevalence of psychiatric comorbidity. In S. Wetzler & W. C. Sanderson (Eds.), *Treatment strategies for patients with psychiatric comorbidity* (pp. 23–48). New York: Wiley.

Kessler, R. C., Berglund, P., Demler, O., Jin, R., Koretz, D., Merikangas, K. R., Rush, A. J., Walters, E. E., & Wang, P. S. (2003). The epidemiology of major depressive disorder: results from the National Comorbidity Survey Replication (NCS-R). *Journal of the American Medical Association, 289*, 3095–3105.

Kessler, R. C., McGonagle, K. A., Zhao, S., Nelson, C. B., Hughes, M., Eshleman, S., Wittchen, H.-U., & Kendler, K. S. (1994). Lifetime and 12-month prevalence of *DSM-III-R* psychiatric disorders in the United States: Results from the National Comorbidity Survey. *Archives of General Psychiatry, 51*, 8–19.

Kessler, R. C., Stein, M. B., & Berglund, P. (1998). Social phobia subtypes in the National Comorbidity Survey. *American Journal of Psychiatry, 155*, 613–619.

Kettunen, J. A., Kujala, U. M., Kaprio, J., Koskenvuo, M., & Sarna, S. (2001). Lower-limb function among former elite male athletes. *American Journal of Sports Medicine, 29*, 2–8.

Kevorkian, J. (1991). *Prescription—medicide: The goodness of planned death*. Buffalo, NY: Prometheus Books.

Khanna, K. V., & Markham, R. B. (1999). A perspective on cellular immunity in the elderly. *Clinical Infectious Diseases, 28*, 710–713.

Khaw, K. T., Bingham, S., Welch, A., Luben, R., Wareham, N., Oakes, S., & Day, N. (2001). Relation between plasma ascorbic acid and mortality in men and women in EPIC-Norfolk prospective study: A prospective population study. European prospective investigation into cancer and nutrition. *Lancet, 357*, 657–663.

Kidder, D. P., Park, D. C., Hertzog, C., & Morrell, R. W. (1997). Prospective memory and aging: The effects of working memory and prospective memory task load. *Aging Neuropsychology and Cognition, 4*, 93–112.

Kidder, T. (1993). *Old friends*. Boston: Houghton Mifflin.

Kiecolt-Glaser, J. K., & Glaser, R. (2002). Depression and immune function: Central pathways to morbidity and mortality. *Journal of Psychosomatic Research, 53*, 873–876.

Kiecolt-Glaser, J. K., McGuire, L., Robles, T. F., & Glaser, R. (2002). Emotions, morbidity, and mortality: New perspectives from psychoneuroimmunology. *Annual Review of Psychology, 53*, 83–107.

Kim, C. H., Chang, J. W., Koo, M. S., Kim, J. W., Suh, H. S., Park, I. H., & Lee, H. S. (2003). Anterior cingulotomy for refractory obsessive-compulsive disorder. *Acta Psychiatrica Scandinavica, 107*, 283–290.

Kim, J. E., & Moen, P. (2001). Is retirement good or bad for subjective well-being? *Current Directions in Psychological Science, 10*, 83–86.

Kim, J. E., & Nesselroade, J. R. (2002). Relationships among social support, self-concept, and wellbeing of older adults: A study of process using dynamic factor models. *International Journal of Behavioral Development, 27*, 49–63.

King, D. A., & Markus, H. E. (2000). Mood disorders in older adults. In S. K. Whitbourne (Ed.), *Psychopathology in later life* (pp. 141–172). New York: Wiley.

Kinoshita, H., & Francis, P. R. (1996). A comparison of prehension force control in young and elderly individuals. *European Journal of Applied Physiology and Occupational Physiology, 74*, 450–460.

Kinsella, K., & Veloff, V. A. (2001). *U.S. Census Bureau, Series P95/01-1. An aging world: 2001*. Washington, DC: U.S. Department of Health and Human Services.

Kirkpatrick, L. A., & Davis, K. E. (1994). Attachment style, gender, and relationship stability: A longitudinal analysis. *Journal of Personality and Social Psychology, 66*, 502–512.

Kisner, S. M., & Fosbroke, D. E. (1994). Injury hazards in the construction industry. *Journal of Occupational Medicine, 36*, 137–143.

Kitagawa, N., Ichikawa, T., Akimoto, S., & Shimazaki, J. (1994). Natural course of human benign prostatic hyperplasia with relation to urinary disturbance. *Prostate, 24*, 279–284.

Kivnick, H. Q. (1982). Grandparenthood: An overview of meaning and mental health. *The Gerontologist, 22*, 59–66.

Klein, R., Klein, B. E., & Linton, K. L. (1992). Prevalence of age-related maculopathy. The Beaver Dam Eye Study. *Ophthalmology, 99*, 933–943.

Klerman, E. B., Duffy, J. F., Dijk, D. J., & Czeisler, C. A. (2001). Circadian phase resetting in older people by ocular bright light exposure. *Journal of Investigative Medicine, 49*, 30–40.

Kligman, A. M., Grove, G. L., & Balin, A. K. (1985). Aging of human skin. In C. E. Finch & E. L. Schneider (Eds.), *Handbook of the biology of aging* (2nd ed.). New York: Van Nostrand Reinhold.

Klohnen, E. C., & Bera, S. (1998). Behavioral and experiential patterns of avoidantly and securely attached women across adulthood: A 31-year longitudinal perspective. *Journal of Personality and Social Psychology, 74*, 211–233.

Kluwer, E., Heesink, J., & Van De Vliert, E. (1997). The marital dynamics of conflict over the division of labor. *Journal of Marriage and the Family, 59*, 635–653.

Klysner, R., Bent-Hansen, J., Hansen, H. L., Lunde, M., Pleidrup, E., Poulsen, D. L., Andersen, M., & Petersen, H. E. (2002). Efficacy of citalopram in the prevention of recurrent depression in elderly patients: placebo-controlled study of maintenance therapy. *British Journal of Psychiatry, 181*, 29–35.

Knight, S., Bermingham, M. A., & Mahajan, D. (1999). Regular non-vigorous physical activity and cholesterol levels in the elderly. *Gerontology, 45*, 213–219.

Knopman, D. S. (2001). An overview of common non-Alzheimer dementias. *Clinical Geriatric Medicine, 17*, 281–301.

Knopman, D., Boland, L. L., Mosley, T., Howard, G., Liao, D., Szklo, M., McGovern, P., & Folsom, A. R. (2001). Cardiovascular risk factors and cognitive decline in middle-aged adults. *Neurology, 56*, 42–48.

Kobak, R. R., & Hazan, C. (1991). Attachment in marriage: Effects of security and accuracy of working models. *Journal of Personality and Social Psychology, 60*, 861–869.

Kohn, A. (1993). Rethinking rewards: What role—if any—should incentives play in the workplace? *Harvard Business Review, 71*, 48–49.

Koropeckyj-Cox, T. (2002). Beyond parental status: Psychological well-being in middle and old age. *Journal of Marriage and the Family, 64*, 957–971.

Kosaka, K. (2000). Diffuse Lewy body disease. *Neuropathology, 20 Supplement*, S73–78.

Kosloski, K., Ekerdt, D., & DeViney, S. (2001). The role of job-related rewards in retirement planning. *Journals of Gerontology: Series B: Psychological Sciences & Social Sciences, 56*, P160–169.

Kotler-Cope, S., & Camp, C. (1990). Memory interventions in aging populations. In E. A. Lovelace (Ed.), *Aging and cognition: Mental processes, self-awareness and interventions* (pp. 231–261). Amsterdam: North Holland.

Kposowa, A. J. (2000). Marital status and suicide in the National Longitudinal Mortality Study. *Journal of Epidemiology and Community Health, 54*, 254–261.

Krach, C. A., & Veloff, V. A. (1999). *Bureau of the Census, Current Population Reports* (Series P23-199RV). *Centenarians in the United States*. (No. P23-199RV). Washington DC: U.S. Govenrment Printing Office.

Krall, E. A., Dawson-Hughes, B., Hirst, K., Gallagher, J. C., Sherman, S. S., & Dalsky, G. (1997). Bone mineral density and biochemical markers of bone turnover in healthy elderly men and women. *Journal of Gerontology: Medical Sciences, 52*, M61–67.

Krall, E. A., Wehler, C., Garcia, R. I., Harris, S. S., & Dawson-Hughes, B. (2001). Calcium and vitamin D supplements reduce tooth loss in the elderly. *American Journal of Medicine, 111*, 452–456.

Krauss, R. M., Eckel, R. H., Howard, B., Appel, L. J., Daniels, S. R., Deckelbaum, R. J., Erdman, J. W., Jr., Kris-Etherton, P., Goldberg, I. J., Kotchen, T. A., Lichtenstein, A. H., Mitch, W. E., Mullis, R., Robinson, K., Wylie-Rosett, J., St Jeor, S., Suttie, J., Tribble, D. L., & Bazzarre, T. L. (2001). Revision 2000: a statement for healthcare professionals from the Nutrition Committee of the American Heart Association. *Journal of Nutrition, 131*, 132–146.

Kreider, R. M., & Fields, J. M. (2002). Number, Timing, and Duration of Marriages and Divorces: 1996. In Current Population Reports P70–80 (Vol. P70–80). Washington, D.C., U.S. Census Bureau.

Kril, J. J., Patel, S., Harding, A. J., & Halliday, G. M. (2002). Neuron loss from the hippocampus of Alzheimer's disease exceeds extracellular neurofibrillary tangle formation. *Acta Neuropathologica (Berlin), 103*, 370–376.

Kripke, D. F., Garfinkel, L., Wingard, D. L., Klauber, M. R., & Marler, M. R. (2002). Mortality associated with sleep duration and insomnia. *Arch Gen Psychiatry, 59*, 131–136.

Krumholz, H. M., Phillips, R. S., Hamel, M. B., Teno, J. M., Bellamy, P., Broste, S. K., Califf, R. M., Vidaillet, H., Davis, R. B., Muhlbaier, L. H., Connors, A. F., Jr., Lynn, J., & Goldman, L. (1998). Resuscitation preferences among patients with severe congestive heart failure: results from the SUPPORT project. Study to Understand Prognoses and Preferences for Outcomes and Risks of Treatments. *Circulation, 98*, 648–655.

Kübler-Ross, E. (1969). *On death and dying.* New York: Macmillan.

Kudielka, B. M., Schmidt-Reinwald, A. K., Hellhammer, D. H., Schurmeyer, T., & Kirschbaum, C. (2000). Psychosocial stress and HPA functioning: No evidence for a reduced resilience in healthy elderly men. *Stress, 3*, 229–240.

Kukull, W. A. (2001). The association between smoking and Alzheimer's disease: effects of study design and bias. *Biological Psychiatry, 49*, 194–199.

Kulik, L. (2002). Marital equality and the quality of long-term marriage in later life. *Ageing and Society, 22*, 459–481.

Kunzmann, U., Little, T., & Smith, J. (2001). Perceiving control: A double-edged sword in old age. *Journals of Gerontology: Series B: Psychological Sciences and Social Sciences, Vol 57B*, P484–P491.

Kurdek, L. A. (1993). The allocation of household labor in gay, lesbian, and heterosexual married couples. *Journal of Social Issues, 49*, 127–139.

Kurdek, L. A. (1995). Developmental changes in relationship quality in gay and lesbian cohabiting couples. *Developmental Psychology, 31*, 86–94.

Kurdek, L. A. (1997). Relation between neuroticism and dimensions of relationship commitment: Evidence from gay, lesbian, and heterosexual couples. *Journal of Family Psychology, 11*, 109–124.

Kwan, C. M., Love, G. D., Ryff, C. D., & Essex, M. J. (2003). The role of self-enhancing evaluations in a successful life transition. *Psychology and Aging, 18*, 3–12.

Kyle, U. G., Gremion, G., Genton, L., Slosman, D. O., Golay, A., & Pichard, C. (2001). Physical activity and fat-free and fat mass by bioelectrical impedance in 3853 adults. *Medicine and Science in Sports and Exercise, 33*, 576–584.

Laaksonen, M., Luoto, R., Helakorpi, S., & Uutela, A. (2002). Associations between health-related behaviors: A 7-year follow-up of adults. *Preventive Medicine: An International Journal Devoted to Practice & Theory, 34*, 162–170.

Laaksonen, M., Prattala, R., & Karisto, A. (2001). Patterns of unhealthy behaviour in Finland. *European Journal of Public Health, 11*, 294–300.

Labouvie-Vief, G., & Hakim-Larson, J. (1989). Development of shifts in adult thought. In S. Hunter & M. Sundel (Eds.), *Midlife myths* (pp. 69–96). Newbury Park, CA: Sage.

Labouvie-Vief, G., & Medler, M. (2002). Affect optimization and affect complexity: Modes and styles of regulation in adulthood. *Psychology and Aging, 17*, 571–588.

Lachman, M. E., Weaver, S. L., Bandura, M., Elliott, E., & Lewkowicz, C. J. (1992). Improving memory and control beliefs through cognitive restructuring and self-generated strategies. *Journal of Gerontology: Psychological Sciences, 47*, P293–299.

Lachs, M. S., Williams, C. S., O'Brien, S., Pillemer, K. A., & Charlson, M. E. (1998). The mortality of elder mistreatment. *Journal of the American Medical Association, 280*, 428–432.

Lamberts, S. W. (2000). The somatopause: To treat or not to treat? *Hormone Research, 53*, 42–43.

Lamberts, S. W. J., van den Beld, A. W., & van der Lely, A.-J. (1997). The endocrinology of aging. *Science, 278*, 419–424.

Lamme, S., Dykstra, P. A., & Broese Van Groenou, M. I. (1996). Rebuilding the network: New relationships in widowhood. *Personal Relationships, 3*, 337–349.

Lang, F. R., & Carstensen, L. L. (1994). Close emotional relationships in late life: Further support for proactive aging in the social domain. *Psychology and Aging, 9*, 315–324.

Lang, F. R., & Carstensen, L. L. (2002). Time counts: Future time perspective, goals, and social relationships. *Psychology and Aging, 17*, 125–139.

Lang, F. R., & Heckhausen, J. (2001). Perceived control over development and subjective well-being: Differential benefits across adulthood. *Journal of Personality and Social Psychology, 81*, 509–523.

Langer, E. J., & Rodin, J. (1976). The effects of choice and enhanced personal responsibility for the aged: A field experiment in an institutional setting. *Journal of Personality and Social Psychology, 34*, 191–198.

Lansford, J. E., Sherman, A. J., & Antonucci, T. C. (1998). Satisfaction with social networks: An examination of socioemotional selectivity theory across cohorts. *Psychology and Aging, 13*, 544–552.

Lantz, P. M., House, J. S., Lepkowski, J. M., Williams, D. R., Mero, R. P., & Chen, J. (1998). Socioeconomic factors, health behaviors, and mortality: Results from a nationally representative prospective study of U.S. adults. *Journal of the American Medical Association, 279*, 1703–1708.

Larson, L. M., Rottinghaus, P. J., & Borgen, F. H. (2002). Meta-analyses of Big Six interests and Big Five personality factors. *Journal of Vocational Behavior, 61*, 217–239.

Lasch, H., Castell, D. O., & Castell, J. A. (1997). Evidence for diminished visceral pain with aging: Studies using graded intraesophageal balloon distension. *American Journal of Physiology, 272*, G1–3.

Latimer, E. J. (1991). Ethical decision-making in the care of the dying and its applications to clinical practice. *Journal of Pain and Symptom Management, 6*, 329–336.

Lattimore, R. R., & Borgen, F. H. (1999). Validity of the 1994 Strong Interest Inventory with racial and ethnic groups in the United States. *Journal of Counseling Psychology, 46*, 185–195.

Lau, A. W., & Gallagher-Thompson, D. (2002). Ethnic minority older adults in clinical and research programs: Issues and recommendations. *Behavior Therapist, 25*, 10–11.

Laub, J. H., & Vaillant, G. E. (2000). Delinquency and mortality: A 50-year follow-up study of 1,000 delinquent and non-delinquent boys. *American Journal of Psychiatry, 157*, 96–102.

Laughlin, G. A., & Barrett-Connor, E. (2000). Sexual dimorphism in the influence of advanced aging on adrenal hormone levels: The Rancho Bernardo Study. *Journal of Clinical Endocrinology and Metabolism, 85*, 3561–3568.

Laumann, E. O., Paik, A., & Rosen, R. C. (1999). Sexual dysfunction in the United States: Prevalence and predictors. *Journal of the American Medical Association, 281*, 537–544.

Laumann, E. O., Paik, A., & Rosen, R. C. (1999). Sexual dysfunction in the United States: Prevalence and predictors. *Journal of the American Medical Association, 281*, 537–544.

Launer, L. J., Masaki, K., Petrovitch, H., Foley, D., & Havlik, R. J. (1995). The association between midlife blood pressure levels and late-life cognitive function. The Honolulu-Asia Aging Study. *Journal of the American Medical Association, 274*, 1846–1851.

Launer, L. J., Ross, G. W., Petrovitch, H., Masaki, K., Foley, D., White, L. R., & Havlik, R. J. (2000). Midlife blood pressure and dementia: The Honolulu-Asia aging study. *Neurobiology of Aging, 21*, 49–55.

Laurenceau, J.-P., Barrett, L. F., & Pietromonaco, P. R. (1998). Intimacy as an interpersonal process: The importance of self-disclosure, partner disclosure, and perceived partner responsiveness in interpersonal exchanges. *Journal of Personality and Social Psychology, 74*, 1238–1251.

Laver, G. D., & Burke, D. M. (1993). Why do semantic priming effects increase in old age? *Psychology and Aging, 8*, 34–43.

Lawton, M. P., & Nahemow, L. (1973). Ecology and the aging process. In C. Eisdorfer & M. P. Lawton (Eds.), *The psychology of adult development and aging*. Washington, DC: American Psychological Association, 619–674.

Lawton, M. P., Kleban, M. H., Rajagopal, D., & Dean, J. (1992). Dimensions of affective experience in three age groups. *Psychology and Aging, 7*, 171–184.

Le, W. D., Xu, P., Jankovic, J., Jiang, H., Appel, S. H., Smith, R. G., & Vassilatis, D. K. (2003). Mutations in NR4A2 associated with familial Parkinson disease. *Nature Genetics, 33*, 85–89.

Lease, S. H. (1998). Annual review, 1993–1997: Work attitudes and outcomes. *Journal of Vocational Behavior, 53*, 154–183.

Lee, K. A., Vaillant, G. E., Torrey, W. C., & Elder, G. H. (1995). A 50-year prospective study of the psychological sequelae of World War II combat. *American Journal of Psychiatry, 152*, 516–522.

Lee, T. R., Mancini, J. A., & Maxwell, J. W. (1987). Sibling relationships in adulthood: Contact patterns and motivations. *Journal of Marriage and the Family, 49*, 431–440.

Lee, V. M., Goedert, M., & Trojanowski, J. Q. (2001). Neurodegenerative tauopathies. *Annual Review of Neuroscience, 24*, 1121–1159.

Lehman, H. C. (1953). *Age and achievement*. Princeton, NJ: Princeton University Press.

Lehtimaki, T., Pirttila, T., Mehta, P. D., Wisniewski, H. M., Frey, H., & Nikkari, T. (1995). Apolipoprotein E (apoE) polymorphism and its influence on ApoE concentrations in the cerebrospinal fluid in Finnish patients with Alzheimer's disease. *Human Genetics, 95*, 39–42.

Lenfant, C. (2001). Can we prevent cardiovascular diseases in low- and middle-income countries? *Bulletin of the World Health Organization, 79*, 980–982.

Lerner, R. M. (2003). What are SES effects effects of? A developmental systems perspective. In M. H. Bornstein & R. H. Bradley (Eds.), *Socioeconomic status, parenting, and child development*. Mahwah, NJ: Erlbaum.

Lerner, R., M. (1995). Developing individuals within changing contexts: Implications of developmental contextualism for human development, research, policy, and programs. In T. J. Kindermann & J. Valsiner (Eds.), *Development of person-context relations* (pp. 13–37). Hillsdale, NJ: Erlbaum.

Lesourd, B. M. (1997). Nutrition and immunity in the elderly: modification of immune responses with nutritional treatments. *American Journal of Clinical Nutrition, 66*, 478S–484S.

Lethbridge-Cejku, M., Scott, W. W., Reichle, R., Ettinger, W. H., Zonderman, A., Costa, P., Plato, C. C., Tobin, J. D., & Hochberg, M. C. (1995). Association of radiographic features of osteoarthritis of the knee with knee pain: Data from the Baltimore Longitudinal Study of Aging. *Arthritis Care and Research, 8*, 182–188.

Leveille, S. G., Bean, J., Bandeen-Roche, K., Jones, R., Hochberg, M., & Guralnik, J. M. (2002). Musculoskeletal pain and risk for falls in older disabled women living in the community. *Journal of the American Geriatrics Society, 50*, 671–678.

Leventhal, A. G., Wang, Y., Pu, M., Zhou, Y., & Ma, Y. (2003). GABA and its agonists improved visual cortical function in senescent monkeys. *Science, 300*, 812–815.

Levinger, G. (1965). Marital cohesiveness and dissolution: An integrative review. *Journal of Marriage and the Family, 27*, 19–28.

Levinger, G., & Huesmann, L. R. (1980). An "incremental exchange" perspective on the pair relationship. In *Social exchange: Advances in theory and research* (pp. 165–188). New York: Plenum.

Levinson, D. J., & Levinson, J. D. (1996). *The seasons of a woman's life*. New York: Knopf.

Levinson, D. J., Darrow, C. N., Klein, E. B., Levinson, M. H., & McKee, B. (1978). *The seasons of a man's life*. New York: Knopf.

Levitt, M. J., Weber, R. A., & Guacci, N. (1993). Convoys of social support: An intergenerational analysis. *Psychology and Aging, 8*, 323–326.

Levy, B. R., Slade, M. D., Kunkel, S. R., & Kasl, S. V. (2002). Longevity increased by positive self-perceptions of aging. *Journal of Personality and Social Psychology, 83*, 261–270.

Lewin, K. (1943). Psychology and the process of group living. *Journal of Social Psychology, 17*, 113–131.

Lewis, J., Dickson, D. W., Lin, W. L., Chisholm, L., Corral, A., Jones, G., Yen, S. H., Sahara, N., Skipper, L., Yager, D., Eckman, C., Hardy, J., Hutton, M., & McGowan, E. (2001). Enhanced neurofibrillary degeneration in transgenic mice expressing mutant tau and APP. *Science, 293*, 1487–1491.

Lichtenburg, P. A., MacNeill, S. E., Lysack, C. L. B., Adam, L., & Neufeld, S. W. (2003). Predicting discharge and long-term outcome patterns for frail elders. *Rehabilitation Psychology, 48*, 37–43.

Lichtenstein, P., Gatz, M., Pedersen, N. L., Berg, S., & McClearn, G. E. (1996). A co-twin–control study of response to widowhood. *Journal of Gerontology: Psychological Sciences, 51*, 279–289.

Lillard, L. A., Brien, M. J., & Waite, L. J. (1995). Premarital cohabitation and subsequent marital dissolution: a matter of self-selection? *Demography, 32*, 437–457.

Lindauer, M. S. (1998). Artists, art, and arts activities: What do they tell us about aging? In C. Adams-Price (Ed.), *Creativity and successful aging: Theoretical and empirical approaches* (pp. 237–250). New York: Springer.

Lindstrom, T. C. (1995a). Anxiety and adaptation in bereavement. *Anxiety, Stress and Coping: An International Journal, 8*, 251–261.

Lindstrom, T. C. (1995b). Experiencing the presence of the dead: Discrepancies in "the sensing experience" and their psychological concomitants. *Omega—Journal of Death and Dying, 31*, 1995.

Linton, P., & Thoman, M. L. (2001). T cell senescence. *Frontiers of Bioscience, 6*, D248–261.

Liu, S., Lee, I. M., Ajani, U., Cole, S. R., Buring, J. E., & Manson, J. E. (2001). Intake of vegetables rich in carotenoids and risk of coronary heart disease in men: The physicians' health study. *International Journal of Epidemiology, 30*, 130–135.

LoConto, D. G. (1998). Death and dreams: A sociological approach to grieving and identity. *Omega—Journal of Death and Dying, 37*, 1998.

Loevinger, J. (1976). *Ego development: Conceptions and theories*. San Francisco: Jossey-Bass.

Loewen, E. R., Shaw, R. J., & Craik, F. I. (1990). Age differences in components of metamemory. *Experimental Aging Research, 16*, 43–48.

Lohr, J. B., Alder, M., Flynn, K., Harris, M. J., & McAdams, L. A. (1997). Minor physical anomalies in older patients with late-onset schizophrenia, early-onset schizophrenia, depression, and Alzheimer's disease. *American Journal of Geriatric Psychiatry, 5, 318–323*.

Longcope, C., Feldman, H. A., McKinlay, J. B., & Araujo, A. B. (2000). Diet and sex hormone-binding globulin. *Journal of Clinical Endocrinology and Metabolism, 85*, 293–296.

Lord, S. R., & Bashford, G. M. (1996). Shoe characteristics and balance in older women. *Journal of the American Geriatrics Society, 44*, 429–433.

Lott, L. A., Schneck, M. E., Haegerstrom-Portnoy, G., Brabyn, J. A., Gildengorin, G. L., & West, C. G. (2001). Reading performance in older adults with good acuity. *Optometry Vision Science, 78*, 316–324.

Lubart, T. I., & Sternberg, R. J. (1998). Life span creativity: An investment theory approach. In C. Adams-Price (Ed.), *Creativity and successful aging: Theoretical and empirical approaches* (pp. 21–41). New York: Springer.

Luborsky, M. R. (1998). Creative challenges and the construction of meaningful life narratives. In C. Adams-Price (Ed.), *Creativity and successful aging: Theoretical and empirical approaches* (pp. 311–337). New York: Springer.

Luborsky, M. R., & McMullen, C. K. (1999). Culture and aging. In J. C. Cavanaugh & S. K. Whitbourne (Eds.), *Gerontology: Interdisciplinary perspectives* (pp. 65–90). New York: Oxford University Press.

Lucas, R. E., Clark, A. E., Georgellis, Y., & Diener, E. (2003). Reexamining adaptation and the set point model of happiness: Reactions to changes in marital status. *Journal of Personality and Social Psychology, 84*, 527–539.

Luoh, M.-C., & Herzog, A. R. (2002). Individual consequences of volunteer and paid work in old age: Health and mortality. *Journal of Health and Social Behavior, 43*, 490–509.

Lupien, S. J., de Leon, M., De Santi, S., Convit, A., Tarshish, C., Nair, N. P. V., Thakur, M., McEwen, B. S., Hauger, R. L., & Meaney, M. J. (1998). Cortisol levels during human aging predict hippocampal atrophy and memory deficits. *Nature Neuroscience, 1*, 69–73.

Lupien, S., Lecours, A. R., Schwartz, G., Sharma, S., Hauger, R. L., Meaney, M. J., et al. (1996). Longitudinal study of basal cortisol levels in healthy elderly subjects: Evidence for subgroups. *Neurobiology of Aging, 17*, 95–105.

Lupsakko, T., Mantyjarvi, M., Kautiainen, H., & Sulkava, R. (2002). Combined hearing and visual impairment and depression in a population aged 75 years and older. *International Journal of Geriatric Psychiatry, 17*, 808–813.

Lykken, D. T. (1998). The genetics of genius. In A. Steptoe (Ed.), *Genius and the mind: Studies of creativity andtemperament in the historical record* (pp. 15–37). New York: Oxford University Press.

Lynn, J. (1996). Caring at the end of our lives. *New England Journal of Medicine, 335*, 201–202.

Lynn, J., Teno, J. M., Phillips, R. S., Wu, A. W., Desbiens, N., Harrold, J., Claessens, M. T., Wenger, N., Kreling, B., & Connors, A. F., Jr. (1997). Perceptions by family members of the dying experience of older and seriously ill patients. SUPPORT Investigators. Study to Understand Prognoses and Preferences for Outcomes and Risks of Treatments. *Annals of Internal Medicine, 126*, 97–106.

Mace, N. L., & Rabins, P. V. (1999). *The 36-hour day: A family guide to caring for persons with Alzheimer's disease, relating dementing illnesses, and memory loss in later life*. Baltimore MD: Johns Hopkins University Press.

Macintyre, S. (1997). The Black report and beyond: What are the issues? *Social Science and Medicine, 44*, 723–745.

MacKay, D. G., & Abrams, L. (1996). Language, memory, and aging: Distributed deficits and the structure of new-versus-old connections. In J. E. Birren, K. W. Schaie, R. P. Abeles, M. Gatz & T. A. Salthouse (Eds.), *Handbook of the psychology of aging* (4th ed.) (pp. 251–265). San Diego, CA: Academic Press.

Madden, D. J., Turkington, T. G., Provenzale, J. M., Denny, L. L., Langley, L. K., Hawk, T. C., & Coleman, R. E. (2002). Aging and attentional guidance during visual search: functional neuroanatomy by positron emission tomography. *Psychology and Aging, 17*, 24–43.

Maentylae, T., & Nilsson, L.-G. (1997). Remembering to remember in adulthood: A population-based study on aging and prospective memory. *Aging Neuropsychology and Cognition, 4*, 81–92.

Magnusson, D. (Ed.). (1996). *The lifespan development of individuals: Behavioral, neurobiological, and psychosocial perspectives: A synthesis*. New York: Cambridge University Press.

Main, M. (1996). Introduction to the special section on attachment and psychopathology: 2. Overview of the field of attachment. *Journal of Consulting and Clinical Psychology, 64*, 237–243.

Mak, Y. T., Chiu, H., Woo, J., Kay, R., Chan, Y. S., Hui, E., Sze, K. H., Lum, C., Kwok, T., & Pang, C. P. (1996). Apolipoprotein E genotype and Alzheimer's disease in Hong Kong elderly Chinese. *Neurology, 46*, 146–149.

Malhi, G. S., Mitchell, P. B., & Salim, S. (2003). Bipolar depression: Management options. *CNS Drugs, 17*, 9–25.

Malmstrom, T., & LaVoie, D. J. (2002). Age differences in inhibition of schema-activated distractors. *Experimental Aging Research, 28*, 281–298.

Mancini, J. A., & Blieszner, R. (1989). Aging parents and adult children: Research themes in intergenerational relations. *Journal of Marriage and the Family, 51*, 275–290.

Manning, J. S. (2003). Difficult-to-treat depressions: a primary care perspective. *Journal of Clinical Psychiatry, 64 (Suppl 1)*, 24–31.

Mannino, D. M., Homa, D. M., Akinbami, L. J., Ford, E. S., & Redd, S. C. (2002). Chronic Obstructive Pulmonary Disease surveillance—United States, 1971–2000. *Morbidity and Mortality Weekly Report, 51, No. SS-6.*

Manton, K. G., Corder, L., & Stallard, E. (1997). Chronic disability trends in elderly United States populations: 1982–1994. *Proceedings of the National Academy of Sciences, USA, 94*, 2593–2598.

Markman, H., & Hahlweg, K. (1993). The prediction and prevention of marital distress. *Clinical Psychology Review, 13*, 29–43.

Markus, H., & Nurius, P. (1986). Possible selves. *American Psychologist, 41*, 954–969.

Marsiglio, W. (1992). Stepfathers with minor children living at home: Parenting perceptions and relationship quality. *Journal of Family Issues, 13*, 195–214.

Marsiglio, W., & Donnelly, D. (1991). Sexual relations in later life: A national study of married persons. *Journal of Gerontology: Social Sciences, 46*, 338–344.

Marsiglio, W., Amato, P., Day, R. D., & Lamb, M. E. (2002). Scholarship on fatherhood in the 1990s and beyond. *Journal of Marriage and the Family, 62*, 1173–1191.

Martin Matthews, A., & Brown, K. H. (1988). Retirement as a critical life event: The differential experiences of women and men. *Research on Aging, 9*, 548–571.

Martin, L. R., Friedman, H. S., Tucker, J. S., Schwartz, J. E., Criqui, M. H., Wingard, D. L., & Tomlinson-Keasey, C. (1995). An archival prospective study of mental health and longevity. *Health Psychology, 5*, 381–387.

Martin, L. R., Friedman, H. S., Tucker, J. S., Tomlinson-Keasey, C., Criqui, M. H., & Schwartz, J. E. (2002). A life course perspective on childhood cheerfulness and its relation to mortality risk. *Personality and Social Psychology Bulletin, 28*, 1155–1165.

Martin, M. D., Hancock, G. A., Richardson, B., Simmons, P., Katona, C., Mullan, E., & Orrell, M. (2002). An evaluation of needs in elderly continuing-care settings. *International Psychogeriatrics, 14*, 379–388.

Martinez, M., Campion, D., Brice, A., Hannequin, D., Dubois, B., Didierjean, O., Michon, A., Thomas-Anterion, C., Puel, M., Frebourg, T., Agid, Y., & Clerget-Darpoux, F. (1998). Apolipoprotein E 4 allele and familial aggregation of Alzheimer disease. *Archives of Neurology, 55,* 810–816.

Martire, L. M., Stephens, M. A. P., & Townsend, A. L. (1998). Emotional support and well-being of midlife women: Role-specific mastery as a mediational mechanism. *Psychology and Aging, 13,* 396–404.

Marx, J. (2001). New leads on the "how" of Alzheimer's. *Science, 293,* 2192–2194.

Masaki, K. H., Losonczy, K. G., Izmirlian, G., Foley, D. J., Ross, G. W., Petrovitch, H., Havlik, R., & White, L. R. (2000). Association of vitamin E and C supplement use with cognitive function and dementia in elderly men. *Neurology, 54,* 1265–1272.

Mast, B. T., Fitzgerald, J., Steinberg, J., MacNeill, S. E., & Lichtenberg, P. A. (2001). Effective screening for Alzheimer's disease among older African Americans. *Clinical Neuropsychologist,* 196–202.

Mast, B. T., MacNeill, S. E., & Lichtenberg, P. A. (2002). A MIMIC model approach to research in geriatric neuropsychology: The case of vascular dementia. *Aging, Neuropsychology, and Cognition, 9,* 21–37.

Masunaga, H., & Horn, J. (2000). Characterizing mature human intelligence: Expertise development. *Learning & Individual Differences, 12,* 5–33.

Matsumae, M., Kikinis, R., Morocz, I. A., Lorenzo, A. V., Sandor, T., Albert, M. S., et al. (1996). Age-related changes in intracranial compartment volumes in normal adults assessed by magnetic resonance imaging. *Journal of Neurosurgery, 84,* 982–991.

Matthews, L., Wickrama, K., & Conger, R. (1996). Predicting marital instability from spouse and observer reports of marital interaction. *Journal of Marriage and the Family, 58,* 641–655.

Matthews, S. H. (1986). *Friendships through the life course.* Beverly Hills, CA: Sage.

Matthews, T. S., & Hamilton, B. E. (2002). *Mean age of mother: 1970–2000. National Vital Statistics Reports, Vol. 51, No 1.* Hyattsville, MD: National Center for Health Statistics.

Mattson, M. P., Duan, W., & Maswood, N. (2002). How does the brain control lifespan? *Ageing Research Reviews, 1,* 155–165.

Maurer, T. J. (2001). Career-relevant learning and development, worker age, and beliefs about self-efficacy for development. *Journal of Management, 27,* 123–140.

May, H., Murphy, S., & Khaw, K. T. (1995). Bone mineral density and its relationship to skin colour in Caucasian females. *European Journal of Clinical Investigation, 25,* 85–89.

Maylor, E. A. (1996). Age-related impairment in an event-based prospective-memory task. *Psychology and Aging, 11,* 74–78.

Mayne, T. J., Acree, M., Chesney, M. A., Folkman, S. (1998). HIV sexual risk behavior following bereavement in gay men. *Health Psychology, 17,* 403–411.

Mazur, A., Mueller, U., Krause, W., & Booth, A. (2002). Causes of sexual decline in aging married men: Germany and America. *International Journal of Impotence Research, 14,* 101–106.

McArdle, J. J., Ferrer-Caja, E., Hamagami, F., & Woodcock, R. W. (2002). Comparative longitudinal structural analyses of the growth and decline of multiple intellectual abilities over the life span. *Developmental Psychology, 38,* 115–142.

McAuley, E., Marquez, D. X., Jerome, G. J., Blissmer, B., & Katula, J. (2002). Physical activity and physique anxiety in older adults: Fitness, and efficacy influences. *Aging and Mental Health, 6,* 222–230.

McCalden, R. W., McGeough, J. A., & Court-Brown, C. M. (1997). Age-related changes in the compressive strength of cancellous bone: The relative importance of changes in density and trabecular architecture. *Journal of Bone and Joint Surgery American, 79,* 421–427.

McCalden, R. W., McGeough, J. A., Barker, M. B., & Court-Brown, C. M. (1993). Age-related changes in the tensile properties of cortical bone. The relative importance of changes in porosity, mineralization, and microstructure. *Journal of Bone and Joint Surgery, 75,* 1193–1205.

McCarthy, E. P., Burns, R. B., Coughlin, S. S., Freund, K. M., Rice, J., Marwill, S. L., Ash, A., Shwartz, M., & Moskowitz, M. A. (1998). Mammography use helps to explain differences in breast cancer stage at diagnosis between older black and white women. *Annals of Internal Medicine, 128,* 729–736.

McCartney, N., Hicks, A. L., Martin, J., & Webber, C. E. (1995). Long-term resistance training in the elderly: Effects on dynamic strength, exercise capacity, muscle, and bone. *Journal of Gerontology: Biological Sciences, 50,* B97–B104.

McCartney, N., Hicks, A. L., Martin, J., & Webber, C. E. (1996). A longitudinal trial of weight training in the elderly: Continued improvements in year 2. *Journal of Gerontology: Biological Sciences, 51,* B425–433.

McCrae, C. S., & Abrams, R. A. (2001). Age-related differences in object- and location-based inhibition of return of attention. *Psychology and Aging, 16,* 437–449.

McCrae, R. R. (2002). The maturation of personality psychology: Adult personality development and psychological well-being. *Journal of Research in Personality, 36,* 307–317.

McCrae, R. R., & Costa, P. T. J. (1990). *Personality in adulthood.* New York: Guilford.

McCrae, R. R., & Costa, P. T. J. (2003). *Personality in adulthood, Personality in adulthood: A five-factor theory perspective* (2nd ed.). New York: Guilford.

McCrae, R. R., Costa, P. T., Jr., de Lima, M. P., Simoes, A., Ostendorf, F., Angleitner, A., Marusic, I., Bratko, D., Caprara, G. V., Barbaranelli, C., Chae, J.-H., & Piedmont, R. L. (1999). Age differences in personality across the adult life span: Parallels in five cultures. *Developmental Psychology, 35,* 466–477.

McDaniel, M. A., & Snell, A. F. (1999). Holland's theory and occupational information. *Journal of Vocational Behavior, 55,* 74–85.

McDonald-Miszczak, L., Hertzog, C., & Hultsch, D. F. (1995). Stability and accuracy of metamemory in adulthood and aging: A longitudinal analysis. *Psychology and Aging, 10,* 553–564.

McGue, M., & Christensen, K. (2002). The heritability of level and rate-of-change in cognitive functioning in Danish twins aged 70 years and older. *Experimental Aging Research, 28,* 435–451.

McGuire, L., Kiecolt-Glaser, J. K., & Glaser, R. (2002). Depressive symptoms and lymphocyte proliferation in older adults. *Journal of Abnormal Psychology, 111,* 192–197.

McKeith, I. G., Galasko, D., Kosaka, K., Perry, E. K., Dickson, D. W., Hansen, L. A., Salmon, D. P., Lowe, J., Mirra, S. S., Byrne, E. J., Lennox, G., Quinn, N. P., Edwardson, J. A., Ince, P. G., Bergeron, C., Burns, A., Miller, B. L., Lovestone, S., Collerton, D., Jansen, E. N., Ballard, C., de Vos, R. A., Wilcock, G. K., Jellinger, K. A., & Perry, R. H. (1996). Consensus guidelines for the clinical and pathologic diagnosis of dementia with Lewy bodies (DLB): report of the consortium on DLB international workshop. *Neurology, 47,* 1113–1124.

McKhann, G., Drachman, D., Folstein, M., Katzman, R., Price, D., & Stadlan, E. M. (1984). Clinical diagnosis of Alzheimer's disease: Report of the NINCDS-ADRDA work group under the auspices of Department of Health and Human Services Task Force on Alzheimer's disease. *Neurology, 34,* 939–944.

McKiernan, F. (1996). Bereavement and attitudes toward death. In R. T. Woods (Ed.), *Handbook of the clinical psychology of ageing* (pp. 159–182). Chichester, UK: Wiley.

Meeks, S. (2000). Schizophrenia and related disorders. In S. K. Whitbourne (Ed.), *Psychopathology in later life* (pp. 189–215). New York: Wiley.

Meinz, E. J., & Salthouse, T. A. (1998). The effects of age and experience on memory for visually presented music. *Journal of Gerontology: Psychological Sciences, 53,* P60–69.

Melov, S. (2000). Mitochondrial oxidative stress. Physiologic consequences and potential for a role in aging. *Annals of the New York Academy of Science, 908,* 219–225.

Melov, S. (2002). "... and C is for Clioquinol"—the AbetaCs of Alzheimer's disease. *Trends in Neuroscience, 25,* 121–123.

Melov, S., Ravenscroft, J., Malik, S., Gill, M. S., Walker, D. W., Clayton, P. E., Wallace, D. C., Malfroy, B., Doctrow, S. R., & Lithgow, G. J. (2000). Extension of life-span with superoxide dismutase/catalase mimetics. *Science, 289,* 1567–1569.

Menninger, J. A. (2002). Assessment and treatment of alcoholism and substance-related disorders in the elderly. *Bulletin of the Menninger Clinic, 66,* 166–183.

Merikangas, K. R., Prusoff, B. A., & Weissman, M. M. (1988). Parental concordance for affective disorders: Psychopathology in offspring. *Journal of Affective Disorders, 15,* 279–290.

Meyer, B. J. F., Russo, C., & Talbot, A. (1995). Discourse comprehension and problem solving: Decisions about the treatment of breast cancer by women across the life span. *Psychology and Aging, 10,* 84–103.

Meyer, J. (2001). *Age 2000: Census 2000 brief.* Washington, DC: U.S. Bureau of the Census.

Michalos, A. C. (1985). Multiple discrepancies theory (MDT). *Social Indicators Research, 16,* 347–413.

Mickelson, K. D., Kessler, R. C., & Shaver, P. R. (1997). Adult attachment in a nationally representative sample. *Journal of Personality and Social Psychology, 73,* 1092–1106.

Midanik, L. T., Soghikian, K., Ransom, L. J., & Tekawa, I. S. (1995). The effect of retirement on mental health and health behaviors: The Kaiser Permanente Retirement Study. *Journal of Gerontology: Social Sciences, 50B,* S59–S61.

Middelkoop, H. A., Smilde-van den Doel, D. A., Neven, A. K., Kamphuisen, H. A., & Springer, C. P. (1996). Subjective sleep characteristics of 1,485 males and females aged 50-93: effects of sex and age, and factors related to self-evaluated quality of sleep. *Journal of Gerontology: Medical Sciences, 51,* M108–115.

Mikulincer, M. (1995). Attachment style and the mental representation of the self. *Journal of Personality and Social Psychology, 69,* 1203–1215.

Mikulincer, M., & Florian, V. (1998). The relationship between adult attachment styles and emotional and cognitive reactions to stressful events. In J. A. Simpson & W. S. Rholes (Eds.), *Attachment theory and close relationships* (pp. 143–165). New York: Guilford Press.

Mikulincer, M., Florian, V., Birnbaum, G., & Malishkevich, S. (2002). The death-anxiety buffering function of close relationships: Exploring the effects of separation reminders on death-thought accessibility. *Personality & Social Psychology Bulletin, 28,* 287–299.

Mikulincer, M., Florian, V., Cowan, P. A., & Cowan, C. P. (2002). Attachment security in couple relationships: A systemic model and its implications for family dynamics. *Family Process, 41,* 405–434.

Miller, R. A. (1996). The aging immune system: Primer and prospectus. *Science, 273*, 70–74.

Miller, T. Q., Smith, T. W., Turner, C. W., Guijarro, M. L., & Hallet, A. J. (1996). Meta-analytic review of research on hostility and physical health. *Psychological Bulletin, 119*, 322–348.

Millon, T. (1994). *Manual for the Millon Clinical Multiaxial Inventory-III*. Minneapolis MN: National Computer Systems.

Minino, A. M., Arias, E., Kochanek, K. D., Murphy, S. L., & Smith, B. L. (2002). *Deaths: Final data for 2000. National vital statistics reports* (Vol. 50, No. 15). Hyattsville MD: National Center for Health Statistics.

Mireles, D. E., & Charness, N. (2002). Computational explorations of the influence of structured knowledge on age-related cognitive decline. *Psychology and Aging, 17*, 245–259.

Mishra, G. D., Ball, K., Dobson, A. J., Byles, J. E., & Warner-Smith, P. (2002). Which aspects of socio-economic status are related to health in mid-aged and older women? *International Journal of Behavioral Medicine, 9*, 263–285.

Moen, P. (1996). A life course perspective on retirement, gender, and well-being. *Journal of Occupational Health Psychology, 1*, 131–144.

Moen, P., Kim, J. E., & Hofmeister, H. (2001). Couples' work/retirement transitions, gender, and marital quality. *Social Psychology Quarterly, 64*, 55–71.

Mohlman, J., Gorenstein, E. E., Kleber, M., de Jesus, M., Gorman, J. M., & Papp, L. A. (2003). Standard and enhanced cognitive-behavior therapy for late-life generalized anxiety disorder: Two pilot investigations. *American Journal of Geriatric Psychiatry, 11*, 24–32.

Monzani, F., Del Guerra, P., Caraccio, N., Del Corso, L., Casolaro, A., Mariotti, S., et al. (1996). Age-related modifications in the regulation of the hypothalamic-pituitary-thyroid axis. *Hormone Research, 46*, 107–112.

Moore, D. E., & Hayward, M. D. (1990). Occupational careers and mortality of elderly men. *Demography, 27*, 31–53.

Moore, P. J., Adler, N. E., Williams, D. R., & Jackson, J. S. (2002). Socioeconomic status and health: the role of sleep. *Psychosomatic Medicine, 64*, 337–344.

Morgan, C. D., & Murray, H. A. (1935). A method for investigating fantasies: The Thematic Apperception test. *American Medical Association Archives of Neurology and Psychiatry, 34*, 289–306.

Morgan, W. K., & Reger, R. B. (2000). Rise and fall of the FEV(1). *Chest, 118*, 1639–1644.

Morishita, R., Tomita, N., & Ogihara, T. (2002). HMG-Co A reductase inhibitors in the treatment of cardiovascular diseases: Stabilization of coronary artery plaque. *Current Drug Targets, 3*, 379–385.

Morley, J. E. (2001). Andropause: Is it time for the geriatrician to treat it? *Journal of Gerontology Series A: Biological Sciences and Medical Sciences, 56*, M263–265.

Morley, J. E., Baumgartner, R. N., Roubenoff, R., Mayer, J., & Nair, K. S. (2001). Sarcopenia. *Journal of Laboratory Clinical Medicine, 137*, 231–243.

Morris, J. C., Cyrus, P. A., Orazem, J., Mas, J., & Bieber, F. (1991). National Institutes of Health Consensus Development Panel on Depression in Late Life. Diagnosis and treatment of depression in late life. *Journal of the American Medical Association, 268*, 1018–1024.

Morrow, D. G., Hier, C. M., Menard, W. E., & Leirer, V. O. (1998). Icons improve older and younger adults' comprehension of medication information. *Journal of Gerontology: Psychological Sciences and Social Sciences, 53B*, P240–P254.

Morrow, D. G., Leirer, V. O., Andrassy, J. M., Hier, C. M., & Menard, W. E. (1998). The influence of list format and category headers on age differences in understanding medication instructions. *Experimental Aging Research, 24*, 231–256.

Morrow, D. G., Menard, W. E., Stine-Morrow, E. A., Teller, T., & Bryant, D. (2001). The influence of expertise and task factors on age differences in pilot communication. *Psychology and Aging, 16*, 31–46.

Morys, J., Bobinski, M., Wegiel, J., Wisniewski, H. M., & Narkiewicz, O. (1996). Alzheimer's disease severely affects areas of the claustrum connected with the entorhinal cortex. *Journal fur Hirnforschung, 37*, 173–180.

Moss, M. S., Resch, N., & Moss, S. Z. (1997). The role of gender in middle-age children's responses to parent death. *Omega—Journal of Death and Dying, 35*, 1997.

Mottram, P. G., Wilson, K. C., Ashworth, L., & Abou-Saleh, M. (2002). The clinical profile of older patients' response to antidepressants—an open trial of sertraline. *International Journal of Geriatric Psychiatry, 17*, 574–578.

Mouloua, M., & Parasuraman, R. (1995). Aging and cognitive vigilance: Effects of spatial uncertainty and event rate. *Experimental Aging Research, 21*, 17–32.

Mozaffarian, D., Kumanyika, S. K., Lemaitre, R. N., Olson, J. L., Burke, G. L., & Siscovick, D. S. (2003). Cereal, fruit, and vegetable fiber intake and the risk of cardiovascular disease in elderly individuals. *Journal of the American Medical Association, 289*, 1659–1666.

Mroczek, D. K., & Kolarz, C. M. (1998). The effect of age on positive and negative affect: A developmental perspective on happiness. *Journal of Personality and Social Psychology, 75*, 1333–1349.

Muchinsky, P. (1999). Application of Holland's theory in industrial and organizational settings. *Journal of Vocational Behavior, 55*, 127–125.

Mueller, M. M., Wilhelm, B., & Elder, G. H., Jr. (2002). Variations in grandparenting. *Research on Aging, 24,* 360–388.

Mukamal, K. J., Conigrave, K. M., Mittleman, M. A., Camargo, C. A., Jr., Stampfer, M. J., Willett, W. C., & Rimm, E. B. (2003). Roles of drinking pattern and type of alcohol consumed in coronary heart disease in men. *New England Journal of Medicine, 348,* 109–118.

Mukamal, K. J., Kuller, L. H., Fitzpatrick, A. L., Longstreth, W. T. J., Mittleman, M. A., & Siscovick, D. S. (2003). Prospective study of alcohol consumption and risk of dementia in older adults. *Journal of the American Medical Association, 289,* 1405–1413.

Multhaup, K. S., Balota, D. A., & Cowan, N. (1996). Implications of aging, lexicality, and item length for the mechanisms underlying memory span. *Psychonomic Bulletin and Review, 3,* 112–120.

Munson, M. L. (1999). Characteristics of elderly home health care users: Data from the 1996 national home and hospice care survey. Advance Data from Vital and Health Statistics of the Centers for Disease Control and Prevention, Number 309, December 22, 1999.

Murialdo, G., Barreca, A., Nobili, F., Rollero, A., Timossi, G., Gianelli, M. V., Copello, F., Rodriguez, G., & Polleri, A. (2001). Relationships between cortisol, dehydroepiandrosterone sulphate and insulin-like growth factor-I system in dementia. *Journal of Endocrinology Investigations, 24,* 139–146.

Murphy, D. G., DeCarli, C., McIntosh, A. R., Daly, E., Mentis, M. J., Pietrini, P., Szczepanik, J., Schapiro, M. B., Grady, C. L., Horwitz, B., & Rapoport, S. I. (1996). Sex differences in human brain morphometry and metabolism: An in vivo quantitative magnetic resonance imaging and positron emission tomography study on the effect of aging. *Archives of General Psychiatry, 53,* 585–594.

Murphy, S., Khaw, K. T., May, H., & Compston, J. E. (1994). Milk consumption and bone mineral density in middle aged and elderly women. *British Medical Journal, 308,* 939–941.

Murray, J. E. (2000). Marital protection and marital selection: Evidence from a historical-prospective sample of American men. *Demography, 37,* 511–521.

Murrell, S. A., & Meeks, S. (2002). Psychological, economic, and social mediators of the education-health relationship in older adults. *Journal of Aging and Health, 14,* 527–550.

Muscarella, F., & Cunningham, M. R. (1996). The evolutionary significance and social perception of male pattern baldness and facial hair. *Ethology and Sociobiology, 17,* 99–117.

Mutchler, J. E., Burr, J. A., Pienta, A. M., & Massagli, M. P. (1997). Pathways to labor force exit: Work transitions and work instability. *Journal of Gerontology: Social Sciences, 52B,* S4–S12.

Mutran, E. J., Reitzes, D. C., & Fernandez, M. E. (1997). Factors that influence attitudes toward retirement. *Research on Aging, 19,* 251–273.

Myerson, J., Hale, S., Wagstaff, D., Poon, L. W., & Smith, G. A. (1990). The information-loss model: A mathematical theory of age-related cognitive slowing. *Psychological Review, 97,* 475–487.

Nakanishi, N., Suzuki, K., & Tatara, K. (2003). Alcohol consumption and risk for development of impaired fasting glucose or type 2 diabetes in middle-aged Japanese men. *Diabetes Care, 26,* 48–54.

Nakazato, M., Endo, S., Yoshimura, I., & Tomita, H. (2002). Influence of aging on electrogustometry thresholds. *Acta Otolaryngolica Supplement,* 16–26.

Natale, V., Albertazzi, P., Zini, M., & Di Micco, R. (2001). Exploration of cyclical changes in memory and mood in postmenopausal women taking sequential combined oestrogen and progestogen preparations. *The British Journal of Obstetrics and Gynaecology, 108,* 286–290.

National Cancer Institute (2004). The science behind the news. http://press2.nci.nih.gov/sciencebehind/cancer/cancer54.htm. Accessed 1/23/04.

National Center for Health Statistics (1998). *Health, United States 1998.* Hyattsville, MD: National Center for Health Statistics.

National Center for Health Statistics (2002). *Births, Marriages, Divorces, and Deaths: Provisional Data for 2001* (No. (PHS) 2002–1120).

National Center for Health Statistics (2002a). *Health, United States, 2002.* Hyattsville, MD: U.S. Department of Health and Human Services, Centers for Disease Control and Prevention.

National Center for Health Statistics (2004). National Nursing Home Survey. http://www.cdc.gov/nchs/about/major/nnhsd/nnhs_chart.htm.

National Center on Elder Abuse at the American Public Human Services Association (1998). *The national elder abuse incidence study.*

National Highway Traffic Safety Administration (2000). Older Drivers. http://www.nhtsa.dot.gov/people/injury/olddrive/. Accessed 1/23/04.

National Institute on Alcohol Abuse and Alcoholism. (1998). Alcohol and aging. *Alcohol Alert, No. 40.*

National Institutes of Health Osteoporosis and Related Bone Diseases National Resource Center. (2002). *Osteoporosis overview.* Retrieved August 2003, from http://www.osteo.org/osteo.html

National Kidney and Urologic Diseases Clearinghouse (2001). Kidney and Urologic Diseases of the United States (Vol. 2003). NIH Publications No. 02-3895.

Naveh-Benjamin, M., Craik, F. I. M., & Ben-Shaul, L. (2002). Age-related differences in cued recall: Effects of support at encoding and retrieval. *Aging, Neuropsychology, & Cognition, 9*, 276–287.

Neder, J. A., Nery, L. E., Silva, A. C., Andreoni, S., & Whipp, B. J. (1999). Maximal aerobic power and leg muscle mass and strength related to age in non-athlethic males and females. *European Journal of Applied Physiology and Occupational Physiology, 79*, 522–530.

Nelson, E. A., & Dannefer, D. (1992). Aged heterogeneity: Fact or fiction? The fate of diversity in gerontological research. *Gerontologist, 32*, 17–23.

Nesselroade, J. R., & Baltes, P. B. (1974). Adolescent personality development and historical change: 1970–1972. *Monographs of the Society for Research in Child Development, 39*.

Neugarten, B. L., & Weinstein, K. K. (1964). The changing American grandparent. *Journal of Marriage and the Family, 26*, 199–204.

Newmann, J. P., Engel, R. J., & Jensen, J. E. (1991). Changes in depressive-symptom experiences among older women. *Psychology and Aging, 6*, 212–222.

Nicolau, C., Greferath, R., Balaban, T. S., Lazarte, J. E., & Hopkins, R. J. (2002). A liposome-based therapeutic vaccine against beta-amyloid plaques on the pancreas of transgenic NORBA mice. *Proceedings of the National Academy of Science USA, 99*, 2332–2337.

Nicolson, N., Storms, C., Ponds, R., & Sulon, J. (1997). Salivary cortisol levels and stress reactivity in human aging. *Journal of Gerontology: Medical Sciences, 52*, M68–75.

Niederehe, G., & Schneider, L. S. (1998). Treatments for depression and anxiety in the aged. In P. E. Nathan & J. M. Gorman (Eds.), *A guide to treatments that work.* (pp. 270–287). New York: Oxford University Press.

Nielsen Bohlman, L., & Knight, R. T. (1995). Prefrontal alterations during memory processing in aging. *Cerebral Cortex, 5*, 541–549.

Nieman, D. C. (2000). Exercise immunology: Future directions for research related to athletes, nutrition, and the elderly. *International Journal of Sports Medicine, 21* (Suppl 1), S61–68.

Nishimura, N., Hongo, M., Yamada, M., Kawakami, H., Ueno, M., Okuno, Y., & Toyota, T. (1996). Effect of aging on the esophageal motor functions. *Journal of Smooth Muscle Research, 32*, 43–50.

Nygaard, I., Turvey, C., Burns, T. L., Crischelles, E., & Wallace, R. (2003). Urinary incontinence and depression in middle-aged United States women. *Obstetrics & Gynecology, 101*, 149–156.

O'Brien, J. T., Schweitzer, I., Ames, D., Tuckwell, V., & Mastwyk, M. (1994). Cortisol suppression by dexamethasone in the healthy elderly: Effects of age, dexamethasone levels, and cognitive function. *Biological Psychiatry, 36*, 389–394.

O'Donnell, C. J., & Kannel, W. B. (2002). Epidemiologic appraisal of hypertension as a coronary risk factor in the elderly. *American Journal of Geriatric Cardiology, 11*, 86–92.

O'Grady, M., Fletcher, J., & Ortiz, S. (2000). Therapeutic and physical fitness exercise prescription for older adults with joint disease: An evidence-based approach. *Rheumatic Disease Clinics North America, 26*, 617–646.

O'Neill, C., Jamison, J., McCulloch, D., & Smith, D. (2001). Age-related macular degeneration: Cost-of-illness issues. *Drugs and Aging, 18*, 233–241.

O'Rourke, K. (1991). Assisted suicide: An evaluation. *Journal of Pain and Symptom Management, 6*, 317–324.

Okatani, Y., Morioka, N., & Wakatsuki, A. (2000). Changes in nocturnal melatonin secretion in perimenopausal women: correlation with endogenous estrogen concentrations. *Journal of Pineal Research, 28*, 111–118.

Orgel, L. E. (1963). The maintenance of the accuracy of protein synthesis and its relevance to aging. *Proceedings of the National Academy of Science of the USA, 49*, 512–517.

Oslin, D. W., Datto, C. J., Kallan, M. J., Katz, I. R., Edell, W. S., & TenHave, T. (2002). Association between medical comorbidity and treatment outcomes in late-life depression. *Journal of the American Geriatrics Society, 50*, 823–828.

Østbye, T., Steenhuis, R., Wolfson, C., Walton, R., & Hill, G. (1999). Predictors of five-year mortality in older Canadians: The Canadian Study of Health and Aging. *Journal of the American Geriatrics Society, 47*, 1249–1254.

Ott, C. H., & Lueger, R. J. (2002). Patterns of change in mental health status during the first two years of spousal bereavement. *Death Studies, 26*, 387–411.

Pacheco, J., Hershberger, P. J., Markert, R. J., & Kumar, G. (2003). A longitudinal study of attitudes toward physician-assisted suicide and euthanasia among patients with noncurable malignancy. *American Journal of Hospital Palliative Care, 20*, 99–104.

Palmer, B. W., Heaton, R. K., Gladsjo, J. A., Evans, J. D., Patterson, T. L., Golshan, S., & Jeste, D. V. (2002). Heterogeneity in functional status among older outpatients with schizophrenia: employment history, living situation, and driving. *Schizophrenia Research, 55*, 205–215.

Palmore, E. B., Fillenbaum, G. G., & George, L. K. (1984). Consequences of retirement. *Journal of Gerontology, 39*, 109–116.

Pamuk, E., Makuc, D., Heck, K., Reuben, C., & Lochner, K. (1998). *Socioeconomic status and health chartbook. Health, United States,1998*. Hyattsville, MD: National Center for Health Statistics.

Pamuk, E., Makuc, D., Heck, K., Reuben, C., & Lochner, K. (1998). *Socioeconomic status and health chartbook. Health, United States,1998.* Hyattsville, MD: National Center for Health Statistics.

Paoletti, A. M., Pilia, I., Nannipieri, F., Bigini, C., & Melis, G. B. (2001). Comparison of pharmacokinetic profiles of a 17 beta-estradiol gel 0.6 mg/g (Gelestra) with a transdermal delivery system (Estraderm TTS 50) in postmenopausal women at steady state. *Maturitas, 40,* 203–209.

Park, D. C., & Jones, T. R. (1997). Medication adherence and aging. In A. D. Fisk & W. A. Rogers (Eds.), *Handbook of human factors and the older adult* (pp. 257–287). San Diego, CA: Academic Press.

Park, D. C., Hertzog, C., Kidder, D. P., Morrell, R. W., & Mayhorn, C. B. (1997). Effect of age on event-based and time-based prospective memory. *Psychology and Aging, 12,* 314–327.

Park, D. C., Lautenschlager, G., Hedden, T., Davidson, N. S., Smith, A. D., & Smith, P. K. (2002). Models of visuospatial and verbal memory across the adult life span. *Psychology and Aging, 17,* 299–320.

Park, D. C., Smith, A. D., & Cavanaugh, J. C. (1990). Metamemories of memory researchers. *Memory and Cognition, 18,* 321–327.

Parnes, H. S., & Sommers, D. G. (1994). Shunning retirement: work experience of men in their seventies and early eighties. *Journal of Gerontology, 49,* S117–124.

Patel, N. V., & Finch, C. E. (2002). The glucocorticoid paradox of caloric restriction in slowing brain aging. *Neurobiology of Aging, 23,* 707–717.

Paterniti, S., Dufouil, C., & Alperovitch, A. (2002). Long-term benzodiazepine use and cognitive decline in the elderly: The Epidemiology of Vascular Aging Study. *Journal of Clinical Psychopharmacology, 22,* 285–293.

Patterson, T. L., McKibbin, C., Taylor, M., Goldman, S., Davila-Fraga, W., Bucardo, J., & Jeste, D. V. (2003). Functional Adaptation Skills Training (FAST): A pilot psychosocial intervention study in middle-aged and older patients with chronic psychotic disorders. *American Journal of Geriatric Psychiatry, 11,* 17–23.

Patterson, T. L., Shaw, W., Semple, S. J., Moscona, S., Harris, M. J., Kaplan, R. M., Grant, I., & Jeste, D. V. (1997). Health-related quality of life in older patients with schizophrenia and other psychoses: Relationships among psychosocial and psychiatric factors. *International Journal of Geriatric Psychiatry, 12,* 452–461.

Pavalko, E. K., Elder, G. H., & Clipp, E. C. (1993). Work lives and longevity: Insights from a life course perspective. *Journal of Health and Social Behavior, 34,* 363–380.

Pawlikowski, M., Kolomecka, M., Wojtczak, A., & Karasek, M. (2002). Effects of six months melatonin treatment on sleep quality and serum concentrations of estradiol, cortisol, dehydroepiandrosterone sulfate, and somatomedin C in elderly women. *Neuroendocrinology Letters, 23 Suppl 1,* 17–19.

Perrig, W. J., Perrig, P., & Stahelin, H. B. (1997). The relation between antioxidants and memory performance in the old and very old. *Journal of the American Geriatrics Society, 45,* 718–724.

Perry, H. M., 3rd, Horowitz, M., Morley, J. E., Fleming, S., Jensen, J., Caccione, P., Miller, D. K., Kaiser, F. E., & Sundarum, M. (1996). Aging and bone metabolism in African American and Caucasian women. *Journal of Clinical Endocrinology and Metabolism, 81,* 1108–1117.

Perry, H. M., 3rd, Miller, D. K., Patrick, P., & Morley, J. E. (2000). Testosterone and leptin in older African-American men: Relationship to age, strength, function, and season. *Metabolism, 49,* 1085–1091.

Persad, C. C., Abeles, N., Zacks, R. T., & Denburg, N. L. (2002). Inhibitory changes after age 60 and their relationship to measures of attention and memory. *Journals of Gerontology Series B: Psychological Sciences and Social Sciences, 57,* P223–232.

Peterson, N. G., Mumford, M. D., Borman, W. C., Jeanneret, P. R., & Fleishman, E. A. (Eds.). (1999). *An occupational information system for the 21st century: The development of O*NET.* Washington, DC: American Psychological Association.

Petrella, R. J., Cunningham, D. A., & Paterson, D. H. (1997). Effects of 5-day exercise training in elderly subjects on resting left ventricular diastolic function and VO2max. *Canadian Journal of Applied Physiology, 22,* 37–47.

Philip, P., Dealberto, M. J., Dartigues, J. F., Guilleminault, C., & Bioulac, B. (1997). Prevalence and correlates of nocturnal desaturations in a sample of elderly people. *Journal of Sleep Research, 6,* 264–271.

Pickering, G., Jourdan, D., Eschalier, A., & Dubray, C. (2002). Impact of age, gender and cognitive functioning on pain perception. *Gerontology, 48,* 112–118.

Pillemer, K., & Suitor, J. J. (1998). Baby boom families: Relations with aging parents. *Generations,* 65–70.

Pini, R., Tonon, E., Cavallini, M. C., Bencini, F., Di Bari, M., Masotti, G., & Marchionni, N. (2001). Accuracy of equations for predicting stature from knee height, and assessment of statural loss in an older Italian population. *Journals of Gerontology: Biological Sciences, 56,* B3–B7.

Pinson-Millburn, N. M., Fabian, E. S., Schlossberg, N. K., & Pyle, M. (1996). Grandparents raising grandchildren. *Journal of Counseling and Development, 74,* 548–554.

Piolino, P., Desgranges, B., Benali, K., & Eustache, F. (2002). Episodic and semantic remote autobiographical memory in ageing. *Memory, 10,* 239–257.

Plassman, B. L., Welsh, K. A., Helms, M., Brandt, J., Page, W. F., & Breitner, J. C. (1995). Intelligence and education as predictors of cognitive state in late life: A 50-year follow-up. *Neurology, 45,* 1446–1450.

Plaut, V. C., Markus, H. R., & Lachman, M. E. (2003). Place matters: Consensual features and regional variation in American well-being and self. *Journal of Personality and Social Psychology, 83*, 160–184.

Pleis, J. R., & Coles, R. (2002). Summary health statistics for U.S. adults: National Health Interview Survey, 1998. *National Center for Health Statistics. Vital Health Statistics, 10*(209).

Plemons, J. K., Willis, S. L., & Baltes, P. B. (1978). Modifiability of fluid intelligence in aging: A short-term longitudinal training approach. *Journal of Gerontology, 33*, 224–231.

Polley, A., Menzel, U., Delabar, J., Kumpf, K., Lehmann, D., Patterson, D., Reichwald, K., Rump, A., Schillhabel, M., Schudy, A., Zimmermann, W., Rosenthal, A., Kudoh, J., Shibuya, K., Kawasaki, I., Asakawa, S., Shintani, A., Sasaki, T., Nagamine, K., Mitsuyama, S., Antonarakis, S. E., Minoshima, S., Shimizu, N., Nordsiek, G., Hornischer, P., Brandt, P., Scharfe, M., Schoen, O., Desario, A., Reichelt, J., Kauer, G., Bloecker, H., Ramser, J., Beck, A., Klage, S., Hennig, S., Riesselmann, L., Dagand, E., Haaf, T., Wehrmeyer, S., Borzym, K., Gardiner, K., Nizetic, D., Francis, F., Lehrach, H., Reinhardt, R., & Yaspo, M.-L. (2000). The DNA sequence of human chromosome 21. *Nature, 405*, 311–319.

Pollock, M. L., Mengelkoch, L. J., Graves, J. E., Lowenthal, D. T., Limacher, M. C., Foster, C., & Wilmore, J. H. (1997). Twenty-year follow-up of aerobic power and body composition of older track athletes. *Journal of Applied Physiology, 82*, 1508–1516.

Popenoe, D., & Whitehead, B. D. (1999). *The state of our unions: The social health of marriage in America.* New Brunswick, NJ: Rutgers University National Marriage Project.

Porta, E. A. (2002). Pigments in aging: An overview. *Annals of the New York Academy of Science, 959*, 57–65.

Porter, V. R., Greendale, G. A., Schocken, M., Zhu, X., & Effros, R. B. (2001). Immune effects of hormone replacement therapy in post-menopausal women. *Experimental Gerontology, 36*, 311–326.

Portin, R., Saarijaervi, S., Joukamaa, M., & Salokangas, R. K. R. (1995). Education, gender and cognitive performance in a 62-year-old normal population: Results from the Turva Project. *Psychological Medicine, 25*, 1295–1298.

President's Commission for the Study of Ethical Problems in Medicine and Biomedical and Behavioral Research (1981). *Defining death.* Washington, DC: U.S. Government Printing Office.

Prevention, Centers for Disease Control and Prevention (2002). Hypothermia-Related Deaths—Utah, 2000, and United States, 1979–1998. *Morbidity and Mortality Weekly Report, 51* (04), 76–78.

Price, D. P. (1997). Organ transplant initiatives: The twilight zone. *Journal of Medical Ethics, 23*, 170–175.

Prinz, P. N., Bailey, S. L., & Woods, D. L. (2000). Sleep impairments in healthy seniors: Roles of stress, cortisol, and interleukin-1 beta. *Chronobiology International, 17*, 391–404.

Prinz, P., Bailey, S., Moe, K., Wilkinson, C., & Scanlan, J. (2001). Urinary free cortisol and sleep under baseline and stressed conditions in healthy senior women: Effects of estrogen replacement therapy. *Journal of Sleep Research, 10*, 19–26.

Pritchard, R. S., Fisher, E. S., Teno, J. M., Sharp, S. M., Reding, D. J., Knaus, W. A., Wennberg, J. E., & Lynn, J. (1998). Influence of patient preferences and local health system characteristics on the place of death. SUPPORT Investigators. Study to Understand Prognoses and Preferences for Risks and Outcomes of Treatment. *Journal of the American Geriatrics Society, 46*, 1242–1250.

Proctor, D. N., Balagopal, P. & Nair, K. S. (1998). Age-related sarcopenia in humans is associated with Centers for Disease Control and Prevention.

Pruchno, R. A., & McKenney, D. (2002). Psychological well-being of Black and White grandmothers raising grandchildren: Examination of a two-factor model. *Journals of Gerontology: Series B: Psychological Sciences and Social Sciences, 57*, P444–452.

Puder, J. J., Freda, P. U., Goland, R. S., & Wardlaw, S. L. (2001). Estrogen modulates the hypothalamic-pituitary-adrenal and inflammatory cytokine responses to endotoxin in women. *Journal of Clinical Endocrinology and Metabolism, 86*, 2403–2408.

Qualls, S. H., Segal, D. L., Norman, S. N., George, & Gallagher-Thompson, D. (2002). Psychologists in practice with older adults: Current patterns, sources of training, and need for continuing education. *Professional Psychology: Research & Practice, 33*, 435–442.

Quetelet, A. (1835/1968). *A treatise on man and the development of his faculties.* New York: Franklin.

Quick, H. E., & Moen, P. (1998). Gender, employment and retirement quality: A life course approach to the differential experiences of men and women. *Journal of Occupational Health Psychology, 3*, 44–64.

Rabbitt, P. (1996). Speed of processing and ageing. In R. T. Woods (Ed.), *Handbook of the Clinical Psychology of Ageing* (pp. 59–72). London: Wiley.

Rabbitt, P., & Abson, V. (1990). "Lost and found": Some logical and methodological limitations of self-report questionnaires as tools to study cognitive ageing. *British Journal of Psychology, 81*, 1–16.

Rahhal, T. A., Colcombe, S. J., & Hasher, L. (2001). Instructional manipulations and age differences in memory: Now you see them, now you don't. *Psychology and Aging, 16*, 697–706.

Ralphs, J. R., & Benjamin, M. (1994). The joint capsule: structure, composition, ageing and disease. *Journal of Anatomy, 184*, 503–509.

Randall, B. B., Fierro, M. F., & Froede, R. C. (1998). Practice guideline for forensic pathology. *Archives of Pathology and Laboratory Medicine, 122*, 1056–1064.

Randell, K. M., Honkanen, R. J., Komulainen, M. H., Tuppurainen, M. T., Kroger, H., & Saarikoski, S. (2001). Hormone replacement therapy and risk of falling in early postmenopausal women—A population-based study. *Clinical Endocrinology (Oxford), 54*, 769–774.

Raudenbush, S. W., & Bryk, A. S. (2002). Hierarchical linear models: *Applications and data analysis methods* (2nd ed.). Newbury Park, CA: Sage.

Ravaglia, G., Forti, P., Maioli, F., Bastagli, L., Facchini, A., Mariani, E., Sararino, L., Sassi, S., Cucinotta, D., & Lenaz, G. (2000). Effect of micronutrient status on natural killer cell immune function in healthy free-living subjects aged ≥90 y. *American Journal of Clinical Nutrition, 71*, 590–598.

Ravaglia, G., Forti, P., Maioli, F., Pratelli, L., Vettori, C., Bastagli, L., Mariani, E., Facchini, A, & Cucinotta, D. (2001). Regular moderate intensity physical activity and blood concentrations of endogenous anabolic hormones and thyroid hormones in aging men. *Mechanisms of Ageing and Development, 122*, 191–203.

Raz, N., Gunning, F. M., Head, D., Dupuis, J. H., McQuain, J., Briggs, S. D., Loken, W. J., Thornton, A. E., & Acker, J. D. (1997). Selective aging of the human cerebral cortex observed in vivo: Differential vulnerability of the prefrontal gray matter. *Cerebral Cortex, 7*, 268–282.

Raz, N., Gunning-Dixon, F. M., Head, D., Dupuis, J. H., & Acker, J. D. (1998). Neuroanatomical correlates of cognitive aging: Evidence from structural magnetic resonance imaging. *Neuropsychology, 12*, 95–114.

Reis, H. T., & Shaver, P. (1988). Intimacy as an interpersonal process. In S. Duck (Ed.), *Handbook of personal relationships.* Chichester, UK: Wiley.

Resnick, S. M., Metter, E. J., & Zonderman, A. B. (1997). Estrogen replacement therapy and longitudinal decline in visual memory: A possible protective effect? *Neurology, 49*, 1491–1497.

Reynolds, C. A., Finkel, D., Gatz, M., & Pedersen, N. L. (2002). Sources of influence on rate of cognitive change over time in Swedish twins: An application of latent growth models. *Experimental Aging Research, 28*, 407–433.

Reynolds, C. F. I., Frank, E., Perel, J. M., Imber, S. D., Cornes, C., Miller, M. D., Mazumdar, S., Houck, P. R., Dew, M. A., Stack, J. A., Pollock, B. G., & Kupfer, D. J. (1999). Nortriptyline and interpersonal psychotherapy as maintenance therapies for recurrent major depression: A randomized controlled trial in patients older than 59 years. *Journal of the American Medical Association, 281*, 39–45.

Reynolds, K., Lewis, L. B., Nolen, J. D. L., Kinney, G. L., Sathya, B., & He, J. (2003). Alcohol consumption and risk of stroke: A meta-analysis. *Journal of the American Medical Association, 289*, 579–588.

Richardson, V., & Kilty, K. (1991). Adjustment to retirement: Continuity versus discontinuity. *International Journal of Aging and Human Development, 32*, 151–169.

Riedel, B., & Lichstein, K. (2000). Insomnia in older adults. In S. K. Whitbourne (Ed.), *Psychopathology in later life* (pp. 299–322). New York: Wiley.

Riggs, K. M., Lachman, M. E., & Wingfield, A. (1997). Taking charge of remembering: Locus of control and older adults' memory for speech. *Experimental Aging Research, 23*, 237–256.

Riordan, C. M., Griffith, R. W., & Weatherly, E. W. (2003). Age and work-related outcomes: The moderating effects of status characteristics. *Journal of Applied Social Psychology, 33*, 37–57.

Robbins, T. W., James, M., Owen, A. M., Sahakian, B. J., Lawrence, A. D., McInnes, L., & Rabbitt, P. M. A. (1998). A study of performance on tests from the CANTAB battery sensitive to frontal lobe dysfunction in a large sample of normal volunteers: Implications for theories of executive functioning and cognitive aging. *Journal of the International Neuropsychological Society, 4*, 474–490.

Roberto, K. A. (1990). Grandparent and grandchild relationships. In T. H. Brubaker (Ed.), *Family relationships in later life* (2nd ed., pp. 100–112). Newbury Park, CA: Sage.

Roberto, K. A., & Stanis, P. I. (1994). Reactions of older women to the death of their close friends. *Omega—Journal of Death and Dying, 29*, 1994.

Roberto, K. A., & Stroes, J. (1992). Grandchildren and grandparents: Roles, influences, and relationships. *International Journal of Aging and Human Development, 34*, 227–239.

Roberts, B. W., & DelVecchio, W. F. (2000). The rank-order consistency of personality traits from childhood to old age: A quantitative review of longitudinal studies. *Psychological Bulletin, 126*, 3–25.

Roberts, B. W., Caspi, A., & Moffitt, T. E. (2003). Work experiences and personality development in young adulthood. *Journal of Personality and Social Psychology, 84, 582–593.*

Robins, L. R., & Regier, D. A. (1991). *Psychiatric disorders in America.* New York: Free Press.

Robinson, G. E. (2001). Psychotic and mood disorders associated with the perimenopausal period: Epidemiology, aetiology and management. *CNS Drugs, 15*, 175–184.

Rodin, J. (1986). Aging and health: Effects of the sense of control. *Science, 233*, 1271–1276.

Rogers, R. G. (1995). Marriage, sex, and mortality. *Journal of Marriage and the Family, 57*, 515–526.

Rogers, S. L., & Friedhoff, L. T. (1998). Long-term efficacy and safety of donepezil in the treatment of Alzheimer's disease: An interim analysis of the results of a US multicentre open label extension study. *European Neuropsychopharmacology, 8*, 67–75.

Rollins, B., & Galligan, R. (1978). The developing child and marital satisfaction of parents. In R. M. Lerner & G. B. Spanier (Eds.), *Child influences on marital and family interaction* (pp. 117–144). New York: Academic Press.

Rosenberg, S. D., Rosenberg, H. J., & Farrell, M. P. (1999). The midlife crisis revisited. In J. D. Reid & S. L. Willis (Eds.), *Life in the middle: Psychological and social development in middle age* (pp. 25–45). San Diego: Academic Press.

Rosow, I. (1967). *Social integration of the aged.* New York: Free Press.

Ross, H. G., & Milgram, J. I. (1982). Important variables in adult sibling relationships: A qualitative study. In M. E. Lamb & B. Sutton-Smith (Eds.), *Sibling relationships: Their significance across the lifespan* (pp. 225–249). Hillsdale, NJ: Erlbaum.

Rossi, A., Ganassini, A., Tantucci, C., & Grassi, V. (1996). Aging and the respiratory system. *Aging, 8,* 143–161.

Rossouw, J. E., Anderson, G. L., Prentice, R. L., LaCroix, A. Z., Kooperberg, C., Stefanick, M. L., Jackson, R. D., Beresford, S. A., Howard, B. V., Johnson, K. C., Kotchen, J. M. & Ockene, J. (2002). Risks and benefits of estrogen plus progestin in healthy postmenopausal women: Principal results from the women's health initiative randomized controlled trial. *Journal of the American Medical Association, 288,* 321–333.

Rothbaum, F., Weisz, J. R., & Snyder, S. S. (1982). Changing the world and changing the self: A two process model of perceived control. *Journal of Personality and Social Psychology, 42,* 5–37.

Roubenoff, R., & Hughes, V. A. (2000). Sarcopenia: Current concepts. Journals of Gerontology: *Medical Sciences, 55,* M716–M724.

Rounds, J., & Tracey, T. J. (1996). Cross-cultural structural equivalence of RIASEC models and measures. *Journal of Counseling Psychology, 43,* 310–329.

Rowe, J. W., & Kahn, R. L. (1987). Human aging: Usual and successful. *Science, 237,* 143–149.

Rowe, J. W., & Kahn, R. L. (1998). *Successful aging.* New York: Pantheon.

Royall, D. R., Chiodo, L. K., Polk, M. S., & Jaramillo, C. J. (2002). Severe dysosmia is specifically associated with Alzheimer-like memory deficits in nondemented elderly retirees. *Neuroepidemiology, 21,* 68–73.

Rubin, D. C., Rahhal, T. A., & Poon, L. W. (1998). Things learned in early adulthood are remembered best. *Memory and Cognition, 26,* 3–19.

Ruhm, C. J. (1996). Gender differences in employment behavior during late middle age. *Journal of Gerontology: Social Sciences, 51,* S11–S17.

Rusbult, C. E. (1983). A longitudinal test of the investment model: The development (and deterioration) of satisfaction and commitment in heterosexual involvements. *Journal of Personality and Social Psychology, 45,* 101–117.

Ruschena, D., Mullen, P. E., Burgess, P., Cordner, S. M., Barry-Walsh, J., Drummer, O. H., Palmer, S., Browne, C., & Wallace, C. (1998). Sudden death in psychiatric patients. *British Journal of Psychiatry, 172,* 331–336.

Russell-Aulet, M., Dimaraki, E. V., Jaffe, C. A., DeMott-Friberg, R., & Barkan, A. L. (2001). Aging-related growth hormone (GH) decrease is a selective hypothalamic GH-releasing hormone pulse amplitude mediated phenomenon. *Journals of Gerontology: Medical Sciences, 56,* M124–129.

Ryan, E. B., & See, S. K. (1993). Age-based beliefs about memory changes for self and others across adulthood. *Journal of Gerontology: Psychological Sciences, 48,* P199–201.

Ryan, E. B., Hummert, M. L., & Boich, L. H. (1995). Communication predicaments of aging: Patronizing behavior toward older adults. *Journal of Language and Social Psychology, 14,* 144–166.

Rybarczyk, B., Lopez, M., Benson, R., Alsten, C., & Stepanski, E. (2002). Efficacy of two behavioral treatment programs for comorbid geriatric insomnia. *Psychology and Aging, 17,* 288–298.

Ryff, C. D., Lee, Y. H., Essex, M. J., & Schmutte, P. S. (1994). My children and me: Midlife evaluations of grown children and self. *Psychology and Aging, 9,* 195–205.

Ryff, C. D., Marshall, V. W., & Clarke, P. J. (1999). Linking the self and society in social gerontology: Crossing new territory via old questions. In C. D. Ryff & V. W. Marshall (Eds.), *The self and society in aging processes* (pp. 3–41). New York: Springer.

Sable, J. A., & Jeste, D. V. (2002). Antipsychotic treatment for late-life schizophrenia. *Current Psychiatry Reports, 4,* 299–306.

Sacher, G. A. (1977). Life table modification and life prolongation. In C. E. Finch & L. Hayflick (Eds.), *Handbook of the biology of aging* (pp. 582–638). New York: Van Nostrand Reinhold.

Saczynski, J. S., Willis, S. L., & Schaie, K. W. (2002). Strategy use in reasoning training with older adults. *Aging, Neuropsychology, & Cognition., 9,* 48–60.

Sadavoy, J., & LeClair, J. K. (1997). Treatment of anxiety disorders in late life. *Canadian Journal of Psychiatry, 42,* 28–34.

Sagiv, M., Vogelaere, P. P., Soudry, M., & Ehrsam, R. (2000). Role of physical activity training in attenuation of height loss through aging. *Gerontology, 46,* 266–270.

Sahyoun, N. R., Pratt, L. A., Lentzner, H., Dey, A., & Robinson, K. N. (2001). *The changing profile of nursing home residents: 1985–1997. Aging Trends; No. 4.* Hyattsville, Maryland: National Center for Health Statistics.

Salari, S. M., & Rich, M. (2001). Social and environmental infantilization of aged persons: Observations in two adult day care centers. *International Journal of Aging and Human Development, 52*, 115–134.

Salmela-Aro, K., Nurmi, J.-E., Saisto, T., & Halmesmaeki, E. (2001). Goal reconstruction and depressive symptoms during the transition to motherhood: Evidence from two cross-lagged longitudinal studies. *Journal of Personality and Social Psychology, 81*, 1144–1159.

Salmon, D. P., Galasko, D., Hansen, L. A., Masliah, E., Butters, N., Thal, L. J., & Katzman, R. (1996). Neuropsychological deficits associated with diffuse Lewy body disease. *Brain and Cognition, 31*, 148–165.

Salthouse, T. A. (1985). Speed of behavior and its implications for cognition. In J. E. Birren & K. W. Schaie (Eds.), *Handbook of the psychology of aging* (2nd ed., pp. 400–426). New York: Van Nostrand Reinhold.

Salthouse, T. A. (1993). Speed and knowledge as determinants of adult age differences in verbal tasks. *Journal of Gerontology: Psychological sciences, 48*, P29–36.

Salthouse, T. A. (1996). The processing-speed theory of adult age differences in cognition. *Psychological Review, 103*, 403–428.

Salthouse, T. A. (2001). Structural models of the relations between age and measures of cognitive functioning. *Intelligence, 29*, 93–115.

Salthouse, T. A., & Ferrer-Caja, E. (2003). What needs to be explained to account for age-related effects on multiple cognitive variables? *Psychology and Aging, 18*, 91–110.

Salthouse, T. A., & Saults, J. S. (1987). Multiple spans in transcription typing. *Journal of Applied Psychology, 72*, 187–196.

Salzman, C. (1992). *Clinical geriatric psychopharmacology* (2nd ed.). Baltimore: Williams & Wilkins.

Samuels, J., Eaton, W. W., Bienvenu, O. J. I., Brown, C., Costa, P. T., Jr, & Nestadt, G. (2002). Prevalence and correlates of personality disorders in a community sample. *British Journal of Psychiatry, 180*, 536–542.

Sandstrom, N. J., & Williams, C. L. (2001). Memory retention is modulated by acute estradiol and progesterone replacement. *Behavioral Neuroscience*, 384–393.

Sasson, Y., Zohar, J., Chopra, M., Lustig, M., Iancu, I., & Hendler, T. (1997). Epidemiology of obsessive-compulsive disorder: A world view. *Journal of Clinical Psychiatry, 12*, 7–10.

Savikas, M. L. (2002). Reinvigorating the study of careers. *Journal of Vocational Behavior, 61*, 381–385.

Scandura, T. A., & Lankau, M. J. (1997). Relationships of gender, family responsibility and flexible work hours to organizational commitment and job satisfaction. *Journal of Organizational Behavior, 18*, 377–391.

Scarr, S., & McCartney, K. (1983). How people make their own environments: A theory of genotype -> environment effects. *Child Development, 54*, 424–435.

Schacter, D. L., Koutstaal, W., Johnson, M. K., Gross, M. S., & Angell, K. E. (1997). False recollection induced by photographs: A comparison of older and younger adults. *Psychology and Aging, 12*, 203–215.

Schacter, D. L., Norman, K. A., & Koutstaal, W. (1998). The cognitive neuroscience of constructive memory. *Annual Review of Psychology, 49*, 289–318.

Schaie, K. W. (1965). A general model for the study of developmental change. *Psychological Bulletin, 64*, 92–107.

Schaie, K. W. (1983). The Seattle Longitudinal Study: A 21-year exploration of psychometric intelligence in adulthood. In K. W. Schaie (Ed.), *Longitudinal studies of adult psychological development* (pp. 64–135). New York: Guilford.

Schaie, K.W. (1989). The hazards of cognitive aging. *Gerontologist, 29*, 484–493.

Schaie, K. W. (1994). The course of adult intellectual development. *American Psychologist, 49*, 304–313.

Schaie, K. W. (1996). Intellectual development in adulthood. In J. E. Birren, K. W. Schaie, R. P. Abeles, M. Gatz & T. A. Salthouse (Eds.), *Handbook of the psychology of aging* (4th ed., pp. 266–286). San Diego CA: Academic Press.

Schaie, K. W., Dutta, R., & Willis, S. L. (1991). Relationship between rigidity-flexibility and cognitive abilities in adulthood. *Psychology and Aging, 6*, 371–383.

Schaie, K. W., Labouvie, G., & Buech, B. U. (1973). Generational and cohort-specific differences in adult cognitive functioning: A fourteen-year study of independent samples. *Developmental Psychology, 9*, 151–166.

Schaie, K. W., Nguyen, H. T., Willis, S. L., Dutta, R., & Yue, G. A. (2001). Environmental factors as a conceptual framework for examining cognitive performance in Chinese adults. *International Journal of Behavioral Development, 25*, 193–202.

Scharffetter-Kochanek, K., Brenneisen, P., Wenk, J., Herrmann, G., Ma, W., Kuhr, L., Meewes, C., & Wlaschek, M. (2000). Photoaging of the skin from phenotype to mechanisms. *Experimental Gerontology, 35*, 307–316.

Scheff, S. W., Price, D. A., & Sparks, D. L. (2001). Quantitative assessment of possible age-related change in synaptic numbers in the human frontal cortex. *Neurobiology of Aging, 22*, 355–365.

Schirmer, L. L., & Lopez, F. G. (2001). Probing the social support and work strain relationship among adult workers: Contributions of adult attachment orientations. *Journal of Vocational Behavior, 59*, 17–33.

Schoenborn, C. A., Vickerie, J. L., & Barnes, P. M. (2003). *Cigarette smoking behavior of adults: United States, 1997–98*. Hyattsville MD: National Center for Health Statistics.

Schoenborn, C. A., Vickerie, J. L., & Barnes, P. M. (2003). *Cigarette smoking behavior of adults: United States, 1997–98*. Hyattsville, MD: National Center for Health Statistics.

Schooler, C., & Mulatu, M. S. (2001). The reciprocal effects of leisure time activities and intellectual functioning in older people: A longitudinal analysis. *Psychology and Aging, 16*, 466–482.

Schooler, C., Mulatu, M. S., & Oates, G. (1999). The continuing effects of substantively complex work on the intellectual functioning of older workers. *Psychology and Aging, 14*, 483–506.

Schugens, M. M., Daum, I., Spindler, M., & Birbaumer, N. (1997). Differential effects of aging on explicit and implicit memory. *Aging Neuropsychology and Cognition, 4*, 33–44.

Schuit, A. J., Feskens, E. J., Launer, L. J., & Kromhout, D. (2001). Physical activity and cognitive decline, the role of the apolipoprotein e4 allele. *Medicine and Science in Sports and Exercise, 33*, 772–777.

Schulman, C., & Lunenfeld, B. (2002). The ageing male. *World Journal of Urology, 20*, 4–10.

Schultz, S. K., Ellingrod, V. L., Moser, D. J., Kutschner, E., Turvey, C., & Arndt, S. (2002). The influence of cognitive impairment and psychiatric symptoms on daily functioning in nursing facilities: A longitudinal study. *Annals of Clinical Psychiatry, 14*, 209–213.

Schulz, R., Beach, S. R., Lind, B., Martire, L. M., Zdaniuk, B., Hirsch, C., Jackson, S., & Burton, L. (2001). Involvement in caregiving and adjustment to death of a spouse: Findings from the caregiver health effects study. *Journal of the American Medical Association, 285*, 3123–3129.

Schwendner, K. I., Mikesky, A. E., Holt, W. S., Jr., Peacock, M., & Burr, D. B. (1997). Differences in muscle endurance and recovery between fallers and nonfallers, and between young and older women. *Journal of Gerontology: Medical Sciences, 52*, M155–160.

Scialfa, C. T. (200). The role of sensory factors in cognitive aging research. *Canadian Journal of Experimental Psychology, 56*, 153–163.

Scogin, F., Floyd, M., & Forde, J. (2000). Anxiety in older adults. In S. K. Whitbourne (Ed.), *Psychopathology in later life* (pp. 117–140). New York: Wiley.

Scogin, F., Storandt, M., & Lott, L. (1985). Memory-skills training, memory complaints, and depression in older adults. *Journal of Gerontology, 40*, 562–568.

Seaton, K. (1995). Cortisol: The aging hormone, the stupid hormone. *Journal of the National Medical Association, 87*, 667–683.

Seccombe, K., & Lee, G. R. (1986). Gender differences in retirement satisfaction and its antecedents. *Research on Aging, 8*, 426–440.

Seddon, J. M., Rosner, B., Sperduto, R. D., Yannuzzi, L., Haller, J. A., Blair, N. P., & Willett, W. (2001). Dietary fat and risk for advanced age-related macular degeneration. *Archives of Ophthalmology, 119*, 1191–1199.

Seeman, T. E., McEwen, B. S., Singer, B. H., Albert, M. S., & Rowe, J. W. (1997). Increase in urinary cortisol excretion and memory declines: MacArthur studies of successful aging. *Journal of Clinical Endocrinology and Metabolism, 82*, 2458–2465.

Seeman, T. E., Singer, B., Wilkinson, C. W., & McEwen, B. (2001). Gender differences in age-related changes in HPA axis reactivity. *Psychoneuroendocrinology, 26*, 225–240.

Seeman, T., & Chen, X. (2002). Risk and protective factors for physical functioning in older adults with and without chronic conditions: MacArthur studies of successful aging. *Journals of Gerontology: Series B: Psychological Sciences & Social Sciences, 57*, S135–144.

Segal, D. L., Coolidge, F. L., & Rosowsky, E. (2000). Personality disorders. In S. K. Whitbourne (Ed.), *Psychopathology in later life* (pp. 89–116). New York: Wiley.

Segal, D. L., Hook, J. N., & Coolidge, F. L. (2001). Personality dysfunction, coping styles, and clinical symptoms in younger and older adults. *Journal of Clinical Geropsychology, 7*, 201–212.

Segal, D. L., Kabacoff, R. I., Hersen, M., Van Hasselt, V. B., & Ryan, C. F. (1995). Update on the reliability of diagnosis in older psychiatric outpatients using the Structured Clinical Interview for DSM-III-R. *Journal of Clinical Geropsychology, 1*, 313–321.

Seibert, S. E., & Kraimer, M. L. (2001). The Five-Factor Model of personality and career success. *Journal of Vocational Behavior, 58*, 1–21.

Seidman, S. N., Araujo, A. B., Roose, S. P., Devanand, D. P., Xie, S., Cooper, T. B., & McKinlay, J. B. (2002). Low testosterone levels in elderly men with dysthymic disorder. *American Journal of Psychiatry, 159*, 456–459.

Selling to seniors. (1999). *Monthly Report on Marketing*.

Semple, S. J., Patterson, T. L., Shaw, W. S., Grant, I., Moscona, S., & Jeste, D. V. (1999). Self-perceived interpersonal competence in older schizophrenia patients: The role of patient characteristics and psychosocial factors. *Acta Psychiatrica Scandinavica, 100*, 126–135.

Shadden, B. B. (1997). Discourse behaviors in older adults. *Seminars in Speech and Language, 18*, 143–156.

Shapiro, A. (2003). Later-life divorce and parent-adult child conduct and proximity: A longitudinal analysis. *Journal of Family Issues, 24*, 264–285.

Sharps, M. J., & Martin, S. S. (1998). Spatial memory in young and older adults: Environmental support and contextual influences at encoding and retrieval. *Journal of Genetic Psychology, 159*, 5–12.

Sharpsteen, D. J., & Kirkpatrick, L. A. (1997). Romantic jealousy and adult romantic attachment. *Journal of Personality and Social Psychology, 72*, 627–640.

Sheehy, G. (1974). *Passages: Predictable passages of adult life.* New York: Dutton.

Sheline, Y. I., Mintun, M. A., Moerlein, S. M., & Snyder, A. Z. (2002). Greater loss of 5-HT(2A) receptors in midlife than in late life. *American Journal of Psychiatry, 159*, 430–435.

Shephard, R. J. (1999). Age and physical work capacity. *Experimental Aging Research, 25*, 331–343.

Sherrington, R., Froelich, S., Sorbi, S., Campion, D., Chi, H., Rogaeva, E. A., Levesque, G., Rogaev, E. I., Lin, C., Liang, Y., Ikeda, M., Mar, L., Brice, A., Agid, Y., Percy, M. E., Clerget-Darpoux, F., Piacentini, S., Marcon, G., Nacmias, B., Amaducci, L., Frebourg, T., Lannfelt, L., Rommens, J. M., & St George-Hyslop, P. H. (1996). Alzheimer's disease associated with mutations in presenilin 2 is rare and variably penetrant. *Human Molecular Genetics, 5*, 985–988.

Shimokata, H., & Kuzuyam, F. (1995). Two-point discrimination test of the skin as an index of sensory aging. *Gerontology, 41*, 267–272.

Ship, J. A., Nolan, N. E., & Puckett, S. A. (1995). Longitudinal analysis of parotid and submandibular salivary flow rates in healthy, different-aged adults. *Journal of Gerontology: Medical Sciences, 50A*, M285–289.

Shumaker, S. A., Legault, C., Rapp, S. R., Thal, L., Wallace, R. B., Ockene, J. K., Hendrix, S. L., Jones, B. N., 3rd, Assaf, A. R., Jackson, R. D., Kotchen, J. M., Wassertheirl-Smoller, S., & Wactawski-Wende, J. (2003). Estrogen plus progestin and the incidence of dementia and mild cognitive impairment in postmenopausal women. The women's health initiative memory study: A randomized controlled trial. *Journal of the American Medical Association, 289*, 2651–2662.

Siebert, D. C., Mutran, E. J., & Reitzes, D. C. (2002). Friendship and social support: The importance of role identity to aging adults. *Social Work, 44*, 522–533.

Siegler, I. C., Bastian, L. A., Steffens, D. C., Bosworth, H. B., & Costa, P. T. (2002). Behavioral medicine and aging. *Journal of Consulting and Clinical Psychology, 70*, 843–851.

Siegler, I. C., George, L. K., & Okun, M. A. (1979). Cross-sequential analysis of adult personality. *Developmental Psychology, 15*, 350–351.

Silverstein, M., & Bengtson, V. L. (1997). Intergenerational solidarity and the structure of adult child-parent relationships in American families. *American Journal of Sociology, 103*, 429–460.

Silverstein, M., & Parker, M. G. (2002). Leisure activities and quality of life among the oldest old in Sweden. *Research on Aging, 24*, 528–547.

Silverstein, M., Conroy, S. J., Wang, H., Giarrusso, R., & Bengtson, V. L. (2002). Reciprocity in parent–child relations over the adult life course. *Journals of Gerontology: Series B: Psychological Sciences & Social Sciences, 57*, S3–13.

Simensky, J. D., & Abeles, N. (2002). Decline in verbal memory performance with advancing age: The role of frontal lobe functioning. *Aging & Mental Health, 6*, 293–303.

Simmons, V., & Hansen, P. D. (1996). Effectiveness of water exercise on postural mobility in the well elderly: An experimental study on balance enhancement. *Journal of Gerontology: Medical Sciences, 51*, M233–238.

Simon, R. (1995). Too damn old. *Money, 25* (7), 118–126.

Simonton, D. K. (1984). Creative productivity and age: A mathematical model based on a two-step cognitive process. *Developmental Review, 4*, 77–111.

Simonton, D. K. (1988). Age and outstanding achievement: What do we know after a century of research? *Psychological Bulletin, 104*, 251–267.

Simonton, D. K. (1989). The swan-song phenomenon: Last-works effects for 172 classical composers. *Psychology and Aging, 4*, 42–47.

Simonton, D. K. (1997). Creative productivity: A predictive and explanatory model of career trajectories and landmarks. *Psychological Review, 104*, 66–89.

Simonton, D. K. (1998a). Achieved eminence in minority and majority cultures: Convergence versus divergence in the assessments of 294 African Americans. *Journal of Personality and Social Psychology, 74*, 804–817.

Simonton, D. K. (1998b). Career paths and creative lives: A theoretical perspective on late-life potential. In C. Adams-Price (Ed.), *Creativity and successful aging: Theoretical and empirical approaches* (pp. 3–18). New York: Springer.

Simonton, D. K. (1999). Personal communication.

Simpson, J. A., & Rholes, W. S. (2002). Attachment orientations, marriage, and the transition to parenthood. *Journal of Research in Personality, 36*, 622–628.

Sinaki, M. (1996). Effect of physical activity on bone mass. *Current Opinions in Rheumatology, 8*, 376–383.

Sinnott, J. D. (1989). A model for solution of ill-structured problems: Implications for everyday and abstract problem-solving. In J. D. Sinnott (Ed.), *Everyday problem solving: Theory and applications* (pp. 72–99). New York: Praeger.

Sinnott, J. D. (1998). Career paths and creative lives: A theoretical perspective on late-life potential. In C. Adams-Price (Ed.), *Creativity and successful aging: Theoretical and empirical approaches* (pp. 43–72). New York: Springer.

Skinner, B. F., & Vaughan, M. E. (1983). *Enjoy old age: A practical guide.* New York: Norton.

Skultety, K., & Whitbourne, S. K. (in press). Gender differences in identity processes. *Journal of Women and Aging.*

Sliwinksi, M. J., & Hall, C. B. (1998). Constraints on general slowing: a meta-analysis using hierarchical linear models with random coefficients. *Psychology and Aging, 13,* 164–175.

Sloane, P. D., Mitchell, C. M., Weisman, G., Zimmerman, S., Foley, K. M., Lynn, M. Calkins, M., Lawton, M. P., Teresi, J., Grant, L., Lindeman, D., & Montgomery, R. (2002). The Therapeutic Environment Screening Survey for Nursing Homes (TESS-NH): An observational instrument for assessing the physical environment of institutional settings for persons with dementia. *Journals of Gerontology Series B: Psychological Sciences and Social Sciences, 57,* S69–78.

Smart, R., & Peterson, C. (1997). Super's career stages and the decision to change careers. *Journal of Vocational Behavior, 51,* 358–374.

Smith, A. D. (1996). Memory. In J. E. Birren, K. W. Schaie, R. P. Abeles, M. Gatz & T. A. Salthouse (Eds.), *Handbook of the psychology of aging* (4th ed., pp. 236–250). San Diego, CA: Academic Press.

Smith, J., & Freund, A. M. (2002). The dynamics of possible selves in old age. *Journals of Gerontology: Series B: Psychological Sciences & Social Sciences, 57,* P492–500.

Smith, S. C., Jr., Blair, S. N., Bonow, R. O., Brass, L. M., Cerqueira, M. D., Dracup, K., Fuster, V., Gotto, A., Grundy, S. M., Miller, N. H., Jacobs, A., Jones, D., Krauss, R. M., Mosca, L., Ockene, I., Pasternak, R. C., Pearson, T., Pfeffer, M. A., Starke, R. D., & Taubert, K. A. (2001). AHA/ACC Scientific Statement: AHA/ACC guidelines for preventing heart attack and death in patients with atherosclerotic cardiovascular disease: 2001 update: A statement for healthcare professionals from the American Heart Association and the American College of Cardiology. *Circulation, 104,* 1577–1579.

Smits, C. H., Smit, J. H., van den Heuvel, N., & Jonker, C. (1997). Norms for an abbreviated Raven's Coloured Progressive Matrices in an older sample. *Journal of Clinical Psychology, 53,* 687–697.

Sneed, J. R. & Whitbourne, S. K. (2003). Identity processing and self-consciousness in middle and later adulthood. *Journals of Gerontology, Psychological Sciences,* 58B, p313–319.

Sneed, J. R., & Whitbourne, S. K. (2001). Identity processing styles and the need for self-esteem in middle-aged and older adults. *International Journal of Aging and Human Development, 52,* 311–321.

Snowdon, D. (2001). *Aging with grace: What the Nun Study teaches us about leading longer, healthier, and more meaningful lives.* New York: Bantam Books.

Soares, C. N., & Cohen, L. S. (2001). The perimenopause, depressive disorders, and hormonal variability. *Sao Paulo Medical Journal, 119,* 78–83.

Social Security Administration (2002). Fast facts and figures about Social Security. Washington, D.C., Social Security Administration.

Sohal, R. S. (2002). Role of oxidative stress and protein oxidation in the aging process. *Free Radical Biology and Medicine, 33,* 37–44.

Sohal, R. S., Mockett, R. J., & Orr, W. C. (2002). Mechanisms of aging: An appraisal of the oxidative stress hypothesis. *Free Radical Biology and Medicine, 33,* 575–586.

Solano, N. H., & Whitbourne, S. K. (2001). Coping with schizophrenia: Patterns in later adulthood. *International Journal of Aging and Human Development, 53,* 1–10.

Soldz, S., & Vaillant, G. E. (1999). The Big Five personality traits and the life course: A 45-year longitudinal study. *Journal of Research in Personality, 33,* 208–232.

Solomon, S., Greenberg, J. & Pyszczynski, T. (1991). In. (1991). A terror management theory of social behavior: The psychological functions of self-esteem and cultural worldviews. In M. P. Zanna (Ed.), *Advances in experimental social psychology* (Vol. 24, pp. 93–159). Orlando, FL: Academic Press.

Somberg, B. L., & Salthouse, T. A. (1982). Divided attention abilities in young and old adults. *Journal of Experimental Psychology: Human Perception and Performance, 8,* 651–663.

Sone, Y. (1995). Age-associated problems in nutrition. *Applied Human Science, 14,* 201–210.

Sonnenberg, C. M., Beekman, A. T., Deeg, D. J., & Van Tilburg, W. (2003). Drug treatment in depressed elderly in the Dutch community. *International Journal of Geriatric Psychiatry, 18,* 99–104.

Sothmann, M. S., Landy, F., & Saupe, K. (1992). Age as a bona fide occupational qualification for firefighting. *Journal of Occupational Medicine, 34,* 26–33.

Spearman, C. (1904). "General intelligence:" Objectively determined and measured. *American Journal of Psychology, 15,* 201–292.

Spearman, C. (1927). *The abilities of man.* New York: Macmillan.

Speilberger, C., Gorsuch, R. C., & Lushene, R. E. (1970). *Manual for the State-Trait Anxiety Inventory.* Palo Alto, CA: Consulting Psychologists Press.

Spiro, A., Schnurr, P. P., & Aldwin, C. M. (1994). Combat-related posttraumatic stress disorder symptoms in older men. *Psychology and Aging, 9*, 17–26.

Sprecher, S. (1988). Investment model, equity, and social support determinants of relationship commitment. *Social Psychology Quarterly, 51*, 318–328.

Squire, L. R. (1989). On the course of forgetting in very long term memory. *Journal of Experimental Psychology: Learning, Memory, and Cognition, 15*, 241–245.

Stallings, M. C., Dunham, C. C., Gatz, M., Baker, L. A., & Bengtson, V. L. (1997). Relationships among life events and psychological well-being: More evidence for a two-factor theory of well-being. *Journal of Applied Gerontology, 16*, 104–119.

Stanley, M. A., Beck, J. G., Novy, D. M., Averill, P. M., Swann, A. C., Diefenbach, G. J., & Hopko, D. R. (2003). Cognitive-behavioral treatment of late-life generalized anxiety disorder. *Journal of Consulting & Clinical Psychology, 71*, 309–319.

Starr, B. D. (1985). Sexuality and aging. In M. P. Lawton & G. L. Maddox (Eds.), *Annual Review of Gerontolgoy and Geriatrics* (Vol. 5, pp. 97–126). New York: Springer.

Starr, B. D., & Weiner, M. B. (1981). *The Starr-Weiner report on sex and sexuality in the mature years.* New York: McGraw-Hill.

Staudinger, U. M., Marsiske, M., & Baltes, P. B. (1995). Resilience and reserve capacity in later adulthood: Potentials and limits of development across the life span. In D. Cicchetti & D. J. Cohen (Eds.), *Developmental psychopathology* (Vol. 2: Risk, disorder, and adaptation, pp. 801–847). New York: Wiley.

Staudinger, U. M., Smith, J., & Baltes, P. B. (1993). Wisdom-related knowledge in a life review task: age differences and role of professional specialization. *Psychology and Aging, 7*, 271–281.

Stebbins, G. T., Carrillo, M. C., Dorfman, J., Dirksen, C., Desmond, J. E., Turner, D. A., Bennett, D. A., Wilson, R. S., Glover, G., & Gabrieli, J. D. E. (2002). Aging effects on memory encoding in the frontal lobes. *Psychology and Aging, 17*, 44–55.

Steen, G., Berg, S., & Steen, B. (1998). Cognitive function in 70-year-old men and women. A 16-year cohort difference population study. *Aging, 10*, 120–126.

Stengel, B., Couchoud, C., Cenee, S., & Hemon, D. (2000). Age, blood pressure and smoking effects on chronic renal failure in primary glomerular nephropathies. *Kidney International, 57*, 2519–2526.

Sternberg, R. J. (1985). *Beyond IQ: A triarchic theory of human intelligence.* New York: Cambridge University Press.

Sternberg, R. J. (1998). A balance theory of wisdom. *Review of General Psychology, 3*, 347–365.

Sternberg, R. J. (1999). The theory of successful intelligence. *Review of General Psychology, 3*, 292–316.

Sterns, H. L., & Gray, J. H. (1999). Work, leisure, and retirement. In J. C. Cavanaugh & S. K. Whitbourne (Eds.), *Gerontology: Interdisciplinary perspectives* (pp. 355–390). New York: Oxford University Press.

Sterns, H. L., & Miklos, S. M. (1995). The aging worker in a changing environment: Organizational and individual issues. *Journal of Vocational Behavior, 47*, 248–268.

Stevens, J. C., & Cruz, L. A. (1996). Spatial acuity of touch: Ubiquitous decline with aging revealed by repeated threshold testing. *Somatosensory and Motor Research, 13*, 1–10.

Stewart, S. A., & Weinberg, R. A. (2002). Senescence: does it all happen at the ends? *Oncogene, 21*, 627–630.

Stewart, W. F., Kawas, C., Corrada, M., & Metter, E. J. (1997). Risk of Alzheimer's disease and duration of NSAID use. *Neurology, 48*, 626–632.

Stine-Morrow, E. A. L., & Miller, L. M. S. (1999). Basic cognitive processes. In J. C. Cavanaugh & S. K. Whitbourne (Eds.), *Gerontology: Interdisciplinary perspectives* (pp. 186–212). New York: Oxford University Press.

Stine-Morrow, E. A., Milinder, L., Pullara, O., & Herman, B. (2001). Patterns of resource allocation are reliable among younger and older readers. *Psychology and Aging, 16*, 69–84.

Stocker, C. M., Lanthier, R. P., & Furman, W. (1997). Sibling relationships in early adulthood. *Journal of Family Psychology, 11*, 210–221.

Strain, L. A., Grabusic, C. C., Searle, M. S., & Dunn, N. J. (2002). Continuing and ceasing leisure activities in later life: A longitudinal study. *Gerontologist, 42*, 217–223.

Stroebe, M. (2001). Gender differences in adjustment to bereavement: An empirical and theoretical review. *Review of General Psychology, 5*, 62–83.

Stroebe, M. S., Stroebe, W., Gergen, K. J., & Gergen, M. (1981). The broken heart: Reality or myth. *Omega, 12*, 87–105.

Stroebe, M., & Schut, H. (1999). The dual process model of coping with bereavement: Rationale and description. *Death Studies, 23*, 197–224.

Stroebe, M., Gergen, M. M., Gergen, K. J., & Stroebe, W. (1992). Broken hearts or broken bonds: Love and death in historical perspective. *American Psychologist., 47*, 1205–1212.

Stroebe, W., & Stroebe, M. S. (1987). *Bereavement and health: The psychological and physical consequences of partner loss.* Cambridge, UK: Cambridge University Press.

Stroebe, W., Stroebe, M. S., & Abakoumkin, G. (1999). Does differential social support cause sex differences in bereavement outcome? *Journal of Community and Applied Social Psychology, 9*, 1–12.

Stroebe, W., Stroebe, M., Abakoumkin, G., & Schut, H. (1996). The role of loneliness and social support in adjustment to loss: A test of attachment versus stress theory. *Journal of Personality and Social Psychology, 70,* 1241–1249.

Substance Abuse and Mental Health Services Administration (2002). *National Household Survey of Drug Abuse Report.* Rockville, MD: SAMHSA, Office of Applied Studies.

Suh, E., Diener, E., & Fujita, F. (1996). Events and subjective well-being: Only recent events matter. *Journal of Personality and Social Psychology, 70,* 1091–1102.

Suitor, J. J., & Pillemer, K. (1988). Explaining intergenerational conflict when adult children and elderly parents live together. *Journal of Marriage and the Family, 50,* 1037–1047.

Sullivan, M. D. (2002). The illusion of patient choice in end-of-life decisions. *American Journal of Geriatric Psychiatry, 10,* 365–372.

Super, D. E. (1957). *The psychology of careers.* New York: Harper.

Super, D. E. (1990). A life span, life-space approach to career development. In D. Brown & L. Brooks (Eds.), *Career choice and development* (2nd ed.). San Francisco: Jossey-Bass.

Swick, D., & Knight, R. T. (1997). Event-related potentials differentiate the effects of aging on word and nonword repetition in explicit and implicit memory tasks. *Journal of Experimental Psychology: Learning, Memory, and Cognition, 23,* 123–142.

Szinovacz, M. E. (1987). Preferred retirement timing and retirement satisfaction in women. *International Journal of Aging & Human Development, 24,* 301–317.

Szinovacz, M. E., DeViney, S., & Davey, A. (2002). Influences of family obligations and relationships on retirement: Variations by gender, race, and marital status. *Journals of Gerontology: Series B: Psychological Sciences & Social Sciences, 56B,* S20-S27.

Szinovacz, M., & Washo, C. (1992). Gender differences in exposure to life events and adaptation to retirement. *Journal of Gerontology: Social Sciences, 47,* S191–S196.

Taaffe, D. R., & Marcus, R. (1997). Dynamic muscle strength alterations to detraining and retraining in elderly men. *Clinical Physiology, 17,* 311–324.

Takema, Y., Yorimoto, Y., Ohsu, H., Osanai, O., & Kawai, M. (1997). Age-related discontinuous changes in the in vivo fluorescence of human facial skin. *Journal of Dermatological Science, 15,* 55–58.

Talaga, J. A., & Beehr, T. A. (1995). Are there gender differences in predicting retirement decisions? *Journal of Applied Psychology, 80,* 16-28.

Tanaka, H., DeSouza, C. A., & Seals, D. R. (1998). Absence of age-related increase in central arterial stiffness in physically active women. *Arteriosclerosis, Thrombosis and Vascular Biology, 18,* 127–132.

Tanaka, H., Seals, D. R., Monahan, K. D., Clevenger, C. M., DeSouza, C. A., & Dinenno, F. A. (2002). Regular aerobic exercise and the age-related increase in carotid artery intima-media thickness in healthy men. *Journal of Applied Physiology, 92,* 1458–1464.

Tang, M.-X., Stern, Y., Marker, K., Bell, K., Gurland, B., Lantigua, R., Andrews, H., Feng, L., Tycko, B., & Mayeux, R. (1998). The APOE-epsilon 4 allele and the risk of Alzheimer disease among African Americans, Whites, and Hispanics. *Journal of the American Medical Association, 279,* 751–755.

Tangri, S. S. (1972). Determinants of occupational role-innovation among college women. *Journal of Social Issues, 28,* 177–200.

Tankersley, C. G., Smolander, J., Kenney, W. L., & Fortney, S. M. (1991). Sweating and skin blood flow during exercise: Effects of age and maximal oxygen uptake. *Journal of Applied Physiology, 71,* 236–242.

Tanzi, R. E., Kovacs, D. M., Kim, T.-W., Moir, R. D., Guenette, S. Y., & Wasco, W. (1996). The presenilin genes and their role in early-onset familial Alzheimer's disease. *Alzheimer's Disease Review, 1,* 91–98.

Tariot, P. N., Farlow, M. R., Grossberg, G. T., Graham, S. M., McDonald, S. M., & Gergel, I. (2004). Memantine treatment in patients with moderate to severe Alzheimer Disease already receiving donepezil. *Journal of the American Medical Association, 291,* 317–324.

Taylor, M. (2001). Psychological consequences of surgical menopause. *Journal of Reproductive Medicine, 46,* 317–324.

Taylor, R. J., & Chatters, L. M. (1991). Non-organizational religious participation among elderly Blacks. *Journal of Gerontology: Social Sciences, 46,* 103–111.

Tekcan, A. I., & Peynircioglu, Z. F. (2002). Effects of age on flashbulb memories. *Psychology and Aging, 17,* 416–422.

Teno, J., Lynn, J., Connors, A. F., Jr., Wenger, N., Phillips, R. S., Alzola, C., Murphy, D. P., Desbiens, N., & Knaus, W. A. (1997). The illusion of end-of-life resource savings with advance directives. SUPPORT Investigators. Study to Understand Prognoses and Preferences for Outcomes and Risks of Treatment. *Journal of the American Geriatrics Society, 45,* 513–518.

Tenover, J. L. (2000). Experience with testosterone replacement in the elderly. *Mayo Clinics Proceedings, 75 Suppl,* S77–81.

Tentori, K., Osherson, D., Hasher, L., & May, C. (2001). Wisdom and aging: Irrational preferences in college students but not older adults. *Cognition, 81,* B87–96.

Teramoto, S., Fukuchi, Y., Nagase, T., Matsuse, T., & Orimo, H. (1995). A comparison of ventilation components in young and elderly men during exercise. *Journal of Gerontology: Biological Sciences, 50A,* B34–39.

Teri, L. (1994). Behavioral treatment of depression in patients with dementia. *Alzheimer's Disease and Associated Disorders, 8,* 66–74.

Thelen, D. G., Schultz, A. B., Alexander, N. B., & Ashton-Miller, J. A. (1996). Effects of age on rapid ankle torque development. *Journal of Gerontology: Medical Sciences, 51,* M226–232.

Thibaut, J. W., & Kelley, H. H. (1959). *The social psychology of groups.* New York: Wiley.

Thomas, G., Fletcher, G. J. O., & Lange, C. (1997). On-line empathic accuracy in marital interaction. *Journal of Personality and Social Psychology, 72,* 839–850.

Thompson, L. W., Coon, D. W., Gallagher-Thompson, D., Sommer, B. R., & Koin, D. (2001). Comparison of desipramine and cognitive/behavioral therapy in the treatment of elderly outpatients with mild-to-moderate depression. *American Journal of Geriatric Psychiatry, 9,* 225–240.

Thompson, L. W., Gallagher-Thompson, D., Futterman, A., Gilewski, M. J., & Peterson, J. (1991). The effects of late-life spousal bereavement over a 30-month interval. *Psychology and Aging, 6,* 434–441.

Thurstone, L. L. (1938). *Primary mental abilities.* Chicago: University of Chicago Press.

Tinetti, M. E., Baker, D., Gallo, W. T., Nanda, A., Charpentier, P., & O'Leary, J. (2002). Evaluation of restorative care vs. usual care for older adults receiving an acute episode of home care. *Journal of the American Medical Association, 287,* 2098–2105.

Tinetti, M. E., Mendes de Leon, C. F., Doucette, J. T., & Baker, D. I. (1994). Fear of falling and fall-related efficacy in relationship to functioning among community-living elders. *Journal of Gerontology, 49,* M140–147.

Tipper, S. (1985). The negative priming effect: Inhibitory priming by ignored objects. *The Quarterly Journal of Experimental Psychology, 37,* 571–590.

Tominaga, K., Olgun, A., Smith, J. R., & Pereira-Smith, O. M. (2002). Genetics of cellular senescence. *Mechanisms of Ageing and Development, 123,* 927–936.

Toogood, A. A., O'Neill, P., & Shalet, S. M. (1996). Beyond the somatopause: Growth hormone deficiency in adults over the age of 60 years. *Journal of Clinical Endocrinology and Metabolism, 81,* 460–465.

Touitou, Y. (2001). Human aging and melatonin. Clinical relevance. *Experimental Gerontology, 36,* 1083–1100.

Townsend, A. L., & Franks, M. M. (1995). Binding ties: Closeness and conflict in adult children's caregiving relationships. *Psychology and Aging, 10,* 343–351.

Travis, S. S., Bernard, M., Dixon, S., McAuley, W. J., Loving, G., & McClanahan, L. (2002). Obstacles to palliation and end-of-life care in a long-term care facility. *Gerontologist, 42,* 342–349.

Troll, L. E. (1985). The contingencies of grandparenting. In V. L. Bengston & J. F. Robertson (Eds.), *Grandparenthood* (pp. 135–149). Beverly Hills, CA: Sage.

Tsevat, J., Dawson, N. V., Wu, A. W., Lynn, J., Soukup, J. R., Cook, E. F., Vidaillet, H., & Phillips, R. S. (1998). Health values of hospitalized patients 80 years or older. HELP Investigators. Hospitalized Elderly Longitudinal Project. *Journal of the American Medical Association, 279,* 371–375.

Tsuji, I., Tamagawa, A., Nagatomi, R., Irie, N., Ohkubo, T., Saito, M., Fujita, K., Ogawa, K., Sauvaget, C., Anzai, Y., Hozawa, A., Watanabe, Y., Sato, A., Ohmori, H., & Hisamichi, S., (2000). Randomized controlled trial of exercise training for older people (Sendai Silver Center Trial; SSCT): Study design and primary outcome. *Journal of Epidemiology, 10,* 55–64.

Tucker, P., Pfefferbaum, B., Nixon, S. J., & Foy, D. W. (1999). Trauma and recovery among adults highly exposed to a community disaster. *Psychiatric Annals, 29,* 78–83.

Tuite, D. J., Renstrom, P. A., & O'Brien, M. (1997). The aging tendon. *Scandinavian Journal of Medicine and Science in Sports, 7,* 72–77.

Tun, P. A., & Wingfield, A. (1997). Language and communication: Fundamentals of speech communication and language processing in old age. In A. D. Fisk & W. A. Rogers (Eds.), *Handbook of human factors and the older adult* (pp. 125–149). San Diego: Academic Press.

Turner, M. J., Spina, R. J., Kohrt, W. M., & Ehsani, A. A. (2000). Effect of endurance exercise training on left ventricular size and remodeling in older adults with hypertension. *Journals of Gerontology Series A: Medical Sciences, 55,* M245–251.

Turvey, C. L., Conwell, Y., Jones, M. P., Phillips, C., Simonsick, E., Pearson, J. L., & Wallace, R. (2002). Risk factors for late-life suicide: A prospective, community-based study. *American Journal of Geriatric Psychiatry, 10,* 398–406.

U.S. Bureau of the Census (1998). *Statistical abstract of the United States.* Washington, DC: U.S. Bureau of the Census.

U.S. Bureau of the Census (2000). Population Projections of the United States by Age, Sex, Race, Hispanic Origin, and Nativity: 1999 to 2100; published January 2000.

U.S. Bureau of the Census (2000a). Percent of High School and College Graduates of the Population 15 Years and Over, by Age, Sex, Race, and Hispanic Origin: March 2000. http://www.census.gov/population/socdemo/education/p20-536/tab01a.txt. Accessed 1/23/04.

U.S. Bureau of the Census (2001a). AD-1. Young Adults Living At Home: 1960 to Present.

U.S. Bureau of the Census (2001a, June 29). *Marital status of the population 15 years old and over, by sex and race: 1950 to present.* Retrieved 3/29/02, from http://www.census.gov/population/socdemo/hh-fam/tabMS-1.txt

U.S. Bureau of the Census (2001b). CH-7. Grandchildren Living in the Home of Their Grandparents: 1970 to Present.

U.S. Bureau of the Census (2001b). *Profiles of General Demographic Characteristics: 2000 Census of Population and Housing, United States.* Washington, DC: U.S. Census Bureau.

U.S. Bureau of the Census (2001c). Families and Living Arrangements.

U.S. Bureau of the Census (2001d). Table MS-2. Estimated Median Age at First Marriage, by Sex: 1890 to the Present.

U.S. Bureau of the Census (2001e). Projections of the Total Resident Population by 5-year Age Groups, and Sex with Special Age Categories: Middle Series, 2050-2070.

U.S. Bureau of the Census (2003a). *Statistical abstract of the United States.* Washington, DC: U.S. Bureau of the Census.

U.S. Bureau of the Census (2003b). Table PINC-01. Selected Characteristics of People 15 Years and Over, by Total Money Income in 2001, Work Experience in 2001, Race, Hispanic Origin, and Sex.

U.S. Department of Health and Human Services (1999). *Mental health: A report of the Surgeon General.* Bethesda, MD: U.S. Public Health Service.

Uchino, B. N., Cacioppo, J. T., & Kiecolt-Glaser, J. K. (1996). The relationship between social support and physiological processes: A review with emphasis on underlying mechanisms and implications for health. *Psychological Bulletin, 119,* 488–531.

Uitti, R. J., Wharen, R. E., Jr., Turk, M. F., Lucas, J. A., Finton, M. J., Graff-Radford, N. R., Boylan, K. B., Goerss, S. J., Kall, B. A., Adler, C. H., Caviness, J. N., & Atkinson, E. J. (1997). Unilateral pallidotomy for Parkinson's disease: Comparison of outcome in younger versus elderly patients. *Neurology, 49,* 1072–1077.

Umberson, D. (1995). Marriage as support or strain: Marital quality following the death of a parent. *Journal of Marriage and the Family, 57,* 709–723.

Umberson, D., & Chen, M. D. (1994). Effects of a parent's death on adult children: Relationship salience and reaction to loss. *American Sociological Review, 59,* 152–168.

United Nations (2002). *Population ageing 2002.* Retrieved August 2003, from http://www.un.org/esa/population/publications/ageing/Graph.pdf

United States Cancer Statistics Working Group (2002). *United States Cancer Statistics: 1999 Incidence.* Atlanta, GA: Centers for Disease Control and Prevention and National Cancer Institute.

Vaillant, C. O., & Vaillant, G. E. (1993). Is the U-curve of marital satisfaction an illusion? A 40-year study of marriage. *Journal of Marriage and the Family, 55,* 230–239.

Vaillant, G. E. (1977). *Adaptation to life.* Boston: Little, Brown.

Vaillant, G. E. (1993). *The wisdom of the ego.* Cambridge MA: Harvard University Press.

Vaillant, G. E. (2000). Adaptive mental mechanisms: Their role in a positive psychology. *American Psychologist, 55,* 89–98.

Vaillant, G. E., & Western, R. J. (2001). Healthy aging among inner-city men. *International Psychogeriatrics, 13,* 425–437.

Vakil, E., & Agmon-Ashkenazi, D. (1997). Baseline performance and learning rate of procedural and declarative memory tasks: Younger versus older adults. *Journal of Gerontology: Psychological Sciences and Social Sciences, 52,* 229–234.

van Boxtel, M. P., Paas, F. G., Houx, P. J., Adam, J. J., Teeken, J. C., & Jolles, J. (1997). Aerobic capacity and cognitive performance in a cross-sectional aging study. *Medicine and Science in Sports and Exercise, 29,* 1357–1365.

Van Cauter, E., Leproult, R., & Kupfer, D. J. (1996). Effects of gender and age on the levels and circadian rhythmicity of plasma cortisol. *Journal of Clinical Endocrinology and Metabolism, 81,* 2468–2473.

van den Beld, A. W., & Lamberts, S. W. (2002). Endocrine aspects of healthy ageing in men. *Novartis Foundation Symposium, 242,* 3–16; discussion 16–25.

van den Beld, A. W., Bots, M. L., Janssen, J. A., Pols, H. A., Lamberts, S. W., & Grobbee, D. E. (2003). Endogenous hormones and carotid atherosclerosis in elderly men. *American Journal of Epidemiology, 157,* 25–31.

van den Beld, A. W., de Jong, F. H., Grobbee, D. E., Pols, H. A., & Lamberts, S. W. (2000). Measures of bioavailable serum testosterone and estradiol and their relationships with muscle strength, bone density, and body composition in elderly men. *Journal of Clinical Endocrinology and Metabolism, 85,* 3276–3282.

Van Manen, K.-J., & Whitbourne, S. K. (1997). Psychosocial development and life experiences in adulthood: A 22-year sequential study. *Psychology and Aging, 12,* 239–246.

Van Ness, P. H., & Larson, D. B. (2002). Religion, senescence, and mental health: The end of life is not the end of hope. *American Journal of Geriatric Psychiatry, 10*(4), 386–397.

Van Someren, E. J., Lijzenga, C., Mirmiran, M., & Swaab, D. F. (1997). Long-term fitness training improves the circadian rest-activity rhythm in healthy elderly males. *Journal of Biological Rhythms, 12,* 146–156.

van Zelst, W., de Beurs, E., & Smit, J. H. (2003). Effects of the September 11th attacks on symptoms of PTSD on community-dwelling older persons in the Netherlands. *International Journal of Geriatric Psychiatry, 18,* p. 190.

Vandewater, E. A., Ostrove, J. M., & Stewart, A. J. (1997). Predicting women's well-being in midlife: The importance of personality development and social role involvements. *Journal of Personality and Social Psychology, 72,* 1147–1160.

Vanhanen, M., Koivisto, K., Kuusisto, J., Mykkanen, L., Helkala, E. L., Hanninen, T., Riekkinen, P., Sr., Soininen, H., & Laakso, M. (1998). Cognitive function in an elderly population with persistent impaired glucose tolerance. *Diabetes Care, 21*, 398–402.

Varani, J., Warner, R. L., Gharaee-Kermani, M., Phan, S. H., Kang, S., Chung, J. H., Wang, Z. Q., Datta, S. C., Fisher, G. J., & Voorhees, J. J. (2000). Vitamin A antagonizes decreased cell growth and elevated collagen-degrading matrix metalloproteinases and stimulates collagen accumulation in naturally aged human skin. *Journal of Investigative Dermatology, 114*, 480–486.

Vassar, R., Bennett, B. D., Babu-Khan, S., Kahn, S., Mendiaz, E. A., Denis, P., Teplow, D. B., Ross, S., Amarante, P., Loeloff, R., Luo, Y., Fisher, S., Fuller, J., Edenson, S., Lile, J., Jarosinki, M. A., Biere, A. L., Curran, E., Burgess, T., Louis, J.-C., Collins, F., Treanor, J., Rogers, G. & Citron, M. (1999). Beta-secretase cleavage of Alzheimer's amyloid precursor protein by the transmembrane aspartic protease BACE. *Science, 288*, 735–740.

Velkoff, V. A., & Lawson, V. A. (1998). *Gender and aging: Caregiving* (No. IB/98-3). Washington, DC: U.S. Department of Commerce.

Verbruggen, G., Cornelissen, M., Almqvist, K. F., Wang, L., Elewaut, D., Broddelez, C., de Ridder, L., & Veys, E. M. (2000). Influence of aging on the synthesis and morphology of the aggrecans synthesized by differentiated human articular chondrocytes. *Osteoarthritis and Cartilage, 8*, 170–179.

Verhaeghen, P., Vandenbroucke, A., & Dierckx, V. (1998). Growing slower and less accurate: Adult age differences in time-accuracy functions for recall and recognition from episodic memory. *Experimental Aging Research, 24*, 3–19.

Vermeulen, A. (2000). Andropause. *Maturitas, 34*, 5–15.

Vermeulen, A., Goemaere, S., & Kaufman, J. M. (1999). Testosterone, body composition and aging. *Journal of Endocrinological Investigation, 22*, 110–116.

Vig, E. K., Davenport, N. A., & Pearlman, R. A. (2002). Good deaths, bad deaths, and preferences for the end of life: A qualitative study of geriatric outpatients. *Journal of the American Geriatrics Society, 50*, 1541–1548.

Villa, M. L., Marcus, R., Ramirez Delay, R., & Kelsey, J. L. (1995). Factors contributing to skeletal health of postmenopausal Mexican-American women. *Journal of Bone and Mineral Research, 10*, 1233–1242.

Villareal, D. T., Binder, E. F., Williams, D. B., Schechtman, K. B., Yarasheski, K. E., & Kohrt, W. M. (2001). Bone mineral density response to estrogen replacement in frail elderly women: A randomized controlled trial. *Journal of the American Medical Association, 286*, 815–820.

Vita, A. J., Terry, R. B., Hubert, H. B., & Fries, J. F. (1998). Aging, health risks, and cumulative disability. *New England Journal of Medicine, 338*, 1035–1041.

Vitiello, M. V. (1997). Sleep disorders and aging: Understanding the causes. *Journal of Gerontology: Medical Sciences, 52*, M189–191.

Vitiello, M. V., Wilkinson, C. W., Merriam, G. R., Moe, K. E., Prinz, P. N., Ralph, D. D., Colasurdo, E. A., & Schwartz, R. S. (1997). Successful 6-month endurance training does not alter insulin-like growth factor-I in healthy older men and women. *Journal of Gerontology: Medical Sciences, 52*, M149–154.

von Zglinicki, T. (2002). Oxidative stress shortens telomeres. *Trends in Biochemical Sciences, 27*, 339–344.

Wagner, A. M., Goodwin, M., Campbell, B., Eskro, S., Frank, S. A., Shephard, P. A., & Wade, M. (1997). Pain prevalence and pain treatments for residents in Oregon nursing homes. *Geriatric Nursing, 18*, 268–272.

Waid, M. O. (1998). Brief Summaries of Medicare and Medicaid, Title XVIII and Title XIX of The Social Security Act as of June 25, 1998 (incorporating the impacts from the Balanced Budget Act of 1997). Office of the Actuary, Health Care Financing Administration, DHHS, Washington, DC.

Waite, L. J., & Gallagher, M. (2000). *The case for marriage: Why married people are happier, healthier, and better off financially.* New York: Doubleday.

Wald, D. S., Bishop, L., Wald, N. J., Law, M., Hennessy, E., Weir, D., McPartlin, J., & Scott, J. (2001). Randomized trial of folic acid supplementation and serum homocysteine levels. *Archives of Internal Medicine, 161*, 695–700.

Walford, R. L., Mock, D., Verdery, R., & MacCallum, T. (2002). Calorie restriction in biosphere 2: Alterations in physiologic, hematologic, hormonal, and biochemical parameters in humans restricted for a 2-year period. *Journal of Gerontology Series A: Biological Sciences and Medical Sciences, 57*, B211–224.

Walster, E., Walster, G. W., & Berscheid, E. (1978). *Equity: Theory and research.* Boston: Allyn & Bacon.

Wang, H. Y., Bashore, T. R., Tran, Z. V., & Friedman, E. (2000). Age-related decreases in lymphocyte protein kinase C activity and translocation are reduced by aerobic fitness. *Journals of Gerontology: Biological Sciences, 55*, B545–B551.

Wang, Q. S., Tian, L., Huang, Y. L., Qin, S., He, L. Q., & Zhou, J. N. (2002). Olfactory identification and apolipoprotein E epsilon 4 allele in mild cognitive impairment. *Brain Research, 951*, 77–81.

Warr, P. (1994). Age and employment. In H. C. Triandis, M. D. Dunnette & L. M. Hough (Eds.), *Handbook of industrial and organizational psychology* (pp. 485–550). Palo Alto, CA: Consulting Psychologists Press.

Wechsler, D. L. (1997). *Wechsler Adult Intelligence Scale—Third Edition.* San Antonio TX: Psychological Corporation.

Wegner, D. M. (1994). Ironic processes of mental control. *Psychological Review,, 101*, 34–52.

Wei, Y. H., & Lee, H. C. (2002). Oxidative stress, mitochondrial DNA mutation, and impairment of antioxidant enzymes in aging. *Experimental Biology and Medicine (Maywood), 227,* 671–682.

Weinstein, B. S., & Ciszek, D. (2002). The reserve-capacity hypothesis: evolutionary origins and modern implications of the trade-off between tumor-suppression and tissue-repair. *Experimental Gerontology, 37,* 615–627.

Weissman, M. M., Bland, R. C., Canino, G. J., Faravelli, C., Greenwald, S., Hwu, H. G., Joyce, P. R., Karam, E. G., Lee, C. K., Lellouch, J., Lepine, J. P., Newman, S. C., Oakley-Browne, M. A., Rubio-Stipec, M., Wells, J. E., Wickramaratne, P. J., Wittchen, H. U., & Yeh, E. K. (1997). The cross-national epidemiology of panic disorder. *Archives of General Psychiatry, 54,* 305–309.

Welten, D. C., Kemper, H. C., Post, G. B., & van Staveren, W. A. (1995). A meta-analysis of the effect of calcium intake on bone mass in young and middle aged females and males. *Journal of Nutrition, 125,* 2802–2813.

Wenger, N. S., Kanouse, D. E., Collins, R. L., Liu, H., Schuster, M. A., Gifford, A. L., Bozzette, S. A., & Shapiro, M. F. (2001). End-of-life discussions and preferences among persons with HIV. *Journal of the American Medical Association, 285,* 2880–2887.

West, S. K., Munoz, B., Rubin, G. S., Schein, O. D., Bandeen-Roche, K., Zeger, S., German, S., & Fried, L. P. (1997). Function and visual impairment in a population-based study of older adults The SEE project Salisbury Eye Evaluation. *Investigative Ophthalmology and Visual Science, 38,* 72–82.

Wetherell, J. L., Gatz, M., & Craske, M. G. (2003). Treatment of generalized anxiety disorder in older adults. *Journal of Consulting & Clinical Psychology, 71,* 31–40.

Wetherell, J. L., Reynolds, C. A., & Gatz, M. P., Nancy L. (2002). Anxiety, cognitive performance, and cognitive decline in normal aging. *Journals of Gerontology: Series B: Psychological Sciences & Social Sciences, 57B,* P246–P255.

Wheeler, I. (2001). Parental bereavement: the crisis of meaning. *Death Studies, 25,* 51–66.

Whitbourne, S. K. (1985). The life-span construct as a model of adaptation in adulthood. In J. E. Birren & K. W. Schaie (Eds.), *Handbook of the psychology of aging* (2nd ed., pp. 594–618). New York: Van Nostrand Reinhold.

Whitbourne, S. K. (1986). *The me I know: A study of adult identity.* New York: Springer-Verlag.

Whitbourne, S. K. (1986a). *Adult development.* New York: Praeger.

Whitbourne, S. K. (1986b). *The me I know: A study of adult identity.* New York: Springer-Verlag.

Whitbourne, S. K. (2002). *The aging individual: Physical and psychological perspectives* (2nd ed.). New York: Springer.

Whitbourne, S. K., & Collins, K. C. (1998). Identity and physical changes in later adulthood: Theoretical and clinical implications. *Psychotherapy, 35,* 519–530.

Whitbourne, S. K., & Connolly, L. A. (1999). The developing self in midlife. In J. D. Reid & S. L. Willis (Eds.), *Life in the middle: Psychological and social development in middle age* (pp. 25–45). San Diego: Academic Press.

Whitbourne, S. K., & Sherry, M. S. (1991). Subjective perceptions of the life span in chronic mental patients. *International Journal of Aging and Human Development, 33,* 65–73.

Whitbourne, S. K., & van Manen, K.-J. (1996). Age differences and correlates of identity status in from college through middle adulthood. *Journal of Adult Development, 3,* 59–70.

Whitbourne, S. K., & Waterman, A. S. (1979). Psychosocial development in young adulthood: Age and cohort comparisons. *Developmental Psychology, 15,* 373–378.

Whitbourne, S. K., & Wills, K.-J. (1993). Psychological issues in institutional care of the aged. In S. B. Goldsmith (Ed.), *Long-term care administration handbook* (pp. 19–32). Gaithersburg, MD: Aspen.

Whitbourne, S. K., Culgin, S., & Cassidy, E. (1995). Evaluation of infantilizing intonation and content of speech directed at the aged. *International Journal of Aging and Human Development, 41,* 107–114.

Whitbourne, S. K., Sneed, J. R., & Skultety, K. M. (2002). Identity processes in adulthood: Theoretical and methodological challenges. *Identity, 2,* 29–45.

Whitbourne, S. K., Zuschlag, M. K., Elliot, L. B., & Waterman, A. S. (1992). Psychosocial development in adulthood: A 22-year sequential study. *Journal of Personality and Social Psychology, 63,* 260–271.

White, L., Petrovitch, H., Ross, G. W., Masaki, K. H., Abbott, R. D., Teng, E. L., Rodriguez, B. L., Blanchette, P. L., Havlik, R. J., Wergowske, G., Chiu, D., Foley, D. J., Murdaugh, C., & Curb, J. D. (1996). Prevalence of dementia in older Japanese-American men in Hawaii: The Honolulu-Asia aging study. *Journal of the American Medical Association, 276,* 955–960.

Wilkinson, C. W., Peskind, E. R., & Raskind, M. A. (1997). Decreased hypothalamic-pituitary-adrenal axis sensitivity to cortisol feedback inhibition in human aging. *Neuroendocrinology, 65,* 79–90.

Wilkniss, S. M., Jones, M. G., Korol, D. L., Gold, P. E., & Manning, C. A. (1997). Age-related differences in an ecologically based study of route learning. *Psychology and Aging, 12,* 372–375.

Willis, S. L. (1996). Everyday problem solving. In J. E. Birren, K. W. Schaie, R. P. Abeles, M. Gatz & T. A. Salthouse (Eds.), *Handbook of the psychology of aging* (4th ed., pp. 287–307). San Diego, CA: Academic Press.

Willis, S. L., Blieszner, R., & Baltes, P. B. (1981). Intellectual training research in aging: Modification of performance on the fluid ability of figural relations. *Journal of Educational Psychology, 73*, 41–50.

Wilson, M. N. (1986). The black extended family : An analytical consideration. *Developmental Psychology, 22*, 246–258.

Wilson, P. W., D'Agostino, R. B., Sullivan, L., Parise, H., & Kannel, W. B. (2002). Overweight and obesity as determinants of cardiovascular risk: The Framingham experience. *Archives of Internal Medicine, 162*, 1867–1872.

Wilson, R. S., Mendes De Leon, C. F., Barnes, L. L., Schneider, J. A., Bienias, J. L., Evans, D. A., et al. (2002). Participation in cognitively stimulating activities and risk of incident Alzheimer disease. *Journal of the American Medical Association, 287*, 742–748.

Wilson, T. M., & Tanaka, H. (2000). Meta-analysis of the age-associated decline in maximal aerobic capacity in men: relation to training status. *American Journal of Physiology—Heart and Circulatory Physiology, 278*, H829–834.

Winch, R. F. (1958). *Mate selection: A study of complementary needs.* New York: Harper & Row.

Wingfield, A., & Kahana, M. J. (2002). The dynamics of memory retrieval in older adulthood. *Canadian Journal of Experimental Psychology, 56*, 187–199.

Wink, P., & Helson, R. (1993). Personality change in women and their partners. *Journal of Personality and Social Psychology, 65*, 597–606.

Wise, P. M., Dubal, D. B., Wilson, M. E., Rau, S. W., & Bottner, M. (2001). Minireview: Neuroprotective effects of estrogen-new insights into mechanisms of action. *Endocrinology, 142*, 969–973.

Wise, P. M., Krajnak, K. M., & Kashon, M. L. (1996). Menopause: The aging of multiple pacemakers. *Science, 273*, 67–74.

Wister, A. V. (1996). The effects of socioeconomic status on exercise and smoking: Age-related differences. *Journal of Aging and Health, 8*, 467–488.

Wiswell, R. A., Jaque, S. V., Marcell, T. J., Hawkins, S. A., Tarpenning, K. M., Constantino, N., & Hyslop, D. M. (2000). Maximal aerobic power, lactate threshold, and running performance in master athletes. *Medicine and Science in Sports and Exercise, 32*, 1165–1170.

Wittchen, H. U., Zhao, S., Kessler, R. C., & Eaton, W. W. (1994). DSM-III--R generalized anxiety disorder in the National Comorbidity Survey. *Archives of General Psychiatry, 51*, 355–364.

Womack, C. J., Harris, D. L., Katzel, L. I., Hagberg, J. M., Bleecker, E. R., & Goldberg, A. P. (2000). Weight loss, not aerobic exercise, improves pulmonary function in older obese men. *Journal of Gerontology Series A: Biological Sciences and Medical Sciences, 55*, M453–457.

Wong, A. M., Lin, Y. C., Chou, S. W., Tang, F. T., & Wong, P. Y. (2001). Coordination exercise and postural stability in elderly people: Effect of Tai Chi Chuan. *Archives of Physical Medicine and Rehabilitation, 82*, 608–612.

World Health Organization (1997). *Composite International Diagnostic Interview (CIDI).*

World Health Organization (2001). *The World Health Report 2001. Mental health: New understanding, new hope.* Retrieved August 2003, from http://www.who.int/whr2001/2001/main/en/index.htm

World Health Organization (2002a). *AIDS epidemic update December 2002.* Geneva, Switzerland: Joint United Nations Programme on HIV/AIDS (UNAIDS), World Health Organization (WHO).

World Health Organization (2002b). *Health and Aging: A Discussion Paper.* Geneva, Switzerland: World Health Organization.

Worzala, K., Hiller, R., Sperduto, R. D., Mutalik, K., Murabito, J. M., Moskowitz, M., D'Agostino, R. B. & Wilson, P. W. (2001). Postmenopausal estrogen use, type of menopause, and lens opacities: The Framingham studies. *Archives of Internal Medicine, 161*, 1448–1454.

Wright, T. A., & Bonett, D. G. (2002). The moderating effects of employee tenure on the relation between organizational commitment and job performance: A meta-analysis. *Journal of Applied Psychology, 87*, 1183–1190.

Wrosch, C., & Heckhausen, J. (2002). Perceived control of life regrets: Good for young and bad for old adults. *Psychology and Aging, 17*, 340–350.

Wrosch, C., Schulz, R., & Heckhausen, J. (2002). Health stresses and depressive symptomatology in the elderly: The importance of health engagement control strategies. *Health Psychology, 21*, 340–348.

Wunderlich, G. S., Kohler, P. O., & Committee on Improving Quality in Long-Term Division of Health Care Services, Institute of Medicine (Eds.). (2001). *Improving the quality of long-term care.* Washington DC: National Academy Press.

Wysocki, C. J., & Gilbert, A. N. (1989). The National Geographic smell survey: Effects of age are heterogenous. *Annals of the New York Academy of Sciences, 561*, 12–28.

Xu, S. Z., Huang, W. M., & Ren, J. Y. (1997). The new model of age-dependent changes in bone mineral density. *Growth, Development, and Aging, 61,* 19–26.

Yan, E., & So-kum, T. C. (2001). Prevalence and psychological impact of Chinese elder abuse. *Journal of Interpersonal Violence, 16,* 1158–1174.

Yesavage, J. A., Brink, T. L., Rose, T. L., Lum, O., Huang, V., Adey, M., & Leirer, V. (1983). Development and validation of a geriatric depression screening scale: A preliminary report. *Journal of Psychiatric Research, 17,* 37–49.

Yesavage, J. A., Rose, T. L., & Bower, G. H. (1983). Interactive imagery and affective judgments improve face-name learning in the elderly. *Journal of Gerontology, 38,* 197–203.

Young, A. J. (1991). Effects of aging on human cold tolerance. *Experimental Aging Research, 17,* 205–213.

Zacks, R. T., Hasher, L., & Li, K. Z. H. (1998). Human memory. In F. I. M. Craik & T. A. Salthouse (Eds.), *Handbook of aging and cognition II.* Mahweh NJ: Erlbaum.

Zacks, R., & Hasher, L. (1997). Cognitive gerontology and attentional inhibition: A reply to Burke and McDowd. *Journal of Gerontology: Psychological Sciences, 52,* P274–283.

Zarit, S. G., & Knight, B. G. (Eds.). (1996). *A guide to psychotherapy and aging.* Washington, DC: American Psychological Association.

Zarit, S. H., & Zarit, J. M. (1998). *Mental disorders in older adults: Fundamentals of assessment and treatment.* New York: Guilford.

Zarit, Ş. H., & Zarit, J. M. (1998). *Mental disorders in older adults: Fundamentals of assessment and treatment.* New York: Guilford.

Zarit, S. H., Reever, K. E., & Bach-Peterson, J. (1980). Relatives of the impaired elderly: Correlates of feelings of burden. *The Gerontologist, 20,* 649–655.

Zeiss, A. M., & Steffan, A. (1996). Behavioral and cognitive-behavioral treatments: An overview of social learning. In S. H. Zarit & B. G. Knight (Eds.), A guide to psychotherapy and aging (pp. 35–60). Washington, DC: American Psychological Association.

Zelinski, E. M., & Burnight, K. P. (1997). Sixteen-year longitudinal and time lag changes in memory and cognition in older adults. *Psychology and Aging, 12,* 503–513.

Zimprich, D., & Martin, M. (2002). Can longitudinal changes in processing speed explain longitudinal age changes in fluid intelligence? *Psychology and Aging, 17,* 690–695.

Zioupos, P., Currey, J. D., & Hamer, A. J. (1999). The role of collagen in the declining mechanical properties of aging human cortical bone. *Journal of Biomedical Materials Research, 45,* 108–116.

Zmuda, J. M., Cauley, J. A., Kriska, A., Glynn, N. W., Gutai, J. P., & Kuller, L. H. (1997). Longitudinal relation between endogenous testosterone and cardiovascular disease risk factors in middle-aged men. A 13-year follow-up of former Multiple Risk Factor Intervention Trial participants. *American Journal of Epidemiology, 146,* 609–617.

Zmuda, J. M., Cauley, J. A., Kriska, A., Glynn, N. W., Gutai, J. P., & Kuller, L. H. (1997). Longitudinal relation between endogenous testosterone and cardiovascular disease risk factors in middle-aged men. A 13-year follow-up of former Multiple Risk Factor Intervention Trial participants. *American Journal of Epidemiology, 146,* 609–-617.

Zubenko, G. S., & Sunderland, T. (2000). Geriatric psychopharmacology: Why does age matter? *Harvard Review of Psychiatry, 7,* 311–333.

Zubenko, G. S., Stiffler, J. S., Hughes, H. B., 3rd, Fatigati, M. J., & Zubenko, W. N. (2002). Genome survey for loci that influence successful aging: sample characterization, method validation, and initial results for the Y chromosome. *American Journal of Geriatric Psychiatry, 10,* 619–630.

Source Notes

Figure 2-2
Sacher, G. A. (1977). Life table modification and life prolongation. In C. E. Finch & L. Hayflick (Eds.), *Handbook of the biology of aging* (pp. 582-638). New York: Van Nostrand Reinhold.

Figure 3-2
Schaie, K. W., Labouvie, G. & Buech, B. U. Generational and cohort-specific differences in adult cognitive functioning: A fourteen-year study of independent samples. *Developmental Psychology*, 9, 151-166, Figure 6, p. 159. Copyright © 1973 by the American Psychological Association. Reprinted by permission.

Figure 3-3
Franks, M. M., Herzog, A. R., Holmberg, D., & Markus, H. R. (1999). Educational attainment and self-making in later life. In C. D. Ryff & V. W. Marshall (Eds.), *The self and society in aging processes*, (pp. 223-246), figure 8.2, p. 238. Springer Publishing Company, Inc., New York 10012. Used by permission.

Figure 4-1
Saladin, K.S. (2001). Essential Study Partner Version 2.0, *Anatomy and physiology: The unity of form and function (2e)*. New York: McGraw-Hill.
http://www.mhhe.com/biosci/esp/2001_saladin/default.htm

Figure 4-3
No longer on web site (was on Medline.gov)

Figure 4-5
Saladin, K.S. (2001). Essential Study Partner Version 2.0, *Anatomy and physiology: The unity of form and function (2e)*. New York: McGraw-Hill.
http://www.mhhe.com/biosci/esp/2001_saladin/default.htm

Figure 4-6
Saladin, K.S. (2001). Essential Study Partner Version 2.0, *Anatomy and physiology: The unity of form and function (2e)*. New York: McGraw-Hill.
http://www.mhhe.com/biosci/esp/2001_saladin/default.htm

Figure 4-7 a and b
Permission not needed. From government web site:
http://www.niaid.nih.gov/final/immun/immun.htm

Figure 4-8
Permission not needed. From government web site:
http://www.cdc.gov/mmwr/preview/mmwrhtml/mm5104a2.htm#fig1

Figure 5-1
From government web site: Centers for Disease Control and Prevention. (2000). Age-specific excess deaths associated with stroke among racial/ethnic minority populations—United States, 1997. *Morbidity and Mortality Weekly Reports, 49(05)*, 94-97.

Figure 5-2
From government web site: Centers for Disease Control and Prevention (2002). Health United States 2002.

Figure 5-3
From government web site: http://www.cdc.gov/nccdphp/aag/aag_dnpa.htm

Figures 5-4 and 5-5
From American Cancer Society web site:
http://www.cancer.org/docroot/STT/stt_0_2001.asp?sitearea=STT&level=1
F&F2001.pdf

Figure 5-6
From government web site:
http://www.cdc.gov/cvh/fs-stroke.htm

Figure 5-7
From government web site:
http://press2.nci.nih.gov/sciencebehind/cancer/cancer54.htm

Figure 5-9
http://jama.ama-assn.org/issues/v289n8/fpdf/jpg0226.pdf

Figure 5-10
Rosen, C. J. (2003). Restoring aging bones. *Scientific American, March,* 71-77.

Figure 5-11
http://www.mayoclinic.com/
invoke.cfm?id=DS00296#Signs%20and%20Symptoms

Figure 5-12
Alzheimer's Disease Research. Program of the American Health Association Foundation.
http://www.ahaf.org/alzdis/about/AmyloidPlaques.htm

Figure 6-4
Sliwinski, M.J. & Hall, C.B. Constraints on general slowing: Using hierarchical linear models with random coefficients. *Psychology and Aging,* 13, 164-175. Copyright © 1998 by the American Psychological Association. Reprinted by permission.

Figure 6-6
Baddeley, Chincotta, D. & Adlam, A. (2001). Working memory and the control of action: Evidence from task switching. *Journal of Experimental Psychology: General, 130,* 641-657, Figure 8.

Figure 7-2
Willis, S. L. (1996). Everyday problem solving. In J. E. Birren, K. W. Schaie, R. P. Abeles, M. Gatz & T. A. Salthouse (Eds.), *Handbook of the psychology of aging* (4th ed.) (pp. 287-307). San Diego, CA: Academic Press.

Figure 7-2
Cattell, R. B. (1971). Abilities: Their structure, growth, and action. Boston: Houghton Mifflin.

Figure 7-4
Horn, J. L. (1970). Organization of data on life-span development of human abilities. In L. R. Goulet & P. B. Baltes (Eds.), *Life-span developmental psychology: Theory and research* (Vol. 1 pp. 211-256). New York: Academic Press.

Figure 7-5
Schaie, K. W. The course of adult intellectual development. *American Psychologist,* 49, 304-313. Copyright © 1994 by the American Psychological Association. Reprinted by permission.

Figure 7-6
Gerontologist by Schaie, K.W.. Copyright 1989 by *Gerontological Society of America.* Reproduced with permission of *Gerontological Society of America* in Textbook format via Copyright Clearance Center.

Figure 7-7
Schaie, K. W. (1996). Intellectual development in adulthood. In J. E. Birren, K. W. Schaie, R. P. Abeles, M. Gatz, & T. A. Salthouse (Eds.), *Handbook of the psychology of aging* (4th ed.) (pp. 266-286). San Diego CA: Academic Press.

Figure 7-8
Schaie, K. W. The course of adult intellectual development. *American Psychologist,* 49, 304-313. Copyright © 1994 by the American Psychological Association. Reprinted by permission.

Figure7-9
Baltes, P. B., & Staudinger, U.M. The search for a psychology of wisdom, *Current Directions in Psychological Science,* 2, 75-80. Copyright © 1993 by Blackwell Publishers, Inc. Reprinted with permission.

Table 7-2
French, J. W., Ekstrom, R. B., & Price, L. A. (1963). Manual for the kit of reference tests for cognitive factors. Princeton NJ: Educational Testing Service. Reprinted by permission of Educational Testing Service the copyright owner.

Ekstrom, R.B., French, J,W., Harman, H. H., & Dirmen, D. (1976). Manual for the Kit of factor-referenced cognitive tests. Princeton NJ: Educational Testing Service. Reprinted by permission of Educational Testing Service the copyright owner.

Figure 8-1
Whitbourne, S. K., Zuschlag, M. K., Elliot, L. B., & Waterman, A. S. Psychosocial development in adulthood: A 22-year sequential study. *Journal of Personality and Social Psychology,* 63, 260-271. Copyright © 1992 by the American Psychological Association. Reprinted by permission.

Figure 8-2
Whitbourne, S. K., Zuschlag, M. K., Elliot, L. B., & Waterman, A. S. Psychosocial development in adulthood: A 22-year sequential study. *Journal of Personality and Social Psychology,* 63, 260-271. Copyright © 1992 by the American Psychological Association. Reprinted by permission.

Figure 8-3
McCrae, R. R. & Costa, P. T., Jr. (1990). Personality in adulthood. New York: Guilford.

Figure 8-4
From THE SEASONS OF A MAN'S LIFE by Daniel Levinson, copyright 1978 by Daniel J. Levinson. Used by permission of Alfred A. Knopf, a division of Random House, Inc.

Figure 8-5
McCrae, R. R. & Costa, P. T., Jr. (1990). Personality in adulthood. New York: Guilford.

Table 8-5
McCrae, R. R., & Costa, P. T., Jr. (1990). *Personality in adulthood.* New York: Guilford.

Figure 9-4
Carstensen, L. L., Gross J. & Fung, H. (1997). The social context of emotion. *Annual Review of Geriatrics & Gerontology* , 17, 325-352. Springer Publishing Company, Inc., New York 10012. Used by permission.

Figure 9-5
Bartholomew, K., & Horowitz, L. M. Attachment styles among young adults: A test of a four-category model. *Journal of Personality and Social Psychology*, 61, 226-244. Copyright © 1991 by the American Psychological Association. Reprinted by permission.

Table 9-1
Mickelson, K. D., Kessler R. C., & Shaver, P. R. Adult attachment in a nationally representative sample. *Journal of Personality and Social Psychology*, 73, 1092-1106. Copyright © 1997 by the American Psychological Association. Reprinted by permission.

Table 9-3
Silverstein, M., & Bengston, V. L. Intergenerational solidarity and the structure of adult child-parent relationships in American families. *American Journal of Sociology*, 103, 429-460. Copyright ©1997 by the University of Chicago. Reprinted by the permission of the University of Chicago Press.

Table 9-4
Stocker, C. M., Lanthier, R. P., & Furman, W. Sibling relationships in early adulthood. *Journal of Family Psychology*, 11, 210-221. Copyright © 1997 by the American Psychological Association. Reprinted by permission.

Table 10-1
Warr, P. (1994). Age and employment. In H. C. Triandis, M. D. Dunnette, & L. M. Hough (Eds.), *Handbook of industrial and organizational psychology* (pp. 485-550). Palo Alto CA: Consulting Psychologists Press. Reprinted with permission of the author.

Figure 11-3
Harpur, T.J. & Hare, R.D. Assessment of psychopathy as a function of age. *Journal of Abnormal Psychology*, 103, 604-609. Copyright © 1994 by the American Psychological Association. Reprinted by permission.

Table 11-3
Segal, D. L., Coolidge, F. L., & Rosowsky, E. (2000). Personality disorders. In S. K. Whitbourne (Ed.), *Psychopathology in later life* (pp. 89-116). New York: Wiley. This material used by permission of John Wiley & Sons, Inc.

Table 11-4
Folstein, M. F., Folstein, S. E., & McHugh, P. R. (1975). Mini-Mental State: A practical method for grading the cognitive state of patients for the clinician. *Journal of Psychiatric Research*, 12, 189-198.

Figure 12-4
Lawton, M. P., & Nahemow, L. Ecology and the aging process. In C. Eisdorfer & M. P. Lawton (Eds.), *The psychology of adult development and aging* . Washington, DC: American Psychological Association. Copyright © 1973 by the American Psychological Association. Reprinted by permission.

Figure 13-3
Field, M. J., Cassel, C. K., & Committee on Care at the End of Life (1997). *Approaching death: Improving care at the end of life, Institute of Medicine, Division of Health Care Services*. Washington, DC: National Academy Press.

Reprinted with permission from *Approaching death: Improving care at the end of life, Institute of Medicine, Division of Health Care Services*. Copyright 1997 by the National Academy of Sciences. Courtesy of the National Academy Press, Washington, DC. (this credit may be edited)

Figure 13-4
Bonanno, G. A., Wortman, C. B., Lehman, D. R., Tweed, R. G., Haring, M., Sonnega , J. Resilience to loss and chronic grief: A prospective study from preloss to 18-months postloss. *Journal of Personality & Social Psychology*, 83, 1150-1164. Figure 1. Copyright © 2002 by the American Psychological Association. Reprinted by permission.

Figure 14-1
Mroczek, D. K., & Kolarz, C. M. The effect of age on positive and negative affect: A developmental perspective on happiness. *Journal of Personality and Social Psychology*, 75 , 1333-1349. Copyright © 1998 by the American Psychological Association. Reprinted by permission.

Figure 14-2
Lehman, H. C.; *Age and Achievement*. Copyright © 1953 by Princeton University Press. Reprinted by permission of Princeton University Press.

Figure 14-3
Simonton, D.K. *Psychology, Science, and History: An Introduction to Histriometry*. New Haven CT: Yale University Press. Copyright © 1990 by Yale University Press.

Figure 14-4
Lehman, H. C.; *Age and Achievement*. Copyright © 1953 by Princeton University Press. Reprinted by permission of Princeton University Press.

Figure 14-6
Simonton, D. K. (1984). Creative productivity and age: A mathematical model based on a two-step cognitive process. *Developmental Review*, 4, 77-111.

Figure 14-7
Simonton, D. K. (1997). Creative productivity: A predictive and explanatory model of career trajectories and landmarks. *Psychological Review*, 104, 66-89.

Photo credits

Name Index

Subject Index